Andrea C. Schalley and Susana A. Eisenchlas (Eds.)
Handbook of Home Language Maintenance and Development

Handbooks of
Applied Linguistics

Communication Competence
Language and Communication Problems
Practical Solutions

Editors
Karlfried Knapp
Daniel Perrin
Marjolijn Verspoor

Volume 18

Handbook of Home Language Maintenance and Development

Social and Affective Factors

Edited by
Andrea C. Schalley and Susana A. Eisenchlas

ISBN 978-1-5015-2721-0
e-ISBN (PDF) 978-1-5015-1017-5
e-ISBN (EPUB) 978-1-5015-1007-6

Library of Congress Control Number: 2019955901

Bibliographic information published by the Deutsche Nationalbibliothek
The Deutsche Nationalbibliothek lists this publication in the Deutsche Nationalbibliografie;
detailed bibliographic data are available on the Internet at http://dnb.dnb.de.

© 2022 Walter de Gruyter GmbH, Berlin/Boston
This volume is text- and page-identical with the hardback published in 2020.
Typesetting: Integra Software Services Pvt. Ltd.
Printing and binding: CPI books GmbH, Leck

www.degruyter.com

Preface

The present handbook constitutes Volume 18 of the De Gruyter Mouton *Handbooks of Applied Linguistics*. This series is based on an understanding of Applied Linguistics as an inter- and transdisciplinary field of academic enquiry. The *Handbooks of Applied Linguistics* provide a state-of-the-art description of established and emerging areas of Applied Linguistics. Each volume gives an overview of the field, identifies most important traditions and their findings, identifies the gaps in current research, and gives perspectives for future directions.

In the late 1990s when the handbook series was planned by its Founding Editors Gerd Antos and Karlfried Knapp, intensive debates were going on as to whether Applied Linguistics should be restricted to applying methods and findings from linguistics only or whether it should be regarded as a field of interdisciplinary synthesis drawing on psychology, sociology, ethnology and similar disciplines that are also dealing with aspects of language and communication. Should it be limited to foreign language teaching or should it widen its scope to language-related issues in general? Thus, what *Applied Linguistics* means and what an Applied Linguist does was highly controversial at the time.

Against this backdrop, Gerd Antos and Karlfried Knapp felt that a series of handbooks of Applied Linguistics could not simply be an accidental selection of descriptions of research findings and practical activities that were or could be published in books and articles labeled as "applied linguistic". Rather, for them such a series had to be based on an epistemological concept that frames the status and scope of the concept of Applied Linguistics. Departing from contemporary Philosophy of Science, which sees academic disciplines under the pressure to successfully solve practical everyday problems encountered by the societies which aliment them, the founding editors emphasized the view that was only emerging at that time – the programmatic view that Applied Linguistics means the solving of real world problems with language and communication. This concept has become mainstream since.

In line with the conviction that Applied Linguistics is for problem solving, we developed a series of handbooks to give representative descriptions of the ability of this field of academic inquiry and to provide accounts, analyses, explanations and, where possible, solutions of everyday problems with language and communication. Each volume of the *Handbooks of Applied Linguistics* series is unique in its explicit focus on topics in language and communication as areas of everyday problems and in pointing out the relevance of Applied Linguistics in dealing with them.

This series has been well received in the academic community and among practitioners. In fact, its success has even triggered competitive handbook series by other publishers. Moreover, we recognized further challenges with language and communication and distinguished colleagues keep on approaching us with proposals to edit further volumes in this handbook series. This motivates both De Gruyter Mouton and the series editors to further develop the *Handbooks of Applied Linguistics*.

Karlfried Knapp (Erfurt), Founding Editor
Daniel Perrin (Zürich), Editor
Marjolijn Verspoor (Groningen), Editor

Acknowledgements

This handbook has been three years in the making, and we are delighted to see the final product. Marjolijn H. Verspoor, one of the editors of the handbook series, first approached and invited us to edit this handbook in May 2017. Plans then started to take shape at the World Congress in Applied Linguistics in Rio de Janeiro, after which we set to work. We would like to express our sincere gratitude to Marjolijn for providing us with this opportunity.

We are tremendously grateful to our 30 collaborating authors, for the stimulating chapters they contributed to this handbook, for the inspiring discussions we had with them along the way, and for their continued support and collaboration throughout the process. We met most of them through the International Association in Applied Linguistics (AILA) Research Network on "Social and Affective Factors in Home Language Maintenance and Development", which we have had the honour of coordinating since 2015. Without our colleagues, this volume would not have come to fruition. Thank you!

We are also greatly indebted to our external reviewers – colleagues from around the world who, while not themselves involved in the handbook, helped us in the reviewing process and who so generously provided invaluable comments and suggestions. The handbook has benefited immensely from their expertise:

> Ajit Mohanty, Alison Crump, Alissa Stern, Ana Maria Relaño Pastor, Angela Scarino, Antonia Rubino, Bahar Otcu-Grillman, Barbara Pini, Belinda Bustos Flores, Bernard Spolsky, Christina Gkonou, Dietha Koster, Durk Gorter, Galina Putjata, Haley De Korne, Ingrid Piller, Jean Conteh, Jean Marc Dewaele, Jill Vaughan, John Edwards, Kaya Oriyama, Ken Cruickshank, Kendall King, Kerry Taylor-Leech, Khadij Gharibi, Lisa Dorner, Liz Ellis, Louisa Willoughby, Loy Lising, Luk Van Menzel, Lyn Fogle, Margaret Kettle, Melanie Revis, Nelleke Van Deusen Scholl, Nicola Yuill, Radosveta Dimitrova, Rose Drury, Ruth Singer, Sarah Prestridge, Sayed Mirvahedi, Shannon Fitzsimmons, Shulamit Kopeliovich, Tej Bhatia, Terese Aceves, Tijana Hirsh, Umberto Ansaldo, Yvette Slaughter, and Zhu Hua.

Along the way, we also received fabulous logistical help: we would like to thank Pernilla Olsson and Alexander Borkowski for their careful and conscientious editorial assistance, and the Mouton de Gruyter team for their unfailing and cheerful support throughout the volume preparation – our thanks in particular go to Birgit Sievert, Katja Lehming, Kirstin Börgen, and Lara Wysong.

Last but not least, we would like to dedicate the volume to our families and especially to our children, who instigated our interest in home language maintenance and development in the first place.

Andrea C. Schalley, Karlstad
Susana A. Eisenchlas, Brisbane

Contents

Preface —— V

Acknowledgements —— VII

Andrea C. Schalley and Susana A. Eisenchlas
1 Social and affective factors in home language maintenance and development: Setting the scene —— 1

Part 1: Terminologies and methodologies

Susana A. Eisenchlas and Andrea C. Schalley
2 Making sense of "home language" and related concepts —— 17

Päivi Juvonen, Susana A. Eisenchlas, Tim Roberts, and Andrea C. Schalley
3 Researching social and affective factors in home language maintenance and development: A methodology overview —— 38

Part 2: Bilingual speakers and their families

Topic area 2.1: Self-conceptions and affective reactions

Annick De Houwer
4 Harmonious Bilingualism: Well-being for families in bilingual settings —— 63

Yeşim Sevinç
5 Anxiety as a negative emotion in home language maintenance and development —— 84

Amelia Tseng
6 Identity in home-language maintenance —— 109

Judith Purkarthofer
7 Intergenerational challenges: Of handing down languages, passing on practices, and bringing multilingual speakers into being —— 130

Topic area 2.2: Family language policy

Elizabeth Lanza and Rafael Lomeu Gomes
8   Family language policy: Foundations, theoretical perspectives and critical approaches —— 153

Xiao Lan Curdt-Christiansen and Jing Huang
9   Factors influencing family language policy —— 174

Mila Schwartz
10 Strategies and practices of home language maintenance —— 194

Cassie Smith-Christmas
11 Child agency and home language maintenance —— 218

Åsa Palviainen
12 Future prospects and visions for family language policy research —— 236

Part 3: Grassroot initiatives

Sabine Little
13 Social media and the use of technology in home language maintenance —— 257

Anikó Hatoss
14 Transnational grassroots language planning in the era of mobility and the Internet —— 274

Janica Nordstrom
15 Community language schools —— 293

Elisabeth Mayer, Liliana Sánchez, José Camacho, and Carolina Rodríguez Alzza
16 The drivers of home language maintenance and development in indigenous communities —— 312

Part 4: **The role of society**

Topic area 4.1: **Social justice and inclusiveness**

Anthony J. Liddicoat
17 Language policy and planning for language maintenance: The macro and meso levels —— 337

Nathan Albury
18 Language attitudes and ideologies on linguistic diversity —— 357

E. Annamalai and Tove Skutnabb-Kangas
19 Social justice and inclusiveness through linguistic human rights in education —— 377

Gregory A. Cheatham and Sumin Lim
20 Disabilities and home language maintenance: Myths, models of disability, and equity —— 401

Topic area 4.2: **Formal education**

Kutlay Yağmur
21 Models of formal education and minority language teaching across countries —— 425

Latisha Mary and Andrea Young
22 Teachers' beliefs and attitudes towards home languages maintenance and their effects —— 444

BethAnne Paulsrud
23 The mainstream classroom and home language maintenance —— 464

About the contributors —— 483

Author Index —— 491

Subject Index —— 509

Language Index —— 521

Andrea C. Schalley and Susana A. Eisenchlas
1 Social and affective factors in home language maintenance and development: Setting the scene

We are delighted to have this volume included in the series *Handbooks of Applied Linguistics*. As a field, applied linguistics investigates language-related real-world issues – particularly those concerning language use, language acquisition and learning, and language teaching – and works towards describing and explaining these processes and suggesting ways to enhance them. It approaches these issues from an interdisciplinary perspective, drawing not only on linguistics but also on neighbouring disciplines such as education, psychology, and sociology. Each of the earlier volumes in the handbook series presents an overview of their chosen field, identifies the most important traditions, their research findings, and gaps in current research, and provides perspectives for future research directions. So too does this volume.

Couched in one of the main branches of applied linguistics research – bilingualism (which in our understanding includes notions of multilingualism and plurilingualism) – this volume focuses on social and affective factors in home language maintenance and development. Bilingualism research has extensively explored linguistic and psycholinguistic perspectives, and educational practices and outcomes. Yet the social and affective perspectives that impact on home language maintenance and development have remained somewhat less researched, a gap that is addressed in this handbook.

This is the first volume that brings together the different strands of research into social and affective factors of home language maintenance and development. Contributors from around the world present a rich harvest of research paradigms and perspectives, providing a comprehensive and constructive overview of the state-of-the-art in this flourishing field.

1 Delimiting the field

First, what do we mean by "the field"? What do we mean by "social and affective factors in home language maintenance and development"? The components of this notion are themselves ambiguous or complex, and so require some clarification. This requirement applies to language – "language maintenance", "home language(s)", "language development" – as well as to factors – "social factors" and "affective factors". In clarifying the meaning of these terms as used in this volume, we also delimit the field of research with which the volume is concerned. Let us begin with "language maintenance" as the first real-world issue which this handbook directs towards, before we turn to the second, "language development".

Mesthrie and Leap (2000: 253) define "language maintenance" as "the continuing use of a language in the face of competition from a regionally and socially more powerful language". As this definition indicates, language maintenance is about *language use*, illuminated here from a sociolinguistic perspective rather than a purely linguistic one, as the notion of "competition from a [...] more powerful language" conveys. In the context of this volume, the more powerful language is typically the language spoken by the majority in society, while the language being "maintained" is a minority or home language. Continued use of the language being "maintained" is by such definition not a given. Rather, it is an assertion of this language, by its users, in a social fabric that relegates the language to "minority" status.

The notion "minority language", in contrast to "majority language", is often used to refer to the language that needs to assert itself, as the very notion itself makes the power imbalance explicit. Yet, whilst we recognise the wide-spread use of "minority language" in bilingualism discourses, as editors of this volume we have chosen to instead refer to these languages as "home languages". Connaughton-Crean and Ó Duibhir (2017: 23) define "home languages" as "languages spoken or used in the home or community but which are not the majority language in the society". As we discuss in the following chapter exploring terminological issues (Eisenchlas and Schalley this vol.), "home language" presents as a relatively neutral term that does not take a stance in regards to, e.g., underlying ideologies or how much societal influence the speaker community may have. While it may be seen as referring to only a restricted usage domain (the "home"), more important for this handbook is, however, that it embraces the contexts where language use is negotiated, which is what concerns the authors in their contributions here. We refer the reader to our chapter for more in-depth discussions of terms.

Secondly, this handbook investigates social and affective factors in "language development", i.e. the development of new linguistic knowledge in all its breadth and hence of *language acquisition*, and/or *language learning*, of the home language. Language development focuses on the processes as much as the outcomes of these processes, and the conditions under which they take place. In line with this handbook's main scope and objectives, the chapters consider these processes, conditions and outcomes particularly in terms of social and affective factors that come into play – in "informal" contexts (such as within the family), "semi-formal" contexts (such as within the community) or "formal" contexts (such as in educational institutions like the school). Whenever instructional learning comes into the picture, *language teaching* and approaches to teaching more generally are inevitably drawn into the discussion. The handbook thus addresses all four major areas of applied linguistics introduced at the beginning of this chapter – use, acquisition, learning, and teaching of language – in relation to home language(s) of bilingual speakers.

As the title conveys, this handbook's lens focuses upon the social and affective factors at play in home language use. "Social factors" are socio-environmental conditions that shape home language maintenance and development as we explore here. These factors include economic, cultural, legal and political constraints and expectations, and societal norms and language ideologies guiding "what a broader community sees as appropriate and expected linguistic practice" (Albury this vol). "Affective factors" are psycho-social conditions that impact on home language maintenance and development. They include individuals' emotions and perspectives on identity, culture and tradition, and impact beliefs and attitudes (cf. Curdt-Christiansen and Huang this vol.). They point to individuals' dispositions and tendencies to react favourably or unfavourably towards particular entities or events (see Sarnoff 1970; Eagly and Chaiken 1993; Albury this vol.).

The overall guiding concern of this handbook is thus not language maintenance and development from a linguistic viewpoint, but the push and pull factors that influence people's affects, behaviours and stances in relation to home language maintenance and development, and what effects these factors have.

2 Three levels of analysis: Macro, meso and micro

As we discussed in the previous section, the factors under consideration here are generally socio-environmental or psycho-social. They are closely related to the society as a whole (the macro level), or to individuals in their direct social contexts (the micro level), and in both cases uncover what impacts on speakers' decisions and efforts when it comes to home language maintenance and development.

Research in the field can thus be roughly organised into these two levels of analysis. Studies at the macro level are often necessarily at a high level of theoretical abstraction and focus on social systems at a large scale (e.g., nationally or globally). Studies at the micro level focus on individuals as members of small social units (such as families and their language policies and practices). A third level of analysis – the meso level – sits amidst the macro and micro levels. It constitutes the grey area in between (Hult 2010), and can be seen as the level of analysis concentrating on community initiatives and efforts in relation to home language maintenance and development. As later discussion makes clear, studies at the meso level reach across a few research foci, but the field still lacks systematic study and coverage of this level (Juvonen et al. this vol.).

We use these three levels of analysis as the organising frame of this handbook. We acknowledge, however, that sociolinguistic reality is more fluid than what this frame may suggest. Although the levels may appear to be discrete, they interact and impact on one another. Neither can they be interpreted as a simple continuum, since the meso level is not a necessary transition point between the micro and the macro levels. For instance, families at the micro level may feel pressures from the macro level (e.g., through educational policies), but may not respond to these pressures by forming a meso level community and taking joint action. On the other hand, macro level policy planners may listen to micro level families' voices directly, without being lobbied by meso level communities. We thus need to be mindful that all levels of analysis are interwoven, and that any representation of real-world complexity can be only a simplified one.

3 Handbook structure and content

The main body of this handbook is structured along the lines of the three levels of analysis explained above. An introductory section discussing terminological and methodological issues and challenges precedes the main body. The handbook is therefore divided into the following four parts: 1 – Terminologies and methodologies; 2 – Bilingual speakers and their families; 3 – Grassroot initiatives; and 4 – The role of society.

Part 1 provides readers with a foundation to the field of study. Parts 2, 3, and 4 each survey perspectives from the three levels of analysis: the micro level (the bilingual individual as part of a family) in part 2; the meso level (the bilingual individual as a member of a speech community) in part 3; and the macro level (the bilingual individual as a member of society) in part 4. Parts 2 and 4 are further subdivided into two topic areas, as outlined below. From here we explain each part and topic area and the kinds of issues discussed in each, thus providing an overview of the contributions to the handbook.

3.1 The basics: Terminologies and methodologies

Part 1, as the handbook's foundation, gives centre stage to terminologies and methodologies. Because the terms used for maintained language(s) are contentious, in chapter 2 we review and distinguish these near-synonyms, including "minority language", "mother tongue", "heritage language", and "home language", and critically evaluate the concepts underlying these terms. We have restricted our discussion to the terms that are of most relevance to this handbook. We compare and contrast the terms on several dimensions, and – as may be expected – conclude that neither a one-size-fits-all term nor a "best" term is workable here, due to the multifaceted nature of the field (see also Wiley 2014). However, through this discussion we explain clearly the reasons for choosing "home language" as the most appropriate umbrella term for this handbook, identifying the term's relative neutrality on social and affective factors in language maintenance and development, while still highlighting social and affective factors as important.

Chapter 3 provides an overview of methodological issues encountered in the field, and explores research aims and foci, research designs and participant populations across this field of research. Juvonen et al. (this vol.) seek to present "a birds-eye view, bringing together, critiquing, and contrasting methodological considerations" across the three levels of analysis in this handbook. The authors discuss pitfalls they have identified for research in the field, including a lack of generalisability of research results, restricted research coverage, limited reporting on the data sets obtained, and a lack of procedural information on data analysis. The authors also discuss some of the field's challenges, including ethical considerations, data management, and the dissemination of research findings. The chapter concludes with an outlook to future developments in the field. The chapter is not intended as a step-by-step guide on how to do research, but rather as providing a snapshot of the current methodological state-of-the-art.

3.2 The micro level: Bilingual speakers and their families

Equipped with the foundational background from part 1, part 2 of the handbook moves to the first level of analysis, the micro level. Here the focus is on the bilingual individual, as member of a family or of other close social groups. The chapters in this part are subsumed under two topic areas. The first topic area illustrates the self-conceptions of bilingual speakers and their affective reactions, casting the spotlight on the affective domain. The second topic area addresses why and how families maintain and develop the home language, placing its chapters squarely within the research field of family language policy.

3.2.1 Self-conceptions and affective reactions

This topic area illuminates a number of affective domains and speakers' reactions to their social experiences. These include the subjective well-being of bilinguals (chapter 4), anxiety as a negative emotion in home language maintenance and development (chapter 5), and the formation of identity (chapter 6). Marking the transition to family language policy research, chapter 7 turns to intergenerational relations and the intergenerational transmission of home language(s).

Chapter 4 directs our attention to the subjective well-being of children and their parents living in bilingual settings. In this chapter, De Houwer (this vol.) reviews empirical studies and shows that young children's well-being is put at risk if their home language is disregarded in early care and they receive no support in learning the societal language. Moreover, the studies show that not speaking the home language has negative effects on family relations, and that a well-developed dual language proficiency is central to both children's and parents' well-being, and hence is conducive to Harmonious Bilingualism.

In contrast, in chapter 5, Sevinç's survey of emotional reactions and psychological dimensions of home language maintenance (or language shift) examines predominantly negative emotions, identifying how bilinguals may, for instance, give up plans to maintain their home language after experiencing negative emotions such as anxiety, shame, or guilt. Exploring a relatively under-studied field, this chapter focuses "specifically on anxiety as a negative emotion in transnational contexts, and its causes and effects" (Sevinç this vol.), to deepen an understanding of the affective challenges bilingual speakers and families experience in their daily lives.

Chapter 6 moves to concepts of self in relationship to others, as constructed through interaction. Tseng's discussion of identity and home language maintenance draws on research from a range of minority language contexts, and addresses key areas of language socialisation and learning. This discussion shows that the relationship between language and identity is "indexical, interactive, and constructed at multiple intersecting scalar levels" (Tseng this vol.), and highlights the importance of identity for home language maintenance. The chapter also ventures into the school as a site of identity negotiations, where social and linguistic hegemonies related to national identities and ideologies may be reproduced. Insights from indigenous communities, and a brief discussion of globalisation and transnationalism conclude the chapter.

Matters of identity also play a role in intergenerational relations, which are not only crucial for transmitting and maintaining languages, but are also laden with affect (as Sevinç identifies in chapter 5). They are the focus of chapter 7, in which Purkarthofer problematises the notions of generation and of language. She posits:

> When talking about languages being passed on, or using terms like language transmission or maintenance, languages are not seen as objects to be handled but as processes requiring active participation from all generations involved. (Purkarthofer this vol.)

The chapter discusses studies of language practices and policies that affect and are negotiated by members of at least two different generations, including some that highlight intergenerational challenges. Hence, while not focussing directly on family language policy, the chapter provides a welcome transition between the two topic areas in this part of the handbook.

3.2.2 Family language policy

The second topic area at the micro level deals with family language policy, which entails the "explicit and overt planning in relation to language use within the home" (King, Fogle, and Logan-Terry 2008: 907) as well as the "implicitly and covertly" implemented practices (Curdt-Christiansen 2009: 352). Family language policy research is a burgeoning field of inquiry so the handbook looks into its past, present, and future, focusing on theoretical concepts and research to date (chapter 8), factors influencing the language policies of families (chapter 9), strategies and practices employed by families (chapter 10), the role of child agency in families' practices (chapter 11), and future prospects and visions for the field (chapter 12).

Chapter 8 traces the field of family language policy back to its roots in the early 20th century. Here Lanza and Lomeu Gomes (this vol.) document five phases of the development of the field. They then overview scholarship published since the landmark article of King, Fogle and Logan-Terry (2008), pointing out the diversity of populations and languages studied. The authors also raise theoretical issues such as the complexity of the notion of family across time and space, and the sociolinguistics of globalisation. Overall, the chapter provides a thorough introduction to the field of family language policy, aspects of which are examined in depth in the chapters that follow it.

In chapter 9, Curdt-Christiansen and Huang present a model that illustrates how internal factors such as emotions, identity, and parental impact beliefs, and external factors such as language status and socio-economic and socio-political realities impact on family language policy. Basing their discussion on empirical studies, they show "how family language policy as a dynamic socio-cultural practice is shaped by both linguistic and non-linguistic forces in different types of families, geopolitical contexts, and macro level policies" (Curdt-Christiansen and Huang this vol.). They also suggest directions for future research into emerging factors that have not, or have only rarely, been taken up, such as the development of new technologies.

While Curdt-Christiansen and Huang focus on what impacts on family language policy, Schwartz turns to the effects of family language policy in chapter 10, and discusses strategies and practices in home language maintenance and development. She considers strategies as part of family language management and hence of (mainly parents') attempts to regulate language use, and home language practices "as the actual routine use of languages in the family regardless of the beliefs or management strategies" (Schwartz this vol.) employed by family members, in line with Spolsky's (2004) definition of language practices. After overviewing early concepts and pioneering contributions, the chapter turns to an analysis of recent studies as the basis for an explicit discussion of home language strategies and practices as currently understood in the field.

The actual use of languages in the family is not determined exclusively by parents, though. Child agency plays an important role in home language maintenance and development, as Smith-Christmas discusses in chapter 11. This chapter explains how research on child agency has evolved over time, arguing that the concept of child agency has come to fruition in family language policy research only recently; previously the child had been seen as merely the "linguistic product" of parents' language maintenance efforts. Smith-Christmas (this vol.) proposes a framework encompassing four intersectional dimensions – compliancy, linguistic competencies, linguistic norms, and power dynamics – to conceptualise how children exert their agency and thus influence family language policy.

The last chapter on family language policy, still at the micro level, is chapter 12 by Palviainen. Taking the current state of research on family language policy as her point of departure, Palviainen (this vol.) explores future research directions in this field. In particular, she asks who constitutes a family and argues that the family needs to be seen as a dynamic and fluid system. She outlines three major topics that need more recognition in the field, namely children's perspectives, (non-linguistic) emotions, and today's mobile digital contexts in which families find themselves. The chapter concludes with practical recommendations on how these perspectives can be implemented in future research, theoretically and methodologically.

3.3 The meso level: Grassroot initiatives for home language maintenance

Part 3 of the handbook widens the perspective to bilingual speakers as members of speech communities. As section 2 indicates, the meso level constitutes the grey area between the micro and macro levels. Here speakers take action – for instance, in response to socio-environmental conditions and hence macro level pressures they encounter – by way of pooling their micro level resources, such as time and knowledge. Consequently, joint action in the form of community or grassroots initiatives directed at home language maintenance and development are in the focus of this part of the volume. Nevertheless, two issues make it difficult to clearly identify efforts at the meso level: (1) what counts as joint action (in contrast to individual reactions) is not clear-cut; and (2) because initiatives are often not driven through official organisations, it remains unclear how the "communities" are delimited and who can and should represent these communities in research (see Juvonen et al. this vol.). Consequently, the meso level has not been researched as systematically and comprehensively as the other levels.

The contributions to this handbook reflect these circumstances. They address rather different topics that have drawn researchers' attention at this level: social media and the use of technology (chapter 13), grassroots language planning in the era of mobility and the Internet (chapter 14), community language schools (chapter 15), and drivers of home language maintenance and development in indigenous communities (chapter 16). These chapters nevertheless exemplify a continuum, from a rather dispersed ad hoc pooling of resources (chapter 13) to joint action of tight-knit communities (chapter 16).

Chapter 13 signals the transition in discussion from micro level family language policy to the meso level. Here Little (this vol.) discusses social media and the use of technology in home language maintenance. Still focussing very much on the family context, Little points out that social media have the power to connect home language speakers to family (in the wider sense) and to virtual language communities more generally, and that the language of social media may influence children's sense of belonging. Little critically evaluates the tension between motivational advantages and developmental affordances of social media and technology in home language development. She advocates for using technology to actively participate in and interact with the wider community, thus drawing on the community as role models for home language use.

Hatoss (this vol.) further extends and develops the idea of virtual connectedness across physical boundaries in chapter 14. Recognising that linguistic resources are drawn and distributed with the help of the Internet, she explores grassroots language planning from a translocal and transnational perspective. The chapter discusses international examples, with a case study from the context of the South Sudanese Australian community, as illustration of bottom-up joint initiatives with little or no involvement of official authorities. It shows that translocal approaches can provide more equitable access to home languages, and argues that these findings call for reconceptualising grassroots planning theoretically and in practice, based on sociolinguistic theories of mobility.

Moving on to more established activities, Nordstrom (this vol.) reports on "community language schools" in chapter 15. Also known as "ethnic", "supplementary", and "heritage" schools, these are one of the best known and reported initiatives. Many were set in motion by parents, and are good examples of meso level communities' efforts to enhance children's target language maintenance and development, and foster a sense of identity and belonging to the parents' community of origin. These schools can provide spaces where children can explore, contest, and negotiate their flexible and multicultural identities, sometimes questioning the identities imposed upon them by mainstream schools' monoglossic language ideologies. This chapter discusses the challenges and opportunities these schools afford children, families, and communities.

While previous chapters in part 3 focus on migrant communities, Mayer et al. (this vol.) take us to minoritised indigenous languages across the globe in chapter 16. They adopt Ruiz' conceptualisation of language as a resource, right, or problem as framework for their discussion and in light of this review a diversity of family language planning and community based activities developed to maintain, transmit and in some instances revitalise indigenous languages. They then focus on a case study based on Peruvian Amazonian and Andean indigenous languages, comparing the linguistic situation across urban and rural contexts. Their study identifies factors conducive to indigenous language maintenance, and concludes with a sober note about the challenges that these languages face. Mayer et al.'s study in this chapter already touches on, and thus establishes links to, the handbook's next topic area of social justice and inclusiveness.

3.4 The macro level: The role of society in home language maintenance and development

The final part of the handbook, part 4, takes the widest perspective, viewing bilingual speakers as members of society at large. As we pointed out in section 1, economic, cultural, legal and political constraints and expectations, as well as societal norms and language ideologies of the broader community, impact on home language maintenance and development at this level. The chapters in part 4 investigate these sources of impact in two topic areas. The first topic area maintains a broad outlook on society as a whole, discussing social justice and inclusiveness from a number of different angles. The second topic area engages specifically with language learning and teaching, which are amongst this handbook's major areas of interest (see section 1), bringing to the fore issues related to home language maintenance and development that arise in the formal educational context.

3.4.1 Social justice and inclusiveness

As this topic area maintains a broad perspective across society as a whole, each chapter centres around a particular topic in the field. These topics are language policy and planning for language maintenance (chapter 17), language attitudes and ideologies on linguistic diversity (chapter 18), social justice and inclusiveness though implementing linguistic human rights in education (chapter 19), and myths and models of disabilities and home language maintenance and development (chapter 20).

Liddicoat (this vol.) provides an overview of language policy and planning for home language maintenance in chapter 17, a topic traditionally deemed to be situated at the macro level. He contends that "[l]anguage maintenance takes place in a context that is shaped by the ideologies (Albury this vol.) and language practices of a wider society and these constitute the policy context in which decisions are made about maintaining a language or shifting to another." He examines both macro level language policies, which predominantly shape the context for language maintenance or shift, and meso level language policies, which can provide resources and social environments for language learning and language use that may not otherwise be available to the actors. While Mayer et al. (chapter 16, this vol.) can thus be seen as a contribution at the meso level that also touches on macro level aspects, Liddicoat's chapter is a macro level contribution that also takes the meso level into account. Both contributions are thus situated at the interface between these two levels of analysis.

Chapter 18 delves more into what lies behind language policies. Here Albury moves the spotlight to language attitudes and ideologies, as two of the main factors impacting on home language maintenance and development. He argues that a home language has "a greater chance of ongoing vitality – and indeed transmission – if it is prized and valued by society more broadly" (Albury this vol.). Drawing on examples from around the world, he delineates very clearly the theoretical constructs of ideologies and attitudes, and explores the importance of research into language ideologies and attitudes in the context of home language research.

In chapter 19, Annamalai and Tove Skutnabb-Kangas draw heavily on studies of both language policy and planning, and language ideologies and attitudes. They discuss the choice of language in education in relation to choosing a medium of instruction and to acquiring further language competence. Traditionally, they argue, speakers of home languages have not been "privileged historically, politically and economically" (Annamalai and Tove Skutnabb-Kangas this vol.) and need special legal and government support at the local, national and international levels. They set out existing international covenants that could provide the scaffolding for national and local policies, and evaluate multilingual education models. They advocate for equity in education, and for trying to reach social justice through linguistic human rights.

The latter is also addressed by Cheatham and Lim (this vol.) in chapter 20, where they explore myths and models of disabilities in the context of home language maintenance and development. They focus specifically on emergent bilingual students diagnosed with learning disabilities, which is the most commonly diagnosed disability for emergent bilingual students in the US context under discussion in this chapter. After introducing the medical model of disability, which is, in connection with deficit discourse, prevalent in schools, the authors advance the social model of disability as an alternative, thereby also advocating for equity in education. They contend that this approach holds promise for emergent bilingual students with and without a disability diagnosis.

3.4.2 Formal education and home language maintenance

The previous topic area has illuminated aspects of education from a social justice and inclusion perspective, mainly that of bilingual students. The handbook's last topic area shifts from learning to teaching, and explores perspectives on formal education systems and their representatives, the teachers. First, it overviews models of formal education and home language teaching across countries (chapter 21), followed by a discussion of teachers' beliefs and attitudes, i.e., their dispositions and tendencies to react favourably or unfavourably towards home language maintenance (chapter 22). The handbook concludes with a practical perspective in chapter 23, addressing how home language maintenance may be managed and supported in the mainstream classroom.

In chapter 21, Yağmur presents models of formal education and home language teaching across mainly European countries. He too takes up the topic of policies, beginning with an outline of policy perspectives on home language education across four main forms of formal education: pluralistic, civic, assimilationist, and ethnist. He then critically evaluates the policy differences of primary and secondary schools in relation to home languages along nine parameters: target groups, arguments, objectives, evaluation, minimal enrolment, curricular status, funding, teaching materials, and teacher qualifications. Following this, he assesses the status of the various models on this basis. The chapter concludes with the sobering note that "only after full social acceptance of 'immigrant' groups, it will be possible to incorporate their languages in school programs as part of school curriculum" (Yağmur this vol.).

This indicates that social acceptance has a crucial role to play. How do teachers position themselves in this regard? In chapter 22, Mary and Young (this vol.) shed light on the importance of teachers' attitudes and beliefs about children's home languages and the impact these have on practiced language policies, classroom practices more generally, and students' bilingual identities. They also explore some factors potentially contributing to teachers' beliefs and attitudes. These include teachers' prior experience with linguistic and cultural diversity both inside and outside of school, their knowledge gained through teacher education, their own language experiences and ethnic background, and the impact of societal language ideologies on their beliefs. The authors conclude with recommendations for teacher education programs.

Paulsrud highlights the aspect of classroom practices even more in chapter 23. In this final chapter of the handbook, she engages with the question of how home language maintenance may be managed and supported in the mainstream classroom. She introduces ideological and implementational spaces, and translanguaging, as two related theoretical key concepts. She builds on these while discussing selected studies, with a focus on the role of the teacher in the mainstream classroom, and on classroom practices where she argues for a transformative translanguaging stance. Paulsrud concludes this chapter with a positive outlook, declaring her ambition "to take a step away from the deficit perspectives often associated with management of students with other home languages than the majority school language" (Paulsrud this vol.) and instead consider how innovative strategies in classroom management can support students' linguistic diversity.

References

Albury, Nathan J. this vol. Language attitudes and ideologies on linguistic diversity.
Annamalai, E. & Tove Skutnabb-Kangas. this vol. Social justice and inclusiveness through linguistic human rights in education.
Cheatham, Gregory A. & Sumin Lim. this vol. Disabilities and home language maintenance: Myths, models of disability, and equity.
Connaughton-Crean, Lorraine & Pádraig Ó Duibhir. 2017. Home language maintenance and development among first generation migrant children in an Irish primary school: An investigation of attitudes. *Journal of Home Language Research* 2. 22–39.

Curdt-Christiansen, Xiao Lan. 2009. Visible and invisible language planning: Ideological factor in the family language policy of Chinese immigrant families in Quebec. *Language Policy* 8(4). 351–375.
Curdt-Christiansen, Xiao Lan & Jing Huang. this vol. Factors influencing family language policy.
De Houwer, Annick. this vol. Harmonious Bilingualism: Well-being for families in bilingual settings.
Eagly, Alice H. & Shelly Chaiken. 1993. *The psychology of attitudes*. Fort Worth, TX: Harcourt Brace Jovanovich College Publishers.
Eisenchlas, Susana A. & Andrea C. Schalley. this vol. Making sense of the notion of "home language" and related concepts.
Hatoss, Anikó. this vol. Transnational grassroots language planning in the era of mobility and the Internet.
Hult, Francis M. 2010. Introduction. *International Journal of the Sociology of Language* 202. 1–6.
Juvonen, Päivi, Susana A. Eisenchlas, Tim Roberts & Andrea C. Schalley. this vol. Researching social and affective factors in home language maintenance: A methodology overview.
King, Kendall A., Lyn Fogle & Aubrey Logan-Terry. 2008. Family language policy. *Language and Linguistics Compass* 2(5). 907–922.
Lanza, Elizabeth & Rafael Lomeu Gomes. this vol. Family language policy: Foundations, theoretical perspectives and critical approaches.
Liddicoat, Anthony J. this vol. Language policy and planning for language maintenance: The macro and meso levels.
Little, Sabine. this vol. Social media and the use of technology in home language maintenance.
Mary, Latisha & Andrea Young. this vol. Teachers' beliefs and attitudes towards home language maintenance and their effects.
Mayer, Elisabeth, Liliana Sánchez, José Camacho & Carolina Rodríguez Alzza. this vol. Drivers of home language maintenance and development in indigenous communities.
Mesthrie, Rajend & Willian L. Leap. 2000. Language contact I: Maintenance, shift and death. In Rajend Mesthrie, Joan Swann, Andrea Deumert & William L. Leap (eds.), *Introducing sociolinguistics*, 248–278. Edinburgh: Edinburgh University Press.
Nordstrom, Janica. this vol. Community language schools.
Palviainen, Åsa. this vol. Future prospects and visions for family language policy research.
Paulsrud, BethAnne. this vol. The mainstream classroom and home language maintenance.
Purkarthofer, Judith. this vol. Intergenerational challenges: Of handing down languages, passing on practices, and bringing multilingual speakers into being.
Sarnoff, Irving. 1970. Social attitudes and the resolution of motivational conflict. In Marie Jahodaand & Neil Warren (eds.), *Attitudes*, 279–284. Harmondsworth: Penguin.
Schwartz, Mila. this vol. Strategies and practices of home language maintenance.
Sevinç, Yeşim. this vol. Anxiety as a negative emotion in home language maintenance and development.
Smith-Christmas, Cassie. this vol. Child agency and home language maintenance.
Spolsky, Bernard. 2004. *Language policy*. Cambridge: Cambridge University Press.
Tseng, Amelia. this vol. Identity in home-language maintenance.
Wiley, Terrence G. 2014. The problem of defining heritage and community languages and their speakers: On the utility and limitations of definitional constructs. In Terrence G. Wiley, Joy Kreeft Peyton, Donna Christian, Sarah Catherine K. Moore & Na Liu (eds.), *Handbook of heritage, community, and native American languages in the United States: Research, policy, and educational practice*, 33–40. New York: Routledge.
Yağmur, Kutlay. this vol. Models of formal education and minority language teaching across countries.

Part 1: **Terminologies and methodologies**

Susana A. Eisenchlas and Andrea C. Schalley
2 Making sense of "home language" and related concepts

1 Introduction

Reviewing the different conceptualisations of terms used in the field of bilingualism is complicated by ambiguity and diverse disciplinary, geographical, and ideological perspectives. Even a cursory look at the literature reveals a plethora of terms referring to bilinguals/multilinguals and the languages they use. Common terms for these languages include "majority" vs. "minority language", "first" vs. "second language", "environment/mainstream" vs. "home/community language", "foreign" vs. "immigrant/heritage/ancestral language", "native language", "dominant language", "language other than X" (X being the "dominant" language of the country) and "mother tongue". Although these terms are frequently used as synonyms in academic and popular debates, they encode subtle (and not so subtle) conceptual distinctions. However, the precise delimitations of these terms are not clear, and none appears to be able to capture the different dimensions encountered in research and practice. There is no one-size-fits-all term that can be drawn upon, in line with Wiley's (2014: 19) remark that "any attempt to apply a single label to a complex situation is problematic."

Despite these definitional challenges, we need to explore and problematise the terms and their underlying concepts. As Skutnabb-Kangas and McCarty (2008: 3) argue:

> The concepts we use are almost never neutral. In contested arenas such as bilingual education, words and concepts frame and construct the phenomena under discussion, making some persons and groups visible, others invisible; some the unmarked norm, others marked and negative. Choice of language can minoritise or distort some individuals, groups, phenomena and relations while majoritising and glorifying others. Concepts also can be defined in ways that hide, expose, rationalise or question power relations.

In this chapter, we use "bilingual" to refer also to "multilingual", as the issues we discuss are relevant to all who operate in more than one language.[1] Bilingualism can be studied as an individual and as a societal phenomenon (Cenoz 2013; Edwards 2013). It has been investigated through diverse disciplinary perspectives,

---

[1] However, we also acknowledge a burgeoning literature suggesting that multilinguals should be studied separately, focusing in particular on the impact of bilingualism on the acquisition of additional languages. See Cenoz (2003) for an overview.

with research drawing on linguistics, psycholinguistics, cognitive psychology, sociology, education, speech pathology, and other related fields. Each discipline raises specific questions and constructs its object of inquiry according to its paradigms, so the absence of both a uniform view of the phenomena under investigation and consistent terminology to refer to them is not surprising.

The lack of terminological consensus has theoretical implications. As Grosjean (1998) noted, research on both bilingualism and its potential benefits is plagued with conflicting results, which may stem partially from imprecision both in terminology and in identifying moderating factors that may impact on bilingual achievement (e.g., age of onset, socioeconomic status, and languages used). This may have deleterious consequences, since many educational decisions at the macro level of language policy planning – including issues such as teacher training and professional development – could be based on misleading research findings.

There are also practical implications, as can be seen in education, clinical practice and other areas (De Houwer and Ortega 2018). Education policies in many Anglophone countries, for instance, have traditionally taken a deficit view of the languages of bilingual children. This can affect teachers' expectations of such students (Pulinx, Van Avermaet, and Agirdag 2015), leading, e.g., to wrong diagnoses of learning difficulties, which are often attributed to the linguistic diversity to which a student is exposed when other non-linguistic factors may be at play (see Cheatham and Lim this vol.). This conceptualises additional languages as handicaps that prevent students from achieving their full potential.

This chapter aims to help set the scene for the handbook by discussing terminological choices in the literature on bilingualism. Research on bilingualism has continued to reach into new contexts, so a single chapter cannot adequately address all the terminological issues raised by the many terms currently in use. We therefore restrict our discussion to the terms used in contexts most relevant to this handbook, and by corollary, to the scholarly fields most closely related to the handbook's topic: (applied) linguistics and education.

We begin by asking, "what does it mean to be bilingual?", and discuss methodological and theoretical difficulties in trying to answer this question without ambiguity (section 2). We then critically evaluate the terms used to refer to the non-mainstream languages in the bilingual's repertoire that are most commonly encountered in the field of home language maintenance and development (section 3). Section 4 compares and contrasts the distinctive characteristics of the selected terms, anchoring them in a multi-dimensional space comprising linguistic and speaker dimensions as well as social and affective ones. Finally, we explain the choice of "home language" for this volume – for lack of a better alternative – in the chapter's conclusion in section 5.

2 What does it mean to be "bilingual"? Definitions and challenges

In his now classic book, *Bilingualism: Basic principles*, Baetens Beardsmore argues that "bilingualism as a concept has open-ended semantics" (1986: 1). He regrets that definitions are continually "being proffered without any real sense of progress being felt as the list extends" (Baetens Beardsmore 1986: 1). Definitions range between maximalist and minimalist perspectives, based on the threshold of linguistic competence a speaker is expected to attain to be considered "bilingual". The maximalist or narrowest view considers bilingualism as "native-like control of two languages" (Bloomfield 1935: 55–56). This is the definition of the mythical, idealised, "true" bilingual.

Yet, most researchers realise that this high expectation is seldom met. They propose more realistic, yet somewhat vague, views of a bilingual, such as "someone who operates during their everyday life in more than one language and does so with some degree of self-confidence" (Miller 1983: x). Similarly, Li (2008: 4) defines a bilingual as "anyone who can communicate in more than one language, be it active (through speaking and writing) or passive (through listening and reading)". Edwards (2004: 7) offers a minimalist perspective, opening his article on the foundations of bilingualism with the claim:

> Everyone is bilingual. That is, there is no one in the world (no adult, anyway) who does not know at least a few words in languages other than the maternal variety. If, as an English speaker, you can say *c'est la vie* or *gracias* or *guten Tag* or *tovarisch* – or even if you only understand them – you clearly have some "command" of a foreign tongue. Such competence, of course, does not lead many to think of bilingualism.

In Edwards' view, incipient bilinguals with minimal competence (cf. Diebold 1961), such as second/foreign language learners in their initial stages of linguistic development, would also be included under the umbrella term "bilingualism". This inclusion embraces the variety of acquisition contexts and linguistic experiences of bilinguals, some of which acquire their language(s) in the home context since birth, while others learn their language(s) in more formal settings, usually later in life. Whether these two populations should be conflated is a matter of debate. A problem with the minimalist perspective is that the definition becomes too encompassing and thus uninformative or unwieldy. The threshold that speakers need to attain to be considered bilingual continues to be contested (Baker and Wright 2017).[2]

---

[2] It is for this reason that we interpret "speaker" broadly in this chapter, to also include, for instance, passive bilinguals.

The degree of linguistic competence in the bilinguals' languages is thus significant. It is the basis upon which speakers have been classified and conceptualised, and has given rise to a number of dichotomies and categories encountered in the literature, such as "balanced" (a.k.a. ambilinguals; equilinguals; ideal or symmetrical bilinguals) vs. "unbalanced" (a.k.a. asymmetrical; semilinguals), or "ascendant" or "active" vs. "recessive" or "passive".

Measuring levels of linguistic competence is not, however, a straightforward process, raising both theoretical and methodological challenges. The narrow definitions above, for instance, assume that "native-like proficiency" is a self-explanatory term, but operationalising it is extremely difficult given the amount of variability monolingual speakers display.[3] Thus Clyne (2005: 30) remarked: "Even a monolingual's 'perfect' command of their 'one' language is undefinable." Moreover, scholars agree there are several areas of abilities, and each of the macro skills (i.e., listening, speaking, reading, and writing) can be subdivided further. Edwards (2004) posits that at least 20 dimensions of language can be assessed to determine bilingual proficiency. He exemplifies his claim with speaking, arguing that speaking involves skills related to the richness (or poverty) of expression in vocabulary, grammatical accuracy, and level of accentedness. Similar subdivisions also apply to the other macro skills. Therefore, decisions need to be made about minimal thresholds for each of the macro skills, and about how to classify users with high levels of proficiency (setting aside the problem of how these are measured) in some skills (typically oral) but not in others (typically written).

Furthermore, knowledge of a language implies much more than mastery of a linguistic system. Speakers need to develop competence in determining what is appropriate to say to whom in particular contexts, and how to interpret meaning beyond what is actually said. However, there is still no consensus on how to operationalise and assess speakers' level of pragmatic or sociocultural competence (Bardovi-Harlig 2012; Grabowsky 2016). Measuring levels of communicative competence, i.e. the ability to use language accurately and appropriately, is complicated in one language, and testing each additional language in the bilingual's repertoire increases the challenge.

The discussion about the degree of bilingualism a speaker needs to attain to be categorised as bilingual appears to assume bilingualism refers mostly to a linguistic phenomenon. It ignores or downplays other influential non-linguistic dimensions of the concept, such as social and affective factors which are the focus of this handbook. As mentioned above, some researchers have recognised other dimensions that impact on bilingual attainment. Some have therefore proposed that any

---

[3] What counts as a distinct language can also be hard to establish in some cases. Current discussions around "named languages" in the translanguaging literature suggest that for some scholars "named languages are social, not linguistic, objects" (Otheguy, García, and Reid 2015: 281).

account of bilingualism needs to recognise the complexity of the phenomenon and resist one-dimensional characterisations. Thus Chin and Wigglesworth (2007: 18) argue that "bilingualism is not a concrete entity that can be quantified or dissected", and that using descriptors (such as age of acquisition, context of acquisition, degree of bilingualism, domain of use of each language) is more appropriate than constructing a general definition of bilingualism.

With this aim, a number of models have been proposed to characterise bilinguals. The precise number and nature of dimensions included in these models are still a matter of debate. Here we do not have space to discuss the different proposals, and can only outline them briefly. The model in Skutnabb-Kangas (1988), one of the most widely cited, proposes four aspects to describe bilinguals: origin – which language the speaker acquired first; competence – which language the speaker knows best; function – which language the speaker uses most; and identification – which language the speaker uses to associate with or disassociate from others. Baker and Wright (2017: 3–4) identify eight: (1) ability; (2) use; (3) balance; (4) age of onset; (5) development (i.e., whether bilingualism is ascendant or recessive); (6) culture; (7) contexts; and (8) choice. Grosjean (1998) identifies six: linguistic history; linguistic abilities; linguistic stability; language functions; language proficiency; language mode (i.e., whether one or two languages are activated); and demographic information. Along similar lines, Leung, Harris, and Rampton (1997) argue for three: language expertise; language inheritance; and language affiliation.

These dimensions are by no means as straightforward as the models cited above suggest. Although usually expressed as categorical constructs, mostly they should be seen as continuous (Butler and Hakuta 2004). Drawing clear boundaries between diverse types of bilinguals within a given dimension is therefore difficult. Furthermore, dimensions interact and impact on one another, and in some instances are interdependent. To give just one example, linguistic competence may be enhanced and further developed through language use, but at the same time, it influences the range of contexts in which each of the languages can be used, which in turn affects the purposes for which a language is used. Consequently, some dimensions appear to cluster together. Instructional domains, for instance, seem to characterise late, elective, additive, probably prestige bilingualism. Finally, it is widely recognised that bilingualism is a dynamic phenomenon and thus a bilingual's profile may change over time. Despite these limitations, categorisations are still useful as a means of framing the discussion, and thus they will serve as the basis for our analysis in section 4.

While the term "bilingualism" is open to different interpretations, further complicating the situation are the different terms used to refer to bilingual speakers' non-mainstream languages. Maintenance and development of these languages are in focus in this handbook, so let us turn to these terms in the next section.

3 Alternative terms to refer to non-mainstream languages spoken by bilingual speakers

Implicitly or explicitly, the terms referring to non-mainstream languages in bilingual repertoires – and their underlying concepts – encode differences in perspectives, along the lines of dimensions such as the ones identified above. In this section we unpack some of these terms, aiming to unveil conceptual and attitudinal implications underpinning their use, as well as the dimensions they foreground. We address the key question: Which term is used when, where, by whom, and with what purpose? Given the plethora of terms in use, we restrict our discussion to the terms most relevant to this handbook, and discuss "minority language", "first language", mother tongue", "heritage language", some commonly used abbreviations and acronyms, and "home language".

3.1 Minority language

We begin with "minority language", since most of the terms used to describe languages of bilingual speakers and contexts hinge on the dichotomy between "majority" and "minority" languages. Skutnabb-Kangas and McCarty (2008: 10) define a minority language as a "[l]anguage that is not the dominant language of a territorial unit such as a state, because the speakers of the language have less power (they have been minoritised), and the language is generally spoken by a smaller number of people." They argue, however, that the defining characteristic of "minority language" is its speakers' lesser power in society rather than its speaker number. As Nelde, Strubell, and Williams (1996: 1) put it, "the concept of minority by reference to language groups does not refer to empirical measures, but rather, to issues of power." They add that these minority groups "lack the political, institutional and ideological structures which can guarantee the relevance of those languages for the everyday life of members of such groups" (Nelde, Strubell, and Williams 1996: 1).

State ideologies, particularly the equation between the nation-state and linguistic homogeneity, serve to legitimise, regulate, and reproduce unequal access to power and resources (Skutnabb-Kangas 1988), entrenching inequality among diverse linguistic groups. Thus, the lack of state support for "minority languages" within a state's territories, including restrictions on both access to allocation of resources and inclusion in educational curricula, further minoritises languages, regardless of the number of speakers. Historical examples in former colonial territories attest to this. Cameroon, for instance, has two official languages (French and English), one lingua franca (Cameroon Pidgin English), and 247 indigenous languages. The two official languages are the languages of instruction, while the indigenous languages and Cameroon Pidgin English are excluded from the education system (Echu 2004).

Two dimensions, both of a social nature, thus appear to be foregrounded by "minority language": the territorial unit (or state) as the restricted social context, and the language group's lack of power and minoritisation in that context.

3.2 First language (L1)

Focusing on the individual, the term "first language" (L1) is probably the most commonly used, but also the most ambiguous and prone to diverse interpretations. L1 is often used as a synonym for "mother tongue" and "home language" and contrasted with second (L2) or foreign language (FL). Naturally, all speakers have a "first language", including speakers of a mainstream language.

Part of the confusion around this term may stem from its inherent ambiguity, since there are several dimensions in which a language can be "first". Skutnabb-Kangas and McCarty (2008: 6) define "first language" as "the language first learnt, best known, and/or most used." This definition entails three aspects: acquisition sequence, proficiency, and extent of use. In bilingual contexts, the "first language" tends to be the "minority language", which may be dominant, and thus the speaker's most proficient language, during the early years of life, but loses its dominance once the speaker begins schooling in the mainstream language. When/if this happens, the first chronological language ceases to be the language that is "known best", and this descriptor then applies to the mainstream language (which may be the second in order of acquisition). Similarly, the first chronological language may be used only in limited contexts, such as the family. This applies particularly in the absence of a community of speakers of that language and/or when there is no institutional support to maintain and develop languages other than the mainstream. Here the mainstream language becomes the "most used", while the "first" chronological language is used in restricted circumstances.

For "first language" to be helpful, then, its meaning needs to be clarified. Some scholars appear to use this term to refer to the dominant language of a speaker, but this assumes that a dominant language in a speaker's life remains dominant throughout their life, a questionable assumption given the dynamic nature of speakers' lives, linguistic repertoires, and language needs.

From this discussion, we suggest that the most salient dimension of "first language" appears to be acquisition sequence: the "first language" is the one acquired first chronologically. This goes hand in hand with the language being acquired in a non-instructional way, as is typically the case with first languages. It follows that the age of onset is early childhood, and during this life period at least some proficiency is guaranteed (which, as we saw in the discussion of the usage domains, could be quite restricted). While the dimensions for "minority language" are social, the dimensions for "first language" thus mainly concern the individual speaker.

3.3 Mother tongue

"Mother tongue" is another commonly used term, particularly in collocations such as "mother tongue instruction". It appears to be prevalent in the education context and in human rights literature. Yet, defining it is not straightforward.

UNESCO uses the term in recommending efforts be made to provide initial education in the mother tongue "because they [students] *understand it best* and because to begin their school life in the mother tongue will make the break between home and school as small as possible" (UNESCO 1951: 691; emphasis added). This description of a mother tongue assumes speakers' proficiency, but the reference to *understanding* seems to privilege oral/aural skills, while disregarding other aspects of communicative competence.

Other definitions of "mother tongue" highlight diverse aspects. Skutnabb-Kangas and McCarty define "mother tongue" as "[l]anguage one *learns first, identifies with,* and/or *is identified by others as a native speaker of*; sometimes also the *language that one is most competent in* or *uses most*" (2008: 11; emphasis added). This definition is problematic, however, as it bundles together separate optional dimensions without problematising them further. Yet, unlike UNESCO's characterisation, this definition recognises that someone may know one language best but feel stronger emotional attachment to another, which they have learned and used at home and associate with their early subjective experiences.

Some in the field object to the use of "mother tongue". Romaine (1995: 18), for example, argues that the term suggests that mothers are "the passive repositories of languages, which they pass on to their children". While this is a very literal reading of the term, one can easily find such interpretations outside the field of bilingualism research. The term's underlying assumption is that mothers, as primary caretakers of children, are ultimately responsible for intergenerational language transmission. Yet this is no longer the case in many modern societies. Furthermore, as several scholars noted (Gupta 1997; Romaine 1995), determining an actual mother tongue is in many instances not a straightforward process, particularly in mixed families where children may not have a single identifiable mother tongue.

At a societal level, deciding which language is the mother tongue has significant real-life implications, including having or being denied the right to receive instruction in a specific language. Countries like Sweden, that offer students supplementary mother tongue instruction, do so for only one "mother tongue". Hence parents must select one "mother tongue", even if their children speak additional languages at home. In Singapore, the state designates the official language of one's ethnic group as the "mother tongue", which students must study as a school subject.⁴ The question thus has to be asked whether the term "mother tongue" is indeed the right term to be used in these societal contexts, as it has acquired a different meaning from the one adopted by UNESCO for individual speakers.

Overall, we can conclude that speakers' identification is the most foregrounded dimension for this term. Generally, a "mother tongue" is seen as transmitted by the parents, and it is contextualised in the family. We see, too, that a substantial level of proficiency is required for a language to be considered a speaker's "mother tongue".

3.4 Heritage language

"Heritage language" has its origins in the education literature and policy circles (Valdés 2001; Wiley 2014) and became prominent in the USA and Canada in the 1990s (Wiley 2014).⁵ It was introduced as a replacement for the language of "quasi-speakers", to move away from the deficit perspective that this term purported. This was an attempt to convey a richer and more accurate account of the "non-mainstream" language component in bilingual repertoires. It sought to cast a more positive light on "heritage" or "background speakers", who were typically contrasted negatively with both native speakers and second language learners. In principle, the concept of "heritage language" includes all languages, since, as Cummins (2005) notes, mainstream speakers also have a heritage. In practice, however, the term is reserved expressly for speakers of languages other than the mainstream. Heritage speakers have been identified as "those whose home or ancestral language is [a language] other than English, including those whose ancestors lived in this country prior to the establishment of the United States and those who have come in recent years" (Alliance for the Advancement of Heritage Languages, n.d., cited in Cummins 2005: 586).

Other definitions, however, downplay the centrality of linguistic proficiency, and instead foreground the affiliative dimension. Van Deusen-Scholl (2003: 221), for instance, defines heritage speakers as "a heterogenous group ranging from fluent native speakers to nonspeakers who may be generations removed but who may feel culturally connected to the language". Valdés (2001: 2) observes similarly, "it is

---

4 The official Singaporean "mother tongues" are Malay, Mandarin and Tamil. Additionally, non-Tamil Indian students have a choice between five Indian languages: Bengali, Gujarati, Hindi, Punjabi, and Urdu (Jain and Wee 2015).
5 Cummins (2005) notes that the term emerged in Canada in 1977 with the inception of the Ontario Heritage Languages, but only became prominent in the USA in the late 1990s in the context of public policy.

the historical and personal connection to the language that is salient and not the actual proficiency of individual speakers". Thus, a speaker may claim – or be ascribed – a "heritage language" because that language has affective family connections for the speaker. This affiliation or attribution neither implies nor excludes actual proficiency in the language. As Gounari (2014: 257) notes, for the heritage language "survival and maintenance is justified upon its historical and personal value, and not on real current societal needs. It follows then that the maintenance of HLs [heritage languages] rests with the individuals and the communities and not with the State or the federal government."

Like all concepts in the field of bilingualism, the term "heritage language" has been challenged by some scholars. Baker and Jones (1998: 509) argue that:

> The danger of the term 'heritage language' is that, relative to powerful majority languages, it points more to the past and less to the future, to traditions rather than to the contemporary. The danger is that the heritage language becomes associated with ancient cultures, past traditions and more 'primitive times.' This is also true of the terms 'ethnic' (used in the US) and 'ancestral.' These terms may fail to give the impression of a modern, international language that is of value in a technological society.

Significantly, scholars may use and understand terms such as "heritage language" purely as academic jargon. Yet those terms could still take on a more "naive" meaning in the public discourse – and/or in policymaking. It is therefore relevant not to ignore the potential impact of such terms on social attitudes.

A further criticism relates to the essentialist view of speech communities that the concept entails, with scholars increasingly challenging the notion of a linguistic inheritance as the basis to classify speakers. As Gounari (2014: 260) asks poignantly, "whose heritage is maintained and who decided on it?". García, Zakharia, and Otcu (2013: 34) argue that "[l]anguage and ethnicity are not simple reflections of 'heritage speech' communities, or of 'practice communities'." Individuals can simultaneously belong to or identify with several groups, and their agency allows them to select which features of their identity to foreground or background in specific contexts. This includes selecting which language in their linguistic repertoire to use, according to time, space, and situation. Rather than being homogeneous entities, communities are composed of individuals that juggle multiple linguistic and cultural identities. And in multilingual contexts, this agency even affords individuals the freedom to engage in "language crossing" and using languages (in addition to the mainstream) that are generally not assumed to "belong" to the speaker (Rampton 1998).

From an educational perspective, scholars (e.g., Polinsky and Kagan 2007; Carreira and Kagan 2011) have distinguished between "broad" and "narrow" definitions of heritage language and heritage language speakers. A broad definition of heritage language emphasises the strong connections between cultural heritage and linguistic heritage, transmitted through family interactions. This perspective highlights the identification dimension, since the individual adopts or is assigned a language as part of their heritage by virtue of being born into a particular community, without implying competence in that language. A narrower definition casts heritage language as a language that "was first in the order of acquisition but was not completely acquired because of the individual's switch to another dominant language" since early childhood (Polinsky and Kagan 2007: 369), which takes us back to the question "what does it mean to be bilingual?".

Different experiences with the heritage language make for wide variation among speakers, ranging from basic (minimally, in aural skills) to advanced levels of competence across skills. Even so, scholars agree that linguistic production and comprehension of heritage speakers fall short of those of the native speaker, who is taken as the yardstick for comparison (Montrul 2002; Polinsky 2006). The view that heritage language speakers acquire their heritage language incompletely entails a negative stance, as evident in discussion about the pedagogical challenges of providing language instruction for heritage learners (Valdés 2005: 410).[6] Ruiz's (1984) perspective of "language as a problem" comes to mind here.

As our discussion reveals, several dimensions come into play for the term "heritage language". Most prominent and hence foregrounded is the felt connection between cultural and linguistic heritage. As to the identification dimension, speakers identify with or are assigned to "heritage languages" for social reasons (e.g., being born into a particular community). Furthermore, some scholars see the term as oriented towards the past, which could have unwanted repercussions in public discourse and policymaking, as indicated above.

3.5 Abbreviations and acronyms

Here we focus briefly on a few of the most commonly used abbreviations and acronyms. These terms are very prominent and influential in the educational discourse of at least some (Anglophone) countries, and education is one of the main fields under discussion in this handbook. As in the previous section (3.4), the terms we discuss here reveal a "language-as-a-problem" orientation in language policy (Ruiz 1984; Skutnabb-Kangas and McCarty 2008), which is also referred to as a deficit perspective (Yağmur 2015). We find that these terms foreground what their speakers lack rather than the competencies they display.

---

[6] See Valdés (2005) for a discussion of problems associated with teaching heritage language speakers. One problem is that many heritage language speakers use stigmatised varieties and thus may face discrimination from teachers of the standard varieties of those languages.

A clear example is the term "Limited English Proficiency" (LEP), found in US language policy documents. Skutnabb-Kangas and McCarty (2008) note a move in 2001 to substitute this term with the term "English Language Learner" (ELL), to convey a more positive association. However, ELL, like LEP, still identifies speakers of other languages by their lack, or limited knowledge, of the mainstream language, while ignoring or devaluing the other language(s) and cultures they know. Similarly, the terms "Languages Other Than English" (LOTE) or "Non-English-Speaking Background" (NESB) have been common in Australian language policies and education documents. Attempts to convey a more inclusive view of languages and speakers have seen these terms replaced by ever more abbreviations and acronyms that rapidly fall out of favour. In a guide produced by the New South Wales Department of Education (2015) for appropriate terminology to refer to people from culturally and linguistically diverse backgrounds, the following terms stand out:
- CALD, "culturally and linguistically diverse backgrounds/communities" (which includes all communities except the Anglo-Saxon);
- LBOTE, "language background other than English"; and
- EAL/D, "English as an additional language or dialect".

Despite the seemingly good intentions, these labels still imply a binary distinction between those who speak Standard Australian English and those who do not. The well-intended guide inadvertently implies that only the latter are (visible) members of communities, belong to ethnic groups, and require "additional support to assist them to develop proficiency in English" (ACARA n.d.). "Additional dialects" refers not to other recognised varieties of English such as New Zealand, British, or Canadian English, but to traditional languages, creoles and related varieties or Aboriginal English, namely, stigmatised varieties.

In terms of dimensions, the deficit or "language-as-a-problem" ideological perspective stands out clearly, and the terms are restricted to the education domain. Moreover, they are understood to apply exclusively to the languages of minority groups, even though some of the notions may try to display a more inclusive attitude, as discussed above.

3.6 Home language

We conclude this overview of selected terms used to refer to bilinguals' non-mainstream languages with the discussion of "home language", the term used in the handbook's title. Unlike most other terms examined in this chapter, "home language" explicitly refers to a specific domain of use, the home. The home language is thus understood as the language spoken in the home environment. But this domain specification is not to imply that participants in family interactions limit the use of their language(s) to the home domain, as some objectors to this term have suggested (cf., e.g., Cunningham 2019).[7] Rather, the home is understood to provide a "point of reference" from which speakers navigate the world; it is the space where negotiations on language use at the micro level predominantly take place. This is highlighted by the field of family language policy research, where studies on "home language" focus on the communicative practices in which families engage, and attempt to document and understand individual and family driven language policy and planning activities.

In this context, "home language" highlights a dynamic outlook built on speakers' agency. Language prominence and use in bilingual families are subject to constant renegotiation, as speakers change their language use in accordance with their perception of the context in which they find themselves at different points in time. Moreover, "home language" implies a sense of contingency; for instance, children will leave the home at some stage, families may disintegrate and blend with others, or particular languages may be abandoned and replaced through migration (cf. also Palviainen this vol.).

It seems obvious that every speaker – of mainstream or other languages – has a "home language". However, as we have seen with previous terms, this term too is generally used in a restricted sense to refer to non-mainstream languages, as is true for many chapters of this handbook. Even so, despite using the term in singular rather than plural, discussion in these chapters recognises that everyday communication in some families is complex and might involve more than one language. The continuous (re)negotiation of language use in everyday communication also shows that, in contrast to "heritage language" potentially being understood as pointing towards the past (rightly or wrongly), "home language" is set in the present.

Beyond this is an under-specification of other dimensions. In terms of linguistic competence, for instance, "home language" accommodates a wide gamut of abilities ranging from limited to native-like proficiency in the language(s). Yet speakers need at least some proficiency for communication to take place. Similarly, in terms of identity and inheritance, speakers, in particular children, vary widely, as some of the chapters that follow illustrate. Some children identify strongly with the home language, as we see in this excerpt from Ahmed, interviewed by Mills (2001) about why he uses the term "home language":

---

[7] Replacing the term *hemspråk* (home language) with *modersmål* (mother tongue) in the Swedish education system (creating the subject *modersmålundervisning*, mother tongue instruction) in 1997 was intended to emphasise that *modersmål* is another language that can be taught in school, rather than used "only" at home. This move also reflected the subject's stronger position in the curriculum (Erica Sandlund; Nihad Bunar, both personal communication).

> Because Pakistan, even though I was born here, I class Pakistan as my home country. That's where the language originates from, so I call it my home language. We speak it at home and like with my family and friends, well some friends. So, I call it my home language because that's one of the languages that I like to express things. (Ahmed, cited in Mills 2001: 398)

Others, however, show no identification with their so-called "home language" and challenge what they perceive as a linguistic imposition from their parents (see Sevinç and Smith-Christmas, both in this volume). This has potential to turn the home into a source of linguistic anxiety, or a linguistic battlefield. Matters of identification are generally dynamic, too, and the above-mentioned sense of contingency suggests that feelings of identity and affiliation may change across speakers' lifespans.

Summing up, the foregrounded dimension appears to be identification. Speakers negotiate their identification in the home, which in turn constitutes the general usage domain of this term. The term's group context is neither the territorial unit nor the community (as it was for "minority language" and "heritage language", respectively), but the family. Moreover, home language speakers are expected to display at least some proficiency in their current home language(s).

4 Comparing and contrasting the terms

So far we have tried to isolate the most prevalent dimensions highlighted by each term. We are aware that these presentations somewhat oversimplify the complexity of bilingualism, but we need to identify them in order to conceptualise the interplay of the dimensions discussed in the previous section. In this section we attempt to systematise the dimensions that contribute to our understanding and usage of each of the terms. Table 1 overviews these dimensions and their respective dimensional values, and indicates how these dimensions differentiate and characterise the terms.

Table 1 identifies a number of different types of dimensions, ranging from linguistic and speaker dimensions to social and affective dimensions. The relevant dimensions for each type are indicated in the columns and displayed in italics across the table (e.g., *proficiency* as linguistic dimension, *acquisition sequence* as speaker dimension, *ideological underpinning* as social dimension, and *identification* as affective dimension). Rows characterise the terms listed in the first column. Empty cells in the table signal that the dimension in question is not relevant to the characterisation or to the definition of that term. Otherwise, cell content indicates the specific value assigned to a particular dimension. Cell values in bold indicate that this dimension is considered the most important specification dimension for a term.

Table 1: Overview of the dimensions and values that differentiate and characterise the terms.

Term	Linguistic dimension	Speaker dimensions				Social dimensions				Affective dimensions	
	proficiency	age of onset	acquisition sequence	initial acquisition type	usage domains	group context	group status	group influence	ideological underpinning	identification	orientation
Minority language						territorial unit		not powerful			
First language	at least some (in early childhood)	early childhood	first	non-instructional							
Mother tongue	substantial					family				transmitted by parents (individual)	
Heritage language						community	minority		cultural	ascribed by the society/community (societal)	past
Abbreviations and acronyms					education		minority		deficit / language as a problem		
Home language	at least some (presently)				home	family	minority			negotiated in the home	present

4.1 Dimensions

We start with some general observations of the dimensions themselves. Only one linguistic dimension, proficiency, plays a role in characterising the terms. However, proficiency does not constitute a primary dimension for any of the terms. Terms such as "home language" and "first language" express the expectation that speakers have at least some proficiency (in contrast to "heritage language"). Yet, this is not foregrounded for any of the terms, since linguistic proficiency is not a determining dimension for the terms discussed here. Instead, a broad range of proficiency levels is accounted for.

In relation to speaker dimensions, three of the four dimensions concern the individual speaker's acquisition history (recording when acquisition started, in which order languages were acquired, and how acquisition took place), while only one dimension relates to the context in which speakers operate, namely, the usage domain. Moreover, for only one term, "first language", is a speaker dimension foregrounded: "first language" is by default defined as the language that is first acquired in life[8] (which in turn results in it being characterised as acquired in a non-instructional way during early childhood).

A similar picture eventuates for the social dimensions, with three of the four sharing a relational perspective on the speaker group (what kind of group it is and in what context it is couched, which status the group has in society, and which level of societal influence the group may have), while the fourth dimension addresses the ideological underpinning stakeholders entertain in relation to a specific term. Matters of influence (i.e., power) and ideology are essential to the definition of terms, indicating (i) relative powerlessness for "minority language", and (ii) a cultural ideological underpinning for "heritage language", and a deficit ("language-as-a-problem") underpinning for abbreviations and acronyms.

Finally, one of the two affective dimensions reaches directly to the core of affective factors (identification), while the other addresses whether the respective terms orient speakers towards their past or situate them in the present. However, the only dimension foregrounded is identification, primarily distinguishing "mother tongue" from "home language". The former is perceived to be associated with the individual speaker (indicating a stable characteristic of the single individual – speakers cannot "loose" their mother tongue from an identification point of view), while for the latter, identification is subject to negotiation (indicating a dynamically adapting, contextual specification, in line with the identification with home languages potentially changing as a result of life experiences and in interactions with others).

---

[8] But see the discussion in section 3.2.

4.2 Terms

We now turn to a more in-depth discussion and comparison of the terms themselves. A quick glance at the table shows that some of the terms are restricted in their definitional dimensions to only some of the types of dimension. For instance, "minority language" is defined exclusively by social dimensions, disregarding the other three dimensional types. This probably results in the term being considered more as a general term, lending itself to a wide variety of discussions, and in particular to those at the meso and macro levels of research.[9]

"First language" functions similarly in that it predominantly displays speaker dimension specifications, with the notion that first language speakers must have had at least some proficiency in their early childhood, which in turn connects tightly to them having acquired the language as their first chronological language. "First language" is thus not specified with regards to social or to affective dimensions, so is likely to be used less often in discussions of social and affective factors in home language maintenance.

"Heritage language" and the abbreviations and acronyms also disregard two types of dimensions, the linguistic dimension for both terms, as well as the speaker dimensions in the case of "heritage language" and the affective dimensions in the case of the abbreviations and acronyms. This can be taken as an indicator that "heritage language" does not make any assumption as to who the speakers are (and whether they speak the language at all), while the abbreviations and acronyms are disconnected from affective aspects, thus emphasising the more managerial perspective often found in educational approaches to bilingualism.

"Mother tongue", in line with "heritage language" and "minority language", disregards speaker dimensions, indicating similarly the wide variety of speaker background characteristics that the term covers. However, of all the terms discussed here, this is the term that assumes the highest level of proficiency. Finally, "home language" displays a breadth in its specification that ranges across all four dimensional types. It shares a number of dimensions (but differing values) with "mother tongue", which indicates a relationship between these two terms. This and sharing the primary dimension of identification (yet with different values, as discussed above) are likely to contribute to the intuition that "mother tongue" and "home language" are not only very closely related, but are also found often in discussions of social and affective factors in home language maintenance.

Some of the terms are uniquely specified, in that they are the only ones for which a particular dimension takes a value. This applies, for instance, to "first language",

---

[9] However, note that the value assignment as "not powerful" may pre-empt use of the term in some social settings, for instance in cases where colonial languages or languages of the ruling class were imposed top-down. Although such speakers may not comprise the majority, it is inappropriate to refer to their language as the "minority language" since they hold the power.

which is the only term for which an acquisition sequence is specified. Similarly, "minority language" appears to be the only term that points to a societal group of speakers perceived as not powerful. These unique specifications impact on when and how scholars use such terms, as they highlight and foreground rather unique characteristics.

Other values assigned to the terms also impact on decisions about using them, with scholars most likely to choose the terms that foreground aspects most relevant for their discussion, while downplaying or disregarding others. For instance, "heritage language" suits best in work on language anxiety (such as in Sevinç this vol.), as it highlights the environment's identification ascription and speakers' cultural community membership, while downplaying any assignment of proficiency and acquisition history.

5 Conclusion

This chapter has illustrated how terms frequently used as synonyms for non-mainstream languages encode their own distinctive concepts. We have compared and contrasted the terms' conceptual dimensions, as well as the values (if any) each term assigns to these dimensions. Clearly, there is no one-size-fits-all term that can be used for nuanced discussion, since bilingualism is multifaceted and perspectives taken in research and practice range widely. Neither is there a single "best" term, as each of these terms foregrounds different dimensions and hence aspects.

This handbook clearly favours one term over the others, though. Both title and many of the chapters use "home language". As we have explained, "home language" is a dynamic term referring to interactional contexts where social units of speakers, the families, negotiate language use in the here and now. This term is therefore highly conducive to work on the micro level, in particular to discussions of family language policy, highlighting the actual practices found in these family units. Moreover, "home language" has no ideological underpinning, in contrast to many other terms used in the field of educational research. It also appears to be a good choice for educational contexts. The term's obvious limitation, however, is that it specifies the domain of language usage, restricting this domain to a speaker's home. Here we have argued that "home" is not the same as "house one lives in" (i.e., the physical space), and should be understood more broadly as referring to a "point of reference" from which speakers navigate the world. As such, the term is also well-suited to meso and macro level discussions, such as those concerned with formal education.

Last but not least, "home language" highlights both social and affective dimensions, without taking a strong stance. This term is not about power relationships, it does not address cultural community membership, and it does not impart a "language-as-problem" perspective. Aspects of identification are not ascribed by others, but are negotiated dynamically by speakers themselves. This is why we see "home language" as a rather neutral term – and the best terminological choice for this handbook.[10]

References

ACARA (Australian Curriculum, Assessment and Reporting Authority). n.d. *Students for whom EAL/D*. https://www.australiancurriculum.edu.au/resources/student-diversity/students-for-whom-eald/ (accessed 3 October 2019).
Alliance for the Advancement of Heritage Languages. n.d. *Guiding principles of the Alliance*. http://www.cal.org/heritage/index (accessed 29 July 2005).
Baetens Beardsmore, Hugo. 1986. *Bilingualism: Basic principles*. 2nd edn. Clevedon: Multilingual Matters.
Baker, Colin & Sylvia P. Jones. 1998. *Encyclopedia of bilingual education and bilingualism*. Clevedon: Multilingual Matters.
Baker, Colin & Wayne E. Wright. 2017. *Foundations of bilingual education and bilingualism*. 6th edn. Clevedon: Multilingual Matters.
Bardovi-Harlig, Kathleen. 2012. Pragmatics in SLA. In Susan. M. Gass & Alison Mackey (eds.), *The Routledge handbook of second language acquisition*, 147–162. New York: Routledge.
Bloomfield, Leonard. 1935. *Language*. London: Allen & Unwin.
Butler, Yuko G. & Kenji Hakuta. 2004. Bilingualism and second language acquisition. In Tej K. Bhatia & William C. Ritchie (eds.), *The handbook of bilingualism*, 114–144. Malden, MA: Blackwell.
Carreira, Maria & Olga Kagan. 2011. The results of the National Heritage Language Survey: Implications for teaching, curriculum design, and professional development. *Foreign Language Annals*. 44(1). 40–64.
Cenoz, Jasone. 2003. The additive effect of bilingualism on third language acquisition: A review. *International Journal of Bilingualism*. 7(1). 71–87.
Cenoz, Jasone. 2013. Defining multilingualism. *Annual Review of Applied Linguistics* 33. 3–18.
Cheatham, Gregory A. & Sumin Lim. this vol. Disabilities and home language maintenance: Myths, models of disability, and equity.
Chin, Ng Bee & Gillian Wigglesworth. 2007. *Bilingualism: An advanced resource book*. London: Routledge.
Clyne, Michael. 2005. *Australia's language potential*. Sydney: University of New South Wales Press.
Cummins, Jim. 2005. A proposal for action: Strategies for recognizing heritage language competence as a learning resource within the mainstream classroom. *Modern Language Journal* 89(4). 585–592.
Cunningham, Clare. 2019. Terminological tussles: Taking issue with "English as an Additional Language" and "Languages Other Than English". *Power and Education* 11(1). 121–128.

---

[10] Nevertheless, we appreciate that some contributors to this handbook prefer to use other terms, and that the terms they have chosen do lend themselves to different purposes in the individual chapters.

De Houwer, Annick & Lourdes Ortega. 2018. Introduction: Learning, using, and unlearning more than one language. In Annick De Houwer & Lourdes Ortega (eds.), *The Cambridge handbook of bilingualism*, 1–12. Cambridge: Cambridge University Press.

Diebold, A. Richard. 1961. Incipient bilingualism. *Language* 37(1). 97–112.

Echu, George. 2004. The language question in Cameroon. *Linguistik Online* 18(1). 19–33.

Edwards, John. 2004. Foundations of bilingualism. In Tej K. Bhatia & William C. Ritchie (eds.), *The handbook of bilingualism*, 7–31. Malden, MA: Blackwell.

Edwards, John. 2013. Bilingualism and multilingualism: Some central concepts. In Tej K. Bhatia & William C. Ritchie (eds.), *The handbook of bilingualism*, 5–25. 2nd edn. Malden, MA: Blackwell.

García, Ofelia, Zeena Zakharia & Bahar Otcu. 2013. Introduction. In Ofelia García, Zeena Zakharia & Bahar Otcu (eds.), *Bilingual community education and multilingualism: Beyond heritage languages in a global city*, 3–42. Bristol: Multilingual Matters.

Gounari, Panayota. 2014. Rethinking heritage language in a critical pedagogy framework. In Peter Pericles Trifonas & Themistoklis Aravossitas (eds.), *Rethinking heritage language education*, 254–268. Cambridge: Cambridge University Press.

Grabowsky, Kirby C. 2016. Assessing pragmatic competence. In Dina Tsagari & Jayanti Banerjee (eds.), *Handbook of second language assessment*, 165–180. Berlin & Boston: De Gruyter.

Grosjean, François 1998. Studying bilinguals: Methodological and conceptual issues. *Bilingualism: Language and Cognition* 1(2). 131–149.

Gupta, Anthea. F. 1997. When mother-tongue education is not preferred. *Journal of Multilingual and Multicultural Development* 18(6). 496–506.

Jain, Ritu & Lionel Wee. 2015. Multilingual education in Singapore: Beyond language communities. In Androula Yiakoumetti (ed.), *Multilingualism and language in education: Sociolinguistic and pedagogical perspectives from Commonwealth countries*, 67–85. Cambridge: Cambridge University Press.

Leung, Constant, Roxy Harris & Ben Rampton. 1997. The idealised native speaker, reified ethnicities and classroom realities. *TESOL Quarterly* 31(3). 543–560.

Li, Wei. 2008. Dimensions of bilingualism. In Li Wei (ed.), *The bilingualism reader*, 3–22. 2nd edn. New York, NY: Routledge.

Miller, Jane. 1983. *Many voices. Bilingualism, culture and education*. London: Routledge.

Mills, Jean. 2001. Being bilingual: Perspectives of third generation Asian children on language, culture and identity. *International Journal of Bilingual Education and Bilingualism* 4(6). 383–402.

Montrul, Silvina. 2002. Incomplete acquisition and attrition of Spanish tense/aspect distinctions in adult bilinguals. *Bilingualism: Language and Cognition* 5(1). 39–68.

Nelde, Peter, Miquel Strubell & Glyn Williams. 1996. *Euromosaic: The production and reproduction of the minority language groups in the European Union*. Luxembourg: Office for Official Publications of the European Communities.

New South Wales Department of Education. 2015. Inclusive language: A guide to appropriate terminology when referring to people from culturally and linguistically diverse backgrounds. https://cpb-ap-se2.wpmucdn.com/learning.schools.nsw.edu.au/dist/c/8/files/2015/12/CALD_terms-1fc2zpl.pdf (accessed 3 October 2019).

Otheguy, Ricardo, Ofelia García & Wallis Reid. 2015. Clarifying translanguaging and deconstructing named languages: A perspective from linguistics. *Applied Linguistics Review* 6(3). 281–307.

Palviainen, Åsa. this vol. Future prospects and visions for family language policy research.

Polinsky, Maria. 2006. Incomplete acquisition: American Russian. *Journal of Slavic Linguistics* 14(2). 161–219.

Polinsky, Maria & Olga Kagan. 2007. Heritage languages: In the "wild" and in the classroom. *Language and Linguistics Compass* 1(5). 368–395.

Pulinx, Reinhilde, Piet Van Avermaet & Orhan Agirdag. 2015. Silencing linguistic diversity: The extent, the determinants and consequences of the monolingual beliefs of Flemish teachers. *International Journal of Bilingual Education and Bilingualism* 20(5). 542–556.

Rampton, Ben. 1998. Language crossing and the redefinition of reality. In Peter Auer (ed.), *Code-switching in conversation: Language, interaction, and identity*, 290–317. London: Routledge.

Romaine, Suzanne. 1995. *Bilingualism*. 2nd edn. Malden, MA: Blackwell.

Ruiz, Richard. 1984. Orientations in language planning. *NABE Journal* 8(2). 15–34.

Sevinç, Yeşim. this vol. Anxiety as a negative emotion in home language maintenance and development.

Skutnabb-Kangas, Tove. 1988. Multilingualism and the education of minority children. In Tove Skutnabb-Kangas & Jim Cummins (eds.), *Minority education: From shame to struggle*, 9–44. Avon: Multilingual Matters.

Skutnabb-Kangas, Tove & Teresa L. McCarty. 2008. Key concepts in bilingual education: Ideological, historical, epistemological, and empirical foundations. In Jim Cummins & Nancy H. Hornberger (eds.), *Encyclopedia of language and education: Bilingual Education*, 3–17. 2nd edn. New York, NY: Springer.

Smith-Christmas, Cassie. this vol. Child agency and home language maintenance.

UNESCO. 1951. The use of vernacular languages in education: The report of the UNESCO Meeting of Specialists. Reprinted in: Joshua A. Fishman (ed.), 1968. *Readings in the sociology of language*, 688–716. The Hague: Mouton de Gruyter.

Valdés, Guadalupe. 2001. Heritage languages students: Profiles and possibilities. In Joy K. Peyton, Donald. A. Ranard & Scott McGinnis (eds.), *Heritage languages in America: Preserving a national resource*, 37–77. Washington, DC: Center for Applied Linguistics and Delta Systems.

Valdés, Guadalupe. 2005. Bilingualism, heritage language learners, and SLA research: Opportunities lost or seized? *The Modern Language Journal* 89(3). 410–426.

Van Deusen-Scholl, Nelleke. 2003. Toward a definition of heritage language: Sociopolitical and pedagogical considerations. *Journal of Language, Identity, and Education* 2(3). 211–230.

Wiley, Terrence G. 2014. The problem of defining heritage and community languages and their speakers: On the utility and limitations of definitional constructs. In Terrence G. Wiley, Joy Kreeft Peyton, Donna Christian, Sarah Catherine K. Moore & Na Liu (eds.), *Handbook of heritage, community, and Native American Languages in the United States: Research, policy, and educational practice*, 33–40. New York: Routledge.

Yağmur, Kutlay. 2015. Multilingualism in immigrant communities. In Jasone Cenoz, Durk Gorter & Stephen May (eds.), *Language awareness and multilingualism*, 347–361. 3rd edn. Cham: Springer.

Päivi Juvonen, Susana A. Eisenchlas, Tim Roberts, and Andrea C. Schalley

3 Researching social and affective factors in home language maintenance and development: A methodology overview

The present handbook is the first volume that brings together the different strands in research on social and affective factors in home language maintenance and development. It therefore presents the first opportunity to explore some of the diverse methodological questions and considerations raised in the field over time, and to discuss how different contexts and foci have impacted on research in this area. This chapter seeks to provide a birds-eye view, bringing together, critiquing, and contrasting methodological considerations across the different sub-areas. The chapter is not intended as a step-by-step guide on how to carry out research. Our focus here concerns what types of research have been conducted on social and affective factors in home language maintenance, and to provide some initial pointers to what we perceive as potential pitfalls and challenges in this research field.

We begin with general observations about the research in this field in section 1, pointing to commonalities and overlaps in research designs and data collection methods. We then organise our discussion across the three levels of analysis set out in the structure of the handbook – micro, meso, and macro. In section 2 we address issues at the micro level, considering research on bilingual speakers and their families. We move to the meso level in section 3, turning to research on home language maintenance and development efforts as initiated and carried out by speaker communities. Section 4 addresses the macro level, and considers societal regulation of minority languages and their use. As these three sections make clear, studies on the micro, meso, and macro levels delimit their participant cohorts and data sources in different ways, according to their distinctive research questions and foci. Section 5 addresses a number of pitfalls researchers can and do encounter in the field, while section 6 discusses general research challenges. Section 7 concludes the chapter with brief summary and an outlook to future developments in this growing research area.

1 Research in the field

The complexity of research in the field is a direct consequence of the diversity of contexts in which this research takes place. This diversity is reflected in the variety of actors who operate in a range of social environments at the micro, meso, and macro levels, each actor with their own particular needs, experiences, and expectations.

At the micro level, actors are individuals (invisible planners, Pakir 1994) such as parents and children. Actors at the macro level are bodies of authority, such as departments of education, which have the power to manage change in language policy and planning (visible planners). The meso level constitutes the grey area between micro and macro levels (Hult 2010). Actors at this level are communities, whose members take joint action in response to pressures from below (at the micro level, such as needs of minoritised families) and from above (at the macro level, such as educational policies and their implications). These actors become research participants for studies in the field, and as we illustrate through the remainder of this chapter, the different factors surrounding participants (e.g., their backgrounds, needs, experiences, expectations) inspire different research aims and foci, and motivate different approaches to data collection and analysis. The overwhelming body of research on social and affective factors in home language maintenance and development aims to explore the personal experiences of participants, to investigate the cultural traditions or praxis of groups in particular contexts, or to examine discourses and policies. This research has a view to not only documenting and understanding current situations, but also to managing linguistic diversity, and/or to advocating for social change.

The last decades have seen a proliferation of research methods in the field, and thus the overview in a single chapter cannot do justice to them all. Readers may find it useful to consult the several comprehensive overviews of relevant research methods that have been employed in bilingualism and second language acquisition research (e.g., Copland and Creese 2015; Dörnyei 2007; Hinkel 2011; Li and Moyer 2009). In the following discussion we focus on some data collection techniques used in the field. These techniques are identified in Table 1. We are mindful to note that these techniques are among many that researchers have used seeking to tap into affective and social aspects of home language maintenance and development. Other techniques include narrative inquiry (Liu and Lin 2018), biographical accounts (Kramsch 2006), linguistic landscapes (Ben-Rafael et al. 2006), linguistic portraits (Wilson 2020), and diary studies and language logs (King and Logan-Terry 2008).

Each row in Table 1 represents a level of analysis: the micro, meso, or macro level. The columns reflect the data analysis continuum from single-method pure qualitative studies to single-method pure quantitative studies. Mixed-method studies are identified along the continuum. These include studies where two or more different types of data are analysed only qualitatively ("mixed qualitative"), only quantitatively ("mixed quantitative"), or both qualitatively and quantitatively ("mixed qualitative–quantitative"). The cells of the table identify the type of data (e.g., "interview", "survey") with a bracketed reference to a study exemplifying this approach.

Table 1: Overview of data collection methods, sorted by level of analysis (rows) and type of data analysis (columns).

	Qualitative	Mixed Qualitative	Mixed Qualitative-Quantitative	Mixed Quantitative	Quantitative
Micro	Observation (Zhu 2008) Interview (Fogle 2013) Focus group (O'Rourke and Nandi 2019)	Ethnographic (Smith-Christmas 2016) Interview + Observation (Curdt-Christiansen 2009)	Survey + Interview (Kaveh 2018)	Survey + Observation (De Houwer and Bornstein 2016)	Survey (Van Mol and de Valk 2018)
Meso	Action research (Patrick, Budach and Muckpaloo 2013) Interview (Yelenevskaya and Fialkova 2003)	Ethnographic (Blackledge and Creese 2009) Interview + Observation (Arnberg 1984) Interview + Focus group (del Puy Ciriza 2019)	Survey + Interview + Observation + Testing + School certificate data (Oriyama 2016)		
Macro	Text analysis (Dovalil 2015)	Ethnographic (Gynne, Bagga-Gupta and Lainio 2016) Interviews + Focus group (Björklund 2013) Interview + Fieldnotes + Linguistic landscaping (Cunningham 2019)		Survey + Card-ranking activity (Lundberg 2019)	Survey (Pulinx, Van Avermaet and Agirdag 2017)

Here it is useful to acknowledge a few challenges in reviewing the methodologies used in the field; we discuss some of these further in the remainder of the chapter. The number of qualitative studies, particularly mixed qualitative studies, far exceeds the number of studies in the other categories. This concentration is arguably related to the area of research, as social and affective factors are well suited to contextualised in-depth qualitative inquiry. Some cells in Table 1 remain empty, as we were unable to locate relevant quantitative studies, particularly at the meso level. We tried to categorise analysis methods more narrowly and to link them to different types of data. However, this proved too difficult to complete, given the dearth of detailed reporting on data analysis methods in many studies and that the same type of data can be analysed from different angles. As Table 1 reveals, for instance, observations can be analysed in both qualitative and quantitative ways. Data collection and data analysis methods thus combine flexibly, eluding clear-cut systematisation.

In the following sections we explore the basic characteristics and peculiarities of research at the three levels of analysis, from micro to macro. In each case, we briefly discuss research participants, research aims and foci, and research designs.

2 The micro level: Researching bilingual speakers and their families

2.1 Research participants

The very notion of what constitutes the "family" in home language contexts has recently undergone critical discussion (Lanza and Lomeu Gomes; Palviainen, both this vol.). A Western idealised conceptualisation of the family containing two married parents and one or more biological children has attracted most research attention to date. Yet this simplified view of a family does not necessarily represent current contexts accurately. In any particular context, single-parent families may be common, as could be separated parents, multi-generational cohabitation, same-sex relationships, and so called "living apart together" couples. Moreover, a family may include adopted as well as biological children. In other environments, the distinction between family and community may not be all that relevant to the research participants themselves. Self-reflection about one's own pre-conceptions on what constitutes a family is necessary before seeking research participants and designing research instruments (Palviainen this vol.). If a researcher implements a research plan that assumes a family consists of two parents, one male and one female, then single-parent or same-sex families are excluded by default. The family unit is not always clearly defined in research, and when delimitation of a family is too narrow to fit families participating in research, relevant data may be overlooked and thus not collected and analysed.

Investigations of language from a familial perspective have drawn participants from a wide range of sociolinguistic environments. However, of all the different language parental constellations, the one that has received most attention is in "WEIRD" (Western, Educated, Industrialised, Rich, and Democratic) contexts

(Henrich, Heine, and Norenzayan 2010; Lanza and Lomeu Gomes this vol.), where one of the parents speaks the societal language, and the other parent has emigrated to that country (e.g., Döpke 1992; Lanza 1992, but see Nakamura 2016 for a non-Western example). A restrictive Western focus is also found in families where parents share the same non-societal language, typically in families with two parents who are migrants to these "WEIRD" countries.

Non-migrant families with parents who share a language but live within inherently multilingual milieus bring a novel set of research contexts to be investigated. Some of these contexts have received considerable research attention, e.g., contexts in Singapore (Curdt-Christiansen 2016), while elsewhere, research published in English has been limited in many of the most multilingual societies in the world, particularly in Central and South America, Africa, and South and Southeast Asia. Further sites of investigation into home language maintenance have focused on families belonging to autochthonous minority communities (Smith Christmas 2016), families with transnationally adopted children (Fogle 2013), and families struggling with disability (Cheatham and Lim this vol.). Contemporaneous families are found in diverse and varied configurations, residing in diverse and varied sociolinguistic environments. Any particular family could contain any constellation of members, drawn from any of the groups mentioned above.

2.2 Aims and foci of research

Studies on home language maintenance from the familial perspective have varied aims and research foci. We have identified two primary strands of research foci, which are also reflected in the handbook structure. These are: (1) affect in multilingual settings; and (2) policies, practices, and ideologies in multilingual families.

The aims within the first strand of affect-focused research are often two-fold: (1) to document affective issues associated with families in varied multilingual contexts, and (2) to discuss and implement these research findings into real-world contexts where deeper understanding of the issues may lead to actual improvements in the quality of life for individuals and their families. Focus areas include socio-emotional well-being (De Houwer this vol.), anxiety (Sevinç this vol.), identity (Tseng this vol.), and intergenerational challenges (Purkarthofer this vol.). Research in the second strand aims to understand how various factors ultimately influence the transmission and maintenance of languages. This is especially relevant to the topic of home language maintenance, as the family domain has been identified as the "critical domain" of intergenerational language transmission (Spolsky 2012), and the rupture of intergenerational language transmission can be seen as a strong indicator of language shift (Fishman 1991). Focus areas of research in this second strand include family language policy (Lanza and Lomeu

Gomes this vol.), home language strategies and practices (Schwartz this vol.), the association between context-specific factors and these practices (Curdt-Christiansen and Huang this vol.), and child agency (Smith-Christmas this vol.).

2.3 Research designs

Typical research designs in family studies draw on various means of data collection. These designs mostly use qualitative approaches based on interviews, observation, or a combination of both. Some have used quantitative approaches, with surveys the most common. Some studies mix qualitative and quantitative methodologies, but there is still a lot of scope for innovative research designs combining qualitative and quantitative approaches. The current focus of family research is overwhelmingly on single-point studies. Longitudinal studies have much to offer to the field, and while potentially difficult to conduct, would create considerable new knowledge on how key issues evolve over time in given contexts.

The focused participants in this research area are often the children of multilingual families. Despite this, research designs often centre their data collection on the parents in such families, particularly mothers, for example by interviewing mothers about home language regimes without including the perspectives of children or fathers. Including all relevant actors in a research design is not always practicable, possible or ethical, but critical evaluation of why a particular study did not include certain family members would both be informative and signal the researcher's awareness of this need.

Studies should also more carefully critique the sources of their data, particularly data collected by self-reports vis-à-vis data of actual language use. Self-reports may differ from actual language use for several reasons (De Houwer 2009; Hult 2014), and the literature has frequently observed discrepancies between stated language policies and actual language practices (Palviainen and Boyd 2013; Schwartz 2008).

3 The meso level: Researching communities

In this section we move our lens on research from the more intimate social unit – the family – to the larger social unit – the community – and hence from the micro to the meso level. We direct our attention to home language maintenance and development efforts as initiated or carried out by speaker communities. As in the previous section, we briefly delimit the key notion and identify the typical participants of such research. We then overview common research aims and foci, and identify key features of research at the meso level, highlighting the inherent difficulty of evaluating it.

3.1 Research participants

In sociology, the notion of "community" is generally defined rather broadly as a social unit whose members share some norms, beliefs, values, or other salient characteristics (Crow 2007). Communities also tend to share a sense of joint delimited space, be this geographical (e.g., a country, region, city, or suburb) or, as more recently acknowledged, virtual (e.g., a joint communication space on a platform such as Facebook). This delimited space enables members of the community to jointly plan and carry out initiatives, and hence to act as a unit, and to form (lasting) relationships with one another.

In the context of home language maintenance research, a community is then understood as a group of people who form a social unit based on shared home language(s) (for a problematisation of the notion of "home language", see Eisenchlas and Schalley this vol.), oftentimes shared cultural practices and values, and a geographical or virtual space affording members opportunities to foster relationships with each other.[1] Communities can differ greatly in their size, level of institutionalisation, and visibility. Examples include church groups, cultural organisations, and community language schools, as well as informal gatherings of people who may share some of the characteristics described above but have not formalised their links with each other (such as informal playgroups and regular get-togethers). Such communities usually cater to their individual linguistic and cultural needs through joint member action.

While the notion of "community" is used widely in research, it is rarely defined clearly, and research studies often do not explicitly delimit who constitutes the focus community. Furthermore, a community comprises an aggregate of actors, but only some of them can be included as participants in research studies. Typically, participants are the members who are seen or position themselves as representatives of the community. Thus, there is no guarantee that these actors' views truly represent the views of the whole community, which may be more heterogeneous than the representatives may portray. An additional issue is that participants usually self-select to some degree (as they have to consent to participating in a study), so researchers can reach only a specific part of a community. Critics claim that this – and researchers' frequent use of convenience sampling – result in biased participant groups. Researchers therefore need to always be very explicit about the criteria guiding selection of research participants, and possible effects of these on research results or findings. Such considerations may lead to improvements in the reporting of research studies (see also section 5).

---

[1] Tyrrell (2015: 13) suggests the notion *translocal* for non-geographical joint spaces, to highlight the "'simultaneous situatedness' across different spaces" that individuals experience. These spaces include "home, school and other social (including virtual) spaces" (Tyrrell 2015: 13).

3.2 Aims and foci of research

Reflecting the diversity of community types, studies on home language maintenance at the community level have a variety of aims and research foci. Research has mostly investigated (1) objectives of the communities; (2) initiatives and programs put in place to achieve these objectives; and (3) the effectiveness of these initiatives and programs.

In the context of home languages, community objectives typically include advocating for community needs, supporting social justice and inclusiveness, developing strategies for home language maintenance at the community level, creating a sense of a cultural identity, and fostering strong links to the home culture.

Studies are conducted in various research contexts and across diverse sites. This handbook illustrates some of the focus areas and research perspectives. Major ones include: (1) motivations, operations, and success of community language schools (Nordstrom this vol.); (2) counteracting geographical and linguistic isolation through new technologies that form translocal virtual communities (Hatoss; Little; Palviainen, all this vol.); (3) revitalising language through community efforts (Mayer et al. this vol.); and (4) effects of macro level policies on the community and its members (Albury; Annamalai and Skutnabb-Kangas; Liddicoat, all this vol.). Yet research in the field is patchy, creating potential – indeed, need – for further systematic inquiries. Part of the research challenge lies in identifying relevant meso level activities and their actors, as many that could helpfully contribute to knowledge pass by unreported (e.g., informal playgroup activities).

3.3 Research designs

As the meso level is a fluid interface between the micro and the macro levels, many research designs and methods used at this level overlap with those used at the two levels on either side (such as ethnographic studies, interviews, surveys, and observations). Here we focus attention on features of research designs that are particularly distinctive to the meso level.

The sharing of norms, values, and beliefs by community members leads to the development of joint goals and actions. Community research often orients to community activities that are transformative and address issues of advocacy, social justice, and inclusiveness. Therefore, in addition to descriptive studies, research is often undertaken through collaboration between researchers and communities, and aims to drive social change. Typical examples of this collaborative approach are action research (e.g., Patrick, Budach, and Muckpaloo 2013) and intervention studies (e.g., Hatoss this vol.). These approaches seek to generate materials and knowledge to benefit the community in the longer term. One of the main challenges, however, is evaluating such research activities, as their impact needs to be measured. This is problematic for two reasons in particular. First, some of the benefits, and costs, are appreciable only in the long term, and second, it is generally difficult to demonstrate a causal relationship between the research activities undertaken and social or other changes that may transpire subsequent to the research. Furthermore, given that collaborative research is always – at least initially – a local response to local issues, the abundance of confounding factors that influence research findings and evaluations makes it hard to generalise from the research, its findings, and its consequences beyond the particular context then under the lens.

4 The macro level: Researching bodies of authority

In this section, we focus on research at the level of society at which actors are bodies of authority governed by common laws and regulations. These macro level authorities exert regulatory power or influence at the nation-state level (e.g., national government) or above (e.g., the European Union or UNESCO, as official bodies of authority), and also below (e.g., through regulating the national education system). Let us give an example here to illustrate the distinction between meso and macro levels. Community language schools and other forms of education arising from community level initiatives for minority language education are grassroots initiated, bottom-up meso level activities, whereas the macro level on the other hand focuses on top-down processes, e.g. the ones that regulate formal education provisions (Shohamy 2006; see also Liddicoat 2014 and May 2015 on interaction between these two levels).

4.1 Research participants

At the macro level, research data are often written documents, such as laws and policies on different levels of organisation of the society. These documents are interpreted to echo the values and ideologies of society. However, individual representatives of bodies of authority (such as representatives of schools or municipalities) also often act as research participants in their capacity as professional stakeholders. Whereas individuals at the micro level represent themselves, and at the meso level position themselves as parts of and actors within a community, individuals at the macro level act as spokespersons for the bodies of authority they represent. Hence, researchers interpret for instance teachers expressing their attitudes and beliefs on multilingualism as representing the prevailing attitudes and beliefs of those in the formal education system (Cunningham 2019; cf. Mary and Young this vol.).

4.2 Aims and foci of research

Research conducted on the macro level also presents a variety of aims and research foci, with studies investigating ideologies, legislation, policies, affordances, practices, and stakeholder attitudes, and the interaction between them. This research aims to: (1) document and critique the current state of affairs; (2) advise on best practice and provide recommendations to stakeholders; and (3) evaluate the effectiveness of policy changes and macro level initiatives.

In the context of home languages, macro level actors' objectives typically concern legislation in relation to minority language policy and language planning, and regulation of educational provisions for minority language speakers. Macro level actors pursue these objectives through regulating, controlling and steering members of society, i.e. these actors simultaneously represent and execute power. Most countries and autonomous regions in the world have legislation regulating the use of languages at some level (Leclerc 2019), for example stating which language(s) can be used in official institutions. However, not all countries acknowledge the linguistic rights of speakers of its indigenous, colonial, and/or immigrant (minority) languages (Fishman 1999). The language of schooling as well as languages taught within formal education have a recognised and profound impact on the maintenance and revitalisation of languages all around the world (e.g., Liddicoat 2008; Annamalai and Skuttnabb-Kangas this vol.). Yet states do not necessarily offer education in or on a minority language. As Annamalai and Skuttnabb-Kangas, Paulsrud, and Yağmur (all this vol.) illustrate, the organisation of minority language education can take almost any guise, from rejection, to indifference, to supporting inclusive education on the grounds of social justice and linguistic rights.

Much of the research conducted and discussed in this volume has legislation and policy documents as a starting point, when, for example, addressing research questions about official institutions implementing policy into practice (Annamalai and Skuttnabb-Kangas; Paulsrud; Yağmur; all this vol.). Studies on multimodal uses and displays of language in public spaces also often take policy documents as a starting point (Buckingham 2018; Gorter 2018), as do studies on educational provisions offered and implemented (Paulsrud this vol.). The social regulative and legislative systems themselves are also subject to extensive research, addressing questions about the content of policy documents or about educational provisions (Liddicoat this vol.), as well as the attitudes and beliefs of stakeholders (Albury; De Houwer; Mary and Young, all this vol.; Lundberg 2019).

4.3 Research designs

Research focusing on the social and affective factors associated with home language maintenance and development on the macro level utilises many of the research designs and methods of data collection used on the other two levels. It thus shares both the benefits and the concerns associated with those levels, as discussed above.

A research design distinctive to the macro level is policy document research. Here, regulations and policy documents are not merely used as supplemental background information as in other studies. Rather, they are analysed in their own right to identify, describe and compare different contexts or to follow longitudinal changes and developments across documents. Macro level policy document research thus specifically studies the values and ideologies of society.

5 Pitfalls

This section summarises some of the pitfalls we encountered in the body of research across the field of social and affective factors of home language maintenance and development. The first pitfall concerns the absence of generalisability of research results, given the uniqueness of each research context. We then focus on the restricted geographical research locations and participant populations. Finally, we discuss the underreporting of both data collection and data analysis methods.

5.1 Lack of generalisability

As we have discussed briefly above, and illustrated in Table 1, much research undertaken within the field at large presents in-depth, small-scale, qualitative descriptions of heterogeneous and complex realities in single-point studies. These studies have identified important social and affective factors in home language maintenance and development, but the effective disentangling of the interplay of these various factors remains a challenge. Moreover, studies with single-point design do not enable researchers to identify correlations between factors, let alone to effectively investigate causes and effects. Thus, the current scarcity of longitudinal studies leaves researchers unable to assess the medium-to-long-term effects of initiatives and practices at the different levels. These issues consequently make generalisations from research data contestable at this time.

A way forward could entail ensuring that qualitative research findings can be aggregated, similar to the aggregation found in meta-analyses carried out on quantitative results. However, this would require careful reporting on study participants and procedures, over and above reporting on the features directly relevant to the research questions of a particular study. It would open up the field for meta-studies that in turn would produce generalisable and quantifiable findings. Only then will researchers be able to provide convincing advice on matters of home language maintenance at the three levels, thus informing non-academic stakeholders as well as other interested academics.

5.2 Restricted research coverage

As we indicated above, research to date has shown a clear bias towards the study of "WEIRD" contexts (Lanza and Lomeu Gomes this vol.), which means that non-Western, non-industrialised contexts remained under-researched. This assessment applies to all three levels. At the micro level, research has typically focused on idealised Western family contexts, ignoring disadvantaged populations in terms of economic resources, educational background, or special needs. At the meso and macro levels, research focuses noticeably on a select number of industrialised countries that traditionally have been strong targets of migration, and where most of the internationally visible researchers in the field are based.

However, studies researching other contexts and participant populations are becoming more common, as evidenced by abstract booklets of recent conferences on bilingualism, and by major international congresses hosted in non-OECD countries. One clear example is the World Congress of the International Association of Applied Linguistics (AILA), held in South America for the first time in 2017. Student and staff mobility are fast becoming another source of cross-fertilisation in research perspectives and interests.

5.3 Data collection: Limited reporting

Underreporting is a limitation noticeable in both qualitative and quantitative studies, mainly in participant sampling, participant demographics, and the sociocultural context in which data collection takes place. This may impact negatively on the interpretability of the research findings and obscure their contribution to existing scholarship. As we mentioned above, for qualitative studies this may also restrict the generalisability of findings. Quantitative studies, on the other hand, risk brushing over important individual background factors. This could skew data by conflating diverse populations, thus negatively affecting studies' credibility and their capacity to truly represent diverse participants.

Another pitfall relates to justifying a researcher's choice of data collection methods. Qualitative studies tend to be labour intensive, even when the pool of participants involved is small, as they often involve collecting multiple types of data, including the use of elaborate ethnographic collection methods. In this context, triangulation (a "mixed qualitative" approach) is often seen as best practice. However, any combination of data collection methods needs to be properly justified. Merely referring to excellent introductions to chosen research methods (such as Copland and Creese 2015) does not suffice as justification for a researcher's choice, nor does merely including a reference to the creator of a data collection method that a researcher wants to apply.

The development of stricter codes of reporting and clear justification guidelines would improve research practices, thus helping to avoid or overcome the abovementioned pitfalls.

5.4 Data analysis: Lack of procedural information

Presentation of data analysis procedures may also have shortcomings through underreporting. Research concerning social and affective factors in home language maintenance seldom adequately explicates its methods of data analysis (e.g., it may just state that a "thematic analysis" has been carried out). This underreporting and vagueness on the analytic steps of research may have unintended consequences. First, the objectivity of the research process and its results may be compromised since the analysis cannot be independently verified (e.g., how excerpts were selected for analysis) and thus the researcher's subjective interpretation can weigh too heavily. Second, lack of transparency in the data analysis process hinders replicability of studies. It is therefore of utmost importance that researchers are explicit and transparent about the data analyses they have conducted.

6 Challenges

In this section, we discuss three particularly significant challenges that impact on research in the field. The first concerns the requirement for ethical conduct at all stages of research, from participant recruitment to data storage and archiving. Parallel to this, and often in tension with ethical considerations, the second challenge concerns data management issues, ranging from questions of data coding to storage and sharing. The third challenge concerns what happens with the findings after research has been conducted, in terms of disseminating results to different stakeholders and across disciplines.

6.1 Ethical considerations

As research in this area is so diverse, every research design can involve specific ethical challenges. We thus concentrate our attention on a few general considerations.

Research in the field often revolves around investigating potentially vulnerable individuals or groups of people, such as children and migrant populations.

Focussing on social and affective factors frequently leads to the collection and handling of sensitive information, which must be treated in an ethically responsible manner. Ethical research needs to be grounded in an honest relationship between researcher and participants. The researcher must obtain participants' informed consent to participate, which is not necessarily a straightforward process since participants need to be made aware of the purpose of the research project and how any data concerning them will be handled. This process is further complicated for those working with children, as children cannot usually consent by themselves to participate in research until they reach a certain age, depending on local laws and regulations. Furthermore, researchers need to take into account potential intercultural differences when working with diverse populations, as ethical concepts may not translate readily between cultures (Copland and Creese 2015).

Ethical research designs critically consider whose interests are being met, and who is really benefiting from a study (Canagarajah and Stanley 2015). Researchers themselves often benefit professionally from any research output generated from a project, but ethical research should be mindful of the well-being of individuals, families, communities and institutions involved, and ensure participants are not harmed in any way. Recognising that research participants may experience anxiety, stress, guilt, and damage to self-esteem during the data collection process (Murphy and Dingwall 2001), researchers should attempt to design research instruments in ways that lessen the likelihood of participants' distress. At the same time, however, we need to acknowledge that the type of research reported in this volume has the potential to give participants a voice and thus an opportunity to redress injustices. Thus, clear benefits may result for the participants involved as well as for the researcher.

6.2 Data management

Management of research data involves questions around the handling, organisation, and storing of data throughout and following the research process. This topic continued to gain traction in recent years, particularly given the opportunities and challenges afforded by ever-developing digital technologies (Berez-Kroeker et al. 2018; Thieberger and Berez 2012). Data management needs to be carefully planned for each stage of the research process, including the data collection, preparation, and analysis phases of a research project as well as general data storage (including archiving the data past the lifetime of the research project). Such considerations are important in relation to not only primary data (e.g., audio and video recordings, observational notes), and secondary data (e.g., transcriptions and annotations), metadata (e.g., contextual/situational information), administrative data (e.g., workflow and data versioning information), but also to tertiary data (e.g., analytical findings) (see Thieberger and Berez 2012).

Researchers are encouraged (or even required, e.g., when applying for research funding, European Commission 2016) to formulate an explicit data management plan that clearly sets out their data management strategies. Although the issue of data management is not near the forefront in this handbook, we expect it will become a serious challenge in the future that researchers will need to address head-on. Calls for replicability – where new data are collected under the same circumstances, and the results are confirmed by a follow-up study – have been superseded by calls for reproducibility – where collected data are made accessible for re-analysis, thus providing scientific accountability of the original results (Berez-Kroeker et al. 2018). The former often appears impossible in our field (due to a multitude of moderating factors), but the latter is most certainly achievable. Moreover, making existing data accessible and achieving comparability across data sets will allow researchers to analyse a larger collection of data, thus moving from small-scale projects and case studies to carrying out comparative larger-scale research. This could be to the benefit of all, also enabling more reliable generalisations to be drawn from the data.

6.3 Dissemination of findings

Research findings surely need to be disseminated. However, researchers working on social and affective factors that impact on home language maintenance and development at times may feel they are caught between a glass ceiling and a "glass floor", in a position from which information flows neither upwards nor downwards. Sometimes they may feel they are between "glass walls" that isolate them from others working on similar matters in related fields. But if researchers want their research to be effective in creating social change, they need to find ways to disseminate research findings beyond academia, to reach a range of diverse stakeholders. This task involves identifying and addressing a number of challenges that seem to hinder the flow of information in every direction.

As to the glass ceiling, research findings need to urgently flow upwards to the macro level of language planning, so policymakers have robust and reliable data to inform decisions about language provision. Yet as we discussed above, much research in the field seems to be qualitative, involving small-scale projects or cases. While this research can undeniably be very sound, it does not have the "numerical power" needed to engage policy makers. Findings from purely quantitative large-scale studies may seem more convincing. However, here we urge caution, since these studies so loved by policy makers may also involve risks. First, Eisenchlas and Schalley (2017) found substantial confounding factors and methodological limitations in meta-analyses of correlates of bilingualism, including a lack of terminological clarity that may lead researchers in the field to inadvertently discuss phenomena that are slightly different while assuming uniformity of interpretations. Second, a publication bias (de Bruin, Treccani, and Della Sala 2015) may often prevent publication in the scholarly literature of papers reporting on negative or no effects, thus providing a misleading picture of a phenomenon.

These two issues may lead policymakers to make decisions based on data that is potentially methodologically flawed or skewed. Furthermore, purely quantitative research may inform about results found on aggregates of participants, but says nothing about what motivates these participants to act as they do. We thus see advantages of mixed methods research combining quantitative and qualitative research methods in a way that the findings validate and reinforce each other – showing not only how much of what, but also how and why. This approach can thus satisfy macro level planners without sacrificing rich insights into the human experience that characterises qualitative research.

As to the "glass floor", we argue that scholars need to find ways to translate their findings to the broader population. Researchers in this field are often motivated by a commitment to social justice and equity (Annamalai and Skutnabb-Kangas this vol.; Eisenchlas and Schalley 2019) and therefore are well-suited to take an activist role in supporting bilingualism. This role could involve a wide variety of activities ranging from lobbying educational institutions and interacting with traditional and social media to amplify the message, to delivering workshops in the community addressing the benefits and challenges of bilingualism and debunking some widespread myths and misinformation.

Finally, we need to deal with the "glass walls" that separate and compartmentalise disciplines. As stated in Eisenchlas and Schalley (this vol.), bilingualism is a complex phenomenon, and as such, it can be, and needs to be, studied from a variety of perspectives. While an impressive amount of research has been conducted following diverse disciplinary traditions, scholars are yet to find a "common language" to engage across disciplinary boundaries. This would entail, among other measures, developing codes of good/best practice that rigorously inform how research in each discipline is conducted, development of reporting procedures that make findings intelligible across fields of study, and identifying and making explicit the disciplinary assumptions and biases under which research in the field is conducted.

7 Conclusion and future directions

In this chapter, we have taken a birds-eye view of the aims and methods of data collection and analysis within research on social and affective factors on home language maintenance and development. We noted there is a motivated methodological bias towards qualitative research designs, data collection methods, and analyses. However, we believe that if research on social and affective factors in home language maintenance is to have an impact on decision makers, the field's future opportunities lie in the use of mixed quantitative–qualitative approaches, aggregation of current research results, careful selection of research participants, and rigorous reporting of data collection and analysis methods, in order to gain generalisable and reliable results. There is also room for more interdisciplinary research, combining sociology, political science and (social) psychology with linguistics in general and with applied and educational linguistics in particular, to account for the complexities of topics researched in this field.

As a specialised area in bilingualism research, the study of social and affective factors in home language maintenance and development is still somewhat underresearched in comparison to the study of linguistic and psycholinguistic aspects of language development and use. For example, during the last decade, less than a quarter of the original research articles published in the *Heritage Language Journal*, which is dedicated to disseminating results on all aspects of heritage language research, focused on social or affective factors. However, the field is growing rapidly. This handbook is a step in that direction, and new dedicated journals are also emerging to disseminate research findings and generate interest more broadly.

As authors of a few chapters in this volume have explored, researchers in this field are experiencing new challenges and realities that will impact on how research in this field is conducted in the future. In particular, technological changes are already transforming actors and their behaviours at the three key levels. At the micro level, new technologies allow families to effectively communicate with others across borders and spaces (Palviainen this vol.) and to take their children's home language development into their own hands by accessing digital resources from around the world (Little this vol.). At the meso level, technological developments foster the creation of translocal communities, whose members are linked through virtual joint spaces (Hatoss this vol.). Finally, at the macro level, digital technologies are now reducing the (often negative) impact of monoglossic language policies, as more individualised educational activities can support children's home language development and thus acknowledge these children's linguistic rights. Such technological advances thus bring with them challenges and opportunities to our data collection methodologies. Communication modes are changing, and participant populations are more dispersed geographically, but the importance of research across all three levels in this field is unlikely to diminish.

References

Albury, Nathan J. this vol. Language attitudes and ideologies on linguistic diversity.
Annamalai, E. & Tove Skutnabb-Kangas. this vol. Social justice and inclusiveness through linguistic human rights in education.
Arnberg, Lenore. 1984. Mother tongue playgroups for pre-school bilingual children. *Journal of Multilingual & Multicultural Development* 5(1). 65–84.

Ben-Rafael, Eliezer, Elana Shohamy, Muhammad Hasan Amara & Nira Trumper-Hecht. 2006. Linguistic landscape as symbolic construction of the public space: The case of Israel. *International Journal of Multilingualism* 3(1). 7–30.
Berez-Kroeker, Andrea L., Lauren Gawne, Susan Smythe Kung, Barbara F. Kelly, Tyler Heston, Gary Holton, Peter Pulsifer, David I. Beaver, Shobhana Chelliah, Stanley Dubinsky, Richard P. Meier, Nick Thieberger, Keren Rice, & Anthony C. Woodbury. 2018. Reproducible research in linguistics: A position statement on data citation and attribution in our field. *Linguistics* 56(1). 1–18.
Blackledge, Adrian & Angela Creese. 2009. "Because tumi Bangali": Inventing and disinventing the national in multilingual communities in the UK. *Ethnicities* 9(4). 451–476.
Björklund, Mikaela. 2013. Multilingualism and multiculturalism in the Swedish-medium primary school classroom in Finland – Some teacher views. *International Electronic Journal of Elementary Education* 6(1). 117–136.
Bruin, Angela de, Barbara Treccani & Sergio Della Sala. 2015. Cognitive advantage in bilingualism: An example of publication bias? *Psychological Science* 26(1). 99–107.
Buckingham, Louisa 2018. Race, space and commerce in multi-ethnic Costa Rica: A linguistic landscape inquiry. *International Journal of the Sociology of Language* 2018(254). 1–27.
Canagarajah, Suresh & Phiona Stanley. 2015. Ethical considerations in language policy research. In David Cassels Johnson (ed.), *Research methods in language policy and planning: A practical guide*, 33–44. Hoboken, New Jersey: John Wiley & Sons.
Cheatham, Gregory A. & Sumin Lim. this vol. Disabilities and home language maintenance: Myths, models of disability, and equity.
Ciriza, María del Puy. 2019. Bringing parents together: An innovative approach for parental involvement in an immersion school in the Basque Autonomous Community. *Journal of Multilingual and Multicultural Development* 40(1). 50–63.
Copland, Fiona & Angela Creese. 2015. *Linguistic ethnography: Collecting, analysing and presenting data*. London: Sage.
Crow, Graham. 2007. Community. In George Ritzer (ed.), *The Blackwell encyclopedia of sociology*, 617–620. New York, NY: Blackwell.
Cunningham, Clare. 2019. "The inappropriateness of language": Discourses of power and control over languages-beyond-English in primary schools. *Language and Education* 33(4). 285–301.
Curdt-Christiansen, Xiao Lan. 2009. Invisible and visible language planning: Ideological factors in the family language policy of Chinese immigrant families in Quebec. *Language Policy* 8(4). 351–375.
Curdt-Christiansen, Xiao Lan. 2016. Conflicting language ideologies and contradictory language practices in Singaporean multilingual families. *Journal of Multilingual and Multicultural Development* 37(7). 694–709.
Curdt-Christiansen, Xiao Lan & Jing Huang. this vol. Factors influencing family language policy.
De Houwer, Annick. 2009. *Bilingual first language acquisition*. Clevedon: Multilingual Matters.
De Houwer, Annick. this vol. Harmonious Bilingualism: Well-being for families in bilingual settings.
De Houwer, Annick & Marc H. Bornstein. 2016. Bilingual mothers' language choice in child-directed speech: Continuity and change. *Journal of Multilingual and Multicultural Development* 37(7). 680–693.
Dovalil, Vít. 2015. Language management theory as a basis for the dynamic concept of EU language law. *Current Issues in Language Planning* 16(4). 360–377.
Döpke, Susanne. 1992. *One parent one language: An interactional approach*. Amsterdam: John Benjamins.
Dörnyei, Zoltán. 2007. *Research methods in applied linguistics: Quantitative, qualitative, and mixed methodologies*. Oxford: Oxford University Press.

Eisenchlas, Susana A. & Andrea C. Schalley. 2017. Comparing like with like? A systematic review of terminology in meta-analytic studies on bilingualism. Paper presented at the 11th International Symposium on Bilingualism, The University of Limerick, Ireland.

Eisenchlas, Susana A. & Andrea C. Schalley. 2019. Reaching out to migrant and refugee communities to support home language maintenance. *International Journal of Bilingual Education and Bilingualism* 22(5). 564–575.

Eisenchlas, Susana A. & Andrea. C. Schalley. this vol. Making sense of the notion of "home language" and related concepts.

European Commission. 2016. *Guidelines on data management in Horizon 2020*. Version 2.1. https://www.fosteropenscience.eu/sites/default/files/pdf/2446.pdf (accessed 21 May 2019).

Fishman, Joshua. A. 1991. *Reversing language shift: Theoretical and empirical foundations of assistance to threatened languages*. Clevedon: Multilingual Matters.

Fishman, Joshua A. 1999. *Handbook of language and ethnic identity*. Oxford: Oxford University Press.

Fogle, Lyn W. 2013. Parental ethnotheories and family language policy in transnational adoptive families. *Language Policy* 12(1). 83–102.

Gorter, Durk. 2018. Linguistic landscapes and trends in the study of schoolscapes. *Linguistics and Education* 44. 80–85.

Gynne, Annaliina, Sangeeta Bagga-Gupta & Jarmo Lainio. 2016. Practiced linguistic-cultural ideologies and educational policies: A case study of a "bilingual Sweden Finnish school". *Journal of Language, Identity & Education* 15(6). 329–343.

Hatoss, Anikó. this vol. Transnational grassroots language planning in the era of mobility and the Internet.

Henrich, Joseph, Steven J. Heine & Ara Norenzayan. 2010. The weirdest people in the world? *Behavioral and Brain Sciences* 33(2–3). 61–83.

Hinkel, Eli (ed.). 2011. *Handbook of research in second language teaching and learning* (Vol. 2). London & New York: Routledge.

Hult, Francis M. 2010. Introduction. *International Journal of the Sociology of Language* 202. 1–6.

Hult, Francis M. 2014. Covert bilingualism and symbolic competence: Analytical reflections on negotiating insider/outsider positionality in Swedish speech situations. *Applied Linguistics* 35. 63–81.

Kaveh, Yalda. M. 2018. Family language policy and maintenance of Persian: The stories of Iranian immigrant families in the northeast, USA. *Language Policy* 17(4). 443–477.

King, Kendall A. & Aubrey Logan-Terry. 2008. Additive bilingualism through family language policy: Strategies, identities and interactional outcomes. *Calidoscópio* 6(1). 5–19.

Kramsch, Claire. 2006. The multilingual subject. *International Journal of Applied Linguistics* 16. 98–110.

Lanza, Elizabeth. 1992. Can bilingual two-year-olds code-switch? *Journal of Child Language* 19(3). 633–658.

Lanza, Elizabeth & Rafael Lomeu Gomes. this vol. Family language policy: Foundations, theoretical perspectives and critical approaches.

Leclerc, Jacques. 2019. *L'aménagement linguistique dans le monde*. [Language planning across the world.] http://www.axl.cefan.ulaval.ca/ (accessed 5 May 2019).

Li, Wei & Melissa G. Moyer (eds.). 2009. *The Blackwell guide to research methods in bilingualism and multilingualism*. New York: John Wiley & Sons.

Liddicoat, Anthony J. 2008. Models of national government language-in-education policy for indigenous minority language groups. In Timothy Jowan Curnow (ed.), *Selected papers from the 2007 Conference of the Australian Linguistic Society*. http://www.als.asn.au/proceedings/als2007/liddicoat.pdf (accessed 22 May 2019).

Liddicoat, Anthony J. 2014. The interface between macro and micro-level language policy and the place of language pedagogies. *International Journal of Pedagogies and Learning* 9(2). 118–129.
Liddicoat, Anthony J. this vol. Language policy and planning for language maintenance: The macro and meso levels.
Little, Sabine. this vol. Social media and the use of technology in home language maintenance.
Liu, Wei & Xiaobing Lin. 2019. Family language policy in English as a foreign language: A case study from China to Canada. *Language Policy* 18(2). 191–207.
Lundberg, Adrian. 2019. Teachers' beliefs about multilingualism: Findings from Q method research. *Current Issues in Language Planning* 20(3). 266–283.
Mary, Latisha & Andrea Young. this vol. Teachers' beliefs and attitudes towards home language maintenance and their effects.
May, Stephen. 2015. Language rights and language policy: Addressing the gap(s) between principles and practices. *Current Issues in Language Planning* 16(4). 355–359.
Mayer, Elisabeth, Liliana Sánchez, José Camacho & Carolina Rodríguez Alzza. this vol. The drivers of home language maintenance and development in indigenous communities.
Murphy, Elizabeth & Robert Dingwall. 2001. The ethics of ethnography. In: Paul Atkinson, Amanda Coffey, Sara Delamont, John Lofland & Lyn Lofland (eds.), *Handbook of ethnography*, 339–351. London: Sage.
Nakamura, Janice. 2016. Hidden bilingualism: Ideological influences on the language practices of multilingual migrant mothers in Japan. *International Multilingual Research Journal* 10(4). 308–323.
Nordstrom, Janica. this vol. Community language schools.
Oriyama, Kaya. 2016. Community of practice and family language policy: Maintaining heritage Japanese in Sydney – ten years later. *International Multilingual Research Journal* 10(4). 289–307.
O'Rourke, Bernadette & Anik Nandi. 2019. New speaker parents as grassroots policy makers in contemporary Galicia: Ideologies, management and practices. *Language Policy* 18(4). 493–511.
Pakir, Anne. 1994. Education and invisible language planning: The case of English in Singapore. In Thiru Kandiah & John Kwan-Terry (eds.), *English and language planning: Southeast Asia contribution*, 158–181. Singapore: Center for Advanced Studies, National University of Singapore.
Palviainen, Åsa. this vol. Future prospects and visions for family language policy research.
Palviainen, Åsa & Sally Boyd. 2013. Unity in discourse, diversity in practice: The one person one language policy in bilingual families. In Mila Schwartz & Anna Verschik (eds.), *Successful Family Language Policy*, 223–248. Dordrecht: Springer.
Patrick, Donna, Gabriele Budach & Igah Muckpaloo. 2013. Multiliteracies and family language policy in an urban Inuit community. *Language Policy* 12(1). 47–62.
Paulsrud, BethAnne. this vol. The mainstream classroom and home language maintenance.
Pulinx, Reinhilde, Piet Van Avermaet & Orhan Agirdag. 2017. Silencing linguistic diversity: The extent, the determinants and consequences of the monolingual beliefs of Flemish teachers. *International Journal of Bilingual Education and Bilingualism* 20(5). 542–556.
Purkarthofer, Judith. this vol. Intergenerational challenges: Of handing down languages, passing on practices, and bringing multilingual speakers into being.
Schalley, Andrea C. & Susana A. Eisenchlas. this vol. Social and affective factors in home language maintenance and development: Setting the scene.

Schwartz, Mila. 2008. Exploring the relationship between family language policy and heritage language knowledge among second generation Russian-Jewish immigrants in Israel. *Journal of Multilingual and Multicultural Development* 29(5). 400–418.

Schwartz, Mila. this vol. Strategies and practices of home language maintenance.

Sevinç, Yeşim. this vol. Anxiety as a negative emotion in home language maintenance and development.

Shohamy, Elana 2006. *Language policy: Hidden agendas and new approaches*. London and New York: Routledge.

Smith-Christmas, Cassie. 2016. *Family language policy. Maintaining an endangered language in the home*. Basingstoke: Palgrave Macmillan.

Smith-Christmas, Cassie. this vol. Child agency and home language maintenance.

Spolsky, Bernard. 2012. Family language policy – the critical domain. *Journal of Multilingual and Multicultural Development* 33(1). 3–11.

Thieberger, Nicholas & Andrea L. Berez. 2012. Linguistic data management. In Nicholas Thieberger (ed.), *The Oxford handbook of linguistic fieldwork*, 90–118. Oxford: Oxford University Press.

Tseng, Amelia. this vol. Identity in home-language maintenance.

Tyrrell, Naomi. 2015. Transnational migrant children's language practices in translocal spaces. *Diskurs Kindheits- und Jugendforschung / Discourse. Journal of Childhood and Adolescence Research* 10(1). 11–23.

Van Mol, Christof & Helga A. G. de Valk. 2018. European movers' language use patterns at home: A case-study of European bi-national families in the Netherlands. *European Societies* 20(4). 665–689.

Wilson, Sonia. 2020. Family language policy through the eyes of bilingual children: The case of French heritage speakers in the UK. *Journal of Multilingual and Multicultural Development* 41(2). 121–139.

Yağmur, Kutlay. this vol. Models of formal education and minority language teaching across countries.

Yelenevskaya, Maria & Larisa Fialkova. 2003. From 'muteness' to eloquence: Immigrants' narratives about languages. *Language Awareness* 12(1). 30–48.

Zhu, Hua. 2008. Duelling languages, duelling values: Codeswitching in bilingual intergenerational conflict talk in diasporic families. *Journal of Pragmatics* 40(10). 1799–1816.

Part 2: Bilingual speakers and their families

Topic area 2.1: **Self-conceptions and affective reactions**

Annick De Houwer

4 Harmonious Bilingualism: Well-being for families in bilingual settings

1 Introduction

1.1 Harmonious Bilingual Development/Harmonious Bilingualism

Home language maintenance, the main topic of this handbook, is a very emotional subject for many parents raising children in bilingual settings. As reviewed in De Houwer (2017), parents feel upset and ashamed when their children do not speak the language that the parents speak to them. On the other hand, growing up in a bilingual setting can lead young children to experience acute feelings of distress (first documented by Dahoun 1995). A bilingual situation can thus influence subjective well-being.

When subjective well-being is not negatively affected by factors relating to a bilingual setting, we can speak of Harmonious Bilingualism. This is an expansion on the notion of Harmonious Bilingual Development proposed earlier in De Houwer (2006, 2015). Harmonious Bilingual Development applies when families with young children in a language contact setting do not generally experience any problems because of that bilingual situation, or have a positive subjective experience with bilingualism. The notion of Harmonious Bilingualism increases the scope to families with children beyond the early childhood stage. Harmonious Bilingualism, then, is the more encompassing term to refer to a subjectively neutral or positive experience that members of a family in a bilingual setting have with aspects of that setting. The counterpart of Harmonious Bilingualism is conflictive bilingualism. Both Harmonious Bilingualism and conflictive bilingualism form two ends of a continuum.

Several studies have specifically assessed aspects of subjective well-being in bilingual situations. Others have revealed aspects of such subjective well-being (or the lack of it) more implicitly. This chapter aims to bring some of these studies together and consider how they contribute to a better understanding of Harmonious Bilingualism and the factors supporting it. First, however, I discuss the notion of subjective well-being.

1.2 Subjective well-being and the role of language

Subjective well-being is a multidimensional concept referring to "a broad category of phenomena that includes people's emotional responses, domain satisfactions, and global judgments of life satisfaction" (Diener et al. 1999: 277). While its precise conceptualization is not clear, the relevant literature tends to define subjective well-being in terms of "the experience of pleasant affect, unpleasant affect, and life satisfaction" (Tov 2018: 3).

Subjective well-being (henceforth: well-being) is inextricably linked with overall physical and mental health, temperament, and personality (Lansford 2018). As reviewed in Diener, Oishi, and Tay (2018), there are many other factors that affect well-being, such as socio-economic status, the political system people live in, and the quality of interpersonal relationships. Newland et al. (2018) studied these extensively for 25,906 9- to 14-year-olds across 14 countries, relying on data collected through the International Survey of Children's Well-Being (ISCWeB), a worldwide research survey on children's well-being that analyzes children's answers to a questionnaire (http://www.isciweb.org).

The general ISCWeB questionnaire does not, however, query anything related to language, except as part of a question about language classes taken outside school time. Also, the comprehensive Diener, Oishi, and Tay (2018) handbook does not mention language as a factor in well-being. Yet, as studies of monolinguals show, it certainly is. For instance, preschoolers with better pragmatic language abilities enjoy higher peer status (Paulus 2017). Adolescents who are proficient speakers have a higher chance of having successful friendships than peers who are not (Durkin and Conti-Ramsden 2007). Low verbal abilities are a risk factor for antisocial and delinquent behavior (Muñoz et al. 2008). People who stammer or who can no longer speak fluently due to dementia or aphasia pay a dear social price. Even receptive language skills impact how others perceive us: A study of 615 children in middle childhood found that children with lower receptive vocabulary skills showed increasingly troublesome behavior and suffered progressively more peer rejection, thus lowering their well-being (Menting, van Lier, and Koot 2011). These results are not surprising, given that we have known at least since Sapir (1927) that language use in interaction is intimately bound with personality, which is a socially ascribed and often verbally expressed construct of how we perceive others and ourselves, with all the biases this may entail (Trofimova 2014). Thus, language plays a fundamental role in well-being (Rose, Ebert, and Weinert 2016).

1.3 Well-being in bilingual settings: Some examples

Except for extreme cases of atypical language use as in aphasia, the role of language in well-being is hard to see in individual interactions in monolingual settings. Perhaps this is why the general well-being literature has not paid much attention to it. In bilingual settings, however, the role of language in well-being is much more immediately visible. Consider the example of my taxi driver in Portland, Oregon, in March 2014. He was born in Ethiopia and had moved to the United States as a young adult. He spoke English fluently. My driver's first language was

Oromiffa, and he self-identified as belonging to the Oromo people. He married an English-speaking American who did not know any Oromiffa. In 2014, my driver was the father of three young children and wanted them to speak Oromiffa. However, after his first son, Ifaa, was born, my driver did not speak Oromiffa to him because he thought it would confuse the child. He just spoke English to the baby. Yet Ifaa grew up with Oromiffa from birth, through input from his aunt, who lived with the family for the first two years of Ifaa's life, and who interacted with Ifaa a lot and did not know any English. Ifaa learned to speak Oromiffa through her, but stopped speaking it when his aunt went back to Ethiopia just before his third birthday. When Ifaa was about 4, his father started to speak Oromiffa to his children because he was alarmed at the fact that Ifaa was not speaking much Oromiffa. At age 6, Ifaa was able to speak some Oromiffa to the family back in Ethiopia (on Skype) but refused to speak it to his father. My driver cited Ifaa as telling him there was no point in speaking Oromiffa to him, because he spoke English anyhow. The father was puzzled by the fact that Ifaa was able and willing to speak some Oromiffa with other Ethiopians, but not with him as his father. Throughout the conversation, my driver was very open about being upset because his son would not speak Oromiffa with him. He expressed his long-held sense of grief about what he saw as his failure as a father to transmit his first language to his elder son. Clearly, my driver's well-being was being affected by specific language choices in the family. He was not experiencing Harmonious Bilingualism.

In another example, a child's sense of belonging in preschool and overall well-being were under attack because of her inability to verbally communicate in a new linguistic environment and the lack of attention from that environment for her predicament. Zerdalia lived in Algeria during the French colonial occupation (Dahoun 1995: 35–36). She spoke Arabic at home. Her first day at a French-speaking nursery school in her neighborhood came as a brutal shock. There was no sweet teacher to greet her in Arabic and pronounce her name correctly. In fact, no-one spoke a language she could understand. When the teacher called on her, she was stifled with fear – in what language should she speak? Zerdalia soon realized that the language spoken in her home and neighborhood was excluded at school. The following months she paid close attention to the sounds coming out of the teacher's and the other children's mouths and to how their mouths opened and closed. She realized she would have to learn to do as they did in order to communicate with them. And there was candy if you found the right words to say. One day, she gathered her courage to get up and address the teacher, in the hope of getting a candy. Instead, she got a cold disapproving stare and a finger pointing at her seat. Zerdalia felt unfairly treated, and her identity and her language crushed (Dahoun 1995 is recounting her own experiences as a child). Thus, already at age 3, Zerdalia experienced a lack of well-being due to the linguistic diversity she was confronted with, or, rather, due to how that linguistic diversity was shaped in her environment. She was not experiencing Harmonious Bilingual Development.

The next example also shows a relation between linguistic factors and well-being, but this time it is a positive one: The young man in this example prides himself on his bilingualism, and his bilingualism seems to contribute to his overall well-being. John lived in Louisiana, United States, with his Canadian-American parents who spoke French to him (Caldas 2006). In Lousiana, John spoke English with his friends. He spent summers in Québec, Canada, and had many French-speaking friends there. When asked how he felt about being bilingual in Canada, he said: "I speak well enough French to be perfectly integrated socially. In fact, my bilingualism and Americanism actually gave me an edge" (Caldas 2006: 158). At age 18, John thus seemed to be experiencing Harmonious Bilingualism, an improvement from 6 years earlier, when he had felt self-conscious and awkward about being bilingual (Caldas 2006: 152–159).

A final example shows a more neutral relation between linguistic factors and well-being: A German mother in Greece admitted that her children did not speak German very well, but she considered this to be normal (Leist-Villis 2004: 166). After all, she said, Greek is the environmental language in Greece, and nobody can be perfectly bilingual. This is also why she did not pressure her children about speaking better German. She found it good enough that they were able to make themselves understood. If her children wanted to speak better German, it was up to themselves to make that happen. This mother attributed no particularly negative or positive aspects to her children's lesser proficiency in the language she spoke to them. She appeared quite satisfied with her bilingual family situation, and was likely experiencing Harmonious Bilingualism.

The examples above show various degrees of well-being in people living in settings where they themselves or a family member are in regular contact with more than a single language variety. As the review below will show, there is indeed a large degree of interindividual variation in how people experience their bilingualism.

2 Scope of the review

The studies selectively reviewed below hail from different disciplines and research perspectives. Similarly to my earlier review of mostly European research (De Houwer 2017), I include both large quantitative and smaller qualitative studies. Their combination can likely tell us more about Harmonious Bilingualism than just a single research perspective. I here widen the scope to studies worldwide. Included are studies published in English, French and German. Most of the quantitative studies, however, are limited to countries where English is the societal language.

One novelty of the present review is that it systematically brings together findings about young children, adolescents and parents who are part of a family with pre-adult children (Sevinç this vol. discusses families with adult children; De Houwer

2017 only considered studies involving families in bilingual settings with children up to age 6). "Family" here means a unit made up of at least one adult who lives with and is responsible for at least one person who has not yet reached legally adult status (excluded are institutions such as orphanages or boarding schools) (for a more in-depth discussion of the notion of "family", see Palviainen this vol.). Families are dynamic systems that are firmly embedded within and influenced by wider society (Treas, Scott, and Richards 2017). Family members are autonomous persons who at the same time are strongly dependent on each other. What happens to one family member will affect the other(s) (Ram et al. 2014). Good child-parent relationships are central to family well-being (Suldo and Fefer 2013).

The review only considers studies yielding information on well-being and language use. Excluded are studies of well-being in bilinguals without a focus on language. The discussion below is limited to links between well-being and aspects of the bilingual setting in which respondents find themselves even if studies investigate additional aspects such as academic achievement.

The bilingual settings covered involve language varieties considered to represent different languages, rather than varieties of the same language. "Home language" here refers to any language not commonly used in public life in the region where the family lives (see Eisenchlas and Schalley this vol. for a more in-depth discussion); "societal language" refers to any language commonly used in public life. Families may speak both a home language and the societal language at home. Often, (pre)schools use the societal language, but some children are in institutions using both the home and the societal language, or just the home language.

Quantitative studies (section 3) often measure aspects of well-being through standardized assessment instruments. Many studies expressly examining well-being in relation to language consider children as individuals, that is, not in relation to their parents (3.1). Several other studies investigating well-being in bilingual settings focus on the child-parent relationship (3.2). So far, I have found only a single study systematically addressing aspects of parental well-being in bilingual families (3.3). Aspects of parental well-being in bilingual settings have mainly become visible through studies that happened to reveal some of those aspects as a result of a more ethnographic approach (section 4).

3 Empirical research explicitly addressing well-being in bilingual settings

3.1 Well-being in children in bilingual settings

When young children are raised with a single home language that is not the societal language, the first place they will meet up with another language in regular interpersonal contact is day care or preschool (De Houwer 2013). Bullying and victimization by monolingual peers are real dangers for these emergent bilingual children who do not yet speak the societal language well (see Chang et al. 2007 in the United States, involving 345 emergent bilinguals between 4.5 and 5.5; and von Grünigen et al. 2012 in Switzerland, involving 203 emergent bilinguals between 6 and 6.5). Importantly, Chang et al. (2007) found that teacher behavior modulates bullying rates: Emergent bilinguals were less likely to be victims of peer aggression in classrooms where teachers spoke more Spanish (the children's home language) compared to classrooms where teachers only spoke English (the societal language). Furthermore, the more teachers spoke English, the more they found their relationships with children to be conflictive. In contrast, the more teachers spoke Spanish, the less they felt that their relationship with the children was conflictive. von Grünigen et al. (2012) found that levels of bullying sharply decreased as emergent bilingual children gained proficiency in the societal language.

Societal language proficiency is important for all children: In a large ($N = 7{,}267$) cohort study in the United Kingdom, low levels of English proficiency at age 5 were associated with social, emotional, and behavioral difficulties for bilingual and monolingual children alike (Whiteside, Gooch, and Norbury 2017). Similarly, an even larger ($N = 261{,}147$) cohort study of 5-year-olds in Australia found that children who were not proficient in the societal language (again English) showed high levels of developmental vulnerability on several measures of well-being, regardless of whether they just heard English at home or another home language (Goldfeld et al. 2014).

It is thus not surprising that bilingual children who have developed good levels of proficiency in the societal language upon (pre)school entry have an advantage over emergent bilingual children in terms of well-being. They may even have an advantage compared to monolingual children who speak just the societal language. 5-year-olds with good proficiency in English but whose main home language was not English experienced fewer social, emotional, and behavioral difficulties than peers from monolingual English-speaking homes (Whiteside, Gooch, and Norbury 2017). Bilingually reared 6-year-olds who did not yet know much English upon entry in English-speaking primary schools ($N = 6{,}361$) were consistently rated by teachers as being in the vulnerable range on several measures of well-being (Goldfeld et al. 2014). In contrast, bilingually reared children who already spoke English fairly well ($N = 37{,}657$) did not show this vulnerability, and had equal or even lower chances of being in the vulnerable range for well-being compared to monolingual English-speaking peers, mirroring Whiteside, Gooch, and Norbury's (2017) findings. Another study from Australia found no bilingual-monolingual differences for socio-emotional outcomes in 8- to 9-year-olds, but did not consider levels of proficiency in the societal language at school entry (McLeod et al. 2016; $N = 3{,}240$). In the U.S., Han and Huang (2010) and Han (2010) found interesting differences amongst 5 types of children. They studied 12,580 and 14,853 children, respectively, who took part in a large cohort study spanning 6 years. Han and Huang's (2010) sample consisted of "Asian origin" children ($N = 1,350$) and "US-born, non-Hispanic White" children; Han's (2010) of "Latino origin" children ($N = 2,888$) and "US-born, non-Hispanic White" children. They categorized children on the basis of language fluency at kindergarten entry (the preparatory year before primary school). Both studies found that language fluency status at kindergarten entry predicted later levels of well-being, viz., children categorized as fluent bilinguals or non-English-dominant bilinguals surpassed monolingual English-speaking children, English-dominant bilinguals and non-English monolinguals on measures of well-being 6 years later. In fact, children who upon school entry did not know any English had the lowest degree of self-control and interpersonal skills, and the highest level of internalizing problems 6 years later.

To prevent such long term negative effects of early developmental vulnerability in emergent bilinguals, Han (2010) proposes that children should have the chance to participate in high quality second language instruction programs as soon as they enter school. While this is no doubt a good recommendation, other factors can help as well. In their study of 2,059 Spanish-speaking Latino/Hispanic children in the United States, Winsler, Kim, and Richards (2014) found that strong skills in children's home language help to fast-develop proficiency in the societal language. Four-and-a-half-year-olds with stronger Spanish and stronger socio-emotional skills made faster gains in English proficiency a year later compared to peers whose Spanish was weaker and who exhibited more behavioral problems, less self-control and lower degrees of initiative. Another U.S. study of somewhat older children ($N = 228$) showed that dual language competence correlated with well-being over and above other factors such as maternal education, levels of poverty, family structure, classroom composition, child non-verbal IQ, or gender (Collins et al. 2011).

The previous studies used teacher and/or parent ratings of aspects of child well-being. Two studies used self-reports to explore links between dual language proficiency and aspects of well-being. Van Der Wildt, Van Avermaet, and Van Hecke (2017) found that bilingual 4th graders ($N = 1,761$) in Belgium who reported knowing one of their languages much better than the other felt less of a sense of school belonging than children who knew both their languages equally well (school belonging supports well-being). In the Netherlands, Vedder (2005; $N = 256$) found interesting differences between two ethnic groups. Turkish origin adolescents experienced slightly better psychological adaptation if they knew both their "ethnic" language and the societal language (Dutch) well. Suriname origin adolescents, on the other hand, showed lower degrees of psychological adaptation if they knew both their "ethnic" language and the societal language well (unfortunately, Vedder does not identify the "ethnic" languages). Vedder explains this discrepancy by differences amongst Turkish and Suriname origin families in the extent to which they emphasize the importance of the societal language. If Suriname origin adolescents try to speak the "ethnic" language well, they are in a sense rebelling against their parents, who tend to emphasize the value of only the societal language, thus contributing to lesser degrees of psychological adaptation. Turkish origin families, on the other hand, consider the home language to be very important. This brings us to the next section, which focuses on studies investigating well-being and adolescent-parent relationships in families in bilingual settings. They were all carried out in North America.

3.2 Well-being of children and parents in bilingual families

Tseng and Fuligni's (2000) was the first quantitative study ($N = 626$) to draw a link between teen well-being and language choice in bilingual families. It showed that adolescents in California who did not speak the same home language as their parents felt more emotionally distant from them and were less likely to engage in conversations with them compared to peers who spoke the same home language as their parents. In a later study of 414 9th graders, Oh and Fuligni (2010) found that in addition to language choice the level of home language proficiency also mattered for the quality of adolescent-parent reationships, reflecting similar earlier findings by Portes and Hao (2002). Similarly, Boutakidis, Chao, and Rodríguez (2011) found positive associations between 611 teens' fluency in their home language and the degree to which they respected their parents. They also found that the more fluent teens were in their home language, the more highly teens rated the communication with their parents.

There have also been studies involving both teens and their parents, all focusing on Chinese as the home language and English as the societal language. These studies used parental and teens' self-reports on language use but included well-being measures only for teens (through self-reports). In Liu et al. (2009; $N = 444$ teens and their mothers) teens who were proficient in their home language (Chinese) and whose mothers were so too reported fewer depressive symptoms compared to teens who were less proficient in their home language or compared to high home language proficient teens with low home language proficient mothers. However, no relation between teen well-being measures and a match in levels of English proficiency between teens and mothers emerged. These findings are consistent with earlier findings by Costigan and Dokis (2006), who studied 89 fathers, 92 mothers and 92 12-year-olds in the same family. Fathers and mothers spoke the home language more frequently than their children. Overall, teens reported relatively low levels of depression and intergenerational conflict. Reported intergenerational conflict and feelings of depression were lowest, however, for children who spoke the home language and had mothers with high levels of home language use. Conversely, in their study of 451 13-year-olds and both their parents, Weaver and Kim (2008) found that teens who reported highest depressive symptoms and who rated their parents as being least supportive had low proficiency in the home language and lived in families where parents had low proficiency in the societal language.

The studies reviewed here strongly suggest that teens feel best in families where there is a match between teens' and parents' language proficiencies.

3.3 Well-being in parents of bilingually reared children

I have been able to find only a single quantitative study investigating aspects of well-being of parents in bilingual families. In her in-depth structured interview and questionnaire study with 100 mothers in Greece and Germany who spoke mostly just German and Greek to their children, respectively, Leist-Villis (2004) included a question about mothers' global satisfaction regarding their bilingual family life. Mothers had first-born children between 4 and 16 years. Most mothers (57) were very satisfied with the bilingual child rearing and development process as a whole, 20 mothers more or less so, and 23 were not satisfied. 12 of these 23 reported feeling they had utterly failed at transmitting their language to their child(ren), and felt very bad about that. Mothers who were highly satisfied with their bilingual family life tended to (1) have children who spoke the home language, (2) only speak the home language to their children regardless of the situation, (3) have children who attended a school that used the home language as a medium of instruction (exclusively, or in addition to the societal language), (4) have a spouse who was able to speak the home language reasonably well, and (5) have more home language speakers in their social networks.

Other interview studies might include questions about how mothers feel about their family's bilingualism, but few do so systematically or in a standardized way. Even if not asked, interviewees may happen to express evaluative feelings towards their bilingual situation. Investigators might also gain insight into aspects of well-being through observation. Section 4 reviews some findings gained through studies that are not explicitly focused on well-being.

4 Empirical research implicitly addressing Harmonious Bilingualism

Observational studies of preschool-age home language speaking children like Zerdalia who did not know the societal language when they first started to attend preschool show extremely high levels of stress and unhappiness in these children, with some withdrawing from engagement and remaining silent in preschool for up to two years (Dahoun 1995, Algeria and France; Drury 2007, United Kingdom; Manigand

1999, France; Kostyuk 2005, Germany; Nap-Kolhoff 2010, the Netherlands). These qualitative studies complement quantitative studies demonstrating that children who do not yet know the societal language when they enter (pre)school are especially vulnerable in terms of overall well-being (section 3.1).

A rare study based on ethnographic interviews with children gives some insights into how they evaluated their bilingualism (Mills 2001). None of the 10 children (aged 5 to 19) were very proficient in their home language (Urdu) but all spoke the societal language (English in the United Kingdom) fluently. None of them appeared to have any particular issues with their bilingualism, and accepted that they needed Urdu for contacts with older relatives and/or with people in Pakistan, even if they did not speak it very well.

If children still speak the home language a bit, its use may, however, become a locus of intergenerational strife, conflict, and power struggle (Danjo 2018; Kheirkhah and Cekaite 2015; Sevinç 2016). Children may actively refuse to speak the home language in particular situations, answer only with single words, or change the topic and with it the language (De Houwer 1999). Eventually, these strategies may lead to children not speaking the home language at all. This negatively affects parents' well-being. Pakistani origin mothers in the United Kingdom expressed feelings of regret, remorse, and guilt at what they saw as their failure to transmit their home language to their children (Mills 2004). Such feelings are shared by parents all over the world (De Houwer 2017). Often, parents mention that if their children were not to be able to speak the home language they would no longer be able to communicate with grandparents and other relatives. Parents shudder at the thought. Rodriguez (1983: 29–30) remembers his relatives' fiercely negative reaction when as a child he could not speak Spanish, his home language (see also Sevinç this vol.). Children are also expected to learn to use polite and respectful language forms when speaking to their home language-speaking grandparents (Mills 2004). If not, parents will be blamed for not raising their children properly. Wong Fillmore (1991) mentions a particularly tragic example where a Korean origin father in the United States felt compelled to physically punish his son for not using appropriate honorifics when the child's Korean-speaking grandfather came to visit. The grandfather had scolded his son for not educating his grandchildren properly so they could speak polite Korean. The children were taken in protective custody. Unfortunately, no-one involved recognized the role that language played in this family drama.

It does not help that in-laws who do not speak the home language may also create tensions. Leist-Villis (2004) reports that societal language-speaking in-laws often voiced negative attitudes towards child bilingualism and/or to the home language, which led to conflicts and made the speaking of the home language by mothers and/or children into a battleground. In these situations, the parental couple relationship may be threatened as well: Spouses face the dilemma of either going against their parents, or against their home-language-speaking spouse, who in turn may not feel sufficiently supported (Leist-Villis 2004).

Conversations in which children speak the societal language and parents the home language involve divergent language choices (De Houwer 2019). The establishment of such conversations may have become a habit since children were preschoolers. Regardless of their feelings about them, parents may have adjusted to such conversations, as shown in Nakamura's (2018) study of an Italian- and an English-speaking father in Japan whose school-aged children spoke mainly Japanese with them. A longitudinal and observational group study of parent-child story-telling interaction in bilingual families in the United States similarly suggests such adjustment. Park et al. (2012) traced home language maintenance (Cantonese or Mandarin) in 68 children who were 6 years old at Time1 and nearly 7.5 years old at Time2. They compared the amount of parental home language support in parent-child interactions with assessments of child home language proficiency. Home language support was defined as a combination of parental home language choice and feedback on child home language use, including the use of "insisting" discourse strategies which socialize children into using the home language. A lack of parental home language support at Time1 was associated with children's home language loss at Time2. Importantly, this study found no evidence that parents decreased their expression of warmth towards their young children with limited home language proficiency. Likewise, fathers' interactions with children in Nakamura (2018) showed evidence of a child-centered and warm parent-child relationship, in spite of divergent language choices. This stands in sharp contrast to findings for adolescents and their parents (3.2), where interpersonal relationships may be strained and conflictive if they speak different languages with each other.

There is less of a chance for conflictive bilingualism when children speak the home language. Parents in recently immigrated Iranian families in the United States mentioned that children started to take pride in knowing the home language (Farsi) when they were asked to translate from English into Farsi for their visiting grandparents (Kaveh 2018). Parents in Greece with school aged children who spoke the home language (Albanian) appeared satisfied with their bilingual family experience (Chatzidaki and Maligkoudi 2013). Indeed, many are quite satisfied if children speak the home language (Leist-Villis 2004). Others may not care much about the home language and are satisfied that their children are highly proficient speakers of other languages (Gogonas and Kirsch 2018), but such reports are rare: Most parents who speak a home language to their children want their children to speak the home language, too. There are no reports of parents or children feeling bad because of fluently conversing in the same home language.

Even if children speak the home language they may not want to use it outside the home. Many maternal reports indicate that somewhat older children are embarrassed when their mothers speak the home language in public (Kaveh 2018; Leist-Villis 2004; Little 2020). Examples abound of children telling their mothers to stop talking the home language in public. This telling off and rejection of their home language makes mothers feel bad. In most cases, though, they comply, and switch to speaking the societal language in public (Chatzidaki and Maligkoudi 2013; De Houwer 2017).

Finally, parents are often insecure about how they should go about ensuring that their children learn both the home language and the societal language (De Houwer 2017). Many are torn between children's need to learn the societal language well, and their desire that children should learn the home language as well (Mills 2004: 184; Kaveh 2018; Sevinç 2016).

5 Research on well-being in families in bilingual settings: A brief assessment and outlook

Research explicitly addressing well-being in families in bilingual settings so far is mostly focused on children. We need more systematic studies like the one conducted by Leist-Villis (2004) that assess parental well-being in bilingual settings. Most of the information on parental well-being in bilingual families is rather scattered and unfocused, given that it usually just happened to come up in an interview. Also, this rather anecdotal information is virtually limited to mothers. We know little about fathers' assessments of their bilingual family life.

The information regarding bilingual children's well-being mostly does not take into account family level processes. Also here the research base needs to be expanded.

Most of the large scale studies of well-being in bilingual family members hail from North America, and are heavily tilted towards children in Hispanic and East Asian origin families. Currently available information on well-being in bilinguals does not indicate different patterns across countries. In particular, the two-country study by Leist-Villis (2004) did not find any differences amongst maternal feelings of satisfaction with their bilingual experience beyond the fact that different languages and societies were involved. Yet, there may be regional or language-specific effects that have thus far gone unnoticed. More comparisons across countries are in order.

Many families in bilingual settings have an immigration background. Recently immigrated individuals may suffer from acculturative stress. Others, also those with a less recent immigration background, may have experiences with non-language related discrimination. It is highly likely that overall processes of acculturation are linked to language. It remains to be investigated, though, to what extent levels of acculturative stress or feelings of societal exclusion are related to linguistic factors. Especially young children's experiences with social exclusion based on lack of intercomprehension (as in Zerdalia's example) may have long lasting effects. These effects may, however, go in either direction: Children may retreat from the new language and society, or they may start focusing only on their new language and reject the home language and all it represents. Only long term longitudinal studies can reveal the effects of either.

The available studies, however, already allow us to formulate some main findings.

6 Well-being in bilingual families: Some main findings

The review above shows that language choice and proficiency relate to well-being in members of families living in bilingual settings. Language use in families living in bilingual settings deeply affects family relationships within the nuclear family and beyond. Furthermore, children's positive or more negative language related experiences in (pre)school are likely to not only affect children as individuals, but also their families.

6.1 Home language use between children and parents

Parents and children may use the same language(s) in speaking to each other, and thus follow the default convergent pattern for language choice (De Houwer 2019). Although same language choice does not guarantee friction-free intergenerational communication, both quantitative and qualitative studies show that well-being is at risk if parents and children address each other in different languages. The pattern whereby children speak the societal language and parents the home language does not serve family members well.

Several surveys show that this divergent choice pattern of intra-family communication is quite common. A quarter of the 5,335 children in 2,250 families in Flanders, Belgium, who heard a home language from one or both parents did not speak that language but solely spoke the societal language, Dutch (De Houwer 2003). Longitudinal findings for 93 infants exposed to an indigenous language in Australia and the societal language, English, show a nearly identical proportion of sole English use by the time children were of preschool age (Verdon and McLeod 2015). A larger longitudinal study of children in Australia, this time including speakers of any non-English home language, found that of the 666 children who spoke a home language at age 2 to 3 only 78% still spoke that language by the time they were 4 to 5 (Verdon, McLeod, and Winsler 2014). Slavkov (2017) reports similar proportions of home language use by school-aged children in bilingual families in Ontario, Canada. A fifth of 626 adolescents with a recent immigration background in the United States reported speaking English to their home language-speaking parents (Tseng and Fuligni 2000). The fact that home language maintenance generally appears to be absent for about a quarter of the families surveyed suggests that many families in a bilingual setting do not experience Harmonious Bilingualism.

A study investigating parent-child language choice in more detail concerns 1,086 families with at least one 5- to 7.5-year-old child in Texas and California where Spanish was the home and English the societal language (Branum-Martin et al. 2014). Amongst others, this study queried whether family members spoke only/mainly Spanish to another family member, Spanish and English equally, or mainly/only English. If we consider just the percentage of parents and children who spoke only Spanish with each other, my comparison of data in Branum-Martin et al. (2014; Table 2) shows that in father-child conversations 52% of fathers spoke just Spanish but only 46% of children did so, and that in mother-child conversations 62% of mothers spoke just Spanish but only 52% of children did so. These comparisons confirm the frequent occurrence of parent-child divergent choice conversations in which parents speak the home language and children the societal language (the reverse pattern has not been reported).

Patterns of divergent language choice may start to occur quite early. Many mothers note that children started to refuse to speak the home language soon after they started attending a preschool in the societal language (Leist-Villis 2004: 187–192; Kaveh 2018; Mills 2004; Wong Fillmore 1991). In response to children's increasing use of the societal language at home, parents may start to speak less and less of the home language, so that eventually the entire family just uses the societal language (e.g., E-Rramdani 2003), with parental feelings of regret and shame as a frequent result.

6.2 Children's dual language proficiency

Apart from what happens with the home language and with intra-family communication, studies demonstrate that children's proficiency in both the home and the societal language is of importance to their well-being, and this from the very start. In this respect children who have been raised with both languages from the very start fare much better than children who have not had the chance to learn the societal language from when they were infants.

Parents are very much aware that dual language proficiency is important for their children's overall well-being and success in life. Society, however, may make it very hard for parents to succeed in raising dual language proficient children. Mothers complained about negative attitudes towards the home language in (pre)schools and blamed these negative attitudes for the fact that children no longer wanted to speak the home language (Leist-Villis 2004: 187–192). All too often, teachers, speech therapists and pediatricians advise parents to solely speak the societal language at home instead of the home language (Bezçioğlu-Göktolga and Yağmur 2018; Kaveh 2018). Such advice is ethically reprehensible and legally unacceptable (De Houwer 2013). As Wong Fillmore (1991) already noted, teachers harm parents and children with this advice. It makes parents feel insecure and thus detracts from Harmonious Bilingualism (De Houwer 2015a; 2017). If home language-speaking parents follow this advice, professionals are co-responsible for taking away the best chance bilingual children have to grow up harmoniously: Supportive and rich language input from expert speakers who love them.

7 Conclusion: The hallmarks of Harmonious Bilingualism and how to support it

How family members experience their bilingual situation is intensely personal (De Houwer 2015a). This implies that individuals with at first sight similar experiences do not necessarily evaluate those experiences the same way. Yet the bulk of the literature that gives "accidental" insights into Harmonious Bilingualism in bilingual families and the large scale studies addressing well-being in bilingual family members does allow for some fundamental generalizations across different individuals, contexts, and languages.

The central finding across all relevant studies is that families in bilingual settings experience Harmonious Bilingualism when children develop good language skills in both the home and the societal language from a young age. This dual language proficiency allows children to develop and continue developing barrier-free communication within and outside the family (Leyendecker et al. 2014).

All children eventually learn the societal language, though not necessarily to high (enough) levels of proficiency. Several surveys of children's and parents' home language use show, however, that home language maintenance is much less of a given. A lack of home language maintenance is linked to a lack of Harmonious Bilingualism in parents and adolescent children alike.

Home language maintenance is threatened when parent-child interactions mainly consist of divergent language choice patterns in which parents speak the home language and children the societal language. Parents tend not to be aware of the importance of convergent choice patterns. Many lack what I have called an "impact belief", that is, a belief that they can influence their child's language development (De Houwer 1999). Yet parents can use conversational practices encouraging very young children's choice of a particular language (Lanza 1997). Such practices tend to be successful. The parents in Greece with children who spoke the home language (Albanian) all insisted that children speak Albanian at home with them and other older relatives (Chatzidaki and Maligkoudi 2013). For many parents such insisting strategies may not suit their parenting style (Currie Armstrong 2014). However, the research evidence suggests that parents (and children) may be spared much sadness and frustration if they socialize children into answering in the same home language that they were addressed in.

In addition to using insisting strategies, the parents in Chatzidaki and Maligkoudi's study tried to expose children to Albanian as much as possible, and actively supported their children's development of home language literacy. The mothers interviewed by Leist-Villis (2004) pointed at the importance for the home language of visits to the country where the home language was a societal language, and of visits of relatives to the country where the family lives. A Greek mother in Germany noted that her Greek mother came to stay with the family 6 months a year. The grandmother did not speak German and this motivated the mother's son to speak Greek (Leist-Villis 2004: 177). My driver was grateful when I gave him tips about how to increase his use of Oromiffa to his children and told him about the importance of joint book reading. I also suggested that he should have his sister record stories and rhymes and songs in Oromiffa that could then be played to the children. The father was aware of having to choose activities that would interest the children and became hopeful that he might be able to turn the tide with Ifaa and do better with his younger children. Indeed, as discussed in other contributions to this volume, there are many more factors supporting home language maintenance besides convergent choice conversations. Frequent and qualitatively high home language input to children is crucial (De Houwer 2018).

Age appropriate proficiency in the societal language is another pillar supporting Harmonious Bilingualism. Many parents raise their children with both a societal and a home language from birth. Parents in such bilingual families hold various ideas about child bilingualism, the languages they should speak to children, the language(s) children should learn, or the best way to teach children two languages (De Houwer 1999). Some of these ideas are likely to support Harmonious Bilingualism (e.g., if parents believe it is possible for young children to learn several languages from early on), whereas others will not (e.g., if parents believe it is harmful to children to learn several languages from early on). Early bilingual acquisition is very much driven by the language input environment children find themselves in, but parents are not always aware of this fact. Frequent and qualitatively high language input is important in any language.

Finally, (pre)schools have a crucial role in supporting Harmonious Bilingualism. They can do so by showing respect for children's home languages and thus bolster children's pride in their home language while children are acquiring the societal language at school (De Houwer 2015b; Robertson, Drury, and Cable 2014). Zerdalia was lucky to have another teacher in the second year of nursery school (Dahoun 1995: 38): Ms. Bruno was new to Algeria and held no linguistic or racial prejudices. She made a patient effort to reach out to the silent Zerdalia, and Zerdalia opened up to her. Ms. Bruno even visited Zerdalia's home and tried to say some things in the local Arab dialect. Because of Ms. Bruno's "intelligence du coeur" (p. 38, intelligence of the heart), Zerdalia started loving school and loving French. She continued to speak

Arabic with her family and in the neighborhood, and describes how she came to evaluate her bilingualism as positive. Chang et al. (2007: 265) note that "The [teacher's] acknowledgement of a child's home language changes and elevates the status of that child within the classroom". School and home are intricately linked: When children feel that their home language is respected at (pre)school, they will show less of a tendency to reject it. This is uniquely shown in a study from Belgium attempting to explain differential levels of self-rated home language proficiency in 312 10- to 12-year-olds (Dekeyser and Stevens 2019). Home language proficiency was not only directly related to parental home language choice and child-rated maternal home language proficiency, but was also higher in students who thought they were allowed to speak the home language at school.

Families in bilingual settings may experience Harmonious Bilingualism most of the time. Others may go through long periods in which they do not. The good news is that Harmonious Bilingualism is possible even after families have had negative experiences. As researchers, we need to investigate the causes of this ebb and flow so that we may furnish families with the tools to help increase their resilience.

References

Bezçioğlu-Göktolga, Irem & Kutlay Yağmur. 2018. The impact of Dutch teachers on family language policy of Turkish immigrant parents. *Language, Culture and Curriculum* 31(3). 220–234.

Boutakidis, Ioakim P., Ruth K. Chao & James L. Rodríguez. 2011. The role of adolescents' native language fluency on quality of communication and respect for parents in Chinese and Korean immigrant families. *Asian American Journal of Psychology* 2(2). 128–139.

Branum-Martin, Lee, Paras D. Mehta, Coleen D. Carlson, David J. Francis & Claude Goldenberg. 2014. The nature of Spanish versus English language use at home. *Journal of Educational Psychology* 106(1). 181–199.

Caldas, Stephen J. 2006. *Raising bilingual-biliterate children in monolingual cultures*. Clevedon: Multilingual Matters.

Chang, Florence, Gisele Crawford, Diane Early, Donna Bryant, Carollee Howes, Margaret Burchinal, Oscar Barbarin, Richard Clifford & Robert Pianta. 2007. Spanish-speaking children's social and language development in pre-kindergarten classrooms. *Early Education and Development* 18(2). 243–269.

Chatzidaki, Aspassia & Christina Maligkoudi. 2013. Family language policies among Albanian immigrants in Greece. *International Journal of Bilingual Education and Bilingualism* 16(6). 675–689.

Collins, Brian A., Claudio O. Toppelberg, Carola Suárez-Orozco, Erin O'Connor & Alfonso Nieto-Castañon. 2011. Cross-sectional associations of Spanish and English competence and well-being in Latino children of immigrants in kindergarten. *International Journal of the Sociology of Language* 208. 5–23.

Costigan, Catherine L. & Daphné P. Dokis. 2006. Relations between parent–child acculturation differences and adjustment within immigrant Chinese families. *Child Development* 77(5). 1252–1267.

Currie Armstrong, Timothy. 2014. Naturalism and ideological work: How is family language policy renegotiated as both parents and children learn a threatened minority language? *International Journal of Bilingual Education and Bilingualism* 17(5). 570–585.

Dahoun, Zerdalia K. S. 1995. *Les couleurs du silence. Le mutisme des enfants de migrants.* Paris: Calmann-Lévy.

Danjo, Chisato. 2018. Making sense of family language policy: Japanese-English bilingual children's creative and strategic translingual practices. *International Journal of Bilingual Education and Bilingualism.* Online first. DOI: 10.1080/13670050.2018.1460302

De Houwer, Annick. 1999. Environmental factors in early bilingual development: The role of parental beliefs and attitudes. In Guus Extra & Ludo Verhoeven (eds.), *Bilingualism and migration*, 75–96. Berlin: Mouton de Gruyter.

De Houwer, Annick. 2003. Home languages spoken in officially monolingual Flanders: A survey. *Plurilingua* 24. 71–87.

De Houwer, Annick. 2006. Le développement harmonieux ou non harmonieux du bilinguisme de l'enfant au sein de la famille. *Langage et Société* 116. 29–49.

De Houwer, Annick. 2013. Early bilingualism. In Carol Chapelle (ed.), *The encyclopedia of applied linguistics*, 1822–1830. Hoboken: John Wiley.

De Houwer, Annick. 2015a. Harmonious bilingual development: Young families' well-being in language contact situations. *International Journal of Bilingualism* 19(2). 169–184.

De Houwer, Annick. 2015b. Integration und Interkulturalität in Kindertagesstätten und in Kindergärten: Die Rolle der Nichtumgebungssprache für das Wohlbefinden von Kleinkindern. In Eva Reichert-Garschhammer, Christa Kieferle, Monika Wertfein & Fabienne Becker-Stoll (eds.), *Inklusion und Partizipation. Vielfalt als Chance und Anspruch*, 113–125. Göttingen: Vandenhoeck & Ruprecht.

De Houwer, Annick. 2017. Minority language parenting in Europe and children's well-being. In Natasha Cabrera & Birgit Leyendecker (eds.), *Handbook on positive development of minority children and youth*, 231–246. Berlin: Springer.

De Houwer, Annick. 2018. The role of language input environments for language outcomes and language acquisition in young bilingual children. In David Miller, Fatih Bayram, Jason Rothman & Ludovica Serratrice (eds.), *Bilingual cognition and language: The state of the science across its subfields*, 127–153. Amsterdam: John Benjamins.

De Houwer, Annick. 2019. Language choice in bilingual interaction. In Annick De Houwer & Lourdes Ortega (eds.), *The Cambridge handbook of bilingualism*, 324–348. Cambridge: Cambridge University Press.

Dekeyser, Graziela & Gillian Stevens. 2019. Maintaining one language while learning another: Moroccan children in Belgium. *Journal of Multilingual and Multicultural Development* 40(2). 143–163.

Diener, Ed, Shigehiro Oishi & Louis Tay (eds.). 2018. *Handbook of well-being.* Salt Lake City, UT: DEF Publishers. https://www.nobascholar.com/books/1 (accessed Dec. 24, 2018).

Diener, Ed, Euncook M. Suh, Richard E. Lucas & Heidi L. Smith. 1999. Subjective well-being: Three decades of progress. *Psychological Bulletin* 125(2). 276–302.

Drury, Rose. 2007. *Young bilingual learners at home and school: Researching multilingual voices.* Stoke on Trent: Trentham Books.

Durkin, Kevin & Gina Conti-Ramsden. 2007. Language, social behavior, and the quality of friendships in adolescents with and without a history of Specific Language Impairment. *Child Development* 78(5). 1441–1457.

Eisenchlas, Susana A. & Andrea C. Schalley. this vol. Making sense of the notion of "home language" and related concepts.

E-Rramdani, Yahya. 2003. *Acquiring Tarifit-Berber by children in the Netherlands and Morocco*. Amsterdam: Aksant Academic Publishers.

Goldfeld, Sharon, Meredith O'Connor, Johanna Mithen, Mary Sayers & Sally Brinkman. 2014. Early developmental outcomes of emerging and English-proficient bilingual children at school entry in an Australian population cohort. *International Journal of Behavioral Development* 38(1). 42–51.

Gogonas, Nikos & Claudine Kirsch. 2018. "In this country my children are learning two of the most important languages in Europe": Ideologies of language as a commodity among Greek migrant families in Luxembourg. *International Journal of Bilingual Education and Bilingualism* 21(4). 426–438.

Grünigen, Renate von, Becky Kochenderfer-Ladd, Sonja Perren & Françoise Alsaker. 2012. Links between local language competence and peer relations among Swiss and immigrant children: The mediating role of social behaviour. *Journal of School Psychology* 50(2). 195–213.

Han, Wen-Jui. 2010. Bilingualism and socioemotional well-being. *Children and Youth Services Review* 32. 720–731.

Han, Wen-Jui & Chien-Chung Huang. 2010. The forgotten treasure: Bilingualism and children's emotional and behavioral health. *American Journal of Public Health* 100(5). 831–838.

Kaveh, Yalda M. 2018. Family language policy and maintenance of Persian: The stories of Iranian immigrant families in the northeast, USA. *Language Policy* 17(4). 443–477.

Kheirkhah, Mina & Asta Cekaite. 2015. Language maintenance in a multilingual family: Informal heritage language lessons in parent–child interactions. *Multilingua* 34(3). 319–346.

Kostyuk, Natalia. 2005. *Der Zweitspracherwerb beim Kind: Eine Studie am Beispiel des Erwerbs des Deutschen durch drei russischsprachige Kinder*. Hamburg: Verlag Dr. Kovač.

Lansford, Jennifer E. 2018. A lifespan perspective on subjective well-being. In Ed Diener, Shigehiro Oishi & Louis Tay (eds.), *Handbook of well-being*. Salt Lake City, UT: DEF Publishers. https://www.nobascholar.com/chapters/25/download.pdf (accessed Dec. 24, 2018).

Lanza, Elizabeth. 1997. *Language mixing in infant bilingualism: A sociolinguistic perspective*. Oxford: Clarendon Press.

Leist-Villis, Anja. 2004. *Zweisprachigkeit im Kontext sozialer Netzwerke. Unterstützende Rahmenbedingungen zweisprachiger Entwicklung und Erziehung am Beispiel griechisch-deutsch*. Münster: Waxmann.

Leyendecker, Birgit, Jessica Willard, Alexandru Agache, Julia Jäkel, Olivia Spiegler & Katharina Kohl. 2014. Learning a host country: A plea to strengthen parents' roles and to encourage children's bilingual development. In Rainer K. Silbereisen, Peter F. Titzmann & Yossi Shavit (eds). *The challenges of diaspora migration: Interdisciplinary perspectives on Israel and Germany*, 291–306. London: Ashgate/Routledge.

Little, Sabine. 2020. Whose heritage? What inheritance?: conceptualising family language identities. *International Journal of Bilingual Education and Bilingualism* 23(2). 198–212.

Liu, Lisa L., Aprile D. Benner, Anna S. Lau & Su Yeong Kim. 2009. Mother-adolescent language proficiency and adolescent academic and emotional adjustment among Chinese American families. *Journal of Youth and Adolescence* 38(4). 572–586.

Manigand, Alain. 1999. Le silence des enfants turcs à l'école. *Psychologie & Éducation* 37. 57–73.

McLeod, Sharynne, Linda Harrison, Chrystal Whiteford & Sue Walker. 2016. Multilingualism and speech-language competence in early childhood: Impact on academic and social-emotional outcomes at school. *Early Childhood Research Quarterly* 34 (1st Quarter). 53–66.

Menting, Barbara, Pol A. C. van Lier & Hans M. Koot. 2011. Language skills, peer rejection, and the development of externalizing behavior from kindergarten to fourth grade. *The Journal of Child Psychology and Psychiatry* 52(1). 72–79.

Mills, Jean. 2001. Being bilingual: Perspectives of third generation Asian children on language, culture and identity. *International Journal of Bilingual Education and Bilingualism* 4(6). 383–402.

Mills, Jean. 2004. Mothers and mother tongue: Perspectives on self-construction by mothers of Pakistani heritage. In Aneta Pavlenko & Adrian Blackledge (eds.), *Negotiation of identities in multilingual contexts*, 161–191. Clevedon: Multilingual Matters.

Muñoz, Luna C., Paul J. Frick, Eva R. Kimonis & Katherine J. Aucoin. 2008. Verbal ability and delinquency: Testing the moderating role of psychopathic traits. *Journal of Child Psychology and Psychiatry* 49(4). 414–421.

Nakamura, Janice. 2018. Parents' use of discourse strategies in dual-lingual interactions with receptive bilingual children. In Elena Babatsouli (ed.), *Crosslinguistic research in monolingual and bilingual speech*, 181–200. Chania: ISMBS.

Nap-Kolhoff, Elma. 2010. *Second language acquisition in early childhood: A longitudinal multiple case study of Turkish-Dutch children*. Utrecht: Netherlands Graduate School of Linguistics LOT.

Newland, Lisa A., Jarod T. Giger, Michael J. Lawler, Soonhee Roh, Barbara L. Brockevelt & Amy Schweinle. 2018. Multilevel analysis of child and adolescent subjective well-being across 14 countries: Child- and country-level predictors. *Child Development* 90(2). 395–413.

Oh, Janet S. & Andrew J. Fuligni. (2010). The role of heritage language development in the ethnic identity and family relationships of adolescents from immigrant backgrounds. *Social Development*, 19(1). 202–220.

Palviainen, Åsa. this vol. Future prospects and visions for family language policy research.

Park, Heejung, Kim M. Tsai, Lisa L. Liu & Anna S. Lau. 2012. Transactional associations between supportive family climate and young children's heritage language proficiency in immigrant families. *International Journal of Behavioral Development* 36(3). 226–236.

Paulus, Markus. 2017. How to Dax? Preschool children's prosocial behavior, but not their social norm enforcement relates to their peer status. *Frontiers in Psychology* 8:1779. DOI: 10.3389/fpsyg.2017.01779

Portes, Alejandro & Lingxin Hao. 2002. The price of uniformity: Language, family and personality adjustment in the immigrant second generation. *Ethnic and Racial Studies* 25(6). 889–912.

Ram, Nilam, Mariya Shiyko, Erika S. Lunkenheimer, Shawna Doerksen & David Conroy. 2014. Families as coordinated symbiotic systems: Making use of nonlinear dynamic models. In Susan M. McHale, Paul R. Amato & Alan Booth (eds.), *Emerging methods in family research*, 19–37. Cham: Springer.

Robertson, Leena H., Rose Drury & Carrie Cable. 2014. Silencing bilingualism. *International Journal of Bilingual Education and Bilingualism* 17(5). 610–623.

Rodriguez, Richard. 1983. *Hunger of memory: The education of Richard Rodriguez*. New York: Bantam.

Rose, Elisabeth, Susanne Ebert & Sabine Weinert. 2016. Zusammenspiel sprachlicher und sozialemotionaler Entwicklung vom vierten bis zum achten Lebensjahr. Eine längsschnittliche Untersuchung. *Frühe Bildung* 5(2). 66–72.

Sapir, Edward. 1927. Speech as a personality trait. *American Journal of Sociology* 32. 894–904.

Sevinç, Yeşim. 2016. Language maintenance and shift under pressure: Three generations of the Turkish immigrant community in the Netherlands. *International Journal of the Sociology of Language* 242. 81–117.

Sevinç, Yeşim. this vol. Anxiety as a negative emotion in home language maintenance and development.

Slavkov, Nikolay. 2017. Family language policy and school language choice: Pathways to bilingualism and multilingualism in a Canadian context. *International Journal of Multilingualism* 14(4). 378–400.

Suldo, Shannon M. & Sarah A. Fefer. 2013. Parent-child relationships and well-being. In Carmel Proctor & P. Alex Linley (eds.), *Research, applications, and interventions for children and adolescents: A positive psychology perspective*, 131–147. Dordrecht: Springer.

Tov, William. 2018. Well-being concepts and components. In Ed Diener, Shigehiro Oishi & Louis Tay (eds.), *Handbook of well-being*. Salt Lake City, UT: DEF Publishers. https://www.nobascholar.com/chapters/12/download.pdf (accessed Dec. 24, 2018)

Treas, Judith, Jacqueline Scott & Martin Richards (eds.). 2017. *The Wiley Blackwell companion to the sociology of families*. Oxford: Wiley Blackwell.

Trofimova, Ira. 2014. Observer bias: An interaction of temperament traits with biases in the semantic perception of lexical material. *PLoS ONE* 9(1): e85677. DOI:10.1371/journal.pone.0085677

Tseng, Vivian & Andrew J. Fuligni. 2000. Parent–adolescent language use and relationships among immigrant families with East Asian, Filipino, and Latin American backgrounds. *Journal of Marriage and the Family* 62(2). 465–476.

Van Der Wildt, Anouk, Piet Van Avermaet & Mieke Van Houtte. 2017. Multilingual school population: Ensuring school belonging by tolerating multilingualism. *International Journal of Bilingual Education and Bilingualism* 20(7). 868–882.

Vedder Paul. 2005. Language, ethnic identity, and the adaptation of immigrant youth in the Netherlands. *Journal of Adolescent Research* 20(3). 396–416.

Verdon, Sarah & Sharynne McLeod. 2015. Indigenous language learning and maintenance among young Australian Aboriginal and Torres Strait Islander children. *International Journal of Early Childhood* 47(1). 153–170.

Verdon, Sarah, Sharynne McLeod & Adam Winsler. 2014. Language maintenance and loss in a population study of young Australian children. *Early Childhood Research Quarterly* 29(2). 168–181.

Weaver, Scott R. & Su Yeong Kim. 2008. A person-centered approach to studying the linkages among parent–child differences in cultural orientation, supportive parenting, and adolescent depressive symptoms in Chinese American families. *Journal of Youth and Adolescence* 37(1). 36–49.

Whiteside, Katie E., Debbe Gooch & Courtenay F. Norbury. 2017. English language proficiency and early school attainment among children learning English as an Additional Language. *Child Development* 88(3). 812–827.

Winsler, Adam, Yoon Kyong Kim & Erin R. Richard. 2014. Socio-emotional skills, behavior problems, and Spanish competence predict the acquisition of English among English language learners in poverty. *Developmental Psychology* 50(9). 2242–2254.

Wong Fillmore, Lily. 1991. When learning a second language means losing the first. *Early Childhood Research Quarterly* 6(3). 232–346.

Yeşim Sevinç
5 Anxiety as a negative emotion in home language maintenance and development

1 Introduction

> (1)[1] My grandfather makes me stressed about my Turkish. He says that I can't speak Turkish very well. I should fix it (...) otherwise, I won't be able to find a husband. He even says even if I find one [husband], I won't be able to communicate with my mother-in-law.

In this excerpt, ET, a 14-year-old third-generation Turkish-Dutch bilingual born in the Netherlands, describes her interaction with her grandfather, when asked to explain why she feels anxious speaking Turkish, her home language, with him. Her words illustrate the contagion of anxiety, spreading from one generation to the next. The three sentences of the grandfather's statement, all contain negatives ('can't' or 'won't') that express his negative opinion about ET's future because of her lack of proficiency in Turkish. In this regard, this anecdote serves as a notable example of a psychologically negative mindset or fixed language mindset – a belief that one's language ability is static and impossible to improve (Lou and Noels 2019). Relevant to transnational and minority contexts, it also highlights that language anxiety is clearly influenced by sociolinguistic and emotional pressure on normative standards, cultural values, beliefs, and practices, such as the tension between home language maintenance and shift (Sevinç 2016).

Negative emotions (e.g., anxiety) are most likely to be shaped by the family group, society, and/or culture in which one lives, as are fixed language mindsets. They can also be cultivated through a "monolingual mindset", or "aggressive monolingualism", a perception that monolingualism is the social norm, as Clyne (2005) defines it. It is present in ET's familial context, particularly her grandfather's world. He strongly believes that all family members must adhere to their heritage cultural norms, in ET's case, finding a Turkish spouse, and hence they should achieve native-like competence in Turkish.

The question arising from ET's experience is whether it is possible to develop and/or maintain home language skills by causing further anxiety or by carrying heavy social and psychological baggage of negative emotions and experience (e.g., pressure, intergenerational tension, and stress). The current chapter aims to answer this question. In particular, it discusses how language anxiety becomes prevalent in everyday communication in transnational communities, as it pertains

---

1 The interview excerpts used in this chapter are translated from either Turkish or Dutch to English. Original texts can be obtained from Sevinç (2017) or by contacting the author at yesim.sevinc@iln.uio.no.

to both the heritage (home) language[2] and the majority language[3] and how anxiety, as a negative emotion, affects home language development in return.

Although the critical role of positive and negative emotions in language acquisition have received considerable attention in second language acquisition (SLA) research, it has not yet been noted in transnational studies. Recent studies on educational contexts highlight the importance of exploring positive emotions as well as negative emotions (e.g., Dewaele and MacIntyre 2014). Given that the current chapter deals with language anxiety as a negative emotion, starting with a general introduction and discussion of emotions (both positive and negative) is fundamental. I therefore begin this chapter with an overview of the link between positive and negative emotions and language acquisition so far as it is examined in SLA, in the educational context. Then, I outline emotional issues and psychological dimensions of home language maintenance, as presented in family language policy (FLP) and transnational studies. For a better understanding of daily emotional challenges confronting transnational families, I then focus on anxiety and its causes and effects as a negative emotion. I elaborate on SLA research conducted on language anxiety in and outside classroom settings, with a particular focus on transnational contexts. Finally, I conclude with a discussion of implications for future research on emotion and emotional reactions (positive and negative) in the study of home language maintenance and development, along with implications for families and practitioners.

2 Research on positive and negative emotions

Emotion has proven remarkably difficult to define, being conceptualized as a complex reaction pattern encompassing several coordinated processes that involve subjective, experiential and behavioral elements, biological responses, and social phenomena (e.g., Izard 2010). Having physical, psychological, social and cognitive dimensions, emotions are reactions to the external world; they express what is going on inside the body to the external world, and they exist for a reason – each emotion has a purpose (MacIntyre and Vincze 2017). Solomon (1980)

---

2 In this chapter, the term "heritage language" is used, as it was preferred over minority or home language by the Turkish immigrants in the Netherlands who participated in the studies summarized in this chapter (i.e., Sevinç 2016, 2017, 2018, in press; Sevinç and Dewaele 2016; Sevinç and Backus 2019). As the Turkish immigrants in these studies put it, the label "heritage language" illustrates the emotional value of Turkish to them better than the other terms, since they often strive to maintain the Turkish language for the sake of their cultural heritage. They consider Turkish not only as their home language but also as their heritage to preserve (Sevinç 2017). See Eisenchlas and Schalley (this vol.) for a further discussion on the term "heritage language".
3 Majority language is the language spoken by the socially or economically dominant group in a national context.

recognizes only two types of emotions at the most basic level, positive (pleasant) (e.g., enjoyment) and negative (aversive)[4] (e.g., anxiety). Since Fredrickson (1998) developed the broaden-and-build theory of positive emotion, potentially rich and powerful avenues for research have flourished in the field of positive psychology. Fredrickson (1998) argues that positive emotions foster creativity and motivate people to try new things, while they actively pursue health and well-being in the absence of negativity (Fredrickson 2001). According to her theory, pleasurable positive emotions can have a long-lasting impact on functional outcomes, leading to enhanced well-being and social connectedness. Notably, positive emotions expand people's mindsets over time in ways that reshape who they are.

The action tendencies produced by negative emotions, on the other hand, powerfully dispose a person to a specific action at the time they are experienced (see Fredrickson 2013). For instance, anxiety leads to the urge to avoid situations that trigger anxiety, anger leads to the urge to impair progress in one's life, and disgust leads to rejection, as in reflexively spitting out spoiled food. More recently, in an effort to show that positive emotions can lead to positive outcomes, scholars have compiled an extensive list of domains in which happier people do better than less happy people (see Lucas and Diener 2008).

Positive and negative emotions in educational contexts have received considerable attention in instructed SLA[5] research. Yet there is a fundamental gap in the literature; no research to date has examined the relationship between positive and negative emotions and the social and linguistic outcomes of home language maintenance and development. The next section (section 2.1) delves into the instructed SLA research on positive and negative emotions and language acquisition to date. Then, the section 2.2 discusses the research related to emotions, migration, and transnational families.

2.1 Positive and negative emotions in instructed SLA

Reflecting on the broaden-and-build theory in psychology (Fredrickson 1998), SLA scholars have recently begun to emphasize the importance of exploring positive emotions as well as negative emotions in educational contexts (Dewaele and MacIntyre 2014; MacIntyre and Gregersen 2012a; MacIntyre and Mercer 2014; MacIntyre and Vincze 2017; Schutz and Pekrun 2007). They eloquently argue for the role of positive emotions in instructed SLA and demonstrate that studies have so far

---

4 Note that beside the terms "positive and negative (aversive) emotions", the terms "pleasant and painful emotions" are also widely used particularly in SLA research (cf. Oxford 2017).
5 The term "instructed SLA", as used in this chapter, refers to language learning in classroom settings, which is influenced by teachers, classmates, pedagogical materials, and so on (cf. Ellis 1991).

ignored this role because they have been too exclusively focused on negative emotions, such as foreign language classroom anxiety.

These studies have generated interest in applications of positive psychology in instructed SLA and in studies of positive emotion (e.g., Arnold and Brown 1999; MacIntyre, Gregersen, and Mercer 2016; Dewaele and MacIntyre 2016; Dewaele and Li 2018). In line with this trend, scholars have compared the effects of foreign language anxiety (FLA) with that of positive emotions such as foreign language enjoyment (FLE) (e.g., Dewaele and MacIntyre 2014, 2016; MacIntyre, Gregersen, and Mercer 2016). Studies have noted a relationship between higher levels of enjoyment and the level of mastery of the foreign language combined with decreased levels of anxiety (Dewaele and MacIntyre 2014). Additionally, Dewaele et al. (2018) have emphasized the relationship between enjoyment and positive attitudes towards the foreign language: Higher levels of foreign language enjoyment are linked to more positive attitudes towards foreign language learning. Conversely, drawing on their research of Mexican language learners' assertions that negative emotions contributed positively to their language learning, Mendéz López and Peña Aguilar (2013) indicate that although negative emotions can be detrimental to foreign language learning, they can also serve as learning enhancers. Given these findings, it is important to note that individual differences in emotion regulation (i.e., habitual tendencies to use reappraisal vs. suppression) and/or attitudes towards negative and positive emotions may play a fundamental role in the outcome of language learning as well. Also, as suggested in MacIntyre and Vincze (2017: 82), "the positivity ratio (Frederickson 2013) provides one way to capture succinctly the notion that positive and negative emotions interact and, to the extent that persons tend to experience positive emotions more often than negative ones, correlate well with language learning motivation".

Emphasizing the power of positive emotions, MacIntyre and Gregersen (2012a) propose that by invoking the imagination and using the power of positive emotion, teachers can stimulate learners to effectively summon the cognition that modifies the emotional schema, especially debilitating negative-narrowing reactions. However, this development also raises the question about the role of concurrent positive and negative emotions, namely mixed emotions, in language learning, considering the fact that it is not always possible for individuals to definitively differentiate between positive and negative emotions and that they can experience both positive and negative emotions at the same time (e.g., joy and guilt, happiness and fear). Drawing on recent narrative research, as Oxford (2016) puts it, language learning situations are often complex and cannot always be simplified to one or two emotions. Dewaele and MacIntyre (2014) argue that positive emotions (e.g., enjoyment) must ideally be more frequent than negative ones (e.g., anxiety) in a language learners' emotional mix. In reality, however, this is often hard to achieve particularly in transnational contexts, given the crucial role of unequal power relations, together with resistance to power, in individuals' negative emotions and language learning situations (cf. Pavlenko 2013; Benesch 2017).

Previous studies on psychological well-being additionally propose that mixed emotions can be a good strategy of "taking the good with the bad", which might benefit individuals during difficult times by allowing them to confront adversity and ultimately find meaning in the stress of life (Hershfield et al. 2013; Larsen et al. 2003). Hence, very relevant to transnational contexts, during difficult situations, a mix of positive and negative emotions, a healthier pattern than pure negative emotions, may be optimal for well-being (Hershfield et al. 2013) and perhaps for the language learning process as well. Note that this argument is at this point only an assumption. The possible effects of mixed emotions on language development are still unclear in language learning and remain largely unexplored.

2.2 Emotion, FLP, and transnational families

Following scholars from various fields such as language and identity (Norton 2013), sociocultural approaches (Garrett and Young 2009), language socialization (Garrett and Baquedano-López 2002), language and desire (Motha and Lin 2013), and narrative perspectives (Pavlenko 2005, 2007; Prior 2011; see Prior 2016: 3 for a complete overview), sociolinguistics has witnessed an increasing interest in emotion-relevant research. Pavlenko (2004) discusses emotional aspects of language use in bilingual families and the link between emotional expressions and language choice and dominance in the family. Pavlenko (2005, 2006) also demonstrates that bilinguals' sociolinguistic histories greatly influence their emotions. Negative experiences, such as discrimination, can result in negative emotions, which can, in turn, result in a person no longer speaking one language (Pavlenko 2005), which will eventually influence the process of home language maintenance and development or lead to language shift.

In recent years, studies in the field of FLP have examined various aspects of home language maintenance from sociocultural, educational, emotional, and cognitive perspectives (e.g., Curdt-Christiansen 2009; King and Fogle 2006; Lanza and Curdt-Christiansen 2018; Lanza and Li 2016; Li 2012; Spolsky 2012; Tannenbaum 2012; see Curdt-Christiansen 2018 for a detailed review). Supporting home language maintenance efforts, many scholars in the field of multilingualism research have been committed to help increase public awareness regarding the benefits of bilingualism and the exposure of the negative consequences of the monolingual mindset (e.g., Eisenchlas and Schalley 2019; Piller and Gerber 2018).

In her contribution to the topic of bilingual first language acquisition, De Houwer (2009, 2015) draws attention to the role of positive attitudes on the part of people in a bilingual child's environment in ensuring that the child grows up to be happy and an expert speaker of two languages (see De Houwer this vol. for a further discussion on harmonious bilingual development). Additionally, De Houwer (2009) notes that bilingual children are often compared to their monolingual peers and say of themselves that "I don't speak either of my languages as well as a monolingual" or "in school I was behind the monolingual children" (De Houwer 2009: 308). These monolingual mindsets based on standard norms can lead bilingual children to form a fixed language mindset about their language skills along with negative emotions such as anxiety, shame, and disappointment. Contrary to a growth mindset which has been found to have a long-lasting positive impact on individuals' motivation, resilience, and achievement in the general academic domain (Noels and Lou 2015 for a discussion), a fixed language mindset can influence children's beliefs about their bilingualism in a negative way (cf. Lou and Noels 2019). Likewise, negative emotions jeopardize bilingual children's language competence, since they often avoid using their languages in particular social contexts because of their negative emotions and experiences (Sevinç in press).

Previous studies have examined the emotional component in FLP in regard to the concepts of language emotionality, emotional need to belong, emotional distance, and family bond (e.g., Fogle 2013; Shin 2014; Zhu and Li 2016; see Hirsch and Lee 2018 for a detailed overview). Affective relationships with extended family members have been noted as key for ideologies that guide FLP management approaches which are supportive of home language maintenance, either through daily language practices or visits to the home countries (e.g., Guardado and Becker 2014). The emotional need to belong in a transnational context is also found to reinforce the learning of the home language over the majority language (cf. Pérez Báez 2013). Although these studies provide ample evidence of the role of emotion in FLP, a solid focus on the concept of emotion in the field has been treated only by Tannenbaum (2012), who takes a psychoanalytic approach to the emotional explanation of FLP.

Tannenbaum (2012) discusses FLP from both sociolinguistic and sociological perspectives, relating language closely to power and identity as well as to emotions. She suggests that emotional aspects should be given a more prominent place in FLP than they currently are, including when not expressed explicitly. Within Tannenbaum's psychoanalytic framework, FLP is seen as either a coping or a defense mechanism; a coping mechanism as a family manages the competing demands of its heritage and of its new environment, and a defense mechanism as it provides security to family members against external pressures. One question that arises out of this framework is what if transnational families fail to cope with these demands and no longer defend themselves against the pressure internal and external to the family. As Canagarajah (2008) suggests, families may forego home language maintenance due to the pressure on them to join mainstream society and the need to resolve intergenerational conflict (see Purkarthofer this vol. for further discussion on intergenerational challenges). Yet perhaps above all, this pressure elicits negative emotions.

Tannenbaum and Yitzhaki (2016) investigated the emotional implications of Arab families' decisions about sending their children to Hebrew preschools in Israel. Importantly, they present their interview findings in three major themes: mixed cities, mixed identities, and mixed feelings. They illustrate that transnational families' language/educational decisions come with an emotional price through mixed feelings, yet they disregard the consequence of this emotional price in relation to family relations, home language maintenance, and/or well-being. All these studies on the emotional aspects of FLP decisions are pivotal, as they assert that the literature on FLP largely ignores significant contributions from psychological and psychoanalytical approaches. However, the role and influence of different types of emotions (i.e., positive, negative, or mixed emotions) in home language maintenance and in FLP are still among the questions remaining to be answered.

As the quotation (1) by ET in the introduction of this chapter illustrates, language anxiety within the family, along with other negative emotions, is simultaneously triggered by social and linguistic factors. Crucially, it is also closely linked to the monolingual mindset formed by family members or society. Drawing on the broaden and build theory, it is safe to propose that anxious behaviors can be decoded by parents and families through positive emotions and experiences. Given that positive emotions expand people's mindsets over time, it is important for transnational families to develop not only linguistic competence but also stimulate positive emotions necessary to overcome negative emotions (e.g., anxiety, shame, disappointment) about home language development. Helping parents and educators become aware of their own and their children's mindsets and articulate interest in applications of positive psychology in their FLP and practice can be a good starting point.

The remainder of the chapter will pay particular attention to anxiety in order to establish the possible role of negative emotions in the processes of home language maintenance and/or shift. The following section begins with a brief review of research on language anxiety in the field of instructed SLA, where language anxiety has been most widely researched. By doing so, the section also draws attention to a fundamental gap in instructed SLA, regarding the investigation of language anxiety in the world outside the classroom, particularly in immigrant and transnational family contexts. Once this task is accomplished, the focus will shift directly to language anxiety in transnational contexts and home language maintenance (cf. section 3.2).

3 Anxiety as a negative emotion

Broadly speaking, anxiety is the subjective feeling of tension, apprehension, nervousness, and worry associated with an arousal of the automatic nervous system (Spielberger 1983). "Anxiety is rooted in fear, one of the most basic of negative human emotions" (Boudreau, MacIntyre, and Dewaele 2018: 150). It is closely related to the emotion fear, which occurs as the result of threats that are perceived to be uncontrollable or unavoidable (Öhman 2000). In the context of foreign language learning, MacIntyre (1999) defines anxiety as "the worry and negative emotional reaction aroused when learning or using a second language" (p. 27).

Anxiety has long been known to narrow the scope of people's attention and thinking, and to debilitate language learners' linguistic development and performance. The debilitating effects of language anxiety has been well documented in applied linguistics, specifically in the educational context (e.g., Rubio-Alcalá 2017, see also Horwitz 2017 for a discussion on facilitating language anxiety). Various studies on classroom contexts have found a negative relationship between language anxiety and language achievement (Dewaele 2007; MacIntyre 1999). MacIntyre and Gregersen (2012b) suggest that language anxiety, which disrupts information processing, causes learners to waste precious cognitive energy. Further negative effects of language anxiety include lowering students' confidence, self-esteem, and level of participation (Horwitz, Horwitz, and Cope 1986), for example, students may avoid using the language through mental blocks when speaking or by skipping class (Gregersen 2003).

As noted in Beatty (1988: 28) for public speaking anxiety, whether referred to as fear, speech fright, speech anxiety, audience anxiety, or state anxiety, "this negative reaction has negative consequences such as an immediate desire to avoid or withdraw from speaking (Beatty, Kruger, & Springhorn, 1976), low verbal output and nonfluency (Lerea, 1956), and physical discomfort (Greenleaf, 1952)". This brings to the surface the critical issue of whether language anxiety is a cause or an effect of compromised language performance (Young 1986). MacIntyre (2017) suggests that along with its academic, social and cognitive manifestations, language anxiety is both the result of insufficient command of the target language and a factor that contributes to further negative effects on linguistic competence. From a social perspective, the low linguistic self-confidence associated with language anxiety may also lead to avoidance of using the target language, as it prevents learners from communicating and being sociable (MacIntyre 2017).

3.1 Language anxiety research in instructed SLA

Language anxiety is widely accepted as a situation-specific psychological phenomenon and is usually linked to the formal learning of a foreign language in a classroom setting (Horwitz, Horwitz, and Cope 1986). In educational contexts, it is thought that the effects of language anxiety spill over into life outside the classroom (Steinberg and Horwitz 1986). Because individual communication attempts are often evaluated according to uncertain or even unknown linguistic and sociocultural standards, second language communication entails risk-taking and provokes anxiety (Horwitz, Horwitz, and Cope 1986). Particularly in transnational contexts where linguistic and socio-cultural standards are more crucial and, in some cases, even more challenging for transnational family members than for language learners in a foreign language classroom setting, language anxiety can effectively invade bilinguals' daily communication (Sevinç and Dewaele 2018).

Therefore, for students with an immigrant or minority background, it is, first of all, reasonable to ask whether classroom anxiety spills into life outside the classroom or language anxiety outside the classroom affects anxiety in the classroom, or whether both dynamics work in tandem.

The literature also bears witness to an increasing trend of exploring heritage language learners' anxiety levels in classroom settings (Spanish: Coryell and Clark 2009; Levine 2003; Tallon 2009, 2011; Chinese: Xiao and Wong 2014; Korean: Jee 2016; Arabic: Odeh 2014). The majority of studies comparing heritage language speakers with non-heritage language learners (i.e., foreign language [FL] learners) have primarily investigated whether or not foreign language anxiety (FLA) affects a specific group of learners like heritage language learners in the same way it impacts traditional FL learners (Tallon 2009; Xiao and Wong 2014). Overall, they conclude that heritage language speakers' anxiety levels tend to be lower than those of nonheritage FL learners in the classroom context.

These studies have extended the scope of language anxiety research to include heritage learners, but another essential question arises as to how accurate the outcome of these studies can be when bilingual students with immigrant or minority backgrounds are compared to FL learners, irrespective of possible pressure and tension that they are exposed to outside the classroom because of their transnational status (e.g., pressure within and outside family). In other words, immigrant/minority students' experiences in the world outside the classroom must be incorporated into the research.

Methodologically, previous research on language anxiety has conventionally been based on individuals' self-reports, most often gathered through Foreign Language Classroom Anxiety Scale, FLCAS, (Horwitz, Horwitz, and Cope 1986), the most commonly used scale particularly in educational studies. According to Woodrow (2006), the existing tools (e.g., the FLCAS) for assessing FLA do not suit the second language environment. Although Woodrow (2006) does not elaborate on the reasons why the existing scales are not appropriate, she offers a new questionnaire – the Second Language Speaking Anxiety Scale, or SLSAS. The SLSAS assesses anxiety of language learners (e.g., international students) studying a language in a country where that language is spoken (e.g., English in Australia) both in and out of the classroom. These two tools, FLCAS and SLSAS, are widely used in language anxiety research, although they mainly target speaking anxiety in classroom settings, leaving out other important dimensions (e.g., the world outside the classroom) and skills (e.g., writing, reading). Finally, Dewaele, Petrides, and Frunham (2008) offer a questionnaire relating to communicative anxiety based on a 5-point Likert scale investigating individuals' language anxiety levels outside the classroom in five different situations, that is, when speaking with friends, with colleagues, with strangers, on the phone, and in public. These scales are useful tools to describe the initial momentum or set of appraisals that a learner brings to a new language-learning situation. However, they neither address the immigrant experience nor the unique elements of the transnational context (e.g., socioemotional outcomes of home language maintenance and/or shift).

More recently, Gkonou, Daubney, and Dewaele (2017) bring together a much-needed collection of theoretical and empirical research in language anxiety, showing that language anxiety should be viewed as a complex and dynamic construct and researched through different methods and frameworks. In his contribution in Gkonou, Daubney, and Dewaele (2017), MacIntyre (2017) introduces the Dynamic Approach, reflecting that anxiety is constantly intertwined with a number of various learner, situational circumstances and other factors such as physiological reactions, linguistic abilities, self-related appraisals, pragmatics, interpersonal relationships, specific contexts and type of setting in which people are interacting, and so on. MacIntyre suggests that new methods must take into consideration the complex and dynamic characteristic of language anxiety and cultural contexts in which the affective forces stemming from physical, emotional, and social components interact dynamically with each other.

All these theoretical frameworks and methodologies from educational contexts have significantly advanced the research on language anxiety, but acquiring a deeper understanding of anxieties experienced in transnational contexts will depend on a more fruitful integration of the psycholinguistic and sociolinguistic factors that concurrently contribute to experiences of transnational families and home language maintenance and/or shift. Immigrant/minority students' experiences in the world outside the classroom should also be integrated into the research. Filling this gap in the field, the following section summarizes recent research on language anxiety in home language maintenance. Drawing on qualitative and quantitative methods, it illustrates various intertwined linguistic, physiological, social and emotional factors in connection with individuals' language anxiety experiences. By doing so, this chapter further contributes to the Dynamic Approach (MacIntyre 2017) and its innovative concepts (see also Gregersen, MacIntyre, and Meza 2014, and Gregersen, MacIntyre, and Olson 2017 in Gkonou, Daubney, and Dewaele 2017).

3.2 Language anxiety in transnational contexts

Compared to the sizable literature on SLA in the classroom context, few studies have examined anxiety outside the classroom in transnational families. Bae (2014), in an ethnographic study of Korean educational migrant families in Singapore, demonstrates that uncertainty and tension serve as an unavoidable aspect of strategic migratory choices and that the fierce pursuit of neoliberal subjectivity through global mobility works to increase family anxiety. By shifting the focus specifically onto language anxiety and relying on questionnaire, interview, and physiological data (i.e., two measures of electrodermal activity – skin conductance level and skin conductance response), Sevinç (2016, 2017, 2018), Sevinç and Dewaele (2018) and Sevinç and Backus (2019) indicate that language anxiety can be pervasive in transnational contexts. Turkish families in the Netherlands face challenges related to the use of their heritage language (Turkish) and the majority language (Dutch) in various daily communicative situations that induce heritage language anxiety (HLA) and/or majority language anxiety (MLA) across three generations.

Sevinç (2016) first reveals a possible ongoing shift that is occurring among third-generation Turkish bilinguals in the Netherlands and discusses socioemotional consequences of this shift in the home language (i.e., a vortex of tension and pressure). The perceived sociolinguistic need to shift to Dutch and/or pressure for full transition to Dutch, as well as immigrant parents' expectations for their children's academic achievements, cause third-generation children to experience tensions and ambiguities in the process of home language maintenance. Similar to the Spanish-speaking community in Puebla, Mexico that Hill and Hill (1986) examined, Sevinç (2016) indicates that due to this tension and pressure, transnational families experience anxiety in their daily lives. Turkish parents are well-aware of the language shift in progress and are discontented with their children's Turkish competence, which inevitably triggers further tension and anxiety in the family. This is, for instance, how DG, a first-generation immigrant married to a second-generation Turkish man, described her third-generation 13-year old daughter's Turkish:

> (2) DG: Her Turkish is terrible. Just now too, I was speaking Turkish outside, she didn't understand me, she was staring blankly. Even if she understands, she doesn't respond in Turkish. Because she finds Dutch easy, and automatically she starts speaking Dutch. In fact, she knows [Turkish] but when she doesn't practice (...) I don't feel that she knows it in practice. (...) I tell her "read Turkish books, watch Turkish channels", she doesn't do any of that. (35-year-old, first-generation)

On the other hand, DG's daughter, IK illustrated her interaction with her mother (DG) regarding their home language use, also noting the tension it created:

> (3) IK: My mother gets angry when I don't understand her. She says "your Turkish is too bad, read Turkish books, watch Turkish channels". Then, we quarrel. Then, I don't speak Turkish with her. She asks in Turkish, I reply in Dutch. (13-year-old, third-generation)

However, when asked whether she or her husband had ever read Turkish books to IK when IK was younger, DG answered "no" and continued emphasizing that maintaining the home language was mostly a stress-triggering process for them, which, building on the research on instructed SLA, can be related to the absence of positive emotions (e.g., enjoyment) within the family. As the consequence of all the tension, pressure, and anxiety associated with negativity, we also see that the third-generation IK consciously refused to speak Turkish with her mother at home.

In order to further explore language anxiety in the Turkish community in the Netherlands, Sevinç and Dewaele (2018), drawing on questionnaire data, compared the levels of heritage language (Turkish) anxiety and majority language (Dutch) anxiety across three generations of the Turkish community (116 Turkish immigrants living in the Netherlands; 76 female, 40 male; 45 were first-generation immigrants, 30 were second generation and 41 were third generation, see Appendix 1, Table 1 for participants' demographic information). They investigated the link between immigrants' language anxiety and sociobiographical (i.e., generation, gender, education) and language background variables (i.e., age of acquisition, self-perceived proficiency, frequency of language use). The study showed that levels of HLA and MLA varied across the three generations in different daily life situations (within the family, outside with friends, outside with/around native speakers). Third-generation children suffer from a high level of HLA in all five social contexts (see above), including the family context, particularly when they speak Turkish with their fathers and grandparents. Interestingly, the majority of the third-generation group in the study reported experiencing medium, high, or extreme HLA with their grandparents, based on a 5-point Likert scale ranging from not at all anxious (1) to extremely anxious (5). First-generation immigrants reported experiencing high levels of MLA particularly when speaking Dutch with or around Dutch people, while the second generation reported experiencing anxiety in both languages, specifically in the so-called native Dutch speaker context. Notably, the study revealed that language anxiety in minority contexts appears to be a response to a variety of issues not easily captured through questionnaires alone, since statistical analysis revealed no significant correlations between language anxiety levels and language background variables in certain social contexts (such as within family and with friends). This finding demonstrates that language background variables and quantitative analyses on their own are insufficient to explain language anxiety in transnational contexts.

As a proof-of-concept study, Sevinç (2018) further evaluated the level of language anxiety among three generations of Turkish immigrants in the Netherlands by assessing autonomic arousal associated with HLA and MLA ($n=30$, 21 female, nine male; six were first-generation bilinguals, eight were second generation, and 16 were third generation, see Appendix 1, Table 2 for participants' demographic information). During a video-retelling task conducted by one Turkish and one Dutch researcher in six experimental phases (i.e., baseline (2x), free (bilingual) mode (2x), monolingual heritage-language (Turkish) mode, and monolingual majority-language (Dutch) mode), two measures of electrodermal activity – skin conductance level (SCL) and skin conductance response (SCR) – were recorded. The two researchers carrying out the experiment first introduced themselves, underlining that one of them came from Turkey and spoke no Dutch, and the other one came from the Netherlands and had no knowledge of Turkish. In monolingual modes, 28 video clips were viewed and described by the participants, in Turkish with the Turkish researcher and in Dutch with the Dutch researcher. The aim here was to examine high levels of language anxiety when the participants spoke Turkish and/or Dutch in monolingual mode with or around so-called natives, as they reported in questionnaire data (Sevinç and Dewaele 2018). Third-generation bilinguals, to a greater extent than first-generation bilinguals, demonstrated greater autonomic arousal during the Turkish monolingual mode than during the Dutch monolingual mode (see Appendix 2, Figure 1 for a sample of raw data from a third-generation bilingual, illustrating high levels of HLA during Turkish monolingual mode). Findings of this study provide evidence for the relationship between anxiety, bilingual speech and physiological reactions. The study also refers to the link between social factors (e.g., tension and power relations between so-called natives and immigrants), language mindsets and anxiety. As it illustrates, in transnational contexts, bilinguals may get their mindset fixed on the idea that they should be able to speak both languages fluently around so-called native speakers.

Following video-retelling experiments, interviews were held with 30 participants (21 female, nine male; six were first-generation bilinguals, eight were second generation, and 16 were third generation, see Appendix 1, Table 2 for participants' demographic information). There were two interviewers – one of Turkish origin, and one Dutch – and the subjects could choose their interviewer: 12 of them chose the Dutch researcher and 18 the Turkish one. Interviewees were informed that they could use both languages freely. All interviews were fully transcribed and translated into English. Procedures for "open coding" i.e., the process of breaking down, examining, comparing, conceptualizing and categorizing the data were applied to provide structure to the interview texts (see Strauss and Corbin 1990). Sevinç and Backus (2019) reported interview results on the causes and effects of language anxiety among Turkish immigrants in the Netherlands in two main categories that are often interrelated: linguistic aspects (language use, practices, self-perceived low proficiency, and language contact phenomena such as frequent code-switching and mixing two languages) and socioemotional aspects (increased tension and pressure and issues of identity and belonging). As MRB describes below, when explaining their reasons for language anxiety, the majority of bilinguals in the study refer to the pressure and stress caused by the monolingual mindset that bilinguals should be able to speak both languages fluently:

> (4) MRB: It is all about the pressure and stress. [It is] because of the wish to speak both languages in the best way. We live in the Netherlands, so they [Dutch people] expect us to speak Dutch properly. Our parents are Turkish, but we were born here, still they [our parents] expect us to speak Turkish accurately. When trying to know two languages perfectly, you get stuck in between the two. It is not easy. (27-year-old, second-generation)

The study also suggested that language anxiety in transnational contexts has to be understood within a larger context of unequal power relationships (cf. Bourdieu 1977; Preston 2013). It revealed the discrimination and social exclusion that Turkish immigrants face because of their bilingual language use both in the Netherlands and when they visit Turkey. In Turkey, an emigrant Turk living in any West European country is labeled as *almancı*, meaning 'German-like', regardless of the country they immigrated to. *Almancı* (var. *alamancı*) has other negative connotations as well, one of them meaning nouveau riche, with the implication that the person has recently and easily become rich and is now flaunting that wealth.

Negative evaluations of emigrants' Turkish linguistic and cultural skills by Turks in Turkey were often cited as one of the main causes of anxiety, along with fear of being mocked and being excluded in Turkey. Taken together, all these factors combine to form the cluster of linguistic and socioemotional causes of language anxiety in this immigrant community.

In the extract below, CC demonstrates that his anxiety while speaking Turkish is closely related to aggressive monolingualism, or the monolingual mindset that is often linked with identity and ethnic allegiances and commitments. These findings also show that research should not ignore immigrants' negative experiences during their visits to their home country and the impact of these experiences on home language maintenance.

> (5) CC: Because they [Turks in Europe] are afraid that they make mistakes (...) as a Turkish person, you do not know the language? (...) I experienced that before that I talked Dutch to my niece unconsciously. She is normal Turkish and lives there. She said: "You Dutch guy! What are you saying?" She laughed at me and said I need to talk Turkish more, then it should get better. It was a joke I know, but it was embarrassing, and this is a common reaction there. (15-year-old, third-generation)

Related to FLP, interview findings showed that first-generation mothers blamed the new generation's anxiety in the home language (i.e., Turkish) partially on the Dutch education system for not providing Turkish classes, but also on themselves for inadequate parenting:

> (6) NVO: Because they [Turkish children in the Netherlands] don't learn Turkish at school, and they can't describe themselves in Turkish. But perhaps, most of all, they lack self-confidence. For instance, many of them constantly speak Turkish, watch Turkish channels, they have Turkish friends but still they think their Turkish is not sufficient. They live in the Netherlands, they go to school in the Netherlands, and they are still not sure about their Dutch level. This [anxiety] is not related to the language levels, it is related to their insecure lifestyle, it is related to how we raised our kids. For instance, the way that we raise children is different from the way that Dutch people do it. We raise our children with prohibitions, fear, and panic. They [Turkish parents] say for instance "if you don't speak Turkish well, you cannot be a Turk" or they say "if you don't know Dutch well, you won't be able to earn money". The children get torn between these two [opinions]. Without letting children try and learn, we expect them to be perfect with fear. That is why they grow up insecure. (43-year-old, first-generation mother)

NVO's comments above also point to the negative mindsets of Turkish families in her description of Turkish parents raising their children with prohibitions, threats, fear, and panic and emphasizing their negative views of their children's future such as "if you don't know Dutch well, you won't be able to earn money". Furthermore, the parents' threat, "if you don't speak Turkish well, you cannot be a Turk", illustrates the link between identity, language use, and language anxiety. In the quotation below, on the other hand, SLD describes her mother's anger and her own fear when she makes mistakes as reasons for her anxiety when speaking Turkish with her mother and grandparents. In this she is like many other Turkish children:

(7) Interviewer: In the questionnaire you reported that you feel anxious, stressed, when speaking Turkish with your mother. Why do you feel anxious?

SLD: Well, she corrects me immediately, sometimes gets angry. For instance, when I say something incorrect, let's say, when she gets angry and corrects me, I am thinking then, if I make the same error again I get scared. As a human being, I mean one gets naturally uncomfortable, stressed.

Interviewer: Well, how about your anxiety with your grandparents?

SLD: With them, it's because our Turkish is insufficient you know. It's because they talk better than us, sometimes you know uhm I can't find Turkish words, Dutch words come to my mouth, and sometimes I can't be sure if the sentence is right. I also consider myself like that and make myself stressed.   (26-year-old, second-generation)

The feeling of having inadequate Turkish skills was prevalent across all three generations and it affected communication and relationships among family members. Many compared themselves unfavorably to Turks in Turkey, citing the attitudes in Turkey towards their linguistic incompetence as negative. Some second-generation bilinguals also blamed their parents' strict monolingual practices at home as it caused tension in their family, wishing that their parents would have spoken Dutch to them as well as Turkish. The majority of this second-generation group believed that their bilingualism was a disadvantage because it often made them feel that their life was a battle-ground, and their bilingual experiences were mostly negative and stressful rather than positive and enjoyable. SLD, for instance, associated her bilingualism with a conflict against two languages, as follows:

(8) SLD: We learned Dutch later at school. Nobody spoke Dutch to us at home. My parents did not even come to school once to talk to my teacher 'cause they did not speak Dutch at all. It has been difficult for us. Although my Dutch has improved at school, there is still that feeling that Dutch people speak it better, 'cause they don't have to fight with another language all the time, like us.   (26-year-old, second-generation)

As Machan (2009) indicates, language anxiety sometimes causes individuals to avoid the issues they find disturbing; when speakers worry about grammar, pronunciation, or vocabulary, the real source of their anxiety is often not the language itself but issues such as their transnational status, ethnic background, immigration, or social instability. Particularly in transnational contexts, language anxiety can often have negative linguistic and socioemotional consequences at individual, family, and societal levels. For instance, due to language anxiety, transnational families may give up on using their home language, which leads to language shift. As proposed in Sevinç and Backus (2019), there is a "vicious circle" that connects immigrants' language knowledge, language use, and language anxiety. Bilingual children may ultimately avoid using the language about which they feel anxious, which, in turn, causes additional anxiety and reduced proficiency in the home language, as DG illustrates when describing the effects of her 13-year-old daughter's anxiety in Turkish:

(9) Interviewer: Well, how do you think IK's stress related to her Turkish is influencing her life?

> DG: (...) She loses herself, she screams, yells, gets aggressive! Then, she shuts herself down, doesn't speak Turkish with me, shakes her head, moves her eyebrows, argh! so annoying sometimes. Seriously, sometimes she doesn't speak with me at all. So I am telling her: her Turkish is not improving, it is not the solution! We will never get rid of these problems like this! Especially for her, she needs to try to speak Turkish, so she doesn't hate it.　　　　　　　　　　　　　　　　　　　　　　　(35-year-old, first-generation)

In the excerpt below, on the other hand, DTB relates how her daughter's avoidance of Turkish has compounded the alienating effects in a socioemotional nature:

> (10) DTB: My daughter for instance last summer, she behaved too ill-tempered in Turkey. She was not affected that much when she was little, but now when she couldn't make herself clear, when she panicked she had nervous breakdowns! And this time she caused many problems. She is ashamed of herself when she can't talk Turkish. Kids [in the neighborhood in Turkey] invited her to play, but (...) because of her Turkish fear and these breakdowns she didn't play with them once the whole summer!
> 　　　　　　　　　　　　　　　　　　　　　(44-year-old, first-generation immigrant)

DTB's daughter ST further elaborates on her experience regarding language anxiety, emphasizing its debilitating effects on her language use.

> (11) ST: I make myself upset, then I can't say what I am supposed to say, I forget uhm the things I know. As this [experience] happens, I get scared more. I don't know, but bad, yes very bad. When it happens, for example, uhm I am forgetting all the words then. Then I give up [speaking].　　　　　　　　　　　(11-year-old, third-generation immigrant)

As the qualitative evidence from Turkish families in the Netherlands discussed in this chapter makes clear, language anxiety can be an ever-present and unavoidable experience in immigrants' daily communication as well as in FLP. Concerning this anxiety, there is plenty of blame going around: Children blame their parents, parents blame their children, parents blame the education or political system and children and parents blame themselves and/or the society, their home or host community members. It should be noted that transnational families around the globe experience home language maintenance in multiple ways because of variations in their value systems (e.g., identity, cultural norms) as well as the diversity of factors contributing to language maintenance and/or shift observed in different countries (e.g., notions of language prestige, linguistic and cultural ideologies). Home language maintenance of transnational families may not always lead to anxiety, yet it is worth examining the psychological baggage of FLP in which negative emotions (e.g., shame, disappointment, frustration, stress, and anxiety) predominate, by comparing transnational families from different backgrounds across different countries. This examination is imperative for a realistic understanding of the link between negative emotions, fixed language mindsets, and home language maintenance in different transnational contexts.

4 Summary, conclusion and future perspectives

I began this chapter by asking whether it was possible to promote and/or maintain the home language by provoking further anxiety or when carrying the heavy social and psychological baggage of negative emotions or experiences (e.g., pressure, intergenerational tension, and stress). Clearly, maintaining the home language can be an anxiety-triggering process for members of a transnational community, which, building on the research on instructed SLA, can be related to the absence of positive emotions (e.g., enjoyment) within the family. Given the adverse effect of negative emotions and fixed language mindsets on children's bilingual language development, as illustrated in this chapter, bilingual children may stop using the home language to avoid experiencing negative emotions, which is likely to cause language shift from the home language to the language of the mainstream community. Yet when examining this question, I further propose that research on transnational contexts and FLP should account for positive emotions as well as negative emotions, as argued in instructed SLA research. Likewise, future research should not underestimate the investigation of mixed emotions, particularly when exploring home language maintenance and language shift in transnational contexts (e.g., Tannenbaum and Yitzhaki 2016). Individuals' attitudes towards negative experiences and emotions also need to be examined, since they may play a fundamental role in the outcome of language learning and FLP (e.g., Mendéz López and Peña Aguilar 2013).

To recap, what is evident from the current review is that we should expand the study of positive and negative emotions in instructed SLA beyond the educational settings to everyday encounters in transnational contexts. Further questions regarding emotion and language anxiety in FLP remain to be explored: What role do different types of emotions (positive, negative, or mixed emotions) play in home language maintenance and in FLP? How do they influence home language maintenance and FLP? Does classroom anxiety spill into life outside the classroom (Steinberg and Horwitz 1986), does language anxiety outside the classroom (heritage language and/or majority language anxiety) affect anxiety in the classroom, or do both dynamics come into play in the case of transnational students? Moreover, for a better understanding of language anxiety and the challenges faced by transnational families across generations, studies should not ignore these families' experiences during their visits to their home country and the impact they have on the families. Crucially, visits to the heritage country may not always support home language maintenance (cf. Guardado and Becker 2014), particularly in the presence of monolingual mindsets or aggressive monolingualism, since they can concurrently trigger anxiety.

Emotions, both positive and negative, are one of the components of FLP and an extremely important domain for maintaining the home language because of their critical role in forming a child's linguistic environment, beliefs about language, as well as their language use and practice. Regarding the investigation of emotions in transnational families, further research should focus attention on the integration of knowledge and methods in sociolinguistics and psycholinguistics. New questionnaire and interview tools should be developed to address the immigrant experience and the unique elements of the transnational context (e.g., socioemotional outcomes of home language maintenance and/or shift, comprising questions related to language mindsets, identity, tension, power relations, pressure within the family, intergenerational conflict, social exclusion and so on). Likewise, drawing on the evidence for the relationship between anxiety, bilingual speech and physiological reactions presented in this chapter, emotional and physiological components of the transnational contexts should not be overlooked. Bridging these gaps in the literature and methodology can favorably advance research in SLA as well as FLP studies. We should draw on methods used in both areas, since many of the research questions that are explored discretely in these areas are often complementary (e.g., questions of language proficiency, language use, language anxiety, and challenges of bilingualism).

5 Implications for families and practitioners

Research on Turkish families in the Netherlands, as discussed in this chapter, has uncovered a link between negative emotions, fixed language mindsets, monolingual mindsets, home language maintenance in transnational contexts, and the vicious circle of language knowledge, language use, and language anxiety. However, as Gkonou, Dewaele, and Daubney (2017: 221) write, "negative emotions such as language anxiety can be counterbalanced by maintaining and increasing the positive ones". Anxious behaviours may therefore be decoded by transnational families through positive emotions such as enjoyment. Rather than combatting and triggering negative emotions and avoiding unpleasant experiences, families should boost positive emotions by fostering greater engagement in language use and increasing the appreciation of multilingualism in their lives through enjoyable activities that are driven by imagination and interaction in tandem. To prevent or break the vicious circle, "it is important to develop not only communicative and intercultural competence but also the resilience necessary to overcome anxiety about failures in intercultural communication" (Lou and Noels 2019: 499). Researchers, speech therapists, and social workers involved with transnational families should focus on developing parental support strategies for language anxiety. In order to lead to a more positive and effective FLP experience, helping parents and their bilingual children become aware of the negative effects of fixed language mindsets may encourage them to use their home language, to reduce the anxiety within the family, and to help families view social interactions as opportunities to improve the home language. Praising children's efforts instead of only their ability and helping bilinguals focus on their language development rather than comparing them with their monolingual peers can facilitate home language maintenance. Suggestions to reduce anxiety provided by Oxford (2017) based on a series of interventions for classroom use and autonomous language learning from positive psychology can also be adapted in transnational contexts and FLP. For instance, an increase in optimism and reduction in anxiety may occur when family members improve their relationships, when bilingual children are taught to focus on success factors and not to view negative situations as permanent, widespread and caused by themselves.

Acknowledgement: This study was financially supported by the Research Council of Norway through its Centres of Excellence funding scheme [project number 223265] and by NTNU [project number 90281100].

References

Arnold, Jane & H. Douglas Brown. 1999. A map of the terrain. In Arnold, Jane (ed.), *Affect in language learning*, 1–24. Cambridge: Cambridge University Press.
Bae, So Hee. 2014. Anxiety, insecurity and complexity of transnational educational migration among Korean middle class families. *Journal of Asian Pacific Communication* 24(2). 152–172.
Beatty, Michael J. 1988. Situational and dispositional correlates of public speaking anxiety. *Communication Education* 37. 28–39.
Beatty, Michael J., Michael W. Kruger & Ron G. Springhorn. 1976. Toward the development of cognitively experienced speech anxiety. *Central States Speech Journal* 27. 181–185.
Benesch Sarah. 2017. *Emotions and English language teaching: Exploring teachers' emotion labor*. New York, NY: Routledge.
Boudreau Carmen, Peter D. MacIntyre & Jean-Marc Dewaele. 2018. Enjoyment and anxiety in second language communication: An idiodynamic approach. *Studies in Second Language Learning and Teaching* 8(1). 149–170.
Bourdieu, Pierre. 1977. Cultural reproduction and social reproduction. In Jerome Karabel & Albert H. Halsey (eds.), *Power and ideology in education*, 487–511. New York: Oxford University Press.
Canagarajah, Suresh A. 2008. Language shift and the family: Questions from the Sri Lankan Tamil diaspora. *Journal of Sociolinguistics* 12(2). 143–176.
Clyne, Michael. 2005. *Australia's language potential*. Sydney: University of New South Wales Press.
Coryell, Joellen E. & M. Carolyn Clark. 2009. One right way, intercultural participation, and language learning anxiety: A qualitative analysis of adult online heritage and nonheritage language learners. *Foreign Language Annals* 42. 483–504.
Curdt-Christiansen, Xiao Lan. 2009. Invisible and visible language planning: Ideological factors in the family language policy of Chinese immigrant families in Quebec. *Language Policy* 8(4). 351–375.
Curdt-Christiansen, Xiao Lan. 2018. Family language policy. In James W. Tollefson & Miguel Pérez-Milans (eds.), *The Oxford Handbook of Language Policy and Planning*, 420–441. Oxford: Oxford University Press.
Dewaele, Jean-Marc. 2007. The effect of multilingualism and socio-situational factors on communicative anxiety and foreign language anxiety of mature language learners. *International Journal of Bilingualism* 11(4). 391–410.
Dewaele, Jean-Marc & Chengchen Li. 2018. Editorial Special Issue 'Emotions in SLA'. *Studies in Second Language Learning and Teaching* 8(1). 15–19.

Dewaele, Jean-Marc & Peter D. MacIntyre. 2014. The two faces of Janus? Anxiety and enjoyment in the foreign language classroom. *Studies in Second Language Learning and Teaching* 4(2). 237–274.

Dewaele, Jean-Marc & Peter D. MacIntyre. 2016. Foreign language enjoyment and anxiety: The right and left feet of the language learner. In Peter D. MacIntyre, Tammy Gregersen & Sarah Mercer (eds.), *Positive psychology in SLA*, 215–236. Bristol: Multilingual Matters.

Dewaele, Jean-Marc, Konstantinos V. Petrides & Adrian Furnham. 2008. Effects of trait emotional intelligence and sociobiographical variables on Communicative Anxiety and Foreign Language Anxiety among adult multilinguals: A review and empirical investigation. *Language Learning* 58. 911–960.

Dewaele, Jean-Marc, John Witney, Kazuya Saito & Livia Dewaele. 2018. Foreign language enjoyment and anxiety in the FL classroom: The effect of teacher and learner variables. *Language Teaching Research* 22(6). 676–697.

De Houwer, Annick. 2009. *Bilingual First Language Acquisition*. Clevedon & Buffalo: Multilingual Matters.

De Houwer, Annick. 2015. Harmonious bilingual development: Young families' well-being in language contact situations. *International Journal of Bilingualism* 19(2). 169–184.

De Houwer, Annick. this vol. Harmonious Bilingualism: Well-being for families in bilingual settings.

Eisenchlas, Susana A. & Andrea C. Schalley. 2019. Reaching out to migrant and refugee communities to support home language maintenance. *International Journal of Bilingual Education and Bilingualism* 22(5). 564–575.

Eisenchlas, Susana A. & Andrea C. Schalley. this vol. Making sense of the notion of "home language" and related concepts.

Ellis, Rod. 1991. *Instructed Second Language Acquisition: Learning in the classroom*. Malden: Wiley-Blackwell.

Fogle, Lyn. 2013. Parental ethnotheories and family language policy in transnational adoptive families. *Language Policy* 12 (1). 83–102.

Fredrickson, Barbara L. 1998. What good are positive emotions? *Review of General Psychology* 2(3). 300–319.

Fredrickson, Barbara L. 2001. The role of positive emotions in positive psychology: The broaden-and-build theory of positive emotions. *American Psychologist* 56. 218–226.

Fredrickson, Barbara L. 2013. Positive emotions broaden and build. *Advances in Experimental Social Psychology* 47. 1–53.

Garrett, Paul B. & Richard F. Young. 2009. Theorizing affect in foreign language learning: An analysis of one learner's response to a communicative Portuguese course. *Modern Language Journal* 93(2). 209–226.

Garrett, Paul B. & Patricia Baquedano-López. 2002. Language socialization: Reproduction and continuity, transformation and change. *Annual Review of Anthropology* 31. 339–361.

Gkonou, Christina, Mark Daubney & Jean-Marc Dewaele (eds.). 2017. *New insights into language anxiety: Theory, research and educational implications*. Bristol: Multilingual Matters.

Gkonou, Christina, Jean-Marc Dewaele & Mark Daubney. 2017. Conclusion. In Christina Gkonou, Mark Daubney & Jean-Marc Dewaele (eds.), *New insights into language anxiety: Theory, research and educational implications*, 219–225. Bristol: Multilingual Matters.

Gregersen, Tammy S. 2003. To err is human: A reminder to teachers of language-anxious students. *Foreign Language Annals* 36. 25–32.

Gregersen, Tammy S., Peter D. MacIntyre & Mario D. Meza. 2014. The motion of emotion: Idiodynamic case studies of learners' foreign language anxiety. *The Modern Language Journal* 98. 574–588.

Gregersen, Tammy S., Peter D. MacIntyre & Tucker Olson. 2017. Do you see what I feel? An idiodynamic assessment of expert and peer's reading of nonverbal language anxiety cues. In Christina Gkonou, Mark Daubney & Jean-Marc Dewaele (eds.), *New insights into language anxiety: Theory, research and educational implications*, 110–134. Bristol: Multilingual Matters.

Greenleaf, Floyd I. 1952. An exploratory study of speech fright. *Quarterly Journal of Speech* 38. 326–330.

Guardado, Martin & Ava Becker. 2014. Glued to the family: The role of familism in heritage language development strategies. *Language, Culture and Curriculum* 27(2). 163–181.

Hershfield, Hal E., Susanne Scheibe, Tamara L. Sims & Laura L. Carstensen. 2013. When feeling bad can be good: Mixed emotions benefit physical health across adulthood. *Social Psychological and Personality Science* 4(1). 54–61.

Hill, Jane H. & Kenneth C. Hill. 1986. *Speaking Mexicano: Dynamics of syncretic language in central Mexico*. Tucson: University of Arizona Press.

Hirsch, Tijana & Jin Sook Lee. 2018. Understanding the complexities of transnational family language policy. *Journal of Multilingual and Multicultural Development* 39(10). 882–894.

Horwitz, Elaine K. 2017. On the misreading of Horwitz, Horwitz, and Cope (1986) and the need to balance anxiety research and the experiences of anxious language learners. An overview of language anxiety research and trends in its development. In Christina Gkonou, Mark Daubney & Jean-Marc Dewaele (eds.), *New insights into language anxiety: Theory, research and educational implications*, 31–47. Bristol: Multilingual Matters.

Horwitz, Elaine K., Michael B. Horwitz & Joann Cope. 1986. Foreign language classroom anxiety. *The Modern Language Journal* 70. 125–132.

Izard, Caroll E. 2010. The many meanings/aspects of emotion: Definitions, functions, activation, and regulation. *Emotion Review* 2. 363–370.

Jee, Min Jung. 2016. Exploring Korean heritage language learners' anxiety: "We are not afraid of Korean!" *Journal of Multilingual and Multicultural Development* 37. 56–74.

King Kendall A. & Lyn Fogle. 2006. Bilingual parenting as good parenting: Parents' perspectives on family language policy for additive bilinguals. *International Journal of Bilingual Education and Bilingualism* 9(6). 685–712.

Lanza, Elizabeth & Xiao Lan Curdt-Christiansen (eds.). 2018. Multilingual families: Aspirations and challenges. *International Journal of Multilingualism* 15(3). 231–232.

Lanza, Elizabeth & Li Wei. 2016. Multilingual encounters in transcultural families. *Journal of Multilingual and Multicultural Development* 37(7). 653–654.

Larsen, Jeff T., Scott H. Hemenover, Catherine J. Norris & John T. Cacioppo. 2003. Turning adversity to advantage: On the virtues of the coactivation of positive and negative emotions. In Lisa G. Aspinwall & Ursula M. Staudinger (eds.), *A psychology of human strengths: Perspectives on an emerging field*, 211–216. Washington, D.C.: American Psychological Association.

Lerea, Louis. 1956. A preliminary study of the verbal behavior of speech fright. *Speech Monographs* 23. 229–233.

Levine, Glenn S. (2003). Student and instructor beliefs and attitudes about target language use, first language use, and anxiety: Report of a questionnaire study. *The Modern Language Journal* 87(3). 343–364.

Li, Wei (ed.). 2012. Special issue: Language policy and practice in multilingual, transnational families and beyond. *Journal of Multilingual and Multicultural Development* 33(1).

Lou, Nigel M. & Kimberly A. Noels. 2019. Sensitivity to language-based rejection in intercultural communication: The role of language mindsets and implications for migrants' cross-cultural adaptation. *Applied Linguistics* 40(3). 478–505.

Lucas, Richard E. & Ed Diener. 2008. Subjective well-being. In Michael Lewis, Jeannette M. Haviland-Jones & Lisa Feldman Barrett (eds.), *Handbook of emotions*, 471–484. 3rd edn. London: The Guilford Press.

Machan, Tim William. 2009. *Language anxiety: Conflict and change in the history of English*. Oxford: Oxford University Press.

MacIntyre, Peter D. 1999. Language anxiety: A review of the research for language teachers. In Dolly Jesusita Young (ed.), *Affect in foreign language and second language teaching: A practical guide to creating a low-anxiety classroom atmosphere*, 24–45. Boston: McGraw-Hill.

MacIntyre, Peter D. 2017. An overview of language anxiety research and trends in its development. In Christina Gkonou, Mark Daubney & Jean-Marc Dewaele (eds.), *New insights into language anxiety: Theory, research and educational implications*, 11–31. Bristol: Multilingual Matters.

MacIntyre, Peter D. & Laszlo Vincze. 2017. Positive and negative emotions underlie motivation for L2 learning. *Studies in Second Language Learning and Teaching* 7(1). 61–88.

MacIntyre, Peter D., Tammy Gregersen & Sarah Mercer (eds.). 2016. *Positive psychology in SLA*. Bristol: Multilingual Matters.

MacIntyre, Peter D. & Sarah Mercer. 2014. Introducing positive psychology to SLA. *Studies in Second Language Learning and Teaching* 4(2). 153–172.

MacIntyre, Peter D. & Tammy Gregersen. 2012a. Emotions that facilitate language learning: The positive-broadening power of the imagination. *Studies in Second Language Learning and Teaching* 2(2). 193–213.

MacIntyre, Peter D. & Tammy Gregersen. 2012b. Affect: The role of language anxiety and other emotions in language learning. In Sarah Mercer, Stephen Ryan & Marion Williams (eds.), *Language learning psychology: Research, theory and pedagogy*, 103–118. Basingstoke: Palgrave.

Méndez López, Mariza G. & Argelia Peña Aguilar. 2013. Emotions as learning enhancers of foreign language learning motivation. *Profile* 15(1). 109–124.

Motha, Suhanthie & Angel Lin. 2013. "Non-coercive rearrangements": Theorizing desire in TESOL. *TESOL Quarterly* 45(3). 453–439.

Noels, Kimberly A. & Nigel M. Lou. 2015. Mindsets, goal orientations and language learning: What we know and where we need to go. *Contact* 41. 41–52.

Norton, Bonny. 2013. *Identity and language learning: Gender, ethnicity and educational change*. London: Longman.

Odeh, Wael. 2014. *Foreign language anxiety and foreign language enjoyment: A study of Arabic heritage and non-heritage language learners*. London: Birkbeck University of London MA thesis.

Oxford, Rebecca. 2016. Toward a psychology of well-being for language learners: The 'EMPATHICS' vision. In Peter D. MacIntyre, Tammy Gregersen & Sarah Mercer (eds.), *Positive psychology in SLA*, 10–87. Bristol: Multilingual Matters.

Oxford, Rebecca. 2017. Anxious language learners can change their minds: Ideas and strategies from traditional psychology and positive psychology. In Christina Gkonou, Mark Daubney & Jean-Marc Dewaele (eds.), *New insights into language anxiety: Theory, research and educational implications*, 177–197. Bristol: Multilingual Matters.

Pavlenko, Aneta. 2004. "Stop Doing That, Ia Komu Skazala!": Language choice and emotions in parent-child communication. *Journal of Multilingual and Multicultural Development* 25(2–3). 179–203.

Pavlenko, Aneta. 2005. *Emotions and multilingualism*. New York: Cambridge University Press.

Pavlenko, Aneta. 2006. Bilingual selves. In Aneta Pavlenko (ed.), *Bilingual minds: Emotional experience, expression, and representation*, 1–33. Clevedon, UK: Multilingual Matters.

Pavlenko, Aneta. 2007. Autobiographical narratives as data in applied linguistics. *Applied Linguistics* 28(2). 162–188.

Pavlenko, Aneta. 2013. Language desire and commodification of affect. In Danuta Gabryś-Barker & Joanna Bielska (eds.), *The affective dimension in second language acquisition*, 3–28. Bristol: Multilingual Matters.

Pérez Báez, Gabriela. 2013. Family language policy, transnationalism, and the diaspora community of San Lucas Quiavinı́ of Oaxaca, Mexico. *Language Policy* 12(1). 27–45.

Piller, Ingrid & Livia Gerber. 2018. Family language policy between the bilingual advantage and the monolingual mindset. *International Journal of Bilingual Education and Bilingualism*. Online First. DOI: 10.1080/13670050.2018.1503227

Preston, Dennis R. 2013. Linguistic insecurity forty years later. *Journal of English Linguistics* 41(4). 304–331.

Prior, Matthew T. 2011. Self-presentation in L2 interview talk: Narrative versions, accountability, and emotionality. *Applied Linguistics* 32(1). 60–76.

Prior, Matthew T. 2016. *Emotion and discourse in L2 narrative research*. Bristol: Multilingual Matters.

Purkarthofer, Judith. this vol. Intergenerational challenges: Of handing down languages, passing on practices, and bringing multilingual speakers into being.

Rubio-Alcalá, Fernando D. 2017. The links between self-esteem and language anxiety and implications for the classroom. In Christina Gkonou, Mark Daubney & Jean-Marc Dewaele (eds.), *New insights into language anxiety: Theory, research and educational implications*, 198–223. Bristol: Multilingual Matters.

Schutz, Paul A. & Reinhard Pekrun (eds.). 2007. *Emotion in education*. San Diego, CA: Elsevier.

Sevinç, Yeşim. 2016. Language maintenance and shift under pressure: Three generations of the Turkish immigrant community in the Netherlands. *International Journal of the Sociology of Language* 242. 81–117.

Sevinç, Yeşim. 2017. *Language anxiety in the immigrant context: An interdisciplinary perspective*. Oslo: University of Oslo PhD thesis.

Sevinç, Yeşim. 2018. Language anxiety in the immigrant context: Sweaty palms? *International Journal of Bilingualism* 22(6). 717–739.

Sevinç, Yeşim. in press. Embodying emotion in migration and in language contact settings. In Gesine Lenore Schiewer, Jeanette Altarriba & Bee Chin Ng (eds.), *Handbook on language and emotion*. Berlin: Mouton de Gruyter.

Sevinç, Yeşim & Jean-Marc Dewaele. 2018. Heritage language anxiety and majority language anxiety among Turkish immigrants in the Netherlands. *International Journal of Bilingualism* 22(2). 159–179.

Sevinç, Yeşim & Ad Backus 2019. Anxiety, language use and linguistic competence in an immigrant context: A vicious circle? *International Journal of Bilingual Education and Bilingualism* 22(6). 706–724.

Shin, Sarah J. 2014. Language learning as culture keeping: Family language policies of transnational adoptive parents. *International Multilingual Research Journal* 8 (3). 189–207.

Solomon, Richard L. 1980. The opponent-process theory of acquired motivation: The costs of pleasure and the benefits of pain. *American Psychologist* 35(8). 691–712.

Spielberger, Charles D. 1983. *Manual for the State-Trait Anxiety Inventory (Form Y)*. Palo Alto, CA: Consulting Psychologists Press.

Spolsky, Bernard. 2012. Family language policy: The critical domain. *Journal of Multilingual and Multicultural Development* 33(1). 3–11.

Steinberg, Faith S. & Elaine K. Horwitz. 1986. The effect of induced anxiety on the denotative and interpretative content of second language speech. *TESOL Quarterly* 20(1). 131–136.

Strauss, Anselm & Juliet Corbin. 1990. *Basics of qualitative research*. Newbury Park, CA: Sage.

Tallon, Michael. 2009. Foreign language anxiety and heritage students of Spanish: A quantitative study. *Foreign Language Annals* 42. 112–137.

Tallon, Michael. 2011. Heritage speakers of Spanish and foreign language anxiety: A pilot study. *Texas Papers in Foreign Language Education* 15. 70–87.
Tannenbaum, Michal. 2012. Family language policy as a form of coping and defence mechanism. *Journal of Multilingual and Multicultural Development* 33(1). 57–66.
Tannenbaum, Michal & Dafna Yitzhaki. 2016. "Everything comes with a price ... "; family language policy in Israeli Arab families in mixed cities. *Language and Intercultural Communication* 16(4). 570–587.
Woodrow, Lindy. 2006. Anxiety and speaking English as a second language. *RELC Journal* 37. 308–328.
Xiao, Yang & Ka F. Wong. 2014. Exploring heritage language anxiety: A study of Chinese heritage language learners. *The Modern Language Journal* 98(2). 589–611.
Young, Dolly Jesusita, 1986. The relationship between anxiety and foreign language oral proficiency ratings. *Foreign Language Annals* 19. 439–445.
Öhman, Arne. 2000. Fear and anxiety: Evolutionary, cognitive, and clinical perspectives. In Michael Lewis & Jeannette M. Haviland-Jones (eds.), *Handbook of emotions*, 573–593. 2nd edn. New York: The Guilford Press.
Zhu, Hua & Li Wei. 2016. Transnational experience, aspiration and family language policy. *Journal of Multilingual and Multicultural Development* 37(7). 655–666.

Appendix 1

Table 1: Questionnaire respondents' demographic information (Sevinç and Dewaele 2016).

	1st Gen. (n = 45)			2nd Gen. (n = 30)			3rd Gen. (n = 41)		
	M	SD	Range	M	SD	Range	M	SD	Range
Age (Years)	50	11.7	(32–85)	33	7.3	(20–42)	15	2.8	(11–21)
Gender									
Female (n = 76)	32			20			24		
Male (n=40)	13			10			17		

Table 2: Interviewees' and experiment participants' demographic information (Sevinç 2016, 2017a).

	1st Gen. (n = 6)			2nd Gen. (n = 8)			3rd Gen. (n = 16)		
	Mean	SD	(Range)	Mean	SD	(Range)	M	SD	(Range)
Age (Years)	41	4.0	(33–43)	26	1.6	(24–28)	14	2.2	(12–19)
Gender									
Female (n = 21)	6			8			7		
Male (n=9)	–			–			9		

Appendix 2

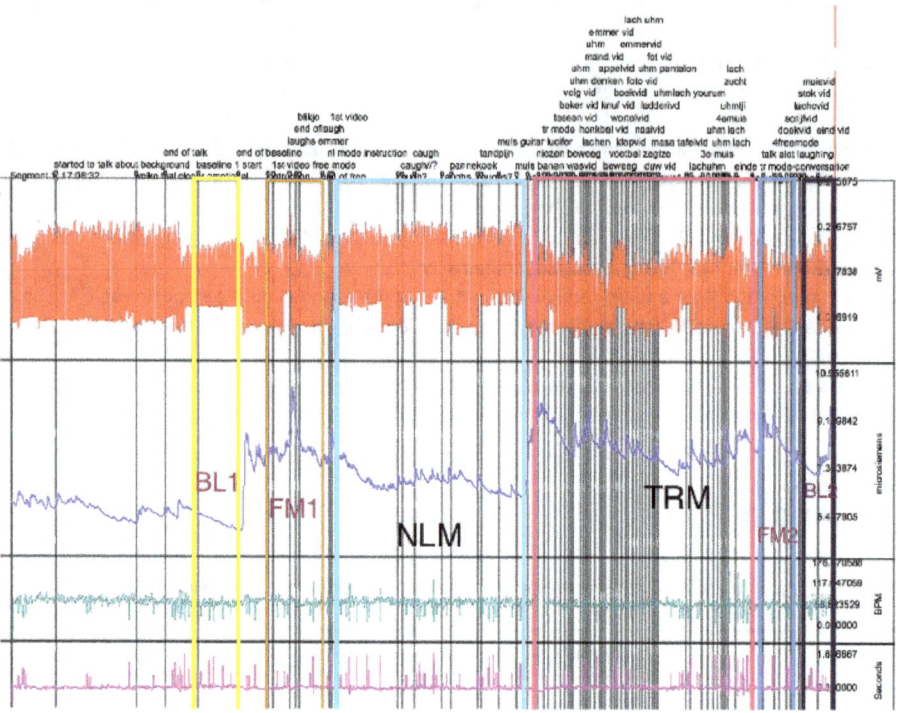

Figure 1: High levels of HLA and electrodermal activity during Turkish monolingual mode. Sample of raw data from a third-generation participant illustrating event markers, skin conductance level and skin conductance responses and the six phases of the experiment, (BL1) baseline1, (FM1) free-mode1, (NLM) Dutch monolingual mode, (TRM) Turkish monolingual mode, (FM2) free-mode2 and (BL2) baseline2, respectively (Sevinç 2017a).

Amelia Tseng
6 Identity in home-language maintenance

This chapter discusses the importance of identity to home language maintenance in several key areas of language learning and socialization: individuals, families, schools, and society. Identity's important role in home language maintenance (also known as community languages, heritage languages,[1] and mother tongues, see Eisenchlas and Schalley this vol. for a detailed discussion of terms) is well-established (Fishman 1972; Kagan 2012). However, the relationship is complex. In sections 1 and 2 of this chapter, I present a brief overview of the relationship between language and identity as indexical, interactive, and constructed at multiple intersecting scalar levels, with particular focus on home languages and ethnocultural identity, (mis)understandings of heritage language speakers, and the relationship between social relations and language discrimination or prestige. In section 3 I address the importance of language and identity in families for home language maintenance, followed by a discussion of schools as sites of language and identity negotiation as well as the reproduction of social and linguistic hegemonies related to national language identities and ideologies (section 4). The chapter concludes with a discussion of critical issues in identity and home language maintenance, such as a Western-centric research bias, insights from indigenous communities, and globalization and transnationalism, and a summary of key points.

1 Language and identity

Sociolinguistic conceptions of identity have evolved from foundational work correlating linguistic variation with social categories (Labov 1972) to fluid, multifaceted concepts of self in relationship to others which are constructed through interaction and grounded in the broader sociocultural environment (Coupland 2007; Le Page and Tabouret-Keller 1986). Identities are constructed at multiple scalar levels: individuals, groups, regions, and nations, among others. Similarly, linguistic identity construction takes place at multiple levels of interaction, from conversations to social roles and

---

[1] The term "heritage languages" encompasses speakers' sociohistorical relationship to a language while avoiding the "balanced bilingual" construct which categorized them as deficient, although the term has been criticized for over-emphasizing a sense of the past (García 2005; Li and Duff 2008; Valdés 2014). In this chapter I follow Eisenchlas and Schalley's (this vol.) useful terminological schema, which distinguishes "home language" and "mother tongue" from "heritage language" based on competence and affective dimensions of learning and use. In contrast, their understanding of "heritage language" emphasizes the language's cultural relationship, community importance, and minoritized social status, without specifying conditions of acquisition and competency.

broader understandings of social groups and categories (Bucholtz and Hall 2005; Bamberg, De Fina, and Schiffrin 2011). Identity construction relies on creating distance and affiliation/alignment (Bucholtz and Hall 2005), or sameness and distinction (Irvine 2001), and is grounded in its sociohistorical context of production, emphasizing or erasing information in line with existing beliefs and political motivations (Irvine and Gal 2009). The languages we speak and the way we speak them index, perpetuate, and redefine social group membership, as do the stories we tell about ourselves and others (De Fina 2003; Pavlenko and Blackledge 2004; Silverstein 2003).

1.1 Language and ethnocultural identity

Language is an important index of ethnocultural identity, since cultural scripts or discourses of habitual language behavior are associated with social groups and qualities (Gee 2015; Goddard and Wierzbicka 2004; Silverstein 2003). Sociolinguistic associations with language range from group membership to general attitudes (e.g. "this accent sounds friendly") and more structured ideologies, or shared sets of beliefs about how language reflects social membership and characteristics (for example, level of education) (Silverstein, 1979; Preston 2002). The beliefs about prestige, privilege, and discrimination, which inform these language ideologies, relate to the broader social context and to power dynamics. For example, Pavlenko (2002) notes that linguistic prejudice parallels political exclusionism, nativism, and xenophobia, This point is echoed by Zentella's (1997) evidence of anti-Latino prejudice in the U.S. English-only movement and Wiley's (2007) overview of the historical ebb and flow of discrimination against minority languages in the United States. In another example, language is often used as an official gate-keeping mechanism to restrict immigration (Blackledge 2009; Hogan-Brun, Mar-Molinero, and Stevenson 2009; Shohamy 2006). Critical raciolinguistic perspectives examining the co-naturalization of race and language within hegemonic racial frameworks (Rosa and Flores 2017; Alim, Rickford, and Ball 2016) demonstrate that U.S. Latinos' Spanish and English are perceived by white Americans as "broken", incorrect, or inferior, while white speakers' second-language Spanish is celebrated (Flores and Rosa 2015; Rosa 2016). This echoes much research where elite bilingualism is positively viewed while minoritized communities' bilingualism is stigmatized and seen as a barrier to assimilation (De Mejía 2002; Menken 2013; Romaine 1999).

1.2 Language ideologies and power

The notion of separate, bounded languages cleanly distributed across social groups and territories is itself a sociopolitically-motivated ideological construct (Anderson 1991; Irvine and Gal 2009). Bilingualism is ideological, in that systems of belief about what it means to speak a language inform beliefs about bilinguals (Heller 2007). Grosjean (1989: 3) cautioned that, contrary to popular belief, "the bilingual is not two monolinguals in one person". However, a monolingual bias persists, in that notions of language proficiency orient to monolingual speech norms and privilege idealized native-speaker language as an index of group membership and authenticity (Coupland 2010; Holliday 2015). Further, language standardization and ideologies of (in)correctness relate to social power (Baker and Prys Jones 1998), elevating certain languages and varieties at the expense of non-prestige ways of speaking, and assume that normal bilingual practices are inferior or impure. For example, code-switching or translanguaging between two or more languages is often stigmatized rather than recognized as an important bilingual practice with its own norms and social significance (Gumperz 1977), and lingering post-colonial insecurity stigmatizes varietal diversity in comparison to an idealized peninsular Spanish (Zentella 2007, 2014). These ideologies are reinforced through social institutions such as schools, subordinating minoritized languages and exacerbating prejudice against their speakers (Lippi Green 2012).

1.3 Dynamism of home-language identities

Language indexicalities extend beyond ethnicity to intersections with gender, social class, etc. and the negotiation of complex situational identities (Mendoza Denton 2002). This is amply attested in the literature. For example, Bailey (2000) demonstrated that Dominican American youth highlight their Afrolatino identities, which are excluded from U.S. racial paradigms, through the use of Spanish. New identities emerge in younger bilingual generations along with new linguistic repertoires. Lee (2002) found that Korean heritage proficiency correlated with bicultural identity rather than a national/ethnic cline. Kagan (2012) observed that respondents to the National Heritage Language Research Center Survey felt hybrid or intercultural identities, and He (2006: 7) demonstrated that Chinese home language speakers enrolled in university heritage courses desired not only heritage language and culture maintenance, but "to transform the heritage language [...] and re-create one's identity".

This section summarized the relationship between language and identity, presenting a brief theoretical overview followed by a discussion of language and ethnocultural identity, language ideology, and dynamic sociolinguistic identities. The next section will address the role of ethnocultural identity in home language maintenance, including a brief discussion of the complications that arise from misunderstanding of bilingual language repertoires and behavior.

2 Identity and heritage language maintenance

In this section I focus on heritage language speakers, a subpopulation of home-language speakers according to Eisenchlas and Schalley's (this vol.) schema, in that they are raised in homes where a minority language is spoken and may have some but not necessarily strong competency in this language (for example, they may understand the language but not have productive ability) (Valdés 2000: 1). Generally speaking, the strong association between language and ethnocultural identity encourages heritage language maintenance (Clyne 1991; Fishman 1972; Giles and Johnson 1987; You 2005). For example, Cho, Cho, and Tse (1997) found that family and community (along with career options) were important motivations in Korean Americans' desire to improve their home language ability. However, cultural distancing and assimilation pressure encourage language loss, as minority languages face stigma and discrimination. Systemic social discrimination and lack of opportunity in South Africa and Peru caused parents to reject community-language education (Banda 2000; García 2005), and Chinese American children perceived their home language as 'useless' due to its lack of representation in social and educational contexts (Zhang and Slaughter-Defoe 2009). On the other hand, minoritized languages can be a source of covert pride and resistance (Blom and Gumperz 2000; Labov 1972), factors which were important in the revitalization of Welsh, among other languages (Williams 2014). However, symbolic importance does not guarantee survival, as demonstrated by the worldwide trend toward minority language loss.

2.1 (Mis)understanding heritage language speakers

The relationship between home language and identity relationship is complex for heritage speakers (Leeman 2015). Heritage speakers often speak stigmatized language varieties and have little exposure to formal registers and to literacy (Valdés 2014). Further, their unique language abilities are often misunderstood through inappropriate comparison with monolingual native speakers despite their different contexts of acquisition (Cabo and Rothman 2012). Heritage speakers typically show characteristics of both second-language learners and native speakers (Lynch 2003), with abilities along a bilingual continuum (Valdés 2014). Communicative practices also change across generations. Clyne et al. (2015) note shifts from community-language pragmatics to Australian English norms and cultural values amongst European migrants to Australia, while Zhu (2008) notes that pronominal choice within and across Mandarin and English, reflecting home-culture norms of collectivism and respect, is both a source of conflict between Chinese parents and their U.K.-raised children and a means by which youth negotiate new diasporic identities (also see Purkarthofer this vol.).

Hybridity and translanguaging are inherent parts of heritage speakers' repertoires as they draw on their full ranges of linguistic resources to communicate in different contexts (Benor 2010; García and Li 2014). New hybrid languages practices can negotiate and mark new identities (Tseng 2015; Spitulnik 1998), as seen in Hurst's (2009) findings that mixed language signaled local, urban township identities for South African youth. Hybridity can also distinguish later generations from the parent/immigrant generation (Auer 2005), marking stances towards modernism or traditionalism (Luke 1998), indicating resistance, and creating third spaces (Bhatt 2008; Lee 2004; Hinnenkamp 2003).

Unfortunately, when viewed through monolingual-normed understandings of proficiency, hybridity is often stigmatized as evidence of deficient or "broken" language (Zentella 2014). This perception is often reproduced within families, communities, and schools (Carruba-Rogel 2018; Tseng, 2018), obfuscating home language abilities. Misunderstanding the fluid, hybrid language practices common to heritage speakers is problematic since delegitimizing language is a powerful way of delegitimizing identity. This pressure is conveyed through the dominant society, for example in a U.S. politician's attack on an activist for "claiming Cuban identity without speaking Spanish" (Vazquez 2018), and reproduced in schools, a theme I will return to in section 4. The belief is also reproduced within communities, with consequences for heritage speakers' acceptance and self-esteem. For example, Cho, Cho and Tse (1997) note that Korean language proficiency was seen as a prerequisite for legitimate Korean/Korean American group membership and that heritage speakers felt "insecure[ity], shame, general uneasiness [...] cultural stress" if they were unable to speak Korean when and as expected by the community (a theme also elaborated by Sevinc this vol.). Similarly, He (2006: 11) notes that Chinese heritage learners (CHL) may "fail to achieve the identity of 'a CHL community member' through failure to act and feel in some way expected by the CHL community or due to the CHL community's failure to ratify the learner's displayed acts and stances", demonstrating that community identity gatekeeping extends beyond proficiency to broader expectations of communication and behavior.

In this section, I have discussed identity as an important factor in home language maintenance (although its symbolic value does not in itself guarantee language survival) and touched upon some complexities of heritage speaker language and identity. The following section will address the importance of language and identity in families for home language maintenance.

3 Language maintenance and identity within families

Families are important sites of home language maintenance, and factors related to identity can support or hinder this. In this section I describe families' motivation to maintain home languages as part of culture and identity, the importance of family interactions, identity concerns of later-generation speakers, and the impact of practical/economic concerns and linguistic prejudice on family language decisions.

3.1 Home language identity and maintenance

While the degree to which minoritized groups view home language as part of their identities can vary, its cultural value and importance in intergenerational communication generally leads families to support language maintenance as part of ethnocultural identity and family solidarity. Ample literature attests to this claim. Curdt-Christiansen (2009) found that Chinese parents in Canada believe in an inseparable relationship between language, culture, and identity, and Phinney et al. (2001) found that families and languages played a key role in adolescent ethnic identity. Zhang and Slaughter-Defoe (2009) found that parental belief in the importance of language maintenance in family cohesion and ethnic identity helped establish a Chinese-speaking family identity and language policy, and Li (1999) discusses explicit parental expression of positive ethnic identity to support child language use in the face of prejudice. Similarly, Melo-Pfeiffer's (2015) research on Portuguese immigrants in Germany found that both the inner and extended family played an important affective role in home-language motivation amongst the younger generation. Guardado and Becker (2014) also emphasize the importance of affect in language transmission in families, aligning it with Latino family-centered cultural values or "familism" in their study of a Peruvian family in Canada. However, actual family speech practices can diverge from their language beliefs and intentions, as in Smith-Christmas's (2014) finding that a Scottish family undermined their strict Gaelic family language policy through extensive English use amongst the parental (as opposed to grandparents') generation, as well as parental use of Gaelic as the language of discipline.

3.2 Home language identity, social roles, and interaction

Family home language maintenance also relates to social identity roles and interaction. Wong Fillmore (1991) noted the negative impact of home-language loss on meaningful parent/child communication, while Cho, Cho, and Tse (1997) found that the desire for better family connection motivated Korean Americans to improve their home language abilities. Parents, grandparents, birth order, and gender can affect language expectations and use (Spolsky 2012). Regarding parents, Morris and Jones (2007) found that mothers' roles as "language decision makers" in mixed Welsh/English households, balanced with politeness concerns about non-Welsh relatives, influenced how much Welsh children received, while Melo-Pfeiffer (2015) noted the important emotional role of grandparents as a motivation for children's home language maintenance. Regarding birth order, Shin (2002) and Wong Fillmore

(1991) found that younger siblings tend to be less home-language proficient than older siblings due to less parental interaction and the influence of majority-language schooling and bilingual older siblings. In terms of gender, Arriagada (2005) found that U.S. Latina girls tend to maintain more Spanish than boys, perhaps due to social roles that expect them to be more involved in the home. Moreover, in terms of interactional identities, Li (1996) demonstrated the importance of home language use and rejection as parents and children negotiate roles and identities, while Weisskirch (2005) found that children's language brokering supported their ethnic identity, which they viewed as part of a family/community relationship.

3.3 Home language insecurity

The strong ideological connection between home language and ethnocultural identity makes it a potent site for heritage speaker identity and insecurity, as later generations' language profiles interact with family and community expectations (see also section 2.1). While families can support home language use, they can also create home language insecurity through criticism (Krashen 1998). Lytra (2012: 95) found that Turkish diasporic parents considered Turkish proficiency "one of the most – if not the most – significant delineator of Turkish identity" and viewed their children's non-native accents as sources of shame, while King's (2013) case study of three Latina sisters in the United States showed that ideologies of idealized bilingualism in their family create anxiety and frustration around both their Spanish and English abilities (also see Sevinc this vol.). Negative messages to youths about their home language abilities and bilingual practices from family and community members can create identity conflict and even language avoidance (Hill and Hill 1986; Littlebear 2003; Tseng 2018; Urciuoli 2008).

3.4 Other identity factors influencing home language maintenance in families

Family language policy, or language use and choice in the home and related domains (King, Fogle, and Logan-Terry 2008; see also Curdt-Christiansen and Huang this vol.), are affected by broader majority/minority dynamics. While raising bilingual children is often considered "good" parenting based on cultural motivations, family language decisions are also affected by linguistic prejudice and economic/practical concerns (Spolsky 2012). These pressures often relate to broader language assimilation or eradication ideologies as part of national identities and policies. U.S. Latino parents who were punished for speaking Spanish at school are hesitant to encourage home language maintenance (Bayley and Schecter 2005). Parents may fear that home languages will prevent their children from learning the dominant-group language (a common myth about bilingualism), underscoring the importance of educating parents on the benefits of home language maintenance (Eisenchlas and Schalley 2019). King (2001) found that Ecuadorian indigenous parents held simultaneous pro- and anti-indigenous ideologies due to discrimination, leading to family language policies that contribute to language shift; and similar patterns have been observed in Ireland (Ó hIfearnáin 2013) and Australia (Simpson 2013). Further, positive identity construction of "good" bilingual parent identity often interacts with instrumentalist ideologies of multilingualism as a valuable resource (Curdt-Christiansen 2009). Both perspectives can be seen in King and Fogle's (2006) findings that parents enrolled their children in dual-language schools to support heritage and prestige bilingualism. While these beliefs can support home language maintenance, they can also reproduce sociolinguistic hegemony by perpetuating the hierarchies identified by Leeman (2006) at home languages' cost. For example, Zhao and Liu (2010) found that English's high practical and prestige value, and associations of Chinese with low socioeconomic status, discourages community-language home use in Singapore despite official bilingual policies. Ideologies of multilingualism as an index of cosmopolitanism (Garrido 2017) also tend to favor elite bilingualism and bilinguals at the expense of minoritized speakers.

In this section, I have reviewed key aspects of identity and language within families as they relate to home language maintenance, and drawn connections to family-external identity factors. The following section presents a brief overview of home language maintenance and identities in education within a broader framework of sociolinguistic hegemony.

4 Home language identity in education

I now turn to another important area: home language identity in education. While the subject is extensive, I present a brief review of key points on several interconnected levels: schools within society, classrooms and communities, and parent and learner identity.

4.1 Imposition of dominant and deficit identities

Schools are sites of interaction between individual, community, institutional, and national identities, and have an important impact on home language loss or maintenance (Cummins 2005; Tse 1997). Ethnic community schools often include home language maintenance as part of cultural continuity. State schools enforce national language identity by enacting national language policy, such as transitional bilingual education encouraging shift to majority languages at the expense of home languages. These educational policies and implementation are affected by often-exclusionary official policies such as "English Only" legislation in the United States (Flores and Murillo 2001). Further, schools often reproduce linguistic discrimination and ascribe deficit identities to heritage speakers through misdiagnosis of bilinguals as linguistically or cognitively impaired; the notion of "semilingualism", or inability to speak either language; high-stakes testing inappropriate to students' language profiles; and biased teacher attitudes and classroom practices (González 2012; Grosjean 2008). The negative impact of this discrimination on students' identity, self-esteem, and home-language maintenance is well-established in the literature. In the United States, for example, "heritage Spanish speakers have drifted about in a linguistic limbo, never quite fitting into the monolingual English speaker or native Spanish speaker categories. Thus, many have been unfairly judged by their lack of 'proper' Spanish skills or, even more unjustly, been forced to abandon their heritage language in the face of the English-only dictum" (Félix 2009: 161). Minoritized students also face systemic discrimination that conflates race and language (see Rosa and Flores 2017), such that they are reprimanded for speaking their home languages while white students are rewarded for practicing "foreign languages", and the linguistic hierarchy of English over Spanish is reproduced within bilingual schools (Potowski 2004).

4.2 Home language and identity in classrooms

Misunderstandings of bilingualism and language and dialect hierarchies are also reproduced at the classroom level. Where home-language support is available, heritage students are often placed in foreign-language classes despite their different learner profiles (Valdés 2014). Foreign-language curriculum overlooks heritage students' language skills and generally high "sociolinguistic and sociocultural communicative competencies" (Kagan and Dillon 2001: 509), creating assumptions that they do not "really" speak the language (Abdi 2011), which negatively impact their linguistic, cultural, and academic identities. Further, based on their ethnicities, heritage students often face unrealistic teacher expectations and are negatively viewed as intimidating to other students (Leeman and Serafini 2017; Li and Duff 2008). Ill-fitting expectations and curriculum can erase heritage speakers' unique abilities and create deficit identities.

Prescriptive attitudes towards "correctness" and non-standard dialects also create identity conflict. Wong and Xiao (2010) note the difficulty of defining heritage languages when it comes to Chinese "dialects" and argue that dialect inclusion in home language education supports positive learner self-identity. However, Li and Duff (2008) found that, rather than expanding learners' linguistic repertoires, programs often offer "standard" varieties irrespective of their relevance to the local community. Doerr and Lee (2009) similarly identified conflict over curricular decisions in a Japanese heritage school, and Showstack (2012) found that monolingual standard

Spanish was privileged over local varieties and translanguaging, both classified as "deficient" Spanish, in heritage classrooms. These examples further demonstrate how heritage students' identities are essentialized in education through the ascription of ethnocultural identities assumed to be homogenous, and the privileging of monolingual prestige norms. However, home language identity within schools as elsewhere is complex. For example, students may resist ascribed identities that are inconsistent with their own senses of selves (Helmer 2013) and negotiate and construct identities as bilinguals, students, and members of local social groups and communities of practice, in addition to ethnicity.

4.3 Minority parental identities at school

The importance of identity in schools extends to family and community relations as parental involvement in education supports home language maintenance (Arriagada 2005). While minority parents are agentive in community schools, their involvement at state schools is often restricted, and negative identities are imposed: even as they are excluded, they are portrayed as uninterested in their children's education (Quiocho and Daoud 2006). Some successful efforts have been made to value and incorporate parental identities: for example, Moll et al.'s (1992) funds of knowledge teaching approach brings parents into classrooms as active intellectual contributors in order to draw upon "historically accumulated and culturally developed bodies of knowledge and skills" (Moll et al. 1992: 133). Furthermore, Harrison and Papa (2005) found that incorporating *kapa haka* (Maori performing arts) in the curriculum creates community connection and parental participation, and supports students' identity development. However, Burns (2017) and Palmer (2010) both note continued identity privilege of white parents over minority parents in U.S. dual language immersion programs even when school policies explicitly attempted to redress power imbalances (Burns 2017), a trend that seems likely to continue with increased interest in elite multilingualism under globalization (Barakos and Selleck 2019).

This section has addressed key factors in the interaction between identity and home language maintenance in education on multiple intersecting levels related to identity, ideology, and power in the broader sociocultural environment. The next section will discuss further considerations for research on identity and home language maintenance in terms of migration, indigeneity, and globalization.

5 Further considerations

This section addresses further considerations for identity and home language maintenance, focusing on underexplored areas of migration and insights from indigenous language identities and revitalization in conversation with new questions raised by globalization and transnationalism.

5.1 Research on home languages, identity, and migration

Much research on language and migration has focused on immigration to Western Europe, North America, Australia/New Zealand, and the United Kingdom. Less research has explored migration to and within Asia, Latin America, Africa, Eastern Europe, and the Middle East (although see Li 2016 on the Chinese diaspora). To give some examples of how research in these areas can add new perspectives on identity and home language maintenance, Gu and Patkin (2013) found that South Asian youth argued for home languages' professional usefulness and importance in identity as a means of resisting the lower social status imposed on them in Hong Kong, and, in a further counter-discourse, argued for the superiority of their English over that of the local Hong Kong Cantonese. This demonstrates a fluid navigation of the complex associations between language and identity within a local social hierarchy as well as English as a post-colonial and global language. In another example, Dyers (2008) found domain-specific home language maintenance related to multilingual identity as well as language-specific identity in families with multiple parental mother tongues in a South African township. However, further research on the relationship between identity and home language in understudied migrant contexts is needed to enrich comparative perspectives and combat Western-centric research bias.

5.2 Insights from indigenous communities

Indigenous communities offer unique insight into identity and home language dynamics. Questions of authenticity, identity, and agency influence the decision to elevate a particular language variety for official endorsement (López 2009), permeate notions of who indigenous speakers are (Zavala 2019), and determine how, when, and by whom languages may be used and/or written down (Currie Armstrong 2013; Whiteley 2003). Indigenous home language and identity are also tied to political sovereignty and cultural survival (Lee and McCarty 2017). Language rights are a key issue in indigenous movements across Latin America (López 2009). However, identity is not enough to sustain indigenous languages in the face of ongoing neglect and discrimination. For example, Australian Aboriginal languages are both salient political/symbolic markers of identity and highly endangered due to a history of state-sponsored linguicide, cultural repression, and forcible separation of children from parents (Nicholls 2005), factors echoed in many other indigenous contexts (Child 1998). López (2009) notes that while indigenous identity politics have advanced bilingual education throughout Latin America, inadequate understanding of multilingualism and of communities limit its effectiveness. Similarly, Mohanty (2006) found that minoritized tribes in India take pride in their home languages and associate them with group identity, but that while some groups have been able to gain language rights through collective identity demands, others are resigned to their marginalization.

5.3 Globalization and transnationalism

Globalization raises new directions for identity and home language maintenance research through increased sociolinguistic contact and expanded power hegemonies. It encourages global languages at the expense of minority languages and increases the scope of instrumental language discourses and discourses associating multilingualism with cosmopolitanism, elitism, and access to the world economy. Globalization also increases migration and language contact, giving rise to superdiverse social contexts (Blommaert 2010, though see Pavlenko's 2014 critique) and to new language forms and sociolinguistic identities which are often studied in terms of youth language, hybridity, and style (e.g. Auer and Dirim 2003; Cheshire et al. 2011; Rampton 2017).

Increased mobility and new means of communication complicate the relationship between home languages and transnational identities (De Fina and Perrino 2013), or identities and communities that transcend national boundaries. For example, multilingual immigrant adolescents use translanguaging and hybrid/multimodal language in digital communication to maintain transnational social networks (Kim 2018; Lam 2009). While transnational indigenous communities can struggle to maintain language in the face of home- and host-society pressure (Falconi 2013), transnationalism also creates new possibilities for identity and home language maintenance. Transnational indigenous identity was a key factor in the emergence of the activists leading demands for language rights in Peru (García 2003). Similarly, transnational Andean hip hop networks support language maintenance and transformation (Hornberger and Swinehart 2012), and Pietikäinen (2008) notes the importance of transnational Sami media in cultural identity, language maintenance, and linguistic hybridization. Further research on home languages, identity, migration, and indigeneity is indicated as globalization and transnationalism continue.

6 Conclusions

In this chapter, I have examined some key aspects of identity's role in home language maintenance. Identity is complex, dynamic, and socially constructed on multiple levels – individual, family, community, institutional, regional/national, and beyond – all of which impact home language maintenance. While language's strong indexical relationship with ethnocultural identity encourages home language maintenance, identity alone is not sufficient support in the face of assimilatory pressure and structural discrimination. These macrolevel factors themselves are part of language identity, in that they pertain to national language ideologies which privilege dominant-group language and culture.

The connection between language and ethnocultural identity motivates home language maintenance in families, as does language's importance in family cohesion. However, assimilatory pressure can influence families to shift away from the home language. Further, the equivalence of language with in-group membership can cause identity tension and discourage heritage language use amongst later-generation speakers whose multilingual abilities and new linguistic identities are criticized in comparison to monolingual norms.

Monolingual-normed and prestige ideology are also at play in classrooms, with negative identity consequences for heritage speakers' identities as home language speakers and as students. Further, schools as a whole do not support positive minoritized identities; dominant-group privilege is reproduced within bilingual education, and minority parents are disempowered. Community schools offer more scope for parental agency, but monolingual norming and prescriptivism remain.

Much remains to be done to understand new complexities of language and identity under globalization. Multilingualism's growing practical and prestige value does not necessarily indicate support for home languages. Nationalism is increasingly fraught, with language as a proxy for identity, legitimacy, and citizenship. Transnationalism offers new directions for research on migrant and indigenous languages and identities. Finally, more research is needed on migration, identity, and home-language maintenance in non-Western contexts to broaden comparative perspectives and correct Western-centric skew.

References

Abdi, Klara. 2011. "She really only speaks English": Positioning, language ideology, and heritage language learners. *Canadian Modern Language Review* 67(2). 161–190.

Alim, H. Samy, John R. Rickford & Arnetha F. Ball. 2016. Introducing raciolinguistics. *Raciolinguistics: How language shapes our ideas about race*, 1–30. Oxford: Oxford University Press.

Anderson, Benedict. 1991. *Imagined communities: reflections on the origin and spread of nationalism*. London: Verso.

Arriagada, Paula A. 2005. Family context and Spanish-language use: A study of Latino children in the United States. *Social Science Quarterly* 86(3). 599–619.

Auer, Peter. 2005. A postscript: Code-switching and social identity. *Journal of Pragmatics* 37(3). 403–410.

Auer, Peter & Inci Dirim. 2003. Socio-cultural orientation, urban youth styles and the spontaneous acquisition of Turkish by non-Turkish adolescents in Germany. In Jannis Androutsopoulos & Alexandra Georgakopoulou (eds.), *Discourse Constructions of Youth Identities*, 223–246. Philadelphia, PA: John Benjamins.

Bailey, Benjamin. 2000. Language and negotiation of ethnic/racial identity among Dominican Americans. *Language in Society* 29(4). 555–582.

Baker, Colin & Sylvia Prys Jones. 1998. Language standardization. In Colin Baker & Sylvia Prys Jones (eds.), *Encyclopedia of bilingualism and bilingual education*, 210–217. Clevedon: Multilingual Matters.

Bamberg, Michael, Anna De Fina & Deborah Schiffrin. 2011. Discourse and identity construction. In Seth Schwartz, Koen Luyckx & Vivian L. Vignoles (eds.), *Handbook of identity theory and research*, 177–199. New York: Springer.

Banda, Felix. 2000. The dilemma of the mother tongue: Prospects for bilingual education in South Africa. *Language Culture and Curriculum* 13(1). 51–66.

Barakos, Elisabeth & Charlotte Selleck. 2019. Elite multilingualism: Discourses, practices, and debates. *Journal of Multilingual and Multicultural Development*. 40(5). 361–374.

Bayley, Robert & Sandra R. Schecter. 2005. Family decisions about schooling and Spanish maintenance: Mexicanos in California and Texas. In Ana Celia Zentella (ed.), *Building on strength: Language and literacy in Latino families and communities*, 31–45. New York: Teachers College Press.

Benor, Sarah Bunin. 2010. Ethnolinguistic repertoire: Shifting the analytic focus in language and ethnicity. *Journal of Sociolinguistics* 14(2). 159–183.

Bhatt, Rakesh. 2008. In other words: Language mixing, identity representations, and third space. *Journal of Sociolinguistics* 12(2). 177–200.

Blackledge, Adrian. 2009. "As a country we do expect": The further extension of language testing regimes in the United Kingdom. *Language Assessment Quarterly* 6(1). 6–16.

Blom, Jan-Petter & John J. Gumperz. 2000. Social meaning in linguistic structure: Code-switching in Norway. In Li Wei (ed.), *The bilingualism reader*, 111–136. New York: Routledge.

Blommaert, Jan. 2010. *The sociolinguistics of globalization*. Cambridge: Cambridge University Press.

Bucholtz, Mary & Kira Hall. 2005. Identity and interaction: A sociocultural linguistic approach. *Discourse Studies* 7(4–5). 585–614.

Burns, Meg. 2017. "Compromises that we make": Whiteness in the dual language context. *Bilingual Research Journal* 40(4). 339–352.

Cabo, Diego P. Y. & Jason Rothman. 2012. The (il)logical problem of heritage speaker bilingualism and incomplete acquisition. *Applied Linguistics* 33(4). 450–455.

Carruba-Rogel, Zuleyma N. 2018. The complexities in *seguir avanzando*: Incongruences between the linguistic ideologies of students and their *familias*. In Mary Bucholtz, Dolores Inés Casillas & Jin Sook Lee (eds.), *Feeling it: Language, race, and affect in Latinx youth learning*, 149–165. New York: Routledge.

Cheshire, Jenny, Paul Kerswill, Sue Fox & Elvind Torgersen. 2011. Contact, the feature pool and the speech community: The emergence of Multicultural London English. *Journal of Sociolinguistics* 15(2). 151–196.

Child, Brenda J. 1998. *Boarding school seasons: American Indian families, 1900–1940*. Lincoln, NE: University of Nebraska Press.

Cho, Grace, Kyung-Sook Cho & Lucy Tse. 1997. Why ethnic minorities want to develop their heritage language: The case of Korean-Americans. *Language, Culture and Curriculum* 10(2). 106–112.

Clyne, Michael. 1991. *Community languages: The Australian experience*. Cambridge: Cambridge University Press.
Clyne, Michael, Yvette Slaughter, John Hajek & Doris Schüpbach. 2015. On the relation between linguistic and social factors in migrant language contact. In Rik De Busser & Randy J. LaPolla (eds.), *Language structure and environment: Social, cultural, and natural factors*, 149–176. Philadelphia, PA: John Benjamins.
Coupland, Nikolas. 2007. *Style: Language variation and identity*. Cambridge: Cambridge University Press.
Coupland, Nikolas. 2010. The authentic speaker and the speech community. In Carmen Llamas & Dominic Watts (eds.), *Language and identities*, 99–112. Edinburgh: Edinburgh University Press.
Cummins, Jim. 2005. A proposal for action: Strategies for recognizing heritage language competence as a learning resource within the mainstream classroom. *Modern Language Journal* 89(4). 585–592.
Curdt-Christiansen, Xiao Lan. 2009. Invisible and visible language planning: Ideological factors in the family language policy of Chinese immigrant families in Quebec. *Language Policy* 8(4). 351–375.
Curdt-Christiansen, Xiao Lan & Jing Huang. this vol. factors influencing family language policy.
Currie Armstrong, Timothy. 2013. "Why won't you speak to me in Gaelic?" Authenticity, integration, and the Heritage Language Learning Project. *Journal of Language, Identity & Education* 12(5). 340–356.
De Fina, Anna. 2003. *Identity in narrative: A study of immigrant discourse*. Philadelphia, PA: John Benjamins.
De Fina, Anna & Sabrina Perrino. 2013. Transnational identities. *Applied Linguistics* 34(5). 509–515.
De Mejía, Anne-Marie. 2002. *Power, prestige, and bilingualism: International perspectives on elite bilingual education*. Bristol, England: Multilingual Matters.
Doerr, Neriko M. & Kiri Lee. 2009. Contesting heritage: Language, legitimacy, and schooling at a weekend Japanese-language school in the United States. *Language and Education* 23(5). 425–441.
Dyers, Charlyn. 2008. Truncated multilingualism or language shift? An examination of language use in intimate domains in a new non-racial working class township in South Africa. *Journal of Multilingual and Multicultural Development* 29(2). 110–126.
Eisenchlas, Susana A. & Andrea C. Schalley. 2019. Reaching out to migrant and refugee communities to support home language maintenance. *International Journal of Bilingual Education and Bilingualism* 22(5). 564–575.
Eisenchlas, Susana A. & Andrea C. Schalley. this vol. Making sense of the notion of "home language" and related concepts.
Falconi, Elizabeth (2013). Storytelling, language shift, and revitalization in a transborder community: "Tell it in Zapotec!". *American Anthropologist* 115(4). 622–636.
Félix, Angela. 2009. The adult heritage Spanish speaker in the foreign language classroom: A phenomenography. *International Journal of Qualitative Studies in Education* 22(2). 145–162.
Fishman, Joshua A. 1972. *Language in sociocultural change*. Stanford, CA: Stanford University Press.
Flores, Susana & Enrique Murillo. 2001. Power, language, and ideology: Historical and contemporary notes on the dismantling of bilingual education. *The Urban Review* 33(3). 183–206.
Flores, Nelson & Jonathan Rosa. 2015. Undoing appropriateness: Raciolinguistic ideologies and language diversity in education. *Harvard Educational Review* 85. 149–171.
García, María Elena. 2003. The Politics of Community: Education, Indigenous Rights, and Ethnic Mobilization in Peru. *Latin American Perspectives* 30(1). 70–95.

García, Ofelia. 2005. Positioning heritage languages in the United States. *The Modern Language Journal* 89(4). 601–605.

García, Ofelia & Li Wei. 2014. Translanguaging and education. In Ofelia García & Li Wei (eds.), *Translanguaging: Language, bilingualism and education*, 63–77. London: Palgrave Macmillan.

Garrido, María Rosa. 2017. Multilingualism and cosmopolitanism in the construction of a humanitarian elite. *Social Semiotics* 27(3). 359–369.

Gee, James P. (2015). Discourse, small d, big D. In Karen Tracy, Cornelia Ilie & Todd Sanders (eds.), *The international encyclopedia of language and social interaction*, 418–422. New York: Wiley-Blackwell.

Giles, Howard & Patricia Johnson. 1987. Ethnolinguistic identity theory: A social psychological approach to language maintenance. *International Journal of the Sociology of Language* 68. 69–100.

Goddard, Cliff & Anna Wierzbicka. 2004. Cultural scripts: What are they and what are they good for? *Intercultural Pragmatics* 1(2). 153–166.

González, Virginia. 2012. Assessment of bilingual/multilingual pre-k–grade 12 students: A critical discussion of past, present, and future issues. *Theory into Practice* 51(4). 290–296.

Grosjean, François. 1989. Neurolinguists, beware! The bilingual is not two monolinguals in one person. *Brain and Language* 36(1). 3–15.

Grosjean, François. 2008. *Studying bilinguals*. Oxford: Oxford University Press.

Gu, Mingyue (Michelle) & John Patkin. 2013. Heritage and identity: Ethnic minority students from South Asia in Hong Kong. *Linguistics and Education* 24(2).131–141.

Guardado, Martin & Ava Becker. 2014. "Glued to the family": The role of familism in heritage language development strategies. *Language, Culture and Curriculum* 27(2). 163–181.

Gumperz, John. 1977. The sociolinguistic significance of conversational code-switching. *RELC Journal* 8(2). 1–34.

Harrison, Barbara & Rahui Papa. 2005. The development of an Indigenous knowledge program in a New Zealand Maori-language immersion school. *Anthropology & Education Quarterly* 36(1). 57–72.

He, Agnes Weiyun. 2006. Toward an identity theory of the development of Chinese as a heritage language. *Heritage Language Journal* 4(1). 1–28.

Heller, Monica. 2007. Bilingualism as ideology and practice. In Heller, Monica (ed.), *Bilingualism: A social approach*, 1–22. London: Palgrave Macmillan.

Helmer, Kimberly A. 2013. A twice-told tale: Voices of resistance in a borderlands Spanish heritage language class. *Anthropology & Education Quarterly* 44(3). 269–285.

Hill, Jane H. & Kenneth C. Hill. 1986. *Speaking Mexicano: Dynamics of syncretic language in central Mexico*. Tucson: University of Arizona Press.

Hinnenkamp, Volker. 2003. Mixed language varieties of migrant adolescents and the discourse of hybridity. *Journal of Multilingual and Multicultural Development* 24(1–2). 12–41.

Hogan-Brun, Gabrielle, Clare Mar-Molinero & Patrick Stevenson (eds.). 2009. *Discourses on language and integration: Critical perspectives on language testing regimes in Europe*. Philadelphia, PA: John Benjamins.

Holliday, Adrian. 2015. Native-speakerism: Taking the concept forward and achieving cultural belief. In Anne Swan, Pamela Aboshiha & Adrian Holliday (eds.), *(En)Countering native-speakerism*, 11–25. London: Palgrave Macmillan.

Hornberger, Nancy H. & Karl F. Swinehart 2012. Bilingual intercultural education and Andean hip hop: Transnational sites for indigenous language and identity. *Language in Society* 41(4). 499–525.

Hurst, Ellen. 2009. Tsotsitaal, global culture and local style: Identity and recontextualisation in twenty-first century South African townships. *Social Dynamics* 35(2). 244–257.

Irvine, Judith T. 2001. "Style" as distinctiveness: The culture and ideology of linguistic differentiation. In Penelope Eckert & John R. Rickford (eds.), *Style and sociolinguistic variation*, 21–43. Cambridge: Cambridge University Press.

Irvine, Judith T. & Susan Gal. 2009. Language ideology and linguistic differentiation. In Alessandro Duranti (ed.), *Linguistic anthropology: A reader*, 402–434. Malden, MA: Blackwell.

Kagan, Olga. 2012. Intercultural competence of heritage language learners: Motivation, identity, language attitudes, and the curriculum. In Beatrice Dupuy & Linda Waugh (eds.), *Proceedings of intercultural competence conference* (vol. 2), 72–84. Tucson, AZ: University of Arizona Center for Educational Resources in Culture, Language & Literacy.

Kagan, Olga & Kathleen Dillon. 2001. A new perspective on teaching Russian: Focus on the heritage learner. *The Slavic and East European Journal* 45(3). 507–518.

Kim, Sujin. 2018. "It was kind of a given that we were all multilingual": Transnational youth identity work in digital translanguaging. *Linguistics and Education* 43. 39–52.

King, Kendall A. 2001. *Language revitalization processes and prospects: Quichua in the Ecuadorian Andes*. Clevedon: Multilingual Matters.

King, Kendall A & Lyn Fogle. 2006. Bilingual parenting as good parenting: Parents' perspectives on family language policy for additive bilingualism. *International Journal of Bilingual Education and Bilingualism* 9(6). 695–712.

King, Kendall A., Lyn Fogle & Aubrey Logan-Terry. 2008. Family language policy. *Language and Linguistics Compass* 2(5). 907–922.

King, Kendall A. 2013. A tale of three sisters: Language ideologies, identities, and negotiations in a bilingual, transnational family. *International Multilingual Research Journal* 7(1). 49–65.

Krashen, Stephen. 1998. Language shyness and heritage language development. In Stephen L. Krashen, Lucy Tse & Jeff McQuillan (eds.), *Heritage language development*, 41–49. Culver City, CA: Language Education Associates.

Labov, William. 1972. *Sociolinguistic patterns*. Philadelphia, PA: University of Pennsylvania Press.

Lam, Wan Shun Eva. 2009. Multiliteracies on instant messaging in negotiating local, translocal, and transnational affiliations: A case of an adolescent immigrant. *Reading Research Quarterly* 44(4). 377–397.

Le Page, Robert & Andreé Tabouret-Keller. 1986. Acts of identity. *English Today* 2(4). 21–24.

Lee, Jamie S. 2004. Linguistic hybridization in K-Pop: Discourse of self-assertion and resistance. *World Englishes*. 23(3). 429–450.

Lee, Jin Sook. 2002. The Korean language in America: The role of cultural identity in heritage language learning. *Language Culture and Curriculum* 15(2). 117–133.

Lee, Tiffany S. & Teresa L. McCarty. 2017. Upholding Indigenous education sovereignty through critical culturally sustaining/revitalizing pedagogy. In Django Paris & Samy Alim (eds.), *Culturally sustaining pedagogies: Teaching and learning for educational justice in a changing world*, 61–82. New York: Teachers College Press.

Leeman, Jennifer. 2006. The value of Spanish: Shifting ideologies in United States language teaching. *AFFL Bulletin* 38(1–2). 32–39.

Leeman, Jennifer. 2015. Heritage language education and identity in the United States. *Annual Review of Applied Linguistics* 35. 100–119.

Leeman, Jennifer & Ellen J. Serafini. 2017. Student perceptions of deficit and difference in "mixed" HL/L2 classes. Paper presented at the Symposium on Spanish as a Heritage Language, University of California, Irvine, 17 February.

Li, Duanduan & Patricia Duff. 2008. Issues in Chinese heritage language education and research at the postsecondary level. In Agnes Weiyun He & Yun Xiao (eds.), *Chinese as a heritage language: Fostering rooted world citizenry*, 13–36. Honolulu, HI: University of Hawai'i Press.

Li, Wei. 1996. *Three generations, two languages, one family: Language choice and language shift in a Chinese community in Britain*. Clevedon: Multilingual Matters.

Li, Wei (ed.). 2016. *Multilingualism in the Chinese diaspora worldwide: Transnational connections and local social realities*. New York: Routledge.

Li, Xiaoxia. 1999. How can language minority parents help their children become bilingual in familial context? A case study of a language minority mother and her daughter. *Bilingual Research Journal* 23(2–3). 211–223.

Lippi-Green, Rosina. 2012. *English with an accent: Language, ideology and discrimination in the United States*. New York: Routledge.

Littlebear, Richard E. 2003. Chief Dull Knife community is strengthening the Northern Cheyenne language and culture. *Journal of American Indian Education* 42 (1). 75–84.

López, Luis E. 2009. *Reaching the unreached: Indigenous intercultural bilingual education in Latin America*. Paper commissioned for the UNESCO Education or All Global Monitoring Report.

Luke, Kang-Kwong. 1998. Why two languages might be better than one: Motivations of language mixing in Hong Kong. In Martha C. Pennington (ed.), *Language in Hong Kong at century's end*, 145–159. Hong Kong: Hong Kong University Press.

Lynch, Andrew. 2003. Toward a theory of heritage language acquisition: Spanish in the United States. In Ana Roca & Cecilia Colombi (eds.), *Mi lengua: Spanish as a heritage language in the United States*, 25–50. Washington, DC: Georgetown University Press.

Lytra, Vally. 2012. Discursive constructions of language and identity: Parents' competing perspectives in London Turkish complementary schools. *Journal of Multilingual and Multicultural Development* 33(1). 85–100.

Melo-Pfeifer, Sílvia. 2015. The role of the family in heritage language use and learning: Impact on heritage language policies. *International Journal of Bilingual Education and Bilingualism* 18(1). 26–44.

Mendoza-Denton, Norma. 2002. Language and identity. In Jack K. Chambers, Peter Trudgill & Natalie Schilling-Estes (eds.), *The handbook of language variation and change*, 475–499. Malden, MA: Blackwell.

Menken, Kate. 2013. (Dis)citizenship or opportunity? The importance of language education policy for access and full participation of emergent bilinguals in the United States. In Vaidehi Ramanthan (ed.), *Language policies and (dis)citizenship: Rights, access, pedagogies*, 209–230. Bristol: Multilingual Matters.

Mohanty, Ajit K. 2006. Multilingualism of the unequals and predicaments of education in India: Mother tongue or other tongue. In Ofelia García, Tove Skutnabb-Kangas & María E. Torres-Guzmán (eds.), *Imagining multilingual schools*, 262–283. Clevedon: Multilingual Matters.

Moll, Luis C., Cathy Amanti, Deborah Neff & Norma González. 1992. Funds of knowledge for teaching: Using a qualitative approach to connect homes and classrooms. *Theory Into Practice* 31(2). 132–141.

Morris, Delyth & Kathryn Jones. 2007. Minority language socialisation within the family: Investigating the early Welsh language socialisation of babies and young children in mixed language families in Wales. *Journal of Multilingual and Multicultural Development* 28(6). 484–501.

Nicholls, Christine. 2005. Death by a thousand cuts: Indigenous language bilingual education programmes in the Northern Territory of Australia, 1972–1998. *International Journal of Bilingual Education and Bilingualism* 8(2–3). 160–177.

Ó hIfearnáin, Tadhg. 2013. Family language policy, first language Irish speaker attitudes and community-based response to language shift. *Journal of Multilingual and Multicultural Development* 34(4). 348–365.

Palmer, Deborah K. 2010. Race, power, and equity in a multiethnic urban elementary school with a dual-language "strand" program. *Anthropology & Education Quarterly* 41(1). 94–114.

Pavlenko, Aneta. 2002. "We have room for but one language here": Language and national identity in the US at the turn of the 20th century. *Multilingua* 21(2/3). 163–196.

Pavlenko, Aneta. 2014. Superdiversity and why it isn't. In Barbara Schmenk, Stephan Breidbach & Lutz Küster (eds.), *Sloganizations in language education discourse*, 142–168. Bristol: Multilingual Matters.

Pavlenko, Aneta & Adrian Blackledge (eds.). 2004. *Negotiation of identities in multilingual contexts*. Clevedon: Multilingual Matters.

Phinney, Jean S., Irma Romero, Monica Nava & Dang Huang. 2001. The role of language, parents, and peers in ethnic identity among adolescents in immigrant families. *Journal of Youth and Adolescence* 30(2). 135–153.

Pietikäinen, Sari. 2008. Sami in the media: Questions of language vitality and cultural hybridisation. *Journal of Multicultural Discourses* 3(1). 22–35.

Potowski, Kim. 2004. Student Spanish use and investment in a dual immersion classroom: Implications for second language acquisition and heritage language maintenance. *The Modern Language Journal* 88(1). 75–101.

Preston, Dennis R. 2002. Language with an attitude. In Jack K. Chambers, Peter Trudgill & Natalie Schilling-Estes (eds.), *The handbook of language variation and change*, 40–66. Malden, MA: Blackwell.

Purkarthofer, Judith. this vol. Intergenerational challenges: Of handing down languages, passing on practices, and bringing multilingual speakers into being.

Quiocho, Alice M. & Annette M. Daoud. 2006. Dispelling myths about Latino parent participation in schools. *The Educational Forum* 70(3). 255–267.

Rampton, Ben. 2017. *Crossing: Language and ethnicity among adolescents*. New York: Routledge.

Romaine, Suzanne. 1999. Early bilingual development: From elite to folk. In Guus Extra & Ludo Verhoeven (eds.), *Bilingualism and migration*, 61–73. Berlin: Mouton de Gruyter.

Rosa, Jonathan. 2016. Racializing language, regimenting Latinas/os: Chronotope, social tense, and American raciolinguistic futures. *Language & Communication* 46. 106–117.

Rosa, Jonathan & Nelson Flores. 2017. Unsettling race and language: Toward a raciolinguistic perspective. *Language in Society* 46(5). 621–647.

Sevinç, Yeşim. this vol. Anxiety as a negative emotion in home language maintenance and development.

Showstack, Rachel E. 2012. Symbolic power in the heritage language classroom: How Spanish heritage speakers sustain and resist hegemonic discourses on language and cultural diversity. *Spanish in Context* 9. 1–26.

Silverstein, Michael. 1979. Language structure and linguistic ideology. In Paul R. Cyne, William F. Hanks & Carol L. Hofbauer (eds.), *The elements: A parasession on linguistic units and levels*, 193–247. Chicago, IL: Chicago Linguistic Society.

Silverstein, Michael. 2003. Indexical order and the dialectics of sociolinguistic life. *Language & Communication* 23(3–4). 193–229.

Simpson, Jane. 2013. What's done and what's said: Language attitudes, public language activities and everyday talk in the Northern Territory of Australia. *Journal of Multilingual and Multicultural Development* 34(4). 383–398.

Shin, Sarah. 2002. Birth order and the language experience of bilingual children. *TESOL Quarterly* 36(1).103–113.

Shohamy, Elana. 2006. *Language policy: Hidden agendas and new approaches*. New York: Routledge.

Smith-Christmas, Cassie. 2014. Being socialised into language shift: The impact of extended family members on family language policy. *Journal of Multilingual and Multicultural Development* 35(5). 511–526.

Spitulnik, Debra. 1998. The language of the city: Town Bemba as urban hybridity. *Journal of Linguistic Anthropology* 8(1). 30–59.

Spolsky, Bernard. 2012. Family language policy – the critical domain. *Journal of Multilingual and Multicultural Development* 33(1). 3–11.

Tse, Lucy. 1997. Affecting affect: the impact of ethnic language programs on students attitudes. *Canadian Modern Language Review* 53(4). 705–728.

Tseng, Amelia. 2015. *Vowel variation, style, and identity construction in the English of Latinos in Washington, D.C.* Washington, DC: Georgetown University dissertation.

Tseng, Amelia. 2018. Bilingualism, ideological recentering, and new Latinx identity construction in the global city. Paper presented at the Latina/o Studies Association 3rd Biennial Conference, Latinx Studies Now: DC 2018+, Washington, D.C. 12–14 July.

Urciuoli, Bonnie. 2008. Whose Spanish?: The tension between linguistic correctness. In Mercedes Niño-Murcia & Jason Rothman (eds.), *Bilingualism and identity: Spanish at the crossroads with other languages*, 257–277. Philadelphia, PA: John Benjamins.

Valdés, Guadalupe. 2000. Introduction. *Spanish for native speakers* (AATSP Professional Development Series Handbook for Teachers K-16 1). New York, NY: Harcourt College Publishers.

Valdés, Guadalupe. 2014. Heritage language students: Profiles and possibilities. In Terrence G. Wiley, Joy Kreeft Peyton, Donna Christian, Sarah Catherine K. Moore & Na Liu (eds.), *Handbook of heritage, community, and native American languages in the United States*, 41–49. New York: Routledge.

Vazquez, Maegan. "Steve King's campaign criticizes Parkland survivor Emma González," CNN, 27 March 2018, https://www.cnn.com/2018/03/26/politics/steve-king-facebook-post-emma-gonzalez/index.html (accessed 2 April 2018).

Weisskirch, Robert S. 2005. The relationship of language brokering to ethnic identity for Latino early adolescents. *Hispanic Journal of Behavioral Sciences* 27(3). 286–299.

Whiteley, Peter. 2003. Do "language rights" serve indigenous interests? Some Hopi and other queries. *American Anthropologist* 105(4). 712–722.

Wiley, Terrence G. 2007. Immigrant language minorities in the United States. In Marlis Hellinger & Anne Pauwels (eds.), *Handbook of language and communication: Diversity and change*, 53–85. Berlin: Mouton de Gruyter.

Williams, Colin H. 2014. The lightening veil: Language revitalization in Wales. *Review of Research in Education* 38(1). 242–272.

Wong, Ka F. & Yang Xiao. 2010. Diversity and difference: Identity issues of Chinese heritage language learners from dialect backgrounds. *Heritage Language Journal* 7(2). 153–187.

Wong Fillmore, Lily. 1991. When learning a second language means losing the first. *Early Childhood Research Quarterly* 6(3). 323–346.

You, Byeong-Keun. 2005. Children negotiating Korean American ethnic identity through their heritage language. *Bilingual Research Journal* 29(3). 711–721.

Zavala, Virginia. (2019). Youth and the repoliticization of Quechua. *Language, Culture, and Society* 1(1). 60–83.

Zentella, Ana Celia. 1997. The Hispanophobia of the Official English movement in the US. *International Journal of the Sociology of Language* 127(1). 71–86.

Zentella, Ana Celia. 2007. "Dime con quién hablas, y te diré quién eres": Linguistic (in)security and Latina/o unity. In Juan Flores & Renato Rosaldo (eds.), *A companion to Latina/o studies*, 25–38. Malden, MA: Blackwell.

Zentella, Ana Celia. 2014. TWB (Talking while bilingual): Linguistic profiling of Latina/os, and other linguistic torquemadas. *Latino Studies* 12(4). 620–635.

Zhang, Donghui & Diana T. Slaughter-Defoe. 2009. Language attitudes and heritage language maintenance among Chinese immigrant families in the USA. *Language, Culture and Curriculum* 22(2). 77–93.

Zhao, Shouhui & Yongbing Liu. 2010. Chinese education in Singapore: Constraints of bilingual policy from the perspectives of status and prestige planning. *Language Problems and Language Planning* 34(3). 236–258.

Zhu, Hua. 2008. Duelling languages, duelling values: Codeswitching in bilingual intergenerational conflict talk in diasporic families. *Journal of Pragmatics* 40(10). 1799–1816.

Judith Purkarthofer
7 Intergenerational challenges: Of handing down languages, passing on practices, and bringing multilingual speakers into being

1 Introduction

There are few topics that are as cross-sectional as intergenerational challenges in language practices. Research in multilingual contexts often has a strong focus on specific age groups while others are treated as "background". Children and parents are the focus in family language policy research, language documentation and revitalization has traditionally focused on elders and has only recently also found an interest in children as emergent speakers. In educational settings, teachers' attitudes can be in the spotlight while children are mainly talked about, or vice-versa, and in most cases teachers and students belong to connected social worlds but have divergent social experiences. The aim of this chapter is to give an overview of studies dealing with more than one generation, but also to question the notion of generations in frameworks of language maintenance.

Within the view on languages as social processes is the understanding of them not being objects that simply emerge or can be handed down (or up for that matter) from generation to generation, but are interactively appropriated, negotiated and changed over time. When talking about languages being passed on or using terms like language transmission or maintenance, languages are not seen as objects to be handled but as processes requiring active participation from all generations involved. Explicitly, intergenerational language transmission refers to a process through which language(s) are taught and learned formally or informally (Borland 2006: 24) and make their way from one generation to the next, in rare cases also bypassing one generation, if the grandparent generation passes a language to the grandchildren generation directly.

In section 2 of this chapter, the notion of "generation" as a concept and how it is relevant for multilingualism research is in focus. Section 3 then presents studies *through a generational lens*, starting with research on language acquisition and in the family context that highlight intergenerational challenges, i.e. multilingual upbringing in transnational contexts or family language policies with multilingual speakers as primary caregivers. This is followed by research on language maintenance in traditional minority contexts and in migration and diaspora, among others in traditionally multilingual rural areas where three to four generations negotiate changes in local language use. Section 3 also deals with multilingualism in institutional language education, and how generational transmission through schooling practices is relevant for children with multilingual repertoires. The final section 4

https://doi.org/10.1515/9781501510175-007

highlights biographical research and how speakers navigate their multilingual language biographies across the lifespan and through different generations. This section also addresses some methodological challenges that relate to intergenerational research and thus adds to the discussion in Juvonen et al. (this vol.). The concluding discussion in section 5 summarises the chapter and proposes future directions for research. Throughout the chapter, I will use notions like home language, family language and minoritized language, and while these terms are largely used as synonymous, they highlight different social qualities (e.g. of being used in the home or else being in a relatively minoritarian status vis-à-vis a majority language, that is just as well used in the home). For an extended discussion, the reader is referred to Eisenchlas and Schalley (this vol.).

2 Intergenerational challenges

2.1 The problem of generations

Generations can be looked at from a biological as well as social perspective. While the lifecycle orientation in biology draws on the succession of individuals as they are born, grow up and produce offspring of their own, the social understanding of generations refers to shared cultural and social experiences that unite individuals born at about the same time.

Generations and their relationships are discussed among the early problems in philosophy and the emerging field of sociology at the end of the 19th century. Dilthey ([1875] 1924), a German empiricist and philosopher, highlighted that the distance between (biological) generations was not to be measured in exact time but rather "internally experienced", while at the same time stressing the simultaneousness of (social) generations. He was interested in the phenomenon of members of the same social generations living through the same important influences, both culturally and socio-politically, which would result in them forming a somewhat coherent group. Mannheim ([1923/1952] 1998: 170) extended Dilthey's thoughts and in his work *The problem of generations* suggested five important characteristics defining the succession of generations:

> (a) New participants in the cultural process are emerging, whilst
> (b) former participants in that process are continually disappearing.
> (c) Members of any one generation can participate only in a temporally limited section of the historical process, and
> (d) it is therefore necessary continually to transmit the accumulated cultural heritage.
> (e) The transition from generation to generation is a continuous process.

The ongoing change that is inherent in the image of generations means that members of generations have to interact continuously (e), in order to welcome new (a) or see off former participants (b, c) or keep up the knowledge that was collected by members of earlier generations (d). Researching any interaction can thus be seen as (only) one moment in the continued sequence of intergenerational interactions. Past, present and future have to be taken into account to understand how transmission and transition are taking place.

However, the understanding of generations is not universal, and researchers in social psychology as well as in communications have researched relevant notions in different countries and regions (Giles et al. 2003; Giles, Makoni, and Dailey 2005; Giles, Khajavy, and Choi 2012). Intergenerational communication has been in focus in publications across cultural contexts (e.g. Nussbaum and Coupland 2004). An interesting finding is the cultural notion of generation and age-group (Giles, Makoni, and Dailey 2005: 196): As the authors have shown for comparable North American, South African and Ghanaian respondents of different age groups, their perception of young adulthood, middle and elderly age differ considerably, seeing a wider span in the North American respondent (young adulthood starting earlier and middle age ending later) than in the other countries. While this does not explain the earlier onset of young adulthood, the regional difference in life expectancy can account for the onset of elderly age around 50 years in both African data sets whereas it was over 60 years for North American respondents. At the same time, findings in this line of research have shown that respondents in different geographical locations perceive intragenerational communication as easier and less problematic (i.e. less risky or face threatening) than intergenerational communication. In all researched geographical contexts, communication with (older) relatives was viewed favourably in comparison to (older) non-family members (Giles et al. 2003).

2.2 The sociolinguistic problem of generations

Frameworks of language revitalization and language classification have used the notion of generation as an important tool to assess the status of languages or their degree of endangerment. Suslak (2009) shows how static notions of generations, as they have been present in sociolinguistic literature, fail to recognise the inherent dynamics and even the options to move between generations. He calls this, in reference to Mannheim's work, the *sociolinguistic problem of generations*.

In Fishman's (1991) scheme of intergenerational disruption of language transmission, four of eight steps are defined by generational relations:[1]

---

[1] Steps 1 to 4, not cited here, make no mention of generations, they apply to languages of little vulnerability.

5: The language is used orally *by all generations* and is effectively used in written form throughout the community;
6: The language is used orally *by all generations* and is being learned by children as their first language;
7: The *child-bearing generation* knows the language well enough to use it *with their elders* but is not transmitting it to their children;
8: The only remaining speakers of the language are *members of the grandparent generation*.
(Fishman 1991, adapted by Lewis and Simons 2010:105, emphasis added by the author)

All of these steps rely on members of older generations to transmit their language(s) to the younger generations – while they need not be biologically related, they are addressed as members of their age-groups, and shared responsibility in the community is constructed.

The UNESCO (2009) Framework of the degree of endangerment of languages builds on similar factors, and intergenerational transmission is seen as the safeguard to keep languages alive. It distinguishes six stages of degree of endangerment:

Safe: The language is spoken by *all generations*; intergenerational transmission is uninterrupted.
Vulnerable: *Most children* speak the language, but it may be restricted to certain domains (e.g., the home).
Definitely endangered: *Children* no longer learn the language as mother tongue in the home.
Severely endangered: The language is spoken by *grandparents and older generations*; while the *parent generation* may understand it, they do not speak it to children or among themselves.
Critically endangered: The youngest speakers are *grandparents and older*, and they speak the language partially and infrequently.
Extinct: There are no speakers left. (italics added by the author)

In both of these frameworks, and others that follow similar patterns (e.g. Schmidt 1990; Krauss 1998), it is understood that each person can be classified as a member of a generation and may grow up to become a member of different generations. However, the speaker's own position is not taken into account when assessing languages with the presented grids, and the prevailing image is that of older speakers talking to younger ones. Repertoires that might overlap and diverse resources that speakers draw on are not mentioned in the frameworks and there is little agency foreseen for younger generations to react to elders.

Meek (2007), researching generational discontinuity among Kaska speakers in Canada, found another possible interpretation of the generational grids discussed above: She reports children perceiving themselves as not being old enough to speak the minority language yet, as it was seen as special knowledge and thus reserved for the elders. In work on Slovene speakers in Austria (Purkarthofer 2016), parents voiced that once their children had learned enough Slovene in school, they would feel confident switching "back" from the majority language, German, and speaking Slovene with their children. While parents and teachers are members of the same generation, parents felt that their own command of the minority language was not sufficient to act as role models for their children and thus, in generational terms, it seemed that they were placing themselves as the (co-)children generation, learning from the adult teachers.

In research dealing with multilingualism, we necessarily encounter issues of intergenerational communication and both biological and social generations can offer a lens to understand relationships and patterns of language use. But generational behaviour is not essentially the same all the time, it is instead made relevant in interactions in different ways, along with other social factors like age, status, power and language competences. In the next section, I will discuss the family, the intergenerational lieu par excellence, and studies on family language policy to point to the intergenerational lens in research on multilingualism and home languages.

3 Challenges seen through a generational lens

3.1 Language acquisition in the family and family language policy

Families are seen as the main site of generational contact, and even if this is not exclusively so, studies on intergenerational transmission usually take families as a starting point. Earlier chapters have already dealt with emotional needs and family relations (e.g. De Houwer; Sevinç, both this vol.), while strategies of home language maintenance (Schwartz this vol.) and the issue of child agency will be discussed later in the handbook (Smith-Christmas this vol.).

Families are seen as dynamic systems, consisting of members of different generations each having their own perspectives on, agency in and ideas about languages and life. One important aspect in research is the experience of multilingual linguistic repertoires of family members developing over time. Definitions about what constitutes a family differ across times and contexts, and do generally transcend the image of (just) two parents and their biological children (Cutas and Chan 2012; Palvainen this vol.). Research on family language policy has gone through four (Fogle and King 2017) or even five phases in the last two decades (Lanza and Lomeu Gomes this vol.), from a focus on language acquisition of children to a more sociolinguistic focus on conditions of language socialisation. In order to study language socialisation, attention should be paid to the linkages between micro and macro levels of analysis: A study design that takes developmental changes over time into account is needed, encompassing an ethnographic perspective, along with field-based naturalistic data collection (Garrett 2017).

Intergenerational challenges in family language policy research can be described as either linked to policies and practices, and divergence between them, or as linked to differences in expectations and perspectives. Other challenges in interpersonal communication do of course also occur in family settings but will not be the focus of this chapter.

Divergence between the policy and practices of a family has been repeatedly reported and this has made it very obvious that research is needed on the models of language distribution (with the most famous being the one-person, one-language model) and plans for exposure and input. But research is also needed on interactions in families, involving different generations, and taking language use and multilingual meaning-making into account. Studies focusing on the emergence of new multilingual speakers have been conducted globally, but with a focus on bilingual families in Europe and North America (for an overview see De Houwer 2017). From the wide body of research, only some examples are given here, dealing with bilingual first-language acquisition in young children (Lanza 2004), multilingual interactions in daily routines (Van Mensel 2018) and interactions around the dinner table (Tannen 2006). Languages come into the families by grandparents (Curdt-Christiansen 2009), adopted children (Fogle 2012), and in and through transnational networks (Zhu and Li 2016). Most studies report the importance of different generations being present in the family, and identify specific strategies of parents and caretakers that might differ from those of grandparents and other members of the extended family. In contrast to the models of language maintenance, the transfer of knowledge happens not only from older to younger generations but is rather negotiated between all interlocutors. Studies from other parts of the world, Africa in particular, are less common, but do emerge and present interesting data, e.g. one study by Coetzee on adolescent parents (2018), raising their children in two extended family settings.

Recently, a focus on child agency is visible (Smith Christmas 2018, this vol.) that has led to more studies on language transmission and learning in families (Said and Zhu 2019), but also to a larger number of studies on older children, among them school-aged children of Rwandan parents in Brussels (Gafaranga 2010) and teenagers of Polish descent in Norway (Obojska 2017, 2018). In Gafaranga's study, the management of family languages is contrasted with face-to-face interactions, and the importance of the children being complicit or resisting intended adult language behaviour is highlighted. In Obojska's studies, the teenagers talk about their language biographies, but their language practices are also observed in relation to their social media activity (see also Little this vol.). The participants in her research reported making conscious choices with regards to the use of Polish outside of the home, mainly targeting an online audience in Poland that followed their Norwegian adventures with great interest.

Among the recent discussions of multilingual intergenerational exchanges is a growing focus on digital interaction and also digital intergenerational interaction (for an overview, see Lanza and Lexander in press). Members of transnational families communicate not only face-to-face, but their linguistic repertoires are widened through diverse digital and mediated practices, from talking on the phone to texting and using social media platforms. The interactions serve as occasions of language use but of course they mainly strengthen the family ties (Szecsi and Szilagyi 2012). Kenner et al. (2008) show how intergenerational learning is happening around a computer and how Bangladeshi grandparents and their grandchildren in the UK mutually use a cultural tool to encourage interactivity and exploration. Akther (2016) analysed a young boy's use of two different scripts (English and Arabic) for literacy and language practices with his grandmother, conveying meaning through hybrid language use in English and Bengali, and found that this intergenerational interaction negotiated the diverging and not congruent repertoires of both participants.

Adult children are rarely the focus of research, with the exception of Soehl (2016) who interprets French data from questionnaires about language behaviour. His study is atypical in the sense that it deals with large data sets that were acquired through telephone interviews as part of a nationwide survey, and that his approach is quantitative in nature. Yet another approach is taken by Leglisé (2019), who traces the trajectories of Brazilian families between French Guyane and Brazil, using commented family genealogies in addition to biographical interviews. Her research offers insights into continued transnational experiences and language choices of women of the grandparent generation, using Portuguese and French along with other resources with their spouses, children and grandchildren.

Challenges in intergenerational relations are also linked to parental expectations, motivations for language use and ideas of transmission. Expectations exist about which languages should be kept in the family's repertoire, which functions need to be filled and which roles each speaker should inhabit, also in relation to genealogies and traditional or modern images of society (Purkarthofer and Steien 2019). How explicit these expectations are is largely dependent on the sociopolitical context and the personal characteristics of the speakers. Parental aspirations and ideologies have been studied and the connection between language choices and good parenting has been pointed out by King and Fogle (2006) in interviews and by Piller and Gerber (2018) in online forums. Van Mensel and Deconinck (2017) focused on desire in the language learning motivations of adults for their children. Purkarthofer (2019b) looked at ideas and conceptions of parents as they were expecting their first child. The research participants were addressed as future parents, but they were relying on their own upbringing and thus their own generational alignment when they offered reasons and evaluations on what success in being a multilingual speaker meant for them. It is thus visible that borders between generations are not clear-cut and that speakers draw on different experiences and changed generational roles as they grow older.

Future research is needed that covers social and geographical contexts that have rarely been in focus. As grandparents, parents and children move along transnational trajectories, their language repertoires differ considerably and conceptions of (only) one family language across generations seem no longer fitting. Expectations regarding languages in family settings are of course also important in relation to these changing repertoires, and questions of communicative functions, symbolic value and the meaning of transmission or language change need to be addressed. The extended family can be seen as a nexus in language policy research, and it is of great interest how it relates to other possible contexts. This will be the topic of the following sections, where I will first focus on minority settings in section 3.2 and then move on to settings of migration and diaspora, while acknowledging that these lines are not clearly drawn.

3.2 A generational effort – language maintenance in minority settings

Multilingual families play an important role in transmitting regional minority languages, or reviving dormant languages. This section focuses on the situation of language users in minority and diasporic settings, where the home language is usually not the majority language (see also Mayer et al. this vol.). Power relations, the ability to participate in societal discourses and to contribute to one's own representation in a majority language setting are part of the specific contexts in which generations are called to action. I will thus discuss studies on efforts to transmit languages that transcend the borders of the family, and I will distinguish traditional regional minority language contexts (this section) from those of speakers in migration and diaspora (next section). Attempting to present a geographical spread, I am aware that European and Northern American researchers and languages are still overrepresented in the studies that I will highlight.

Intergenerational transmission is considered an important predictor of language survival and researchers dealing with minoritised languages have taken efforts to research and highlight successful stories of transmission and revival (e.g. Hinton 2013). While families have been the focus of research, many communities world-wide have developed approaches to support the language acquisition of children. New Zealand's Ministry of Māori Development provides booklets, newsletter and a website with what is considered relevant information for parents who want to raise their children bilingually (Chrisp 2005). In this way, family efforts are met with community or in this case state initiatives. Wales has started the distribution of information material on early bilingual development via midwives taking care of new-born children and their parents (Edwards and Pritchard Newcombe 2006). However, a follow-up study (Tranter et al. 2010) showed that midwives were not perceived as language professionals by parents and did not see themselves in this role. Bilingual child-rearing would be brought up mostly in families that were already quite outspoken about it and met with midwives who were speakers of Welsh. It can be assumed that there is a supportive effect of this kind of marketing material, but given the experiences of midwives, it seemed less successful than has been expected. While in the Welsh case parents no longer feared disadvantages for their children, in other contexts these initiatives still compete with societal pressure, i.e. parents who are afraid that their minority language would put their children at risk, as Lane (2010) has shown for speakers of Kven in 20th century Norway.

Throughout the world, schools have been an important place for language transmission, and chapters in this volume discuss formal education and home language maintenance in more detail, focusing on models of formal education (Yağmur this vol.), teacher attitudes (Mary and Young this vol.) and the mainstream classroom (Paulsrud this vol.). Māori speakers in New Zealand have developed the concept of language nests (*kōhanga reo*), pre-school childcare that immerses children into the desired minority language (Lourie 2011). Hinton (2011: 312) reminds us that "it is also a sweet irony to use schools for language revitalization since they have played such a large role in language death." For teachers and students, as they are also members of their respective generations, educational institutions provide a meeting ground and, especially in smaller communities, might be among the limited places where children and adults are exposed to a minoritised language. Teachers are inscribed in complex social schemes, meandering between grading and standardizing, acting as role models for minority or majority languages and as encouraging advocates of language learning. Their training, however, often does not prepare them for these roles in an appropriate way (Valdés 2017). De Korne (2017) presents two teachers, one in her 20s and the other in his 60s, who each adopt a collaborative way of working towards achieving communicative competence in Isthmus Zapotec, thus practising language reclamation as self-definition. Both are taking the inner dialect variation and the multilingual realities of the region into account when welcoming new members into the Zapotec speech community, but they are doing so by using their different generational positions and personalities. Apart from the personality of the teachers (as highlighted in De Korne's study 2017), the wider policy plays its role in the relations between generations of language users and learners: Lourie (2011) demonstrates how changes in the curriculum for language education influence perceived responsibility of non-Māori and Māori learners, leaving the latter with the task to keep up biculturalism and keep using the lesser-used language.

Generational expectations about who should learn in which way and to which goal need to be answered in all contexts of learning. Todal (2006) describes a project in Eastern Norway, which makes use of the Southern Saami language in school. He highlights the positive effects on the children's competences that were possible by being able to hire a qualified speaker – but at the same time the difficulties to find such a speaker in the area. Still, he also makes an interesting observation for our topic: The children learned to speak Saami, but they would only ever use it with adults and stick to Norwegian for peer interactions. This example also brings another immanent problem to the fore: A few years after the project ended, the whole school was closed down due to lack of students. Across the world, it seems to be a shared experience that adults and elders complain about the perceived loss or infrequent use of minoritised languages by children. As Purkarthofer and De Korne (2019) have shown for Slovene speakers in Austria and Zapotec speakers in the Isthmus of Tehuantepec, this might not be the view of the children who see themselves as speakers of the minority language. In other contexts, children are even seen to be the driving force behind language differentiation and thus the emergence of "new" indigenous languages (e.g. in the case of Light Warlpiri in Australia, O'Shannessy 2012, 2015). In this case, after having had input in a baby talk register of Warlpiri and Australian-English/Kriol from the adults in the community, the language was used in the peer-group of children and developed into a new paradigm distinct from the input languages.

Yet another strategy of intergenerational learning is used in Mentor-Apprentice programs, mostly employed in the revitalisation of Indigenous languages with adult learners. Canadian researchers found well-being effects in participants of a said program (Jenni et al. 2017), among them a sense of reconnection after experienced trauma through forced attendance at boarding schools, healing effects of becoming a language mentor in elders, as well as a strengthening of the apprentices through a more positive outlook and by taking on a leading role in the community. Basham and Fathman (2008), in an earlier study about latent speakers that despite growing up in a multilingual household never acquired the minoritised language, come to comparable conclusions as they highlight how the fear of being ridiculed and not having a trusting relationship to proficient speakers can keep latent speakers from using their language, even if they have a certain intuitive knowledge of it. But they also describe how even for successful learners, communication and the use of languages outside of formal domains is an issue well into advanced stages of learning. While children are "naturally" perceived as language learners, adults have to be more explicit about their will to learn (Chrisp 2005), which might be facilitated through explicit programs (Basham and Fathman 2008). Terms like "new speakers" (Smith-Christmas et al. 2018) can address some of the assumptions about who is supposed to know what and how speakers of a minority language can re-connect with the language well after having reached adult age.

In all of the described settings, generational roles mix with other social roles. Singer (2018) illustrates with her data from an anniversary ceremony on Australia's Northern coast how complex generational and societal patterns can lead to speakers being identified with right or wrong T-shirts, used as an expression of belonging and of alignment with clans, heritage, and language groups. Languages are in her context not completely congruent with clans, but through a set of identification processes, mostly along the lines of belonging to the coast or the inland people, families do arrive at a shared understanding of which distinctions should be made relevant in a given performance.

3.3 Multilingual connections – languages across generations in migration and diaspora

Languages of migration and languages of diasporic communities are subject to change and may eventually move to the periphery of their speakers' linguistic repertoires. In the example of the Maltese community in Melbourne, Australia, Borland (2006) describes facilitating and motivating factors that work together to enable language maintenance and intergenerational transmission. While the facilitating factors are a favourable environment and opportunities for interaction (both in the diaspora and with the homeland), she strongly links the motivating factors to intergenerational exchange, in the form of upholding family communications and fostering familial ties. A third factor, not necessarily linked to generational lineage, is the perceived benefit of bilingualism. Borland identifies a crucial moment when the children generation reaches adulthood and leaves the family home: Only in some of her participants' families, the practice of speaking Maltese (or a mix of Maltese and English) was upheld past this point. In cases where the parents expressed a feeling of their language being stigmatized, and at times a preference for English themselves, the children were more likely to switch to English or to speak less and less Maltese.

Sevinç and Backus (2017; also Sevinç this vol.) present an interesting approach by analysing interviews with members of three generations of Turkish immigrants in the Netherlands, talking about their feelings of anxiety in relation to their heritage language but also the majority language in their country of residence. The authors highlight how anxiety leads to less language use and thus no improvements in language knowledge which in turn contributes to a further increase of language anxiety.

In the case of Bangladeshi families in the London, the grandparents are crucial in providing environments for their grandchildren to use Bangla in different ways (Gregory, Ruby, and Kenner 2010): They model language behaviour, including literacy and religious practices, and they shape spaces of observation and learning for children of all ages. Ruby (2012) discusses in detail how one pair of grandmother and granddaughter uses strategies of teaching and learning, and successfully engages in Bangla literacy, and she concludes with the remark that those instances of learning are rarely acknowledged in formal schooling, and that grandparents and their resources are not sufficiently recognised.

This remark already points to intergenerational challenges that are present in contexts where speakers encounter institutions or are met with official language policy (e.g. Hornberger 2014). Schools and formal environments for languages are in focus in part 4.2 of this volume, and thus, only some aspects will be highlighted in this section. Putjata (2017) analyses policy changes in Israeli schools, aiming at establishing a multilingualism friendly climate, and discusses how Russian speakers experienced both the former, monolingual, and the more recent, multilingual, policy. Her findings show a reduction in overtly negative feedback on the use of Russian and thus success in the policy goals. The reports from her participants, however, also indicate that change was not that apparent in all schools or not perceived as a major change in practice.

Research on students and schools dealing with different languages should be aware of the challenges that arise from intergenerational contact. Reath Warren (2017) analyses curricula for mother tongue instruction in Sweden and Australia and shows how aims and values are contradicted or constrained in some cases. Monoglossic expectations hinder multilingual students to develop literacies in several of their languages. Bigelow (2010) demonstrates with a careful study on Somali youth in Minnesota how language use and literacy practices in Somali and English are negotiated in the peer group but also with adult teachers and the researcher. While Somali is used with family and peers, it is rarely used as a written language and only a few of the teenagers have had schooling experience in Somali, not usually offered in the area.

Yet another case is described by Rienzner (2010) in her paper on Somali mother tongue education entering the Austrian school system: A health professional drew attention to the fact that intergenerational problems were encountered by Somali mothers and their teenage daughters when it came to discussing bodily changes and health prevention activities during puberty. While the mothers had acquired German to some extent, they had not necessarily discussed health topics in their German language classes, even less as they are surrounded by taboo and hardly spoken about in mixed classrooms. The daughters (and sons, obviously) had had their health education in the Austrian school system and were thus more proficient in these topics in German. Their Somali, while being adequate for family interactions, did reportedly not cover technical terms like specific body parts and biological functions. In conjunction with a research project at the university, the Somali community with a women's association as the driving force, initiated Somali mother tongue education in Austrian mainstream schools and the expectation is that this helps to prevent the interruption of communication in a period where health issues and personal development call for personal exchange (Purkarthofer 2019a). If the mainstream school system is not open for such proposals, grassroots initiatives that take on schooling and education in migrant languages can offer relief (see Nordstrom this vol.).

The case of Somali/German exchanges around puberty highlights interruptions in transmission – but it also demonstrates the failure to recognise intergenerational challenges that parents and their children face at times. In the above mentioned situation, both sides were able to address each other in two languages and if using the frameworks of language maintenance (as cited in section 2), transmission would be regarded as successful. However, the communicative needs of the teenagers and of the parents could not be fulfilled in any of the languages at hand. I would thus consider this an example that accounts for language transmission that is not either happening or not happening (in a binary opposition) but is instead partially successful. Such complex, partial or combined transmission practices, inherently multilingual, are not represented in frameworks of language maintenance, and revisions might be needed.

4 Becoming different generations – biographical research, intergenerational understanding and methodological challenges

The multilingual speaker can be seen from very different angles, as a rather solitary individual through the lens of competence and testing, in relation to one or more groups as a user of certain linguistic resources, and as a bearer of identities, affectively linked to languages and speech styles. Furthermore, she is also linked to other speakers through generational links. While early publications on language transmission and shift focused on certain, relatively delimited languages, more recent publications have problematised the notion of language as an abstract construct and instead focus on the speaker as a whole person.

Speaker-centred approaches focus on multilingual speakers and their developing language biographies (Busch 2017; Purkarthofer 2019b). Such approaches take the multilingual subject (Kramsch 2009), and its identity and language learning (Norton 2013) as a focal point and highlight the importance of the diversity of resources that speakers employ, transcending binary categories such as majority and minority or home language. Over time, multilingual speakers form their communicative or linguistic repertoire (Gumperz 1964; Busch 2012), consisting of language competence; the individual's biography including the history of language learning and use; metalinguistic knowledge; speech styles, registers and the contexts of use, and the ability to understand the social meaning of those; as well as aspirations, ideologies and attitudes about languages. As speakers experience changes in their lives, i.e. moving between speech communities, entering school or having children, their repertoire is often changing as well. Changes in the linguistic repertoire can be perceived as positive and liberating, opening new communicative worlds, but they can also be frightening as in the case of forced language shifts.

Busch (2012) presents an example of a teacher living in the borderlands of Germany and France, as the child of a French-German couple, moving repeatedly between the countries. He describes his two main languages as they put him in an exposed position in either language community, he sees himself "as belonging to two language worlds but never entirely. Something always remains foreign and, as such, suspect" (Busch 2012: 514). He expresses positive feelings towards both his languages, emotions shared by many multilingual speakers, but also ambivalent feelings about the social evaluations of one's languages. As a child, his experiences were different from the one's he is having as an adult, and his generational position influences the subject positions that he can inhabit as a multilingual speaker.

Speakers are perceived as members of different generations as they participate in research projects, but in biographical research the aim is to understand how speakers become different generations and how they make sense of their experiences across the lifespan. Dilthey ([1905–1910] 1990: 307) has called for recognising the importance of the interdependency or "Wirkungszusammenhang" in autobiographies and the retrospective evaluation of experiences as they are linked to different roles, ages and social positions. In a speaker-centred approach, the speaking subject is conceptualized as one that uses a wide range of communicative resources and draws on different meaning making systems, not necessarily attributable to one or the other "language". However, as Blackledge and Creese (2008: 535) note, it is necessary to highlight the very real effects of languages as social constructs:

> If languages are invented, and languages and identities are socially constructed, we nevertheless need to account for the fact that at least some language users, at least some of the time, hold passionate beliefs about the importance and significance of a particular language to their sense of 'identity'.

Researchers in speaker-centred approaches tend to explicitly take their positioning into account and the role of the researcher, who is also situated along the generational continuum, is thought to have an influence on the topics and the interactions more broadly. Being a researcher comes with being a daughter, a father or an elder (Giampapa 2011), it is linked to being a professional and sometimes a professional stranger (Agar 1980), and the cultural and societal expectations of research, age, gender, religion, ethnicity, positioning, language(s) and professional status cannot be ignored. Relations to the research participants are influenced by power relations, questions of authority and previous experiences with research (Singer 2018; Maquire 2005). As knowledge and use of languages come with social hierarchies, these will also play a role in the choice of medium of data collection or in the multilingual set-up of encounters. Securing understanding and integrating strategies to ensure that participants and researchers are on the same page seems necessary in the research process.

As most researchers enter the field as adults, working with children becomes another important point in intergenerational research: Clark (2011) calls for methods that take children's voices into account, while Mayall (2002) highlights the need for a sociology of childhood that thinks of children's worlds using their relevant categories. Researchers in different fields have called for and developed methods to collect data with children, using creative methods involving speech and drawing (Prasad 2018), photographs and video formats, storytelling techniques and identity texts (Cummins and Early 2011).

5 Conclusions

Intergenerational challenges need to be addressed not so much as a research field on its own but rather as a necessity in research that involves speakers. I argue that we need to be more explicit about the generational positions of research participants, but also mention their *sense of generations*, that is, their understanding of social relationships linked to biological and social generations. An explicit focus on intergenerational relations, as in a workshop at the 20th International Congress for Linguists in Cape Town in 2018,[2] can be a good starting point to review one's own categories and re-examine assumptions about roles and competences linked to members of generations. Being able to describe social relations and using terminology that has meaning in a given context can be steps to enhanced awareness of generational challenges. It will be important to take speakers' own categories (i.e. kinship terms, heritage and alignment with languages) into account, but at the same time be open for non-traditional family structures and relationships between generations.

In multilingualism research and with a focus on home languages, generational transmission needs to be seen as the meeting of repertoires – not one language that is passed on but instead speakers meeting with and in several of their linguistic resources. King (2016) makes a passionate case for looking both at learners of minoritised or endangered languages, and mostly at those who are eager to learn despite being outside of institutional contexts, and at migrant learners who are on the verge of passing the age of schooling. From the point of view of intergenerational challenges, I find these learners to be of particular interest: While they might have been considered learners "on the margins", they are central actors in a generational line. They are parents, aunts and uncles, teachers and educators – or in the case of just-out-of-school youths, they will be soon. Their interactions are likely to reach those younger as well as those older than them and thus their language use is likely to influence other speakers. Research on their experiences, their circumstances and motivations for learning, and how they are linked to expectations for other generations, is needed.

Attention to the generational set-up of learning opportunities can help to work along cultural or social expectations that might facilitate the integration of emergent speakers, adult learners or speakers who perceive themselves as peripheral members of a speech community. Breeching expectations can on the other hand open non-traditional learning opportunities, i.e. for minoritised languages in urban centres.

References

Agar, Michael H. 1980. *The professional stranger. An informal introduction to ethnography.* New York: Academic Press.

Akhter, Parven. 2016. A young child's intergenerational practices through the use of visual screen-based multimodal communication to acquire Qur'anic literacy. *Language and Education* 30(6). 500–518.

Basham, Charlotte & Ann K. Fathman. 2008. The latent speaker: Attaining adult fluency in an endangered language. *International Journal of Bilingual Education and Bilingualism* 11(5). 577–597.

---

[2] Several of the authors mentioned in this chapter presented their research at this workshop.

Bigelow, Martha H. 2010. *Mogadishu on the Mississippi: Language, racialized identity, and education in a new land*. Oxford: Wiley-Blackwell.
Blackledge, Adrian & Angela Creese. 2008. Contesting "language" as "heritage": Negotiation of identities in late modernity. *Applied Linguistics* 29(4). 533–554.
Borland, Helen. 2006. Intergenerational language transmission in an established Australian migrant community: What makes the difference? *International Journal of the Sociology of Language* 180. 23–41.
Busch, Brigitta. 2012. The linguistic repertoire revisited. *Applied Linguistics* 33(5). 503–523.
Busch, Brigitta. 2017. Biographical approaches to research in multilingual settings Exploring linguistic repertoires. In Marilyn Martin-Jones & Deirdre Martin (eds.), *Researching Multilingualism*, 46–59. London: Routledge.
Chrisp, Steven. 2005. Māori intergenerational language transmission. *International Journal of the Sociology of Language* 172. 149–181.
Clark, Cindy D. 2011. *In a younger voice. Doing child-centered qualitative research*. New York: Oxford University Press.
Coetzee, Frieda. 2018. Hy leer dit nie hier nie ('He doesn't learn it here'): Talking about children's swearing in extended families in multilingual South Africa. *International Journal of Multilingualism* 15(3). 291–305.
Cummins, Jim & Margaret Early. 2011. *Identity texts: The collaborative creation of power in multilingual schools*. London: Trentham.
Curdt-Christiansen, Xiao Lan. 2009. Invisible and visible language planning: Ideological factors in the family language policy of Chinese immigrant families in Quebec. *Language Policy* 8. 351–375.
Cutas, Daniela & Sarah Chan. 2012. Introduction: Perspectives on private and family life. In Daniela Cutas & Sarah Chan (eds.), *Families – Beyond the nuclear ideal*, 1–12. London: Bloomsbury Academic.
De Houwer, Annick. 2017. Minority language parenting in Europe and children's well-being. In Natasha J. Cabrera & Birgit Leyendecker (eds.), *Handbook on positive development of minority children and youth*, 231–246. Cham: Springer.
De Houwer, Annick. this vol. Harmonious Bilingualism: Well-being for families in bilingual settings.
De Korne, Haley. 2017. The multilingual realities of language reclamation: Working with language contact, diversity, and change in endangered language education. In Wesley Y. Leonard & Haley De Korne (eds.), *Language Documentation and Description*, 111–135. London: EL Publishing.
Dilthey, Wilhelm. [1875] 1924. Über das Studium der Geschichte der Wissenschaften vom Menschen, der Gesellschaft und dem Staat. In Wilhelm Dilthey, *Gesammelte Schriften, Band* 5, 36–41. Leipzig & Berlin: Teubner.
Dilthey, Wilhelm. [1905–1910] 1990. *Der Aufbau der geschichtlichen Welt in den Geisteswissenschaften*. Frankfurt/Main: Suhrkamp.
Edwards, Viv & Lynda Pritchard Newcombe. 2006. Back to basics: Marketing the benefits of bilingualism to parents. In Ofelia García, Tove Skutnabb-Kangas & María E. Torres-Guzmán (eds.), *Imagining multilingual schools. Language in education and glocalization*, 137–149. Bristol: Multilingual Matters.
Eisenchlas, Susana A. & Andrea C. Schalley. this vol. Making sense of the notion of "home language" and related concepts.
Fishman, Joshua A. 1991. *Reversing language shift*. Clevedon: Multilingual Matters.
Fogle, Lyn Wright. 2012. *Second language socialization and learner agency: Adoptive family talk*. Bristol: Multilingual Matters.

Fogle, Lyn Wright & Kendall King. 2017. Bi- and multilingual family language socialization. In Patricia A. Duff & Stephen May (eds.), *Language socialization. Encyclopedia of language and education*, 79–95. Cham: Springer.

Gafaranga, Joseph. 2010. Medium request: Talking language shift into being. *Language in Society* 39. 118–135.

Garrett, Peter B. 2017. Researching language socialization. In Kendall A. King, Yi-Ju Lai & Stephen May (eds.), *Research methods in language and education. Encyclopaedia of language and education*. Boston: Springer.

Giampapa, Frances. 2011. The politics of "being and becoming" a researcher: Identity, power, and negotiating the field. *Journal of Language, Identity & Education* 10(3). 132–144.

Giles, Howard, Gholam H. Khajavy & Charles W. Choi. 2012. Intergenerational communication satisfaction and age boundaries: Comparative Middle Eastern data. *Journal of Cross-Cultural Gerontology* 27. 357–371.

Giles, Howard, Sinfree Makoni & René M. Dailey. 2005. Intergenerational communication beliefs across the lifespan: Comparative data from West and South Africa. *Journal of Cross-Cultural Gerontology* 20. 191–211.

Giles, Howard, Kimberley Noels, Angie Williams, Hiroshi Ota, Tae-Seop Lim, Sik Ng, Ellen Ryan & Lilnabeth Somera. 2003. Intergenerational communication across cultures: Young people's perceptions of conversations with family elders, non-family elders, and same-age peers. *Journal of Cross-Cultural Gerontology* 18. 1–30.

Gregory, Eve, Mahera Ruby & Charmian Kenner. 2010. Modelling and close observation: Ways of teaching and learning between third-generation Bangladeshi British children and their grandparents in London. *Early Years* 30(2). 161–173.

Gumperz, John J. 1964. Linguistic and social interaction in two communities. *American Anthropologist* 66(6). 137–153.

Hinton, Leanne. 2011. Language revitalization and language pedagogy: New teaching and learning strategies. *Language and Education* 25(4). 307–318.

Hinton, Leanne (ed.). 2013. *Bringing our languages home: Language revitalization for families*. Berkeley, CA: Heyday.

Hornberger, Nancy H. 2014. On not taking language inequality for granted: Hymesian traces in ethnographic monitoring of South Africa's multilingual language policy. *Multilingua* 33(5–6). 623–645.

Jenni, Barbara, Adar Anisman, Onowa McIvor & Peter Jacobs. 2017. An exploration of the effects of mentor-apprentice programs on mentors' and apprentices' wellbeing. *International Journal of Indigenous Health* 12(2). 25–42.

Juvonen, Päivi, Susana A. Eisenchlas, Tim Roberts & Andrea C. Schalley. this vol. Researching social and affective factors in home language maintenance: A methodology overview.

Kenner, Charmian, Mahera Ruby, John Jessel, Eve Gregory & Tahera Arju. 2008. Intergenerational learning events around the computer: A site for linguistic and cultural exchange. *Language and Education* 22(4). 298–319.

King, Kendall A. 2016. Who and what is the field of Applied Linguistics overlooking?: Why this matters and how Educational Linguistics can help. *Working papers in Educational Linguistics* 31(2). 1–18. https://repository.upenn.edu/wpel/vol31/iss2/1 (accessed 30 October 2018).

King, Kendall A. & Lyn Fogle. 2006. Bilingual parenting as good parenting: Parents' perspectives on family language policy for additive bilingualism. *International Journal of Bilingual Education and Bilingualism* 9(6). 695–712.

Kramsch, Claire. 2009. *The multilingual subject*. Oxford: Oxford University Press.

Krauss, Michael. 1998. The condition of native North American languages: The need for realistic assessment and action. *International Journal of the Sociology of Language* 132. 9–21.

Lane, Pia. 2010. "We did what we thought was best for our children": A nexus analysis of language shift in a Kven community. *International Journal of the Sociology of Language* 202. 63–78.

Lanza, Elizabeth. 2004. *Language mixing in infant bilingualism. A sociolinguistic approach*. Oxford: Oxford University Press.

Lanza, Elizabeth & Rafael Lomeu Gomes. this vol. Family language policy: Foundations, theoretical perspectives and critical approaches.

Lanza, Elizabeth & Kristin Vold Lexander. in press. Family language practices in multilingual transcultural families. In Simona Montanari & Suzanne Quay (eds.), *Multidisciplinary perspectives on multilingualism*. Berlin: Mouton de Gruyter.

Léglise, Isabelle. 2019. Documenter les parcours de familles transnationales: généalogies, biographies langagières et pratiques langagières familiales. In Shahzaman Haque & Françoise Le Lièvre (eds), *Politique linguistique familiale: Enjeux dynamiques de la transmission linguistique dans un contexte migratoire, LINCOM*, 159–182. Paris: Éditions des Archives Contemporaines.

Lewis, Paul M. & Gary F. Simons. 2010. Assessing endangerment: Expanding Fishman's GIDS. *Revue Roumaine de Linguistique* 55(2). 103–120.

Little, Sabine. this vol. Social media and the use of technology in home language maintenance.

Lourie, Megan. 2011. "Canaries in the coal mine": The reframing of biculturalism and non-Māori participation in Māori language learning. *International Studies in Sociology of Education* 21(3). 217–230.

Maguire, Mary H. 2005. What if you talked to me? I could be interesting! Ethical research considerations in engaging with bilingual / multilingual child participants in human inquiry. *Forum Qualitative Sozialforschung* 6 (1).Art. 4. DOI: 10.17169/fqs-6.1.530.

Mannheim, Karl. [1923/1952] 1998. *Essays on the sociology of knowledge*. London: Taylor & Francis.

Mary, Latisha & Andrea Young. this vol. Teachers' beliefs and attitudes towards home language maintenance and their effects.

Mayall, Berry. 2002. *Towards a sociology of childhood. Thinking from children's lives*. Buckingham: Open University Press.

Mayer, Elisabeth, Liliana Sánchez, José Camacho & Carolina Rodríguez Alzza. this vol. The drivers of home language maintenance and development in indigenous communities.

Meek, Barbra A. 2007. Respecting the language of elders: Ideological shift and linguistic discontinuity in a Northern Athapascan community. *Journal of Linguistic Anthropology* 17(1). 23–43.

Nordstrom, Janica. this vol. Community language schools.

Norton, Bonny. 2013. *Identity and language learning. Extending the conversation*. Bristol: Multilingual Matters.

Nussbaum, Jon F. & Justine Coupland. 2004. *Handbook of communication and aging research*. Mahwah, NJ: Lawrence Erlbaum.

O'Shannessy, Carmel. 2012. The role of codeswitched input to children in the origin of a new mixed language. *Linguistics* 50(2). 305–340.

O'Shannessy, Carmel. 2015. Multilingual children increase language differentiation by indexing communities of practice. *First Language* 35(4–5). 305–326.

Obojska, Maria A. 2017. "Are you so ashamed to come from Poland and to speak your mother tongue?" – Metalinguistic talk, identities and language ideologies in teenagers' interactions on ASKfm. *Multilingual Margins* 4(1). 27–39.

Obojska, Maria A. 2018. Between duty and neglect: Language ideologies and stancetaking among Polish adolescents in Norway. *Lingua* 208. 82–97.

Palviainen, Åsa. this vol. Future prospects and visions for family language policy research.

Paulsrud, BethAnne. this vol. The mainstream classroom and home language maintenance.

Piller, Ingrid & Livia Gerber. 2018. Family language policy between the bilingual advantage and the monolingual mindset. *International Journal of Bilingual Education and Bilingualism*. 1–14. Online First. DOI 10.1080/13670050.2018.1503227

Prasad, Gail Lori. 2018. "But do monolingual people really exist?" Analysing elementary students' contrasting representations of plurilingualism through sequential reflexive drawing. *Language and Intercultural Communication* 18(3). 315–334.

Purkarthofer, Judith. 2016. *Sprachort Schule. Zur Konstruktion von mehrsprachigen sozialen Räumen und Praktiken in einer zweisprachigen Volksschule*. Klagenfurt: Drava.

Purkarthofer, Judith. 2019a. Austria's curriculum for heritage language education across languages: A case study in balancing speakers' needs on the local, national and international level. In Corinne A. Seals & Vincent Ieni Olsen-Reeder (eds.), *Embracing multilingualism across educational contexts*, 152–181. Wellington: Victoria University Press.

Purkarthofer, Judith. 2019b. Building expectations: Imagining family languages policy and heteroglossic social spaces. *International Journal of Bilingualism* 23(3). 724–739.

Purkarthofer, Judith & Guri B. Steien. 2019. "Comme si on connaît pas une autre langue que le swahili": Multilingual parents in Norway on change and continuity in their family language policies. *International Journal of the Sociology of Language* 155. 109–131.

Purkarthofer, Judith & Haley De Korne. 2019. Learning language regimes: Children's representations of minority language education. *Journal of Sociolinguistics*. Online First. DOI 10.1111/josl.12346

Putjata, Galina. 2017. "New Language Education Policy" – Policy making and enhancement of migrant-related multilingualism in student's own perception. A case study with Russian speaking Israelis. *Zeitschrift für Erziehungswissenschaft* 20. 259–278.

Reath Warren, Anne. 2017. *Developing multilingual literacies in Sweden and Australia: Opportunities and challenges in mother tongue instruction and multilingual study guidance in Sweden and community language education in Australia*. Stockholm: University of Stockholm PhD thesis. http://su.diva-portal.org/smash/get/diva2:1116085/FULLTEXT01.pdf (accessed 8 August 2019).

Rienzner, Martina. 2010. „Platz machen" und Schule (mit)gestalten. Muttersprachlicher Unterricht in Somali. In Judith Purkarthofer & Brigitta Busch (eds.), *Schulsprachen – Sprachen in und um und durch die Schule* (Schulheft 151), 28–42. Innsbruck: Studienverlag.

Ruby, Mahera. 2012. The role of a grandmother in maintaining Bangla with her granddaughter in East London. *Journal of Multilingual and Multicultural Development* 33(1). 67–83.

Said, Fatma & Zhu Hua. 2019. "No, no Maama! Say 'Shaatir ya Ouledee Shaatir'!" Children's agency in language use and socialisation. *International Journal of Bilingualism* 23(3). 771–785.

Schmidt, Annette. 1990. *The loss of Australia's Aboriginal language heritage*. Canberra: Aboriginal Studies Press.

Schwartz, Mila. this vol. Strategies and practices of home language maintenance.

Sevinç, Yeşim. this vol. Anxiety as a negative emotion in home language maintenance and development.

Sevinç, Yeşim & Ad Backus. 2017. Anxiety, language use and linguistic competence in an immigrant context: A vicious circle? *International Journal of Bilingual Education and Bilingualism* 22(6). 706–724.

Singer, Ruth. 2018. The wrong t-shirt: Configurations of language and identity at Warruwi Community. *Australian Journal of Anthropology* 29(1). 70–88.

Smith-Christmas, Cassie. 2018. "One 'Cas,' Two 'Cas'": Exploring the affective dimensions of family language policy. *Multilingua: Journal of Cross-Cultural and Interlanguage Communication* 37(2). 131–152.

Smith-Christmas, Cassie. this vol. Child agency and home language maintenance.

Smith-Christmas, Cassie, Noel P. Ó Murchadha, Michael Hornsby & Máiréad Moriarty (eds.). 2018. *New speakers of minority languages. Linguistic ideologies and practices*. London: Palgrave Macmillan.

Soehl, Thomas. 2016. But do they speak it? The intergenerational transmission of home-country language in migrant families in France. *Journal of Ethnic and Migration Studies* 42(9). 1513–1535.

Suslak, Daniel F. 2009. The sociolinguistic problem of generations. *Language & Communication* 29(3). 199–209.

Szecsi, Tunde & Janka Szilagyi. 2012. Immigrant Hungarian families' perceptions of new media technologies in the transmission of heritage language and culture. *Language, Culture and Curriculum* 25(3). 265–281.

Tannen, Deborah. 2006. Intertextuality in interaction: Reframing family arguments in public and private. *Text & Talk* 26(4/5). 597–617.

Todal, Jon. 2006. Small languages and small language communities: The Southern Saami language in Svahken Sijte. *International Journal of the Sociology of Language* 180. 147–158.

Tranter, Siobhan, Fiona Irvine, Gwerfyl Roberts, Llinos Spencer & Peter Jones. 2010. The role of midwives and health visitors in promoting intergenerational language maintenance in the bilingual setting: Perceptions of parents and health professionals. *Journal of Clinical Nursing* 20. 204–213.

UNESCO. 2009. *UNESCO atlas of the world's languages in danger*. http://www.unesco.org/languages-atlas/ and http://www.unesco.org/new/en/culture/themes/endangered-languages/atlas-of-languages-in-danger/ (accessed 8 August 2019).

Valdés, Guadalupe. 2017. From language maintenance and intergenerational transmission to language *survivance*: Will "heritage language" education help or hinder? *International Journal of the Sociology of Language* 243. 67–95.

Van Mensel, Luk. 2018. "Quiere koffie?" The multilingual familylect of transcultural families. *International Journal of Multilingualism* 15(3). 233–248.

Van Mensel, Luk & Julie Deconinck. 2017. Language learning motivation and projected desire: An interview study with parents of young language learners. *International Journal of Bilingual Education and Bilingualism* 22(5). 535–550.

Yağmur, Kutlay. this vol. Models of formal education and minority language teaching across countries.

Zhu, Hua & Wei Li. 2016. Transnational experience, aspiration and family language policy. *Journal of Multilingual and Multicultural Development* 37(7). 655–666.

Topic area 2.2: **Family language policy**

Elizabeth Lanza and Rafael Lomeu Gomes

8 Family language policy: Foundations, theoretical perspectives and critical approaches

1 Introduction

The family has come into sharp focus in recent sociolinguistic inquiry, spearheaded by the burgeoning field of "Family Language Policy". While the name was originally coined by Luykx (2003) in her study of family language policy and gender socialization in bilingual Aymara households, it was through the now classic article by King, Fogle, and Logan-Terry (2008) that it gained currency in the establishment of a key field of scholarship. This field did not evolve in a vacuum, yet its clear profile in scientific inquiry is witnessed by the myriad of publications bearing the title of *family language policy*. The importance of investigating family language policies is clearly articulated in King, Fogle, and Logan-Terry (2008: 907): "they shape children's developmental trajectories, connect in significant ways with children's formal school success, and collectively determine the maintenance and future status of minority languages". Today the study of family language policy (hereafter FLP) has indeed become a catalyst in promoting the sociolinguistic inquiry of language practices and policies in multilingual transnational families, although not all such studies actually refer to themselves as studies of FLP (Lanza and Lexander 2019). Emanating from the field of language policy, FLP was originally narrowly defined as "explicit and overt planning in relation to language use within the home among family members" (King, Fogle, and Logan-Terry 2008: 907), with a firm anchoring onto the decision-making processes families undertake in the home and how these may relate to child language learning outcomes. Inspired by Spolsky's (2009) tripartite model of language policy, attention has been given to language ideologies, language practices and language management in the family with Spolsky (2012) himself referring to the family as "the critical domain" of language policy.

While firmly rooted in language policy research in its incipient days, FLP research initially defined its purview in relation to work on child language acquisition, pointing out the need to assess the impact of language ideologies on language use to the child, such as the one-person–one-language policy, and how this impacted the child's language development. Currently, however, studies of FLP encompass not only investigations of actual policies in the home but also language practices, in other words, not only "explicit and overt planning" but also implicit

---

Note: This work was supported by the Research Council of Norway through its Centres of Excellence funding scheme, project number 223265.

https://doi.org/10.1515/9781501510175-008

and covert language practices, including literacy (Curdt-Christiansen 2013). This is an approach that is along the lines of contemporary language policy research (cf. Hult and Johnson 2015; Tollefson and Pérez-Milans 2018) through which language practices may be seen as de facto grassroots language policy (King and Lanza 2019a). As King and Fogle (2013: 172) state, "FLP addresses child language learning and use as functions of parental ideologies, decision-making and strategies concerning languages and literacies, as well as the broader social and cultural context of family life." Accordingly, underlying language ideologies have been investigated through the study of family language practices in multilingual transcultural families (see Curdt-Christiansen and Huang this vol.) and in educational environments (see Mary and Young this vol.). Whereas earlier FLP studies attempted to "draw clear causal links across ideologies, practices, and outcomes" (King 2016: 731), more recent work focuses on meaning-making, experiences, agency, and identity constructions in transnational families (Zhu and Li 2016; King and Lanza 2019a; Li and Zhu 2019; Purkarthofer and Steien 2019; Smith-Christmas 2019). Hence in the course of about ten years, we have witnessed the establishment, transformation and shift in focus of a field of inquiry that can provide an important key to understanding the role language plays for family members, not only in regards to children's language development by the time they enter into the educational system of a society, but also in the construction of a family's identity, including both children and adults.

There are reviews of research on FLP that highlight various factors contributing to, and impacting, family language policy (see for example, Caldas 2012; Curdt-Christiansen 2018; Lanza and Lexander 2019; Curdt-Christiansen and Jing Huang this vol.). The goal of this chapter is rather to provide an overview of the development of the field of "family language policy" and its theoretical perspectives, tracing its epistemological roots from the early 20th century and onward to the flourishing field of inquiry in the new millennium. This involves crossing disciplinary borders to encompass research on child language acquisition, bilingual upbringing, language socialization, and language maintenance and shift – all of which have contributed to FLP as we know it today. We also aim to present a critical approach to the field with an eye to its future.

In the following, we first give an overview of the roots of the study of FLP in child bilingual acquisition research (section 2), covering both psycholinguistic and sociolinguistic scholarship. Subsequently, we document the growth of the field from 2008 to the present, presenting an overview of publications, indicating the diversity of populations and languages studied (section 3), and finally before concluding (section 5), we provide an overview of relevant theoretical perspectives and critical approaches to the field as it has developed thus far (section 4), in the hope of paving the path for future innovative and socially grounded approaches to the study of multilingual transnational families.

2 Foundations: The family in research on home language development

Home language maintenance and development pinpoints the family as the primary social and affective unit for the language-learning child. However, in any study of family language policies and practices, an important question to address is actually how one may define *family*. In an article on family studies published 20 years ago, Holstein and Gubrium (1999: 3) open by stating "The question 'What is family?' is still controversial". Twenty years later, this question is still controversial or at least debatable in today's highly connected society. Holstein and Gubrium (1999: 5) proposed a social constructionist approach and argued for the importance of analyzing the family as "interpretive practice", positing that "[t]his view of interpretive practice is quite different from the conventional vision of family as a group or object to be described and explained". This is in line with shifts that have taken place in sociological understandings of family from traditional approaches that see "the family as a *social institution* governed by rigid moral conventions to an idea of family and wider personal life as diverse sets of *practices*" (Chambers 2012: 33). Correspondingly, while the home may be the locus of the family and the hub for language maintenance and development, the complexity of the notion of family is accentuated by the different types of family with some as transcultural families resulting from immigration and transnational movement, while others are from intercultural marriages and bonds; some are recently established, and others have existed for generations. Globalization only serves to intensify the encounters of different traditions, values and languages of the various members of the family (Lanza and Li 2016). We return to the complexity of families in sections 3 and 4 below (see also Palviainen this vol.), and now turn to the development of the field of FLP.

In a commentary to a special issue on multilingual transcultural families (Lanza and Li 2016), King (2016) points out the historical context of FLP research anchoring it within a long line of research traditions, by sketching various phases in its development. These may be summarized as follows:
1. Classic diary studies by linguist parents
2. Bilingual language acquisition studies focused on central psycholinguistic questions
3. A turn to a more sociolinguistic approach: the establishment of FLP as a field of inquiry
4. A turn to include a more diverse range of family types, languages, and contexts
5. A focus on globally dispersed, transnational, multilingual populations, and ever-greater heterogeneity and adaptability in research methods.

While phase 3 marks the discernible onset of what is now called FLP (King, Fogle, and Logan-Terry 2008), phases 4 and 5 are in progress, addressing researchers' increasing awareness of, and concern for, the shortcomings of earlier studies of FLP. In this section, we examine in particular the roots of FLP, that is, phases 1 and 2, as well as the impact of other closely related established fields, namely those of language socialization and language maintenance and shift, in the turn to sociolinguistic approaches to the family in phase 3. FLP initially took issue with studies of child bilingual acquisition and second language learning, posing questions regarding the impact of language policy on language learning. FLP differs, however, from more psycholinguistically oriented investigations of childhood bilingualism: "rather than targeting the child, the emphasis of FLP is on the balance between and use of languages within the family unit" (King and Fogle 2013: 172).

In the first phase of FLP, the role of the family and social life is highlighted. Classic diary studies on bilingual children have provided important insights into the study of bilingual first language acquisition (BFLA) and early second language learning in a home context. Indeed, the very first documented study of FLP in a bilingual family is Ronjat's (1913) carefully detailed account of his son Louis' bilingual acquisition of French and German through age 4;10, with a French-speaking father and German-speaking mother, living in France. Ronjat was advised by linguist Maurice Grammont to employ what is referred to as the One person–One language ("une personne, une langue") method or policy, the impact of which is still studied today (for example, Döpke 1992; Palviainen and Boyd 2013; Venables, Eisenchlas, and Schalley 2014). Louis' father spoke only French to him in the home while his mother kept to German, and as predicted by Grammont, the child developed both languages and kept them separated. Another relevant diary study is Leopold's (1939–1949) four volumes focusing on his daughter Hildegarde's simultaneous acquisition of English and German in the US, also using the One person–One language policy. In Leopold's work there is more emphasis on meticulous descriptions of the child's linguistic forms; however, language use in the family receives due attention. His claim that the young child exposed to two languages from birth does not learn bilingually but rather welds the dual presentation into one unified system would come to have a strong impact on child language scholars in the years to come (cf. Lanza [1997] 2004: 18–23).

In the second phase of FLP, the family took on a backstage role in the study of bilingual and multilingual acquisition in developmental psycholinguistics, which subsequently dominated research on bilingual and multilingual acquisition in children. During this second phase, a focus was on the language-internal and individual cognitive mechanisms at play in the acquisition process (cf. Volterra and Taeschner 1978), and what was called "input" was *not* seen as relevant for studying the bilingual child's purported transition to language differentiation from a stage in which the two languages were welded, a claim forwarded by Leopold (1939–1949). The interaction between the two languages, or language mixing, was at the heart of the one system vs. two system hypothesis of bilingual acquisition. Lanza (1992, [1997] 2004) took a sociolinguistic and discourse analytic approach in order to address this classic psycholinguistic question concerning early language differentiation, arguing for the importance of studying parent–child interaction in evaluating the child's language mixing and positing that the question of *one system or two* was not the right question to ask in regards to language mixing. The theoretical perspective employed was that of language socialization (cf. Duranti, Ochs, and Schieffelin 2011), which is at the very foundation of FLP work today. Children are socialized to use language and socialization occurs through the use of language. That is, language learning and socialization go hand in hand, and this occurs within interactional contexts, as socialization is an interactive process, with the child as an active agent (Schieffelin and Ochs 1986).

While developmental psycholinguistics moved away from the one system vs. two system hypothesis with studies validating the separate development of two languages morphologically and syntactically (Genesee 1989; Meisel 1989; De Houwer 1990), an interest in the role of input in BFLA gradually evolved. It took time, however, before the claim was accepted that quantity or quality of linguistic input might be relevant to the course of language acquisition (Snow 2014: 117). Today issues concerning input and experience in bilingual acquisition have received increasing attention with a focus on variation in input and the effect on language acquisition (Grüter and Paradis 2014; Unsworth 2013). The family per se has not been in focus, rather the quantity of input in each language and the quality of that input defined and measured as various factors such as the variety of speakers providing language input, and the types of activities for which the language is used. Nonetheless the importance of the family in bilingual development was clearly articulated in Carroll (2017) in her appeal to developmental psycholinguists to consider language socialization; she states that "the realities of bilingual family life are complex and patterns of language use in the home, including patterns of parental language use (studied via recordings), merit detailed examination" (Carroll 2017: 8). Although developmental psycholinguistics gave impetus to the onset of FLP research, it appears that there is mutual impact across both fields. As noted by Quay and Montanari (2016: 37), "The trend to study BFLA as part of FLP is expected to increase awareness that the varied learning environments in which bilingual children are raised in the home in the early years and outside the home in child care facilities and educational institutions strongly affect their language and academic learning".

Hence two different approaches contribute to the study of the bilingual/multilingual child in the family, as noted in the second phase of FLP: developmental psycholinguistics and sociolinguistics. Both have distinct theoretical and methodological origins and distinct analytical foci. And within sociolinguistics, we see the impact of research in both language socialization, and language maintenance and shift, as we turn to phase 3. Each of these approaches has distinct origins and foci. As Ochs and Schieffelin (2011: 1) state, "language socialization research integrates discourse and ethnographic methods to capture the social structurings and cultural interpretations of semiotic forms, practices, and ideologies that inform novices' practical engagements with others". Thus anchored in anthropology, this research views cultural beliefs linked to child-rearing practices in the interactional process of language socialization (cf. Okita 2002). Studying this requires an analysis over time and hence ethnographic methods. The family is a "community of practice" (Wenger 1998), a social unit that has its norms for speaking, acting and believing and hence "provides a focus on praxis, the cornerstone for language socialization" (Lanza 2007: 47). The sociology of language and the seminal work of Joshua Fishman (1991) are the driving forces behind the study of language maintenance and shift in communities, including work on heritage languages (e.g. Döpke 1992; Higgins 2019) and encompassing a variety of research methods. Fishman himself pointed out that it is the micro-level of face-to-face interaction and social life within the intimate family that plays a decisive role for language maintenance and language shift.

Hence various research traditions have contributed to the field of FLP, as we know it today. It has, as noted above, its origins in language policy research yet has discernible influence in current studies from research traditions investigating both language socialization, and language maintenance and shift (see for example Caldas and Caron-Caldas 2000; Tannenbaum and Howie 2002). Moreover, the child's agency in socialization, language maintenance and shift, and language policy in the family has also received increasing attention in studies of multilingual families (Gafaranga 2010; Kheirkhah and Cekaite 2017; see Smith Christmas this vol.).

3 The establishment of family language policy (FLP) as a field of inquiry

FLP as a field of inquiry bearing this name dates back to King, Fogle, and Logan-Terry's (2008) seminal article, as noted above, and the ever-growing interest in family language policies and practices is demonstrated by an increasing number of publications, including books (for example, Fogle 2012; Schwartz and Verschik 2013; Smith-Christmas 2016; Macalister and Mirvahedi 2017) in addition to overview articles in handbooks, anthologies, and encyclopedias (Curdt-Christiansen 2018; King and Fogle 2016; Smith-Christmas 2017; Lanza and Lexander 2019). There has also been a rise in the number of special issues of journals that have focused on family language practices and policies (Curdt-Christiansen and Lanza 2018a; Higgins 2019; King and Lanza 2019a; Lanza and Curdt-Christiansen 2018; Lanza and Li 2016; Li 2012). The individual studies in these contributions illustrate on the whole the myriad of methods used in research to document family language policies and practices, encompassing both qualitative and quantitative methods: large scale language use surveys, online questionnaires, interviews, language portraits, focus group conversations, ethnography, diaries, and interactional analyses of video recordings.

To trace the development of the field, Figure 1 presents an overview of the growing number of publications self-identifying as studies of "family language policy". While there are still many studies that deal with what may be considered the scope of FLP and yet are not entitled "family language policy", in our overviews we focus exclusively on those studies purporting to be FLP. In order to get an overview of these publications, we utilized the search engine Oria,[1] which covers the well-stocked university and research libraries of Norway, yielding results such as books, articles, magazines, music, movies and online resources. Our focus was on books, special issues of journals, and journal articles. Our search criteria required the mention of *family language policy* in the title or abstract of the named work. We took 2008 as a point of departure given the publication of King, Fogle, and Logan-Terry (2008), and set May 2019, the time of writing of this chapter, as the end cutoff point. As we see in Figure 1, there has been an increase over time of publications with various degrees of intensity over the past decade.

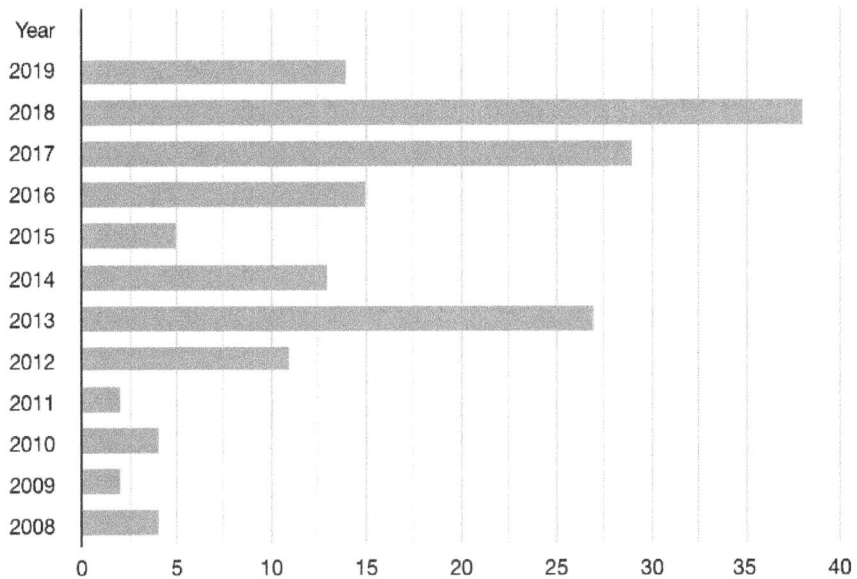

Figure 1: Number of FLP publications per year January 2008 – May 2019 (N = 164).[2]

---

[1] https://www.oria.no.
[2] We thank Research Assistant Mari J. Wikhaug Andersen for her indispensable assistance in finding and documenting all of the relevant FLP studies and for constructing the figures and table.

In tracing these publications over time, one may discern shifts in focus in FLP research, as noted by King and Lanza (2019b). Initial research questions aimed to discern the link between explicit planning and parental language use, and language learning outcomes in multilingual children, similar to the call to action in King, Fogle, and Logan-Terry (2008). More recent studies, however, focus on (1) language as a means through which multilingual adults and children define themselves and their families; (2) globally dispersed, transnational or multilingual populations beyond the traditional, two-parent family; and (3) research methods that attend to meaning-making in interaction as well as the broader context. In other words, referring back to King's (2016) phases in the development of FLP, we see that FLP studies have moved into phases 4 and 5. The field has increasingly seen the need to probe the impact of a diversity of family configurations, going beyond traditional understandings of the nuclear family to investigate, for example, adoptive families (Fogle 2012), families with co-located grandparents (Ruby 2012), and LGBT families (see Goldberg and Allen 2012) in various contexts. The complexity of parenting is clearly illustrated in Coetzee (2018) who emphasizes the processes of "family making" *across* households. She documented the socialization of two young boys born to adolescent mothers living in socio-economically marginalized neighborhoods in Cape Town in a multilingual South African community. In contrast to the home environment typically portrayed in FLP studies, these children's young parents do not live together, but rather with their respective extended families and the children.

An overview of the FLP literature published between 2008 and 2019 indicates a diversity of geographical locations reported as the context for the individual study (Figure 2) and the languages investigated (Table 1). While Figure 1 lists all of the studies self-designated as FLP studies, including overviews and theoretical discussions, Figure 2 is more narrowly focused on actual empirical studies. It should be noted that some publications were based on data collected in more than one country. In such cases, each country was counted separately. Smith-Christmas (2017: 18) justly pointed out that "there is a dearth of research situated within Africa or the Middle East (apart from Israel)", and this we see clearly in Figure 2. In fact, Figure 2 illustrates that most studies, although not all, address FLP in what may be referred to as "WEIRD" countries (Western, Educated, Industrialized, Rich, and Democratic; Henrich, Heine, and Norenzayan 2010). We may ask: What about low-status languages in economically marginalized societies, as well as indigenous and endangered language communities? And what about such languages in diaspora in "WEIRD" locations? There is clearly a need to examine FLP in light of sociopolitical parameters. This opens the discussion for critical approaches to the study of FLP, to which we return in 4.2 below.

The language most often represented in the empirical studies covered in Figure 2 is English ($N = 82$). A wide variety of languages, however, is addressed in the surveyed FLP studies from 2008 to 2019, as noted in Table 1. While this list does not provide any information on how the individual languages were paired in particular

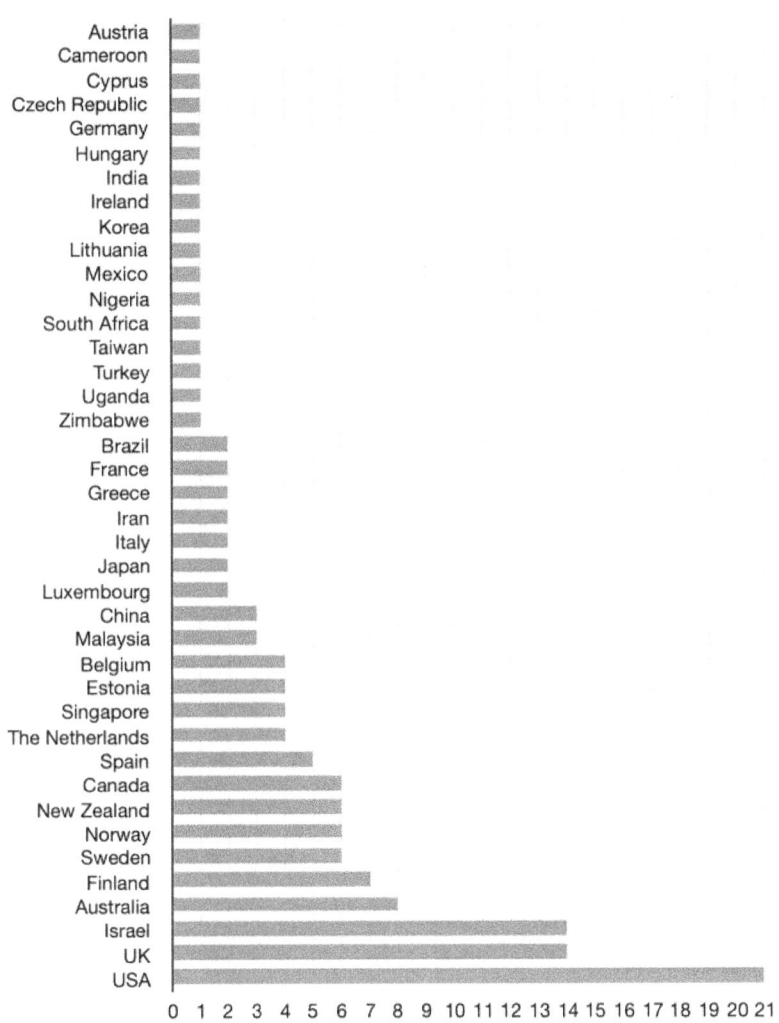

Figure 2: Overview of the number of FLP publications by country (*N* = 146).

geographical locations nor how they ranked in a sociolinguistic hierarchy in the specified geographical location, it nonetheless indicates a representation of speakers of languages usually associated with certain geographical locations from across the globe. Furthermore, it is interesting to note the terms that are used to account for the languages used at home. For example, Curdt-Christiansen (2016), in her study of language ideologies and practices of three multilingual families in Singapore, distinguishes between Hokkien and Mandarin as opposed to employing the cover term Chinese, used in turn in her 2009 study on the languages used by Chinese parents in Quebec, Canada (Curdt-Christiansen 2009).

Table 1: An overview of languages (as named by researchers in their own studies) investigated in FLP studies (2008–2019).

Afrikaans	Greek	Latvian	Russian
Albanian	Gujarati	Lithuanian	San Lucas Quiaviní Zapotec
American Sign Language	Hakka	Lokaa	Scottish Gaelic
Amharic	Haryanvi	Luganda	Sinhala
Arabic	Hebrew	Luxembourgish	Slovakian
Azerbaijani	Hindi	Malacca Portuguese Creole	Spanish
Bengali	Hokkien	Malay	Swahili
Cantonese	Hungarian	Malayalam	Swedish
Castilian	Ibibio	Mandarin	Tagalog
Catalan	Igbo	Maori	Tagalog/Visayan
Chinese	Indonesian	Marathi	Taiwanese
Czech	Inuktitut	Marwari	Tamil
Dutch	Irish	Ndebele	Telugu
Efik	Italian	New Zealand Sign Language	Teochew
English	Japanese	Nigerian Pidgin	Tetum
Estonian	Javanese	Norwegian	Thai
Farsi	Judeo-Spanish	'Ōlelo Hawai'i	Tibetan
Filipino	Kalanga	Persian	Turkish
Finnish	Khmer	Polish	Ukrainian
French	Korean	Portuguese	Urdu
Fulfulde	Kurdish	Punjabi	Veneto dialect
Galician	Kutchi	Putonghua	Vietnamese
German	Lao	Qur'anic Arabic	Zapotec

The use of *named* languages, as illustrated in Table 1, also brings into question the extent to which FLP engages with current sociolinguistic theorizing concerning the nature of language and language in practice, with an emphasis on the multilingual speaker's linguistic repertoire and engagement with translanguaging. We return to this in section 4.2 below.

4 Theoretical perspectives and critical approaches to the field

FLP research has, as noted above, followed developments in the field of language policy and planning through its shift in focus from explicit planning in relation to language use in the family to including bottom up language policies through practices. We may evaluate to what extent other current theoretical perspectives may contribute to enhancing the field.

There are two broad processes of change in the transformation of current sociolinguistic research on multilingualism, as pointed out by Martin-Jones and Martin (2017: 1), including (1) "broad epistemological shifts in the field of sociolinguistics to ethnographic and critical approaches"; and (2) "increasing focus on the study of the social, cultural and linguistic changes ushered in by globalization". These changes encompass the escalation of transnational population movements, the introduction of new communication technologies and their intensified use, and changes taking place in the political and economic landscape of different regions of the world. All of these factors will impact on families and their linguistic heritage, with current scholarship in the field demonstrating the turbulence of contemporary globalization. For example, Gallo and Hornberger's (2017) three-year ethnographic study traces the experiences of an eight-year-old girl following her father's deportation from the US, and poignantly illustrates how she engages with FLP within her routine daily interactions, shadowed by the threat of deportation.

More generally, recent language-related scholarship has attended to certain developments in the social sciences – for example, decoloniality (Castro-Gómez and Grosfoguel 2007; Mignolo and Walsh 2018), epistemologies of the South (Santos 2018), and southern theory (Connell 2014) – which challenge not only well-received concepts about language and language use, but also foundational epistemological and ontological assumptions behind the elaboration and reception of these concepts. Heugh and Stroud (2019), for example, propose a southern lens through which multilingualisms can be better understood. Pointing to the limitations of northern literature to account for multilingual practices of peoples from the Global South (including those in diaspora), Heugh and Stroud (2019: 7) suggest that "careful listening to the voices of people of the south and close observation of their agency and indeed ownership of linguistic citizenship, indicate that attempts to define and delimit the nature, variability and scholarship of multilingualisms found in some enthusiastic northern literature are misplaced". Another pivotal contribution to redressing the imbalance between northern and southern perspectives in sociolinguistics is Milani and Lazar's (2017) special issue on discourse, gender, and sexuality. An important consequence of such approaches is also the expressed engagement with southern literature. How this impacts FLP will be discussed below.

In the following, we delineate some theoretical perspectives and critical approaches that address the changes outlined above, and illustrate how these perspectives and approaches may play out in family multilingualism research.

4.1 The complexity of family across time and space

As pointed out in 1, the notion of family is indeed complex as is communication within families. Growing transnationalism is an earmark of contemporary society with families often making many moves across geographical spaces. FLP studies tend to capture a family's policies and practices at any given point in time, while these are indeed dynamic and change over time. Hence there is a need to trace transnational families' policies and practices across time, as emphasized by Hirsch and Lee (2018). Decisions about language policies in the home may be rooted in visions to return to the home country or to make a future move, for whatever reason. The family can be conceptualized as a dynamic temporal body and FLP should be analyzed accordingly.

Technological advances have greatly transformed communication with social media allowing transnational families to be multi-sited, or "stretched" (Porter et al. 2018), and yet interact intimately. Research on multilingual transnational families has shown increasing attention to the interface between language use and media use, that is, how families are constructed through multilingual language practices "in contexts of transmigration, social media and technology saturation, and hypermobility" (King and Lanza 2019b: 2). Nonetheless, this interest has so far not brought about a substantial body of research on how linguistic practices in interpersonal mediated communication affect family language policy and practices in transcultural families. A number of investigations from digital anthropology and media studies have zoomed in on the transnational family to study how the use of media shapes the migration experience and contributes to the management of interpersonal relationships. For example, in work on transnational family communication, Madianou and Miller (2012) introduced the term *polymedia* to highlight the impact of a variety of media technologies on particular interpersonal relationships (see Lanza and Lexander 2019, for an overview of work on digitally mediated language practices in multilingual families; see also Palviainen this vol.).

Digital communication opens up a wide vista for the study of family language practices and inherent family language policies across space. At the same time, such mediated communication forces us to rethink theoretical conceptions of the family as a space, particularly in regards to other digital and online media, for example, online news media's representations of families in periods of intensified migration. Lanza (2020) points to a salient debate in the Norwegian media prompted by an article published in a national newspaper concerning the poor school success of children with a particular immigrant background. This led to a prominent Labor party politician advocating in the media that parents speak Norwegian in the family and not their home language. The idea that politicians could regulate language use in the home is against all Norwegian traditions, as Lanza (2020) points out. Political pressure on family language policies ensued in the following months after the politician's profiled remarks. This incident calls into question the very notion of the family as a private space.

In classic sociolinguistic theorizing, the family has been considered a private *domain,* a cluster of settings and relationships affecting language choice (Fishman 1991). However, as scholars working on space have maintained, space is constantly negotiated between various social actors having different discursive power, material constraints, and spatial practices (Lefebvre 1991; Massey 2005). As such, the family can be conceptualized as a space along the private – public continuum of arenas of social life. The notion of the family as a "space" has been advanced in applied linguistics – as a space for language learning (Canagarajah 2013) and a potential *safe* space for the family's language learning and use, especially important for children (Purkarthofer 2019). Mediatized discourses on migrant families have thrust the family into the public eye, and hence to be constructed as a public space that can be commented upon, accepted and/or rejected. However, the family is also negotiated as a public space in online media by parents themselves, especially through online blogging (Lanza 2018a). The media of parenting websites, online discussion forums, and blogs are a growing setting for exchanging experiences and advice on raising children, with so-called 'Mommy blogging' as a specific type of social media usage that is a common and growing phenomenon. Blum-Ross and Livingstone (2017) take up intensive parenting in the digital age and note that "sharenting", that is, sharing parenting experiences, has become ever more digital, visible, and scrutinized. FLP has been conceptualized as an important element of good parenting, yet there is a scarcity of studies addressing the multitude of online blogs/vlogs and online parental forums that focus on the raising of children multilingually (but see Bello-Rodzen 2016; Piller and Gerber 2018). A close look at the many multilingual parenting online blogs reveals that several offer consultancy services in addition to advice to families aiming to raise their children bilingually/multilingually. Furthermore, an innovative study of the "language consultant" as "a new professional service for multilingual families" in expat situations (Daussa and Limacher-Riebold 2018) illustrates how FLP can and has become a commodity in late modernity, similar to online parenting blogs offering services for families. Hence the family can be negotiated as a public space open for scrutiny and amenable to change, as advised by public actors. In some cases, families are constructed as public space by the media while in other cases, families actually choose to go public.

4.2 Critical approaches to family multilingualism

While there is increasing attention to mobility and linguistic diversity resulting in widespread multilingualism in a European and North American context, there is a growing interest and need to draw attention to Southern experiences of multilingualism, mobility and diversity (cf. Léglise 2017; Skutnabb-Kangas and Heugh 2012). This was also documented in Figure 2 above. Discourses of multilingualism have been circulating in Africa, Asia and Latin America for the past century or more and have been appropriated into Northern debates in Europe and North America and then returned, reconfigured, to Southern contexts (cf. Comaroff and Comaroff 2012; Connell 2014). Dialogue between northern and southern conceptions and practices of multilingualism is paramount for advancing the field of multilingualism (see Kerfoot and Hyltenstam 2017; Guilherme and Souza 2019) and this includes the field of FLP.

Lomeu Gomes (2018) points out how many of the studies of FLP build ostensibly on Spolsky's seminal work on language policy and planning (for example, Spolsky 2004, 2009). While this model has elucidated many interesting aspects of FLP predominantly in the global North, it falls short in addressing important issues relevant for the global South. Following Santos (2018), the global South refers not only to the geographical South, whose populations have had the weight of domination from the global North, but also areas in the global North where certain groups of people struggle against oppression and injustice. Lomeu Gomes (2018: 51) proposes "a decolonial approach to family multilingualism" in order to advance the study of FLP theoretically by moving beyond theoretical frameworks that can be understood as "Western-centric, canonic epistemologies". Accordingly, such a critical approach to family multilingualism may provide a more robust theoretical framework to anchor social categorizations (such as class), and shed light on various migratory trajectories across the North and South. Such an approach may unpack the discursive reproduction of how gender, race/ethnicity and social class are hierarchized in intercultural encounters of parents from the global South living in the global North (Lomeu Gomes forthcoming). Moreover, it may reveal the affective dimensions of being othered as people attempt to make sense of themselves as belonging to and constructing multilingual families (cf. Tannenbaum and Yitzhaki 2016).

A decolonial approach to family multilingualism would also challenge canonic understandings of central concepts such as *family*, *language* and *policy*, which are often taken for granted in various studies. While the notion of family is gaining increased attention in FLP studies, the very conceptualization of language so central to current sociolinguistic thinking (for example, "metrolinguism", Pennycook and Otsuji 2015; "translanguaging", García and Li 2014; Li 2018; for a critical discussion about "home language", see Eisenchlas and Schalley this vol.) has not received sufficient attention, as noted above in regards to Table 1 in which named languages are listed as more or less autonomous systems that can be separated into discrete units and counted. Multilingual families seem, however, to orient to named languages while their activity is indeed translanguaging. There is a tension between the purported need to maintain names for languages, as in the fight for language rights of endangered languages, and the need to acknowledge the fluid borders of named languages. Nonetheless, FLP has the potential to contribute to the theory of language by engaging in the theoretical debates of named languages.

A critical approach to the study of *policy* and the extent to which certain practices can be conceived of as management (or policy) involves a tension in "the blurred distinction between the concepts of language practices and language management" (Curdt-Christiansen and Lanza 2018b: 126). As noted above, in researching contemporary multilingualism, Martin-Jones and Martin (2017) call for critical and ethnographic perspectives. Our understanding of the relationship between policy and practice can be enhanced through more ethnographic perspectives and interactional analyses revealing actual language practices in the family.

Many FLP studies are in fact already engaging in these critical discussions and debates that go beyond the impact of Spolsky's model, as Lomeu Gomes (2018) points out. Pertinent examples that draw on concepts and debates from critical research traditions include Revis' (2016) employment of a Bourdieusian framework to analyze child agency in FLP, and Nandi's (2018) use of the Foucauldian concept of governmentality to examine the language practices of parents. While drawing on the works of Bourdieu and Foucault yields a necessary development in FLP, these dialogues remain within the Eurocentric canon of critical research (see Mignolo and Walsh 2018; Santos 2018). In order to capture the social reality of contemporary multilingualism, the study of multilingual families needs to draw on Southern perspectives and realities of multilingualism and not only those of the global North.

5 Conclusion

In this chapter, we initially presented an overview of the foundations and development of the field of family language policy, drawing on King's (2016) phases of its historical context. We then highlighted the scholarship in the field since the publication of King, Fogle, and Logan-Terry (2008), which marks the beginning of the field identifying itself as "Family Language Policy". Finally, we raised theoretical issues relevant for the sociolinguistics of globalization, and culminated our discussion in a presentation of a critical approach to the study of family multilingualism.

Research on FLP has demonstrated that family matters, not only for the multilingual child's language development, as revealed in earlier studies, but also for the family's identity and meaning-making. The family is embedded in society as the context for home language development and maintenance with discourses on transnational families and heritage languages (Smith-Christmas 2019) potentially playing a significant role for promoting or dissuading multilingualism through heritage language maintenance.

While FLP acted as a magnet to attract scholars to give more serious attention to the family in sociolinguistic scholarship, time will tell whether the name will prevail as an index to the field in future studies of multilingual families' policies and practices, or whether the field as initially proposed will "splinter", which King (2016: 731) foresees as potential. Although many current studies do not use the term *family language policy*, they have been motivated by the wave of sociolinguistic studies focusing on the family and home language maintenance. Returning to the foundations of FLP research, the call for attention to the family as having explanatory value in developmental psycholinguistics may in fact be seen as an impact of the field since its development. Hence a potential future sixth phase in King's taxonomy of phases in the development of FLP (see section 2) may witness a returned focus to the impact of FLP on child language learning outcomes. In order to effectively study and understand the multilingual child's language development, we need to draw on insights from both FLP and multilingual acquisition research, both sociolinguistic and developmental psycholinguistic approaches (Lanza 2018b). A socially real study of FLP, however, must draw on the perspectives of a critical approach to family multilingualism. Indeed, the evolving complexity of the field of FLP in the past decade bears witness to the complexities of families in the new millennium and the dynamic nature of home language maintenance and development as manifested in family language policies and practices.

References

Bello-Rodzen, Ingrid. 2016. Multilingual upbringing as portrayed in the blogosphere: On parent-bloggers' profile. *Theory and Practice of Second Language Acquisition* 2(2). 27–46.

Blum-Ross, Alicia & Sonia Livingstone. 2017. "Sharenting," parent blogging, and the boundaries of the digital self. *Popular Communication* 15(2). 110–125.

Caldas, Stephen. 2012. Language policy in the family. In Bernard Spolsky (ed.), *The Cambridge handbook of language policy*, 351–373. Cambridge: Cambridge University Press.

Caldas, Stephen & Suzanne Caron-Caldas. 2000. The influence of family, school, and community on bilingual preference: Results from a Louisiana/Quebec case study. *Applied Psycholinguistics* 21(3). 365–381.

Canagarajah, Suresh. 2013. Agency and power in intercultural communication: Negotiating English in translocal spaces. *Language and Intercultural Communication* 13(2). 202–224.

Carroll, Susanne. 2017. Exposure and input in bilingual development. *Bilingualism: Language and Cognition* 20(1). 3–16.

Castro-Gómez, Santiago & Ramón Grosfoguel (eds.). 2007. *El giro decolonial: Reflexiones para una diversidad epistémica más allá del capitalismo global*. Bogotá: Siglo del Hombre Editores.

Chambers, Debora. 2012. *A sociology of family life: Change and diversity in intimate relations*. Cambridge: Polity.

Coetzee, Frieda. 2018. *Hy leer dit nie hier nie* ('He doesn't learn it here'): Talking about children's swearing in extended families in multilingual South Africa. *International Journal of Multilingualism* 15(3). 291–305.

Comaroff, Jean & John L. Comaroff. 2012. Theory from the South: Or, how Euro-America is evolving toward Africa. *Anthropological Forum: A Journal of Social Anthropology and Comparative Sociology* 22 (2). 113–131.

Connell, Raewyn. 2014. Using southern theory: Decolonizing social thought in theory, research and application. *Planning Theory* 13(2). 210–223.

Curdt-Christiansen, Xiao Lan. 2009. Invisible and visible language planning: Ideological factors in the family language policy of Chinese immigrant families in Quebec. *Language Policy* 8(4). 351–375.

Curdt-Christiansen, Xiao Lan (ed.). 2013. Family language policy. (Special issue.) *Language Policy* 12.

Curdt-Christiansen, Xiao Lan. 2016. Conflicting language ideologies and contradictory language practices in Singaporean multilingual families. *Journal of Multilingual and Multicultural Development* 37(7). 694–709.

Curdt-Christiansen, Xiao Lan. 2018. Family language policy. In James W. Tollefson & Miguel Pérez-Milans (eds.), *The Oxford handbook of language policy and planning*, 420–461. Oxford: Oxford University Press.

Curdt-Christiansen, Xiao Lan & Jing Huang. this vol. Factors influencing family language policy.

Curdt-Christiansen, Xiao Lan & Elizabeth Lanza (eds.). 2018a. Multilingual family language management: Efforts, measures and choices. (Special issue.) *Multilingua* 37(2).

Curdt-Christiansen, Xiao Lan & Elizabeth Lanza. 2018b. Language management in multilingual families: Efforts, measures and challenges. *Multilingua* 37(2). 123–130.

Daussa, Eva & Ulrike Limacher-Riebold. 2018. Helping multilingual families: Internet forums and personal language counselors. Paper presented at *Third International Conference on Language, Identity and Education in Multilingual Contexts (LIEMC18)*, Dublin, 1 February.

De Houwer, Annick. 1990. *The acquisition of two languages from birth: A case study*. Cambridge: Cambridge University Press.

Duranti, Alessandro, Elinor Ochs & Bambi Schieffelin (eds.). 2011. *The handbook of language socialization*. Malden, MA: Wiley-Blackwell.

Döpke, Susanne. 1992. *One parent–One language. An interactional approach*. Amsterdam: John Benjamins.

Eisenchlas, Susana A. & Andrea C. Schalley. this vol. Making sense of the notion of "home language" and related concepts.

Fishman, Joshua. 1991. *Reversing language shift*. Multilingual Matters.

Fogle, Lyn Wright. 2012. *Second language socialization and learner agency: Talk in three adoptive families*. Bristol: Multilingual Matters.

Gafaranga, Joseph. 2010. Medium request: Talking language shift into being. *Language in Society* 39. 241–270.

Gallo, Sarah & Nancy Hornberger. 2017. Immigration policy as family language policy: Mexican immigrant children and families in search of biliteracy. *International Journal of Bilingualism* 23(2). 757–770.

García, Ofelia & Li Wei. 2014. *Translanguaging: Language, bilingualism and education*. Basingstoke: Palgrave Macmillian.

Genesee, Fred. 1989. Early bilingual development: One language or two? *Journal of Child Language* 16. 161–179.

Goldberg, Abbie E. and Katherine R. Allen. 2012. *LGBT-parent families: Innovations in research and implications for practice*. New York: Springer.

Grüter, Therese & Johanne Paradis (eds.). 2014. *Input and experience in bilingual development.* Amsterdam: John Benjamins.

Guilherme, Manuela & Lynn Mario T. Menezes de Souza (eds.). 2019. *Glocal languages and critical intercultural awareness: The South answers back.* New York: Routledge.

Henrich, Joseph, Steven Heine & Ara Norenzayan (2010). The weirdest people in the world? *Behavioral and Brain Sciences* 33(2–3). 61–135.

Heugh, Kathleen & Christopher Stroud. 2019. Diversities, affinities and diasporas: A southern lens and methodology for understanding multilingualisms. *Current Issues in Language Planning* 20(1). 1–15.

Higgins, Christina (ed.). 2019. Language, heritage, and family – a dynamic perspective. (Special issue.) *International Journal of the Sociology of Language* 255.

Hirsch, Tijana & Jin Sook Lee. 2018. Understanding the complexities of transnational family language policy. *Journal of Multilingual and Multicultural Development* 39(10). 882–894.

Holstein, James A. & Jay Gubrium. 1999. What is family? Further thoughts on a social constructionist approach. *Marriage & Family Review* 28. 3–20.

Hult, Francis M. & David C. Johnson. 2015. *Research methods in language policy and planning: A practical guide.* Malden, MA: Wiley.

Kerfoot, Caroline & Kenneth Hyltenstam (eds.). 2017. *Entangled discourses: South-north orders of visibility.* Oxfordshire: Taylor & Francis.

Kheirkhah, Mina & Asta Cekaite. 2017. Siblings as language socialization agents in bilingual families. *International Multilingual Research Journal* 12(4). 255–272.

King, Kendall. 2016. Language policy, multilingual encounters, and transnational families. *Journal of Multilingual and Multicultural Development* 7(7). 726–733.

King, Kendall A. & Lyn Wright Fogle. 2013. Family language policy and bilingual parenting. *Language Teaching* 46(2). 172–194.

King, Kendall A. & Lyn Wright Fogle. 2016. Family language policy. In Teresa McCarty & Stephen May (eds.), *Language policy and political issues in education. Encyclopedia of language and education*, 315–327. 3rd edn. New York: Springer.

King, Kendall & Elizabeth Lanza (eds.). 2019a. Ideology, agency and imagination in multilingual families. (Special issue.) *International Journal of Bilingualism* 23(3).

King, Kendall & Elizabeth Lanza. 2019b. Ideology, agency and imagination in multilingual families: An introduction. *International Journal of Bilingualism* 23(3). 717–723.

King, Kendall A., Lyn Wright Fogle & Aubrey Logan-Terry. 2008. Family language policy. *Language and Linguistics Compass* 2(5). 907–922.

Lanza, Elizabeth. 1992. Can bilingual two-year-olds code-switch? *Journal of Child Language* 19(3). 633–658.

Lanza, Elizabeth. [1997] 2004. *Language mixing in infant bilingualism: A sociolinguistic perspective.* Oxford: Oxford University Press.

Lanza, Elizabeth. 2007. Multilingualism and the family. In Peter Auer & Li Wei (eds.), *Handbook of multilingualism and multilingual communication*, 45–67. Berlin: Mouton de Gruyter.

Lanza, Elizabeth. 2018a. Raising children multilingually: Family language policies and online blogging. Paper presented at Sociolinguistics Symposium 22, Auckland, New Zealand, 27–30 June.

Lanza, Elizabeth. 2018b. Multilingualism across the lifespan: Competence, practices and policies. In David Bradley & Rajend Mesthrie (eds.), *The dynamics of language: Plenary and focus papers from the 20th International Conference of Linguists.* Cape Town: University of Cape Town Press.

Lanza, Elizabeth. 2020. Urban multilingualism and family language policy. In Giuditta Caliendo, Rudi Janssens, Stef Slembrouck & Piet Van Avermaet (eds.), *Urban multilingualism in Europe:*

Bridging the gap between language policies and language practices, 121–140. Berlin: Mouton De Gruyter.

Lanza, Elizabeth & Xiao Lan Curdt-Christiansen (eds.). 2018. Multilingual families. Aspirations and challenges. (Special issue.) *International Journal of Multilingualism* 15(3).

Lanza, Elizabeth & Kristin Vold Lexander. 2019. Family language practices in multilingual transcultural families. In Simona Montanari & Suzanne Quay (eds.), *Multidisciplinary Perspectives on Multilingualism*, 229–251. Berlin: Mouton De Gruyter.

Lanza, Elizabeth & Li Wei (eds.). 2016. Multilingual encounters in transcultural families. (Special issue.) *Journal of Multilingual and Multicultural Development* 7(7).

Lefebvre, Henri. 1991. *The production of space.* Malden, MA: Blackwell.

Léglise, Isabelle. 2017. Multilinguisme et hétérogénéité des pratiques langagières. Nouveaux chantiers et enjeux du *Global South. Langage et société* 160–161(2). 251–266.

Leopold, Werner. 1939–1949. *Speech development of a bilingual child: A linguist's record.* Volumes 1–4. Bloomington: Indiana University Press.

Li, Wei (ed.). 2012. Family language policy in multilingual transnational families and beyond. (Special issue.) *Journal of Multilingual and Multicultural Development* 33(1).

Li, Wei. 2018. Translanguaging as a practical theory of language. *Applied Linguistics* 39(1). 9–30.

Li, Wei & Zhu Hua. 2019. Imagination as a key factor in LMLS in transnational families. *International Journal of the Sociology of Language* 255. 73–107.

Lomeu Gomes, Rafael. 2018. Family language policy ten years on: A critical approach to family multilingualism. *Multilingual Margins* 5(2). 51–72.

Lomeu Gomes, Rafael. Forthcoming. Family multilingualism. Language practices and ideologies of Brazilian-Norwegian families in Norway. Oslo: University of Oslo dissertation.

Luykx, Aurolyn. 2003. Weaving languages together: Family language policy and gender socialization in bilingual Aymara households. In Robert Bayley & Sandra Schecter (eds.), *Language socialization in bilingual and multilingual societies*, 10–25. Bristol: Multilingual Matters.

Macalister, John & Seyed Hadi Mirvahedi (eds.). 2017. *Family language policies in a multilingual world. Opportunities, challenges, and consequences.* London: Routledge.

Madianou, Mirca & Daniel Miller. 2012. *Migration and new media. Transnational families and polymedia.* London: Routledge.

Martin-Jones, Marilyn & Deidre Martin (eds.). 2017. *Researching multilingualism: Critical and ethnographic perspectives.* London: Routledge.

Mary, Latisha & Andrea Young. this vol. Teachers' attitudes towards home language maintenance and their effects.

Massey, Doreen. 2005. *For space.* London: Sage.

Meisel, Jürgen. 1989. Early differentiation of languages in bilingual children. In Kenneth Hyltenstam & Loraine Obler (eds.), *Bilingualism across the lifespan*, 13–40. Cambridge: Cambridge University Press.

Mignolo, Walter D. & Catherine E. Walsh. 2018. *On decoloniality: Concepts, analytics, praxis.* Durham: Duke University Press.

Milani, Tommaso M. & Michelle M. Lazar. 2017. (Special issue.) Discourse, gender and sexuality from the Global South. *Journal of Sociolinguistics* 21(3).

Nandi, Anik. 2018. Parents as stakeholders: Language management in urban Galician homes. *Multilingua* 37(2). 201–223.

Ochs, Elinor & Bambi Schieffelin. 2011. The theory of language socialization. In Alessandro Duranti, Elinor Ochs & Bambi Schieffelin (eds.), *The handbook of language socialization*, 1–21. Malden, MA: Wiley-Blackwell.

Okita, Toshie. 2002. *Invisible work. Bilingualism, language choice and childrearing in intermarried families*. Amsterdam: John Benjamins.
Palviainen, Åsa. this vol. Future prospects and visions for family language policy research.
Palviainen, Åsa & Sally Boyd. 2013. Unity in discourse, diversity in practice: The One Person One Language policy in bilingual families. In Mila Schwartz & Anna Verschik (eds.), *Successful family language policy. Parents, children and educators in interaction*, 223–248. Dordrecht: Springer.
Pennycook, Alastair & Emi Otsuji. 2015. *Metrolingualism: Language in the city*. London: Routledge.
Piller, Ingrid & Livia Gerber. 2018. Family language policy between the bilingual advantage and the monolingual mindset. *International Journal of Bilingual Education and Bilingualism*, 1–14. Online First. DOI:10.1080/13670050.2018.1503227
Porter, Gina, Kate Hampshire, Albert Abane, Alister Munthali, Elsbeth Robson, Augustine Tanle, Samuel Owusu, Ariane De Lannoy & Andisiwe Bango. 2018. Connecting with home, keeping in touch: Physical and virtual mobility across stretched families in sub-Saharan Africa. *Africa* 88(2). 404–424.
Purkarthofer, Judith. 2019. Building expectations: Imagining family language policy and heteroglossic social spaces. *International Journal of Bilingualism* 23(3). 724–739.
Purkhartofer, Judith & Guri B. Steien. 2019. "Prétendre comme si on connaît pas une autre langue que le swahili": Multilingual parents in Norway on change and continuity in their family language policies. *International Journal of the Sociology of Language* 255. 109–131.
Quay, Suzanne & Simona Montanari. 2016. Early bilingualism: From differentiation to the impact of family language practices. In Elena Nicoladis & Simona Montanari (eds.), *Lifespan perspectives on bilingualism*, 23–42. Washington, D.C.: American Psychological Association; Berlin: De Gruyter Mouton.
Revis, Melanie. 2016. A Bourdieusian perspective on child agency in family language policy. *International Journal of Bilingual Education and Bilingualism* 22(2). 177–191.
Ronjat, Jules. 1913. *Le développement du langage observé chez un enfant bilingue*. Paris: Champion.
Ruby, Mahera. 2012. The role of a grandmother in maintaining Bangla with her granddaughter in East London. *Journal of Multilingual and Multicultural Development* 33(1). 67–83.
Santos, Boaventura de Sousa. 2018. *The end of the cognitive empire: The coming of age of epistemologies of the South*. Durham: Duke University Press.
Schieffelin, Bambi & Elinor Ochs. 1986. Language socialization. *Annual Review of Anthropology* 15. 163–191.
Schwartz, Mila & Anna Verschik (eds.). 2013. *Successful family language policy. Parents, children and educators in interaction*. Dordrecht: Springer.
Skutnabb-Kangas, Tove & Kathleen Heugh (eds.). 2012. *Multilingual education and sustainable diversity work. From periphery to center*. New York & London: Routledge.
Smith-Christmas, Cassie. 2016. *Family language policy. Maintaining an endangered language in the home*. Basingstoke: Palgrave Macmillan.
Smith-Christmas, Cassie. 2017. Family language policy: New directions. In John Macalister & Seyed Hadi Mirvahedi (eds.), *Family language policies in a multilingual world. Opportunities, challenges, and consequences*, 13–29. New York & London: Routledge.
Smith-Christmas, Cassie. 2019. When X doesn't mark the spot: The intersection of language shift, identity and family language policy. *International Journal of the Sociology of Language* 255. 133–158.
Smith-Christmas, Cassie. this vol. Child agency and home language maintenance.
Snow, Catherine. 2014. Input to interaction to instruction: Three key shifts in the history of child language research. *Journal of Child Language* 41(S1: Reflections – 40 years of JCL). 117–123.

Spolsky, Bernard. 2004. *Language policy*. Cambridge: Cambridge University Press.
Spolsky, Bernard. 2009. *Language management*. Cambridge: Cambridge University Press.
Spolsky, Bernard. 2012. Family language policy – the critical domain. *Journal of Multilingual and Multicultural Development* 33(1). 3–11.
Tannenbaum, Michal & Pauline Howie. 2002. The association between language maintenance and family relations: Chinese immigrant children in Australia. *Journal of Multilingual and Multicultural Development* 23(5). 408–424.
Tannenbaum, Michal & Dafna Yitzhaki. 2016. "Everything comes with a price ... ": Family language policy in Israeli Arab families in mixed cities. *Language and Intercultural Communication* 16(4). 570–587.
Tollefson, James W. & Miguel Pérez-Milans (eds.). 2018. *The Oxford handbook of language policy and planning*. Oxford: Oxford University Press.
Unsworth, Sharon. 2013. Current issues in multilingual first language acquisition. *Annual Review of Applied Linguistics* 33. 21–50.
Venables, Elizabeth, Susana A. Eisenchlas & Andrea C. Schalley. 2014. One-Parent-One- Language (OPOL) families: Is the majority language-speaking parent instrumental in the minority language development? *International Journal of Bilingual Education and Bilingualism* 17(4). 429–448.
Volterra, Virginia & Traute Taeschner. 1978. The acquisition and development of language by bilingual children. *Journal of Child Language* 5(2). 311–326.
Wenger, Etienne. 1998. *Communities of Practice: Learning, meaning, and identity*. Cambridge: Cambridge University Press.
Zhu, Hua & Li Wei. 2016. Transnational experience, aspiration and family language policy. *Journal of Multilingual and Multicultural Development* 37(7). 655–666.

Xiao Lan Curdt-Christiansen and Jing Huang
9 Factors influencing family language policy

1 Introduction

Family language policy (FLP), a critical element in home language maintenance in ethnic minority contexts, is dynamically influenced by "a wide range of linguistic and non-linguistic elements, variables, and factors" (Spolsky 2004: 41). As families are a microcosm of a macro society, reflecting the larger sociocultural environment in which they are situated, they constantly interact with others in socio-linguistic, socio-cultural, socio-economic and socio-political contexts (Curdt-Christiansen 2018). Because of the social nature of families, the study of home language maintenance with regard to FLP goes beyond parenting at home to encompass different domains related to family decisions, such as education, and the public linguistic space (Spolsky 2009) as well as many different aspects in individual family members' everyday life, including emotions, identity, and cultural and political allegiances (Curdt-Christiansen 2009, 2014, 2016; de Houwer 1999; King, Fogle, and Logan-Terry 2008; Pavlenko 2004; Piller 2002; Tannenbaum 2012).

Recently, a number of important volumes and studies have addressed not only how families navigate the use of language in the home, but also what impact social, economic and political forces have on family language practices (for examples, see Curdt-Christiansen and Lanza 2018; Curdt-Christiansen and Wang 2018; Macalister and Mirvahedi 2017; Lanza and Curdt-Christiansen 2018; Lanza and Li 2016; Revis 2019; Smith-Christmas 2016; Fogle 2012).

This chapter starts with a brief introduction outlining the recent developments of FLP. In section 2, the theoretical model of FLP is introduced to illustrate how internal and external forces interact to influence the formation of FLP, and definitions are provided together with a critical discussion of the different types of these internal and external factors. Following that, in sections 3 and 4, major contributions to the field are discussed with focus on a few major studies that examine internal factors such as emotions, identity, and parental impact beliefs, and external factors such as language status, socio-economic and socio-political realities. By using empirical studies, the chapter illustrates how family language policy as a dynamic socio-cultural practice is shaped by both linguistic and non-linguistic forces in different types of families, geopolitical contexts, and macro-level policies. Section 5 outlines suggestions for future research into factors that have not been or are rarely included in the field as they are related to recent development of new technologies and depend on emerging variables resulting from increasing transnational migration and evolving language policies.

2 Family language policy – a dynamic model

Research on family language policy (FLP) has developed considerably over the past decade (see Lanza and Lomeu Gomes this vol.). Apart from examining what types of practices were best for language transmission outcomes, more recent lines of FLP scholarship have reframed key questions on FLP by recognising the family as a dynamic system in a changing world (King 2016). While language policies at large are set to change or influence social structures and processes, language policies enacted in a family domain are based on the individual family's perception of social structures and social changes (Curdt-Christiansen 2009). Immigrant parents often encounter the dilemma of either raising their children bilingually or only in the societal language. While they often desire that their children maintain the home language and at the same time learn the school language to succeed at school subjects (De Angelis 2011), the dilemma to raise children bilingually or only in the societal language is never a fading issue. There are many factors that influence parents' choices about "what will strengthen their family's social standing and best serve and support the family members' goal in life" (Curdt-Christiansen 2009: 326).

Curdt-Christiansen (2009, 2014, 2018) developed an FLP model illustrating the complex interplay of FLP and its socio-cultural-political-linguistic environment (see Figure 1). Building on Spolsky (2009)'s triadic model of language policy (see Lanza and Lomeu Gomes; Palviainen; Smith-Christmas, all this vol.) and language socialisation theory (Duranti, Ochs and Schieffelin 2011; Lanza 2007), this FLP model provides a theoretical conceptualisation to depict how different factors influence family language decisions in dynamic ways.

2.1 The inner core

Situated within the broader socio-cultural, socio-economic, socio-political and socio-linguistic context, the inner core represents the three interrelated components of FLP. According to Spolsky (2004, 2009), language ideology, made up of beliefs, refers to how family members perceive particular languages; language practices refer to what individuals actually do with languages; and language management is the interventional measures used to maintain and develop a particular language.

Within a family, there are rules and norms for speaking, acting and believing. Making rules and decisions on what language(s) to practice and encourage, or to discourage or abandon, depends largely on the beliefs and values that family members ascribe to certain languages. Curdt-Christiansen (2009, 2012) contends that this decision-making process is not only related to parental beliefs and goals for their children's multilingual development and educational success, it is also related to the emotional and identity needs of family members.

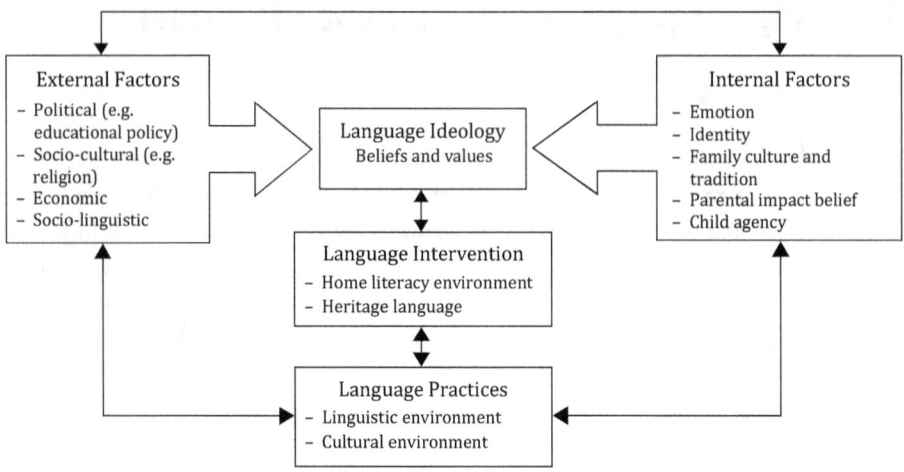

Figure 1: Dynamic model of family language policy (adapted from Curdt-Christiansen 2009:335, 2014:37).

These beliefs and goals are driving forces for caregivers to provide language and cultural environments as well as facilities, accessible to family members, for language socialisation and maintenance. As deliberate and explicit efforts (language management), these environments include literacy-related resources in the home language, parental involvement/investment and different forms of capital in engaging home language development. As implicit language socialization practices (language practices), these environments refer to the linguistic and cultural resources for language use and practices. These environments are crucial for home language maintenance and development because they provide the natural "speech resources" (Blommaert 2008) to which children are exposed within and outside a family. In other words, without an adequate linguistic and cultural environment, it is unrealistic to expect any children to maintain and develop a home language. Therefore, FLP decisions are influenced by language ideologies, the nature of intergenerational speech resources, parents' educational background, their own language learning experience, their migration history, and the family's economic resources.

In this regard, the influencing variables can be divided into two major types of forces or factors: internal factors and external factors. Although the two types of factors are categorised as two distinct entities, they are actually closely related and sometimes blurred together; they form the ideological bedrock for language choices, linguistic practices and language investments at home (see Curdt-Christiansen, 2009, 2014, 2018). In the following section, we provide a discussion of the two types of factors.

2.2 Internal factors

Internal factors refer broadly to language-related variables that can maintain or break a close family bond and intimate relationship between family members. These factors include "emotion", "sense of identity", "cultural practices and social norms" that parents or caregivers perceive as important and valuable for family ties. Concomitantly, "parental impact beliefs" and "child agency" also play a crucial role in home language maintenance (see Smith-Christmas this vol.).

The **emotional factor** concerns the role home language plays in the relationship between the generations in a family. Research into emotions and language shows that home language serves not only for heritage maintenance but also for strengthening the emotional ties between family members (de Houwer 1999, 2015; Okita 2002; Pavlenko 2004; Tannenbaum 2012). Pavlenko (2004, 2012) points out that intimacy and emotional development take place in two parallel processes during primary language acquisition. The first is related to *perceptual development* where children form their emotional concepts of all sensory modalities, such as visual, auditory, tactile and visceral, through language socialisation. The second process involves *linguistic affective conditioning* where children develop linguistic associations with emotionally charged experiences and memories. During this process, words and phrases take on affective connotations and have deep personal meanings in that some are linked to love, others linked to fear, and others again linked to taboos. As a result, using the primary language can invoke deep emotional reactions and make family members feel "closer" in daily interactions. Home language fluency also enables meaningful communication between generations (Wong Fillmore 1991).

The **identity factor** is related to an individual's perception of self as a member of a family. This identity is related to the ethnolinguistic origins of the family (see Tseng this vol.). As a symbolic representation, home language is, in some families, the most significant cultural and ethnic feature reflecting family roots and heritage, despite the fact that family members may simultaneously take on other identities related to their profession and have membership of multiple communities (e.g. Little 2020). Heritage identity, in the context of intergenerational transmission, can be a contested issue that may cause conflicts between family members (Blackledge and Creese 2010; Zhu 2008).

The **cultural factor** refers to cultural practices and social norms to which a family adheres. Like identity, culture can be interpreted and experienced differently from one member of a family to the other and from one generation to the next (Little 2020; Mu 2014). Within a family, some parents/caregivers may expect their children to learn the home language in order to maintain a cultural "loyalty" to the home country and continue to maintain certain cultural values and social practices which may or may not be consistent with those of the host society. As a consequence, the home language may be lost or altered because of conflicting values attached to it (Curdt-Christiansen 2016).

Parental impact beliefs (de Houwer 1999) refers to parental convictions about their own capability and responsibility for raising children in a home language or bilingually. Such beliefs are motivated by parents' past educational experiences, cultural upbringing and disposition, migration experiences, and knowledge of raising bilingual children. All of them are reflected through parental expectations of their children's linguistic and educational development (Curdt-Christiansen 2009). This factor is one of the most crucial factors in home language maintenance as it is directly related to parental involvement and investment in the process of language learning and development.

Child agency, in the context of FLP, can be defined as children's active role in making decisions about patterns of family language use (see also Smith-Christmas this vol.). While child agency is noticeable in immigrant families, the notion is complex because generational gaps in cultural values and social norms exist inherently between the parent/grandparent generation and the child generation (Fogle 2012; Revis 2019; Said and Zhu 2019; Smith-Christmas 2016, 2018). Language socialisation practices between mainstream society (including school and peer culture) and home can be drastically different oftentimes involving competing social and cultural values as well as political affiliations. Such competing forces can lead to emotional, psychological and ideological consequences that may or may not lead to home language loss (Little 2020; Pavlenko 2012). Therefore, child agency should be treated with careful consideration in specific cultural or linguistic contexts (Ahearn 2001).

2.3 External factors

While internal factors tend to focus on close analysis of face-to-face interactions and social life within the family (Curdt-Christiansen 2009, 2016; Curdt-Christiansen and Wang 2018; Fogle 2012; Gafaranga 2010; Lanza 2004, 2007; Li 1994), families do not live in a vacuum, isolated from the larger socio-cultural environment. On the contrary, they are always influenced by external factors, including socio-linguistic, socio-cultural, socio-economic and socio-political factors (Spolsky 2004, 2012).

Socio-economic factors refer to the economic forces or linguistic capital that a particular language evokes or vice versa (Bourdieu 1996). In other words, they are the interconnections between languages and the economy (Grin 2006). Language economics is a field of study that seeks to address whether and, if so, to what degree language variables affect economic variables, such as earnings and salaries. Tollefson and Tsui (2018) argue that economic forces are central in most language policies. FLP decisions on whether to continue developing a home language are often related to the economic benefits to which the language can provide access.

Socio-political factors concern individuals' rights, resources and access to education (e.g. language-in-education policy), civil activities, and political decisions.

FLP is often influenced by parents' concerns about their children's education in the societal/mainstream language. If immigrant families see their home language as an educational barrier or problem, preventing them from accessing educational information and their children from participating in education, then the chances of maintaining this home language are very small.

Socio-cultural factors refer to the symbolic cultural values that particular languages represent. In this perspective, languages are viewed as manifestations of culture. As mentioned earlier (see child agency), mainstream culture and school culture as well as peer culture can be strong forces that compete against or strengthen the home culture (c.f. Tse 2001; Oriyama 2016). Therefore, FLP often faces challenges and may struggle with the mainstream ideology to resist language loss.

Socio-linguistic factors provide resources for parents to form beliefs about what kind of languages are good/acceptable or bad/unacceptable. Such beliefs are typically reflected in parents' attitudes towards mixing mainstream language with home language or their preference for a particular language variety. In immigrant contexts, many Chinese parents, for example, decide to teach their children Mandarin rather than their home dialect because of the prestige and instrumental value of Mandarin in today's world.

While the above discussion may present the factors as internal and external, there is, in reality, no clear distinction between the two types of factors. Language-in-education policy as an external factor, for example, influences parental decisions on whether to (dis)continue home language development which is reflected in their impact beliefs. Child agency is also a blurred factor between internal and external categories as child agency is often related to school culture, peer culture as well as mainstream culture. These cultures, by category, are external factors that shape children's agentive role in FLP. In this regard, internal and external factors are inherently related.

These factors, as evidenced in above discussion, act as driving forces for family members to make critical decisions about continuity or discontinuity of home languages. Unpacking the influences of these factors can "enhance our understanding of the power relationships between linguistic varieties and cultural and symbolic values" (Curdt-Christiansen 2013: 4). In the following section, we present empirical studies to demonstrate how these factors are interconnected and crucially shape language ideologies and practices in different types of families.

3 Internal factors: Changing cultures, evolving identities and conflicting views

When combating language shift and loss, immigrant families encounter tremendous challenges from mainstream ideologies, children's culture, and peer influence on children's social values, as well as from public education and macro language policies (Curdt-Christiansen 2009, 2016, 2018; Little 2020). In recent years, scholars have paid particular attention to emotions, parental impact beliefs and child agency (e.g. Fogle 2012; Pavlenko 2012; Smith-Christmas 2016; Tannenbaum 2012). These shaping factors turn families into contested fields with conflicting views from different policy actors (family members) within the same families.

3.1 Harmonious family relationship

Home language maintenance, as argued by some scholars (de Houwer 2009, 2015; Okita 2002; Pavlenko 2004, 2012; Tannenbaum 2012), can be an important element for a harmonious and cohesive family relationship. De Houwer (2009), for example, studied a bilingual Dutch-English child (Lauren) in Belgium. At age three, Lauren spoke fluent Dutch and understood some English. Her productive English, however, was restricted to "yes" and "no", which is understandable as her exposure to English was limited and the input came only from her father who often traveled. Her father perceived this linguistic behaviour as a "rejection" of him. De Houwer argues that by not speaking the parents' language, a child may affect the harmonious relationship in a family. Similar cases have also been reported by other scholars where parents feel guilty for not passing on their heritage language (Curdt-Christiansen 2016; Okita 2002). Okita (2002), in her study of children of Japanese and English heritage in the UK, reported Japanese mothers' conflicting feelings about not using Japanese with their children when they started schooling in English. Curdt-Christiansen (2016), in her study of Singaporean families, also illustrated the parents' conflicting emotions and regrets for not passing on their heritage language.

In addition to the conflicting feelings expressed by parents, studies have shown that emotional expressions used by parents in their L1 emerge as more authentic, natural and genuine (Pavlenko 2004). Therefore, terms of endearment or other strong emotions expressed in L1(s) offer an opportunity for language maintenance. The relationship between emotions and home language maintenance has been reported by Tannenbaum and Berkovich (2005) in their studies of 180 adolescents from families that immigrated to Israel from the former USSR. Focusing on attitudes and other emotional aspects, they found that home language maintenance in the second generation is associated with harmonious family relations which lead to the well-being of immigrant parents and children. They concluded that successful home language maintenance is largely attributable to children's internalisation of the emotional dimensions that their parents attach to the L1.

3.2 Parental impact beliefs

While children's emotional identification with their parents has a strong influence on home language maintenance, parents' impact beliefs (De Houwer 1999) about their children's ability to learn the home language can be a decisive factor, informing their FLP decisions and thus affecting the linguistic environment they provide for their children. Such beliefs are often instantiated through parents' expectations of their children's bilingual development. Pérez Báez (2013) studied language shift of speakers of San Lucas Quiavini Zapotec within the home and in the diaspora context in Mexico and California. She found that parents held weak impact beliefs in their ability to support their children's bilingual development leading to ineffective FLPs and language shift in both home context and diaspora community. These weak impact beliefs were derived from the strong external forces associated with the assimilation ideology in the US. The example provides evidence for the close relationship and blurred characteristics of internal and external factors.

In contrast to the weak impact beliefs, *strong impact beliefs* held by parents have been found in diaspora context with regard to minority home language maintenance. Curdt-Christiansen (2009) studied Chinese immigrant families in Quebec where Chinese, English and French were part of the children's language repertoires. Believing that "language is a window to the world" (Curdt-Christiansen 2009: 367), the parents in her study provided rich linguistic resources for home language development. The findings revealed that parents' perceptions of maintaining Chinese and developing French and English simultaneously (multilingual proficiency) were clearly related to their past educational and migration experiences, and beliefs in the market values of the different languages in Canada and beyond (Curdt-Christiansen 2009; Zhu and Li 2016). Similar findings have been reported in studies of immigrant families in other parts of the world, demonstrating that impact beliefs are contributing factors that inform FLPs (Curdt-Christiansen and LaMorgia 2018; Kang 2015; Li 2007; Ren and Hu 2013).

3.3 Child agency and home language maintenance

A harmonious and cohesive family relationship is not always easy to achieve in immigrant families. Migration background and experiences have crucial effects not only on individual family members' language practices but also on relational factors such as culture and identity. As family members have different encounters and experiences during their migration trajectory, conflicts of identity and culture between generations may arise.

Zhu (2008) studied family language talk between parents and children in Chinese diasporic families in the UK. Using a detailed analysis of sequential movement in conversations, she demonstrated that "conflicts in values and identities are negotiated, mediated and managed" (2008: 1799). Family language policy in these participating families is thus negotiated through intergenerational conflict talk as a result of different life experiences, socio-cultural values and linguistic practices between members of different generations. Critically, Zhu points out that family dynamics and family values are changing because societies are changing; such changes, however, have crucial effects on home language maintenance.

Also looking at the evolving sociolinguistic environment of immigrant families in the UK, Little (2020) explored families' attitudes towards home language development and their efforts to support or develop the home language in their families. Involving 212 families from a wide variety of cultural and linguistic contexts, she looked into how attitudes towards heritage language may be linked to identity. By asking "Whose heritage? What inheritance?" she drew attention to the notions of peripheral vs. essential and pragmatic vs. emotional aspects of heritage language learning. While parents may have an "essential/emotional" attitude to their home language and view it as an essential aspect of their identity, children may struggle to identify with their parents and find it difficult to understand their parent's deep emotional need. She points out that because of the external influence from school and society, and because of the lack of resources for home language learning and use, children tend to regard their home languages as peripheral. The study, again, demonstrates the influences of blurred internal and external forces, which together contribute to the incomplete home language development.

While the outcome of children's home language development may not have been as the parents expected, recent studies reveal that children can exert their agency to make creative use of their heritage language and the mainstream language (Said and Zhu 2019; Mu 2014; Zhu 2008; Smith-Christmas 2016, 2018). Said and Zhu (2019: 773) reported a case of third generation Arabic speaking bilingual children who "mobilise their multiple (and developing) linguistic repertoires creatively to assert their agency in language use and socialisation". By analysing mealtime interactions, they argue that the acts of agency are enacted through the children's knowledge and manipulation of their parents' preference for Arabic. These "bottom up" (child negotiation of parental decisions) vs. "top down" (explicit parental decisions) language negotiations are conducive for successful development or maintenance of home language. They demonstrate that the children's clever manipulation of their metalinguistic knowledge contributes to their language learning and cultural appreciation of the "home" linguistic environment, because family values go hand-in-hand with language development through socialisation processes. They finally contend that a flexible FLP may encourage active involvement in language learning and create positive experiences related to home language development which, in turn, invite children to assert their agency to develop a close family relationship. This positive perspective on the value of children's agentive role is congruent with De Houwer's (2015) harmonious bilingualism and Schwartz's (2008) co-existence of L1 and L2 environment for bilingual development.

However, child agency does not always result in a positive home-language learning experience. Very often, child agency can go against parental language decisions for home language maintenance, thus causing conflicts within families. Fogle (2102), for example, found three types of agency in children's heritage language development in adoptive families: resistance through 'nothing' response, interaction through the frequent use of wh-questions, and influencing their parents' language choice. Revis (2019) also studied child agency in Ethiopian and Colombian refugee families and communities in New Zealand. Employing a Bourdieusian theory as conceptual framework, she illustrated that there are gaps between ethnic values and norms of parents and those with which the children grow up in their new living context. As children are immersed in the educational field where the prevalent cultural and linguistic norms of the broader society shape their habitus, they bring such "embodied predisposition from the societal field to their home environment" (Revis 2019: 188). In this regard, children act on their habitus and make decisions about changes in their cultural and linguistic practices in their families. Such changes are evidenced in their metalinguistic evaluations of their parents' ethnic language and the host country language (Said and Zhu 2019), in their "medium requests", demanding adults to repeat questions in the societal language (Gafaranga, 2010; Smith-Christmas, 2016), in their sociocultural socialisation, and in their teaching of the mainstream language to their parents (Revis 2019).

These above-mentioned conflicting issues in families provide evidence of the ways in which children contest their parents' decisions with regard to their top-down FLPs. As Mu and Dooley (2015) have observed, children do not just reproduce their home language and culture, rather they establish a bi/multilingual space where the languages and cultures of both the ethnic home and the mainstream society co-exist. They may also establish a monolingual space where only the mainstream language and culture are practiced. The latter illustrates a case of language loss in intergenerational transmission which has critical implications for identity, cultural continuity and societal cohesion. Home language maintenance and development, thus, are not private matters confined to family and community domains. Instead, they are closely related to external forces exemplified by broader sociopolitical policies and public ideologies, which will be explored in the next section.

4 External forces in FLP: Competing for space for home language development

As illustrated in the above review, FLP tends to be competing for space with the mainstream society and sociological ideologies. The competing forces are most visible in language status, political allegiance, educational goals and economic benefits brought forth by home languages. In what follows, we present some empirical studies that illuminate the influence of these external forces on FLP formation.

4.1 Language status

The status of a home/minority language is a critical factor for its survival in a given society (Curdt-Christianen and LaMorgia 2018; Curdt-Christiansen and Wang 2018; Lane 2010; Ren and Hu 2013). Walls (2018) examined how immigrant Anglophone parents, based in the metropolitan region of Barcelona, Catalonia, Spain, raised their children in English by competing with the two official languages in the region: Catalan and Castilian (Spanish). Because of the powerful status of English as valuable linguistic capital, both in its socio-economic capacity and as a global lingua franca, all participating parents (*n* = 331) recounted deliberate and ambitious FLP decisions for their children to attain a high level of English proficiency as well as native or native-like levels of Castilian and Catalan.

In the same vein, Curdt-Christiansen (2009, 2014, 2016, 2018) found in Chinese diasporic communities that parental decisions on maintaining Chinese are related to the economic and political power brought forth by the language as well as to the powerful position of China on the global economic-political stage. One of the Quebec parents expressed her view this way (data from Curdt-Christiansen 2009: 364):

看中国的这个经济改革，有一种局势，那个那个经济中心会移向东方。所以那你要是会英文又会中文，你工作上的机会会多很多。现在已经很明显，如果你有一门技术，又懂几门语言，那你就可以跨越很多障碍。	Look at the economic changes in China, there is a tendency that the center [of finance] will move to the East. There will be ample opportunities if you know English and Chinese, the job opportunities will be abundant. It is very obvious now, if you have a skill and know a few languages, you can overcome many barriers.

The positive view of Chinese language in this quote reflects its economic value and powerful political status. When linguistic and human capital is ascribed to a home language (Bourdieu 1996), FLP decisions for home language development can be made with assertion, which can be directly reflected in their impact beliefs.

While the "high" status of a minority language has motivated parents to implement home language development policies, a "low" status of a language could force parents to make the opposite decisions (Curdt-Christiansen 2014, 2016; Curdt-Christiansen and Wang 2018; Wang 2017). Lane (2010), for example, studied a group of Kven (a Finnic language) speakers in northern Norway. Aiming to understand the macro (external)-micro (internal) connections contributing to the massive language shift in this ethnic minority group, Lane conducted this longitudinal study through sociolinguistic interviews, participant observation, and feedback discussion with participants. The research was situated within the context of the official Norwegianisation Policy of the 1970s. The entire process of Norwegianisation had imparted a sense of inferiority and shame to the Kven speakers, who had little choice but to stop language transmission. In their own words, "[w]e did what we thought was best for our children" (Lane 2010: 63).

These examples illustrate that in multilingual societies where minority/home and majority/mainstream languages and cultures co-exist, "language ranking and ideological conflicts can invoke complex systems of power relations that may or can inhibit intergenerational language transmission" (Curdt-Christiansen 2018: 431). This is particularly crucial for minority/home language maintenance in societies with an explicit and strong monolingual ideology in public discourse, such as the UK and the US. Kirsch (2012), for instance, studied Luxembourgish families in Britain, in which she demonstrated the unbalanced power relationship between English, the dominant societal and powerful global language, and Luxembourgish, the non-dominant European home language. Although Luxembourgish is perceived as a European language with a "high status" in Luxembourg, it struggles in vain on the linguistic battleground of the United Kingdom. Similarly, in multilingual Singapore and Malaysia, Curdt-Christiansen (2014, 2016) and Wang (2017) have shown that even when home languages are given official languages status (such as Malay, Tamil and Mandarin), they are hierarchically ranked and placed below English. These studies are not unique cases as illustrated by other researchers (e.g. Sevinç 2016; Curdt-Christiansen and LaMorgia 2018). Many immigrant families have encountered similar issues when trying to raise multilingual children in a new, monolingual society where peer pressure, the political discourse and school policy are generating various pressures or difficulties for home language maintenance. In the following section, we discuss the influence of public education and language-in-education policy on FLP.

4.2 Public education

Education is one of the most important factors – if not *the* most important – that shape immigrant families' decisions on whether to continue or to discontinue home language practices for intergenerational transmission. It is understandable, as Curdt-Christiansen (2009: 352) has argued, that parents usually want what "will strengthen the family's social standing" and usually do their best to support their children. However, very often this best interest tends to make parents sacrifice their home language and give way to the dominant school language. In this regard, FLPs have to compete with language-in-education policy, and home languages have to compete for space with school languages. In addition, parents' inner voice that speaks for the heritage language has to compete with the teacher's advice on developing only school language (Curdt-Christiansen 2014; Curdt-Christiansen and

LaMorgia 2018; Bezçioğlu-Göktolga and Yağmur 2018; Gkaintartzi, Chatzidaki, and Tsokalidou 2014).

To understand how external factors underlie the process of language decisions in families, Baldauf (2005: 961) argues that "language-in-education planning, through schooling can become the sole language change agent". Curdt-Christiansen (2014, 2015, 2016) studied how language-in-education policy affects Singaporean families' FLP. In Singapore, despite the fact that the state language policy recognises four official languages – English, Mandarin, Malay, and Tamil – which are also the home languages of some of the recent and past immigrants from China, Malaysia and India, the language-in-education policy has adopted English as the language of instruction across all subjects in all schools at all levels. This political decision has resulted in much less curriculum time allocated to the teaching of Mandarin, Malay and Tamil (also referred to as the mother tongues) as a subject in schools. In her study of bilingual Chinese families, Curdt-Christiansen found that there are competing ideologies with regard to developing Chinese and English simultaneously. Concerned about "losing out to English in a competitive society and a meritocratic educational system" that emphasizes high proficiency in English, the parents had little choice other than to place Chinese and English in opposing positions (Curdt-Christiansen 2014: 48). This has resulted in their lower expectations for their children's Chinese proficiency and less sufficient provision of Chinese literacy resources at home.

Socio-cultural and socio-political realities are driving families to make difficult decisions about their language practices. On the one hand, they desire to maintain their cultural loyalty and linguistic continuity through intergenerational transmission. On the other hand, they have to negotiate social pressure and public educational demands. In a recent special issue on family language management, edited by Curdt-Christiansen and Lanza (2018), researchers from different geopolitical contexts, such as England, Scotland and Luxembourg, showed that family language management measures often encounter obstacles from public educational systems where immigrant parents are forced to prioritise school languages and academic matters (Curdt-Christiansen and LaMorgia 2018; Gogonas and Kirsch 2018; Smith-Christmas 2018).

In a study of Chinese, Italian and Urdu-speaking families in the UK, Curdt-Christiansen and LaMorgia (2018) showed the importance of the "conscious choice" of the linguistic measures and literacy practices in shaping the "unconscious process" of linguistic and cultural transmission in transnational families. While the study shows that parents provide an environment and various language resources that enable their children to maintain their home language and develop additive bilingualism, it also shows the dilemma that parents encounter in their everyday life and the challenges parents have as they struggle to keep up with social and educational pressures and the demands of the educational system. As one of the parents stated about choice of language at home (Curdt-Christiansen and LaMorgia 2018: 19):

> First of all, she [daughter] has to complete her school work. Currently, she is in a private primary school, so she has homework to do every day. When that is completed, it's already eight, time for bed. To read in Chinese, we really don't have time for it. Because we both work and have to make sure that one of us gets home before seven, so we take turns to bathe her and supervise her homework. This is the main reason. Ideally, we should read to her in English and do the same in Chinese.

This narrative illustrates one of the challenges that parents encounter when raising bilingual children. The authors highlight that educational demands from the public educational system have "coerced" the parents to promote English in the family domain, and that leaves them little time and energy to keep up with the children's home language development.

Within the educational context, language-in-education and space for home language development are not the only competing forces determining parental decisions. The teachers' advice to parents regarding language practices at home, and their expectations of the parental role in the schooling of immigrant children play a key factor in shaping parental language choices and practices at home. Bezçioğlu-Göktolga and Yağmur (2018) studied the impact of Dutch teachers on the FLP of Turkish immigrant parents. By observing 20 families and interviewing 35 parents and five classroom teachers, they found that there is a major mismatch between teachers' perceptions of the parental role in education and parents' beliefs about the language use at home, as illustrated in one of the interviews with a teacher (Bezçioğlu-Göktolga and Yağmur 2018: 227):

> You have to choose one language. I know a Turkish intern, she knew two languages but neither is good. She told me her parents speak only Turkish, so she has to choose between languages. I think if she lives here, she has to choose Dutch.

Although research in recent years shows that bilingualism does not cause confusion and is not the cause of school failure, in this study the Dutch teachers still believe that monolingualism should be the norm. In this regard, parents are influenced by teachers' beliefs and act upon teachers' advice to watch Dutch TV with their children, ask their children to play with Dutch schoolmates, and hire private tutors to support children's language learning in Dutch. The authors suggest that more research into teachers' knowledge of multilingualism and beliefs about bilingual education is needed as it can facilitate immigrant students' educational achievement and language development (Palviainen and Mård-Miettinen 2015; Schwartz 2008).

The studies above show that in order to ensure more positive examples of bilingual development, the public educational system and schools need to provide adequate structures and facilities for heritage language development as well as ideological support for families battling against language shift and loss.

5 Outlook

The last ten years of empirical research has enriched the field of FLP with increased emphasis on seeing each family as a dynamic unit in society. Language decisions made in such a unit are always contextually situated and therefore shaped by the broader context of the society. Accordingly, FLP research must look beyond family confines in order to effectively investigate and interpret the home decisions made by family members. It is evident from our review that internal and external factors are not discrete and independent categories, rather they influence each other, and together they form the ideological underpinnings of FLP.

In this final section of the chapter, we would like to point out, alongside the internal and external factors which we have discussed above, some recently generated new factors that have not been or are only rarely included in the discussion of FLP factors. These new factors are related to recent development of new technology (see Palviainen; Hatoss both this vol.) and the changing social structure resulting from increasing transnational mobility of people, resources, and capital.

An increasingly relevant force affecting FLP, which we would like to highlight in this conclusion, is the digital media. The growing exposure to global satellite broadcasting and easy access to the Internet have enabled immigrants to establish instant contact and affiliation with religious, ethnic, and political practises happening in their countries of origin and other places around the world. The wide distribution of computer-mediated online language learning and teaching, the free access to digital language resources, and the constant connection with peer parents from various settings around the world are all playing increasingly salient roles in parents' decision-making for FLP (Piller and Gerber 2018). For example, in our ongoing research project on British minority communities and FLP, we are observing parents' social media practices and the influence of such practices on their home language use. Being a member of a parent chat group of 200 people on a social media platform where hundreds of messages are daily exchanged can greatly influence a parent's ideas and practices regarding home language use. Moreover, this constant online connection with peer parents involves collective practices with regard to language learning, home language maintenance, and language socialisation. A parent may easily start or reform an FLP under peer influence from such a chat group.

To address this new phenomenon, we would like to call for more attention to the cross-boundary connectedness, to being in a network and to being digitally networked. Perhaps a new term – "Networked FLP" – would be of use for us to further investigate the cross-boundary connectedness and its influence on FLP, such as "how would grandparents' weekly video chats with a grandchild affect the parents' language planning and the child's motivation to learn the home language?"

Secondly, we would like to call for further attention to the term "hybrid urbanism" (Rabinowitz and Monterescu 2008) in research on FLP and FLP factors. This hybrid urban norm of language use reinforces the earlier conceptualisation of FLP as a complex, multilevel process of formulating, interpreting, and appropriating certain plans and practices. We suggest further research on FLP to shed light on this urban complexity and ensuing challenges, particularly in the lives of cosmopolitan families, to investigate how contextualised FLP links to national and regional level political and economic forces, and how such a link is being negotiated, adopted, and reproduced among parents, children, and other family members.

Thirdly, we would like to suggest that further FLP research devotes more attention to how neoliberal language ideology and policy (Piller and Cho 2015) and the commodification of language influence FLP in our discussion of external factors. Under the neoliberal language policy, the commodification of language has resulted in new conceptualisations of individual parents and children, their reasons for language planning and learning, and the ideologies that give meaning to their everyday family routine and language use. Neoliberal language policy inevitably affects parent's FLP decision-making. Questions like "What language(s) will bring my child a financially advantaged future?"; "Is my home language still useful in the global market?"; or "Am I paying too much money and spending too much energy on the maintenance of my home language?" are often heard from parents when they talk about their FLPs. Thus, it will contribute to the field if specific investigations can be conducted with a focus on the impact of neoliberal ideology on FLP.

References

Ahearn, Laura. M. 2001. Language and agency. *Annual Review of Anthropology* 30.109–137.
Baldauf, Richard B. Jr. 2005. Language planning and policy research: An overview. In Eli Hinkel (ed.), *Handbook of research in second language teaching and learning*, 957–970. Mahwah, NJ: Erlbaum.
Bezçioğlu-Göktolga, Irem & Kuylay Yağmur. 2018. Home language policy of second-generation Turkish families in the Netherlands. *Journal of Multilingual and Multicultural Development* 39(1). 44–59.
Blackledge, Adrian & Angela Creese. 2010. *Multilingualism: A critical perspective*. London: Continuum.
Blommaert, Jan. 2008. *Grassroots literacy: Writing, identity and voice in central Africa*. London & New York: Routledge.
Bourdieu, Pierre. 1996. *Distinction. A social critique of the judgement of taste*. London: Routledge.
Curdt-Christiansen, Xiao Lan. 2009. Visible and invisible language planning: Ideological factor in the family language policy of Chinese immigrant families in Quebec. *Language Policy* 8(4). 351–375.
Curdt-Christiansen, Xiao Lan. 2012. Private language management in Singapore: Which language to practice and how? In Alexander S. Yeung, Elinor L. Brown & Cynthia Lee (eds.), *Communication and language*, 55–77. Scottsdale, AZ: Information Age Publishing.
Curdt-Christiansen, Xiao Lan. 2013. Editorial: Family language policy: realities and continuities. *Language Policy* 13(1). 1–7.

Curdt-Christiansen, Xiao Lan. 2014. Family language policy: Is learning Chinese at odds with learning English in Singapore? In Xiao Lan Curdt-Christiansen & Andy Hancock (eds.), *Learning Chinese in diasporic communities: Many pathways to being Chinese*, 35–58. Amsterdam: John Benjamins.

Curdt-Christiansen, Xiao Lan. 2015. Family language policy in the Chinese community in Singapore: A question of balance? In Li Wei (ed.), *Multilingualism in the Chinese diaspora worldwide*, 255–275. Routledge: London.

Curdt-Christiansen, Xiao Lan. 2016. Conflicting language ideologies and contradictory language practices in Singaporean multilingual families. *Journal of Multilingual and Multicultural Development* 37(7). 694–709.

Curdt-Christiansen, Xiao Lan. 2018. Family language policy. In James Tollefson & Miguel Perez-Milans (eds.), *The Oxford handbook of language policy and planning*, 420–441. Oxford: Oxford University Press.

Curdt-Christiansen, Xiao Lan & Francesca LaMorgia. 2018. Managing heritage language development: Opportunities and challenges for Chinese, Italian and Urdu speaking families in the UK. *Multilingua: Journal of Cross-Cultural and Interlanguage Communication* 37(2). 177–210.

Curdt-Christiansen, Xiao Lan & Elizabeth Lanza (eds.). 2018. Special Issue: Multilingual family language management: Efforts, measures and choices. *Multilingua: Journal of Cross-Cultural and Interlanguage Communication* 37 (2).

Curdt-Christiansen, Xiao Lan & Weihong Wang. 2018. Parents as agents of multilingual education: Family language planning in China. *Language, Culture and Curriculum* 31(3). 235–254.

De Angelis, Gessica. 2011. Teachers' beliefs about the role of prior language knowledge in learning and how these influence teaching practices. *International Journal of Multilingualism* 8(3). 216–234.

De Houwer, Annick. 1999. Environmental factors in early bilingual development: The role of parental beliefs and attitudes. In Guus Extra & Ludo Verhoeven (eds.), *Bilingualism and migration*, 75–95. Berlin: Mouton de Gruyter.

De Houwer, Annick. 2009. *Bilingual first language acquisition*. Bristol: Multilingual Matters.

De Houwer, Annick. 2015. Harmonious bilingual development: Young families' well-being in language contact situations. *International Journal of Bilingualism* 19(2). 169–184.

Duranti, Alessandro, Elinor Ochs & Bambi B. Schieffelin (eds.). 2011. *The handbook of language socialization*. Malden: Wiley-Blackwell.

Fishman, Joshua. A. 1972. The relationship between micro- and macro-sociolinguistics in the study of who speaks what language to whom and when. In John B. Pride & Janet Holmes (eds.), *Sociolinguistics: Selected readings*, 15–32. New York: Penguin Books.

Fogle, Lyn Wright. 2012. *Second language socialization and learner agency*. Bristol: Multilingual Matters.

Gafaranga, Joseph. 2010. Medium request: talking language shift into being. *Language in Society* 39(2). 241–270.

Gkaintartzi, Anastasia, Aspasia Chatzidaki & Roula Tsokalidou. 2014. Albanian parents and the Greek educational context: Who is willing to fight for the home language? *International Multilingual Research Journal* 8(4). 291–308.

Gogonas, Nikos & Claudine Kirsch. 2018. "In this country my children are learning two of the most important languages in Europe": Ideologies of language as a commodity among Greek migrant families in Luxembourg. *International Journal of Bilingual Education and Bilingualism* 21(4). 426–438.

Grin, François. 2006. Economic considerations in language policy. In Thomas Ricento (ed.), *An introduction to language policy: Theory and method*, 77–94. Malden: Blackwell.

Hatoss, Anikó. this vol. Transnational grassroots language planning in the era of mobility and the Internet.

Kang, Hyun-Sook. 2015. Korean families in America: Their family language policies and home-language maintenance. *Bilingual Research Journal* 38(3). 275–291.

King, Kendall. 2016. Language policy, multilingual encounters, and transnational families. *Journal of Multilingual and Multicultural Development* 37(7). 726–733.

King, Kendall, Lyn Fogle & Aubrey Logan-Terry. 2008. Family language policy. *Language and Linguistics Compass* 2(5). 907–922.

Kirsch, Claudine. 2012. Ideologies, struggles and contradictions: An account of mothers raising their children bilingually in Luxembourgish and English in Great Britain. *International Journal of Bilingual Education and Bilingualism* 15 (1). 95–112.

Lane, Pia. 2010. We did what we thought was best for our children: A nexus analysis of language shift in a Kven community. *International Journal of Social Language* 202. 63–78.

Lanza, Elizabeth. 2004. *Language mixing in infant bilingualism: A sociolinguistic perspective*. Oxford: Oxford University Press.

Lanza, Elizabeth. 2007. Multilingualism in the family. In Peter Auer & Li Wei (eds.), *Handbook of Multilingualism and Multilingual Communication*, 45–69. Berlin: Walter de Gruyter.

Lanza, Elizabeth & Xiao Lan Curdt-Christiansen (eds.). 2018. Multilingual families: Aspirations and challenges. *International Journal of Multilingualism* 15. 231–232.

Lanza, Elizabeth & Li Wei (eds.). 2016. Special Issue: Multilingual encounters in transcultural families. *Journal of Multilingual and Multicultural Development* 37(7).

Lanza, Elizabeth & Rafael Lomeu Gomes. this vol. Family language policy: Foundations, theoretical perspectives and critical approaches.

Li, Xuemei. 2007. Souls in exile: identities of bilingual writers. *Journal of Language, Identity, and Education* 6(4). 259–275.

Li, Wei. 1994. *Three generations two languages one family*. Clevedon: Multilingual Matters.

Little, Sabine. 2020. Whose heritage? What inheritance?: conceptualising family language identities. *International Journal of Bilingual Education and Bilingualism* 23(2). 198–212.

Macalister, John & Seyed H. Mirvahedi. 2017. *Family language policies in a multilingual world: Opportunities, challenges, and consequences*. London: Taylor & Francis.

Mu, Guanglun M. 2014. Heritage language learning for Chinese Australians: The role of habitus. *Journal of Multilingual and Multicultural Communication* 35(5). 497–510.

Mu, Guanglun M. & Karen Dooley. 2015. Coming into an inheritance: Family support and Chinese heritage language learning. *International Journal of Bilingual Education and Bilingualism* 18(4). 501–515.

Okita, Toshie. 2002. *Invisible work: Bilingualism, language choice and childrearing in intermarried families*. Amsterdam: Benjamins.

Oriyama, Kaya. 2016. Community of practice and family language policy: Maintaining heritage Japanese in Sydney – ten years later. *International Multilingual Research Journal* 10(4). 289–307.

Pavlenko, Aneta. 2004. "Stop doing that, Ia Komu Skazala!": Language choice and emotions in parent–child communication. *Journal of Multilingual and Multicultural Development* 25 (2–3). 179–203.

Pavlenko, Aneta. 2012. Affecting processing in bilingual speakers: Disembodied cognition? *International Journal of Psychology* 47(6). 405–428.

Palviainen, Åsa. this vol. Future prospects and visions for family language policy research.

Palviainen, Åsa & Kartia Mård-Miettinen. 2015. Creating a bilingual pre-school classroom: The multilayered discourses of a bilingual teacher. *Language and Education* 29(5). 381–399.

Pérez Báez, Gabriela. 2013. Family language policy, transnationalism, and the diaspora community of San Lucas Quiaviní of Oaxaca, Mexico. *Language Policy* 12(1). 27–45.

Piller, Ingrid. 2002. Passing for a native speaker: Identity and success in second language learning. *Journal of Sociolinguistics* 6(2). 179–206.

Piller, Ingrid & Jinhyun Cho. 2015. Neoliberalism as language policy. In Thomas Ricento (ed.), *Language policy and political economy: English in a global context*, 162–186. New York: Oxford University Press.

Piller, Ingrid & Livia Gerber. 2018. Family language policy between the bilingual advantage and the monolingual mindset. *International Journal of Bilingual Education and Bilingualism*. Online First. DOI: 10.1080/13670050.2018.1503227

Rabinowitz, Dan & Daniel Monterescu. 2008. Reconfiguring the "mixed town": Urban transformations of ethnonational relations in Palestine and Israel. *International Journal of Middle East Studies* 40. 195–226.

Ren, Li & Guangwei Hu. 2013. Prolepsis, syncretism, and synergy in early language and literacy practices: A case study of family language policy in Singapore. *Language Policy* 12(1). 63–82.

Revis, Melanie. 2019. A Bourdieusian perspective on child agency in family language policy. *International Journal of Bilingual Education and Bilingualism* 22(2). 177–191.

Said, Fatima & Zhu Hua. 2019. "No, no Maama! Say '*Shaatir ya Ouledee Shaatir*'!" Children's agency in language use and socialisation. *International Journal of Bilingualism* 23(3). 771–785.

Schwartz, Mila. 2008. Exploring the relationship between family language policy and heritage language knowledge among second generation Russian–Jewish immigrants in Israel. *Journal of Multilingual and Multicultural Development* 29(5). 400–418.

Sevinç, Yeşim. 2016. Language maintenance and shift under pressure: Three generations of the Turkish immigrant community in the Netherlands. *International Journal of Sociology of Language* 242. 81–117.

Smith-Christmas, Cassie. 2016. *Family language policy: Maintaining an endangered language in the home*. Basingstoke: Palgrave Macmillan.

Smith-Christmas, Cassie. 2018. "One *Cas*, Two *Cas*": Exploring the affective dimensions of family language policy. *Multilingua: Journal of Cross-Cultural and Interlanguage Communication* 37(2). 211–230.

Smith-Christmas, Cassie. this vol. Child agency and home language maintenance.

Spolsky, Bernard. 2004. *Language policy*. Cambridge: Cambridge University Press.

Spolsky, Bernard. 2009. *Language management*. Cambridge: Cambridge University Press.

Spolsky, Bernard. 2012. Family language policy – the critical domain. *Journal of Multilingual and Multicultural Development* 33(1). 3–11.

Tannenbaum, Michal. 2012. Family language policy as a form of coping or defence mechanism. *Journal of Multilingual and Multicultural Development* 33. 57–66.

Tannenbaum, Michal & Marina Berkovich. 2005. Family relations and language maintenance: Implications for language education policies. *Language Policy* 4(3). 287–309.

Tollefson, James & Amy Tsui. 2018. Medium of instruction policy. In James Tollefson & Miguel Perez-Milans (eds.), *The Oxford handbook of language policy and planning*, 257–279. Oxford: Oxford University Press.

Tse, Lucy. 2001. Resisting and reversing language shift: Heritage language resilience among U.S. native biliterates. *Harvard Educational Review* 71(4). 676–706.

Tseng, Amelia. this vol. Identity in home-language maintenance.

Walls, Francesca. 2018. *Transmitting English abroad: Transnational Anglophone parents raising children in Barcelona*. Barcelona: University of Barcelona doctoral thesis.

Wang, Xiaomei. 2017. Family language policy by Hakkas in Balik Pulau, Penang. *International Journal of the Sociology of Language* 244. 87–118.

Wong Fillmore, Lily. 1991. When learning a second language means losing the first. *Early Childhood Research Quarterly* 6. 323–346.

Zhu, Hua 2008. Duelling languages, duelling values. Codeswitching in bilingual intergenerational conflict talk in diasporic families. *Journal of Pragmatics* 40. 1799–1816.

Zhu, Hua & Li Wei. 2016. Transnational experience, aspiration and family language policy. *Journal of Multilingual and Multicultural Development* 37(7). 655–666.

Mila Schwartz
10 Strategies and practices of home language maintenance

> The more we know about micro-level features of the interaction between parent and child and their correlation with the successful acquisition of an otherwise unsupported minority language, the better we can give parents practical advice on factors which they have the power to manipulate.
> (Döpke 1998: 46)

1 Introduction

De Houwer (1999: 75) raised an important sociolinguistic question: "why it is that some children, regularly exposed to two languages from a very young age, actually start to speak and continue to actively use these languages, and why other children, in what are apparently very similar circumstances, do not". This chapter seeks to answer this question, at least to some extent, by zooming in on research on home language strategies and practices, their purpose and meaning for home language maintenance.

Globalization has changed world demographics in recent decades, creating multilingual and multicultural societies, communities, and families. Today, within the context of multilingual societies, no single home language exists in isolation from other community, state, or world languages. In addition, in light of the concept of the home language theorized by the editors in the current volume, this notion will be used as an umbrella concept for terms such as minority language, heritage language, first language, or mother tongue. In addition, this chapter does not profess to provide a broad meta-analysis of the available empirical evidence related to the field of home language strategies and practices but presents an overview of its key theoretical concepts and their empirical support. Thus, studies that have discerned a link between home language strategies and practices and sociolinguistic aspects such as family's socioeconomic status, family type and structure, parental education, and family cultural and ethnic background, are not included in the current analysis. Curdt-Christiansen and Huang (this vol.) provide an overview of these relations.

This chapter is divided into six sections. After this introductory section 1, section 2 presents a brief overview of prominent theoretical frameworks that outline home language strategies and practices. In addition, this section aims to clarify the difference between two primary concepts of the chapter's topic: language strategies and language practices. Section 3 includes a description of the major pioneering contributions to the field of parental discourse strategies and children's bilingual development in early childhood. The chapter continues with section 4, which analyzes some relatively recent studies with focus on distinctive data on home language strategies and practices. The chapter concludes with section 5, which addresses some challenges in current research and recommends directions for future research, and section 6, which summarises the main points presented in this chapter.

2 Theoretical framework

This section briefly addresses the main theoretical concepts that ground the family's role in intergenerational home language transmission, and then raises important distinctions between the chapter's key notions: language strategies and practices. The family is considered an extremely important domain for studying home language strategies and practices because of its critical role in forming children's linguistic environment. Educators are frequently unaware of the family's efforts to maintain the home language while supporting children's acquisition of the societal dominant language. Important questions arise when classroom teachers try to understand children from diverse cultural and linguistic backgrounds. What do home language environments look like and in what ways are languages and literacies in the children's environment supported at home? How do home language practices differ from school experiences? To seek answers to these questions, we need to address the concept of *funds of knowledge*. This concept refers to "historically accumulated and culturally developed bodies of knowledge and skills essential for household or individual functioning and well-being" (Moll et al. 1992: 133). One can view home language strategies and practices as family *funds of knowledge*, i.e., part of the experience and traditions stored and maintained by the family. The chapter will illustrate how home language strategies and practices, as family *funds of knowledge*, influence children's home language acquisition and development in interaction with their wider linguistic environment.

Fishman (1991), an early proponent of proactive language maintenance research, put forward a model for *Reversing Language Shift* through efforts to retain non-mainstream societal languages at family and community levels. According to Fishman (1991), the family acts as a natural boundary, a bulwark against outside pressures. Connection to intimacy and privacy makes the family particularly resistant to outside competition and substitution. In this context, Fishman (1991) identified the most important point of intergenerational language transmission as being use of the home language between family members. This is because the family context is a critical initial stage in children's language socialization and is their closest *language ecology*.[1]

Furthermore, this role of the family was conceptualized within the notion of *family language policy* (hereafter FLP, see Lanza and Lomeu Gomes this vol.).

---

[1] Language ecology has been defined as "the study of interactions between any given language and its environment" (Haugen 1972: 325).

Kopeliovich (2006) and Schwartz (2008) suggested adapting Spolsky's language policy model to the family level. Spolsky (2004) distinguished between three components in the language policy of a speech community: "its language practices – the habitual pattern of selecting among the varieties that make up its linguistic repertoire; its language beliefs or ideology – the beliefs about language and language use; and any specific efforts to modify or influence that practice by any kind of language intervention, planning or management" (Spolsky 2004: 5). Spolsky argued that, as in any other social unit, language policy at the family level may be analyzed with reference to language ideology, practice, and management.

Concerning family language management, Schwartz (2010) defined two main directions: first, internal control of the home language environment at the micro level (e.g., establishing cultural family traditions and rituals associated with home language, strict monitoring of home language strategies and practices); second, seeking external control to maintain the home language by searching for a supporting sociolinguistic environment (e.g., community education setting). In this chapter, the focus is on the first direction of family language management at the micro level of the home environment.

Additionally, recent research on FLP has paved the way to a new concept – *child's language-based agency* (e.g., Fogle 2012; King and Fogle 2013). Child agency in language use refers to the child's actions and linguistic choices performed in a given context or conversation, as a result of the child's identity, culture, social ties, environment, family, and language (Said and Zhu 2019). Accordingly, any discussion on home language maintenance must take the child's language-based agency into account, as it is an essential component of the FLP (e.g., Schwartz 2010; Smith-Christmas this vol.).

Finally, since the primary concepts of this contribution are the notions of "strategies" and "practices", clarifying the differences between these two notions is of high importance to this chapter. Notably, in some cases, scholars who contributed fundamental research on family language s did not make a clear distinction between home language strategies and practices (Okita 2002). Thus, for example, Okita (2002) coined the term "language work" or "invisible work" to denote all the strategies and practices undertaken by mothers in the bilingual rearing of their children. To address this terminological ambiguity, this chapter suggests differentiating between strategy and practice by defining home language strategies as a part of family language management and home language practices as a part of family language practices. This component is characterized by applying certain strategies planned to directly regulating language input, and to control its quality and quantity in a given family context. For example, the strategy of "the maximum engagement principle" is characterized by significantly increasing the minority language input at home through parents' purposeful use of this language between them and directly with the child (see subsection 4.2). At the same time, drawing on Spolsky's definition of language practices (2004), we can address the home language practices as the actual routine use of languages in the family, regardless of the beliefs or management strategies explicitly or implicitly designed by the parents or siblings.

3 Pioneering contributions

This section will begin with the discussion of two important contributions in the field of home language strategies, namely, pioneer studies by Döpke (1988, 1992) and Lanza (1997, 2004). These four studies lead the way in our understanding of genuine interactional processes through which the family realizes, negotiates, and modifies its language policy in daily interaction, and highlight the role of home language strategies. This section will end by addressing a pioneer study of De Houwer (1999), who proposed a distinction between four dimensions that can help conceptualise the use of laguages in bilingual families.

3.1 Parents as minority language teachers

Döpke's (1992) research focused on in-depth analyses of parent–child communication techniques in six mixed German-English-speaking middle-class families in Australia. These families chose the One Parent One Language (OPOL) framework whereby each parent speaks a different language to the child (Döpke 1988, 1992). An advantage of this strategy is that the children learn to associate a specific language with each parent and are, therefore, better able to decide which language to use when addressing each parent. The OPOL strategy invokes principles of language maintenance and is particularly relevant for parents who are striving to maintain their home language in the context of individual bilingualism, where outside societal support is either minimal or nonexistent (Döpke 1988).

Döpke gained the following insights regarding the specific teaching techniques applied by parents whose children were willing to make active use of the home language, German. First, that the quality of input, i.e., creating a language-conducive context[2] – a joyful, playful atmosphere and diverse sources of language input, providing positive feedback, is more important than quantity in parent–child interaction. Second, parents' personalities and their ability to apply various creative language teaching strategies, such as where-is and what-doing questions and elicit verbalization in the home language, are essential to language acquisition. Alongside the playful elements, these parents explicitly asked their children to use the home language, and their joint

---

[2] Recently, Schwartz (2018: 6) defined a language-conducive context as a learning environment that is "rich in multisensory activities with a wide array of semiotic resources" and diverse interactions.

activities were structured and more didactic than in other families. Thus, the parent played the role of language teacher, who applied diverse teaching techniques, e.g., perseverance with vocabulary, rehearsing routines, modeling, and patterning techniques. Finally, the author's analyses revealed that successful intergenerational transmission of the home language is strongly related to the degree of child-centeredness during parent–child interaction that current research discusses in terms of parents' sensitivity to child's language-based agency.

3.2 Parental discourse strategies

Döpke (1998: 49) argued that OPOL, as a language choice framework, "provides a macrostructure, which needs to be realized through micro-structure" strategies of daily parent–child interactions, creating a *continuum between monolingual and bilingual development*. This continuum was investigated and defined by Lanza (1997) in her study of two 2-year-old bilingual English-Norwegian-speaking children in Norway, who were socialized at home within the OPOL framework. Their mothers communicated with the children in English and the fathers used Norwegian. The key research question addressed how parents' reactions expressed in their discourse strategies were related to their children's code-mixing patterns. Lanza identified five types of discourse strategies that parents use to socialize their children into a particular linguistic behavior: *minimal grasp*, *expressed guess*, *repetition*, *move on*, and *code-switch*. Adults use the *minimal grasp strategy* to indicate their lack of comprehension of the children's language choice; in the *expressed guess strategy*, they pose yes/no questions in the other language and accept a simple confirmation as an answer; in the *repetition strategy*, adults repeat the children's utterance in the other language; in the *move-on strategy*, they indicate comprehension and acceptance of the children's language choice so that the conversation continues without any implicit and explicit "disruptions"; finally, adults using *code-switch* either switch over completely to the other language or use intra-sentential change of language. Parents who regularly employed the monolingual strategies – *minimal grasp* or *expressed guess* – to respond to their children's code-mixing, indicated their apparent failure to understand the children's code-mixed utterances. In contrast, parents who employed the bilingual strategies, by providing a translation equivalent or by code-switching, indicated their implicit acceptance of their child's language choice as the suitable communication medium during parent–child interactions.

De Houwer (1999: 79–80) proposed a distinction between four dimensions in the ways two languages (one societal dominant language and one non-societal language, e.g. home language) might be used in familial language practices. The first dimension is whether parents use one or two languages in communication with their child, namely how parents position themselves as monolingual or as bilingual speakers. The second dimension refers to the degree to which parents share a specific societal or non-societal language, namely, if there is a "shared language space" (1999: 79) between the parents or not. The third dimension addresses the question of the minimal amount of input required for language acquisition by the child to occur. Finally, the fourth dimension raises a question of the relative frequency of a particular language use in communication with the child. De Houwer (1999) claimed that each of these dimensions might contribute to explaining whether a home language will be transmitted intergenerationally or not. Further, in a large-scale survey study, De Houwer (2007) showed that in a case where parents share the non-societal language and both of them use this language in communication with their child, there is a greater chance that the child will speak both of their parents' languages, but in a situation where both parents use the societal language alongside the OPOL strategy, a child's chance of growing up actively using both languages is minimal.

In summary, in these ground-breaking studies which are of particular interest to researchers, parents and practitioners, explored parental discourse strategies and configurations of language(s) use at home, in a case where one language was a non-societally dominant language. They concluded that a thorough analysis of the link between discourse strategies and patterns of language use at home would enhance, to some extent, our understanding of children's willingness as well as ability to communicate in the minority language in the future.

4 Recent contributions

During the last 20 years, research has focused on the management of home language strategies and practices in families with immigrant and intermarriage backgrounds and explored the nature of relationships between their home language practices and children's bi/multilingual experiences in both oral and written modalities. Before starting a description of key strategies and practices, the role of parental beliefs in designing the home language strategies and practices will be addressed.

4.1 Parental beliefs and home language strategies and practices

Home language strategies and practices are inevitably related to the family language ideology (Spolsky, 2004). Many immigrant and minority language speaking parents feel strongly about teaching their children the home language as a way of transmitting their values and traditions, strengthening their ethnic identity, and keeping in touch with monolingual relatives (e.g., Kopeliovich 2010; Riches and Curdt-Christiansen 2010; Schwartz 2010). To illustrate, in an 11-year-long ethnographic research project, Kopeliovich (2013), as a parent-researcher, presented her own and her husband's experience of raising a bilingual L1-Russian-L2-Hebrew-speaking family in Israel. She incorporated a new perspective, of parents as language teachers in the bilingual family. Drawing on an ecological approach (Haugen 1972), Kopeliovich coined the notion of the *Happylingual approach* as a manifestation of flexible home language practices. The *Happylingual approach* is an outcome of the longitudinal search for parental strategies of how to bring up truly happy bilingual children.[3] The *Happylingual approach* reveals "the positive emotional coloring of the complex processes related to the heritage language transmission, a special emphasis on the linguistic aspects of childrearing, unbiased attitude to diverse languages that enter the household and respect for the language preferences of the children" (Kopeliovich 2013: 250–251). The study showed that the parents' belief in the *Happylingual approach* towards childhood bilingualism, enhanced by planned and systematic language and literacy activities (e.g., home lessons in the home language, thematic units of study, creative writing projects), resulted in the children's willingness to use the home language. To recap, parents' language beliefs inevitably play a critical role in designing their home language strategies and practices; those in turn play a powerful role in the children's language use at home and in their general linguistic development (De Houwer 1999).

4.2 Home language strategies and practices

Tables 1 and 2 present studies illustrating key strategies and practices that have been identified and described in the literature. Due to space limitations, the number of illustrations of each strategy and practice was restricted to two. In addition to data novelty criteria, to give a more comprehensive and authoritative picture of recent research on home language strategies and practices, the inclusion criteria were diversity of socio-linguistic and geographic contexts, and the research methodology used.

4.2.1 Home language strategies

As mentioned above, home language strategies refer to family language management. The following main strategies have been addressed below: OPOL, diverse discourse strategies (minimal grasp, expressed guess, repetition, move on, and code-switch), maximal engagement with the minority language, and design of home language environment. A selected number of studies using these strategies are listed and described in Table 1.

---

[3] Negative emotions in home language maintenance, manifested by children/adolescents whose parents adopt a very strict family language policy and expect high levels of proficiency, are discussed by Sevinç (this vol.).

Table 1: Selected studies on home language strategies.

Strategy	Study	Context	Annotations
OPOL	Okita (2002)	Okita (2002) conducted a two-stage approach to data collection: (1) investigating the distinctive features of the target community (Japanese-British intermarried families in the UK) in a general sense through an exploratory survey; (2) providing in-depth, qualitative insight into family language policy and childrearing, using the life story method in separate, semi-structured interviews of mothers and fathers.	The book introduces a concept of "invisible work" and includes the term "pro-activist mothers" who are highly motivated to transfer Japanese to their children within the OPOL strategy of language management at home. These mothers reported having difficulty in coping with conflicting language demands, especially when they felt personally responsibility for their children's perceived limitations in English because of the Japanese language maintenance. Another outcome of active Japanese nurturing has been discouraging their English-speaking partners from actively participating in childrearing. Okita discusses the emotional demands involved in raising bilingual children in intermarried families.
	Doyle (2013)	Doyle focused on 11 intermarried families living in Tallinn, Estonia, which follow OPOL principles. Through semi-structured interviews the family members, including 18 children ranging in age from 10;9 to 21 years old, discussed the formation and application of home language ideology, management and practices.	The analysis of interviews with parents and adolescent children showed that 10 of the intermarried families in this study have been successful in raising at least one adolescent child with productive competence in both Estonian and the non-Estonian languages, while concurrently maintaining a harmonious environment in the family. This success was attributed by the participants, in part, to *move on* and *code-switching* home language strategies and an avoidance of overwhelming children with overambitious goal of bilingualism to develop a *"super linguist"*. Doyle argued for the need to take a long-term perspective when investigating changes over the course of childhood and to be attentive to adolescents' reflections on their bilingual competence and family language management.

(continued)

Table 1 (continued)

Strategy	Study	Context	Annotations
Diverse discourse strategies: (minimal grasp, expressed guess, repetition, move on, and code-switch)	Juan-Garau and Pérez-Vidal (2001)	This longitudinal case study focused on a Catalan-English bilingual boy from 1;3 to 4;2 years of age. The child was brought up in Barcelona, Catalonia, by his English-speaking father and Catalan-speaking mother who applied the OPOL principle. Data were collected by means of audio-recordings, note-taking, video-recordings and parental diary keeping.	The study showed that parental strategies varied significantly with changes in the child's sociolinguistic environments and with his growing up and linguistic development. In line with Lanza's data (1997), strategies such as *minimal grasp* and *expressed guess*, played a critical role in the child's development of productive bilingualism. The authors argued that simply following to the OPOL principle by the minority language-speaking parent would not have been sufficient to achieve productive minority language use if the parent had not insisted on getting responses in the target language from the child.
	Curdt-Christiansen (2013)	Ethnographic observations of three mothers' discourse strategies with their school age children during their help with the children's routine homework in bilingual English–Chinese families in multilingual Singapore.	The following three types of parental discourse strategies were observed: (1) highly organized family language policy, with regular monitoring of children's bilingual development and adherence to Chinese as a "threatened" language; (2) unreflective parental adaptation, which is characterized by a *move on* strategy (Lanza 1997) signifying acknowledgement of code-mixing policy, and (3) total laissez-faire policy, which permits code-mixing practice in mother–child interaction. The different linguistic strategies used by the mothers reflected their varied language ideologies, moving from a strong tendency towards balanced bilingualism in Chinese and English to the "English only" attitude signalling a strong conviction for the benefits of using English.

Maximal engagement with the minority language	Yamamoto (2001)	Survey regarding how languages are used in 188 inter-lingual families in Japan using Japanese as a majority language and English as a minority language.	Yamamoto (2001) shows how the majority-language speaking parents' support for bilingual childrearing can also be expressed through their use of the minority language with their spouses and children. The study points out that if the linguistic environment of the child is characterized by the principle of *maximal engagement with the minority language*, the child receives not only more input in the minority language, but also an implicit message from the parents that the minority language is supposed to be the means of communication in the family. It should be noted that this conclusion is contrary to the advice of the OPOL strategy.
	Venables, Eisenchlas, and Schalley (2014)	This case study focused on three bilingual families with the minority language being either French or Spanish, in Brisbane, Australia, who reported applying the OPOL principle. To collect data on the home language strategies and practices, video and audio recordings of natural and spontaneous interactions were taken, along with interviews using an elicited recall task based on the recordings.	In line with the principle of *maximum engagement with the minority language*, the majority language-speaking parents played a significant role in fostering minority language development and maintenance. Diverse home language strategies were used by the majority language-speaking parents to facilitate the minority language-speaking parents' interactions with children and to provide affective support for the minority language at home, e.g., providing contextual clues to help with comprehension of utterance in the minority language.

(continued)

Table 1 (continued)

Strategy	Study	Context	Annotations
Design of home language environment	Riches and Curdt-Christiansen (2010)	Riches and Curdt-Christiansen focused on 13 anglophone families and 10 Chinese immigrant families in multilingual Montreal to compare the children's bilingual (in English and French), and multilingual development in the case of the anglophone community, and their multilingual development (in Chinese, French, and English) in the Chinese community. This ethnographic study documented an important observation of family efforts to create a home language environment in a multilingual context in a situation where some of the immigrant parents in the Chinese community had only limited proficiency in English and French.	Riches and Curdt-Christiansen found that in both types of families, the home language and literacy environment reflected Montreal's multilingual nature, including visible reading materials for children in all contextual languages. In addition, to promote the children's literacy in French, the Chinese parents not only hired tutors to help their children learn French as an external support strategy, but some even took French classes to help their children, assisting them with their French homework with the help of a dictionary.
	Little (2018)	This is one of the few studies investigating the use of games-based digital technology as a part of home language environment for language development. The data were drawn from 212 web-based questionnaires with more than 40 different languages spoken among the responding families and 10 in-depth interviews with heritage language families in the UK. In seven interviews, children were present and offered their own views.	Concerning the design of the home language environment, overall, 25% of families responded that they used technology-based games or apps to support home language development. In the majority of these families, the use of technology co-existed with book reading, providing additional sources of children's exposure to the home language. Interestingly, in their interviews most parents did not view a use of online materials as shared home language practices but rather as technology-enhanced language resources that motivated children to learn language, often independently of the parents.

The following paragraphs will briefly discuss the above presented strategies.[4]

As noted above, OPOL refers to long-term home language management strategies, where in inter-lingual families, parents clearly assert in advance which parent will speak which of the family's languages in a consistent manner. As in the studies by Döpke (1988) and Lanza (1997) addressed above, in most cases, one parent speaks the societal dominant or majority language while the other speaks the non-societal or minority language. Despite the popularity of this strategy, research shows that this approach cannot guarantee successful inter-generational language transmission in a case of minority language because, in many situations, the parents declaring to follow OPOL strategy do not in fact implement it very consistently (De Houwer 2007; Yamamoto 2001). Thus, it appears that parents who are supposed to use a minority language in communication with children often switch to their non-designated language.

Maximal engagement with the minority language: Yamamoto (2001:128) has proposed the "principle of maximal engagement with the minority language" claiming a necessity of more input in the minority language in the context of inter-lingual families: "the more engagement the child has with the minority language, the greater her or his likelihood of using it". Further, De Houwer (2011: 227) stressed that the maximum engagement principle "may create much more of an environment conducive to using that minority language" in particular in a case when parents tend to use the minority language amongst themselves.

Design of home language environment: One of the parental strategies aimed at adding to a quality of the home language input involves designing of the home language environment through practices such as joint book reading in a joyful atmosphere (see also above description of Döpke's findings), and the use of devices (e.g., storybooks, educational literacy-based games, computer games, and educational TV programs), which promote bilingual development. Family managing of such language practices, such as joint parent–child book reading, are particularly important, since they arise children's interest in language, develop meta-linguistic awareness, and provide them with family *funds of knowledge*. In addition, the concept of joint parent–child book reading encompasses a socioemotional aspect of parent–child interactions and time spent together, which has an inevitable impact on the child's emotional development as well as on cognitive and linguistic development (de la Piedra 2011).

---

[4] Note that the diverse discourse strategies were defined above (see sub-section 3.2 "Parental discourse strategies").

4.2.2 Home language practices

As defined above, home language practices refer to routines and traditions in actual language use at home in interaction between family members. The following main practices have been examined in the literature: goal directed code-mixing, flexible language use, ritual language use, and reciprocal bidirectional learning. These practices could be strategic, such as ritual book reading, as well as spontaneous and routine, such as faith practices "embedded in meaningful contexts" of daily interactions (Reyes and Azuara 2008: 392). Apart of the maintenance and enrichment of the home language as a desirable outcome, these practices scaffold children's bilingual development in both oral and written modalities by developing metalinguistic awareness through inducing children to compare the prominent characteristics of their languages and notice different aspects of oral language (phonemes, morphemes) and print (e.g., Reyes 2006; Schwarzer 2001). Representative studies using these practices are listed and described in Table 2.

In the following paragraphs, the above presented home language practices will be outlined.

Goal-directed code-switching: Parents who usually adhere to use one language at home, e.g., home language in immigrant families, or who generally stick to the OPOL strategy in the context of inter-lingual families, might sometimes code-switch and use mixed utterances in communication with children due to a specific pragmatic goal. By crossing the language boundaries (Baker 2000) from time to time, the parents create an effect of unexpectedness and even confusion, thereby eliciting the child's attention. Although this code-switching practice occurs infrequently, it happens in salient situations and therefore indicates a new and authoritative model of home language use.

Flexible language use and translanguaging at home: the Happylingual approach towards childhood bilingualism/multilingualism means that parental management of flexible language practices assumes a positive emotional coloring of home language activities and an "unbiased attitude to diverse languages that enter the household and respect for the language preferences of the children" (Kopeliovich 2013: 251). This approach reflects on translingual practices that have recently been researched within a framework of family language practices (e.g., Alvarez 2014; Lindquist and Gram Garmann 2019). Translingual practices take place in "translingual spaces" (Li 2018: 23), where "different languages are brought together", and where speakers use linguistic resources from all the languages they know for meaning-making (García and Li 2014). A more detailed discussion of translanguaging is presented by Paulsrud (this vol.).

Ritual language practices: Family language management involves controlling the home language environment by establishing family cultural traditions and rituals strongly associated with home language(s) (Schwartz 2010). Ritual language practices are frequently observed during inter-generational learning where grandparents and

Table 2: Summary of major studies on home language practices.

Practice	Study	Context	Annotations
Goal-directed code-switching	Goodz (1989)	Goodz's study of four 1st-born children aged 14, 21, 22 and 28 months (at the beginning of the study) and their parents, one of whom spoke French and the other English as a native language in Canada. The families applied the OPOL principle. Naturally occurring children's interactions with each parent were recorded for a period of 19 to 36 months.	The study questioned the main principle of the OPOL strategy, namely, parent's adhering to one language. Goodz found that parents use to switch to their non-designated language to attract children's attention, to discipline them or to stress parental intentions. This practice served as a behavioral model for children who understood that code-switching in a single utterance is acceptable.
	Schwartz, Moin, and Leikin (2011)	Schwartz et al. addressed the question of how eight immigrant Russian-speaking parents in Israel describe and explain their home language strategies and practices. The study was based on semi-structured interviews with each parent separately.	Parents reported use of goal-directed code-mixing and shifting from Russian to Hebrew as an important strategy in their interaction with their child. They used code-switching as a powerful tool to achieve such childrearing objectives as discipline and emphasis on specific task/demand as well as for linguistic enrichment.

(continued)

Table 2 (continued)

Practice	Study	Context	Annotations
Flexible language use and translanguaging at home	Alvarez (2014)	Alvarez investigated the language-brokering[5] practices of the volunteering mentors who were involved with homework at the Mexican American Network of Students after-school homework assistance program as translanguaging events. The data were collected during six yearlong ethnographic observations and included field notes, video and audio recordings, and photographs.	Alvarez's empirically rich project on the language-brokering practices during mentoring of homework provided evidence for how language-brokering and translanguaging events assists Spanish-speaking immigrant mothers in helping their children with homework. The mentors modelling of the translanguaging practices encouraged children to try the role of language brokers by themselves in their communication with less competence in L2 mothers.
	Lindquist and Gram Garmann, (2019)	Lindquist and Gram Garmann examined the home language strategies and practices in communication with toddlers in multilingual families in Norway. Data were obtained from parentally administered video recordings of everyday family communications during the toddlers' first year in a Norwegian-speaking preschool setting and three interviews with each couple of parents during the research year.	Lindquist and Gram Garmann demonstrated the concept of translingual practices into contact with language use with toddlers in multilingual families. All three cases illustrated that the multilingual families used their translingual space, and some of the varieties of translingual practices, as a natural part of everyday interactions between toddlers, parents, and siblings. Although the families differed in terms of their home language ideology and management, the parents let their toddlers make their own choices regarding language use, and in the translingual space the toddlers' agency influenced which language was spoken.

---

5 Language brokering is the sociolinguistic practice of bilingual children who function as significant language mediators in the negotiating of family members' understanding of L2 by translating in diverse social institutions, such as hospitals and stores within an immigrant context (Orellana 2010).

Ritual language practices	De la Piedra (2011)	Focus on transnational literacy practices that were conducted ritually together by mothers and daughters in Mexican-origin transnational families living between the border of the United States and Mexico. The data were collected through individual interviews in a conversational format with the 11 low-income transnational mothers.	De la Piedra found that ritual reading together in Spanish, called *Leer juntas*, as a home practice, was an activity that transnational mothers frequently performed on both sides of the border. In addition to intergenerational language transmission of the Spanish language, *Leer juntas* helped maintain close relationships between mothers and daughters and contributed to family unity. Since this literacy practice was conducted also by relatives across the border, it was a transnational digital literacy practice that allowed the mothers and daughters, together, to connect with relatives in Mexico across time and space.
	Kopeliovich (2013)	Kopeliovich presented a twelve-year-long action research of FLP based on her own experience as a parent-researcher raising a Russian-Hebrew bilingual family in Israel.	In this empirically rich longitudinal study, Kopeliovich showed how through daily ritual exposure to literature in home languages, Russian and Hebrew, children became fascinated by bilingual humour based on Hebrew-Russian word puns, linguistic games, rhymes, intermingling the two languages in joyful play. These ritual practices were a part of the *Happylingual approach* towards childhood bilingualism and facilitated creating a positive emotional attitude towards languages in their environment among children.

(continued)

Table 2 (continued)

Practice	Study	Context	Annotations
Reciprocal bidirectional learning	Kenner et al. (2004)	Kenner et al. (2004) conducted a large-scale project exploring transmission of funds of knowledge between generations in Sylheti/Bengali-speaking families of Bangladeshi origin in East London.	The project showed that the grandparent–grandchild interactions were diverse and bidirectional, ranging from storytelling in Bengali to computer activities in English. Grandparents often placed a hand over their grandchildren to demonstrate an action physically, and children sometimes guided their grandparents in a similar way, by directing their grandparents' hand while moving the computer mouse.
	Reyes (2006)	Reyes (2006) conducted a longitudinal ethnographic study exploring language and emergent literacy practices at home and at bilingual preschool among three four-year-old children of first-generation Mexican Spanish-speaking families living in Arizona. The data were gathered through observations of family members' interactions, field notes, collection of 'writing' samples, and informal conversations with children and their parents.	Reyes (2006) revealed that, through participating in diverse language and literacy practices, family members supported not only the child but also each other in biliteracy development. This role was defined by Reyes as bidirectional. Thus, parents and older siblings served as experts and scaffolded Spanish (L1) print knowledge, yet they became novice learners when they carried out English (L2) practices together.

children share daily religious activities, telling stories, reading stories and poems in a home language as in a case of traditional reading and reciting Bengali poetry in Bengali-speaking families in London. This day-to-day routine supported by grandparents give children a sense of security and self-esteem as home language speakers (Kenner et al. 2004).

Bidirectional reciprocal learning: Of importance to our understanding of home language practices is the concept of *bidirectional learning*. Recent research shows that in immigrant families, home language support might be bidirectional, that is, parents and grandparents serve as experts, scaffolding the knowledge of home language and print, but become novice learners of the society's dominant language when performing language and literacy practices together with their children and grandchildren (e.g., Kenner et al. 2004; Reyes 2006). In addition, *bidirectional reciprocal learning* was observed in interaction between siblings whenever both siblings teach and learn from each other.

To summarize, the studies discussed above show that home language strategies and practices are a result of the FLP with proactive bilingual management rooted in the ecological perspective. This management could be strategic, such as planned language activities initiated by family members, as well as spontaneous and routine, such as faith practices "embedded in meaningful contexts" of daily interactions (Reyes and Azuara 2008: 392). Children's exposure to the concept of print in different languages at home helps them to develop hypotheses about scripts around them, and as a result, their cross-linguistic awareness. The interactions with parents, siblings, and grandparents during ritual language and literacy activities are characterized by their bidirectional nature, a mutual exchange of family funds of knowledge, modeling, and synergies.

5 Evaluation of the current research landscape and future research directions

This final section of the chapter raises some critical points about the study of strategies and practices of home language maintenance and addresses future directions for research. Attention will be drawn to three problematic issues in the empirical study of home language strategies and practices which require proper attention in future research. First, in most cases, ethnographic observation of the home language strategies and practices has focused on family members' interaction with preschool or elementary school children within a relatively brief period in their life that does not extend beyond one year. Today, almost nothing is known about the long-term impact of home language management on children's linguistic, cognitive, social, and emotional development in general, and their bilingual development in particular. Although there is no question that additional factors, besides parental language use, play a role in intergenerational language transmission, there is still very limited data about how successful strategies and practices are for intergenerational home language transmission. We do not yet know the optimal proportions of minority and majority language use at home, in order to provide the necessary conditions for children to speak both languages in their future (De Houwer 2007). Do both parents need to support the minority language use by increasing its input, to apply the "principle of maximal engagement with the minority language" (Yamamoto, 2001), or should they stick strongly to the OPOL strategy as has been advised by practitioners for years? Drawing on De Houwer's and Yamamoto's data, it appears that both parents' aspiration to provide maximal input in non-societal language sets the ground for the child's productive command of both languages in the future. Still, the strategy of "maximal engagement" contradicts a flexible language use (*move on* and *code-switching* strategies). Today, however, to the best of the author's knowledge, there is little, if any, research on how these contradictory strategies impact on children's language development in the long run. This void leaves us with many open questions relating to the actual long-term effects of the discussed strategies, on the changes a child undergoes in the transition from childhood to adolescence, as well as the influence they may have on their bilingual competence and family language management in their future. In addition, few studies to date have addressed the question of how home language strategies and practices change over time when children grow older. Finally, some scholars have made a connection between family cultural values and home language strategies and practices (e.g., Riches and Curdt-Christiansen 2010), which may, to a large extent, affect the developmental domains as well.

The second important issue in research on home language strategies and practices is the incorporation of children's and adolescents' perspectives in the studies, alongside parental data. Few studies to date have addressed these potential participants' reflections on home language strategies and practices (e.g., Juvonen et al. this vol.; Fogle 2013; Kopeliovich 2006). Using the children's and adolescents' reports on home language strategies and practices could considerably strengthen the validity of data collected through observations of home language and literacy activities. While considering the strengths and limitations of addressing the children's reflections on home language strategies and practices, Schwartz (2010) emphasized that "we should take into account that (a) even if we cannot assume that the children's views are fully reflected in what they say, they are not likely to try to please the researcher by providing expected answers during the interviews (i.e., the halo effect), and (b) the children's language ideology seems to be affected considerably both by parental language ideology and by the actual implementation of the language policy at home" (Schwartz 2010: 186). Listening to the children's voices could provide us with understanding of a novel concept of child's language-based agency and agentic behavior in the process of language learning. As for the adolescents' retrospective reflections on their family language management, they may shed light on the longitudinal effect of the home language strategies and practices and their modifications over time (see Fogle 2013).

The third point addresses the methodological challenges in the study of home language strategies and practices. Even though research into home language strategies and practices has grown exponentially over the last two decades, it has primarily resorted to the use of qualitative data collection instruments (see also Juvonen et al. this vol.). How can such overwhelming use of the qualitative methodology be explained? First, the diversity and heterogeneity of the family's background characteristics limits our ability to construct a large homogeneous sample for study. Therefore, researchers have difficulty applying quantitative data collection methods such as standardized tests for children and parental questionnaires, to perform statistical analysis revealing the magnitude of the impact of the home language strategies and practices on children's bilingual development. Second, the use of qualitative analysis might permit detailed observations of both the form and content of verbal interaction (e.g., scaffolding questions, reading mediation, praise) and nonverbal interactions (e.g., affectionate touch, gestures, smiling) between family members and their patterns of language and literacy activities (Gregory 1998). Nonetheless, we can find promise in current efforts to apply quantitative methods (e.g., Minkov 2019) and mixed methods data analysis. As noted by Mackey and Gass (2005), in qualitative research, quantification permits a more precise examination of phenomenon occurrence and facilitates the subsequent drawing of inferences. Frequency analysis of the observed home language strategies and practices may pinpoint the strategies and practices regularly used by family members versus those that are rarely used. As a result, we may obtain a deeper understanding of the rationale behind the observed home language and literacy interactions.

As a final point, in an era of globalization, an important question for future research is how home language management navigates between conflicting expectations and demands concerning multiple languages in the family environment. More specifically, the question is how family expectations to bring up children as global citizens through their exposure to English in non-English speaking countries, for instance, are negotiated with the emotional aspects of home language maintenance or loss. Such a case of societal bilingualism exists in Malta, where Maltese and English are the official languages. The picture may be complicated in cases where the home language is either a local dialect or a regional language endangered by the society's dominant language. This is the case in China, where Putonghua is a standard common language, English is a global language, and the local dialects are gradually disappearing.

Another issue resulting from globalization is a growing number of the transnational families. Transnationalism as the "phenomenon of living locally with global connection" (Sarroub 2009: 64) created the novel concept of transnational literacies that are utilized by families living across borders and are defined as "the written language practices of people who are involved in activities that span national boundaries"

(Jiménez, Smith, and Teague 2009: 17). Recent research shows that these new types of home language practices develop due to the use of technology (see Little; Hatoss; Palviainen, all this vol.). In this case, the availability of multimodal communication technologies seems to significantly modify the ways in which traditionally family members use languages in communication with each other.

6 Summary of the main points

Research on home language strategies and practices is grounded within diverse theoretical perspectives, such as *funds of knowledge*, Fishman's *Reversing language Shift* model, *language ecology,* Sposky's *FLP* model and the Kopeliovich's *Happylingual approach* towards home language management. The chapter explored the concept of the family language management at the micro level of the home environment and suggested a clear-cut distinction between two central notions: home language strategies and practices. The chapter analysed how current research rooted in pioneering studies of Döpke (1988, 1992), Lanza (1997, 2004) and De Houwer (1999), questions such traditional strategies as OPOL via a more flexible and pragmatic use of language at home and claims for taking into consideration a child's language-based agency and agentic behavior in the home language management. With regards to methodology, although the analysed research on home language maintenance employs diverse methodologies, linguistic ethnography is the leading approach to the study of strategies and practices as it allows observing them in a naturalistic home environment. Concerning the pedagogical implication of the overviewed data, it seems undisputable that in order to understand children's cognitive, linguistic and emotional language development, teachers, speech and language therapists, as well as policy makers, need to explore the strategies and practices that parents use at home to support their children's home language maintenance.

References

Alvarez, Steven. 2014. Translanguaging tareas: Emergent bilingual youth as language brokers for homework in immigrant families. *Language Arts* 91. 326–339.
Baker, Colin. 2000. *The care and education of young bilinguals*. Clevedon: Multilingual Matters.
Curdt-Christiansen, Xiao Lan. 2013. Negotiating family language policy: Doing homework. In Mila Schwartz & Anna Verschik (eds.), *Successful family language policy*, 277–295. New York & London: Springer.
Curdt-Christiansen, Xiao Lan & Jing Huang. this vol. Factors influencing family language policy.
De Houwer, Annick. 1999. Environmental factors in early bilingual development: The role of parental beliefs and attitudes. In Guus Extra & Ludo Verhoeven (eds.), *Bilingualism and migration*, 75–95. Berlin: Mouton de Gruyter.

De Houwer, Annick. 2007. Parental language input patterns and children's bilingual use. *Applied Psycholinguistics* 28. 411–424.

De Houwer, Annick. 2011. Language input environments and language development in bilingual acquisition. *Applied Linguistics Review* 2. 221–240.

Doyle, Colm. 2013. To make the root stronger: Language policies and experiences of successful multilingual intermarried families with adolescent children in Tallinn. In Mila Schwartz & Anna Verschik (eds.), *Successful family language policy*, 145–175. New York & London: Springer.

Döpke, Susanne. 1988. The role of parental teaching techniques in bilingual German–English families. *International Journal of the Sociology of Language* 72. 101–112.

Döpke, Susanne. 1992. *One parent one language: An interactional approach*. Amsterdam and Philadelphia, PA: John Benjamins.

Döpke, Susanne. 1998. Can the principle of 'one person – one language' be disregarded as unrealistically elitist? *Australian Review of Applied Linguistics* 21(1). 41–56.

Fishman, Joshua A. 1991. *Reversing language shift: Theoretical and empirical foundations of assistance to threatened languages*. Clevedon: Multilingual Matters.

Fogle, Lyn. 2012. *Second language socialization and learner agency: Adoptive family talk*. Bristol: Multilingual Matters.

Fogle, Lyn. 2013. Family language policy from the children's point of view: Bilingualism in place and time. In Mila Schwartz & Anna Verschik (eds.), *Successful family language policy*, 177–200. New York & London: Springer.

García, Ofelia & Li Wei. 2014. *Translanguaging: Language, bilingualism and education*. Houndmills: Palgrave Macmillan.

Goodz, Naomi. 1989. Parental language mixing in bilingual families. *Journal of Infant Mental Health* 10. 25–44.

Gregory, Eve. 1998. Siblings as mediators of literacy in linguistic minority communities. *Language and Education* 1(12). 33–55.

Hatoss, Anikó. this vol. Transnational grassroots language planning in the era of mobility and the Internet.

Haugen, Einar. 1972. *The ecology of language*. Stanford, California: Stanford University Press.

Jiménez, Robert T., Patrick H. Smith & Brad L. Teague. 2009. Transnational and community literacies. *Journal of Adolescent and Adult Literacy* 53(1). 16–26.

Juan-Garau, María & Carmen Pérez-Vidal. 2001. Mixing and pragmatic parental strategies in early bilingual acquisition. *Journal of Child Language* 28. 59–86.

Juvonen, Päivi, Susana A. Eisenchlas, Tim Roberts, & Andrea C. Schalley. this vol. Researching social and affective factors in home language maintenance: A methodology overview.

Kenner, Charmian, Eve Gregory, John Jessel, Mahera Ruby & Tahera Arju. 2004. *Intergenerational learning between children and grandparents in East London*. Project Report. ESRC, Swindon: Goldsmiths Research Online.

King, Kendall A. & Lyn Fogle. 2013. Family language policy and bilingual parenting. *Language Teaching* 46(2). 172–194.

Kopeliovich, Shulamit. 2006. *Reversing language shift in the immigrant family: A case-study of a Russian speaking community in Israel*. Ramat-Gan: Bar-Ilan University PhD thesis.

Kopeliovich, Shulamit. 2010. Family language policy: From a case study of a Russian-Hebrew bilingual family towards a theoretical framework. *Diaspora, Indigenous, and Minority Education* 4(3). 162–178.

Kopeliovich, Shulamit. 2013. Happylingual: A family project for enhancing and balancing multilingual development. In Mila Schwartz & Anna Verschik (eds.), *Successful Family Language Policy*, 249–276. New York & London: Springer.

Lanza, Elizabeth. 1997. Language contact in bilingual two-year-olds and code-switching: Language encounters of a different kind? *The International Journal of Bilingualism* 1(2). 135–162.

Lanza, Elizabeth. 2004. *Language mixing in infant bilingualism: A sociolinguistic perspective.* Oxford: Oxford University Press.

Lanza, Elizabeth & Rafael Lomeu Gomes. this vol. Family language policy: Foundations, theoretical perspectives and critical approaches.

Lindquist, Hein & Nina Gram Garmann. 2019. Toddlers and their translingual practicing homes. *International Journal of Multilingualism.* Online First. DOI: 10.1080/14790718.2019.1604712.

Little, Sabine. 2018. "Is there an app for that?" Exploring games and apps among heritage language families. *Journal of Multilingual and Multicultural Development* 40(3). 218–229.

Little, Sabine. this vol. Social media and the use of technology in home language maintenance.

Li, Wei. 2018. Translanguaging as a practical theory of language. *Applied Linguistics* 31(1). 9–30.

Mackey, Alison & Susan M. Gass. 2005. *Second language research: Methodology and design.* Mahwah, NJ: Lawrence Erlbaum.

Minkov, Miriam. 2019. *Early literacy development in immigrant families: How bilingual ideology, management and practice predict children's early literacy.* Tel-Aviv: Tel-Aviv University PhD thesis.

Moll, Luis C., Cathy Amanti, Deborah Neff & Norma González. 1992. Funds of knowledge for teaching: A qualitative approach to developing strategic connections between homes and classrooms. *Theory into Practice* 31. 132–141.

Okita, Toshie. 2002. *Invisible work: Bilingualism, language choice and childrearing in intermarried families.* Amsterdam: John Benjamins.

Orellana, Marjorie Faulstich. 2010. From here to there: On the progress of ethnography of language brokering. *mediAzioni. Rivista online di studi interdisciplinari su lingue e culture* 10. http://mediazioni.sitlec.unibo.it (accessed 28 January 2020).

Palviainen, Åsa. this vol. Future prospects and visions for family language policy research.

Paulsrud, BethAnne. this vol. The mainstream classroom and home language maintenance.

Piedra, María Teresa de la. 2011. "Tanto necesitamos de aquí como necesitamos de allá": Leer juntas among Mexican transnational mothers and daughters. *Language and Education* 25(1). 65–72.

Reyes, Illiana. 2006. Exploring connections between emergent biliteracy and bilingualism. *Journal of Early Childhood Literacy* 6. 267–292.

Reyes, Illiana, & Patricia Azuara. 2008. Emergent biliteracy in young Mexican immigrant children. *Reading Research Quarterly* 43(4). 374–398.

Riches, Caroline & Xiao Lan Curdt-Christiansen. 2010. A tale of two Montreal communities: Parents' perspectives on their children's language and literacy development in a multilingual context. *The Canadian Modern Language Review* 66(4). 525–555.

Said, Fatma & Zhu Hua. 2019. "No, no Maama! Say 'Shaatir ya Ouledee Shaatir'!" Children's agency in language use and socialisation. *International Journal of Bilingualism* 23(3). 771–785.

Sarroub, Loukia K. 2009. Glocalism in literacy and marriage in transnational lives. *Critical Inquiry in Language Studies* 6(1–2). 63–80.

Schwartz, Mila. 2008. Exploring the relationship between family language policy and heritage language knowledge among second generation Russian-Jewish immigrants in Israel. *Journal of Multilingual and Multicultural Development* 29(5). 400–418.

Schwartz, Mila. 2010. Family language policy: Core issues of an emerging field. *Applied Linguistics Review* 1(1). 171–192.

Schwartz, Mila. 2018. Preschool bilingual education: Agency in interactions between children, teachers, and parents. In Mila Schwartz (ed.), *Preschool bilingual education: Agency in interactions between children, teachers, and parents*, 1–24. Dordrecht: Springer.

Schwartz, Mila, Viktor Moin & Mark Leikin. 2011. Parents' discourses about language strategies for the child's preschool bilingual development. *Diaspora, Indigenous, and Minority Education: An International Journal 5*. 149–166.

Schwarzer, David. 2001. *Noah'sArk: One child's voyage into multiliteracy*. Portsmouth, NH: Heinemann.

Sevinç, Yeşim. this vol. Anxiety as a negative emotion in home language maintenance and development.

Smith-Christmas, Cassie. this vol. Child agency and home language maintenance.

Spolsky, Bernard. 2004. *Language Policy*. Cambridge: Cambridge University Press.

Venables, Elizabeth, Susana A. Eisenchlas & Andrea C. Schalley. 2014. One-parent-one-language (OPOL) families: Is the majority language-speaking parent instrumental in the minority language development? *International Journal of Bilingual Education and Bilingualism* 17(4). 429–448.

Yamamoto, Masayo. 2001. *Language use in interlingual families: A Japanese – English sociolinguistic study*. Clevedon: Multilingual Matters.

Cassie Smith-Christmas
11 Child agency and home language maintenance

1 Introduction

This chapter discusses child agency and its role in home language maintenance. The concept of child agency has been orbiting "Family Language Policy" "FLP" (King, Fogle, and Logan-Terry 2008; Lanza and Lomeu Gomes this vol.) for some time now. In the first introduction of the term "Family Language Policy" as such, Luykx (2003: 41) emphasises that "in the 'language ecology' of the family, children are agents as much as objects. For this reason, socialization should be viewed in terms of 'participation' rather than merely 'transmission'." Similarly, Tuominen (1999: 71) characterises her findings of multilingual families in the US as suggesting "that children in multilingual families not only 'test' their parents but often 'run the show'." The import of child agency is also reflected in caregivers' comments, often as a rationalisation for undesirable outcomes, such as language shift (e.g. Kulick 1992; Kroskrity 2009) or use of swearwords (Coetzee 2018). Yet, as Fogle and King (2013) rightly point out, the concept of child agency has not gained much traction in FLP research until recently. Exactly *what* agency means and *how* it operates remain much-debated questions among some of social sciences' most prominent figures (e.g. Giddens 1979; Taylor 1985; Bourdieu 1997, to name just a few). Emergent through these discussions is "agency" on the one hand and "structures" on the other, yet crucially, an emphasis on the highly reflexive relationship between the two entities: as Giddens and Turner (1987: 8) put it for example: "agents, action, and interaction are constrained by, yet generative of, the structural dimension of social reality." In exploring this reflexivity, a number of FLP researchers whose work looks at child agency (e.g. Fogle and King 2013; Gyogi 2015; Bergroth and Palviainen 2017; Said and Zhu 2019) anchor their analysis in Ahearn's (2001: 112) definition of agency as "the socioculturally mediated capacity to act." Invoking this definition, however, points to the potentially paradoxical challenge of discussing *child* agency specifically in so far as the child is *still in the process* of acquiring the sociocultural knowledge (including *language*) requisite for their capacity to act. As Meek (2007: 36) puts it: "the degree to which a novice must 'understand' the constitutive potential of language (Ochs 1996: 431) in order to reproduce, disrupt, or transform the world around him or her remains uncharted and ambiguous."

In grappling with the added challenge of considering *child* agency specifically, FLP researchers have turned to other fields that focus on aspects of childhood and especially child-caregiver relations. In her work on the FLPs of refugees in New Zealand, Revis (2016) for instance draws on developmental psychology in centring her analysis in Kuczynski's (2002: 9) definition of agency as "individuals as actors with the ability to make sense of the environment, initiate change, and make choices." Like FLP research, other related fields, such as developmental psychology and sociology, tended initially to apply a unidirectional lens to caregiver-parent relations (Cummings and Schermerhorn 2003; Morrow 2003). Strauss (1992) for instance likens earlier developmental conceptualisations of children's socialisation to a fax machine, where parents were seen to transmit a copy of particular beliefs and behaviours to their children. Similarly, as Fogle and King (2013: 2) point out, early child language socialisation research – one of the main fields from which FLP research emerged – "tended to emphasize caretakers' roles in socializing children *to* and *through* language to culture-specific norms" before advancing more reciprocal views of the socialisation process (see Schieffiin and Ochs 1986; Garrett and Baquedano-López 2002; Kulick and Schieffiin 2004; Duranti, Ochs, and Schieffiin 2011). Echoing this sentiment, Morrow (2003: 113) highlights how across various disciplines, the child is often seen as an *outcome*: children are the proverbial "products" of their caregivers in both the biological and the social sense.

It is this emphasis on outcome that is argued to account largely for the orbiting nature of child agency in FLP research described earlier. As King (2016: 728) notes, the initial phases of FLP research centred on the key question of "What beliefs, practices, and conditions lead to what child language *outcomes*?" (emphasis my own). With this focus on outcomes, FLP research has illustrated *how* and *why* a language may be maintained in the family, which is in turn crucial to understanding the processes of language shift and social change more generally (see Döpke 1992; Lanza 1997; Curdt-Christiansen 2009; Ó hIfearnáin 2013, Bezçioğlu-Göktolga and Yağmur 2018, to name just a few examples). However, this outlook unintentionally privileged a unidirectional perspective. FLP's early focus on language maintenance meant interest was – and going back to Strauss' fax machine analogy – in *how* the child was (or was not) a copy of the caregivers' linguistic practices. What was of concern was whether or not the language was maintained, to what degree, and what led to this reality, such as the amount of input both in terms of *quality* and *quantity*, and the ideologies underpinning the caregivers' language practices (see for example, De Houwer 1990; Kasuya 1998). It was not until Gafaranga's (2010, 2011) work based in Conversational Analysis therefore that FLP began to orbit back towards looking at the crucial role children can play in shaping language use within the family. Situated in the Rwandan community in Belgium, Gafaranga's work illustrates how children resist their caregivers' use of Kinyarwanda by initiating what he refers to as "medium requests". Here the child's use of French is a bid for French as medium-of-interaction, not Kinyarwanda. This alongside caregivers' acquiescence to these bids is responsible for widespread language shift in the Rwandan community. Thus, FLP research began to take a more active interest in children's role in thwarting language maintenance and in how children actively shape the contexts for their own language input.

The other key work that played a role in initiating what can be seen as the "agentive turn" in FLP is Fogle's (2012) study of transnational adoptive families (US caregivers adopting Russian children). Fogle situates her analysis within an understanding of agency from second language socialisation (e.g. van Lier 2007; see also chapters in Deters et al. 2015) and discourse analytic perspectives which privilege the co-constructed, *in-situ* nature of agency (e.g. Al Zidjaly 2009). She identifies resistance, participation, and negotiation as the three main ways in which the adopted Russian children in her study enact their agency as speakers and in turn shape the contexts for language learning in their new environment. Like Gafaranga, Fogle emphasises how analysing child agency in the context of family language use is not simply a matter of examining what the children are *doing* (e.g. resisting their caregivers' linguistic regimes) but understanding *how* these actions impact current and future family language practices. Aligning with Kuczynski's (2002: 9) emphasis on change as discussed earlier, Fogle argues that (2012: 41) the key question concerning child agency in FLP is: "at what point can children have an influence on the construction of family language policies?"

Following Gafaranga and Fogle's landmark studies in the shift towards a more agentive view of the child in FLP research, several studies (e.g. Gyogi 2015; Revis 2016; Antonini 2016) discussed agency from a perspective of cases where the child takes on the role of expert vis-à-vis their caregivers' novice role due to the children's greater linguistic and sociocultural competence in the majority language than their caregivers', for example such as sometimes occurs in immigrant families (see also Kuczynski, Marshall and Schnell 1997: 36). With this agentive turn also came a perceptible shift in focus, which King and Lanza (2019: 718) characterise as "increasingly interested in how families are constructed *through* multilingual language practices, and how language functions as a resource for this process of familymaking and meaning-making in contexts of transmigration, social media and technology saturation, and hypermobility" (see also Lomeu Gomes 2018; Lanza and Lomeu Gomes; Palviainen, both this vol.).

We are now in this most recent wave of FLP research. Home language maintenance is still of certain import, not only from a theoretical perspective but also from the perspectives of caregivers going to great lengths to transmit their language to their children (for very recent examples of this premise, see for instance Higgins 2019; Purkarthofer and Steien 2019). However, agency now appears in a different light: The playing field has been levelled, so to speak, and children are now generally considered as equal co-participants in constructing the various and diverse ways in which a language may (or may not) be maintained in the home (*cf.* Luykx 2003: 41, quote provided earlier). In doing so, FLP has highlighted the creative and multifarious linguistic and paralinguistic resources through which children enact their agency in everyday interactions, and ultimately, how these agentive acts shape how individual families engage in the process of "doing being" a family (*cf.* Auer's 1984 term of "doing being bilingual").

The purpose of this chapter is to trace this trajectory of FLP research from its initial focus on agency from a resistance lens to the more multidirectional focus which characterises this most recent wave of FLP research. The chapter will thus critically evaluate *how* certain acts are agentive, and what this means in the family's evolving interactions with each other and within the wider society. In making these evaluations, the chapter will draw on a conceptualisation of child agency in FLP as outlined in Figure 1.

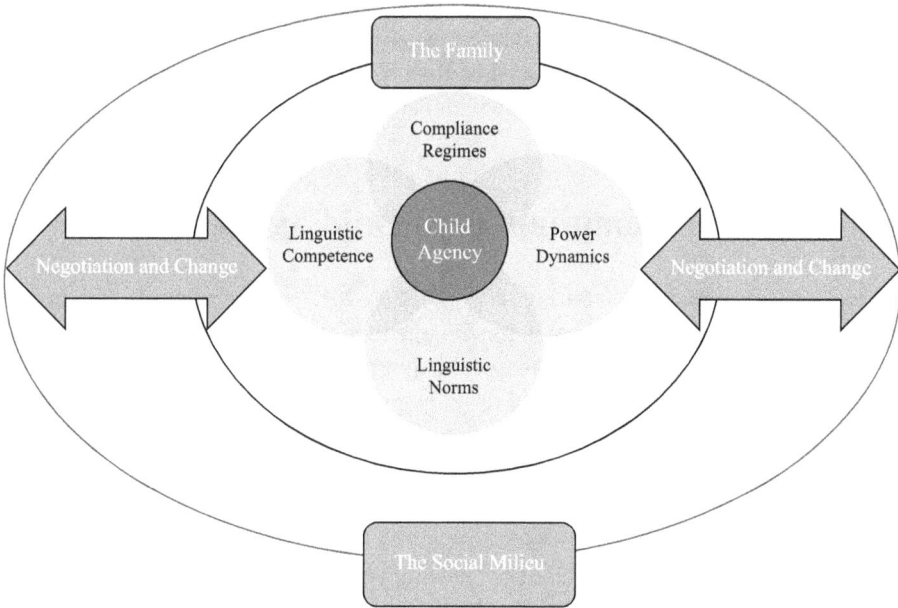

Figure 1: The intersectional, multidimensional, and multilayered nature of child agency in FLP.

Figure 1 illustrates the intersectional, multidimensional, and multi-layered nature of conceptualising child agency in FLP. All four main dimensions ("Compliance Regimes"; "Linguistic Competence;" "Linguistic Norms" and "Power Dynamics") are seen to intersect with *each other* in the convergence of the centre circle "Child Agency." For instance, as will be discussed at length in the chapter, both compliance regimes and linguistic competence contribute to the formation of linguistic norms within the family. The figure therefore does not imply these dimensions can be easily disentangled from one another. Rather, it illustrates how their convergence provides a meaningful starting point for examining the various ways in which children can enact their agency in family interactions. As Revis (2016) discusses in her application of a Bourdesian framework to FLP, these diverse acts of agency in turn are both the product *of* negotiation within the family and also contribute *to* the process of change within the family (the inner layer); similarly, interactions within the family are also circumscribed by, and also play a role in shaping, the existent structures (e.g. linguistic and cultural norms; institutions such as schools and government bodies) that constitute the fabric of the family's wider social milieu (the outer layer). It is argued that this intersectional, multidimensional and multi-layered conceptualisation is necessary if we are take into account that, as Canagarajah (2008: 173) states, the family[1] is a "dynamic social unit, situated in space and time, open to socio-political processes". The remainder of this chapter therefore centres on the four main intersectional dimensions in this model to discuss the multifarious and creative ways in which children can enact their agency in everyday conversation, and in turn bring about changes in communication within the family and the family's wider social milieu.

2 The role of 'compliance' in child agency

As previously mentioned, Gafaranga's work (2010, 2011) on Rwandans in Belgium is seen as one of the main impetuses for the agentive turn within FLP research. This key study raises a number of theoretical questions about *what counts* as child agency in FLP, especially in terms of the specific task of looking at *language* in conjunction with child agency. One issue is that of *compliance*, which Kuczynski and Hildebrandt (1997: 240) define in the developmental tradition as the child's acquiescence to a caregiver's command (e.g. "Pick up that toy") within a certain timeframe. In essence, as described in the introduction to this chapter, earlier FLP research centred on the linguistic equivalent of "pick up your toy": "Speak Language X;" the ideologies underpinning this directive (that Language X is important for social/cultural/heritage reasons; that it benefits the child to be bilingual, etc.); and *how* this directive is indexed and reified in everyday interactions. This synthesis in turn aligns closely with Spolsky's (2004) tripartite model of language policy, which in turn has been very influential in FLP studies (see for example King, Fogle, and Logan-Terry 2008; Schwartz and Verschik 2013; Altman et al. 2014). At the basic level, therefore, agency in the form of resistance is seen as the child *not* speaking Language X.

Whereas in the developmental tradition the directive "Pick up your toy" appears clear-cut, in the FLP tradition the parallel directive "Speak Language X" can be reified in multiple ways on multiple levels. One study which clearly demonstrates this

---

[1] In this chapter, the term "family" is used to refer to adult caregivers and their children, as this is the implicit definition in most FLP work. For FLP work which widens the scope of this definition, see for example Kendrick and Namazzi's (2017) work on orphan families, where older children play the role of caregiver to younger children.

premise is Lanza's (1997) landmark FLP study of caregivers in Norway who decide to follow the "one-parent one-language" (OPOL) strategy, with the father speaking Norwegian and the mother speaking English. This decision implicitly therefore sets up Norwegian as the compliant code to use with the father and English as the compliant code to use with the mother; in other words, the *very act* of setting up this particular family language policy means that there is an underlying expectation of compliance being related to language and interlocutor (*cf.* Palviainen and Boyd 2013). How this expectation is then brought to fruition hinges on how compliance is established both synchronically (in the moment of interaction) and diachronically (accreted over a series of interactions), an observation which aligns with the developmental tradition and the concept that what children understand as compliance and caregivers in turn accept as compliance is usually a matter of negotiation over time and space through multiple interactions (Kuczynski and Hildebrandt 1997). Lanza (1997) views this negotiation process in terms of a continuum of the discourse strategies that a parent may use in initial response to the non-compliant choice (in this case, English to the father, Norwegian to the mother) and how caregivers *overtly mark* an utterance as a non-compliant code choice. Overt marking may include for instance ignoring the child's use of the non-compliant language until he or she uses the compliant language with that particular interlocutor. Conversely, the caregiver may choose *not* to overtly mark the child's language choice in a particular utterance as non-compliant: it might be glossed over in conversation, or the caregiver might indeed code-switch to the non-compliant code choice, thus not reifying it as non-compliant at all.

In direct reference to Lanza's (1997) continuum, Gafaranga (2010: 257) illustrates how caregivers in the Rwandan diaspora community tend to use the latter strategies, by either glossing over the children's use of French or in fact code-switching to French themselves. Parents therefore are not overtly reifying Kinyarwanda as the compliant code choice, which in turn raises an important question about compliancy and its relationship to agency: to what extent can the children's habitual linguistic choices of French be considered an act of resistance if the parameters of compliance have not been set in place? In other words, is the adult's use of Kinyarwanda in *the first place* equivalent to asking the child to pick up the toy, and is the child's reply in French the equivalent of the child refusing to pick up the toy, or does the fact that the adult will then gloss over this use of French render this analogy incompatible? As Gafaranga shows, the children's use of French is *indeed* an act of child agency on several fronts, even if the caregivers have not strongly established the parameters for compliance. First of all, by marking the adult's utterance in Kinyarwanda as "faultable" (*cf.* Goffman 1981) through what Gafaranga (2010) refers to as a "medium request," the child assumes an agentive role in the interaction, and manipulates the power dichotomy between caregiver and child. Secondly, thinking back to the importance of *choice* and *change* as per Kuczynski's (2002: 9) definition of agency, the child has made their decision based on particular environmental factors (the fact that they prefer French; the fact that the use of French will, at worst, simply be glossed over, or at best, accommodated – in other words, it will not be marked as faultable). Finally, the child initiates a change within the environment, notably from Kinyarwanda as medium-of-interaction to either parallel mode or French-as-language-of-interaction. As Gafaranga shows, the accretion of these negotiations of language-of-interaction, where again, the child "runs the show" (*cf.* Tuominen 1999: 71) is leading to widespread language shift within wider social milieu of the Kinyarwanda community in Belgium. Thus, the children are indeed engaging in resistance, thereby participating in one form of agency,[2] even if the caregivers are not setting in place the paradigm for compliance in linguistic terms. A recent example of this can also be found in Canagarajah's (2019: 29) study of Sri Lankan Tamil diaspora families, in which some caregivers accommodated their children's English dominance by adopting mixed language strategies in the home.

There is also substantial evidence of course of caregivers' deep concern that their children *are not* speaking Language X. For instance, in Higgins' (2019: 63) study of the FLPs of "new" speakers (see Smith-Christmas et al. 2018) of Hawaiian, a mother describes how her son sees English as a "forbidden fruit," and how notwithstanding the strongly Hawaiian-only policy of his caregivers, he is now using more English. The mother, however, fears that if she is to "force" him to "talk more Hawaiian," it would only whet his appetite for more active resistance in the form of using more English. A similar example is recounted in Kopeliovich's (2013: 260) study of her four children's bilingual development in Russian and Hebrew in Israel. Here, she describes how although her eldest child Yotam was initially very compliant in terms of language choice, this shifted after he spent more time in the Hebrew environment of the school:

> However, at the age of 5, he was reluctant to switch to Russian even several hours after coming home! He started to express clear preferences towards Hebrew over Russian. The ethnographic log registered his frequent phrases like "I love Hebrew more", "It is boring to speak Russian". He started to use only Hebrew when he played alone with his toys, he actively resisted our attempts to switch the family conversation from Hebrew to Russian; he completely switched to Hebrew in his communication with his friends from Russian-speaking families with whom he had previously communicated in Russian. It was very hard for us to accept this behavior. [...] We chose to avoid arguments and reproaches, as we were afraid to stick a label that could later force the child into the role of a "linguistic rebel".

Here it is clear to see the agentive nature of Yotam's refusal to speak Russian, best encapsulated by the phrase "linguistic rebel." Yotam is not adhering to the compliance regimes set forth by his parents, where Russian operates as the language-of-interaction in the home. Going back to Kuczynski's definition of agency, this example

---

2 As Ahearn (2001:115) emphasises, it is crucial that researchers not simply use agency as a synonym for resistance.

clearly shows how Yotam is able to "make choices" (in this case, the choice to use Hebrew instead of Russian). This choice is mediated by different factors, which in this case, appear to relate to his language attitudes. These are evidenced for example through his metalinguistic comments, such as "I love Hebrew more" which in turn resonates with other FLP research such as Revis' (2016: 7) example in which an Ethopian child in New Zealand insists on only speaking English because she feels "Kiwi". This type of language choice initiates change, not only in terms of the language-of-interaction, but as seen from Kopeliovich's framing of "hard to accept this" and having to "avoid arguments and reproaches," this type of choice is also emotionally challenging (*cf.* Smith-Christmas 2016). Continuing with the theme of *choice* and how it can lead to change in family language dynamics over time, the next section examines the interface between language competence and choice, and the role this relationship plays in conceptualising child agency in FLP.

3 Muddying the waters: The issue of language competence and choice

In addition to raising issues of compliancy and its relation to agency, Gafaranga's study (2010: 248) also raises the question of how competency relates to choice, and therefore, to agency. For example, the children's preference for French over Kinyarwanda was related to their greater competence over the former as opposed to the latter. This observation prompts us to consider the question: to what extent can a child's use of a particular language be considered a *choice* if the child appears to *lack* the choice (i.e. does not have the requisite linguistic skills) to say the utterance in a particular language? My own eight year study (2016) of a family on the Isle of Skye, Scotland provides a good case and point. The repercussive effects of language shift in this family meant that the third generation – and especially the youngest member of the third generation, Jacob, who was 4;0 when I recorded him in 2014 – lacked much productive use in Gaelic and, like the children in Gafaranga's study, answered in the majority language (in this case, English) when addressed in the minority language (Scottish Gaelic). In a recent article examining how Jacob's grandmother Nana makes concerted efforts to embed the language in child-centred contexts as part of her overall language maintenance strategy (Smith-Christmas 2018), I contend that in many interactions, even if he *wants* to, Jacob in fact lacks the linguistic capability to respond in Gaelic. However, I posit that even in the absence of choice in many instances (as I suggest is the case for Jacob), the child is still exercising their agency. First of all, it is well-established within the literature on language choice, and particularly on code-switching, that an interlocutor's choice of one language over the other for (or within) a particular utterance often relates to their competence in that particular language (Auer 1984). A specific language choice in a particular instance is in turn the result of the interface of each interlocutor's own linguistic trajectory and the interactional milieu that they are navigating at that very moment, and in that sense, even if a speech act *is constrained* by competency, in interactional terms, it is still a choice. Secondly, these choices do not exist in a vacuum: in Jacob's case, his answering in English is just one of the many ways through which he actively resists his caregivers' pro-Gaelic FLP. For example, as described in the 2018 article, in one interaction in which Nana, Jacob and I went to a seafood restaurant, Jacob asked the names for various items on the wall (such as a fish, a crab, etc.) and after Nana or I would supply him the answer in Gaelic, he asserted "no, not *iasg*" ("fish"), thereby enacting his agency not only though his use of English, but also implicitly telling *us* not to speak Gaelic. In another incident (Smith-Christmas 2016: 71), Jacob's great-aunt attempts to read him a story in Gaelic, but he is so vociferous in his refusal to have the story read in Gaelic, that again, he constrains the adults in the language *they* must use. Jacob accomplishes this through metalinguistic comments such as "No I want it in English," thus clearly enacting his agency even though, as discussed earlier, in many ways he lacks the linguistic means to make a choice between Gaelic and English. His *overall* choice is English, and he makes this point loud and clear.

In her study of two Japanese bilingual adolescents in the UK, Gyogi (2015: 258) noticeably demonstrates the interrelated nature of competence and preference. Writing about one of the two girls in her study, "Naomi's interview suggests that her language shift is mostly a competence-based one; the growing gap between her English and Japanese proficiencies has pressed her towards this language shift, rather than a conscious desire to challenge her mother's beliefs." Gyogi also shows how Naomi incorporates these lapses in linguistic competency into a skilful way of code-switching, masking her gaps and making it appear that rather than *lacking* competency, she deliberately inserts English into utterances as a means to "show off" that she knows English. Similarly, Boyd, Huss, and Ottesjö's (2017: 523) analysis of play sequence among children in an English-medium pre-school in Sweden, shows how one child, Rose, speaks a nonsense language following her classmates' use of Swedish in preceding turns, which according to the authors, is a means for Rose to ratify her participation in the conversation, despite her lack of Swedish. Thus, notwithstanding the potential of competence to place constraints on agency (such that the *choice* dimension might be absent from children's language acts), it is clear that children employ multiple strategies to navigate the conversation, and use what skills they *do* have in varied and creative ways, thereby enacting their agency.

Further, in some instances, the child's lack of competency may in fact be the source of the child's enactment of agency in the conversation, rather than an agentive strategy to mask the lack of competence. In their study of an Arabic-English family in the UK, Said and Zhu (2019: 776–777) demonstrate how six year-old Hamid has been trying to make a bid for his father's attention, but to little avail. He then uses Arabic as a strategy in this endeavour, and a grammatical error in his utterance then serves as an opportunity for his father to verbally attend to this lack of competency. Hamid is therefore successful in his attempt to gain a response from his father while his grammatical error – although not necessarily intentional – serves as a means for Hamid to further hold his father's attention. Thus, in enacting his agency by speaking Arabic, Hamid is able to attain his desired conversational goals. Similarly, in my own work (Smith-Christmas 2016), one of my main observations about Maggie – Jacob's older sister aged 3:4 when I recorded the family in 2009 – is that she tends to use Gaelic specifically when she wants to mitigate trouble between her and her caregivers. This usually consists of single lexical mixes (e.g. "I am *modhail*" in asserting that she is indeed being polite). Much of the efficacy of this strategy essentially lies in the reflexive relationship between preference and competence. Because Maggie does *not* use Gaelic very often, instances in which she *does* use Gaelic become marked (*cf.* Myers-Scotton 1993), and in many ways, constrains *how* she can use the language (i.e. lexical mixes versus full sentences). Both of these often contribute to her caregivers' affective softening towards the strife at hand, normally through their overt amusement at her utterances. Thus, although Maggie is constrained linguistically by *what* she can accomplish in Gaelic, it is in fact this lack of competency that makes her use of Gaelic such a potent tool for enacting her agency vis-à-vis her caregivers. It also resonates with her caregivers – especially her grandparents' generation – high use of code-switching and mixing for effect, which is one of the hallmarks of Maggie's family's communicative practices. It one of the key ways the family participates in "doing being" a family, the concept of which is investigated in more depth in the next section.

4 "Doing being" a family: The negotiation of linguistic norms

As illustrated in Figure 1, both compliancy regimes and issues of linguistic competence contribute to the formation of linguistic norms within the family. Again to return to Gafaranga's landmark study, the accretion of the children's answering in French leads to the community norm of Kinyarwanda for adults and French for children and therefore adults do not expect children to answer in Kinyarwanda; in fact, hypothetically-speaking, the child's reply in Kinyarwanda could be seen as a breach in interactional norms and may result in a breakdown in communication (see Kulick 1992; Smith-Christmas 2016). This highlights another challenge in conceptualising child agency in FLP, especially in terms of Fogle's (2012: 32) question of "at *what point* can children have an influence on the construction of family language policies": to what extent can we see any speech act (in this case, language choice) as an act of agency versus a reification of linguistic norms at work, and how does this relate to the reflexive nature of agency, as both *shaped* by and integral in *shaping* particular norms?

In order to discuss this question, we will begin by exploring how children's accreted acts of linguistic compliance can become agentive, and in doing so, shape linguistic norms within the family. The concept of compliancy as a form of agency is well-established within developmental psychology (Kuczynski 2002), and in embarking on this exploration, I draw on my recent work in the Corca Dhuibhne Gaeltacht in Ireland (see Smith-Christmas, under review) in illustrating how compliancy can be a form of agency. In the following excerpt, the mother Mia explains how she invoked discourse strategies, such as ignoring her daughters if they addressed her in English, in setting up Irish as the compliant choice, thereby firmly establishing the language as the language-of-interaction between Mia and her daughters. Here, Mia describes what happens when *she* breaks this interactional norm:

Excerpt 1: Mia and her daughters.
1 Mia   yeah yeah (.) yeah it doesn't enter their heads not to speak to me in Irish no matter who is in the company (.) and sometimes I recently decided (.) oh God (.) I should make an effort when we are in company (.) and address something to them in English so that the other person knows what I'm on about (.) and they find that uncomfortable, they don't like that
2 Cassie that's great
3 Mia   yeah
4 Cassie that's great
5 Mia   I know yeah, yeah it's, it's great (.) I've noticed that, they just kind of go (.) they look at me weird (.) and they speak to me in Irish as if to say (.) come on

This example clearly highlights the reflexive nature of child agency and language choice. Irish is firmly established as the language-of-interaction between Mia and her daughters; however, Mia occasionally tries to re-negotiate this norm in the company of interlocutors who do not speak Irish. Her attempts are unsuccessful, however, due to her daughters' agency: they do not allow Mia to breach this norm. Thus, even though their actions are compliant with Mia's *overall* FLP, they are still an act of agency, and in fact an act of agency that curtails Mia's own agency. Her use of English is sanctioned, therefore reflexively strengthening the norm of Irish as the language of interaction in this family.

Similarly, Boyd and Palviainen (2013: 238, 241) show how children in Swedish-Finnish OPOL families translate accreted compliance into agency. Like Mia's daughters, they actively sanction their parents' use of the "wrong" language. In one example (Boyd and Palviainen 2013: 241) the daughter Sara takes a teacher-like tone in informing her Finnish-speaking father that his use of the lexical item *åtta* (eight) is "mother's language." The authors write that "this is a nice example of child agency in that Sara effectively confirms her adherence to the interaction order of

OPOL". This sentiment is echoed in Palviainen's work with Bergroth (2017) on the pre-school-family interface, which demonstrates how children's linguistic compliance to pre-school linguistic regimes also can be seen as a type of agency. It is clear therefore that there is a highly reflexive relationship between compliancy, norms, and child agency. Children not only enact their agency in FLP in their *choice* to use the code the caregiver has set up as the compliant choice, but also by enforcing these compliancy regimes, i.e. by sanctioning their parents' non-compliant choices. The children therefore play a key role in how linguistic norms are established and in turn how the language can be maintained in various ways. Further, children may enact their agency by participating in normative practices in other ways that support language maintenance. In their study of multilingual families in Norway, Obojska and Purkarthofer (2018: 257) show how one adult participant positioned gifts of Polish books each time her father returned from Poland as a reflex of her *own* agency. When she was younger, she would specifically request Polish books, and therefore, in addition to participating in her family's strongly pro-Polish FLP, she took an active role in maintaining Polish in other domains. Similarly, Nyikos (2014: 33) gives another example of a child enacting her agency by actively seeking to promote her own language maintenance, a decision precipitated by a visit to the home country (Slovakia) where the child was teased for speaking Slovak "with an American accent."

Van Mensel's (2018) recent work on familylects of multilingual families in Brussels is also highly illustrative of the way in which children play an active role in shaping family linguistic norms. Firmly situated in the most recent wave of FLP research, Van Mensel's study takes a more resource-oriented approach, showing how in spite of various asymmetries in individual family members' linguistic competencies (in one of the families, both parents – Ann and Ricardo – speak Spanish but Ricardo cannot speak much Dutch), all family members exploit a variety of linguistic resources in "doing being" a family (*cf.* Auer 1984). Multilingualism therefore plays a large role in the creation of these families' particular familylects, and the norms associated with these familylects are constantly being re-negotiated. For example, in one instance (Van Mensel 2018: 243), Ann and Ricardo's daughter Daniela repeatedly asks her parents in Spanish if they would like more coffee, but inserts the Dutch word "koffie" for instead of the Spanish "*café*." Both parents index that at some level, this instance of use is incorrect, but their motivations appear different, with Ricardo's stance seeming to relate to politeness norms and Ann's to the use of mixing. Daniela, however, asserts in Spanish that she speaks "really well" and van Mensel (2018: 244) concludes that Daniela is not resisting her parents' language choices per se, but instead is "resisting the 'delimiting' and 'policing' of her language as she exploits the linguistic resources in her repertoire in a playful and creative way." In other words, she is actively shaping the norm of multilingualism-within-the-family. However, this does not mean that the parameters for language norms are boundless. For example, in one instance (van Mensel 2018: 242),

Ricardo uses the wrong Dutch diminutive suffix (*-etje* when it should be *–je*) on the word "*boek*" (book). His daughter then overtly corrects this, and van Mensel concludes that "family repertoire thus appears to follow certain rules as well, and in this case it is one of the children who imposes a normative restriction on what can be said, thus illustrating how the family language policy is co-constructed by both children and parents." Thus, members – including children – work together in establishing the parameters for linguistic norms in FLP as they evolve over space and time.

5 Re-negotiation of roles: Children's empowerment through linguistic and cultural capital

The last example – in which the child enacted a expert role vis-à-vis the caregiver – resonates with the theme of this section: children's empowerment through linguistic and cultural capital. As Revis (2016) discusses in her Bourdesian approach to FLP in refugee families in New Zealand, immigrant children's experiences at school mean that they often acquire linguistic capital more swiftly than their caregivers, and thus are in a position to act as interpreters. This language brokering in turn may occur in a number of different situations in both the public and private sphere, from doctor visits and shopping, to informal visits with acquaintances (Antonini 2016). Some of these situations might require the child to navigate challenging spheres of communication (e.g. medical terminology in doctor's visits) or might be particularly distressing, as illustrated in Gallo's (2017: 77) study where a child has to broker a conversation between her father and a policeman at the door. In this case, the stakes are particularly high, as in the context of Mexicans in the US, any encounter with authorities had the potential to lead to deportation. The gravity of these situations compounds the child's relative power vis-à-vis the adult's disenfranchisement; even in situations not of this nature (e.g. a social visit), we see a clear inversion of the expected caregiver-child relationship. As Revis (2016: 8) discusses, this inversion can cause discomfort for caregivers, and the accretion of language brokering interactions has the potential to cause a shift in parent-child relations: "while some families only expressed concern about the reversed order of authority, others added that this represented a challenge to them as authorities in the home." Thus, we see the child's agency operating at two different levels: first, in the child's action (i.e. the act of performing language brokering) and then at the *change* it brings about in the family – in this case, inverting traditional power dynamics. Language brokering in the case of FLP very clearly highlights how linguistic competency adds another dimension to the bidirectional nature of language socialisation. Not only are the children socialising the caregivers into being caregivers, but in the case of transnational families, children also have the potential to socialise their parents into the sociocultural milieu of their wider environment.

In addition to language brokering, the linguistic competence asymmetry that can exist between children and their caregivers may take other forms in opening up avenues for children to use language to enact their agency in everyday interactions. Zhu (2008) for example shows how the children of Chinese immigrants in the UK use their greater linguistic competency in English to subvert traditional power structures in managing conflict talk. The growth of minority language immersion education is another means by which children may attain greater linguistic competency than their caregivers. In such instances, while the child may not normally play the role of interpreter – as situations such as going to the doctor's etc. are conducted through the majority language – the child is still able to subvert caregiver-child power relations. This often takes the form of the child overtly marking the adult's lack of linguistic competence, as seen in van Mensel's example discussed earlier, where the child corrected her father's use of the diminutive suffix. This also surfaced in my most recent research in the Outer Hebrides of Scotland (Smith-Christmas, under review) where the mother in each family spoke Gaelic but the father did not, and the children all attended Gaelic immersion education. In one of the families, the father had acquired a moderate level of fluency in Gaelic, and would try and speak it to me as the researcher when I was recording some of the interactions. His sons were eager to correct any lapses in fluency and were very animated in their corrections, thus subverting the traditional caregiver-child power relationship. Later in one of the interactions, the father capitalised on this power reversal and used it to pedagogical effect by engaging the children in homework activities, actively taking on the role of student while the children took on the role of teacher. It therefore became a way for the father to play a role in enacting the pro-Gaelic FLP that was typically his wife's remit. His emphasis on his sons' agency also provided a way in which he could facilitate and further their linguistic and academic skills acquisition.

6 Conclusion

The purpose of this chapter has been to raise questions about conceptualising child agency in the context of FLP. In doing so, we have focused on critically examining what counts as agency and have explored the intricacies of the reflexive relationship between agency on the one hand and structures on the other. The chapter has illustrated how the concept of agency is "layered, complex, and at times contradictory" (Fogle 2012: 41). In trying to untangle these interwoven complexities and surfacing conundrums, the chapter has centred on four main intersectional dimensions of child agency in FLP research: compliancy; linguistic competencies; linguistic norms; and power dynamics. It has explored these dimensions through the main criteria of *choice* and *change,* focusing on how children can have an "influence on the construction of family language policies" (Fogle 2012: 32). It has examined how certain factors – such as linguistic competency – may appear to constrain choice, while at the same time demonstrating how the child employs a variety of strategies to circumnavigate these constraints, thereby reifying his or her linguistic act as agentive. In addressing the issue of compliancy and especially its relation to linguistic norms, this chapter has also critically examined whether certain acts exemplify agency or not, underscoring that when applying the criteria of choice and change, these acts are indeed agentive. This is especially true in terms of change: the children's linguistic agency has the potential to shape not only language practices in the family, but to induce change beyond the bounds of the family. In sum, the chapter has shown that there are many and varied points in which, at some level, children may influence FLP. It has shown the value of critically exploring the mechanisms by which these influences can happen and of continually questioning *how* a particular speech act is indeed an act of agency. As emphasised in the introduction, FLP is only just now circling back to the importance of child agency, and it is hoped that this critical examination will be fruitful in further explorations of this important topic.

References

Ahearn, Laura M. 2001. Language and agency. *Annual Review of Anthropology* 30(1). 109–137.
Altman, Carmit, Zhanna Burstein Feldman, Dafna Yitzhaki, Sharon Armon Lotem & Joel Walters. 2014. Family language policies, reported language use and proficiency in Russian – Hebrew bilingual children in Israel. *Journal of Multilingual and Multicultural Development* 35(3). 216–234.
Al Zidjaly, Najma. 2009. Agency as an interactive achievement. *Language in Society* 38(2). 177–200.
Antonini, Rachele. 2016. Caught in the middle: Child language brokering as a form of unrecognised language service. *Journal of Multilingual and Multicultural Development* 37(7). 710–725.
Auer, Peter. 1984. *Bilingual conversation*. Amsterdam: Johns Benjamins.
Bergroth, Mari & Åsa Palviainen. 2017. Bilingual children as policy agents: Language policy and education policy in minority language medium Early Childhood Education and Care. *Multilingua* 36(4). 375–399.
Bezçioğlu-Göktolga, Irem & Kutlay Yağmur. 2018. Home language policy of second-generation Turkish families in the Netherlands. *Journal of Multilingual and Multicultural Development* 39(1). 44–59.
Bourdieu, Pierre. 1997. *Outline of a theory of practice*. Cambridge: Cambridge University Press.
Boyd, Sally, Leena Huss & Cajsa Ottesjö. 2017. Children's agency in creating and maintaining language policy in practice in two "language profile" preschools in Sweden. *Multilingua* 36(4). 501–531.
Canagarajah, Suresh. (2008). Language shift and the family: Questions from the Sri Lankan Tamil diaspora. *Journal of Sociolinguistics* 12(2). 143–176.
Canagarajah, Suresh. 2019. Changing orientations to heritage language: The practice-based ideology of Sri Lankan Tamil diaspora families. *International Journal of the Sociology of Language* 2019(255). 9–44.

Coetzee, Frieda. 2018. *"Hy leer dit nie hier nie"* ('He doesn't learn it here'): Talking about children's swearing in extended families in multilingual South Africa. *International Journal of Multilingualism* 15(3). 291–305.
Cummings, E. Mark & Alice C. Schermerhorn. 2003. A Developmental perspective on children as agents in the family. In Leon Kuczynski (ed.), *Handbook of dynamics in parent-child relations*, 91–108. London: Sage Publications.
Curdt-Christiansen, Xiao Lan. 2009. Invisible and visible language planning: Ideological factors in the family language policy of Chinese immigrant families in Quebec. *Language Policy* 8(4). 351–375.
De Houwer, Annick. 1990. *The acquisition of two languages from birth: A case study*. Cambridge: Cambridge University Press.
Deters, Ping, Xuesong Gao, Elizabeth R. Miller & Gergana Vitanova. 2015. *Theorizing and analyzing agency in second language learning: Interdisciplinary approaches*. Bristol: Multilingual Matters.
Döpke, Suzanne. 1992. *One parent, one language: An interactional approach*. Amsterdam: John Benjamins.
Duranti, Alessandro, Elinor Ochs & Bambi Schieffiin (eds.). 2011. *The handbook of language socialization*. Malden, MA: Wiley-Blackwell.
Fogle, Lyn W. 2012. *Second language socialization and learner agency: Adoptive family talk*. Bristol: Multilingual Matters.
Fogle, Lyn W. & Kendall A. King. 2013. Child agency and language policy in transnational families. *Issues in Applied Linguistics* 19. 1–25.
Gafaranga, Joseph. 2010. Medium request: Talking language shift into being. *Language in Society* 39(2). 241–270.
Gafaranga, Joseph. 2011. Transition space medium repair: Language shift talked into being. *Journal of Pragmatics* 43(1). 118–135.
Gallo, Sarah. 2017. *Mi Padre: Mexican immigrant fathers and their children's education*. New York: Teachers College Press.
Garrett, Paul B. & Patricia Baquedano-López. 2002. Language socialization: Reproduction and continuity, transformation and change. *Annual Review of Anthropology* 31(1). 339–361.
Giddens, Anthony. 1979. *Central problems in social theory: Action, structure, and contradiction in social analysis*. Berkeley: University of California Press.
Giddens, Anthony & Jonathan Turner. 1987. Introduction. In Anthony Giddens & Jonathan Turner (eds.), *Social theory today*, 1–11. Stanford: Stanford University Press.
Goffman, Erving. 1981. *Forms of talk*. Philadelphia: University of Pennsylvania Press.
Gyogi, Eiko. 2015. Children's agency in language choice: A case study of two Japanese-English bilingual children in London. *International Journal of Bilingual Education and Bilingualism* 18(6). 749–764.
Higgins, Christina. 2019. The dynamics of Hawaiian speakerhood in the family. *International Journal of the Sociology of Language* 2019(255). 45–72.
Kasuya, Hiroko. 1998. Determinants of language choice in bilingual children: The role of input. *International Journal of Bilingualism* 2(3). 327–346.
Kendrick, Maureen & Elizabeth Namazzi. 2017. Family language practices as emergent policies in child-headed households in rural Uganda. In John Macalister & Seyed H. Mirvahedi (eds.), *Family language policies in a multilingual world: Opportunities, challenges, and consequences*, 56–73. London: Routledge.
King, Kendall A. 2016. Language policy, multilingual encounters, and transnational families. *Journal of Multilingual and Multicultural Development* 37(7). 726–733.

King, Kendall A., Lyn Fogle & Aubrey Logan-Terry. 2008. Family Language Policy. *Language and Linguistics Compass* 2(5). 907–922.

King, Kendall. A. & Lanza, Elizabeth. 2019. Ideology, agency, and imagination in multilingual families: An introduction. *International Journal of Bilingualism* 23(3). 717–723.

Kopeliovich, Shulamit. 2013. Happylingual: A family project for enhancing and balancing multilingual development. In Mila Schwartz & Anna Verschik (eds.), *Successful family language policy: Parents, children and educators in interaction*, 249–276. Dordrecht: Springer.

Kroskrity, Paul V. 2009. Narrative reproductions: Ideologies of storytelling, authoritative words, and generic regimentation in the village of Tewa. *Journal of Linguistic Anthropology* 19(1). 40–56.

Kuczynski, Leon. 2002. Beyond bidirectionality: Bilateral conceptual frameworks for studying dynamics in parent-child relations. In Leon Kuczynski (ed.), *Handbook of dynamics in parent-child relations*, 3–24. London: Sage.

Kuczynski, Leon & Neil Hildebrandt. 1997. Models of conformity and resistance in socialization theory. In Joan E. Grusec & Leon Kuczynski (eds.), *Parenting and children's internalization of values: A handbook of contemporary theory*, 227–256. Hoboken: John Wiley & Sons.

Kuczynski, Leon, Sheila Marshall & Kathleen Schell. 1997. Value socialization in a bidirectional context. In Joan E. Grusec & Leon Kuczynski (eds.), *Parenting and children's internalization of values: A handbook of contemporary theory*, 23–50. Hoboeken: John Wiley & Sons.

Kulick, Don. 1992. *Language shift and cultural reproduction: Socialization, self, and syncretism in a Papua New Guinean village*. Cambridge: Cambridge University Press.

Kulick, Don & Bambi Schiefflin. 2004. Language socialization. In Alessandro Duranti (ed.), *A companion to linguistic anthropology*, 349–368. Oxford: Blackwell.

Lanza, Elizabeth. 1997. *Language mixing in infant bilingualism: A sociolinguistic perspective*. Oxford: Oxford University Press.

Lanza, Elizabeth & Rafael Lomeu Gomes. this vol. Family language policy: Foundations, theoretical perspectives and critical approaches.

Lier, Leo van. 2007. Action-based teaching, autonomy and identity. *Innovation in Language Learning and Teaching* 1(1). 46–65.

Lomeu Gomes, Rafael. 2018. Family language policy ten years on: A critical approach to family multilingualism. *Multilingual Margins* 5(2). 50–71.

Luykx, Aurolyn. 2003. Weaving languages together: Family language policy and gender socialisation in bilingual Aymara households. In Robert Bayley & Sandra Schecter (eds.), *Language socialisation in bilingual and multilingual societies*, 10–25. Clevedon: Multilingual Matters.

Meek, Barbra A. 2007. Respecting the language of elders: Ideological shift and linguistic discontinuity in a Northern Athapascan Community. *Journal of Linguistic Anthropology* 17(1). 23–43.

Morrow, Virginia. 2003. Perspectives on children's agency within families: A view from the sociology of childhood. In Leon Kuczynski (ed.), *Handbook of dynamics in parent-child relations*, 109–130. London: Sage.

Myers-Scotton, Carol. 1993. *Duelling languages: Grammatical structure in code-switching*. Oxford: Clarendon Press.

Nyikos, Martha. 2014. Bilingualism and family: Parental beliefs; child agency. *Sustainable Multilingualism* 5. 18–40.

Obojska, Maria A. & Judith Purkarthofer. 2018. "And all of a sudden, it became my rescue": Language and agency in transnational families in Norway. *International Journal of Multilingualism* 15(3). 249–261.

Ochs, E. (1996). Linguistic resources for socializing humanity. In John J. Gumperz & Stephen C. Levinson (eds.), *Rethinking linguistic relativity*, 407–437. Cambridge: Cambridge University Press.

Ó hIfearnáin, Tadhg. 2013. Family language policy, first language Irish speaker attitudes and community-based response to language shift. *Journal of Multilingual and Multicultural Development* 34(4). 348–365.

Palviainen, Åsa. this vol. Future prospects and visions for family language policy research.

Palviainen, Åsa & Sally Boyd. 2013. Unity in discourse, diversity in practice: The one person one language policy in bilingual families. In Mila Schwartz & Anna Verschik (eds.), *Successful family language policy: Parents, children and educators in interaction*, 223–248. Dordrecht: Springer.

Purkarthofer, Judith & Guri B. Steien. 2019. "Pretendre comme si on connaît pas une autre langue que le swahili": Multilingual parents in Norway on change and continuity in their family language policies. *International Journal of the Sociology of Language* 2019 (255). 109–132.

Revis, M. (2016). A Bourdieusian perspective on child agency in family language policy. *International Journal of Bilingual Education and Bilingualism* 22(2). 177–191.

Said, Fatma, & Zhu Hua. 2019. "No, no Maama! Say 'Shaatir ya Ouledee Shaatir'!" Children's agency in language use and socialisation. *International Journal of Bilingualism* 23(3). 771–785.

Schieffelin, Bambi & Elinor Ochs. 1986. Language socialization. *Annual Review of Anthropology* 15. 163–191.

Schwartz, Mila & Anna Verschik (eds.). 2013. *Successful family language policy: Parents, children and educators in interaction*. Dordecht: Springer.

Smith-Christmas, Cassie. 2016. *Family language policy: Maintaining an endangered language in the home*. Basingstoke: Palgrave Macmillan.

Smith-Christmas, Cassie. 2018. "One *Cas*, Two *Cas*": Exploring the affective dimensions of family language policy. *Multilingua – Journal of Cross-Cultural and Interlanguage Communication* 37(2). 131–152.

Smith-Christmas, Cassie. under review. Do sheans: Children's agency in integrating Scottish Gaelic and Irish into 'Happy Families.' In Aengus Finnegan & Gordon Ó Riain (eds.), *Léann na Sionainne*. Uppsala: University of Uppsala Press.

Smith-Christmas, Cassie, Noel P. Ó Murchadha, Michael Hornsby & Máiréad Moriarty (eds.). 2018. *New speakers of minority languages: Linguistic ideologies and practices*. Basingstoke: Palgrave Macmillan.

Spolsky, Bernard. (2004). *Language policy*. Cambridge: Cambridge University Press.

Strauss, Claudia. 1992. Models and motives. In Roy D'Andrade & Claudia Strauss (eds.), *Human motives and cultural models*, 1–20. Cambridge: Cambridge University Press.

Taylor, Charles. 1985. *Human agency and language: Philosophical papers*, Vol. 1. Cambridge: Cambridge University Press.

Tuominen, Anne. 1999. Who decides the home language? A look at multilingual families. *International Journal of the Sociology of Language* 1999(140). 59–76.

Van Mensel, Luk. 2018. "Quiere koffie?" The multilingual familylect of transcultural families. *International Journal of Multilingualism* 15(3). 233–248.

Zhu, Hua. 2008. Duelling languages, duelling values: Codeswitching in bilingual intergenerational conflict talk in diasporic families. *Journal of Pragmatics* 40. 1799–1816.

Åsa Palviainen
12 Future prospects and visions for family language policy research

1 Introduction

Although the roots of the field of family language policy (FLP) can be traced about one hundred years back in time, it was after the seminal article by King, Fogle, and Logan-Terry (2008) – in which the term FLP was introduced and defined – that the FLP research field started to grow exponentially. The idea of combining previous insights from psycholinguistic research on bilingual language acquisition and sociolinguistic studies on family interaction with theory and concepts from the field of language policy and planning (LPP) obviously filled a gap: Researchers were provided with conceptual tools to better understand processes of language maintenance and change as a function of explicit (or implicit) language planning within families, and they were able to apply a wider range of methodologies to empirically examine these processes. (For more detailed descriptions of the development of the field, see King and Fogle 2013; King 2016; King and Fogle 2017; Lanza and Lomeu Gomes this vol.; Schwartz 2010; Smith-Christmas 2017).

In the first chapter on the topic area "Family Language Policy" in this handbook, Lanza and Lomeu (this vol.) present an overview of the field. Their conclusion is that much of the current FLP research revolves around making sense of multilingual family language practices and ideologies, often in transnational populations, and covers an ever-increasing range of languages and family types. The following three chapters all provide different current perspectives from the FLP field. Curdt-Christiansen and Huang (this vol.) show the importance of understanding the multilayered, complex and dynamic sociopolitical contexts in which individual transnational family language policy-making is situated, whereas Schwartz (this vol.) examines family language management at the micro level of the home environment. Finally, Smith-Christmas (this vol.) focuses on child agency, and children's displayed actions of resistance to or compliance with the use of a minority language.

The aim of the current chapter is to envision future research directions within the FLP field. I will discuss topics that need further recognition in future studies, to better understand and do justice to multilingual family constellations and the conditions they are formed by as we enter the 2020s. I will therefore discuss the inclusion of child perspectives in the research (section 3) and the role of emotions in family language policy-making (section 4), as well as point to the need for the study of families in today's mobile digital context (section 5). The final part of the

---

Note: The writing of the chapter was supported by Academy of Finland Grant No. 315478.

https://doi.org/10.1515/9781501510175-012

chapter (section 6) puts forward some practical suggestions as to how these perspectives can be implemented in research: how to define the family as an object of study, what research questions may be asked, and what methodologies can be used. In the following (section 2), I will discuss the theoretical argument that runs through the chapter that families, as well as the FLPs they negotiate and develop, are dynamic across time and space.

2 FLP-making across time and space

The "family" is at the core of FLP research, and for this reason it is important for the researcher to clearly establish what exactly this object under study is. As a unit based on kin membership, which can vary in size, the notion sometimes tends to be taken for granted (cf. Lanza and Lomeu Gomes this vol.). The objective of research is often to describe *the* FLP of one or more separate family unit(s). These types of study tend to be based on "snapshot" descriptions rooted in a given point in time.

The argument I put forward in this chapter is the need to see the family as a dynamic and fluid system – rather than a fixed unit – where the individual is residing at the centre of his or her own universe of networks (Stern and Messer 2009). Family systems as such are affected by external factors as well as individual ones (Curdt-Christiansen 2016; Lanigan 2009; Tannenbaum 2012). Rather than mapping one unified FLP of a particular family, I think it is important to acknowledge the "multiple individual policies that include individual ideologies, management approaches, and practices within a single family unit" (Hirsch and Lee 2018: 890) and as a researcher to assign similar weight to the different individual policy-makers. Together, these agents make up the complex FLP web.

I further argue for the need to see FLP-making as a process that takes place across time and space (Hirsch and Lee 2018). The temporal aspect is crucial; the negotiation of different aspects of the FLP occurs on multiple time scales and all individual members bring along their own historical bodies (He 2014; Hirsch and Lee 2018; Scollon and Scollon 2004). Introducing a new linguistic variety into a family system, processes of migration, family member re-configurations (such as new siblings, restructured families, transnational adoption), individuals growing and ageing, the introduction of new communication technologies, the start or change of school, and so on, all potentially affect FLP-making, as a function of time. As for space, the concept of home (domain) is often seen as crucial for – or even as equalling – the family (Fishman 1991; Spolsky 2012). Eisenchlas and Schalley (this vol.) argue that home does not necessarily imply a (physical) space, but rather serves as a point of reference from which speakers navigate the world and negotiate language use at the micro level. Following this line of interpretation, the points of reference may vary for individual family members as they can experience many different significant "home spaces" and have multiple senses of belonging (Hirsch and Lee 2018; Tyrrell 2015). The traditional conceptualisation of home (domain) is complicated by the fact that in our post-modern society the boundaries between the private and public spheres have become blurred (Zhu and Li 2016). Today's transglobal family realities, saturated with social media and communication technology, make it necessary to rethink more traditional concepts of space (Hatoss; Lanza and Lomeu Gomes both this vol.).

These understandings lead inevitably to a reconsideration of the conceptualisation of FLP. In the original definition put forward by King, Fogle, and Logan-Terry in 2008, the focus was on explicit and overt planning carried out in relation to language use within the home among family members. Gradually this has been extended to include also implicit and covert planning, as well as literacy practices (Curdt-Christiansen 2009; King and Fogle 2013; Spolsky 2012). In order to include the dynamicity of language negotiation over time and space(s) that takes place among individual members of a network who define themselves as of familial significance, FLP is here understood as explicit and overt, as well as implicit and covert, planning among the members in a family network in relation to their language use and literacy practices across time and space. Importantly, literacy practices also then encompass digital practices, not only as an outcome of planning but also as a significant mediational tool.

3 Including child perspectives

The field of FLP has certain epistemological traditions which have also had an effect on how children have been looked at and what methodologies have been applied to research them. Theories of language socialisation, language transmission and early language acquisition tend to see the child as a fairly passive receiver of language(s). From this perspective, parents' (and other [older] socialising agents') language practices, strategies and ideologies serve – in interaction with environmental factors such as the quantity and quality of language input and societal ideologies – as determining factors for language development. Moreover, as a consequence of the fact that the FLP field links studies of child language acquisition, early second language learning and bilingualism (King and Fogle 2013), the focus has often been on parents and children during their very first years of life (Juvonen et al. this vol.).

An increasing number of FLP studies have appeared with a focus on child agency, including those in which the child is recognised as an active co-producer of the FLP with the mandate to shape, reject and change policies (e.g., Bergroth and Palviainen 2017; Fogle 2012; Kheirkhah 2016; Luykx 2005; Said and Zhu 2019; Smith-Christmas this vol.; Zhu 2008). Acknowledging child agency does not, however, necessarily mean that children's own perspectives are taken into account, for example, in choosing data collection methodologies which give children a voice. Within the field of new sociology (or anthropology) of childhoods (e.g. Prout 2011), childhood is seen as socially constructed and it is argued that children's worlds should be studied in their own right, not in relation to adults. In processes of family migration, children have shown to be key actors in transnational social practices, such as serving as language brokers and contributing to family divisions of labour and relations of care (Orellana 2009). Olwig's (1999) research on Caribbean children who are cared for by relatives rather than parents who have left for work elsewhere (also Madianou and Miller 2012; Parreñas 2014), as well as Tyrrell's (2015) study on the experiences of Spanish migrant children in the UK, are examples where children's voices and experiences are being heard, theoretically as well as methodologically.

In many Western contexts, close family members and home settings play a significant role in the child's life during the preschool years; during the elementary school years the child's independence and access to out-of-home spaces and social networks increase, and the teenager is seen as autonomous in many respects (Lim 2016). Although there have recently been studies on language practices and policies focusing on older children (e.g. Caldas 2006; De Houwer 2015; Doyle 2013; Fiorentino 2017; Kayam and Hirsch 2014; Kheirkhah 2016), more research is needed to understand the processes of language maintenance and change along life's trajectories (He 2014), including the role of others such as peers and siblings (Parada 2013). As Zhu and Li (2016) show, individuals of different generations within the same transnational family may have very different sociocultural experiences. Moreover, across different cultural contexts there may be other assumptions and expectations about the needs, capacities and appropriate activities of children at different ages, as well as different child-rearing practices (Orellana et al. 2001). Therefore we need a more thorough understanding of FLP formation as a dynamic process, involving the multiple individuals of the family, and as situated in a certain sociocultural context.

As for methodologies within the FLP field, there is a long tradition of observing parent-child interactions in home settings as well as of collecting data on children's language practices and ideologies by means of sociolinguistic surveys or interviews with the parents (typically the mother). This means that the data on children's language practices are mediated and filtered through the experiences and eyes of a parent, and/or interpreted by an adult researcher (Boivin and Cohenmiller 2018; see also Juvonen et al. this vol.). The (adult) researcher also makes informed (and ideological) decisions on what situations to record and observe, how to formulate question items and categories in a survey, and which questions to ask as part of an interview protocol. It is an inescapable fact that the researcher is a subject (and adult), and in ethnographic research it is important for the researcher to establish his/her own zone of identification (Scollon and Scollon 2004: 11). In her article on how to listen to children's voices in ethnographic fieldwork, Almér (2017: 404) asks the thought-provoking question of "whether anyone who has reached adulthood can ever find out what a child experiences and thus understand their perspective."

This is a critical question for FLP researchers interested in the perspectives and voices of the young: how do we, for example, avoid asking typically adult questions and mediating adult perceptions of how things are? How do we really explore and examine children's language practices, ideologies and life experiences in their own terms? How do we reverse perspectives and learn from the young?

4 Making sense of (non-linguistic) emotions

Tempting as it is for a linguist to rely on language-based models to explain children's (bilingual) language development and processes of language maintenance and change – a natural consequence of the FLP field's emergence from the traditions of socio- and psycholinguistics, applied linguistics, language socialisation, language learning, and language planning and policy – we must bear in mind that language is only one of many dimensions affecting family life. There is a risk that we will apply a linguacentrist perspective, i.e., we will exaggerate the role of language(s), in the lives of multilingual families. To date we have a fairly large body of knowledge on the impact of language attitudes, linguistic input, language ideologies, parental language strategies and the ascribed values of different languages in minority/majority/endangered/sociocultural/educational etc. contexts on language learning, transmission and revitalisation. We know less about the impact of other aspects not directly related to language on these processes, aspects such as family communication style, child and parent personality characteristics, or parent-child connectedness (Van den Bulck, Custers, and Nelissen 2016).

The relationships between socio-emotional factors and language developmental outcomes cannot be reduced to simplistic models of cause and effect, simply because the human being is a fairly unpredictable and autonomous subject with emotions and personality at the same time as (s)he is social and adaptive and part of complex dynamic systems (De Houwer 2015). As Tannenbaum (2012: 58) contends, FLP differs from broader national and societal policies in that it involves emotional issues and psychological dimensions such as a person's "[p]ast and present experiences, hopes and worries about the future, close interactions, attraction, aversion, love, hate, dependency, alienation, closeness." Along similar lines, Hirsch and Lee (2018: 890) explain that a family ideology can be in favour of a certain language practice, but that individual ideologies may differ considerably, depending on "the intricate interplay of past and present experiences, agency, desires, emotions, future plans, personality traits."

From migration studies we have learned how children have been emotionally impacted by growing up with biological parents living elsewhere, at a great geographical distance (Madianou and Miller 2012; Olwig 1999), and about the emotional work and power dynamics involved in family cases where children serve as language experts and language brokers for the parents (Orellana 2009), or when children are sent abroad to study (Hirsch and Lee 2018; Orellana et al. 2001). Migration can be an emotionally dramatic – or even traumatic – experience and in many cases this forces a shift to a new language and the (re)shaping of the FLP (Revis 2017; Tannenbaum 2012). Other significant changes of condition that have been described in the literature as affecting formulations of FLP are on the adoption of children (Fiorentino 2017; Fogle 2012; Shin 2013), and on coming out as LGBTQ, which was shown to affect bilingual identity and practices (Cashman 2017). Taking into account the large number of reconstituted families nowadays, there are, however, still surprisingly few studies examining how changed family member constellations – e.g., when parents divorce and members live apart (Levin 2004) – affect FLP. When new families are formed, the linguistic ecologies may change, as well as the social and power relationships within the family systems. Emotional dimensions touching each individual member separately also affect the system as a whole (Tannenbaum 2012).

Tannenbaum (2012) proposes a conceptual framework in which the psychoanalytical concepts of coping and defence mechanisms can be used to understand and explain how family members negotiate their FLP. She criticises FLP research for tending to leave out psycho-emotional dimensions and points out that the literature to a large extent ignores significant contributions, conceptions and methodologies from psychology, psychoanalysis and psychodynamics. Opening up to cross-fertilisation between the disciplines could provide new tools for analysis and create new insights in our understanding of FLP processes and family dynamics, particularly from the point of view of the emotions. Smith-Christmas (2017), in outlining future directions in the FLP field, indeed proposes that explorations of the psychological/affective realm are the next step in the field.

5 Connecting the family

The availability of and easy access to communication technologies have radically transformed ways of keeping contact across time and space (Madianou and Miller 2012), and these changes have direct implications for how contemporary families form and maintain social and emotional relationships (King O'Riain 2014). Whereas research strands such as computer-mediated communication have tended to focus on the linguistic content of online communication (e.g., Lee 2017), others have kept their focus on the emotional consequences of choosing between the plethora of digitally mediated tools now available for keeping in contact within transnational families (Madianou and Miller 2012), and on the complex issue of acting as a parent at a distance (Parreñas 2014). Communication technologies are, however, not only central to transnational multilingual families; they are also used to mediate, coordinate and synchronise the daily lives of individually networked family members who live in the same household (Christensen 2009). The perspective of the children is particularly crucial. Although parents in contemporary Western families tend to have a more decisive role in the purchasing of media products, in helping children to navigate media use and in setting the rules (Lim 2016), it is the children who are often the key agents and take the lead when it comes to introducing new technologies and changing media practices in families, in the literature known as the child-effect (Van den Bulck, Custers, and Nelissen 2016). This includes changing the language practices mediated through them.

Despite the significant role technology-mediated communication potentially plays in processes of language transmission and change across generations in multilingual families, research on it is still scarce within the FLP field. One exception is Hirsch (2017), who presents unique longitudinal data over 7 years of one mother who had moved from Great Britain to Israel with her family. Hirsch could follow the (re)formulations of FLP over time by tracking the mother's postings in different groups on social media (Facebook). Social media also turned out to be an important space for the mother to reflect on her evolving language ideologies, management and practices together with other mothers. In another study, Little (2019) examined how parents of different cultural and linguistic backgrounds used digital technology to support their children's language development. It gives examples of explicit parental management strategies for using technology to promote home language maintenance (see also Hatoss; Little, both this vol.).

In order to get a better picture of how multilingualism, digitally mediated communication and emotional relationships interact in contemporary families across time and space, combined insights from different research disciplines are needed. A notion from sociology that is potentially helpful for FLP researchers is *the digital family*, by which Taipale (2019: 2–3) refers to everyone – from grandchildren to grandparents – who has at least some basic familiarity with communication technologies and with some social media, and access to basic communication devices (such as a mobile phone and the internet), and uses these to stay in touch with other family and extended family members. A digital family is in these terms defined as a social structure based on the technologically mediated communication practices and routines that take place between its individual members across generations and geographical spaces. Lanigan (2009), in turn, suggests a socio-technological family framework model in which familial, extra-familial and individual characteristics influence how technologies are incorporated within the family context.

Sociological frameworks like Taipale's (2019) and Lanigan's (2009) have great analytical potential. However, they often lack the language dimension, which is where linguists come in. In order to develop "innovative research protocols that can make sense of the mobile multi-screen, multi-app, multi-media and multi-modal environment that surrounds families today," which Lim (2016: 27) calls for, we need to add issues that come with multilingualism.

6 Topics for future enquiry

In order to expand our knowledge about FLP processes we need further empirical evidence from a wider range of family types, languages, and contexts (Lanza and Lomeu Gomes this vol.). However, simply adding more cases to the cumulative body of FLP data is not enough; we should also have the courage to raise new issues, ask new types of research questions, be open to unconventional research methodologies, and challenge our own conceptual as well as epistemological traditions. In the following I start by suggesting different perspectives that the researcher can take on what is a family, i.e., the object of study. After that I propose a number of research questions, and methodologies that can be applied to respond to questions like these.

6.1 Who is in the family?

When conducting FLP studies, the researcher needs to define for themselves what is meant by family in that particular study, to identify his/her own position and ideological underpinnings, and determine how family is going to be examined (Wright forthcoming). This orientation informs the analytical stances and methodological choices, the questions that can be asked as well as the conclusions that can ultimately be drawn from the data.

Family, seen as a fixed unit and defined in terms of the members it consists of, is a common category in FLP research. Hence, in finding his/her research target, the ethnographer may decide to search for a family unit that meets certain pre-set criteria of membership and roles (e.g. a mother, a father and a child under school age in ethnolinguistic community X, speaking languages Y and Z). In administering a survey, a sociolinguist might include boxes to be ticked for family roles (e.g. mother, father), to be used as statistical variables to explain specific language outcomes. These are straightforward and powerful means of conducting research. Yet one needs to be careful with the pre-conceptions that are involved in the procedures: One gets what one asks for. In other words, defining and setting the criteria for what counts as a family beforehand is a deductive and top-down process, including the risk of implementing normative flaws (Ericsson 2017).

A more inductive and bottom-up perspective on what makes a family is to depart from the individual and focus on social and personal relationships and interconnected individual networks (Pahl and Spencer 2004). The observation of family communities and examination of their practices and interpersonal ties of different types and strengths can, for example, be done through social network analysis (Milroy and Gordon 2003). Although Western notions of family stress kinship relations, there may be other personal relationships that are significant (Budgeon and Roseneil 2004; Cashman 2017) and represent different types of ties, contacts, choices and commitments (Milroy and Gordon 2003; Pahl and Spencer 2004). It is a challenge to decide where to draw the lines in these webs of relational links and identify not only which these significant relationships are, but also *how* and *why* they are significant. Lanza and Svendsen (2007) have suggested that social network analysis should be supplemented with interpretative and constructivist approaches in order to account for issues of identity and ideology. Moreover, in digital families (Taipale 2019) the networked practices and the use of communication technologies between members need to be mapped. Applying multilingual practices to the digital family adds further dimensions into the complex family web.

A third way of viewing the family is to see the family as an ecological and dynamic system. In this view, we should be able to capture family dynamics and changes over time and space, at the same time taking individual as well as external factors into account. This way of modelling the family is challenging but can be informed by theories in related fields, such as dynamic systems theory in applied linguistics (Larsen-Freeman 2012) or family systems theory in sociology (e.g., Lanigan 2009). In order to examine the family as dynamic, emotional and built on interpersonal relationships, we can learn from different branches of psychology (Tannenbaum 2012). If we see the family as a complex and dynamic ecosystem, we may be informed by theories from the natural sciences or even mathematical modelling. If the focus is on technology-mediated communication and FLP, we can learn from communication theory, computer-mediated communication as well as IT, and so on.

As FLP researchers – whether individuals or a community – we need to make clear how we conceptually understand family and what the consequences are of this understanding in terms of theorising, the questions we ask, the factors, targets or phenomena we choose to examine, and the methodologies we apply. Some researchers have argued that reliance on a family-based model of intergenerational language transmission is a dominant narrative within sociolinguistics that needs to be challenged (Cashman 2017). The ultimate critical question will be whether we need a concept of family at all, challenging the validity of the construct. This in turn will have important epistemological implications for the research field of FLP.

6.2 Potential research questions

Based on the discussion in this chapter, I will suggest some research issues that could be further explored as part of the FLP field. In Table 1 a number of potential research questions are formulated. The list is neither exhaustive – there are many important aspects I have not been able to address in this chapter (see e.g. Lanza and Lomeu Gomes this vol.) – nor does it necessarily present entirely new or unexplored issues. Rather, the list presents a collection of issues that deserve further attention and that I propose could inform future studies.

Table 1: Suggestions for research questions that may be asked and explored further as part of FLP research.

Research questions
– How is "family" understood and researched by other related scientific disciplines such as psychology, sociology, anthropology, economics, communication studies, or the natural sciences, and to what extent can (and should?) FLP be informed by multidisciplinary approaches, bringing in new epistemologies, perspectives and interpretations?
– How is family conceptualised, politicised, brought into the ideology and realised in practice, in and by different states, and in different political, religious and community contexts across the globe? How do these facts affect the way we pose research issues and understand our objects of study?
– How do divorce and reconstituted family configurations affect a child's (language) world? How do changes in emotional landscapes and relationships in connection with reconstituted family settings affect language practices and FLP?
– How do single-parent families navigate in multilingual contexts and how is family multilingualism managed in sociocultural contexts where family membership is more fluid or non-normative?
– How do we, as (adult) researchers, cross age barriers and mediate true perspectives of the young and their experiences? How can we learn from the young and their life worlds and collaborate with them in the development of appropriate data collection methodologies? How do we capture phenomena such as the child-effect (Van den Bulck, Custers, and Nelissen 2016), reverse questions and examine FLP processes as multi-way interactions?
– How is child agency perceived in family contexts in different parts of the world, in different ideological, socio-economic, educational and religious contexts, and what are its consequences for FLP? What is the impact of different cultural (or individual) practices of child-rearing on processes of language transmission and change?
– In the negotiation and formation of FLPs, what is the role of inter-personal emotions and power relations that are not necessarily linguistically encoded? How do we refrain from being "linguacentric" (cf. discussion above) in our explanatory models of multilingual families?
– How do flight from war, experiencing a split family, and emotional turmoil affect different members of the family and aspects of their FLP, and over time?
– What is the role of languages in emotional endeavours such as emotional streaming (King O'Riain 2014) and intimate labour parenting (Parreñas 2014)?
– How do family members use different modes of technological communication to maintain their networks (cf., Madianou and Miller 2012; Rudi et al. 2015; Stern and Messer 2009), over time and space, and as mediated by language(s)?
– How can we, in Lim's (2016: 27) wording, "develop innovative research protocols that can make sense of the mobile multi-screen, multi-app, multi-media and multi-modal environment that surrounds families today", and add multilingualism to these protocols?
– How do technology-mediated communicative affordances serve to empower and transmit home languages and identities within families, across (and within) generations? Do they hinder language transmission in any way and if so, how and why?

In each of these cases we need to critically examine to what extent they are relevant to the key issues of FLP research (such as how home languages are transmitted, learned, or changed in a family context), and the implications for policymaking (cf. King 2016: 731) and (re)formulate our questions accordingly. Still we should be able to pose questions in new ways too, not limited to a certain paradigm of questions.

6.3 Methodological approaches

The FLP field has always been defined by methodological and interdisciplinary diversity (King 2016) and this diversity has become even more significant in recent years, along with new research interests. Curdt-Christiansen (2018) divides the methods used in FLP into three broad categories: quantitative approaches (such as survey studies), qualitative and interpretative approaches (e.g. interview, narrative and ethnographic data), and sociolinguistic ethnography (including audio- and video-recorded family interactional data). In the following I will suggest some methodological and analytical (primarily qualitative and interpretative) approaches that might be helpful in understanding and examining the sort of issues discussed in the previous sections.

To connect with the issue of how the notion of family is understood across different sociocultural, political or disciplinary contexts, critical discourse analysis (e.g., Wodak and Meyer 2009) is helpful. The analysis of linguistic landscapes (Gorter 2006), e.g., how family is reflected in public signage, may yield enlightening results. Linguistic-oriented approaches are also possible, such as corpus analysis, concept, or the lexical analysis (Litosseliti 2010) of, for example, official (policy) texts. If the focus is rather on the individual and his/her perceived family and relationships, an informant can be asked, "Who is in your family? Could you make a list?" or "Could you place your family on this sheet of paper according to closeness and distance to you?" (Levin 2004: 229). Prieto-Blanco (2016) has used photographs to elicit members' "circle of reference" in transnational families and Ericsson (2017) developed an app to elicit discursive constructions of cisnormativity in interactions between parents and 5–8-year-old children.

If families are looked at in terms what members come together and *do* (rather than who they *are*), mediated discourse analysis (Scollon 2001), nexus analysis (Scollon and Scollon 2004) or Moment Analysis (Zhu and Li 2016) can be useful. The point of departure in mediated discourse analysis and nexus analysis is social action, i.e., "any social action taken by an individual with reference to a social network, also called a mediated action" (Scollon and Scollon 2004: 11). All social actions are mediated; this means that all practices – linguistically encoded or not – are shaped by and filtered through subjective and collective experiences, beliefs, ideologies, interaction orders, expectations, and physical environments. Moment Analysis focuses on frequent and regular patterns of linguistic behaviour and creative actions that have immediate as well as long-term consequences (Zhu and Li 2016). In mediated discourse analysis terms, these moments of repeated actions are called nexus of practice. The researcher cannot presuppose which actions, discourses and data are relevant and need closer study. It is therefore up to the (FLP) researcher to identify and recognise the relevant components of and agents in the nexus of practice.

Mediated discourse analysis is particularly powerful in unpacking multilayered and complex social phenomena and understanding FLP-making processes on different scales of time and space (see Curdt-Christiansen and Huang this vol.), and in describing FLP processes and discourses in single families (Palviainen and Boyd 2013; Palviainen and Bergroth 2018). When the conceptual and analytical perspective is social action – rather than a fixed social unit, interconnected personal networks, or space – the analysis of e.g. digitally mediated relationships in multilingual, transnational or reconstituted family configurations becomes particularly fruitful. Applying linguistic analyses of digitally mediated messages (e.g., Lexander 2018) or multimodal conversational analysis (Mondada 2016) to video call interactions can give us information about processes of language transmission across time and space.

A strong argument throughout this chapter has been that we should see FLP as a dynamic phenomenon and analysis should take into account that family configurations, language ecologies, and significant relationships and memberships change over time. The calls for true longitudinal studies of families (e.g., King and Fogle 2017) are challenging time-wise, as they might require the researcher to follow one or more families for several years (see Smith-Christmas. this vol.). The time aspect can, however, also be captured through, for example, retrospective interviews (Palviainen and Bergroth 2018), or life cycle analysis (He 2014), or by tracing FLP changes in social media (Hirsch 2017). Olwig's (1999) study on the life stories of four adults who reflected on their experiences of growing up in the Caribbean without one or both parents focuses particularly on emotions and memories as a function of time.

In the technologically saturated world of today, where time and space are conflated, we need to try to understand the role of technical mediation in contemporary family life, emotions and communication. As FLP researchers, we should particularly aim to understand the role of languages in these digitally mediated processes, as they carry the potential for language transmission and learning (Little this vol.). As has been strongly urged in this chapter, every member of the family should have their voice heard from their own perspective, including children of all ages. Taking part, as FLP researchers do, in sociolinguistic ethnography and qualitative and interpretative inquiries (Curdt-Christiansen 2018), we want to know what individuals do with language and also what they think about what they do. The data collection can be researcher-led, participant-led or co-constructed combinations of these. Methods include shadowing or mobile ethnography (Czarniawska 2007), visual methods and visual ethnography (Kalaja and Pitkänen-Huhta 2018; Pauwels 2015; Pink et al. 2016), mixtures of observations, chatlogs and interviews (Androutsopoulos 2008), online ethnographies (Markham and Baym 2009), and participant-generated videos/recordings/diaries (Boivin and Cohenmiller 2018).

Boivin and Cohenmiller (2018: 589) encourage ethnographic researchers to move away from the use of technology only as a simple data collection device and propose "moving into a greater co-constructed dialogue between participants, observers, researchers, teachers, and community members with the use of digital technology used by participants during ethnographic observations." A good example of this type of research is the study by Noppari, Uusitalo, and Kumpulainen (2017). In their study, the researchers carried out activity-oriented interviewing (an approach in which materials prepared by the participants and clues found in the home environment guide the interviews) with children aged 5, 8 and 11 years, wherever they chose in their homes, about their media use. When data are co-constructed and participants become researchers and choose their data, unexpected results, insights and developments are made possible. In this way we can advance and develop the FLP field methodologically by asking: What can we as professional researchers learn from young informants in whose lives digital media is deeply integrated? What happens when we put lab coats on children, empowering them as researchers? Engaging with even younger, pre-school and pre-literate children can be challenging, but for example Crump and Phipps (2013) and Almér (2017) have provided some methodological ideas, and Ericsson and Boyd (2017) reflect on how to engage such children in research in an ethically appropriate way.

Other possible methodologies include quantitative surveys (e.g., De Houwer 2007; Kayam and Hirsch 2012) and experimental designs. One ethical as well as methodological challenge is how to examine the relationships between non-linguistic personal and emotional characteristics, such as shyness, introversion/extroversion or self-confidence, and language practices. As De Houwer (2015) points out, it is in practice impossible for third persons, such as researchers, to decide on subjective well-being – including affective information about how one feels – in a particular situation, but it ought to be of significance. In this sense we can probably learn from psychoanalytical and psychodynamic protocols, as pointed out by Tannenbaum (2012).

7 Conclusion

In this chapter I have sought to map topics that I consider need further attention in future FLP research, I have suggested research questions to be posed and offered ideas on how to empirically conduct the studies. I have also put forward a conceptual understanding of the family context as dynamic and the family as comprised of individuals who each have their own (changing) emotions, agency and ideologies. In order to research and understand these complexities, cross-disciplinary initiatives and the courage to think outside the box theoretically as well as methodologically are required.

The question is whether the application of too diverse approaches, cross-disciplinary initiatives and methodologies will lead to the FLP field losing its foundation, its identity and its raison d'être, and a risk of being subsumed into other fields (cf. King and Fogle 2017). King (2016: 731) argues for the need of a shared body of central research questions and methodologies to be able to definitively and collectively answer the questions and move the field forward. King (2016) further identifies as a problem the fact that a research focus on meaning-making in families rather than outcomes tends not to provide findings that are productive or responsive to policy-making. Consequently, Lanza and Lomeu Gomes (this vol.) predict that the FLP field will return to a language outcome focus in the future. In the context of the current handbook, it is worth remembering home language transmission and including that in the research issues. As Hirsch and Lee (2018: 885) conclude, "[a]lthough FLP examines relationships with all languages in the life of a family, FLP regarding HLs [=Heritage Languages] is particularly important to understand as it bears lasting influences on identity development, self-esteem, and academic achievement on children."

The concerns raised are relevant and as FLP researchers we need to acknowledge and discuss them. I do, however, think that in order for the field to advance it is necessary to allow for a stage characterised by diversity and experimentation, and to be ready to approach the topic with new ideas and in innovative ways. As Smith-Christmas (2017: 25) puts it: "there is much at stake in FLP research, and it is our job as researchers to see that we move the field forward." As for future prospects and visions for FLP, despite the risks and challenges associated with a fast-expanding and diverse field, I am confident that FLP as an academic field is here to stay. Regardless of how families are defined, language policy and practices within multilingual families across time and space will continue to be important for our understanding of the processes of language transmission and change. However, as with all academic fields, in order to find its future identity FLP needs to grow, develop and adapt in step with the changing times.

References

Almér, Elin. 2017. Children's beliefs about bilingualism and language use as expressed in child-adult conversations. *Multilingua – Journal of Cross-cultural and Interlanguage Communication* 36(4). 401–424.

Androutsopoulos, Jannis. 2008. Potentials and limitations of Discourse-Centred Online Ethnography. *Language@Internet* 5(8). 1–20.

Bergroth, Mari & Åsa Palviainen. 2017. Bilingual children as policy agents: Language policy and education policy in minority language medium Early Childhood Education and Care. *Multilingua* 36(4). 375–399.

Boivin, Nettie & Anna Cohenmiller. 2018. Breaking the "fourth wall" in qualitative research: Participant-led digital data construction. *The Qualitative Report* 23(3). 581–592.

Budgeon, Shelley & Sasha Roseneil. 2004. Editors' introduction: Beyond the conventional family. *Current Sociology* 52(2). 127–134.

Caldas, Stephen J. 2006. *Raising bilingual-biliterate children in monolingual cultures*. Clevedon: Multilingual Matters.

Cashman, Holly R. 2017. *Queer, latinx, and bilingual: Narrative resources in the negotiation of identities*. New York: Routledge.

Christensen, Toke H. 2009. "Connected presence" in distributed family life. *New Media & Society* 11(3). 433–451.

Crump, Alison & Heather Phipps. 2013. Listening to children's voices: Reflections on researching with children in multilingual Montreal. *Learning Landscapes* 7(1). 129–148.

Curdt-Christiansen, Xiao Lan. 2009. Invisible and visible language planning: Ideological factors in the family language policy of Chinese immigrant families in Quebec. *Language Policy* 8(4). 351–375.

Curdt-Christiansen, Xiao Lan. 2016. Conflicting language ideologies and contradictory language practices in Singaporean multilingual families. *Journal of Multilingual and Multicultural Development* 37(7). 694–709.

Curdt-Christiansen, Xiao Lan. 2018. Family Language Policy. In James W. Tollefson & Miguel Pérez-Milans (eds.), *The Oxford handbook of language policy and planning*, 420–441. Oxford: Oxford University Press.

Curdt-Christiansen Xiao Lan & Jing Huang. this vol. Factors influencing family language policy.

Czarniawska, Barbara. 2007. *Shadowing and other techniques for doing fieldwork in modern societies*. Malmö: Liber.

De Houwer, Annick. 2007. Parental language input patterns and children's bilingual use. *Applied Psycholinguistics* 28(3). 411–424.

De Houwer, Annick. 2015. Harmonious bilingual development: Young families' well-being in language contact situations. *International Journal of Bilingualism* 19(2). 169–184.

Doyle, Conan. 2013. To make the root stronger: Language policies and experiences of successful multilingual intermarried families with adolescent children in Tallinn. In Mila Schwartz & Anna Verschik (eds.), *Successful family language policy: Parents, children and educators in interaction*, 145–175. Dordrecht: Springer.

Eisenchlas, Susana A. & Andrea C. Schalley. this vol. Making sense of the notion of "home language" and related concepts.

Ericsson, Stina. 2017. The language of cisnormativity: Children and parents in interaction with a multimodal app. *Gender and Language* 12(2). 139–167.

Ericsson, Stina & Sally Boyd. 2017. Children's ongoing and relational negotiation of informed assent in child–researcher, child–child and child–parent interaction. *Childhood* 24(3). 300–315.

Fiorentino, Alice. 2017. Strategies for language maintenance in transnational adoption: Which role for the parents? *Journal of Home Language Research* 2. 5–22.

Fishman, Joshua A. 1991. *Reversing language shift*. Clevedon: Multilingual Matters.

Fogle, Lyn W. 2012. *Second language socialization and learner agency: Talk in three adoptive families*. Clevedon: Multilingual Matters.

Gorter, Durk (ed.). 2006. *Linguistic landscape: A new approach to multilingualism*. Clevedon & Buffalo: Multilingual Matters.

Hatoss Anikó. this vol. Transnational grassroots language planning in the era of mobility and the Internet.

He, Weigun A. 2014. Heritage language development and identity construction throughout the life cycle. In Terrence G. Wiley, Joy K. Peyton, Donna Christian, Sarah C. K. Moore & Na Liu (eds.), *Handbook of heritage, community, and native American languages in the United States. Research, policy and educational practice*, 324–332. New York, NY: Routledge.

Hirsch, Tijana. 2017. *An ethnographic study of transnational family language policy in Facebook communities across time*. Santa Barbara: University of California PhD dissertation.

Hirsch, Tijana & Jin S. Lee. 2018. Understanding the complexities of transnational family language policy. *Journal of Multilingual and Multicultural Development* 39(10). 882–894.

Juvonen, Päivi, Susana A. Eisenchlas, Tim Roberts & Andrea C. Schalley. this vol. Researching social and affective factors in home language maintenance: A methodology overview.

Kalaja, Paula & Anne Pitkänen-Huhta. 2018. ALR special issue: Visual methods in applied language studies. *Applied Linguistics Review* 9(2–3). 157–176.

Kayam, Orly & Tijana Hirsch. 2012. Using social media networks to conduct questionnaire based research in social studies case study: Family language policy. *Journal of Sociological Research* 3(2). 57–67.

Kayam, Orly & Tijana Hirsch. 2014. Socialization of language through family language policy: A case study. *Psychology of Language and Communication* 18(1). 53–66.

Kheirkhah, Mina. 2016. *From family language practices to family language policies*. Linköping: Linköping University PhD dissertation.

King, Kendall A. 2016. Language policy, multilingual encounters, and transnational families. *Journal of Multilingual and Multicultural Development* 37(7). 726–733.

King, Kendall A. & Lyn W. Fogle. 2013. Family language policy and bilingual parenting. *Language Teaching* 46(2). 172–194.

King, Kendall A. & Lyn W. Fogle. 2017. Family language policy. In Theresa McCarty & Stephen May (eds.), Language policy and political issues in education. Encyclopedia of language and education, 315–326. Cham: Springer.

King, Kendall A., Lyn Fogle & Aubrey Logan-Terry. 2008. Family language policy. *Language and Linguistics Compass* 2(5). 907–922.

King O'Riain, Rebecca. 2014. Transconnective space, emotions and skype: The transnational emotional practices of mixed international couples in the republic of Ireland. In Eran Fisher & Tova Benski (eds.), *Internet and emotions*, 131–143. New York: Routledge.

Lanigan, Jane D. 2009. A sociotechnological model for family research and intervention: How information and communication technologies affect family life. *Marriage & Family Review* 45(6–8). 587–609.

Lanza, Elizabeth & Rafael Lomeu Gomes. this vol. Family language policy: Foundations, theoretical perspectives and critical approaches.

Lanza, Elizabeth & Bente A. Svendsen. 2007. Tell me who your friends are and I might be able to tell you what language(s) you speak: Social network analysis, multilingualism, and identity. *International Journal of Bilingualism* 11(3). 275–300.

Larsen-Freeman, Diane. 2012. Complex, dynamic systems: A new transdisciplinary theme for applied linguistics? *Language Teaching* 45(2). 202–214.

Lee, Carmen. 2017. *Multilingualism online*. Milton Park, Abingdon, Oxon: Routledge.

Levin, Irene. 2004. Living apart together: A new family form. *Current Sociology* 52(2). 223–240.

Lexander, Kristin V. 2018. Nuancing the Jaxase – young and urban texting in Senegal. In Cece Cutler & Unn Røyneland (eds.), *Analyzing multilingual youth practices in computer mediated communication (CMC)*, 68–86. Cambridge: Cambridge University Press.

Lim, Sun S. 2016. Through the tablet glass: Transcendent parenting in an era of mobile media and cloud computing. *Journal of Children and Media* 10(1). 21–29.

Litosseliti, Lia (ed.). 2010. *Research methods in linguistics*. London: Continuum.

Little, Sabine. 2019. "Is there an app for that?" Exploring games and apps among heritage language families. *Journal of Multilingual and Multicultural Development* 40(3). 218–229.

Little, Sabine. this vol. Social media and the use of technology in home language maintenance.

Luykx, Aurolyn. 2005. *Children as socializing agents: Family language policy in situations of language shift*. Somerville, MA: Cascadilla Press.

Madianou, Mirca & Daniel Miller. 2012. *Migration and new media: Transnational families and polymedia*. Abingdon, Oxon, New York: Routledge.

Markham, Annette N. & Nancy K. Baym (eds.). 2009. *Internet inquiry: Conversations about method*. Los Angeles: Sage

Milroy, Lesley & Matthew Gordon. 2003. *Sociolinguistics. Method and Interpretation*. Oxford: Blackwell Publishing

Mondada, Lorenza. 2016. Challenges of multimodality: Language and the body in social interaction. *Journal of Sociolinguistics* 20(3). 336–366.

Noppari, Elina, Niina Uusitalo & Reijo Kupiainen. 2017. Talk to me! Possibilities of constructing children's voices in the domestic research context. *Childhood* 24(1). 68–83.

Olwig, Karen F. 1999. Narratives of the children left behind: Home and identity in globalised Caribbean families. *Journal of Ethnic and Migration Studies* 25(2). 267–284.

Orellana, Marjorie F. 2009. *Translating childhoods*. New Brunswick, N.J: Rutgers University Press.

Orellana, Marjorie F., Barrie Thorne, Anna Chee & Wan S. E. Lam. 2001. Transnational childhoods: The participation of children in processes of family migration. *Social Problems* 48(4). 572–591.

Pahl, Ray & Liz Spencer. 2004. Personal communities: Not simply families of 'fate' or 'choice'. *Current Sociology* 52(2). 199–221.

Palviainen, Åsa & Mari Bergroth. 2018. Parental discourses of language ideology and linguistic identity in multilingual Finland. *International Journal of Multilingualism* 15(3). 262–275.

Palviainen, Åsa & Sally Boyd. 2013. Unity in discourse, diversity in practice. The one-person one-language policy in bilingual families. In Mila Schwartz & Anna Verschik (eds.), *Successful family language policy: Parents, children and educators in interaction*, 223–248. Dordrecht: Springer.

Parada, Maryann. 2013. Sibling variation and family language policy: The role of birth order in the Spanish proficiency and first names of second-generation Latinos. *Journal of Language, Identity & Education* 12(5). 299–320.

Parreñas, Rachel S. 2014. The intimate labour of transnational communication. *Families, Relationships and Societies* 3(3). 425–442.

Pauwels, Luc. 2015. *Reframing visual social science: Towards a more visual sociology and anthropology*. Cambridge, United Kingdom: Cambridge University Press.

Pink, Sarah, Heather Horst, John Postill, Larissa Hjorth, Tania Lewis & Jo Tacchi. 2016. *Digital ethnography. Principles and practice*. Los Angeles: Sage.

Prieto-Blanco, Patricia. 2016. (Digital) photography, experience and space in transnational families. A case study of Spanish-Irish families living in Ireland. In Edgar Gómez Cruz & Asko Lehmuskallio (eds.), *Digital photography and everyday life. Empirical studies on material visual practices*, 122–140. New York, NY: Routledge.

Prout, Alan. 2011. Taking a step away from modernity: Reconsidering the new sociology of childhood. *Global Studies of Childhood* 1(1). 4–14.

Revis, Melanie. 2017. Family language policy in refugee-background communities: Towards a model of language management and practices. *Journal of Home Language Research* 2. 40–62.

Rudi, Jessie, Jodi Dworkin, Susan Walker & Jennifer Doty. 2015. Parents' use of information and communications technologies for family communication: differences by age of children. *Information, Communication & Society* 18(1). 78–93.

Said, Fatma & Zhu Hua. 2019. "No, no Maama! Say 'Shaatir ya Ouledee Shaatir'!" Children's agency in language use and socialisation. *International Journal of Bilingualism* 23(3). 771–785.

Schwartz, Mila. 2010. Family language policy: Core issues of an emerging field. *Applied Linguistics Review* 1(1). 171–192.
Schwartz, Mila. this vol. Strategies and practices of home language maintenance.
Scollon, Ron. 2001. *Mediated discourse: The nexus of practice*. London: Routledge.
Scollon, Ron & Suzie W. Scollon. 2004. *Nexus analysis. Discourse and the emerging Internet*. London: Routledge.
Shin, Sarah J. 2013. Transforming culture and identity: Transnational adoptive families and heritage language learning. *Language, Culture and Curriculum* 26(2). 161–178.
Smith-Christmas, Cassie. 2017. Family language policy: New directions. In John Macalister & Seyed H. Mirvahedi (eds.), *Family language policies in a multilingual world. Opportunities, challenges, and consequences*, 13–29. London: Routledge.
Smith-Christmas, Cassie. this vol. Child agency and home language maintenance.
Spolsky, Bernard. 2012. Family language policy – the critical domain. *Journal of Multilingual and Multicultural Development* 33(1). 3–11.
Stern, Michael J. & Chris Messer. 2009. How family members stay in touch: A quantitative investigation of core family networks. *Marriage & Family Review* 45(6–8). 654–676.
Taipale, Sakari. 2019. *Intergenerational connections in digital families*. Cham: Springer International.
Tannenbaum, Michal. 2012. Family language policy as a form of coping or defence mechanism. *Journal of Multilingual and Multicultural Development* 33(1). 57–66.
Tyrrell, Naomi. 2015. Transnational migrant children's language practices in translocal spaces. *Diskurs Kindheits- und Jugendforschung* 10(1). 11–23.
Van den Bulck, Jan, Kathleen Custers & Sara Nelissen. 2016. The child-effect in the new media environment: Challenges and opportunities for communication research. *Journal of Children and Media* 10(1). 30–38.
Wodak, Ruth & Michael Meyer (eds.). 2009. *Methods of critical discourse analysis*. Los Angeles, CA: Sage.
Wright, Lyn. forthcoming. *Critical perspectives on language and kinship in multilingual families*. London: Bloomsbury.
Zhu, Hua. 2008. Duelling languages, duelling values: Codeswitching in bilingual intergenerational conflict talk in diasporic families. *Journal of Pragmatics* 40(10). 1799–1816.
Zhu, Hua & Li Wei. 2016. Transnational experience, aspiration and family language policy. *Journal of Multilingual and Multicultural Development* 37(7). 655–666.

Part 3: **Grassroot initiatives**

Sabine Little

13 Social media and the use of technology in home language maintenance

1 Introduction

The ubiquity of technology has led to the re-classification and expansion of many terms used in the context of family and language research. Marsh et al. (2017), for example, propose an expansion of the term "family literacy", first coined by Taylor (1983), ensuring that digital practices inherent in modern family life are more explicitly included in research and policy. A thus expanded notion of "family digital literacy" is then distinct from the notions used in the existing research in the field of digital literacy, with the former providing a specific focus on family digital practices, while the latter is more closely related to skills development linked to digital practices, both internal and external to the family context.

Within the realm of multilingual families, the notion of family language policy (Lanza and Lomeu Gomes; Palviainen, both this vol.) may require a similar "digital" addendum, taking into account recent technological developments in the family context. With uptake and availability of technology still continuing to rise, social understandings of family language, with respect to policies and education, need to consider family language policy from a technological perspective: What media are accessed within the family, specifically by the children, and how access is actioned within the family setting. Further questions need to be asked, such as: To what extent does the availability of media and the ability to access and navigate them influence the child's attitude and use of the home language? In contemporary families, technology facilitates a significant proportion of daily language input, especially as children grow older. It is therefore of vital importance to critically explore and understand both the affordances and barriers technology puts in place, specifically for multilingual families.

This chapter explores the use of technology and social media in multilingual families, particularly those with younger children of primary school age. The focus is first on a detailed exploration of motivational factors of technology, and how these may be utilised for home language development (section 2), before it shifts to how the language of social media and popular culture may influence children's sense of belonging (section 3). The research literature around screen time is then critically evaluated (section 4), before this chapter looks at the affordances of specific technologies in relation to home language maintenance (sections 5 and 6). The difference between consumption of, and participation in, media is discussed in section 7, while the role of parents as gatekeepers is outlined in section 8. Finally, the chapter offers conclusions on how technology may become more integrated into family digital practices, supporting home language development through parent-child collaboration (section 9).

2 Motivational aspects of technology

Understanding how multilingual children view themselves both as individuals and within their family, school, and social context, is an important consideration when seeking to understand multilingual identities (Little 2020). Technology forms a significant part of our lives, and the way we access, use, and relate to technology forms an important aspect of our sense of self. Operating on the principles of autonomy, competence, and relatedness, self-determination theory (Ryan and Deci 2008) seeks to understand motivational factors that may influence behaviour. Borrowing from the notion of self-determination theory and curated identity, or the notion of how we choose to display ourselves online (Potter 2012), we can conclude that our lives online are as much part of our identity as our lives offline. Among multilingual children, this "determination of the self" is arguably more complex, balancing composite identities (Tseng this vol.) which have emotional links to the children's and the parents' heritage, thus necessitating a careful examination of the place that multiple languages have in the children's life, and – in the context of this chapter – how technology relates to this.

The increase in technology over recent years undoubtedly means increased access for children to a large variety of both suitable and unsuitable online experiences (Blackwell et al. 2014). However, the links between technology and motivation require critical consideration. Early on in the literature around motivation and online environments, Katz (2002) suggested that there might be a "'psychological suitability" for the medium, particularly among those

> who held attitudes such as positive self-image, independence in the learning process, self-confidence in the learning process, satisfaction with learning, internal locus of control, level of control of learning, creativity, and motivation for study (Katz 2002: 5).

This was among the first publications highlighting the notion of an inherently motivational pull of technology, at a time when many still saw the medium as being particularly suitable to work with disaffected learners (see e.g. Franklin 2001). In a study on the relationship between the motivation to engage in online games and the motivation to engage with the home language (Little 2019a), background information provided by 212 participating families showed that 82% of children had a generic interest in online or mobile games, and an encouraging 78% of the families declared that children were, in principle, interested in the home language. These figures, and the resulting overlap amongst the two groups, highlight the potential affordances of the medium specifically within the home language context, although the dichotomy of children as language learners versus children as game players needs to be further explored (Little 2019a). Whitton (2013), for example, points out that the enjoyment of playing games does not necessarily correlate with the motivation to engage in games-based learning, and that online games and access to technology raise complex tensions around equity and social inclusion. Just because a child likes playing 'Fortnite' (an online multi-player game which rewards strategy and collaboration) does not mean that the same child will happily engage with a points-based vocabulary test, or a kanji writing app, and we need to be careful not to oversimplify children's interests, and instead as agents capable of expressing their own digital preferences (Smith-Christmas this vol.).

At the same time, this distinction between different types of games does not necessarily mean that there will be a clearly designated split between engagement for entertainment and engagement for language learning. In fact, Kalantzis and Cope (2012) discuss ubiquitous learning among the current generation of children, whose learning, thanks to technological access and multiliteracies, is not confined to the classroom or even to the family context, but may instead take place at any time, through a variety of media, both formally and informally. With many opportunities for online language engagement, then, it becomes ever more important to understand the complexities facing multilingual families, seeking to develop a holistic approach to online technology and social media, which has the potential to embrace and support all family languages.

Looking at these complexities more closely, there are several important considerations linked to expertise, knowledge, and power: While children may be comfortable in the world of social media and online technologies, younger children in particular may not necessarily have either the language skills or the ability to navigate resources in the home language. Similarly, fully grasping financial implications of online resources – which ones need payment, which ones need subscriptions, which ones are free, and which ones have hidden costs – may be difficult for children and/or parents. Parents and children may also have very different views on the kinds of games and apps that they find motivating, desirable, or useful, leading to interfamily tensions. As a result, parents may prioritise "edutainment" games aimed at language learning (Little 2019a). These games are often thinly veiled learning apps, focusing on vocabulary learning or developing literacy skills. On the other hand, games which have been designed purely for game play have been shown to include up to 36 different types of learning opportunities, including semiotics, situated meaning, cultural models, and textual and intertextual understanding (Gee 2004). As such, they have the potential to support several forms of action-based language acquisition (Glenberg and Gallese 2012). Nevertheless, they are often viewed by parents as secondary or negative, and disregarded in favour of more obvious educational games, which may hold little appeal for the children.

It is rare to find custom-made environments specifically for children who have little confidence in their home language, and those that do exist are often tied to specific funding streams (e.g. research grants) which make it difficult to maintain and update resources. Edwards et al. (2002) report on an interface enabling children independently, or families collaboratively, to create their own books in a minority language, while Eisenchlas, Schalley, and Moyes (2016) explore the affordances of three custom-designed games played by nine children from German home language backgrounds, reporting improvement in motivation to engage with the home language, as well as advanced literacy development. While the resources created for these studies are successful, they lack the funds to make them commercially viable, and thus they often become unavailable once research funding finishes. Looking at the commercial market, and being able to navigate it successfully, therefore becomes a vital component in the search for sustainable and engaging opportunities for language use.

Smith-Christmas (2018) explores how playful language engagement on the child's terms can help with the affective aspects of home language management, assisting children in forming positive associations with the language, and ultimately transferring these associations to attitudes and language use. Understanding the children's world view here is a vital enabler for a positive motivational relationship between the child and the home language, and facilitating the child to lead their own gaming explorations according to preference can have vital motivational impact in terms of language engagement, even if language learning in and of itself is not a core function of the game or app in question. A sense of identity and belonging can be an important factor in children's digital practices, making this a relevant focus for the following section.

3 Social media and popular culture as belonging

Among children, access to social media and technology fulfils not only the role of entertainment, but also has important social connotations, allowing them to access playground conversations, and feeling a sense of belonging among their peers (González 2005; González, Moll, and Amanti 2005). These social interactions form an important part of identity construction, a way of negotiating the self as part of social participation (Lave and Wenger 1991). Even in the early years, this identity construction and social participation is influenced by media, as popular culture informs children's conversations and play (Arthur 2001; Marsh 2005), and children frequently access a variety of media on the basis of their interests (Marsh 2009). Among multilingual families, this can lead to a split between two language selves (Orellana 1994), where one self fits in with that of peers and the majority language speakers, whereas another is relegated to the family home. Understanding how multilingual children negotiate their various interests and languages within a multimedia context is therefore an important step in facilitating language development, as well as identity construction. While Potter (2012) discusses the notion of a curated identity in terms of how and what we choose to share online, this notion can helpfully be extended by seeking to understand how children's multilingual, multimedia experiences, sometimes curated by parents, sometimes incidentally or formally introduced in educational settings, can have an impact on identity construction.

One aspect of the construction of a multilingual identity is an understanding of the cultural and social capital (Bourdieu 1986) children gain in their multilingual lives. Similar to the notion of funds of knowledge (González 2005; González, Moll, and Amanti 2005), Ashton (2005) warns that cultural capital which does not conform to the norms of the dominant society may potentially be seen as having little value in that society. While her argument is presented as a call to include more popular culture in formal literacy contexts, it throws light on the complexities experienced by multilingual families, whose cultural experiences – both online and offline – may involve multiple cultural references ranging from *babushkas* to Bollywood. For children, these experiences may provide cultural capital within the home context, but may not necessarily offer much to enhance their social standing in the playground. While parents may rightly argue that engagement with the home language is not meant to improve social standing in the playground, it is nevertheless important to seek to understand children's lives from their perspective. Although Ashton (2005: 38) concludes that

> using popular culture to build on children's existing capital gives children of all social and economic strata, racial and language groups the currency needed for full participation with their peers and in academic pursuits,

this conclusion implies that all popular culture is universally popular, foregrounding Anglophone Western cultural capital and treating popular culture as a singular concept, rather than as relevant to and popular among very different populations. But even in shared popular culture, language can make a difference, with key vocabulary being different from that of peers and preventing access to a fund of knowledge that is shared among peers. For children inhabiting multiple "cultural niches" (Boyd, Richerson, and Henrich 2011), this inhabitation of multiple cultural and social spheres requires continual maintenance and effort, potentially involving a multiple workload, such as learning the names of all Pokémon in multiple languages, or learning multiple names of Harry Potter creatures or spells. While this, of course, also has multiple benefits, and maximises development of their social capital, not all children view the effort as worthwhile (Little 2019b).

The previous sections discussed access, motivation, and negotiating multiple or composite identities in different social spheres; however, screen time remains the single most constant concern raised by parents (Little 2019a), thus warranting a dedicated section in this chapter, highlighting key literature, and juxtaposing opposing views and ideals among families.

4 Screen time

What kind of technology children should access, via what media, and how long they should spend in front of this technology has caused much debate. While some view screen time as a distraction from learning, others argue for media supporting learning, facilitating both language and literacy development (Robinson and Mackey 2003). Wright et al. (2001), for example, point to the benefits of educational content for children; however, little is known about the viewing habits of multilingual children, where arguably accessing media in the home language can be said to have educational potential, regardless of educational content, by increasing exposure and access. Similar to the previous problematisation of motivation to play versus motivation to learn, in a multilingual context, we therefore need to re-define existing classifications, and consider carefully what potential technology has for home language development.

One recurring issue is that screen time is frequently used as a singular term, while it actually incorporates a large number of potential interactions with media, both active and passive, and the term "screen" being used synonymously with many different types of screen, without critically exploring context or use. Today, screens are used in many multifaceted contexts, with increasing opportunities to mix online and real-world engagement. Some games, such as Pokémon Go, for example, are mainly played outside, by walking around, and several television programmes encourage physical activity. Leblanc et al. (2015) point out that this mis-association works in two ways – not only is screen time seen as passive, but sedentary time outside of school is typically viewed as mainly screen time, when screens actually account for only one third of overall sedentary time, which also includes eating, passive transport, and reading a book. With many studies around screen time among children focusing on obesity (see e.g. Leblanc et al. 2015) and sleep patterns (see e.g. Tzischinsky and Haimov 2017), a more nuanced understanding is required when we consider what devices children use, what they access, the reasons they access it, and other situational details. Only recently have governmental recommendations in the United States begun to take the context and content of screen engagement into account (American Academy of Pediatrics Council on Communications and Media, AAP, 2016). What is important here is to consider the correlation/causation complexities – the American Academy of Pediatrics Council on Communications and Media (2016) finds, for example, that any speech delays among children who use screens excessively are likely due to decreased parent-child interaction. This finding, then, draws into sharp focus how technology and social media may be used constructively, socially, and collaboratively, making it part of targeted parent-child interaction, rather than a solitary, passive pursuit.

Cultural differences linked to screen time have been reviewed in terms of both how sedentary habits may differ across countries (see e.g. Leblanc et al. 2015) and how parental education and socio-economic background may affect access (see e.g.

Atkin et al. 2014), but there has been little research into how cultural attitudes affect children's use of technology. Tzischinsky and Haimov (2017) explore the viewing habits and sleep patterns of Muslim and Jewish children in Israel and discovered that Muslim children in the study had longer viewing habits, earlier sleep times, and more sleep disturbances than their Jewish counterparts. However, as a quantitative study, the reasons for this could only be hypothesised, and require further critical exploration before arriving at generalised conclusions based on language or cultural differences.

In exploring children's use of screen time, then, it is important to differentiate between various uses but also the potential it has to facilitate greater language development. In particular, this chapter focuses not on providing one-size-fits all answers to the issue of screen time, instead suggesting facilitatory, collaborative and family-oriented contexts for parents and children to explore issues together, and arrive at personalised solutions. In the following, this chapter explores screen time from the perspectives of accessing films or programmes, engaging with games and apps, and participating in online social media practices, in each case exploring the specific affordances linked to multilingual families.

5 Television, films, DVDs, streamed television, YouTube and co

As outlined above, the definition of screen time is becoming ever more complex, and nowhere is this more evident than in the context of watching filmed content. While there used to be three or four channels at a family's disposal, there is now almost unlimited potential to access filmed materials, free and paid-for, in real-time or on-demand, created by professionals or amateurs at a variety of levels, with several media bridging the gap between consumption and engagement both online and offline. Several programmes (including children's programmes) offer opportunities for interaction, through discussion boards, or posting images of work created by viewers of the programme. This blurring of consumption versus engagement makes it difficult to discuss some aspects of technology use without also discussing others.

In a study conducted among bilingually educated pupils in Melbourne, Australia, Molineux and Aliani (2012) found that TV and DVD watching at home was seen as the most common bilingual practice among students in two of the three schools under investigation. However, a repeated study today may shift these results to online practices, especially with the rapid development of streaming and online content. A differentiation according to devices may therefore not be the most helpful, instead, a focus on the type of medium (i.e. filmed content) may be more appropriate. In this respect, filmed content remains widely accessible, enabling multilingual children to access content in their multiple languages, which may ultimately help with at least passive language development. One study explicitly explored and compared TV watching habits in both English and the home language (Curdt-Christiansen and La Morgia 2018). Working with families with Italian, Chinese and Pakistani backgrounds, they identified varying practices in terms of both English and home language TV watching. Half of the Italian families provided home language programmes for children (14 out of 28), while the number was much smaller among the participating Chinese families (4 out of 28), and non-existent among Pakistani families (0 out of 10). While some of this may be due to availability, at least some of the viewing habits are attitudinal, since all languages are represented in some form or another on online streaming platforms. Curdt-Christiansen and La Morgia (2018) suggest that Urdu may have a diminished function in family life, since families were often second or third-generation immigrants. However, it is often exactly these families that are actively making efforts to keep the home language alive (Little 2017). Such differences show how difficult it is to identify a one-size-fits-all approach for multilingual contexts, which may be one reason why related studies tend to be small size and qualitative, focusing on individual families rather than larger groups (Juvonen et al. this vol.).

In one such study, located in a bilingual context in the United States, Orellana (1994) explores young children's language choices in relation to their viewing habits. The data showed that children switched to English when engaging in play about superheroes, since their experience with relevant media (superhero films, comic books, etc.) were English dominant, while they were playing in Spanish at other times. Orellana's findings link TV viewing habits to both funds of knowledge (González 2005; González, Moll, and Amanti 2005) and real-life play (Marsh 2005), again highlighting the complexities families face when wanting to facilitate both their children's language and social development. This link between viewing and real-life play and engagement is important, because it highlights just one of many opportunities for language use. Real-life play further encourages physical action, linked to improved language acquisition (Glenberg and Gallese 2012; Adams, Glenberg, and Restrepo 2018), and challenges the perception of screen time as a purely passive phenomenon. Understanding the links between the language children use to access content, and the language children use to discuss content in their various social spheres is a vital consideration for parents, especially since they may be the only people in the child's life to offer opportunities to discuss and engage with viewing content in the home language. Co-viewing and considering activities that link viewing habits to real life situations can create occasions for family communication, bringing content to life, and bridging passive and active domains. For older children, creating as well as consuming video content may be an option, something that is further explored in section 7 which focuses on social media.

6 Games and apps

The use of games and apps in multilingual families is among the least explored when it comes to examining the affordances of different resources for language development. While there is a considerable market of games and apps, accessing them can be problematic for financial as well as technological reasons. Many parents are reluctant to provide access to computer games for younger children (Hamilton et al. 2016), making the medium mainly relevant for children of primary school age and upwards. Yet again, however, the literature remains dominated by studies in the contexts of English as an Additional Language and foreign language learning, often focusing specifically on learning outcomes. One example is presented by Ashraf, Motlagh, and Salami (2014), who evaluate the impact of online vocabulary games on language learners' vocabulary retention in Iran, reporting positive results, a finding echoed by Sundqvist and Wikström's (2015) research among teenagers in Sweden, involved in digital gameplay. These studies are useful in showing the learning potential of games and apps, but do not necessarily address previously outlined issues concerning asynchronous language development among home language learners. The difficulty in developing a solid research base in the home language context is similar to the difficulties faced by developers who might consider catering to this specific niche: Since each multilingual family is a microcosm that is unique in its language composition, family composition, family language policy and choices, there is simply no homogenous market that would make it viable for games developers to cater for the specific needs of all multilingual families (Little 2019a). Therefore, the best way forward for multilingual families is to develop an awareness of available apps and games, and to consider whether, where and how these may fit into family life.

Games may exist at a number of levels: commonly available games that have been localised/translated into multiple languages, games aimed at language learners of the home language (e.g. foreign language learners), games aimed at young native speakers looking to develop early literacy (early years market), and games which originate in the country the language is spoken, specific to the local market. Each has their own shortcomings and benefits. The easiest games to access, and arguably most likely to fit in with a child's fund of knowledge (González 2005; González, Moll, and Amanti 2005), are games that are translated into multiple languages. These translations, however, depend on marketability, and will only exist in languages where it makes financial sense to localise the game. Similarly, translations that only take into account language, rather than a sensitive cultural localisation, may be inappropriate in many contexts. Games aimed at foreign language learners are often gamified learning apps, consisting largely of vocabulary lists which are learnt in a number of playful settings, but which rarely offer a true gameplay experience. Games aimed at young learners for literacy development may be suitable if the home language speaker is young, but can create tensions with children's sense of identity if they feel the content and visuals are too childish for them (Little 2019a). Finally, games which are aimed at native speakers may arguably offer the best potential gameplay, in the most natural setting, but the language may be inaccessible to less confident speakers, especially because a number of games require high literacy skills.

Finding appropriate games and deciding which may be a good fit for any particular child can thus be problematic – parents may need to browse suitable websites in the home language to identify suitable games, and then, in some cases, navigate complex settings to enable access. Again, the home language may greatly limit the choice and availability, but parents choosing to jointly access and discuss resources with their children (AAP 2016) will not only widen the range of resources accessible to them, but also be able to model language use and monitor their child's gaming habits simultaneously. Through co-playing, children who are less confident in the language can therefore access more complex, and potentially more engaging, resources, creating not only opportunities for more advanced language use, but, again, facilitate a bridge between online and offline engagement, since parents will be familiar with content and rules, and thus able to converse with children about aspects important to them.

7 Online/social media consumption and participation

As outlined previously, there is an increasing overlap between consumption of media (whether viewing filmed content or playing games and apps), and online participation, since many programmes, films, and games offer social interaction opportunities via the Internet. The use of social media thus potentially encroaches on all virtual media use, and essentially represents any and all opportunities to use media to take part in online activities. This may range from commenting on video content, communicating via social media platforms, and actively creating content for others to consume and engage with. Although English has long been viewed as the lingua franca of the Internet (Crystal 2003), it has been in steady decline, from 75% of all Internet pages in 1998, to 45% in 2009 (Pimienta, Prado, and Blanco 2009). By 2018, it had become impossible to analyse the Internet as a whole, and although English accounts for 54% of the 100 million most accessed websites in 2019 (W3Techs 2019), this only serves to problematise the attempts to linguistically homogenise a medium that is both fast-evolving and flexible. With the Internet becoming more multilingual, opportunities for multilingual families are also on the rise.

In fact, language use and prevalence of languages online are becoming ever more complex (Kern 2014), incorporating truncated and stylised language, both spoken and written, as well as multiple versions of language mash-ups. Accessed content may be generated by native speakers or non-native speakers, in a multitude of genres and for multiple purposes, including dialects and language variants. These can be a useful opportunity to expose children to language variety and develop confidence across linguistic genres, however, they can also become a barrier to engagement. Social media, in particular, will feature code-switching or stylised codes and acronyms (e.g. the "brb" = "be right back" sign-off in English), many of which require existing familiarity with language and culture. Particularly for younger children, or those developing their skills in the home language, such environments may be confusing, and speak to parental fears in terms of what kinds of language models children may access online (Little 2019a).

This section looks both at parental attitudes towards social media use specifically, and the affordances of social media in the language-learning context. Multilingual families and support for the minority languages are again under-represented in the literature, necessitating continued "borrowing" from monolingual, foreign language learning and English as an Additional Language contexts, as well as exploring the generic literature around access and online participation across various countries.

The complexities of social media and the Internet are rarely fully explored in studies. Instead, research frequently focuses on prevailing generic opinions, seeking to gain an overview of a specific target population. In a qualitative study among the parents of primary-school-aged children in Spain, for example, Bartau-Rojas, Aierbe-Barandiaran, and Oregui-González (2018) explored parental attitudes towards children's Internet usage, and highlighted common fears and negative emotions linked to inappropriate content and use, impact on social development, and a mentality of instant gratification. More concretely, though, parents acknowledged positive aspects linked to accessing information, developing digital literacy skills, and, again, social development, through digital communication. Language was not a focus in this study, nor was it specifically mentioned. Nevertheless, Bartau-Rojas, Aierbe-Barandiaran, and Oregui-González (2018) identified a need for parental training and awareness-raising, since many parents admitted to having little knowledge of when, how, and for which purposes their children used the Internet. There appears to be a sense of lack of control, similar to that discovered by Little (2019a), with parents feeling disempowered regarding their children's Internet use. Just like this chapter, Bartau-Rojas, Aierbe-Barandiaran, and Oregui-González (2018) recommend a participatory parenting style, authoritative in modelling good practice and engaging children in communication early on, rather than being authoritarian and simply forbidding Internet use.

Rama et al. (2012) explore older teenagers' use of massively multiplayer online games (MMOGs), specifically World of Warcraft, and its impact on language learning and socialisation, finding that it had considerable motivational impact. Their study highlights the potential of online gaming and more generic social media use, as technology provides access to an extensive network of other speakers of the language, expanding opportunities for communication and giving language use a relevance and "relatedness" (Ryan and Deci 2008) which can affect positive language engagement, use, and learning. While undoubtedly mainly relevant for older learners (since social media use across many platforms is limited to children 13+ years of age), parents of younger children can borrow from the notion of relevance to seek out age-appropriate opportunities for language engagement. Many languages will be represented on online platforms that allow user-generated content, enabling children to access films or content produced by native speakers on their topics of interest, allowing home language speaking children to fit their language use around their identity.

One aspect of language development which may challenge parents is the topic of active language use, rather than mere language consumption. Just like technology itself may be used both passively and actively, so are the opportunities for language engagement on a sliding scale, from consumer (e.g. watching content) to participant (e.g. commenting on content) to creator. These different stages obviously require different levels of language use, and hold genuine potential for extended engagement with the language, and for further exploring a bilingual or multilingual identity online (Potter 2012). Public participation on the Internet, however, has certain consequences and implications, not least taking into account aspects of privacy and online safety. It is beyond this chapter to discuss these in full. Instead, the focus will shift to specific considerations linked to language and multilingual identity when it comes to actively participating in, or creating content for, social media contexts. This is particularly true of online content, since having an Internet presence comes with a certain sense of permanence – although content can be deleted, it is never quite certain whether it is truly gone. Most parents will have ready-formed opinions on whether their children should contribute to, as well as consume, the Internet, and the purpose of this chapter is not to influence that opinion. Instead, it suggests the opportunities for families to discuss child agency and parent-child interaction as linked to online participation. Children may, for example, create a film or poster where they do not necessarily show themselves, but which allows them to speak or write the home language. Accessing media suitable for children in the home language, which often includes age-appropriate platforms (such as monitored discussion boards), may offer another opportunity. Once more, parental collaboration is most certainly helpful in helping children grow in confidence, and in ensuring safety online. Younger children most certainly should collaborate with parents to use parental accounts, rather than having access to their own, and a monitored email address can help to keep track of account messages and communications.

For families with younger children, or families less willing to engage fully online, privacy settings make it possible to use only a small part of social media, for controlled use among family members and trusted friends. In balancing their role as both gatekeepers and enablers, it becomes important also to consider the parental role specifically in the context of technology and social media use, which is what the next section addresses.

8 Parents as gatekeepers, families as creators

To the reader of this chapter, it may appear that co-watching and co-playing comes across as the panacea, which will make children willingly access, learn and use the home language through technology. While this is a very simplistic view, it is true that parents have a vital role to play in ensuring their children have access to high-quality technology experiences in the home language, working collaboratively to develop an understanding of accessing, evaluating, financing, and using appropriate resources, since children will likely not be able to navigate the various barriers identified in this chapter.

Parents function as gatekeepers at a variety of levels, ultimately controlling access to both hardware and software. When and how children are able to access technology is therefore linked to a combination of parental beliefs, family finances, and technological awareness. Within families, it is therefore important to understand what drives parental decisions around technology use, and training and discussions involving both parents and children will help each family to find a personalised solution, which will likely be as individual as any family language policy. A positive, playful relationship of family communication which involves all family members (Smith-Christmas 2018) allows children to bring in their expertise, preferences and understanding. In being able to share, discuss, and potentially drive access to suitable technology, children are able to take a leading role in their home language development, potentially facilitating agency and engagement. Through negotiation, for example, children who are excited about creating content such as video game walkthroughs or toy reviews may be encouraged to do so in the home language, with the extended family as the immediate audience.

With advancing technology, creating content in the home language is therefore a genuine possibility for families, facilitating active and creative use of the home language. And this content need not be limited to video only. The online book writing interface reported on by Edwards et al. (2002) earlier in this chapter, for example, has its parallel today in openly available story-writing apps, many of which facilitate multiple languages, use of original photos, and a variety of dissemination options. With the help of parents, children might use such an app to create a lasting memory of a family holiday, using family photos, written titles and short narratives, and audio-recorded content, turning technology use into a creative and joint family endeavour. Writing of fanfiction may offer a similar outlet for older children.

9 Conclusion: Parents and children as collaborators in technology use

One of the most important guidelines from the American Academy of Pediatrics concerns social and collaborative technology use, encouraging parents to take an interest, test apps before the child accesses them, play them with the child, and engage the child in conversation about them. This not only helps bridge the gap between the "online" and the "real" world, but, particularly in the context of multilingual families, crucially enables children to engage with content which may otherwise be too advanced to access. Parents here can take on a scaffolding role, facilitating true game play and shared enjoyment by providing access to higher-level language. Taking into account the child's preferences (availability allowing) can help the child bring their own funds of knowledge (González 2005; González, Moll, and Amanti 2005) to the relationship. A joint exploration of what languages certain apps are available in may help parents and children negotiate common ground, possibly even allowing for increased access if this is in the home language.

Yuill and Martin (2016) demonstrated that the difference between electronic books and paper-based books is in the reduced warmth and parent-child interaction. What is yet unclear is where and how such lack of warmth might originate. Potentially, however, it may simply be that, inherently and traditionally, electronic media are not ingrained in the current *parent* generation as something that is shared, whereas the current generation of *children* is much more used to viewing technology as a social medium. It is therefore not only parenting practices but also attitudes that will need to change, with parents acknowledging their status as learner in the child's digital world. The question is how this tension will evolve, as this generation grows older and becomes parents themselves, especially as technologies continue to change, already facilitating game design and creation at user level.

In the meantime, working collaboratively with their children will enable parents to take their lead from and build on their children's interests, thus utilising technology's affordances for both active and passive language development. Jointly exploring and discussing children's interests and how these may be furthered using both technology and the home language encourages not only ongoing family communication, but also opportunities for shared and creative media use. Throughout this engagement, parents will be able to scaffold and model language, monitor children's access to age-appropriate technology and enhancing language skills. Seeing technology and social media in all their variety, and with all their possibilities, both passive and active, can help parents in building on existing family "funds of knowledge" (González 2005; González, Moll, and Amanti 2005), expanding cultural and linguistic understanding, as well as creating opportunities for children to lead with their own expertise, and building on motivational affordances of technology.

References

Adams, Ashley, Arthur Glenberg & Ma Adelaida Restrepo. 2018. Moved by reading in a Spanish-speaking, dual language learner population. *Language, Speech & Hearing Services in Schools* 9(3). 582–594.
American Academy of Pediatrics Council on Communications and Media (AAP). 2016. Media and young minds. *Pediatrics* 138(5). 1–6.
Arthur, Leonie. 2001. Popular culture and early literacy learning. *Contemporary Issues in Early Childhood* 2(3). 295–308.
Ashraf, Hamid, Fateme G. Motlagh & Maryam Salami. 2014. the impact of online games on learning English vocabulary by Iranian (low-intermediate) EFL learners. *Procedia – Social and Behavioral Sciences* 98. 286–291.
Ashton, Jean. 2005. Barbie, the Wiggles and Harry Potter. Can popular culture really support young children's literacy development? *European Early Childhood Education Research Journal* 13(1). 31–40.
Atkin, Andrew J., Stephen J. Sharp, Kirsten Corder & Esther M. F. van Sluijs. 2014. Prevalence and correlates of screen time in youth: An international perspective. *American Journal of Preventive Medicine* 47(6). 803–807.
Bartau-Rojas, Isabel, Ana Aierbe-Barandiaran & Eider Oregui-González. 2018. Parental mediation of the Internet use of primary students: Beliefs, strategies and difficulties. *Comunicar: Media Education Research Journal* 26(54). 71–79.
Blackwell, Courtney K., Alexis R. Lauricella, Annie Conway & Ellen Wartella. 2014. Children and the Internet: Developmental implications of web site preferences among 8- to 12-year-old children. *Journal of Broadcasting & Electronic Media* 58(1). 1–20.
Bourdieu, Pierre. 1986. Forms of capital. In John G. Richardson (ed.), *Handbook of Theory and Research for the Sociology of Education*, 241–258. New York: Greenwood Press.
Boyd, Robert, Peter J. Richerson & Joseph Henrich. 2011. The cultural niche: Why social learning is essential for human adaptation. *Proceedings of the National Academy of Sciences* 108. 10918–10925.
Crystal, David. 2003. *English as a global language*. 2nd edn. Cambridge, UK: Cambridge University Press.
Curdt-Christiansen, Xiao Lan & Francesca La Morgia. 2018. Managing heritage language development: Opportunities and challenges for Chinese, Italian and Pakistani Urdu-speaking families in the UK. *Multilingua* 37(2). 177–200.
Edwards, Viv, Lyn Pemberton, John Knight & Frank Monaghan (2002). Fabula: A bilingual multimedia authoring environment for children exploring minority languages. *Language Learning & Technology: A Refereed Journal for Second and Foreign Language Educators* 6(2). 59–69.
Eisenchlas, Susana A., Andrea C. Schalley & Gordon Moyes. 2016. Play to learn: Self-directed home language literacy acquisition through online games. *International Journal of Bilingual Education and Bilingualism* 19(2). 136–152.
Franklin, Glendon. 2001. Special educational needs issues and ICT. In Marilyn Leask (ed.) *Issues in teaching using ICT*, 105–116. London: Routledge.
Gee, James P. 2004. *What video games have to teach us about learning and literacy*. New York: Palgrave Macmillan.
Glenberg, Arthur & Vittorio Gallese. 2012. Action-based language: A theory of language acquisition, comprehension, and production. *Cortex* 48(7). 905–922.

González, Norma. 2005. Beyond culture: The hybridity of funds of knowledge. In Norma González, Luis C. Moll & Cathy Amanti (eds.), *Funds of knowledge. Theorizing practices in households, communities and classrooms*, 29–47. London: Routledge.

González, Norma, Luis C. Moll & Cathy Amanti. 2005. Preface. In Norma González, Luis C. Moll & Cathy Amanti (eds.), *Funds of knowledge. Theorizing practices in households, communities and classrooms*, ix. London: Routledge.

Hamilton, Kyra, Teagan Spinks, Katherine M. White, David J. Kavanagh & Anne M. Walsh. 2016. A psychosocial analysis of parents' decisions for limiting their young child's screen time: An examination of attitudes, social norms and roles, and control perceptions. *British Journal of Health Psychology* (21). 285–301.

Juvonen, Päivi, Susana A. Eisenchlas, Tim Roberts & Andrea C. Schalley. this vol. Researching social and affective factors in home language maintenance: A methodology overview.

Kalantzis, Mary & Bill Cope. 2012. *Literacies*. Port Melbourne: Cambridge University Press.

Katz, Yaakov. 2002. Attitudes affecting college students' preferences for distance learning. *Journal of Computer Assisted Learning* 18. 2–9.

Kern, Richard. 2014. Technology as pharmakon: The promise and perils of the Internet for foreign language education. *The Modern Language Journal* 98(1). 340–357.

Lanza, Elizabeth & Rafael Lomeu Gomes. this vol. Family language policy: Foundations, theoretical perspectives and critical approaches.

Lave, Jean & Etienne Wenger. 1991. *Situated learning: Legitimate peripheral participation*. Cambridge, MA: Cambridge University Press.

Leblanc, Allana G., Peter T. Katzmarzyk, Tiago V. Barreira, Stephanie T. Broyles, Jean-Philippe Chaput, Timothy S. Church, Mikael Fogelholm, Deirdre M. Harrington, Gang Hu, Rebecca Kuriyan, Anura Kurpad, Estelle V. Lambert, Carol Maher, José Maia, Victor Matsudo, Timothy Olds, Vincent Onywera, Olga L. Sarmiento, Martyn Standage, Catrine Tudor-Locke, Pei Zhao & Mark S. Tremblay. 2015. Correlates of total sedentary time and screen time in 9–11 year-old children around the world: The international study of childhood obesity, lifestyle and the environment. *PLoS ONE* 10(6). 1–20.

Little, Sabine. 2017. A generational arc: Early literacy practices among Pakistani and Indian heritage language families. *International Journal of Early Years Education* 25(4). 424–438.

Little, Sabine. 2019a. "Is there an app for that?" Exploring games and apps among heritage language families. *Journal of Multilingual and Multicultural Development* 40(3). 218–229.

Little, Sabine. 2019b. Great aunt Edna's vase – metaphor use in working with heritage language families. *The Family Journal* 27(2). 150–155.

Little, Sabine. 2020. Whose heritage? What inheritance?: conceptualising family language identities. *International Journal of Bilingual Education and Bilingualism*. 23(2). 198–212.

Marsh, Jackie. 2005. Ritual, performance and identity construction: Young children's engagement with popular cultural and media texts. In Jackie Marsh (ed.) *Popular culture, new media and digital literacy in early childhood*, 28–50. London: Routledge Falmer.

Marsh, Jackie. 2009. Digital beginnings: Young children's use of popular culture, media and new technologies in homes and early years settings. In Adriana G. Bus & Susan B. Neuman (eds.), *Multimedia and literacy development: Improving achievement for young learners*, 28–43. New York: Routledge.

Marsh, Jackie, Peter Hannon, Margaret Lewis & Louise Ritchie. 2017. Young children's initiation into family literacy practices in the digital age. *Journal of Early Childhood Research* 15(1). 47–60.

Molyneux, Paul & Renata Aliani. 2016. Texts, talk and technology: The literacy practices of bilingually-educated students. *Trabalhos em Linguística Aplicada* 55(2). 263–291.

Orellana, Marjorie F. 1994. Appropriating the voice of the superheroes: Three preschoolers' bilingual language uses in play. *Early Childhood Research Quarterly* 9. 171–193.

Palviainen, Åsa. this vol. Future prospects and visions for family language policy research.

Pimienta, Daniel, Daniel Prado & Álvaro Blanco. 2009. *Twelve years of measuring linguistic diversity in the Internet: balance and perspectives*. United Nations Educational, Scientific and Cultural Organization.

Potter, John. 2012. *Digital media and learner identity: The new curatorship*. New York, NY: Palgrave Macmillan.

Rama, Paul S., Rebecca W. Black, Elisabeth van Es & Mark Warschauer. 2012. Affordances for second language learning in World of Warcraft. *ReCALL* 24. 322–338.

Robinson, Muriel & Margaret Mackey. 2003. Film and television. In Nigel Hall, Joanne Larson & Jackie Marsh (eds.), *Handbook of early childhood literacy*, 126–141. Thousand Oaks, CA: Sage.

Ryan, Richard M. & Edward L. Deci. 2008. Self-determination theory and the role of basic psychological needs in personality and the organization of behavior. In Oliver P. John, Richard W. Robbins & Lawrence A. Pervin (eds.), *Handbook of personality: Theory and research*, 654–678. New York: The Guilford Press.

Smith-Christmas, Cassie. this vol. Child agency and home language maintenance.

Smith-Christmas, Cassie. 2018. "One Cas, Two Cas": Exploring the affective dimensions of family language policy. Multilingua 37(2). 131–152.

Sundqvist, Pia & Peter Wikström. 2015. Out-of-school digital gameplay and in-school L2 English vocabulary outcomes. *System* 51. 65–76.

Taylor, Denny. 1983. *Family literacy: Young children learning to read and write*. Exeter, New Hampshire: Heinemann.

Tseng, Amelia. this vol. Identity in home-language maintenance.

Tzischinsky, Orna & Iris Haimov. 2017. Comparative study shows differences in screen exposure, sleep patterns and sleep disturbances between Jewish and Muslim children in Israel. *Acta Paediatrica* 106(10). 1642–1650.

W3Techs. 2019. *Historical trends in the usage of content languages for websites*. https://w3techs.com/technologies/history_overview/content_language (accessed 20 May 2019).

Whitton, Nicola. 2013. Games for learning creating a level playing field or stacking the deck? *International Review of Qualitative Research* 6(3). 424–439.

Wright, John C., Aletha C. Huston, Kimberlee C. Murphy, Michelle St. Peters, Marites Piñon, Ronda Scantlin & Jennifer Kotler. 2001. The relations of early television viewing to school readiness and vocabulary of children from low-income families: The early window project. *Child Development* 72. 1347–1366.

Yuill, Nicola & Alex Martin. 2016. Curling up with a good e-book: Mother-child shared story reading on screen or paper affects embodied interaction and warmth. *Frontiers in Psychology* 7. 1–12.

Anikó Hatoss
14 Transnational grassroots language planning in the era of mobility and the Internet

The purpose of this chapter is to theorise grassroots language planning in the context of globalisation from below (Appadurai 2001). Grassroots language planning is defined here as bottom-up initiatives to influence the language use of minority language speakers without or with little involvement of official authorities. The chapter provides international examples of bottom-up planning to demonstrate how processes and sites of grassroots language planning have moved beyond the local to the translocal and transnational space, and how grassroots planning is linked with wider processes of transnational activism (Lacroix 2014). While locality of language practices is recognised as equally important, the chapter showcases the way grassroots globalisation and activism mobilises social actors in the transnational space. These changed contexts call for a theoretical shift in language planning and policy (LPP) and for studies to reconceptualise grassroots planning as a translocal activity using sociolinguistic theories of mobility. The chapter aims to provide a brief overview of these developments and focus researchers' attention on recent conceptual shifts. The discussion draws on selected studies from international contexts but has a specific focus on the South Sudanese Australian community in which the author has conducted empirical research. This chapter is divided into three main sections guided by three research questions. Section 1 is a theoretical overview of grassroots language planning in the context of mobility, globalisation and the Internet; section 2 addresses the methodological challenge of exploring grassroots planning in transnational and translocal contexts; and section 3 provides a case study from the context of the South Sudanese community in Australia to showcase how theory works in practice, including the challenges of using technology for implementing a grassroots literacy class.

1 Language planning from bottom-up

1.1 Why grassroot planning?

Language planning and policy has traditionally been conceived as a top-down activity with involvement of government authorities, and the scope of such planning was bounded to the state as per modernist ideologies of the nation state (Moriarty 2015). According to Ager (2001: 5), language planning refers to the "ways in which organised communities [...] consciously attempt to influence the language(s) their members use". It is widely accepted in the language planning and policy literature that there are multiple levels of planning involving different actors which exert different levels of influence on language. Kaplan and Baldauf (1997) identified three main levels of planning: macro, meso and micro. While the distinction between these levels has been subject to theoretical debate (see Liddicoat this vol.; Schalley and Eisenchlas this vol.), in this chapter macro refers to top-down government policy, meso to policies applied on institutional level (e.g. school) and micro to grassroots or bottom-up processes initiated from the community or by individuals.

Bottom-up planning has received increasing focus of attention with scholars turning to explore how minority communities act to protect and promote their languages through their grassroots movements (Blommaert 2008; Hornberger 1999). This shift has occurred in parallel with the development of globalisation, and this is well reflected in current language planning and policy scholarship. For example, *The Oxford Handbook of Language Planning and Policy* (Tollefson and Pérez-Milans 2018) lists some of the following key words: globalisation, governmentality, inequality, late modernity, nationalism, and social media. Indeed, these words capture the most significant themes in the field, and this chapter will touch on some of these. However, the discussion here is necessarily selective and focuses on exploring grassroot language planning in the context of global mobility. Family language policy is not discussed here (see Lanza and Lomeu Gomes this vol. for discussion on family language policy). First, the chapter discusses how globalization has impacted the field of language planning and the implications for grassroots activism research.

1.2 Globalization from bottom up

While globalisation means different things to different people, it is generally associated with "global flows" and the "world in motion" (Appadurai 2001). Linguistic diversity in immigrant contexts is on the rise, but sadly, globalisation has brought the decline of indigenous minority languages, and there is a general consensus that global forces threaten to eradicate the local and the distinctive, such as endangered indigenous languages (McCarty, Nicholas, and Wyman 2012: 51; Mayer et al. this vol.). These processes, therefore, point towards a homogenisation of linguistic diversity as far as the global linguistic landscape is concerned.

However, flows are not coeval, convergent, isomorphic, or spatially consistent (Appadurai 2001: 5), but multidimensional, fluid and poly-scalar (Lacroix 2014: 653), and they impact local linguistic ecologies in diverse ways. Against the global process of homogenisation emerges a parallel process of "globalisation from bottom-up" or "grassroots globalisation". These bottom-up processes contest top-down globalisation and create new forms of knowledge transfer and social mobilisation independently of the nation-state (Appadurai 2001: 3). Grassroots language activism in linguistic minority communities, particularly immigrant groups, is a good example of such social mobilisation from bottom-up.

While nation-states have been perceived to be stable, globalisation is characterised by disjunctures which produce fundamental problems of livelihood, equity, suffering, justice, and governance (Appadurai 2001: 5). Therefore, there are two main lessons for researchers in home language maintenance: (1) language use and language choices need to be contextualised within these new transnational social fields (Levitt and Glick Schiller 2004); and (2) research should focus on bottom-up processes as they hold a deeper "ecological stance" (Coupland 2010: 17). Keeping these broad challenges in mind, three general questions arise which have guided this chapter:

1. How can we conceptualise grassroot language planning in transnational social fields? (section 1)
2. How can we theorise grassroots language planning from a post-modern and critical lens? (section 2)
3. How can technology support the building and maintenance of transnational networks and grassroot language planning? (section 3)

1.3 New social fields of grassroots language planning: Locality and the transnational space

In order to address the first question, we need to consider what locality means in language planning. The notion of locality has been subject to international theoretical debate. According to scholars in human geography, places are social constructions created through actions performed in a particular space (Cresswell 2004; Harvey 1996; Murray and Lamb 2018). As Murray and Lamb (2018: 1) argue "we appropriate spaces, embody them, impose our identities on them and at the same time have our identities shaped by the places we inhabit and the practices we engage in". In language planning, this means that language use can only be planned to the extent that language users appropriate the spaces around them and to the extent that they engage in activities which will allow them to mobilise their language resources in complex multilingual spaces.

While language planning and policy sites have moved beyond the local, this does not mean that locality is replaced by translocality. Local knowledge is an essential part of translocal initiatives. Local knowledge is "context-bound, community-specific, and nonsystematic because it is generated ground-up through social practice in everyday life" (Canagarajah 2005: 4). While the locality is not questioned in this chapter, the term "local" has become problematic in the context of language activism which transcends geographical and national borders. It is particularly problematic to conceive locality in describing second-generation speakers. While children of immigrants have traditionally been referred to as second-generation migrants, they are also first-generation locals, and researchers have increasingly conceptualised their language maintenance alignments and identities in the "third space" (Winter and Pauwels 2007: 181) which is somewhere in-between their parents' source country and their own. The term "poly-centric" has also been used to conceptualise language planning and policy as a multisite social process (Halwachs 2011: 398). Considering these points, grassroots planning is thus best described not just in physical locality but in transnational social fields where actors and actions span cross geographical boundaries.

Contemporary speech communities are local and global at the same time (Canagarajah 2005), as they are interconnected through new media (Internet, Facebook, Twitter, YouTube, etc.). In fact, traditional notions of "speech community" have been contested as a result of new translocal communication technologies (Varis and Nuenen 2017), and communities have, instead, been described as having multiple boundaries, being increasingly connected and being sites and generators of grassroots responsibilities and power (Li 2018). Migration research refers to transnational migrants who connect with their homeland and do not necessarily stay in their country of migration. An example is given from the US context by Levitt:

> Over the past 20 years, Indian immigrants from Gujarat State have moved from villages and small towns in western India, first to rental apartment complexes in northeastern Massachusetts, and then to their own homes in subdivisions outside Boston. Watching these suburban dwellers work, attend school, and build religious congregations here, casual observers might conclude that yet another wave of immigrants has successfully joined in the pursuit of the American dream.
>
> A closer look, however, reveals they are pursuing Gujarati dreams as well. They send money back to India to open businesses or improve family homes and farms. They work closely with religious leaders to establish Hindu groups in the United States, to strengthen religious life in their homeland, and to build a global Hindu community transcending national borders.
> (Levitt 2004, paragraphs 4–5)

Indeed, contemporary migrant families are less local, more transitory and their language practices and membership status are contingent on relatively unpredictable future trajectories (Song 2016). As families simultaneously operate in the "here and now" of their adopted country as well as the "back at home" (Hatoss 2013), researchers have used the term *glocalisation* (García, Skutnabb-Kangas, and Torres-Guzmán 2006), and the notion of *simultaneity* to capture participation across multiple spaces and over various periods of time (Warriner and Wyman 2013). On the other hand, researchers have stressed that global forces should not deter us from the importance of *locality* and *situatedness* of language practices (Pennycook 2017), notwithstanding the emerging transnational space (Li and Zhu 2013).

Language choices are governed by complex factors, as language resources are "stratified and distributed across time, space, and place in sociolinguistic ecologies" (Hornberger and McCarty 2012: 3). Languages come to contact and live side by side, as different speakers share the same neighbourhood. However, languages are not equal in terms of power and, therefore, we need to think of them as being stratified, with the more powerful ones being at the top. This is why theorists have argued that space is both horizontal and vertical in which language choices are governed by scales (vertical space) of indexicality (Blommaert 2010; Blommaert, Collins, and Slembrouck 2005). Indexicality means that language choices signal the speaker's position about what the expected code is in a given situation. These expectations are shaped by multiple levels (scales) of connections in the actual local context as well as in the imagined broader space of where people have come from and what they are doing in that context. For example, case studies in indigenous minority contexts have provided evidence for temporal and spatial scales governing language use (Hornberger and McCarty 2012), and such temporal and spatial dimensions have also been shown to impact immigrant communities' language practices (Hatoss 2013).

Spaces of multilingualism are transformed by the dialogic (Bakhtin 1981) relationship between immigrants and their hosts, as immigrants do not arrive to empty spaces, but to spaces which are already shaped by the norms of interaction set by the people who participate in them (Blommaert 2010; Blommaert, Collins, and Slembrouck 2005; Blommaert and Rampton 2011). These spaces are shaped as newcomers add their linguistic repertoire and negotiate language use through language games (Habermas 2002). In summary, immigrants' language ecology is filled with complex power structures and language use extends beyond the physical space. A significant new domain – discussed in the following – is the use of new media (social media, You Tube, the Internet), which provide new spaces for language planning.

1.4 New forms of connectedness and the Internet

With the spread of new media and technology, new types of diaspora, termed here as "cyberspora" (Hatoss 2013), emerge. According to Appadurai (1996), global flows do not just refer to people on the move (ethnoscapes), but also to the dissemination of information (mediascapes), technology (technoscapes), global capital (financescapes) and ideas (ideoscapes). The development of technology had a major impact on the way languages are used across the globe and through technology language communities are more interconnected than ever before.

For example, in the German context, Internet-based fora were found to provide an opportunity for home language usage and vernacular digital literacies played an important role in creating local content for local audiences (Androutsopoulos 2010: 206). In addition, scholars working within the frame of critical multilingualism have pointed out connections between transnationalism and transnational identities (Blackledge 2010; Block 2004; De Fina and Perrino 2013; Mazzaferro 2018; Owusu 2003; Song 2012) as well as transnational aspects of home language maintenance (Hatoss 2006, 2013; Kwon 2017).

The Internet has, therefore, become an important medium in grassroots language planning, language documentation, and language maintenance (Hatoss 2019b; Jany 2018; Jones 2014), and numerous case studies have provided evidence for the use of social media for language revitalisation, such as the use of Facebook for the revival of Yucatec Maya (Cru 2015) and Balinese (Stern 2017). Jany (2018) has argued that technology is beneficial for smaller languages and attributes this to the fact that the new generation is highly computer literate and its members are determined to connect with the friends they leave behind when they move to another country (Jany 2018: 75). Similarly, Eisenlohr (2004) has emphasised the practical benefits of computer technology for language revitalisation, stating that these techniques do not need to be tied to a particular locale and they can be available to relatively small groups of geographically dispersed language learners (Eisenlohr 2004: 24). Most importantly, in addition to these practical benefits, computer technology was identified as a tool in increasing the prestige of minority languages and "ideologically moving them away from peripheral, rural, and obsolete positions in space and time" (Eisenlohr 2004: 24). The use of electronic mediation is an important tool to "contest ideologies of contempt and to formulate alternative ways of ideologically mapping linguistic differentiation on time and space" (Eisenlohr 2004: 33). According to Eisenlohr (2004), electronic mediation of lesser used languages can help remove stereotypes of backwardness and create new iconicity where languages become indexical of modernity.

In another study (Reershemius 2017), Facebook was shown to provide a useful channel for the maintenance of low German, an autochthonous heritage language. In another context, Matras stated: "the virtual space serves as an organic transnational network through which a shared Romani cultural identity is celebrated via the medium of a shared language" (Matras 2015: 302). Matras (2015) attributes the spread of Romani to key developments of global nature, such as "increased networking and mobility opportunities, the rise of digital communication technology, the role of social media in facilitating virtual communities, the strengthening of transnational forms of governance especially in connection with safeguarding regional and minority rights, and the growing acceptance of multiple identities or 'scapes'" (Matras 2015: 313). As touched on above, another example, in the context of indigenous minorities, is provided by Cru (2015), who reports that the use of Yucatec Maya on Facebook has had a much greater impact on the vitality of the language than top-down government policy, as it has led to an ideological shift of legitimacy of Mayan language from the ground up. Cru argues that its presence on Facebook also led to the deterritorialised use of Mayan in a globalised and transnational context with Maya speakers living outside the local area of Yucatán. A success story in a migrant context was the case study of Latino immigrants in the United States (Noguerón-Liu 2013) where adult immigrants engaged with technology to develop digital literacies. The study concluded that as a result of the creation of an online space Spanish was more valued, and community members used their agency to materialize the delivery of the content (Noguerón-Liu 2013: 46). In this study the key to success was that "multiple social fields that spanned national borders overlapped and allowed the flow of educational resources across microlevel networks such as family relationships and macrolevel structures such as the binational institutional agreement that made computer classes in Spanish possible" (Noguerón-Liu 2013: 45).

Another study from the European context (Pelliccia 2013) has reported how Greek students maintain their language and identity through online media while living in Italy:

> Equipped with technological know-how, people interviewed use all manner of technology such as the internet, computers, software ('Skype'), webcams, smartphones and all means which allow for audio-visual communication in real time with friends and family both in Italy and Greece. Through the internet they read the most important Greek daily newspapers or online news portals such as 'H Kathimeriní', 'To Víma', 'Ta Néa', 'Tromaktikó', 'Elefterotipía', as well as Italian and international ones ('BBC' and 'CNN') from which they collect information on what is happening in Greece. Some even have satellite TV in their homes that gives them the feeling of being in Greece while staying in Italy. (Pelliccia 2013: 75)

In summary, as the examples above have shown, language communities connect translocally and participate in transnational social networks. They utilise technology for building and maintaining these connections and to further their language activism. Therefore, researchers have an emerging rich ground to theorise activism in these new spaces. This challenge is discussed in the next section.

2 The theoretical challenge: New social spaces require new concepts and methods

Considering the shifts in social spaces of language use and the increasing interconnectedness through technology, there are a number of methodological challenges facing researchers of language planning. In this section I will propose cosmopolitanism as a new theoretical frame used in sociology to capture the transnational connectedness of communities involved in planning their language. I will contrast this with traditional nation-state-based (or nationalist) theories of language planning.

2.1 From nationalism to cosmopolitanism

Globalisation theorists and critical sociolinguists (Appadurai 1996, 2001; Block 2004; Blommaert 2010; Giddens 2000; Habermas 2000; Ricento 2010) have argued for new social theories which are better suited to describe social processes in our contemporary post-modern world. One direction in sociology is provided through the concept of cosmopolitanism, which offers useful methodological insights for the study of language planning. Cosmopolitanism has been critiqued for being a western concept and it has been largely used to refer to cross-cultural tolerance: cosmopolitanism might be best understood as a way forward toward a more just world (Levitt 2016: 276). However, cosmopolitanism is also a useful analytical lens in sociology. Traditional social research based on the nation-state idea has become unfit for the study of contemporary society (Beck and Sznaider 2006). Instead, a cosmopolitan outlook which moves away from bounded territoriality is more suitable to describe grassroots actions involving transnational movements. The key tenets of cosmopolitanism are summarised in Table 1 and contrasted with nation-based approaches to the study of society, that is methodological nationalism.

Table 1: Contrasting methodological nationalism and cosmopolitanism (Hatoss 2013).

Methodological nationalism	Cosmopolitan outlook
– clear distinction between national and international	– blurred boundaries between national and international
– contrasting stable and homogenous units	– exploring dynamic and heterogeneous units
– unit of analysis: the nation state	– unit of analysis: the cosmopolitan space
– categories of analysis are rigid and static	– categories of analysis are characterized by 'fluidity', 'liquidity' and 'mobility'
– social actors are treated as separate and belonging to one nation state	– recognition of interdependency among social actors across national boundaries
– focussed on national	– focussed on transnational
– uses national statistical indicators: mono-perspectival – one 'lens'	– uses multi-perspectival – multiple 'lenses'

In summary, the cosmopolitan outlook provides a useful theoretical tool to conceptualise transnational language planning and policy.

While the discussion so far has focussed on the sites of language planning and policy, the next section will focus on motives and agency as the underlying forces in grassroots language planning and consider why communities engage in planning from bottom up, what constraints they face and how structure and agency come together to shape the social fields in which they aim to maintain their home languages.

2.2 Agency and equity

While the focus thus far has been on sites of language planning, this section turns its attention to three important sub-questions: Who does the planning? With what power? What does this mean for equity in language planning? Language planning and policy has been increasingly theorised as involving complex interactions between structural, cultural and agentive processes (Glasgow and Bouchard 2019). With the development of the ecological approach to language planning and policy (Baldauf 2006; Mühlhäusler 2000; Pennycook 2004), researchers have turned their attention to decipher how communities exercise their agency to manage their linguistic resources and how such processes can be conceptualised with theories of language planning and policy. While past language planning and policy theory saw individuals and communities as victims or beneficiaries of certain historical and structural factors (Tollefson 1991), in current language planning and policy literature there has been more recognition of the active role individuals and communities play in shaping their linguistic future. Concepts of grassroots planning, agency, advocacy, and activism are just a few which have become some of the keywords in the study of language planning and policy.

Thus, the post-modern turn brought greater attention to agency in language planning and policy (Baynham 2006; Bouchard and Glasgow 2019; Carter and Sealey 2000; Hatoss 2019a; Sikoli 2011; Šimičić 2019). While early language planning and policy was criticised for being devoid of agency (Ricento 2000, 2006), there is a current consensus in the literature that agency is relevant to every level of language planning and policy, and not only top-down authorities (such as governments) but also individuals can engage in agentive behaviour and influence language outcomes. Agency research in language planning and policy, however, is divided between social realism which recognises the cause and effect relations between agentive action and linguistic consequences, and the discursive approach which argues that social reality does not exist in its objective form but is partly conditioned and partly constructed through discourse (Hatoss 2019a). No matter which side we accept, it is essential for language planning and policy researchers to apply methodologies which "situate evidence of agentive processes in relation to broader structural and cultural forces, which act as constraints and enablements upon agentive movements" (Glasgow and Bouchard 2019: 4).

Furthermore, critical theorists in language planning and policy have increasingly turned their attention to social justice (see e.g. Piller 2016; Annamalai and Skutnabb-Kangas this vol.). The linguistic human rights argument in language policy discourse is not new; however, it has mainly concentrated on traditional indigenous minorities and the protection of their language rights (Kymlicka and Patten 2003; May 2011; Phillipson 2000; Skutnabb-Kangas 2000, 2008). Yet, equity and social justice are also central to immigrant communities and grassroots language planning, as language inequities impact on community wellbeing and need to be examined in light of social, political, demographic and power inequities. While linguistic diversity *per se* is not a political problem, it becomes a problem when linguistic diversity is ignored (Makoni and Trudell 2006: 21). According to Makoni and Trudell, while less powerful groups are often the users of minority languages, "national unity need not imply cultural or linguistic uniformity" (Makoni and Trudell 2006: 21). On the contrary, a stronger and more equitable unity is achieved when national authorities recognise "the right of individual communities to distinct language and cultural practices, and do not withhold resources or power from such communities" (Makoni and Trudell 2006: 21).

Contrary to the moral and ethical obligation to support equity in language provision, top-down national policies rarely address the needs of all immigrant communities. For example, in Australia immigrant communities have three ways to maintain their heritage language, but none of these programs cater for the needs of smaller languages. The first option is the Saturday Schools managed through the Ethnic Schools Council of Australia (see also Nordstrom this vol.). Within this program, approximately over 100,000 students participate in learning 69 languages (CLA 2019). However, these ethnic schools are dependent on the numerical strength in the ethnic community, and smaller and more dispersed language communities struggle to run sustainable programs. While ethnic schools have traditionally been viewed as bastions of conservatism, they have been shown to respond to new trends in technology, travel and migration (Cruickshank 2019). Secondly, children of immigrant backgrounds can attend Languages Other Than English (LOTE) classes as part of the mainstream education system, but language offerings are limited to prestigious and economically useful, mainly European and Asian languages, and the levels are often limited to beginners, which does not suit the immigrant children who are already conversant in the language. Therefore, smaller communities are left with the third option, that is to set up their own grassroots programs. The next section explains why these programs fill an important gap and respond better to local needs.

2.3 Local initiatives are more responsive to local needs and more equitable

Several studies have illustrated that local initiatives can be more effective in language planning than top down policies. For example, in a study in the European context, Halwachs (2011) illustrates that more localised approaches to planning Romani, such as the national Macedonian and the local Burgenland Romani approaches, have been more successful than the international standardisation initiatives, as local initiatives were more responsive to the on-going developments in the respective speech community and catered better for the needs and wishes of both the speakers and their representatives. Therefore, the more language planning initiatives are rooted in the respective speech communities, the more successful they are, as the lack of an authorised body to implement or to impose language-planning efforts is thus compensated (Halwachs 2011: 388).

Heterogeneity has been shown to be a key factor in the success of grassroots planning initiatives. In traditional language planning and policy, ethnic communities were often seen as homogenous, though, and home language maintenance studies typically aimed to describe trends of intergenerational language maintenance of a given speech community with tools designed for describing stable and homogeneous conditions (Clyne 2003). Drawing on the case of Romani, again, Halwachs (2011) described the challenges of language planning on supranational and national levels for Romani speakers, as the Romani groups are highly heterogeneous, speaking different varieties, and groups also compete on the political level. Romani is mainly used for symbolic purposes and there is no authority which could take charge of corpus planning. As Halwachs (2011: 384) argues, it is impossible to initiate language planning activities which aim at a unified variety in such heterogenous groups, and without a robust corpus planning, acquisition planning is doomed to fail.

As we have seen there are a number of factors impacting community language initiatives, and top-down policy rarely solves the problem of small languages. Grassroots planning plays an important role, but these programs are challenging to set up and to make sustainable, as section 3 will discuss.

3 Case study of Cyberspora: Dinka literacy online in Australia

In this section, I draw on a case study of an online Dinka literacy class (Hatoss 2013, 2019b) to illustrate the theoretical points raised in this chapter. The study is an example of a bottom-up initiative using technology and illustrates the translocal nature of grassroots language planning in a specific diasporic context. While the project was initiated as part of a broader research agenda exploring intergenerational language maintenance in the South Sudanese community in Australia (Hatoss 2013), the Dinka literacy class was an unplanned outcome, resulting from the ongoing dialogue between the research team and the community. The next section explains how the project came about, its aims and how it was implemented.

3.1 The project

During the ethnographic stage of the larger sociolinguistic project conducted in the local South Sudanese and other African communities in regional South East Queensland (Australia), one of the key findings that surfaced was that various local Dinka language schools were initiated by individuals as the community was keen to maintain their heritage language (the majority were Dinka speakers from South Sudan). However, these programs proved to be unsustainable due to poor attendance and shortage of resources. For example, most families did not have access to transport and the volunteer teacher drove children to the Saturday classes back and forth, which proved to be an onerous task. As the teacher explained, his whole Saturday was occupied with collecting kids and then dropping them back to their homes. In addition, the teaching resources were rather limited, and the community relied on schoolbooks transported across from South Sudan. There was a need to make the program more engaging for children and to make it easier for them to participate. There was also a need to share the teaching task across more volunteers, which meant involving people across various geographical locations.

The project developed from bottom-up, as the community was involved in formulating the aims and the processes from the beginning. According to cultural traditions, the research team set up an initial meeting with the community leaders, where the current state of affairs was discussed. A group of elders were invited and asked to share their thoughts on the status of language maintenance activities in the community. These discussions were in addition to a community-wide sociolinguistic survey about language use and maintenance. After discussing the issues, the group decided to create a learning opportunity where children could use computers and learn Dinka in their own homes. This would solve the problem of sustainability as children from different parts of Australia could engage with the program. The idea of having an online program was also attractive, as language and teaching resources could be shared across various locations.

As a result, and with help from the research team, an online program was designed to teach basic Dinka literacy skills such as the Dinka alphabet and reading short texts. However, there was a shortage of Dinka literacy materials, and as parents emphasised the need to teach their children the traditional Dinka stories, it was decided that the best way to generate content was to ask parents to record their stories, which could be then written down and uploaded to the online platform for all children to read and share. These texts were then placed online to be used in an asynchronous learning environment. The recorded content was introduced by two teachers: a Dinka speaker and an English speaker using a Voki-animated character. In addition, a synchronous class component was added using the WizIQ platform. This platform used a whiteboard and allowed teachers to write letters and words, while children also shared their Dinka words online. Children from across two different states (Queensland and New South Wales) engaged in these weekly classes. The pilot project ran for a period of eight weeks. The researchers, including one from the Dinka community, were engaged as volunteer teachers. These researchers reflected on the experience and asked participants about their views on the program. The main outcomes are summarised in the next section.

3.2 The project outcomes

As previously explained, the aim of the project was to engage Dinka speakers from different locations as they had difficulty attending traditional classes due to the geographical distances. We also aimed to make the project bottom-up by making sure that all community members participated in the decision making and in all planning stages, which included deciding on content, materials, material developers, and teachers,

Based on participants' feedback, the following benefits for home language maintenance were identified. Participants reported that the project
- engaged all age groups in the community (i.e., children, youth, adults, grandparents and elders) in the local as well as in transnational communities;
- encouraged a whole family approach to the development of materials: parents recorded oral stories in Dinka, children created picture books, etc.;
- enhanced participants' identity engagement, reaffirming their own ethnic and linguistic identity and cultural traditions;
- empowered parents in terms of their capacity to assist their children in their literacy development;
- enhanced the visibility and audibility of Dinka in the community and beyond;
- raised the status of Dinka as a language of literacy and of educational value;
- enhanced the feeling of belonging in the diaspora transnationally;
- developed participants' sense of agency and empowerment vis-à-vis the way to learn and teach their language to the next generation; and
- allowed for the use of dialects and removed the sense of censorship associated with prescriptive grammar and the ideology of language as uniform and monolithic.

Overall, the project proved to be a useful pilot to explore the possibilities provided by technology in terms of grassroots language initiatives. As mentioned above, children engaged with the project materials across two Australian states, namely, Queensland and New South Wales. This demonstrates the translocal aspect of planning, as the materials produced in New South Wales were also utilised by Queensland-based families and vice versa. Since the project required active engagement from parents across two states, it became a translocal site of grassroots planning where parents used their agency to mobilise their linguistic resources. Parents were highly motivated to transfer their heritage language to their children, and they were keen for their children to participate. As these families came from refugee background, the project served an additional purpose of community building, particularly, in resilience building. In contrast with top-down planning where community members were told what to do, the project allowed them to use their agentive role to increase their sense of self-efficacy.

The sociolinguistic survey (Hatoss 2013) conducted in the community showed that South Sudanese families were strongly motivated to maintain their home languages in Australia. This motivation was linked to complex translocal spatio-temporal relations such as the "here and now" in Australia, the "back home and now" in South Sudan, and the "imagined future" either in Australia or in their homeland (Hatoss 2013). Parents considered it important that their children maintained their home language for cultural and identity reasons, but also for their potential future return to South Sudan. They considered their home language critical for keeping ties with family members and friends left behind in Africa as well as those who settled across the globe, e.g. in the United States and Canada. This illustrates that transnational ties are not only channels for the dissemination of linguistic resources (agency as action) but constitute important motivational factors for home language maintenance (agency as motive) (Hatoss 2019a). These transnational aspects of language planning need attention in research. Researchers of language planning must look beyond who does what in language planning in one locality and explore the actions and motives translocally.

Notwithstanding its positive outcomes, the project faced numerous challenges. In terms of agency, it was difficult to come to agreement in the community about who should fulfil which roles. Some participants had the view that the government should be responsible for providing Dinka classes for their children rather than the parents, as they were busy seeking employment and supporting their families. It was also a challenge to keep the program running after the official project was over. In terms of equity, the community valued that everyone had the opportunity to participate regardless of their location. However, as previously discussed, heterogeneity proved to be a key challenge, as four different dialects of Dinka were competing in the local and the translocal (across cities in Australia) linguistic ecology. While there was a high level of mutual intelligibility across the various dialects of Dinka, the various dialect groups have attached strong symbolic value to their local dialect and insisted on their dialect being used for the development of learning and teaching materials. For example, the teaching materials sent from South Sudan were written in Dinka Rek, and were thus judged as unsuitable by Dinka Bor speakers due to the vocabulary and spelling differences (Hatoss 2013).

Access to computers and the Internet was also a major challenge and curtailed the success of the program. Even though most households had a computer in the home, there were several children competing for access, and adults were also using the same computer for their study and work purposes. Therefore, the so-called "digital divide" (Noguerón-Liu 2013) was evident and this was consistent with other studies (see e.g. Noguerón-Liu 2013) which argued that computer access was a major obstacle in the development of online digital literacy programs for minority learners. Also, the digital disadvantage was a factor at both ends of the migrant journey. This means that families did not have computer access in their country of origin and continued to have limited access in their country of residence. Overall, the project was a useful endeavour to map the possibilities and challenges in developing a grassroots literacy program online, and the lessons learnt from this project are potentially useful for other minority language communities also. These main lessons are summed up in the conclusion.

4 Conclusion

This chapter has provided a brief overview of current theoretical development in the area of grassroots language planning, with a specific focus on conceptualising translocal, transnational initiatives assisted by the use of technology. There are three main points that are essential for future studies of home language maintenance. Firstly, the analytical shift from the local to the translocal is essential, as sites of grassroots language planning transgress national boundaries and connect communities across cities, states, and nations. That is, grassroot language planning needs to be interpreted, analysed and evaluated as performed by transnational actors in transnational social fields. Cosmopolitanism, as outlined in this chapter (also see Hatoss 2013), provides useful conceptual tools and keeps scholarly attention on the fluidity, translocality and transnational dynamics of contemporary speech communities and their language planning initiatives. Secondly, grassroots language planning initiatives play a crucial role in addressing issues of equity and social justice for diasporic speech communities. As numerical strength (or weakness) of a language community is often a determining factor in access to government funded top-down support for minority languages, bottom-up planning is more responsive to small minorities' local needs, their heterogeneity, and resulting initiatives are more inclusive and more likely to be sustainable. Migrants' agency and motivation to maintain their home language is linked to transnational social fields such as the projected and imagined return to the home country in the future. Thirdly, as we have seen through the online Dinka literacy program, grassroots language planning is likely to be successful if it involves engagement of the community from the very beginning. The bottom-up language planning allows communities to enhance their transnational identity and cultural affirmation. The use of technology is a catalyst in this process and provides new spaces for language maintenance and language activism in diasporic and "cybersporic" contexts. The obstacles of the digital divide can be overcome by the involvement of government support from both the source and the host countries.

Researchers of grassroot language planning must not lose sight of the emerging new media of language planning and must explore the transnational aspects of language use, language motives, agency and language planning. Policy research trajectories focussing solely on the national and top-down level lose sight of globalisation from bottom up. Minority communities, however, are equipped with agency and transnational motives to influence the future of their languages within their own community as well as transnationally. They also have the capacity to make a change symbolically through shifting old-fashioned ideologies and by creating new spaces for minority languages in new media. For this, they need support from other agencies, but these should remain secondary to the community-led initiatives.

As top-down policies do not always achieve their objectives (Ricento 2000), and it is increasingly difficult for governments to accommodate the cultural and linguistic diversity within state systems, grassroots activism continues to be key to language maintenance in minority language communities. For this, technology provides exciting new opportunities. Globalization from the top may lead towards linguistic homogeneity, globalization from bottom-up leads to the emergence of small languages in wider spaces of communication, such as the Internet. These are exciting news for language planning as action and research.

References

Ager, Denis. 2001. *Motivation in language planning and language policy*. Clevedon: Multilingual Matters.
Androutsopoulos, Jannis. 2010. Localizing the global on the participatory web. In Nikolas Coupland (ed.), *The handbook of language and globalisation*, 203–231. Oxford: Blackwell.
Annamalai, E. & Tove Skutnabb-Kangas. this vol. Social justice and inclusiveness through linguistic human rights in education.
Appadurai, Arjun. 1996. *Modernity at large: Cultural dimensions of globalization*. Minneapolis: University of Minnesota Press.
Appadurai, Arjun. 2001. Grassroots globalization and the research imagination. In Arjun Appadurai (ed.), *Globalization*, 1–21. Durham, NC: Duke University Press.
Bakhtin, Mikhail M. 1981. *The dialogic imagination: Four essays*. Edited by Michael Holquist. Austin: University of Texas Press.
Baldauf, Richard B. 2006. Rearticulating the case for micro language planning in a language ecology context. *Current Issues in Language Planning* 7(2&3). 147–170.
Baynham, Michael. 2006. Agency and contingency in the language learning of refugees and asylum seekers. *Linguistics and Education* 17(1). 24–39.
Beck, Ulrich & Nathan Sznaider. 2006. Unpacking cosmopolitanism for the social sciences: A research agenda. *British Journal of Sociology* 57(1). 2–23.
Blackledge, Adrian & Angela Creese 2010. *Multilingualism. A critical perspective*. London: Continuum.
Block, David. 2004. Globalization, transnational communication and the Internet. *International Journal of Multicultural Societies* 6(1). 13–28.
Blommaert, Jan. 2008. *Grassroots literacy: Writing, identity and voice in Central Africa*. Hoboken: Routledge.
Blommaert, Jan. 2010. *Sociolinguistics of globalization*. Cambridge: Cambridge University Press.
Blommaert, Jan, James Collins & Stef Slembrouck. 2005. Spaces of multilingualism. *Language & Communication* 25. 197–216.
Blommaert, Jan & Ben Rampton. 2011. Language and superdiversity. *Diversities* 13(2). 1–23.
Bouchard, Jeremie & Gregory P. Glasgow. 2019. *Agency in language policy and planning: Critical inquiries*. London: Routledge.
Canagarajah, A. Suresh. 2005. *Reclaiming the local in language policy and practice*. Mahwah, NJ: Lawrence Erlbaum.
Carter, Bob, & Alison Sealey. 2000. Language, structure and agency: What can realist social theory offer to sociolinguistics? *Journal of Sociolinguistics* 4(1). 3–20.
CLA. 2019. Community Languages Australia. http://www.communitylanguagesaustralia.org.au/aboutus/ (accessed 12 June 2019).
Clyne, Michael. 2003. *Dynamics of language contact*. Cambridge: Cambridge University Press.
Coupland, Nikolas. 2010. Introduction: Sociolinguistics in the global era. In Nikolas Coupland (ed.), *The handbook of language and globalization*, 1–27. Oxford: Blackwell Publishing.
Cresswell, Tim. 2004. *Place: A short introduction*. Oxford: Blackwell Publishing.
Cru, Josep. 2015. Language revitalisation from the ground up: Promoting Yucatec Maya on Facebook. *Journal of Multilingual and Multicultural Development* 36(3). 284–296.
Cruickshank, Ken. 2019. Community language schools: Bucking the trend? In Alice Chick, Phil Benson & Robyn Moloney (eds.), *Multilingual Sydney*, 129–140. New York: Routledge.
De Fina, Anna & Sabina Perrino. 2013. Transnational identities. *Applied Linguistics* 34(5). 509–515.
Eisenlohr, Patrick. 2004. Language revitalization and new technologies: Cultures of electronic mediation and the refiguring of communities. *Annual Review of Anthropology* 33. 21–45.

García, Ofelia, Tove Skutnabb-Kangas & María Torres-Guzmán (eds.). 2006. *Imagining multilingual schools: Languages in education and glocalization*. Clevedon: Multilingual Matters.

Giddens, Anthony. 2000. *Runaway world: How globalization is reshaping our lives*. London: Routledge.

Glasgow, Gregory P. & Jeremie Bouchard. 2019. *Researching agency in language policy and planning*. New York & London: Routledge.

Habermas, Jürgen. 2000. Beyond the nation-state? On some consequences of economic globalization. In Erik Oddvar Eriksen & John Erik Fossum (eds.), *Democracy in the European Union: Integration through deliberation?*, 29–41. London: Routledge.

Habermas, Jürgen. 2002. *The pragmatics of communication*. Cambridge: Polity Press.

Halwachs, Dieter W. (2011). Language planning and media: The case of Romani. *Current Issues in Language Planning* 12(3). 381–401.

Harvey, David. 1996. *Justice, nature and the geography of difference*. Cambridge, MA.: Blackwell.

Hatoss, Anikó. 2006. Community-level approaches in language planning: The case of Hungarian in Australia. *Current Issues in Language Planning* 7(2–3). 287–306.

Hatoss, Anikó. 2013. *Displacement, language maintenance and identity: Sudanese refugees in Australia*. Amsterdam & Philadelphia: John Benjamins.

Hatoss, Anikó. 2019a. Agency in bottom-up language planning: Motives of language maintenance in the south Sudanese community of Australia. In Gregory P. Glasgow & Jeremie Bouchard (eds.), *Researching agency in language policy and planning*, 35–60. New York: Routledge.

Hatoss, Anikó. 2019b. Technology and language planning for minority languages. In Michael K. Allred & Theresa M. Pesavento (eds.), *From personal to policy: Multidimensional perspectives on technology in language education policy*, 38–63. Blue Mounds, WI: Deep Education Press.

Hornberger, Nancy H. 1999. Maintaining and revitalising indigenous languages in Latin America: State planning vs. grassroots initiatives. *International Journal of Bilingual Education and Bilingualism* 2(3). 159–165.

Hornberger, Nancy H. & Teresa L. McCarty. 2012. Globalization from the bottom up: Indigenous language planning and policy across time, space, and place. *International Multilingual Research Journal* 6(1). 1–7.

Jany, Carmen. 2018. The role of new technology and social media in reversing language loss. *Speech, Language and Hearing* 21(2). 73–76.

Jones, Mari C. 2014. *Endangered languages and new technologies*. Cambridge: Cambridge University Press.

Kaplan, Robert B. & Richard B. Baldauf. 1997. *Language planning: From practice to theory*. Clevedon: Multilingual Matters.

Kwon, Jungmin. 2017. Immigrant mothers' beliefs and transnational strategies for their children's heritage language maintenance. *Language and Education* 31(6). 495–508.

Kymlicka, Will & Alan Patten (eds.). 2003. *Language rights and political theory*. Oxford: Oxford University Press.

Lacroix, Thomas. 2014. Conceptualizing transnational engagements: A structure and agency perspective on (hometown) transnationalism. *International Migration Review* 48(3). 643–679.

Lanza, Elizabeth & Rafael Lomeu Gomes. this vol. Family language policy: Foundations, theoretical perspectives and critical approaches.

Levitt, Peggy. 2004. Transnational migrants: When "home" means more than one country. *Migration Information Source*. https://www.migrationpolicy.org/article/transnational-migrants-when-home-means-more-one-country (accessed 18 June 2019).

Levitt, Peggy. 2016. Understanding immigration through icons, images, and institutions: The politics and poetics of putting the globe on display. *Journal of Anthropological Research* 73(2). 272–288.

Levitt, Peggy & Nina Glick Schiller. 2004. Conceptualizing simultaneity: A transnational social field perspective on society. *International Migration Review* 3. 1002–1039.

Li, Wei. 2018. Community languages in late modernity. In James W. Tollefson & Miguel Pérez-Milans (eds.), *The Oxford handbook of language policy and planning*, 591–609. Oxford: Oxford University Press.

Li, Wei & Zhu Hua. 2013. Translanguaging identities and ideologies: Creating transnational space through flexible multilingual practices amongst Chinese university students in the UK. *Applied Linguistics* 34(50). 516–535.

Liddicoat, Anthony J. this vol. Language policy and planning for language maintenance: The macro and meso levels.

Makoni, Sinfree & Barbara Trudell. 2006. Complementary and conflicting discourses of linguistic diversity: Implications for language planning. *Per Linguam* 22(2). 507–524.

Matras, Yaron. 2015. Transnational policy and 'authenticity' discourses on Romani language and identity. *Language in Society* 44(3). 295–316.

May, Stephen. 2011. *Language and minority rights: Ethnicity, nationalism and the politics of language*. 2nd edn. New York: Routledge.

Mayer, Elisabeth, Liliana Sánchez, José Camacho & Carolina Rodríguez Alzza. this vol. The drivers of home language maintenance and development in indigenous communities.

Mazzaferro, Gerardo. 2018. Language maintenance and shift within new linguistic minorities in Italy: A translanguaging perspective. In Gerardo Mazzaferro (ed.), *Translanguaging as everyday practice*, 87–106. Cham: Springer International.

McCarty, Teresa L., Sheilah E. Nicholas & Leisy T. Wyman. 2012. Re-emplacing place in the "global here and now" – Critical ethnographic case studies of native American language planning and policy. *International Multilingual Research Journal* 6(1). 50–63.

Moriarty, Máiréad. 2015. Globalization and minority language policy and planning. In Máiréad Moriarty (ed.), *Globalizing language policy and planning: An Irish language perspective*, 9–23. London: Palgrave Macmillan.

Mühlhäusler, Peter. 2000. Language planning and language ecology. *Current Issues in Language Planning* 1(3). 306–367.

Murray, Garold & Terry Lamb (eds.). 2018. *Space, place and autonomy in language learning*. London: Routledge.

Noguerón-Liu, Silvia. 2013. Access to technology in transnational social fields: Simultaneity and digital literacy socialization of adult immigrants. *International Multilingual Research Journal* 7(1). 33–48.

Nordstrom, Janica. this vol. Community language schools.

Owusu, Thomas. 2003. Transnationalism among African immigrants in North America: The case of Ghanaians in Canada. *Journal of International Migration and Integration* 4(3). 395–413.

Pelliccia, Andrea. 2013. Greek students in Italy from a transnational perspective. *Diaspora Studies* 6(2). 67–79.

Pennycook, Alastair. 2004. Language policy and the ecological turn. *Language Policy* 3. 213–239.

Pennycook, Alastair. 2017. Language policy and local practices. In Ofelia García, Nelson Flores & Massimiliano Spotti (eds.), *The Oxford handbook of language and society*, 125–140. Oxford: Oxford University Press.

Phillipson, Robert (ed.) 2000. *Rights to language: Equity, power and education*. Mahwah, NJ: Lawrence Erlbaum.

Piller, Ingrid. 2016. *Linguistic diversity and social justice: An introduction to applied sociolinguistics*. Oxford: Oxford University Press.

Reershemius, Gertrud. 2017. Autochthonous heritage languages and social media: Writing and bilingual practices in Low German on Facebook. *Journal of Multilingual and Multicultural Development* 38(1). 35–49.

Ricento, Thomas. 2000. Historical and theoretical perspectives in language policy and planning. In Thomas Ricento (ed.), *Ideology, politics and language policies: Focus on English*, 9–24. Philadelphia, PA: John Benjamins.

Ricento, Thomas. 2010. Language policy and globalization. In Nikolas Coupland (ed.), *The handbook of language and globalization*, 123–141. Oxford: Blackwell.

Ricento, Thomas. (ed.) (2006). *Introduction to language policy: Theory and method*. Oxford: Blackwell.

Schalley, Andrea C. & Susana A. Eisenchlas. this vol. Social and affective factors in home language maintenance and development: Setting the scene.

Sikoli, Mark A. 2011. Agency and ideology in language shift and language maintenance. In Tania Granadillo & Heidi A. Orcutt-Gachiri (eds.), *Ethnographic Contributions to the Study of Endangered Languages*, 161–176. Tucson, AZ: University of Arizona Press.

Šimičić, Lucija. 2019. Torn between two nation-states. In Gregory P. Glasgow & Jeremie Bouchard (eds.), *Researching agency in language policy and planning*, 12–34. New York & London: Routledge.

Skutnabb-Kangas, Tove. 2000. *Linguistic genocide in education – or worldwide diversity and human rights?* London: Lawrence Erlbaum.

Skutnabb-Kangas, Tove 2008. Human rights and language policy in education. In Stephen May & Nancy H. Hornberger (eds.), *Language policy and political issues in education: Encyclopedia of language and education*, 107–120. New York: Springer.

Song, Juyoung. 2012. Imagined communities and language socialization practices in transnational space: A case study of two Korean "study abroad" families in the United States. *The Modern Language Journal* 96(4). 507–524.

Song, Juyoung. 2016. Language socialization and code-switching: A case study of a Korean–English bilingual child in a Korean transnational family. *International Journal of Bilingual Education and Bilingualism* 22(2). 91–106.

Stern, Alissa J. 2017. How Facebook can revitalise local languages: Lessons from Bali. *Journal of Multilingual and Multicultural Development* 38(9). 788–796.

Tollefson, James W. 1991. *Planning language, planning inequality. Language policy in the community*. London: Longman.

Tollefson, James W. & Miguel Pérez-Milans (eds.). 2018. *The Oxford handbook of language planning and policy*. New York: Oxford University Press.

Varis, Piia & Tom van Nuenen. 2017. The Internet, language, and virtual interactions. In Ofelia García, Nelson Flores & Massimiliano Spotti (eds.), *The Oxford handbook of language and society*, 473–488. Oxford: Oxford University Press.

Warriner, Doris S. & Leisy T. Wyman. 2013. Experiences of simultaneity in complex linguistic ecologies: Implications for theory, method, and practice. *International Multilingual Research Journal* 7(1). 1–14.

Winter, Joanne & Anne Pauwels. 2007. Language maintenance and the second generation: Policies and practices. In Anne Pauwels, Joanne Winter & Joseph Lo Bianco (eds.), *Maintaining minority languages in transnational contexts*, 180–200. London & New York: Palgrave.

Janica Nordstrom
15 Community language schools

1 Introduction

Around the world, millions of families are raising their children to become speakers of two or more languages, thereby continuing to create linguistically diverse societies worldwide. In Australia, for example, 21% of the population speak a language other than English at home, with the most common languages being Mandarin, Arabic, Cantonese, and Vietnamese (Australian Bureau of Statistics 2017). Similar figures are reported for the UK, where 20.6% of primary school aged students are exposed to a language other than English at home (Department of Education [UK] 2017), and in the U.S., where 21.6% of the population speak a language other than English at home (The United States Census Bureau 2017).

The importance of maintaining the home languages of children of migrants[1] has been long acknowledged for its social, cognitive, economic, and educational benefits (e.g. Conteh and Meier 2014; Ginsburgh and Weber 2011). Yet, while many societies recognise the importance and possible benefits of language diversity, efforts to assist migrant communities and their families with successful intergenerational language transmission are often limited. Rather, around the world, migrant communities are largely left to rely on their own expertise, creativity, and good-will when striving to maintain and promote their children's home languages and customs (Fee, Rhodes, and Wiley 2014; Fishman 1991; García, Zakharia, and Otcu 2013). Having identified a need for structured language learning that is not met by formal education systems, many minority communities have come to set up their own schools, teaching languages and cultures on evenings and weekends to school-aged children who are descendants of migrants. These community language schools (also known as "heritage", "ethnic", "supplementary", "complementary", and sometimes "Saturday" schools) are thus global grassroots initiatives, examples of what Liddicoat (this vol.) describes as meso-level planning where actors in-between the micro-level of the family and the macro-level of the state become agents to meet particular local needs perceivably not met in mainstream education policies (see also Liddicoat and Taylor-Leech 2014).

In English speaking countries, these schools date back some 150 years to the mid-1800s. While it is difficult to pinpoint the first attempts of structured home language schooling, records show that schools were established by Russian settlers as early as the late 19th century in the UK (Simon 2018), by Germans in 1886 in the U.S. (Fishman 2014), and by Jewish communities as early as 1865 in Australia (Norst

---

1 Following common Australian practice, the term 'migrant' is used instead of 'immigrant'.

1982). In the Australian context, as migration has continued, and socio-political affordability has arisen, these schools and their enrolments have continued to increase: from teaching approximately 61,000 students in one of 53 languages in 1982 (Norst 1982), to teaching over 100,000 students in approximately 70 different languages in 2018 (Australian Federation of Ethnic Schools Associations Inc. 2015). Community language schools thus represent communities from all corners of the world: Europe (e.g. Portuguese, German, Hungarian, Latvian, Spanish, Finnish, and Swedish schools), Middle-Eastern (e.g. Arabic, Assyrian, and Dari schools), East Asia (e.g. Chinese, Japanese, and Filipino schools), and Africa (e.g. Somali schools), to name a few (Australian Federation of Ethnic Schools Association Inc. 2015; Cardona, Noble, and Di Biase 2008).

Despite community language schools being major providers of languages education worldwide, most countries do not gather systematic data about the schools that operate within their borders (see Hancock 2018 for a Scottish example, or Fishman 2014 for a discussion in the U.S. context). Australia seems to be the exception to this widespread lack of oversight. In Australia, state and territory government offers annual per capita grants to eligible[2] schools based on student enrolments, and many schools thus provide their educational department with regular information regarding student enrolments, teacher data, and school information. In many other countries, however, it is difficult to gain an accurate or estimate overview of how many schools exist or how many students are enrolled. In the UK, The National Resource Centre for Supplementary Education (NRCSE) estimate that there are 3,000–5,000 "supplementary" schools, thus including not only schools teaching home languages and cultures, but also other schools that focus on supporting and tutoring in mainstream curriculum subjects (NRCSE 2019). In other countries, there are seemingly no umbrella organisations for community language schools but schools are instead affiliated with language specific associations, such as the Korean Schools Association of Northern California, or the Chinese Schools Association in the United States (Wang 2017).

This lack of political and governmental acknowledgement, partly due to lack of funding, reinforces the idea of these schools as "invisible" institutions, with mainstream governing bodies and policy makers (and the public alike) having little knowledge about the practices in these schools, how many schools operate in their country, how many teachers are involved, or how many students are enrolled. Indeed, Fishman (2014: 39) recalls how he twice attempted to scope the number of

---

2 To be eligible for state and territory funding in Australia, community language schools need to meet a range of criteria. In NSW, for example, schools need to be registered as "incorporate associations" with insurance, have at least 20 students enrolled, teach a "sound educational program" for a minimum of 2 hours per week for 35 weeks, and they must be open to all school aged children regardless of their language background (NSW Department of Education 2017). Thus, enrolment numbers provided often exclude playgroups and adult learners, as well as those schools that for various reasons have not applied, or do not meet the criteria, for funding.

heritage language schools in the U.S. "to determine [himself] what the government had studiously ignored". In his first attempt (in the 1950s and 60s) he located 1,885 schools, although he argued that there undoubtedly were hundreds more. Despite attracting the attention of the FBI querying him if any of these schools had any communist agendas (none to his knowledge), Fishman repeated his count in the 1980s. This time he identified more than 6,500 schools, but again he argued that there were thousands that he had not been able to locate. Since that last count in the 1980s, there seem to have been no further nationwide studies of community language schools in the United States (Fishman 2014: 40). Rightly so, Fishman concludes that:

> The determination of immigrants to develop and maintain heritage language schools for their children should have been documented by the U.S. Department of Education or by the separate state departments of education. However, as far as these official agencies were concerned, no such schools have existed, unless they have been cited [i.e. criticised] for lack of bathrooms, windows or fire escapes. (Fishman 2014: 38)

Nonetheless, it is evident through the emerging research that community language schools represent many different communities from all corners of the world. With diversity in language, heritage, migration trajectories, and host communities, any attempt to theorising the aim and purpose of these schools needs to carefully consider the historical, political and social contexts in which each school operates. Some similarities in structure and operation however emerge. For example, community language schools worldwide are often run by community members and parent volunteers. They are primarily self-funded and typically operate for a few hours on weeknights or weekends offering complementary language education to school aged children and adolescents. Depending on the host country, some financial support may be available. For instance, as mentioned above, state governments in Australia offer minor funding to support eligible schools based on student enrollments (e.g. NSW Department of Education 2017), and there is charity and non-government funding available in the UK (Simon 2018). Some schools also receive funding from governments of the home country, for example, Korean schools in the U.S. can apply for funding from the Korean government (Kim 2017b). Classes are often held in borrowed mainstream classrooms or community facilities such as churches. In the late 1990s however, some community language schools in Australia also began offering online or blended (alternating between face-to-face and online) learning environments in attempts to overcome some of the challenges these schools face, such as lack of classrooms, resources, geographically dispersed communities, and decreased student enrolments and motivation (see for example Nordstrom 2015a). While little is documented about online teaching in community language schools elsewhere, findings from studies focusing on computer-mediated communication and use of weblogs among adult community language learners have shown that Internet based communication might increase opportunities for language use, authenticity of language use, as well as vocabulary development (Fitzgerald and Debski 2006; Hatoss this vol.;

Little this vol.; Little, Meskill and Anthony 2008; Lee 2006), suggesting that offering online learning environments might have pedagogical benefits for students in community language schools.

This chapter will provide an in-depth understanding of community language schools and the main contemporary issues emerging from studies focusing on these schools in different geographical contexts around the world. Although community language schools exist worldwide, research has primarily emerged from North America, the UK, Australia, and (to some extent) from wider Europe. The chapter will describe parents' and students' perceptions of, and attitudes towards, the schools (section 2), as well as ideologies and language practices often observed by researchers visiting these sites of learning (section 3). One of the key findings in current research is that students and teachers alike often use their languages in flexible ways and contest some of the teaching practices, issues that are discussed in section 4. Although community language teachers (section 5) are rarely the focus of community language school research, some emerging findings suggests that more attention is needed that focus on teachers' sense of teacher identity and professionalism, in order to fully understand why schools operate as they do. Finally, in section 6, an overview and forward-looking perspective of research into community language schools is provided before the chapter is concluded in section 7.

2 Parents' and students' perceptions of community language schools

Despite diversity among community language schools, some common findings have emerged from research across the world and from different communities. A first main finding is that these schools, at least in English speaking countries, have the important function to strengthen the cultural and/or religious identities of migrant children and to foster a sense of belonging to a community and/or nation (Archer, Francis, and Mau 2010; Arthur 2003; Blackledge and Creese 2010a; Borland 2005; Cardona, Noble, and Di Biase 2008; Choudhury 2013; Conteh, Riasat, and Begum 2013; Francis, Archer, and Mau 2010b; Ghaffar-Kucher and Mahajan 2013; Otcu 2010; Tsolidis and Kostogriz 2008; Walters 2011; Wu 2006). These schools thus differ from other second and foreign language learning providers, in that parents, educators, and students alike, often contextualise their perceptions of their community language school around notions of "belonging" with other native speakers and with a distant heritage nation. For example, parents and educators in a large-scale UK study of four different community language schools expressed that a sense of belonging was a driving force behind these schools, where "teaching of affiliation to the homeland is one of the motivating principles of the schools" (Blackledge and Creese 2010a: 198). Also in the UK, Francis, Archer, and Mau (2010b) found in interviews with 21 teachers and

24 parents in Chinese schools that underlying reasons for home language acquisition were embedded in an idea of "being" someone. Asked why learning the Chinese language was important, the informants commonly explained that it was important for their children and students to learn Chinese, because they *are* Chinese. Similarly, parents and community language school staff in a study by Walters (2011), emphasized notions of identity when constructing their reasons for complementary schooling, with the Bengali language being described as "ours" and intertwined with the students' "roots", and parents of Swedish community language school learners in Australia argued that it was important that their children learnt Swedish because it encouraged them to "feel" Swedish and being "accepted" as Swedes (Nordstrom 2015b).

However, it seems that this notion of "belonging" is equivocal because it is not clear if it is the learning and teaching of the home language and culture that encourages this sense of belonging, or if being surrounded by people alike enhances a feeling of membership. That is, students' sense of "ethnic membership" may be more the result of being surrounded by others alike (as found by Archer, Francis, and Mau 2010) where individuals create a community of practice (Lave and Wenger 1991) rather than the result of what is taught in the classrooms. Attending a community language school might thus alleviate feelings of segregation that some students are subjected to in mainstream education and offer refuge from racism sometimes encountered in their everyday life (Creese et al. 2006; Francis, Archer, and Mau 2010b; Hall et al. 2002; Kim 2017b). For example, students in a Korean community language school in the U.S. explained how they can be "normal", "legitimate", and can "relate to each other more" (Kim 2017b) in the Korean school than in their mainstream school. Similarly, Chinese community language school students in the UK told Francis, Archer, and Mau (2010b) that they felt more comfortable in their community language schools where they could be "noisier" and "cheekier" than in their mainstream school. Francis, Archer, and Mau propose that this may "perhaps [be] in relation to different interpellations and expectations by teachers and other spectators" (2010b: 90) and that an absence of racism and pressure to achieve can lead students to negotiate and construct different identities to those in mainstream schools.

Similar to their parents, many community language school students learn the home language (at least partly) to create or maintain a strong sense of ethnic or cultural identity. Both Chinese students in Francis, Archer, and Mau's (2010a) study and young 11–12 year-old Somali learners in the UK (Arthur 2003) explained that learning their home language was important because of who they were, e.g. "because they are Chinese" and because Somali was "their" language. A lack of proficiency was, to learners in both studies, associated with notions such as shame, outsiderness, and disgrace, while learning Somali came "with the advantage of avoiding a challenge to the perception, in their own eyes or in those of others, that they are native speakers [of Somali]" (Arthur 2003: 260).

It is increasingly argued, however, that perpetuating the home language and education in community language schools is about more than creating a sense of belonging with other home language speakers and with a heritage community. García, Zakharia, and Otcu (2013: 19) describe these schools (and other bilingual programs) as providing contexts where students "live the language other than English, not as heritage, but as life [...] in present and a global future". Indeed, parents from a range of communities around the world are echoing such claims. For example, Chinese parents in the UK (Francis, Archer, and Mau 2010b), Persian parents in the U.S. (Shirazi and Borjian 2009) and Swedish parents in Australia (Nordstrom 2016) have emphasised home language learning and bilingualism as having merit in academic and tertiary contexts outside of the community language school, with parents and students alike arguing that being bilingual would be good for their CVs, future work and travels.

Although students often agree with the overall aims and perceptions of community language schooling, it is nonetheless worth noting that attending these schools, for many students, is the parents' decision (Francis, Archer, and Mau 2009; Kim 2017b; Mu and Dooley 2015; Tereshchenko and Cárdenas 2013). Interviewing 60 students aged 11 to 13 at a UK Chinese community language school, Francis, Archer, and Mau (2009) found that 37% of students claimed that attending the Chinese school was their parents' decision. A further 28% stated that although it initially was their parents' choice, they now chose to come themselves, with only 27% of students said it was solely their decision to attend. Reluctance towards community language schooling has also been noted by teachers, in particular as students approach their teenage years. For example, Japanese teachers in Kano's (2013) study explained that while many young learners were seemingly content at their community language school, students in early teenage years began "to display negative attitudes toward learning Japanese, as their other interests and social lives develop" (2013: 110). This was also confirmed by Mu and Dooley (2015). Asking five young adults to recollect their memories of attending a Chinese community language school when younger, Mu and Dooley (2015: 509) quote the participants stating that they "hated learning Chinese with a passion" and that they perceived there to be "no point" in attending community language school when they were younger. However, as years went by and they became young adults, they again became interested in learning their home language. Drawing on Bourdieu's notion of *habitus* (Bourdieu 1977), Mu and Dooley (2015: 510) intriguingly argue that this change in attitudes towards home language maintenance may have been taught rather than inherited, where "constant and ongoing family inculcation comes to shape participants' internal attitudes, values, perceptions and dispositions in a largely unconscious way".

3 Monoglossic language ideologies and contradictory practices

Community language schools are often described as having some kind of one-language-only policy; an agreed understanding (explicit or implicit) that the home language is to be used (preferably exclusively) in the classrooms (see for example Blackledge and Creese 2010a; Choudhury 2013; Chung 2013). This is often embedded in monoglossic ideologies of languages, in particular in a perception that languages are separate entities where each language can be measured against a monolingual standard (Blackledge and Creese 2010a; García 2009). In community language schools, such ideologies often translate to teachers expecting students to use the target language exclusively while at the community language school (regardless of students varying proficiencies) and/or a belief that the mainstream language is to be avoided as much as possible by both the teacher and the students (e.g. Blackledge and Creese 2010a; Chung 2013; Kim 2017b; Otcu-Grillman 2016; Otcu 2010). Although English (or the dominant language) may be accepted in the classrooms for pragmatic reasons, it is rarely valued as highly as the home language (Otcu 2013; Nordstrom 2015a). Instead, several community language teachers from a variety of studies and communities have argued that because the home language is an intrinsic part of who the students are (or at least who the teachers perceive the students to be), students should keep their languages separate and only speak the home language at school, despite students being more proficient in English than in their community language (e.g. Blackledge and Creese 2010a; Otcu 2010; Wu 2006). The enforcement of such one-language-only policies however differed, ranging from teachers ignoring or pretending not to understand students when they speak the mainstream language (Choudhury 2013; Chung 2013) to explicitly discouraging it by reprimanding students when they speak the "wrong" language (Blackledge and Creese 2010a; Kim 2017b; Wu 2006). Although little is known about the implications in terms of student learning and attitudes of one-language-only policies and practices in community language schools, some research (e.g. Nordstrom 2015b) has highlighted that policies and practices that favour one language over the other can result in the pragmatic exclusion of less proficient students, where the teacher avoids directing questions to less-proficient students in whole-class discussions, or in other ways limits their participation (see also Duff 2002 for similar findings).

Furthermore, there also appears to be a general trend where community language teachers believe that maximising target language use in the classroom is the most appropriate way to teach languages (Blackledge and Creese 2010a, 2010b; Choudhury 2013). Such beliefs in keeping languages separate to optimise learning are of course not unique to community language teachers. Cook (2001: 403) describes how teachers' "assumptions" that students' first language (L1) should be discouraged in the language learning classroom have "affected many generations of students and teachers", ranging from explicit policies that L1 is banned from the classroom to a more positive framing of maximising the target language. However, to explain beliefs around separate ideologies in community language schools, Blackledge and Creese (2010b) draw on Jaffe's (2007) argument that when a minority community experiences language shift to the extent that there is "a tip" (Jaffe 2007: 53) in the direction of the mainstream language, fear of language loss causes the community to construct a "fictive unity" (Blackledge and Creese 2010b: 9) that is embedded in an idea of dual or balanced bilingualism (Jaffe 2007), thus starting to produce "structures of hegemony similar to those against which they struggle" (Blackledge and Creese 2010b: 9). That is, monoglossic policies and ideologies that value each language according to monolingual standards (García 2009) might not be the result of pedagogical considerations, but embedded in notions of fear for language loss, identity, and belonging.

Despite language ideologies and policies that favour one language over the other, research into language use in these schools have shown that students and teachers indeed use languages in flexible ways (Blackledge and Creese 2010a; Chung 2013; Hancock 2012; Li 2009; Otcu 2013; Wu 2006). For example, in a large-scale study in the UK led by Angela Creese (e.g. Blackledge and Creese 2009, 2010a), as well as in a separate study by Choudhury (2013), it was frequently observed how students challenged and questioned monolingual ideologies and school policies by arguing for, and using, both English and the community language in the classrooms. Blackledge and Creese (2010a) sum up these dichotomies in the notions of "separate" and "flexible" bilingualism where separate bilingualism emphasises a view of languages as systems clearly defined and separate from each other, while flexible bilingualism relates to the view of multiple languages as semiotic resources, used in normative, flexible, ways.

These findings, highlighting the discrepancy between beliefs and practices in community language schools, have in turn sparked a pedagogical discussion around the use of language in community language school teaching. While using languages in flexible ways is often perceived as "non-legitimate" actions (García and Li 2014: 58), it has been increasingly argued that pedagogical practices in these schools would benefit from a "bilingual pedagogy, with two or more languages used alongside each other" (Blackledge and Creese 2010a: 201) to meet the expectations and experiences of young learners. For this purpose, García and Li (2014) use the notion of "translanguaging", described as "*multiple discursive practice* in which bilinguals engage in order to *make sense of their bilingual worlds*" (García 2009: 45, italics in original), and as a construct which "liberates language from structuralist-only or mentalist-only or even social-only definitions" (García and Li 2014: 42). While little research has focused on the pedagogical benefits of deliberate translanguaging practices in community language schools, Nordstrom (2015a) found that less proficient students who attended online community language school classes were able to overcome the school's monoglossic language ideologies and increase their participation through translanguaging practices that were hidden from teachers and peers. That is, when students and their teacher interacted with each other through text-based computer mediated communication (i.e. "chatting") without the use of video, less proficient students were found to draw on all their languages in flexible ways to construct their participation (including interaction(s) with parents and the use of bilingual dictionaries), unknown to the other participants.

4 Pedagogy and curricula

Despite many students valuing the idea of home language learning and maintenance for identity reasons and for their future travels and careers, findings continuously report that students across school years and communities nonetheless contest part of the curricula, teaching, and pedagogy within these schools by objecting to teachers, being disengaged in classrooms, refusing to do homework, and mocking content (Creese and Blackledge 2011; Li and Wu 2010; Otcu 2010). Several researchers have observed this resistance in classrooms, noting that it is often linked to the teaching of *culture* and *cultural values and behaviour*[3] as static and fixed constructs existing more in the past than being fluid in the present, thus rarely resonating with the experiences and expectations of the students (Archer, Francis, and Mau 2010; Blackledge and Creese 2009; Curdt-Christiansen 2008; Duff and Li 2014; Hancock 2012; Li and Wu 2010). When exploring social and cultural knowledge embedded in classroom resources in a Canadian-Chinese community language school, Hancock (2012: 109) found that teaching resources for the young learners were "laden with ideological under- and overtones" where cultural knowledge and ideologies were constructed, emphasising notions of obedience, perseverance, diligence, patriotism, conformity, achievement, modesty, and altruism. Blackledge and Creese (2009, 2010a), similarly, found that teachers across different language groups often taught the language through stories of martyrdom and heroic events in attempts to foster "a sense of national belonging that is firmly rooted in narratives of collective memories" (Blackledge and Creese 2009: 462) and functioning to "remind students of shared cultural heritage" (Blackledge and Creese 2010a: 149). Moreover, Choudhury (2013) and Archer, Francis, and Mau (2010), for Bengali and Chinese community language schools respectively, found that schools had a strong focus on teaching social values tied to an idea of "correct" Bengali and Chinese behaviour, echoed in Otcu's (2010) research where teachers and administrators complained that students did not behave in ways expected of "Turkish children", and reprimanded them thereafter. While students often express interest in learning about more contemporary issues and pop culture (Archer, Francis, and Mau 2010; Kim 2017a; Li and Wu 2010; Nordstrom 2015b), such topics are

---

[3] The use of italics emphasises the schools' perceptions of *cultures* as static and fixed, rather than fluid and continuously constructed.

nonetheless rarely included in curricula and materials used in community language schools.

Focussing on pedagogy and curricula is important in the discussion of how well these schools serve their communities, because students' attitudes towards their home language and motivation for home language maintenance have been found to correlate with their perceptions of their community language school classes (Chow 2001; Kim 2017b). For example, Chow (2001) found in a large survey of 510 Chinese community language school students in Canada (with a mean age of 14.24) that positive experiences of the Chinese community language school correlated with engagement with, inter alia, Chinese media, ethnic pride, and self-assessed proficiency. It should be noted, however, that students' perceptions of their community language schooling also correlated with age of migration, with students who arrived in the host country at an older age being more positive to their community language schooling than those who were born in the country or were very young at the time of migration (Chow 2001). This suggests that current teaching practices in these schools may better suit students who migrated at an older age but may not align with the experiences and expectations of other children and adolescents who have lived most of their lives in the host community (Duff and Li 2014). It is therefore suggested that schools and teachers need to strive to focus their teaching around common reference points that are motivating for students (Blackledge and Creese 2010a; Duff and Li 2014; García 2009). That is, language use, pedagogy, and curricula need to adapt to the uses and practices of languages in today's global society where languages are not idealised representations of heritage (Blackledge and Pavlenko 2001; García and Li 2014; Makoni and Pennycook 2007). However, some findings have suggested that this "socialisation teaching"[4] (Li and Wu 2010), at least partly, is the result of teachers' insecurity and a lack of available resources and professional development, and that teachers themselves often recognise the issues while striving towards engaging in more motivating teaching practices that aligns with the lives of the students (Hancock 2012; Walters 2011). Such issues thus point to the importance of available professional development for this group of teachers.

5 The "marginalised" community language teacher

Although there is a dearth of research focussing on the needs and working conditions of community language school teachers, common findings worldwide highlight that some of the challenges this group of teachers experience include a lack of relevant

---

[4] Li and Wu (2010: 37) use the term "socialisation teaching" to describe teaching practices where "the teaching of specific linguistic structures" is routinely embedded in the teaching of broader socio-cultural issues such as moral duties, socio-cultural ideals, or solidarity and unity with a homeland.

qualifications, training, and access to appropriate resources (Cardona, Noble, and Di Biase 2008; Hall et al. 2002; Hancock 2012; McPake, Tinsley, and James 2007; Ruby et al. 2010; Wu 2006). Teachers are often described as parents or community volunteers (Archer, Francis, and Mau 2009; Choudhury 2013; Chung 2013; Hall et al. 2002; Otcu 2010; Walters 2011) or as native speakers of the target language with limited bilingual proficiency (Hall et al. 2002; Walters 2011).

However, emerging evidence are suggesting that the stereotypical description of community language school teachers as uneducated volunteers might be changing. A recent study by Cruickshank, Ellsmore, and Brownlee (2018) focussing on community language teachers in NSW, Australia, found that the typical community language teacher in NSW was a female who has been in Australia for more than 10 years, and who has full-time commitments outside of her teaching in community language schools (see also Otcu 2013 for similar findings). The study furthermore showed that these community language teachers have high qualifications: 87% had tertiary qualifications, with 44.3% of these having qualifications in education, and 54.9% having international teaching experience (Cruickshank, Ellsmore, and Brownlee 2018).

A key emerging issue, however, is that community language teachers routinely feel marginalised in educational contexts. They are described as "invisible adjuncts" (Cruickshank, Ellsmore, and Brownlee 2018: 7), quoted feeling tense relationships with mainstream educators, and not perceiving themselves as "real" teachers (Baldauf 2005; Cardona, Noble, and Di Biase 2008). This perceived lack of recognition in mainstream education systems is often amalgamated by poor working conditions. Many community language schools worldwide operate in "borrowed" mainstream classrooms that are "clearly intended for other times, people, and purposes" (Tsolidis and Kostogriz 2008: 324). Furthermore, teachers rarely have access to school resources such as the internet, whiteboards, and places used for storage (Archer, Francis, and Mau 2009; Cruiskshank, Ellsmore, and Brownlee 2018; Tsolidis and Kostogriz 2008), resulting in the community language school teachers feeling "like unwelcome guests" at the mainstream school (Cruickshank, Ellsmore, and Brownlee 2018: 26).

This perception of being marginalised in educational contexts is also sometimes compounded by power relations between parents and teachers within the community language school itself. For example, a Swedish community language teacher in Australia concluded that she felt more "accepted" by parents and approached more as a "professional teacher" in her role as a mainstream teacher, mainly because she felt that parents in community language schools have a unique position and ability to influence curriculum and classroom practices in ways that she did not always found pedagogically sound (Nordstrom 2015b). Levels of parental engagement in community language schools however appear to differ. In some schools, parents have been found to have a strong and active influence on the school curricula (e.g. Tsolidis and Kostogriz 2008), while at other schools, lack of parental engagement is a concern of principals and teachers (e.g. Aravossitas and Oikonomakou 2018).

6 Current and future research trends

Despite community language schools dating back some 150 years, our knowledge and research focussing on these schools is still relatively new. Most available scholarly works have emerged in the last 20 years, providing foundational insights and snapshot of how schools operate and why. However, with each new insight, a new question also seems to emerge, often asking how particular findings relate to other community language schools. As seen throughout this chapter, a strong body of scholarly work has emerged primarily from North America, the UK, Australia, and to lesser extent from wider Europe. Nonetheless, research is still unevenly distributed, primarily focussing Turkish (e.g. Creese et al. 2007; Lytra 2012; Otcu 2010; 2013; Otcu-Grillman 2016) or Asian languages such as Chinese (Archer, Francis, and Mau 2010; Blackledge and Creese 2010a; Chow 2001; Creese, Wu, and Li 2007; Curdt-Christiansen 2008; Hancock 2012; Li and Wu 2010), Bengali (Blackledge and Creese 2010a; Choudhury 2013; Creese, Blackledge, and Hamid 2007), Gujarati (Blackledge and Creese 2010a; Creese, Bhatt, and Martin 2007; Creese 2009; Martin et al. 2006), Vietnamese (Reath Warren 2018), and Korean (Chung 2013; Kim 2017b). Emerging research focussing on smaller, less visible minority communities such as Ukrainian schools in Portugal (Tereshchenko and Cárdenas 2013) and Swedish schools in Australia (Nordstrom 2015a, 2015b, 2016) are thus increasingly important in order to achieve a broader and more holistic understanding of how different community language schools serve their communities in the 21st century.

To date, much focus on community language schools has aimed to understand classroom practices as well as students' and parents' perceptions of schools and languages. Slowly emerging, however, is a discussion on how we can use this knowledge to help community language schools overcome challenges related to resources, pedagogy, and staffing. With resources being sparse and sometimes outdated or irrelevant for community language school purposes, some researchers have begun working with schools to develop quality teaching material that aligns with students' authentic and contemporary use of language(s) (e.g. Sydney Institute for Community Languages 2018). Similarly, drawing on observations in classrooms of flexible language use, convincing arguments urge teachers to draw on bilingual scaffolding and translanguaging as deliberate pedagogical practices to improve language learning in community language schools (see also section 14.3). Importantly, home language learners differ from second language learners both in their needs and experiences (Carreira and Kagan 2018). For example, home language learners tend to be more proficient in informal, every day vocabulary and have good pronunciation, and their reasons for language learning are often embedded in notions of identity and community (Carreira and Kagan 2018). Thus, it becomes a natural step for researchers to work closely together with schools and communities to assist them in developing sustainable teaching resources and language policies that meet the needs of their students.

Furthermore, few studies so far focus explicitly on teachers. A sturdy research base in the field of mainstream education argues that understanding teacher identity is important because it influences teachers' self-esteem, efficiency, quality of teaching, ability, and commitment, as well as effort in teaching (Beauchamp and Thomas 2009; Beijaard, Verloop, and Vermunt 2000; Hammerness, Darling-Hammond, and Bransford 2005). Emerging research (such as those described in section 5) highlight that these are prevalent issues in community language schools, where community language teachers often struggle with their perceptions of themselves as teachers. The issues are twofold. On the one hand, many community language teachers struggle to feel confident in their own teaching and pedagogy, and thus it becomes crucial to offer more and better professional development tailored to meet the needs of community language school teachers. While many teachers are first generation migrants and highly proficient in their home language, they often lack pedagogical foundations suitable for this distinct group of learners, who are often second-generation migrants and less proficient in the home language. On the other hand, teachers also struggle with for legitimacy in broader mainstream educational contexts, often feeling marginalised in their roles as language teachers in community language schools. Yet Cruickshank, Ellsmore, and Brownlee (2018) found that although many community language teachers struggled with claiming space in the mainstream educational context, the majority of the teachers interviewed wanted to become accredited to teach in mainstream education, and it thus becomes crucial to find pathways for this group of teachers. Indeed, at the launch of the Sydney Institute for Community Languages Education, Cruickshank (2018) claimed that finding pathways for overseas trained teachers to become accredited can result in an astounding $182 million economic benefit for Australia, although he did not provide details as to how this was calculated. Nonetheless, this highlights that there may be political incentives to invest more research into community language teachers and teacher training.

7 Conclusion

Community language schools represent minority communities from all corners of the world and they have grown to be significant (albeit often invisible) language education providers worldwide. Nonetheless, it is evident that these schools differ from other language providers who teach second or foreign languages in their aims and purposes, and that they are important institutions where students can come together with others alike, creating "safe" places that are free from racism (Francis, Archer, and Mau 2010b; Hall et al. 2002).

Research into community language schools is still in its infancy, and findings from second and foreign language learning research may not be easily transferable to the context of community language schools. Some of the key findings from emerging research in community language schools, highlighted throughout this chapter, have shown that these schools face their own unique challenges, often in relation to teacher qualification, resources, available professional development, and student motivations. Furthermore, despite large enrolment numbers worldwide, schools still struggle for legitimacy and are (at best) peripheral in the educational sector. It thus becomes utterly important that educational departments worldwide recognise these schools as valid sites for learning and the important work done by both students and teachers. For students, this may be stronger recognition of community language learning in their mainstream academic transcripts or for tertiary admission, thus emphasising the educational value of community language school learning as part of holistic education. For teachers, this could be recognition, in the eyes of the educational departments, as professional teachers in the field of community language schooling. This, of course, may require tertiary institutions and educational departments working closely together to offer pathways and professional development that focus on evidence-based approaches to language teaching in community language schools, thus also assisting schools meeting the needs of their communities and continue to encourage home language learning and maintenance.

References

Aravossitas, Themistoklis & Marianthi Oikonomakou. 2018. Professional development of heritage language instructors: Profiles, needs, and course evaluation. In Peter Pericles Trifonas & Themistoklis Aravossitas (eds.), *Handbook of research and practice in heritage language education*, 263–284. Cham: Springer.

Archer, Louise, Becky Francis & Ada Mau. 2009. 'Boring and stressful' or 'ideal' learning spaces? Pupils' constructions of teaching and learning in Chinese supplementary schools. *Research Papers in Education* 24(4). 477–497.

Archer, Louise, Becky Francis & Ada Mau. 2010. The culture project: Diasporic negotiations of ethnicity, identity and culture among teachers, pupils and parents in Chinese language schools. *Oxford Review of Education* 36(4). 407–426.

Arthur, Jo. 2003. "Baaro afkaaga hooyo!" A case of Somali literacy teaching in Liverpool. *International Journal of Bilingual Education and Bilingualism* 6(3–4). 253–266.

Australian Bureau of Statistics. 2017. Census reveals a fast changing, culturally diverse nation. http://www.abs.gov.au/ausstats/abs@.nsf/lookup/Media%20Release3 (accessed 7 August, 2018).

Australian Federation of Ethnic Schools Associations Inc. 2015. *Ethnic schools – Statistical data*. http://www.communitylanguages.org.au/ (accessed 2 June 2015).

Baldauf, Richard B. 2005. Coordinating government and community support for community language teaching in Australia: Overview with special attention to New South Wales. *International Journal of Bilingual Education & Bilingualism* 8(2–3). 132–144.

Beauchamp, Catherine & Lynn Thomas. 2009. Understanding teacher identity: An overview of issues in the literature and implications for teacher education. *Cambridge Journal of Education* 39(2). 175–189.

Beijaard, Douwe, Nico Verloop & Jan D. Vermunt. 2000. Teachers' perceptions of professional identity: An exploratory study from a personal knowledge perspective. *Teaching and Teacher Education* 16(7). 749–765.

Blackledge, Adrian & Aneta Pavlenko. 2001. Negotiation of identities in multilingual contexts. *International Journal of Bilingualism* 5(3). 243–257.

Blackledge, Adrian & Angela Creese. 2009. "Because tumi Bangali": Inventing and disinventing the national in multilingual communities in UK. *Ethnicities* 9(4). 451–476.

Blackledge, Adrian & Angela Creese. 2010a. *Multilingualism: A critical perspective*. London: Continuum.

Blackledge, Adrian & Angela Creese. 2010b. Opening up flexible spaces: Ideology and practice in complementary schools. In Vally Lytra & Peter Martin (eds.), *Sites of multilingualism. Complementary schools in Britain today*, 3–18. Stoke on Trent: Trentham Books.

Borland, Helen. 2005. Heritage languages and community identity building: The case of a language of lesser status. *International Journal of Bilingual Education and Bilingualism* 8(2–3). 109–123.

Bourdieu, Pierre. 1977. *Outline of a theory of practice*. Cambridge: Cambridge University Press.

Cardona, Beatriz, Greg Noble & Bruno Di Biase. 2008. *Community languages matter: Challenges and opportunities facing the community language program in New South Wales*. Penrith: University of Western Sydney.

Carreira, Maria & Olga Kagan. 2018. Heritage language education. A proposal for the next 50 years. *Foreign Language Annals* 51. 152–168.

Choudhury, Ruhma. 2013. Raising bilingual and bicultural Bangladeshi-American children in New York City: Perspectives from educators and parents in a Bengali community program. In Ofelia García, Zeena Zakharia & Bahar Otcu (eds.), *Bilingual community education and multilingualism: Beyond heritage languages in a global city*, 60–73. Bristol: Multilingual Matters.

Chow, Henry P. 2001. Learning the Chinese language in a multicultural milieu: Factors affecting Chinese-Canadian adolescent's ethnic language school experience. *Alberta Journal of Educational Research* 47(4). 369–374.

Chung, Jeehyae. 2013. Hidden efforts, visible challenges: Promoting bilingualism in Korean-America. In Ofelia García, Zeena Zakharia & Bahar Otcu (eds.), *Bilingual community education and multilingualism: Beyond heritage languages in a global city*, 87–98. Bristol: Multilingual Matters.

Conteh, Jean & Gabriella Meier (eds.). 2014. *The multilingual turn in education: Opportunities and challenges*. Bristol: Multilingual Matters.

Conteh, Jean, Saiqa Riasat & Shila Begum. 2013. Children learning multilingually in home, community and school contexts in Britain. In Mila Schwartz & Anna Verschik (eds.), *Successful family language policy: Parents, children and educators in interaction*, 83–102. London: Springer.

Cook, Vivian. 2001. Using the first language in the classroom. *Canadian Modern Language Review* 57(3). 402–423.

Creese, Angela. 2009. Building on young people's linguistic and cultural continuity: Complementary schools in the United Kingdom. *Theory Into Practice* 48(4). 267–273.

Creese, Angela & Adrian Blackledge. 2011. Separate and flexible bilingualism in complementary schools: Multiple language practices in interrelationship. *Journal of Pragmatics* 43(5). 1196–1208.

Creese, Angela, Arvind Bhatt & Peter Martin. 2007. *Investigating multilingualism in Gujarati complimentary school in Leicester*. University of Birmingham. https://www.researchcatalogue.esrc.ac.uk/grants/RES-000-23-1180/read (accessed 27 May 2019).

Creese, Angela, Adrian Blackledge & Shahela Hamid. 2007. *Investigating multilingualism in Bengali complementary schools in Birmingham*. University of Birmingham. https://www.researchcatalogue.esrc.ac.uk/grants/RES-000-23-1180/read (accessed 27 May 2019).

Creese, Angela, Chao-Jung Wu & Li Wei. 2007. *Investigating multilingualism in Chinese complementary schools in Manchester*. University of Birmingham. https://www.researchcatalogue.esrc.ac.uk/grants/RES-000-23-1180/read (accessed 27 May 2019).

Creese, Angela, Taskin Baraç, Vally Lytra & Dilek Yagcioglu-Ali. 2007. *Investigating multilingualism in Turkish complementary schools in London*. University of Birmingham. https://www.researchcatalogue.esrc.ac.uk/grants/RES-000-23-1180/read (accessed 27 May 2019).

Creese, Angela, Arvind Bhatt, Nirmala Bhojani & Peter Martin. 2006. Multicultural, heritage and learner identities in complementary schools. *Language and Education* 20(1). 23–43.

Cruickshank, Ken. 2018. Community language teaching offers migrant women pathways to work. Sydney Institute for Community Language Education. https://sydney.edu.au/news-opinion/news/2018/09/12/-community-language-teaching-offers-migrant-women-pathways-to-wo.html (accessed 28 May 2019).

Cruickshank, Ken, Marjory Ellsmore & Patrick Brownlee. 2018. *The skills in question: Report on the professional learning strengths and needs of teachers in the NSW Community Language Schools*. University of Sydney: Sydney Institute for Community Languages Education.

Curdt-Christiansen, Xiao Lan. 2008. Reading the world through words: Culture themes in heritage Chinese language texbooks. *Language and Education* 22(2). 95–113.

Department of Education [UK]. 2017. *Schools, students and their characteristics: January 2017*. https://www.gov.uk/government/statistics/schools-pupils-and-their-characteristics-january-2017 (accessed 20 August, 2018).

Duff, Patricia A. 2002. The discursive co-construction of knowledge, identity and difference: An ethnography of communication in the High School Mainstream. *Applied Linguistics* 23(3). 289–322.

Duff, Patricia A. & Duanduan Li. 2014. Rethinking heritage languages: Ideologies, identities, practices and priorities in Canada and China. In Peter Pericles Trifonas & Themistoklis Aravossitas (eds.), *Rethinking heritage language education*, 45–65. Cambridge: Cambridge University Press.

Fee, Molly, Nancy C. Rhodes & Terrence G. Wiley. 2014. Demographic realities, challenges, and opportunities. In Terrence G. Wiley, Joy Kreeft Peyton, Donna Christian, Sarah Catherine K. Moore & Na Liu (eds.), *Handbook of heritage, community, and native American languages in the United States: Research, policy, and educational practice*, 6–18. New York: Routledge.

Fishman, Joshua A. 1991. *Reversing language shift: Theoretical and empirical foundations of assistance to threatened languages*. Clevedon: Multilingual Matters.

Fishman, Joshua A. 2014. Three hundred-plus years of heritage language education in the United States. In Terrence G. Wiley, Joy Kreeft Peyton, Donna Christian, Sarah Catherine K. Moore & Na Liu (eds.), *Handbook of heritage, community, and native American languages in the United States: Research, policy, and educational practice*, 36–44. New York: Routledge.

Fitzgerald, Michael & Robert Debski. 2006. Internet use of Polish by Polish Melburnians: Implications for maintenance and teaching. *Language Learning and Technology* 10(1). 87–109.

Francis, Beckly, Louise Archer & Ada Mau. 2009. Language as capital, or language as identity? Chinese complementary school pupils' perspectives on the purposes and benefits of complementary schools. *British Educational Research Journal* 35(4). 519–538.

Francis, Becky, Louise Archer & Ada Mau. 2010a. Chinese complementary school pupils' social and educational subjectives. In Vally Lytra & Peter Martin (eds.), *Sites of multilingualism: Complementary schools in Britain today*, 85–96. Stoke on Trent: Trentham Books.

Francis, Becky, Louise Archer & Ada Mau. 2010b. Parents' and teachers' constructions of the purpose of Chinese complementary schooling: 'Culture', identity and power. *Race Ethnicity and Education* 13(1). 101–117.

García, Ofelia. 2009. *Bilingual education in the 21st Century: A global perspective*. Malden, MA: Wiley-Blackwell.

García, Ofelia & Li Wei. 2014. *Translanguaging: Language, bilingualism and education*. New York: Palgrave Macmillan.

García, Ofelia, Zeena Zakharia & Bahar Otcu. 2013. Bilingual community education: Beyond heritage language education and biingual education in New York. In Ofelia García, Zeena Zakharia & Bahar Otcu (eds.), *Bilingual community education and multilingualism: Beyond heritage languages in a global city*, 3–44. Bristol: Multilingual Matters.

Ghaffar-Kucher, Ameena & Anup P. Mahajan. 2013. *Salaam! Namaste!:* Indian and Pakistani community-based efforts towards mother tongue language maintenance. In Ofelia García, Zeena Zakharia & Bahar Otcu (eds.), *Bilingual community education and multilingualism: Beyond heritage languages in a global city*, 74–86. Bristol: Multilingual Matters.

Ginsburgh, Victor & Shlomo Weber. 2011. *How many languages do we need? The economics of linguistic diversity*. New Jersey: Princeton University Press.

Hall, Kathy A., Kamil Özerk, Mohsin Zulfiqar & Jon E. C. Tan. 2002. "This is our school": Provision, purpose and pedagogy of supplementary schooling in Leeds and Oslo. *British Educational Research Journal* 28(3). 399–418.

Hammerness, Karen, Linda Darling-Hammond & John Bransford. 2005. How teachers learn and develop. In Linda Darling-Hammond & John Bransford (eds.), *Preparing teachers for a changing world: What teachers should learn and be able to do*, 358–389. San Francisco: Jossey-Bass.

Hancock, Andy. 2012. Unpacking mundane practices: Children's experiences of learning literacy at a Chinese complementary school in Scotland. *Language and Education* 26(1). 1–17.

Hancock, Andy. 2018. *Extending the 1+2 language strategy: Complementary schools and their role in heritage language learning in Scotland*. University of Edinburgh.

Hatoss, Anikó. this vol. Transnational grassroots language planning in the era of mobility and the Internet.

Jaffe, Alexandra. 2007. Minority language movements. In Monica Heller (ed.), *Bilingualism: A social approach*, 50–70. Hampshire: Palgrave Macmillian.

Kano, Naomi. 2013. Japanese community schools: New pedagogy for a changing population. In Ofelia García, Zeena Zakharia & Bahar Otcu (eds.), *Bilingual community education and multilingualism: Beyond heritage languages in a global world*, 99–112. Bristol: Multilingual Matters.

Kim, Jung-In. 2017a. Immigrant adolescents investing in Korean heritage language: Exploring motivation, identities, and capital. *The Canadian Modern Language Review* 73(2). 183–207.

Kim, Jung-In. 2017b. Issues of motivation and identity positioning: Two teachers' motivational practices for engaging immigrant children in learning heritage languages. *International Journal of Bilingual Education and Bilingualism* 20(6). 638–651.

Lave, Jean & Etienne Wenger. 1991. *Situated learning: Legitimate peripheral participation*. Cambridge: Cambridge University Press.

Lee, Jin S. 2006. Exploring the relationship between electronic literacy and heritage language maintenance. *Language Learning and Technology* 10(2). 93–113.

Li, Wei. 2009. Polite Chinese children revisited: Creativity and the use of codeswitching in the Chinese complementary school classroom. *International Journal of Bilingual Education and Bilingualism*. 12(2). 193–211.

Li, Wei & Chao-Jung Wu. 2010. Literacy and socialisational teaching in Chinese complementary schools. In Vally Lytra & Peter Martin (eds.), *Sites of multilingualism: Complementary schools in Britain today*, 33–44. Stoke on Trent: Trentham Books.

Liddicoat, Anthony J. this vol. Language policy and planning for language maintenance: The macro and meso levels.

Liddicoat, Anthony & Kerry Taylor-Leech. 2014. Micro language planning for multilingual education: Agency in local contexts. *Current Issues In Language Planning* 15(3). 237–244.

Little, Sabine. this vol. Social media and the use of technology in home language maintenance.

Lytra, Vally. 2012. Discursive constructions of language and identity: Parents' competing perspectives in London Turkish complementary schools. *Journal of Multilingual and Multicultural Development*. 33(1). 85–100.

Makoni, Sinfree & Alastair Pennycook. 2007. Disinventing and reconstructing languages. In Sinfree Makoni & Alastair Pennycook (eds.), *Disinventing and reconstructing languages*, 1–41. Clevedon: Multilingual Matters.

Martin, Peter, Arvind Bhatt, Nirmala Bhojani & Angela Creese. 2006. Managing bilingual interaction in a Gujarati Complementary School in Leicester. *Language and Education* 20(1). 5–22.

McPake, Joanna, Teresa Tinsley & Ceri James. 2007. Making provision for community languages: Issues for teacher education in the UK. *The Language Learning Journal* 35(2). 99–112.

Meskill, Carla & Natasha Anthony. 2008. Computer mediated communication: Tools for instructing Russian heritage language learners. *Heritage Language Journal* 6(1). 1–22.

Mu, Guanglun M. & Karen Dooley. 2015. Coming into an inheritance: Family support and Chinese Heritage Language learning. *International Journal of Bilingual Education and Bilingualism* 18(4). 501–515.

Nordstrom, Janica. 2015a. Flexible bilingualism through multimodal practices: Studying K–12 community languages online. *International Journal of Bilingual Education and Bilingualism* 18(4). 395–408.

Nordstrom, Janica. 2015b. *Re-thinking community language schools: Moving from in-between the beyond the nation-states*. Sydney: The University of Sydney PhD Thesis.

Nordstrom, Janica. 2016. Parents' reasons for community language schools: Insight from a high-shift, non-visible, middle-class community. *Language and Education* 30(6). 1–17.

Norst, Marlene. 1982. Ethnic schools: What they are and what they would like to be. *Journal of Intercutural Studies* 3(1). 6–16.

NRCSE. 2019. Supplementary Education. National Resource Centre for Supplementary Education [UK] http://www.supplementaryeducation.org.uk/supplementary-education-the-nrc/ (accessed 1 February 2019).

NSW Department of Education. 2017. Community languages school grants. https://education.nsw.gov.au/public-schools/community-languages-schools/community-languages-school-grants (accessed 10 August 2018).

Otcu, Bahar. 2010. Heritage language maintenance and cultural identity formation: The case of a Turkish Saturday schools in New York City. *Heritage Language Journal* 7(2). 112–137.

Otcu, Bahar. 2013. Turkishness in New York: Languages, ideologies and identities in a community-based school. In Ofelia García, Zeena Zakharia & Bahar Otcu (eds.), *Bilingual community education and multilingualism: Beyond heritage languages in a global city*, 113–127. Bristol: Multilingual Matters.

Otcu-Grillman, Bahar. 2016. "Speak Turkish!" or not? Language choices, identities and relationship building within New York's Turkish community. *International Journal of the Socioloqy of Language: Middle Eastern Languages in Diasporit USA Communities* 237. 161–181.

Reath Warren, Anne. 2018. Monoglossic echoes in multilingual spaces: Language narratives from a Vietnamese community language school in Australia. *Current Issues in Language Planning*. 19(1). 42–61.

Ruby, Mahera, Eve Gregory, Charmian Kenner & Salman Al-Azami. 2010. Grandmothers as orchestrators of early language and literacy practices. In Vally Lytra & Peter Martin (eds.), *Sites of multilingualism: Complementary schools in Britain today*, 57–68. Stoke on Trent: Trentham Books.

Shirazi, Roozbeh & Maryam Borjian. 2009. Persian bilingual and community education among Iranian-Americans in New York City. In Ofelia García, Zeena Zakharia & Bahar Otcu (eds.), *Bilingual community education and multilingualism: Beyond heritage langauges in a global city*, 154–168. Bristol: Multilingual Matters.

Simon, Amanda. 2018. *Supplementary schools and ethnic minority communities: A social positioning perspective*: Palgrave Macmillan.

Sydney Institute for Community Languages. 2018. https://sydney.edu.au/arts/our-research/centres-institutes-and-groups/sydney-institute-community-languages-education.html (accesssed 28 May 2019).

Tereshchenko, Antonia & Valeska Grau Cárdenas. 2013. Immigration and supplementary ethnic schooling: Ukrainian students in Portugal. *Educational Studies* 39(4). 455–467.

The United States Census Bureau. 2017. New American community survey statistics for income, poverty and health insurance available for states and local areas. https://www.census.gov/newsroom/press-releases/2017/acs-single-year.html?CID=CBSM+ACS16 (accessed 3 February 2019).

Tsolidis, Georgina & Alex Kostogriz. 2008. "After hours" schools as core to the spatial politics of "in-betweenness". *Race Ethnicity and Education* 11(3). 319–328.

Walters, Sue. 2011. Provision, purpose and pedagogy in a Bengali supplementary school. *The Language Learning Journal* 39(2). 163–175.

Wang, Nan. 2017. *Heritage language schools in the U.S.: Administration, sustainability and school operations*. University of Nebraska PhD Thesis.

Wu, Chao-Jung. 2006. Look who's talking: Language choice and culture of learning in UK Chinese classrooms. *Language and Education* 20(1). 62–75.

Elisabeth Mayer, Liliana Sánchez, José Camacho, and Carolina Rodríguez Alzza

16 The drivers of home language maintenance and development in indigenous communities

1 Introduction

Indigenous and tribal peoples represent 5% of the 7.7 billion world population, with roughly 370 million worldwide distributed over 70 countries and accounting for the bulk of the world's linguistic and cultural diversity. According to The World Bank (2019), while indigenous peoples own, cultivate or occupy almost a quarter of the world's surface, they embody 15% of the world's extreme poor and face problems of marginalization and other human rights violations. Indigenous people speak roughly three quarters of the approximate 7000 known spoken languages today (McCarty, Nicholas, and Wigglesworth 2019). Despite the fact that language rights for indigenous and tribal peoples are enshrined in articles 13 and 14 of the *United Nations Declaration on the Rights of Indigenous Peoples*, indigenous languages across the world continue to have a minoritized status, despite efforts from indigenous communities, regional and in some cases even national governments to secure policies and practices to turn this status around (Annamalai and Skutnabb-Kangas this vol.). The development and maintenance of indigenous languages exhibit great variability around the globe. It is driven by multiple factors, such as numbers of first and second language speakers, access to intercultural bilingual education, and adequate language policies and their implementation (Lo Bianco 1987; McCarty, Nicholas, and Wigglesworth 2019; Coronel-Molina and McCarty 2016).

Traditionally, indigenous communities have been characterized by extensive multilingualism on a global scale, dating back to premodern and precolonial times (Boas 1940; McCarty, Wyman, and Nicholas 2014; Simpson and Wigglesworth 2008; Vaughan and Singer 2018). In many modern and postcolonial societies their language rights as well as the use of their indigenous languages are under threat or critically endangered (Patrick 2012). Indigenous languages across the world exhibit different configurations and vary in relation to the challenges these bring. For instance, indigenous languages in Australia and the USA are usually spoken and used in very small communities, and most of these are endangered. In Latin America, however, these languages may be spoken by a larger percentage of the population and enjoy different degrees of vitality. However, despite having larger numbers of speakers, they remain minoritized and may encounter negative attitudes that lead to discrimination of their speakers.

This chapter will first engage in a global discussion of the major challenges faced by indigenous languages' maintenance and development, as well as revitalization efforts in indigenous communities. This will be followed by an in-depth country-study (Peru). The issues to be discussed include conflicting perspectives in language policies about minoritized indigenous languages as a resource, as a right or as a problem, as well as local and family language planning, educational practices, language attitudes and community-based activities.

We will use the following terminology throughout the chapter "minority language" refers to a language spoken by a minority of the population within a larger national or regional context, whereas "minoritized language" refers to their minimized status in the larger society either in terms of legitimization or actual language planning (Groff 2017: 136). A "local language" is "a language spoken in a fairly restricted geographical area, and usually not learned as a second language by people outside the immediate language community" (Kosonen and Young 2009: 12). A "national language" is "a language that is considered to be the chief language of a nation state" (Crystal 1999: 227), and an "official language" is "used in such public domains as the law courts, government, and broadcasting. In many countries, there is no difference between the national and official language" (Crystal 1999: 227). We will use the term "indigenous" to refer to peoples, groups or communities that have coexisted since colonial times within and across national boundaries. Importantly, indigenous peoples possess their own cultures, institutions, customs, economic and political systems and languages (see ILO 2017 for definitions and legal conditions).[1] We acknowledge that the term "indigenous" to refer to peoples, groups or communities is controversial in some areas of the world (African Commission on Human and Peoples' Rights 2006).

2 Language-as-problem and language-as-right perspectives on indigenous language policies

Ruiz (1984) originally articulated three orientations in language planning: language-as-problem, language-as-right, and language-as-resource (Hult and Hornberger 2016 present further developments). The first concept arises from a monolingual ideal and assimilationist mindset (Hornberger 1990) that results in limiting or eliminating multilingualism. The notion of language-as-right relies on the idea that language is an essential factor in enabling full access to healthcare, employment, legal rights, among others. We should also note that the language-as-right perspective is not always

---

[1] Australians refer to their indigenous populations as Aboriginal people or First Nations people, in the United States they are referred to as Native American People, in Canada as First Nations and in Latin America all groups that inhabited the continents before colonization are named indigenous.

implemented in meaningful planning and practice policies. We first discuss these two perspectives, and then turn to initiatives that shift the perspective to language-as-a-resource.

2.1 Language-as-problem perspectives

National language policies tend to oscillate between the language-as-problem and the language-as-right perspectives. Language-as-problem perspectives were pervasive in legislation of many newly independent postcolonial states in the 19th and 20th centuries. Simpson (2008) notes that many countries faced the challenge of continuing with colonial languages as official languages or choosing some of the many indigenous languages spoken in their territories as official languages creating a marginalization of indigenous languages. In many cases, the result was the selection of a single national language, using it at all levels of administration and in the educational system, and ensuring that it is employed as the official means of interaction in the country. In the extreme case, minority languages have no official status, for example in Honduras, where only Spanish is considered a national language while indigenous languages such as Mískito and Mayangna are not (Lewis, Simons, and Fennig 2015). Similarly, other Latin American countries fail to recognize indigenous languages as official languages (Zajíková 2017). Among them are countries where indigenous languages are no longer spoken, such as Cuba, the Dominican Republic, Uruguay and Puerto Rico, as well as countries such as El Salvador where indigenous languages are spoken but the constitution does not mention them. This group further includes Costa Rica, Panama, and Guatemala. The latter two countries have constitutions that acknowledge indigenous languages but do not declare them official.

The United States has no official language, although several states have implemented English-only legislation at the state level which reflects the language-as-planning perspective (Menken 2013). Arguably, the transitional language education programs that have dominated bilingual education in the US throughout the past 60 years also had as a goal to incorporate speakers of minority languages into a society conceived of as essentially monolingual.

South-East Asian nations also faced the challenge of establishing official languages after independence in a linguistically diverse region with over one thousand languages (Kosonen 2005; Kosonen and Young 2009). These nations faced a difficult balance between promoting a single official language as a symbol of national identity and the fact that a significant percentage of the population speaks a local language (Bradley 1985, 2007, 2019). The result has put pressure on the maintenance of local languages. In many countries, English, as the former colonial language of current international importance also remains in the educational system.[2]

The *Australian Language and Literacy Policy* of 1991 reversed the perspective of the previous 1987 law (see below) to a language-as-problem perspective that lead to "an almost exclusive emphasis on English" enforcing national literacy standards (McKay 2001: 297). This policy resulted in the decline of the use of Aboriginal and Torres Strait Islander languages, which can be seen as "a result of repressive policies, both explicit and implicit" (McKay 2001: 297).

Although national language policies built on the language-as-problem perspective constructed multilingualism as a practical obstacle to overcome, this perspective is rooted in social, emotional and ideological factors that relate to the powerful role of language as a cultural and national identity symbol.

2.2 Recognition of minority languages as a right

Minority languages may have different degrees of legal recognition Furthermore, legal recognition usually does not entail equal social status (Hinton and Hale 2001). International agreements, such as the ILO *Convention 169*, have an important role in elevating the legal status of indigenous languages. For example, many countries in Latin America have passed legislation to protect indigenous languages rights at the central government level inspired by *Convention 169*. Countries that recognize indigenous languages as official languages with some territorial restrictions in Latin America are Nicaragua, Ecuador, Peru, and Bolivia. Argentina and Chile recognize indigenous languages as co-official languages along with Spanish at the level of regional, but not national, legislation.

Mexico does not have *de jure* official languages but gives indigenous languages the same status as Spanish as national languages. Venezuela recognizes indigenous languages for indigenous peoples, and, in Paraguay, despite there being other indigenous languages recognized by the Language Act of 2010 (Lewis, Simons, and Fennig 2015), only Paraguayan Guaraní is a co-official language with Spanish spoken by indigenous and non-indigenous speakers in a unique diglossic situation in Latin America.

---

[2] The promotion of a majority language as a national symbol can be seen in the case of Tagalog in the Philippines, Lao in Laos, Malay in Malaysia, Burmese in Myanmar, Khmer in Cambodia and Thai in Thailand, with some variations in each case. In the case of Indonesia, for example, the national language (Malay or Bahasa Indonesia) was different from the ethnic majority's language, Javanese (Guan and Suryadinata 2007). Sometimes national languages, as is the case of Bahasa Malaysia, are used as lingua franca to communicate across indigenous language groups given their mutual unintelligibility (Ting and Ling 2012).

In the United States, some federal legislation in the United States protects and promotes indigenous languages as rights: The *Native American Languages Act* (McCarty 2003: 160) and the *Native American Languages Reauthorization Act*.[3]

In some African countries like Cameroon and Sudan, indigenous languages achieved official status after independence, representing examples of the implementation of inclusive postcolonial language policies.

India also represents an interesting attempt to promote minority languages as official in a very complex linguistic landscape (Pandharipande 2002; Bhatt and Mahboob 2008; Groff 2017). Estimates of the number of languages in India vary from 270 reported in the 2011 census (Kidwai 2019) to 447 reported in the *Ethnologue* (Lewis, Simons, and Fennig 2015). Hindi, the national language, is spoken only by about one third of the population but the Indian constitution also provides strong safeguards for minority languages. It explicitly lists two sets of languages: 18 so-called "scheduled" languages, later extended to 22, and 48 minority languages (Pandharipande 2002).

In multi-ethnic Singapore, bilingualism in English and a home language is one of the pillars of the country's strategy, indicating recognition of language as a vehicle for ethnic cultures, and economic considerations. For example, Mandarin was initially marginalized after independence, but has become much more prominent as China's economic rise made it more relevant for the Singaporean economy (Guan and Suryadinata 2007: 79).

3 Minority and indigenous languages as resources

In parallel with the inclusion of language as a legal right, minority and indigenous languages are now increasingly seen as resources. This shift in perspective has produced new revitalization efforts whose results can be classified at the national level and at the local and regional level.

The *Australian National Policy on Languages* (Lo Bianco 1987; Moore 1996) illustrates a shift in national policy that unfortunately only lasted for four years. This national language framework, which was locally developed by all States and Territories and was adopted by the Australian Government, gave Aboriginal and Torres Strait Islander languages significant recognition as an important social and cultural resource. This policy pioneered very successfully the establishment of Regional Aboriginal Language Centres as well as language management committees (McConvell and Thieberger 2001). The introduction of bilingual education in the Northern Territory was also highly valued by indigenous communities. Regrettably, it has been marred by policy failures based on multifaceted misunderstandings and miscalculations, a deficiency of appropriate training for Indigenous educators and English as

---

3 https://www.congress.gov/bill/113th-congress/senate-bill/2299/text

a second language teachers (Simpson, Caffery, and McConvell 2009; McKay 2001; Simpson and Wigglesworth 2018). The introduction of the English-speaking policy labeled "First Four Hours" in addition to other negative changes all but wiped out Bilingual Education for indigenous languages (Devlin 2011; Disbray 2014). As reported by the Australian Bureau of Statistics (2017), of the estimated 250 Aboriginal and Torres Strait Islander languages, less than half are still spoken in homes with 90% of the indigenous languages in a critically endangered state.

3.1 Indigenous languages in national education policy

Education policies have a large impact on Indigenous home-language maintenance, so it is no surprise that most changes in language policy have focused on local, regional or national educational systems. We will begin the discussion with India's program, which is perhaps the most comprehensive attempt at incorporating Indigenous languages into the educational system.

For several decades, India has developed an innovative language education policy that factors in its complex linguistic landscape and the recognition of linguistic rights of its citizens. India's constitution includes the right to maintain one's culture and language, and to develop minority languages through education, particularly at primary levels (Bhatt and Mahboob 2008; Kidwai 2019). In addition to the introduction of a home or regional language at the primary level, two additional languages chosen among Hindi, English or some other Indian languages are planned to be introduced at later stages. However, as Bhatt and Mahboob (2008) point out, not all states have implemented the three-languages policy equally. The goal of introducing home languages poses a challenge for languages that lack scripts, or use scripts that differ from the mainstream language.

In addition, the generalized three-languages policy and the increasing urbanization and development of rural communities has resulted in reduced functional domains for local languages in favor of regional ones. Some communities have reacted against language regulations, demanding greater autonomy in setting their educational or linguistic policies, as in the case of Bengali speakers in Assam (Pandharipande 2002). In other cases, minority communities have segregated from majority communities, elevating the symbolic status of their language, as in the case of Konkani speakers in Maharastra and Karnataka. In most cases, however, minority linguistic communities have assimilated (Pandharipande 2002). As in other situations around the world, local languages face familiar challenges such as lack of educational materials, teachers, and exclusion from many social contexts. As a result, Razz and Ahmed (1990, quoted in Pandharipande 2002) suggest that half of India's tribal population have already lost their languages.

Kosonen (2005) notes that in South East Asia, many children who are minority language speakers only have minimal knowledge of the national language in which education is typically delivered. These gaps potentially hinder their achievement and their access to further educational levels. Kosonen (2005) and Kosonen and Young (2009) describe several initiatives in which minority language education is an opportunity to bridge the gap between the minority home-language and the national language. For these projects to be successful, local community involvement is a crucial factor. At the same time, the unavailability of trained teachers who can speak minority languages raises a big challenge for these programs.

Kosonen (2005) describes four different patterns in South East Asia: countries in which local languages are used in education to a great extent, and all activities are provided by the government, as in China. Second, countries like Vietnam, where the government provides education in local languages, but these are not widely used. Third, countries where both the government and non-governmental groups provide education in local languages to different degrees, as in Malaysia, Indonesia and the Philippines, and fourth, countries where non-governmental organizations carry the bulk of local language education, as in Thailand, Cambodia and Myanmar.

Morocco's language policy represents an interesting example of how language policies have evolved from the non-inclusive postcolonial language-as-problem status quo: Morocco's traditional linguistic identity has been built on French and Arabic. More recently, the country's official stance has shifted, allowing for the introduction of Berber in elementary education. Berber is one of the indigenous languages spoken, in addition to French as a colonial language, Classical and Moroccan Arabic (Zouhir 2014). However, this shift in national-level policy still faces challenges in the language ideologies and practices of some Berber parents, who, according to Zouhir (2014: 46), "seem to distance themselves from their Berber roots in an attempt to be socially accepted into mainstream Moroccan linguistic culture." In this case, the strong symbolic status of French and Arabic as prestigious national languages challenges the affective connection to Berber as a family language for the Berber community.

In sum, the survey of minority language education policy and practice reveals several common threads: the need to involve local communities for initiatives to be successful, the challenge of finding appropriate curricular materials and qualified teachers, the need for political support. In some cases, we find increasingly urbanized and mobile populations whose connection to the symbolic identity of the indigenous language may be diminished. Finally, smaller indigenous languages have a difficult challenge in expanding their social prestige and functionality in the larger national context.

3.2 Local initiatives: Indigenous language education

Ash, Fermino, and Hale (2001: 20) point out that "local language projects operate independent of one another" as a result of the fact that "the structure of a local language program is determined by local considerations." In this sense, local programs are unique, sometimes adapting methodologies developed for other populations, other times developing original programs that stem from their local realities. Language immersion schools in Hawaiian, Ojibwe, Mohawk, Maori, Navajo (Bishop 2003; Harrison and Papa 2005; McCarty 2003) are examples of local initiatives. However, immersion schools are difficult to implement in communities with few speakers or little control of the educational system. Other options include summer immersion programs e.g. Acoma, Cochiti (McCarty 2003), language classes in a system that operates in the majority language e.g. Hupa, Acoma, and Master-Apprentice language learning programs (MALLP) that pair a master, a speaker fluent in the language, and a dedicated learner, who is guided by the master through regular phone calls and visits. This model has been implemented in Sauk and Chickasaw and many other languages in the US (Hinton 2001), and in Canada, Brazil and Australia (Tom, Huaman, and McCarty 2019). McCarty (2003) also discusses the Navajo Nation immersion schools' program, and the language reclamation efforts of the Keres-speaking Pueblos of Acoma and Cochiti as examples of community-based efforts at promoting immersion education in native languages.

Increasingly, minority communities have been questioning Western education paradigms and incorporating traditional indigenous educational perspectives and epistemologies (McCarty, Nicholas, and Wigglesworth 2019). These initiatives also take different shapes. In some cases, traditional knowledge is included within Western-style educational structures (cf. the Maori-language immersion school in New Zealand as described in Harrison and Papa 2005); in other cases, indigenous educational practices challenge formal educational practices more directly, as described in contributions to McCarty, Nicholas, and Wigglesworth (2019) and Lee and McCarty (2017). Or, as in the case of the urban Inuktitut in Canada, where state-driven language policies void of appropriate cultural content, paved the way for community-based "Indigenous-defined language and literacy learning activities" targeting not only children but including families across several generations. Two long-term community projects "Photovoice" and "Sculpin fishing song" aimed at bringing back cultural knowledge from the rural into the urban domain and extending it to cultural and linguistic practices through literacy material prepared in multiple workshops (Patrick, Budach, and Muckpaloo 2013).

In Australia, due to a small and shrinking indigenous population in conjunction with a steady increase in urbanization (now 79%) with half of the rural population living in remote or isolated areas in the Northern Territory, the promotion and valorization of indigenous languages depends heavily on national language policies and strongly on community-based support. The introduction of bilingual education in the

1970s was highly successful at first but failed to address cultural and language needs of aboriginal people. For example, for the Yolŋu people, the struggle for "Both Ways" bilingual and multilingual education and teacher training for indigenous teachers continues to present a challenge. Additionally, "aboriginalization" of the curriculum, i.e. ownership of educational content of the Yolŋu people as well as representation at the School Council and integration of the wider community, remain outstanding issues (Stockley et al. 2017). Community involvement also came up as the top theme in responses for key elements of language activities in the 2014 Indigenous Language activity and Language attitude survey (Marmion, Kazuko, and Troy 2014).

3.3 Community-based initiatives

Across the globe, the lack of appropriate support for indigenous languages has given rise to community-based efforts to develop and maintain their home languages globally, showing an increasing awareness of the language-as-resources perspective. Here a distinction has to be drawn between urban and rural contexts due to different opportunities and needs, although, in most cases both, urban and rural communities, profit from most efforts through continuous connection, specifically in a digital age.

In urban environments, community-driven activities, raised from indigenous people's agency as a reaction to living in environments where they lack representation, may serve as incentives to pass on their language and culture to their children. Patrick, Budach, and Muckpaloo (2013) link Inuit-centered literacy activities developed between an Inuit Children's Center in Ottawa and a Family Literacy Program to drivers of family language policy. This creates a link between urban Inuit and an educational center for Arctic Inuit families in their homeland. At the core of this collaboration was the exchange of travelling objects and cultural artefacts that helped create a greater understanding of traditional Inuit culture and language in the context of migration.

Rural remoteness worldwide poses enormous challenges for language vitality and intergenerational transmission, calling for everyday language policies and practices in and out of school to counter language loss. In the Australian Western Desert, Elders use narratives and cultural activities to teach language, speech styles, registers and traditional knowledge within the extended family setting on country.[4] Storytelling practices are filmed in order to document and promote indigenous languages and cultures, to counter loss of oral practices, and to pass on traditional knowledge and culture to the next generation (Kral and Ellis 2019).

---

[4] Aboriginal Australians have a strong social, cultural and spiritual connection to their homeland and to land- and waterways management.

The availability of modern digital communication technologies across the world has created invisible learning spaces without borders or socio-spatial confines (Hatoss this vol.; Palviainen this vol.). Access to such technologies unites globally Indigenous youth as they explore and share new / hybrid modes of cultural production through song-writing and recording and film-making on media such as Facebook and Youtube. Although oral and written language use is impacted by daily communication practices of online messaging, SMS and WhatsApp text and visual messages, the new practice is an invaluable addition to corpus building not only in Australia but also worldwide (Kral 2010). Other Australia-wide online resources such as National Indigenous Television on Demand (NITV), Indigenous Community Television (ICTV), IndigiTUBE—featuring language and culture, ABC Indigenous Radio for news and current affairs, TV and iview are fundamental instruments of and for Aboriginal voices and promotion of aboriginal cultures and languages. The introduction of *narrangunnawali* — Reconciliation in schools, and early learning and access to online resources from AIATSIS (Australian Institute of Aboriginal and Torres Strait Islander Studies).[5]

Finally, an important factor globally across urban and rural domains is raising the status of indigenous languages through professionalization. Translation and interpreting as public services serve multiple purposes and are often seen just as "*social lubricants* that prevent social tensions" (Serrano and Fouces 2018: 8). Although this may be true to a certain extent, professionalizing these services raises not only the status of indigenous languages, but also their economic value by creating professional paid workplaces. Additionally, extending the practice of indigenous languages from the private into the public domain by regulation and certification helps to ensure ethnolinguistic vitality of indigenous languages (Spolsky 2004). Shifting from community-based voluntary work to paid professional work also improves the status of indigenous languages by raising their economic value.

4 Language attitudes

An important factor that impacts minority language home maintenance relates to language attitudes (Albury this vol.). We can distinguish several related threads. Speakers of "pure" varieties are seen as more prestigious than those understood to be influenced by the majority language. Since purer varieties tend to be identified with older speakers, one unintended consequence of this ideology is that younger generations of speakers, who may speak varieties more influenced by the majority language,

---

[5] AIATSIS is an independent Australian Government statutory authority that has been instrumental in raising awareness and connecting indigenous culture Australia-wide (AIATSIS n.d.).

and sometimes may also be perceived as less proficient speakers, may feel less confident in their ability to use the minority language (Dorian 1994).

In some cases, communities that used to be monolingual in an indigenous language and that lacked access to majority/socially dominant languages, have become bilingual (Arguedas 1966) and have come to terms with the idea of indigenous languages becoming heritage languages (Hornberger 2005). In recent years, minority language planning has begun to incorporate the notion of heritage speakers (Valdés 2000) and adult L2 speakers (Hornberger 2005). Heritage learners are exposed to input that includes more frequent use of the majority language, and the resulting linguistic abilities may be markedly different from those of older speakers, and in this sense minority languages share aspects of heritage varieties (Eisenchlas and Schalley this vol.). In states that have invested in revitalization efforts of indigenous and minoritized languages, differences between "new speakers", namely second language speakers of these languages, on the one hand, and heritage and native speakers, on the other, have opened the door to the debate of what constitutes being a native speaker of a minoritized language (O'Rourke and Pujolar 2013; O'Rourke and Ramallo 2015).

Another dimension related to language attitudes involves the urban/rural divide. Traditional population patterns tended to associate higher density of minority languages with rural areas. However, increased migration to cities means that large numbers of minority language speakers are now located in urban centers, sometimes creating more complex linguistic interactions as well as the need to redefine what constitutes an indigenous linguistic identity in an urban environment (May 2014; Davis 2018; Shulist 2018; Ferguson 2019). Sánchez et al. (2018) describe how attitudes towards languages have changed over fifteen years in a community of speakers of Shipibo who migrated from the Amazonian region of Pucallpa to the city of Lima, Peru. Away from the traditional rural areas where minority languages were based, some groups have begun to develop innovative initiatives where minority languages may be rooted. These initiatives, however, face a multiplicity of challenges such as lack of support from central governments and urban administrations that do not view revitalization efforts as a priority. This is especially the case in the area of education in indigenous languages (Hornberger 2008).

The case of local languages in India also illustrates the importance of attitudes connected to the broader geographic divide. Most local languages tend to be rural, whereas regional and national languages are associated with urban centers, with economic mobility and progress. Even co-official indigenous languages such as Guaraní in Paraguay are subject to this perception. Despite being considered central in Paraguayan identity, Guaraní is at the same time associated with ruralness and ignorance (Mortimer 2013). As a result of these assumptions, as local languages become less functional, speakers perceive them as less valuable.

In the last section, we turn to the case of indigenous languages in Peru, which show a clear example of how the changing urban/rural divide is altering the traditional perspectives on indigenous language maintenance. Peru also exemplifies the case of a country where, while legislation recognizes indigenous languages, maintenance depends on a combination of government policies, NGOs and community initiatives.

5 Peruvian Amazonian and Andean languages across urban and rural conditions

Peru currently has 19 language families, and 48 indigenous languages actively spoken (Ministerio de Educación, Perú 2019). In the 2017 General Census (INEI 2017a), 22,209,686 individuals 5 and older (82,6%) declared Spanish to be the language they acquired in childhood, followed by 3,735,682 Quechua speakers (13,9%), 444,389 Aymara speakers (1,7%) and 210,017 speakers of other indigenous languages (0,8%).

Language acquisition differs in the urban and rural contexts. In the urban context, 87,9% of the population acquired Spanish in childhood, 9.7% acquired Quechua, 1.1% acquired Aymara and 1.3%, all other indigenous languages. In rural communities, on the other hand, more children acquire indigenous languages than in cities: 61.8% acquire Spanish, 30.3% Quechua 3.9% Aymara, and 3.2% other indigenous languages. This distribution indicates that indigenous languages, while present in urban centers, continue to have a stronger presence in rural areas.

Rural communities, usually not much larger than a town, are basic, officially recognized territorial organizations with title to communal lands. 64% of the 6682 rural communities identified as belonging to one of the 20 indigenous people. The most frequently spoken indigenous languages in those communities are Quechua (69.9%) and Aymara (9.3%). Additionally, 17 other indigenous languages are also spoken (all under 1%), as well as Spanish (21%, INEI 2017b).

Indigenous languages in the Andean and Amazonian regions of Peru have been historically minoritized and their speakers have been traditionally discriminated against. Their use is associated with indigenous and rural backgrounds. Given that most of their speakers reside in rural areas, it is not surprising that the majority of language planning and educational efforts are focused on rural populations.

Early efforts to gain official recognition for indigenous language rights started in the late 1960s and early 1970s. In the 1980s intercultural bilingual education was overseen by a low-level unit within the Division of Elementary Education. As Sánchez, Lucero and Córdova (2012) point out, the unit was promoted to a higher rank only in 1989, demoted again in the 1990s, and finally converted to a Division again in 2000.

Currently, the Ministry of Culture and the Ministry of Education are the main sources of language planning dedicated to protecting the language rights guaranteed by the Constitution and the *Language Rights Bill* (*Ley de Lenguas*, Congreso del la República 2011). The *National Policy of Original Languages, Oral Tradition and Interculturality*, approved in 2017, has resulted in several initiatives, including

(Ministerio de Cultura, Perú 2019): the program "Voces Vivas" (Living Voices), which aims to revitalize the endangered languages Jaqaru, Kukama, Isconahua, Shiwilu, Uro and Iquitu, the Technical Committee on Indigenous Languages (Comité Técnico Especializado en Lenguas Indígenas, CTELI), which develops language policies, and the program "Estado Multilingüe" (Multilingual State), which implements linguistic rights in public administration currently focused on the Cuzco region and to a lesser extent on the regions of Loreto, Ucayali, Junín y San Martín. A very successful initiative has been the training of indigenous language translators and interpreters to assist indigenous people in administrative processes. Graduates of this training program are listed in the National Register of Translators and Interpreters of Indigenous Languages created in 2014. In April 2019, the Peruvian Institute of Indigenous Languages, was formally established, with the charge to promote research, documentation, preservation, development and teaching of indigenous languages in Peru.

5.1 Educational policies

Several initiatives in the early 1990s developed programs in intercultural bilingual education at the Elementary school level, before the current legal framework was created. As noted by Sánchez, Lucero and Córdova (2012), intercultural bilingual education in indigenous languages and Spanish was already recognized as a fundamental right of indigenous peoples both by the *Language Rights Bill* (Congreso del la República 2011) and by Peru's Ombudsman Office (Defensor del Pueblo 2011) and further developed by law as a right from kindergarten to 12th grade. This law promotes the use of indigenous languages by teachers and it seeks to ensure indigenous peoples' participation in the formulation and implementation of educational and language planning in indigenous languages (DIGEIBIR 2005–2007).

The 2015 *National Plan of Intercultural Bilingual Education* (Ministerio de Educación, Perú 2015) aims to expand the number of indigenous children and youth attending intercultural bilingual schools. These schools are defined as having an intercultural bilingual education curriculum and materials in the indigenous language, and at least one teacher with knowledge of the relevant indigenous culture and language. The policy aims to expand the percentage of children receiving pre-school intercultural bilingual education, from 52% in 2015 to 90% in 2021. It also aims to increase the percentage of students receiving elementary intercultural bilingual education, from 52.6% in 2015 to 90% in 2021 and the percentage of students who receive intercultural bilingual education at the secondary education level from 0% to 50%. Some regions with high percentages of indigenous population and with indigenous teachers and administrators such as Puno have made significant progress in developing an indigenous approach to curricular development (Ministerio de Educación and CARE Perú 2009). In 2009, the Huancavelica region also characterized by strong indigenous leadership approved an ordinance that prohibits discrimination on the basis of many factors that typically identify indigenous peoples, among them language. In the region of La Libertad in Northern Peru, several programs for the revitalization of Muchik, an extinct language have begun to gain strength in recent years.

5.2 NGOs and local initiatives

Throughout the years, and even before the creation of an intercultural bilingual education unit within the Ministry of Education, a succession of non-profit organizations initiated and implemented indigenous bilingual education. Sánchez (2016) notes the existence of multiple NGOs, many of them with indigenous leadership and membership, whose work focuses on indigenous rights, among them language rights, revitalization, and intercultural bilingual education in many regions of Peru.

In the Amazonian region, AIDESEP (Asociación Interétnica de Desarrollo de la Selva Peruana 'Interethnic Association for the Development of the Peruvian Rainforest', 2019) is a macro-level organization. It represents indigenous organizations from the northern, central, and southern parts of the Amazonian region (65 federations representing 1,500 communities, around 650,000 indigenous people, and 16 language families) (Sánchez 2016). It collaborates in teacher training efforts with the Programa de Formación de Maestros Bilingües de la Amazonía Peruana (Institute for the Education of Bilingual Teachers in the Peruvian Amazonian Region, FORMABIAP). Efforts to revitalize the Kukama language through communal schools are promoted by indigenous people in the Loreto region, too. More recently, the Wampis indigenous people established their "Autonomous Territorial Government of the Wampis Nation" declaring the necessity to guarantee education in the Wampis language which in their view is a mechanism to transmit their culture (GTANW 2015).

In the Andean macroregion, regions such as Apurimac, Ayacucho, Cusco, Huancavelica, Junín, and Puno have either NGOs or regional efforts to support intercultural bilingual education. Some like the Asociación Pukllasunchis' (2016) educational projects focus on intercultural bilingual education in Quechua in an urban school and a Pedagogical Institute for bilingual teachers. The HOPE Foundation supports a network of four intercultural bilingual education schools in the community of Tiracancha, Cusco, where teachers and indigenous parents work together to generate a participative and cooperative educational organization that has Quechua language and culture at the center of their endeavors. In addition to intercultural bilingual education, radio channels and social media play an important role in the promotion and use of indigenous languages (IWGIA 'International Working Group on Indigenous Affairs' 2016). IWGIA supports, along with Servindi, La Voz Indigena a radio station in Shipibo in the Ucayali region and the Aymara radio program Wiñay Pankara in Radio Pachamama in the Puno region (Servindi n.d.). Since 2016, the Peruvian State is promoting news programs in Quechua, Aymara and Ashaninka.

There are multiple radio programs that transmit exclusively in indigenous languages. One of those is Axenon Ikanwe, a radio program in Shipibo-Konibo that started in 2017 and has as its main objective to strengthen the Shipibo-Konibo language from the perspective of traditional indigenous knowledge and to promote the end of language shift towards Spanish (Axenon Ikanwe n.d.). Despite governmental, NGO and community efforts, and even when indigenous communities have positive attitudes towards home language maintenance, the road to widespread implementation of intercultural bilingual education and to a complete reversal of language shift from indigenous languages to Spanish in Peru is still paved with obstacles. An example of the difficulties of promoting and sustaining home language maintenance in indigenous languages is Sánchez et al.'s (2018) study of Shipibo speakers in the city of Lima. The study shows how despite positive attitudes among urban speakers of the indigenous language Shipibo living in the city of Lima, language shift is still likely to take place given the lack of intergenerational transmission of Shipibo. Such cases show that without sustained efforts from the whole society, indigenous languages revitalization, maintenance and development will continue to be a challenge.

While there has been progress at the local and the state institutional level, for intercultural bilingual education to reach the majority of indigenous communities in Peru further progress is needed in terms of generalized teacher training and development, indigenous language standardization, and the development of culturally appropriate assessment techniques that also respond to national assessment standards.

6 Conclusion

Indigenous communities across the world have been multilingual societies for millennia, free of the confines of monolingual nation-states and with very different language planning, management and practices from the explicit top-down monolingual language policies employed by the latter. Therefore, in many postcolonial societies, the coexistence of top-down monolingual language policies and traditional language practices including linguistic repertoires consisting of indigenous and other languages have given rise in many cases to language shift, posing challenges to home language maintenance. Sadly, few tangible improvements have been registered despite the growing global focus and interest in indigenous languages.

In this chapter we have endeavoured to present a synoptic view of the challenges indigenous and minority languages face in maintaining and passing on their languages to the next generation globally and locally, in a detailed case study from Peru. We have shown how indigenous languages are seen as a problem, a right and a resource (Ruiz 1984). Across the globe, we see national shortcomings in terms of bringing indigenous languages into the public sphere and raising thus their status which would make them desirable to learn and practice in all domains. However, we also witness a growing interaction between national policies and local and communal efforts for home language maintenance reflecting positive language attitudes and ideologies and allowing for group and language and culture-specific practices across urban and rural domains.

Home language maintenance and development will continue to depend strongly on recognising and actively supporting the fact that it is "the inherent human right to learn, use and transmit a language of heritage and birth" (McCarty, Nicholas, and Wigglesworth 2019: 4). A huge task that requires good will and action from all parts of society.

References

African Commission on Human and Peoples' Rights (ACHPR). 2006. *Indigenous peoples in Africa: The forgotten peoples? The African Commission's work on indigenous peoples in Africa*. Copenhagen: International Work Group for Indigenous Affairs.

AIATSIS (Australian Institute of Aboriginal and Torres Strait Islander Studies). n.d. https://aiatsis.gov.au/ (accessed 27 June 2019).

AIDESEP (Asociación Interétnica de Desarrollo de la Selva Peruana). 2019. http://www.aidesep.org.pe/index.php/ (accessed 26 June 2019).

Albury, Nathan J. this vol. Language attitudes and ideologies on linguistic diversity.

Annamalai, E. & Tove Skutnabb-Kangas. this vol. Social justice and inclusiveness through linguistic human rights in education.

Arguedas, José María. 1966. *Mesa redonda sobre el monolingüismo quechua y aymara y la educación en el Perú*. Lima: Casa de la Cultura.

Ash, Anna, Jessie Little Doe Fermino & Ken Hale. 2001. Diversity in local language maintenance and restoration: A reason for optimism. In Leanne Hinton & Ken Hale (eds.), *The green book of language revitalization in practice*, 19–37. Leiden: Brill.

Asociación Pukllasunchis. 2016. *Educación Intercultural Bilingüe*. https://www.pukllasunchis.org/educacion-intercultural (accessed 6 October 2016).

Australian Bureau of Statistics. 2017. Aboriginal and Torres Strait Islander population, 2016. In Australian Bureau of Statistics, *2071.0 – Census of Population and Housing: Reflecting Australia – Stories from the Census 2016*. https://www.abs.gov.au/ausstats/abs@.nsf/Lookup/by%20Subject/2071.0~2016~Main%20Features~Aboriginal%20and%20Torres%20Strait%20islander%20Population%20Article~12 (accessed 28 June 2019).

Axenon Ikanwe. n.d. https://alianzaarkana.org/es/work/axenon-inkanwe (accessed 29 June 2019).

Bhatt, Rakesh & Ahmar Mahboob. 2008. Minority languages and their status. In Braj Kachru, Yamuna Kachru & S. N. Sridhar (eds.), *Language in South Asia*, 132–152. Cambridge: Cambridge University Press.

Bishop, Russell. 2003. Changing power relations in education: Kaupapa Ma¥ori messages for "mainstream" education in Aotearoa/New Zealand. *Comparative Education* 39(2). 221–238.

Boas, Franz. 1940. *Race, language and culture*. New York, NY: Macmillan.

Bradley, David (ed.). 1985. *Language policy, language planning and sociolinguistics in South-East Asia* (Papers in Southeast Asian Linguistics 9/Pacific Linguistics A–67). Canberra: Department of Linguistics, Australian National University.

Bradley, David. 2007. Language policy and language rights. In Osahito Miyaoka, Osamu Sakiyama & Michael Krauss (eds.), *Vanishing languages of the Pacific Rim*, 77–90. Oxford: Oxford University Press.

Bradley, David. 2019. Minority language learning in mainland Southeast Asia. In Andy Kirkpatrick & Anthony Liddicoat (eds.), *The Routledge international handbook of language education policy in Asia*, 14–28. London: Routledge.

Congreso del la República. 2011. *Ley que regula el uso, preservación, desarrollo, recuperación, fomento y difusión de las lenguas originarias del Perú* (Ley N° 29735).

Coronel-Molina, Serafin & Teresa L. McCarty. 2016. *Indigenous language revitalization in the Americas*. New York, NY: Routledge.

Crystal, David. 1999. *The Penguin dictionary of language*. 2nd edn. London: Penguin.

Davis, Jenny L. 2018. *Talking Indian: Identity and language revitalization in the Chickasaw renaissance*. Tucson, AZ: University of Arizona Press.

Defensor del Pueblo. 2011. *Informe anual 2011: Mecanismo nacional de prevención de la tortura*. Madrid: Defensor del Pueblo. https://www.defensordelpueblo.es/informe-mnp/mecanismo-nacional-de-prevencion-de-la-tortura-informe-anual-2011/ (accessed 27 June 2019).

Devlin, Brian. 2011. The status and future of bilingual education for remote indigenous students in the Northern Territory. *Australian Review of Applied Linguistics* 34(3). 260–279.

DIGEIBIR (Dirección General de Educación Intercultural Bilingüe y Rural). 2005–2007. http://centroderecursos.cultura.pe/es/editorial/ministerio-de-educaci%C3%B3n (accessed 27 June 2019).

Disbray, Samantha. 2014. Evaluating the bilingual education program in Warlpiri schools. In Rob Pensalfini, Myfany Turpin & Diana Guillemin (eds.), *Language description informed by theory*, 25–46. Amsterdam: Johns Benjamins.

Dorian, Nancy. 1994. Purism vs. compromise in language revitalization and language revival. *Language in Society* 23(4). 479–494.

Eisenchlas, Susana A. & Andrea C. Schalley. this vol. Making sense of the notion of "home language" and related concepts.

Ferguson, Jean. 2019. *Words like birds: Sakha language discourses and practises in the city*. Lincoln, NE: University of Nebraska Press.

Groff, Cynthia. 2017. Language and language-in-education planning in multilingual India: A minoritized language perspective. *Language Policy* 16. 135–164.

GTANW (Gobierno Territorial Autónomo de la Nación Wampís). 2015. https://www.forestpeoples.org/en/node/50347 (accessed 27 June 2019).

Guan, Lee H. & Leo Suryadinata Leo (eds.). 2007. *Language, nation and development in Southeast Asia*. Singapore: ISEAS (Institute of Southeast Asian Studies).

Harrison, Barbara & Rahui Papa. 2005. The development of an indigenous knowledge program in a New Zealand Maori-language immersion school. *Anthropology & Education Quarterly* 36(1). 57–72.

Hatoss, Anikó. this vol. Transnational grassroots language planning in the era of mobility and the Internet.

Hinton, Leanne. 2001. The master-apprentice language learning program. In Leanne Hinton & Ken Hale (eds.), *The green book of language revitalization in practice*, 217–226. Leiden: Brill.

Hinton, Leanne & Ken Hale (eds.). 2001. *The green book of language revitalization in practice*. Leiden: Brill.

Hornberger, Nancy H. 1990. Bilingual education and English-only: A language-planning framework. *The Annals of the American Academy of Political and Social Science* 508(1). 12–26.

Hornberger, Nancy H. 2005. Opening and filling up implementational and ideological spaces in heritage language education. *Modern Language Journal* 89(4). 605–609.
Hornberger, Nancy H. 2008. Introduction: Can schools save indigenous languages? Policy and practice on four continents. In Nancy H. Hornberger (ed.), *Can schools save indigenous languages?* (Palgrave Studies in Minority Languages and Communities), 1–12. London: Palgrave Macmillan.
Hult, Francis M. & Nancy H. Hornberger. 2016. Revisiting orientations in language planning: Problem, right, and resource as an analytical heuristic. *Bilingual Review/Revista Bilingüe* 33 (3). http://bilingualreview.utsa.edu/index.php/br/article/view/118 (accessed 26 August 2019).
ILO (International Labor Organization). 2017. *C169 – Indigenous and Tribal Peoples Convention, 1989 (No. 169)*. https://www.ilo.org/dyn/normlex/en/f?p=NORMLEXPUB:12100:0::NO::P12100_INSTRUMENT_ID:312314 (accessed 12 June 2019).
INEI (Instituto Nacional de Estadística e Informática). 2017a. *Perú: Perfil sociodemográfico. Informe Nacional*. https://www.inei.gob.pe/media/MenuRecursivo/publicaciones_digitales/Est/Lib1539/libro.pdf (accessed 8 August 2019).
INEI (Instituto Nacional de Estadística e Informática). 2017b. *Resultados definitivos del Censo de Comunidades Campesinas*. https://www.inei.gob.pe/media/MenuRecursivo/publicaciones_digitales/Est/Lib1599/ (accessed 28 June 2019).
IWGIA (International Working Group on Indigenous Affairs). 2016. *Emisoras indígenas en Perú: el derecho a la comunicación*. https://www.iwgia.org/es/peru/2351-emisoras-indigenas-en-peru-el-derecho-a-la-comunic (accessed 27 June 2019).
Kidwai, Aysha. 2019. The people's linguistic survey of India volumes: Neither linguistics, nor a successor to Grierson's LSI, but still a point of reference. *Social Change* 49(1). 154–159.
Kosonen, Kimmo. 2005. Education in local languages: Policy and practice in South-East Asia. In UNESCO (ed.), *First language first: Community-based literacy programmes for minority language contexts in Asia*, 96–134. Bangkok: UNESCO Asia and Pacific Regional Bureau for Education.
Kosonen, Kimmo & Catherine Young (eds.). 2009. *Mother tongue as bridge language of instruction: Policies and experiences in Southeast Asia*. Bangkok: SEAMEO (Southeast Asian Ministers of Education Organization).
Kral, Inge. 2010. Plugged in: Remote Australian Indigenous youth and digital culture. *CAPER (Centre for Aboriginal Economic Policy Research) Working paper* 69/2010. Canberra: Centre for Aboriginal Economic Policy Research, Australian National University.
Kral, Inge & Elizabeth M. Ellis. 2019. Language vitality in and out of school in a remote indigenous Australian context. In Teresa L. McCarty, Sheilah E. Nicholas & Gillian Wigglesworth (eds.), *A world of indigenous languages: Resurgence, reclamation, revitalization and resilience*, 115–133. Bristol: Multilingual Matters.
Lee, Tiffany S. & Teresa L. McCarty. 2017. Upholding indigenous education sovereignty through critical culturally sustaining/revitalizing pedagogy. In Django Paris & H. Samy Alim (eds.), *Culturally sustaining pedagogies: Teaching and learning for justice in a changing world*, 61–82. New York, NY: Teachers College Press.
Lewis, M. Paul, Gary F. Simons & Charles D. Fennig (eds.). 2015. *Ethnologue: Languages of the World*. 18th edn. Dallas, TX: SIL International. https://www.ethnologue.com/ (accessed 26 June 2019).
Lo Bianco, Jo. 1987. *National policy on languages*. Canberra: Australian Government Publishing Service.

Marmion, Doug, Obata Kazuko & Jakelin Tory. 2014. *Community, identity, wellbeing: The report of the Second National Indigenous Languages Survey*. Canberra: Australian Institute of Aboriginal and Torres Strait Islander Studies.

May, Stephen. 2014. Contesting metronormativity: Exploring indigenous language dynamism across the urban-rural divide. *Journal of Language, Identity & Education* 13(4). 229–235.

McCarty, Teresa L. 2003. Revitalising indigenous languages in homogenising times. *Comparative Education* 39(2). 147–163.

McCarty, Teresa L., Sheilah E. Nicholas & Gillian Wigglesworth (eds.). 2019. *A world of indigenous languages: Resurgence, reclamation, revitalization and resilience*. Bristol: Multilingual Matters.

McCarty, Teresa L., Leisy T. Wyman & Sheila E. Nicholas. 2014. Activist ethnography with indigenous youth. In Django Paris & Maisha T. Winn (eds.), *Humanizing research: Decolonizing qualitative inquiry with youth and communities*, 81–104. Thousand Oaks: SAGE.

McConvell, Patrick & Nicholas Thieberger. 2001. State of indigenous languages in Australia – 2001. *Australia State of the Environment Second Technical Paper Series (Natural and Cultural Heritage)*. Canberra: Department of the Environment and Heritage.

McKay, Penny. 2001. National literacy benchmarks and the outstreaming of ESL learners. In Jo Lo Bianco & Rosie Wickert (eds.), *Australian policy activism in language and literacy*, 221–237. Melbourne: Language Australia.

Menken, Kate. 2013. Restrictive language education policies and emergent bilingual youth: A perfect storm with imperfect outcomes. *Theory into Practice* 52 (3). 160–168.

Ministerio de Cultura, Perú. 2019. *Lenguas indígenas*. http://www.cultura.gob.pe/es/interculturalidad/programas-y-proyectos (accessed 28 June 2019).

Ministerio de Educación & CARE Perú. 2009. Proyecto Curricular Regional Puno. Puno: Ministerio de Educación.

Ministerio de Educación, Perú. 2015. *Plan Nacional de Educación Intercultural Bilingüe*. Lima: Ministerio de Educación. http://www.minedu.gob.pe/campanias/pdf/eib-planes/plan_nacional_eib_castellano.pdf (accessed 7 October 2019).

Ministerio de Educación, Perú. 2019. *Lenguas originarias del Perú*. Lima: Ministerio de Educación. http://www.minedu.gob.pe/campanias/lenguas-originarias-del-peru.php (accessed 28 June 2019).

Moore, Helen. 1996. Language policies as virtual reality: Two Australian examples. *TESOL Quarterly* 30. 473–497.

Mortimer, Katherine S. 2013. Communicative event chains in an ethnography of Paraguayan language policy. *International Journal of the Sociology of Language* 219. 67–99.

O'Rourke, Bernadette & Joan Pujolar. 2013. From native speakers to "new speakers" – problematizing nativeness in language revitalization contexts. *Histoire Épistémologie Langage* 35(2). 47–67.

O'Rourke, Bernadette & Fernando Ramallo. 2015. Neofalantes as an active minority: Understanding language practices and motivations for change amongst new speakers of Galician. *International Journal of the Sociology of Language* 2015(231). 147–165.

Palviainen, Åsa. this vol. Future prospects and visions for family language policy research.

Pandharipande, Rajeshwari. 2002. Minority matters: Issues in minority languages in India. *International Journal on Multicultural Societies* 4(2). 213–234.

Patrick, Donna. 2012. Indigenous contexts. In Marilyn Martin Jones, Adrian Blackledge & Angela Creese (eds.), *The Routledge handbook of multilingualism*, 29–48. New York, NY: Routledge.

Patrick, Donna, Gabriele Budach & Igah Muckpaloo. 2013. Multiliteracies and family language policy in an urban Inuit community. *Language Policy* 12(1). 47–62.

Razz, Moonis & Aijazuddin Ahmed. 1990. *An atlas of tribal India*. New Delhi: Concept.

Ruiz, Richard. 1984. Orientations in language planning. *NABE Journal* 8(2). 15–34.
Sánchez, Liliana. 2016. The linguist gaining access to the indigenous populations: Sharing cultural and linguistic knowledge in South America. In Gabriela Pérez Báez, Chris Rogers & Jorge E. Rosés Labrada (eds.), *Language documentation and revitalization in Latin American contexts*, 195–214. Berlin: Mouton de Gruyter.
Sánchez, Liliana, Milagros Lucero & Paola Córdova. 2012. *Análisis comparativo e interpretativo de propuestas de Educación Intercultural Bilingüe como base para una elaboración de estándares de evaluación en EIB*. Lima: Instituto Peruano de Evaluación, Acreditación y Certificación de la Calidad de la Educación Básica (Ipeba).
Sánchez, Liliana, Elisabeth Mayer, José Camacho & Carolina Rodríguez Alzza. 2018. Linguistic attitudes towards Shipibo in Cantagallo: Reshaping indigenous language and identity in an urban setting. *International Journal of Bilingualism* 22(4). 466–487.
Serrano, María-Sierra Córdoba & Oscar Diaz Fouces. 2018. Building a field: Translation policies and minority languages. *International Journal of the Sociology of Language* 2018(251). 1–17.
Servindi. n.d. https://www.servindi.org/ (accessed 28 June 2019).
Shulist, Sarah. 2018. *Transforming indigeneity: Urbanization and language revitalization in the Brazilian Amazon*. Toronto: University of Toronto Press.
Simpson, Andrew (ed.). 2008. *Language and national identity in Africa*. New York, NY: Oxford University Press.
Simpson, Jane H., Jo Caffery & Patrick McConvell. 2009. Gaps in Australia's indigenous language policy: Dismantling bilingual education in the Northern Territory. *AIATSIS Discussion Paper* 24.
Simpson, Jane H. & Gillian Wigglesworth. 2008. *Children's language and multilingualism: Indigenous language use at home and school*. New York, NY: Continuum Intl Pub Group.
Simpson, Jane H. & Gillian Wigglesworth. 2018. Language diversity in Indigenous Australia in the 21st century. *Current Issues in Language Planning* 20(1). 67–80.
Spolsky, Bernard. 2004. *Language policy*. Cambridge: Cambridge University Press.
Stockley, Trevor, Banbapuy Ganambarr, Dhuŋgala Munuŋgurr, Multhara Munuŋgurr, Greg Wearne, W.W. Wunuŋmurra, Leon White & Yalmay Yunupiṉu. 2017. The quest for community control at Yirrkala. In Brian Devlin, Samantha Disbray & Nancy Devlin (eds.), *History of bilingual education in the Northern Territory: People, programs and policies*, 141–148. Singapore: Springer.
The World Bank. 2019. *Indigenous Peoples*. https://www.worldbank.org/en/topic/indigenouspeoples (accessed 29 June 2019).
Ting, Su-Hie & Teck-Yee Ling. 2012. Language use and sustainability status of indigenous languages in Sarawak, Malaysia. *Journal of Multilingual and Multicultural Development* 34(1). 77–93.
Tom, Miye N., Elizabeth S. Huaman & Teresa L. McCarty. 2019. Indigenous knowledges as vital contributions to sustainability. *International Review of Education* 65(1). 1–18.
Valdés, Guadalupe. 2000. The teaching of heritage languages: An introduction for Slavic-teaching professionals. In Olga Kagan & Benjamin Rifkin (eds.), *The learning and teaching of Slavic languages and cultures*, 375–403. Bloomington, IN: Slavica.
Vaughan, Jill & Ruth Singer. 2018. Indigenous multilingualisms past and present. *Language and Communication* 62, part B. 83–90.
Zajíková, Lenka. 2017. Lenguas indígenas en la legislación de los países hispanoamericanos. *Onomázein* (Número especial: Las lenguas amerindias en Iberoamérica: Retos para el siglo XXI). 171–203.
Zouhir, Abderrahman. 2014. Language policy and state in Morocco. *Domes* 23. 37–53.

Part 4: **The role of society**

Topic area 4.1: **Social justice and inclusiveness**

Anthony J. Liddicoat
17 Language policy and planning for language maintenance: The macro and meso levels

1 Language policy and planning (LPP) as a field of study

Language policy and planning (LPP) has often been considered as an important factor in language maintenance (e.g. Hornberger and Coronel-Molina 2004). However, the position of LPP scholarship in language maintenance research has been ambiguous and it has often been omitted from studies of language maintenance – for example, García (2003) explicitly excludes language policy research from her state-of-the-art survey. Part of the cause of this ambiguity appears to come from an understanding of LPP as an activity solely of nation-states and governments. This view constructs LPP as of limited relevance to language maintenance, as much language maintenance happens without specific government policy.

In discussions of LPP, there is often disagreement about the relationship between the terms "policy" and "planning". For some, language planning is subsumed in language policy (Schiffman 1996), for others policy is part of planning (Kaplan and Baldauf 1997), and for yet others they are separate but related activities (Djité 1994), or the two have coalesced in such a way that making a distinction is no longer useful (Hornberger 2006). In this chapter I will use LPP as a general term, acknowledging Hornberger's arguments about the coalescing of the field, but sometimes use the more specific terms "policy" or "planning" to emphasise different aspects of action around language. Where "planning" refers to decision-making processes and "policy" refers to decisions, principles or guiding ideas that result from some explicit or implicit decision-making process.

LPP scholarship has developed a more nuanced understanding of LPP as a focus of study and considers LPP as a wide range of activities relating to language use, not just in formal policy and planning documents. LPP needs to be considered in two interrelated ways: as text and as discourse (Ball 1993). LPP documents are "textual interventions into practice" (Ball 1993: 12) and they intervene by constructing representations of a particular future state of society (aspects of future language learning or language use) that is to be enacted through the implementation of the actions the planning and policy requires. In articulating desired future states, planning and policy actors seek to control agendas and constrain the field of interpretation of their texts. However, they cannot control the ways in which documents are interpreted by readers, as any interpretation happens within systems of values, priorities, beliefs and contexts. As a result,

LPP is changing and contested representations. Different readers are likely to have different interpretations and may seek to shape implementation of provisions to achieve their own valued aims. Implementation therefore needs to be negotiated by those involved in its enactment in specific contexts. Therefore, local actors have forms of agency in implementing LPP provisions in their local contexts (Baldauf 2006; Glasgow and Bouchard 2019). Such agency does not amount to free will, but rather is constrained by aspects of society and context (Liddicoat 2019).

LPP does not just exercise authority by requiring people to act in particular ways, but also by shaping how the phenomena they address are understood in the society; for languages, LPP can state and shape beliefs and values about languages, their utility and the criteria against which their utility, their place in the social fabric, etc. will be evaluated. Thus, LPP documents are not simply administrative documents, they are ideological constructs. As ideologies are inherent in any form of language use (Voloshinov 1929), LPP is not confined to administrative documents but is also present in other texts (both written and spoken) and in practices that construct beliefs about languages and how they are used, and that create affordances or constraints on language-related practice (Lo Bianco 2005). Such a view opens up the scope of what can constitute LPP and recognises that LPP is not only overtly expressed in documents but also covertly expressed in decisions taken at any level of society that influence languages, their learning and their use (Shohamy 2006). In this way, it is possible and useful to treat practices around language learning and language use as forms of LPP, whether they are formally articulated or not.

Kaplan and Baldauf (1997) argue that LPP work operates at a number of different levels within any society: macro, meso and micro. This more nuanced view of LPP is useful for understanding the field when studying language maintenance, as it brings to light the complex, interacting, and often conflicting policy positionings that occur at different social levels as they are enacted by different actors. While the terms macro-, meso- and micro-level have come to be widely used in LLP studies, the distinction between the levels is not fixed, and what any particular author may mean by a term often has much to do with the context and point of view of a particular study. The macro-level in LPP is most typically the work of government and government agencies (Kaplan and Baldauf 1997). This has been the classical focus of LPP scholarship. The place of government will vary according to the ways that societies are structured. In countries with strong centralisation, such as France or Japan, the macro-level may be the national government. However, in federal systems, such as Australia, the United States or Belgium, where some aspects of government responsibility are located at regional levels (states, provinces, etc.), these levels may also be considered part of the macro-level. The macro-level may also include supranational bodies, such as the United Nations or the European Union. The influence of such bodies may be less direct and less immediate than that of governments, but they may nonetheless represent an important part of the context in which national level policies are articulated and implemented. Often macro-level LPP is represented by explicit texts, such as constitutions, laws and policy documents, but may also be covert, existing in ideologies and cultural assumptions (Schiffman 1996) or in the silences in which languages and their speakers are passed over and thus have no place in representations of language learning and use in a particular polity.

The meso-level has not been well conceptualised in LPP research and has been treated as different things by different authors. Kaplan and Baldauf (1997) focus on the targets of LPP and define the meso-level as LPP for a sector of society or for a particular group of individuals. However, they do not focus on who the actors are at meso-levels. This means that while macro-level actors are usually identified as governments and micro-level actors are understood as agents acting in local contexts (Liddicoat and Baldauf 2008), there is less clarity about who meso-level actors are. Miranda, Berdugo, and Tejada (2016), studying university language policy, attempt to resolve this issue by understanding the meso-level as a fluid concept, with the macro being represented by actors outside the university, the micro-level by academics and students and the meso-level by all actors between the two. This more fluid conceptualisation is quite sensitive to context with the micro-level being the most local level of actors and the meso-level those actors that intervene between the macro- and the micro-level. Following from this conceptualisation, for language maintenance, the micro-level can be considered to be language users themselves, especially families, the macro-level is the level of government, and the meso-level are entities intermediate the two. Each level of policy interacts with language maintenance in different ways and, in any attempt to understand LPP and language maintenance, it is important to consider how the various layers work. This issue of family LPP is addressed elsewhere in the present volume (Curdt-Christiansen and Huang; Lanza and Lomeu Gomes; Schwartz; Smith Christmas; Palviainen, all this vol.) and will not be developed further here. Rather this chapter will focus on the macro- and meso-levels that provide a backdrop against which family LPP is enacted.

Across the three levels, there are two main types of LPP that have implications for home language maintenance (see Kaplan and Baldauf 1997). These are language status LPP, which deals with the use and functions of language varieties, and language-in-education LPP, which deals with language teaching and learning. Status planning may open or close spaces for the public use of language (van Els 2005). Language-in-education planning may open or close spaces for languages in educational contexts and foster or inhibit opportunities for development of literacy or expanded registers in particular language varieties and for overall educational success (Liddicoat 2013). However, other forms of LPP, such as corpus LPP involving the development of scripts, orthography, lexicon, codified grammar, etc., and prestige or image planning, which seeks to address issues of perception of language varieties, can also influence language maintenance. Where languages have not created scripts, orthographies or specialised lexicon, these may be seen as motivations to exclude such languages from valued contexts, especially education (Liddicoat 2005). Prestige planning may alter how particular languages varieties are seen by speakers and so promote or impede language maintenance (Baldauf 2004). This chapter will; now turn to considering how macro and meso level LPP can influence home language maintenance.

2 Macro-level LPP

Macro-level LPP provide a socio-political context in which language maintenance occurs. They do this by expressing the value that is given to language maintenance (e.g. through status planning) and secondly by providing support (e.g. through language-in-education planning).

Arguably, declaring a language to be an official or national language at national or regional level provides the potential for strong support for a minority language at risk of shift or loss, e.g. Irish in Ireland, Māori in New Zealand, Sámi in parts of Norway. Such policies are usually status policies (van Els 2005) that identify the functions a language will have in society, rather than focusing specifically on questions of maintenance. Granting a language official status is a symbolic act of recognition of the language and its place in the nation and a positive affirmation of the language and its speakers, and therefore can provide a positive context for the transmission of a language to future generations. Such policies may also provide for resources, educational programmes and other forms of support for the language maintenance effort. However, what is entailed in making a language official can mean very different things in terms of how such documents address language maintenance. In some cases, status planning documents may only relate to language use. Article 8 of the Irish Constitution recognises Irish as the national and first official language and makes provision for its possible exclusive use in official communication. Thus, it gives recognition of the language as a symbol of Irish identity and allocates to it possible functions but makes no comment on language maintenance or the role of the Irish state in this. Instead, language maintenance is addressed primarily through language-in-education policy, which has strongly supported the provision of Irish-medium education and Irish language lessons in schools. In other contexts, there may be reference to language maintenance in status planning documents. In the case of Sámi, Norway has integrated a responsibility for language maintenance in Article 108 of the Constitution: "It is the responsibility of the authorities of the State to create conditions enabling the Sámi people to preserve and develop its language, culture and way of life". That is, the text has an explicit statement of state responsibility for language maintenance but details of how this will be done are operationalised in other laws and policy documents. Macro-level documents such as constitutions and language laws are usually very succinct statements about the language and do little more than frame the general context for language use. More developed policy for language maintenance usually occurs in other forms of policy, especially for language education.

Language-in-education policy provisions for education in minority languages is a common way in which macro-level policy has supported maintenance. There are different ways in which macro-level language-in-education policy can provide for language maintenance. In some cases, policies for language maintenance may involve the teaching and learning of minority languages in schools. In Colombia, the government policy of *etnoeducación* (ethnoeducation) aimed at making access to indigenous languages a normal part of schooling for indigenous children (Liddicoat and Curnow 2007). Access to education in indigenous languages is recognised as a right in Article 10 of the constitution. While the policy was originally intended only for indigenous groups, Afro-Colombian groups have since argued that they too should have access to such programs as ethnolinguistic minorities, and the policy has since been extended to cover them (Castillo Guzmán 2016). In laws developed to implement the constitutional provision, ethnoeducation is represented as a primary school program that aims to assist children in their early educational development and facilitate their transition to Spanish-medium education. While Colombia's policy guarantees access to indigenous language education, local conditions, such as teacher supply, availability of materials, etc. often mean that provision of programs may be limited or problematic (Liddicoat and Curnow 2007). Alternatively, language maintenance programs may be provided through complementary provision. Australia's adoption of a policy of multiculturalism led to the introduction in 1981 of the Ethnic Schools Program[1] (see Baldauf 2005). The program provided financial support for schools run by ethnic communities as part of their language maintenance work. Government-funded ethnic schools are organized outside normal school provision and usually take the form of after-hours or weekend classes. The policy provides resources for communities to offer education in their languages, but leaves responsibility for maintenance programmes with community groups; language maintenance is therefore a task for individual communities rather than part of schooling (Liddicoat 2013). These examples of macro-level policy from Colombia and Australia represent rather formal, explicit and funded interventions into language maintenance work, but macro-level policy may also be much vaguer and general in the way it states a government's commitment and responsibility for maintaining minority languages. Japan's policy relating to Ainu states only that the government supports the promotion and teaching of Ainu culture, but gives little direction to this (Maher 2001). These examples show that officially articulated policies may not be enough in themselves to ensure provision and that support is needed in their implementation to turn the rhetoric into a reality.

At the international level, LPP favouring language maintenance has received some support in documents relating to human rights (see Annamalai and Skuttnab-Kangas, this vol.), such as the 1966 International Covenant on Civil and Political Rights, which includes in Article 27 a provision for minorities to "use their own

---

[1] Later renamed the Community Languages Element

language". This covenant provides a negative right to use language free from government interference. The 1992 Declaration on the Rights of Persons Belonging to National or Ethnic, Religious and Linguistic Minorities further strengthens the possibilities for language maintenance stating in Article 1 that governments should "encourage" conditions for the promotion and protection of linguistic identities. Such documents provide a form of international level support for language maintenance as a legitimate activity for minority groups, but are often quite remote from the realities of individual groups seeking to maintain their languages (Romaine 2015).

Macro-level policies may also be antagonist to language maintenance and seek to prevent it. In Spain, LPP under Franco represented a hostile environment for language maintenance as minority languages were treated as a threat to national identity and stability, and policy was aimed at removing these languages from the national language ecology (Vallverdú 1991). The explicit policy of Franco's regime was to remove the languages from the cultural sphere, close down minority language media newspapers, and forbid the use of minority languages in everyday contexts: names of children, commerce and even in telephone conversations (Ben-Ami 1991). Further, the minority languages were stigmatized and ridiculed in public discourse: e.g. *No ladres: habla el idioma del Imperio* [Don't bark: speak the language of the empire], which equates minority language use with a sub-human form of behaviour. More recently, Kurdish language maintenance in Turkey has been associated with terrorist activity; it has been constructed in law as a form of material support for the Kurdistan Workers Party (PKK) and militant Kurdish separatism (Liddicoat 2018b). Skutnabb-Kangas and Fernandes (2008) reported a number of court cases where supporters of Kurdish language education were found guilty of terrorist offenses for activities such as speaking publicly in favour of Kurdish language education for Kurdish children, demanding Kurdish language tuition, and asking for optional Kurdish language courses. In such contexts, language maintenance may become highly politicized as a form of resistance to the state, be carried out covertly, or be allowed to lapse in favour of safer linguistic practices.

In most cases, however, macro-level LPP may be ambivalent. Educational policy in Bhutan (Dukpa 2019) states that multilingualism in local minority languages, Dzongkha and English is a key educational goal: "This plan of transition from home language to Dzongkha to English can be seen as a golden balance between the goals of multicultural identity, multilingual competence" (School Education and Research Unit 2012: 133). However, it allocates no place for minority languages in the school curriculum: "students acquire their home languages at home and Dzongkha and English language in the school" (School Education and Research Unit 2012: 103). Thus, Bhutan's education policy gives value to home language maintenance but allocates responsibility entirely to the home context.

Even where policies may appear to be supportive of language maintenance, the actual situation is more complex as language maintenance is enacted within contexts of covert policy that construct less supportive discourses (Liddicoat and Curnow 2014). Liddicoat and Curnow argue that there are three prevailing discourses that threaten the place of minorities' languages in school education: Discourses about social cohesion, about competition between languages in the school curriculum, and about language maintenance as a private matter. The discourse of language maintenance as contrary to social cohesion is a manifestation of an enduring one nation–one language ideology on understandings of national identity and citizenship (see also Chiro 2014; Heugh 2014). Linguistic diversity can be seen as a threat to national unity and stability and thus language maintenance programmes can be perceived as in conflict with the nation-building role of schooling. This view is behind the bans on Kurdish and minority languages in Spain discussed above. Similar discourses can be present in even nominally supportive contexts as can be seen in some framings of the debate over the recent (re)introduction of mother tongue education in Kenya. The response of the Kenyan National Teachers Union, as articulated by its chairperson Mudzo Nzili, rejected mother tongue education as contrary to the social role of schooling:

> "As already indicated, the country is moving towards social integration and this cannot be achieved when at the same time we have policies with tribal references as mother tongue shall always prioritise tribes," he [Nzili] said. "Education in Kenya is to promote unity within the community". (Waweru 2014)

Language maintenance can thus be constructed as contrary to the core purpose of education and so even where overt policy is supportive of language maintenance, covert policy may not be.

LPP for language maintenance may also be in conflict with a "common sense" belief (Ferris and Politzer 1981) that more time spent on learning a dominant language will lead to better acquisition of that language. Language maintenance and LPP that support it may thus be conceived as problematic for the learning of the dominant language and viewed as problematic for the future life choices of language minority students. As Liddicoat and Curnow (2014: 282) argue this is "a view of language that denies the possibility of any inter-relationship between languages in the learning process and sees languages as fundamentally in competition". It leads to a discursive construction of linguistic abilities in a minority language as a deficit to be overcome through education rather than as a social, educational or identity resource, and thus sees little value in the development of that language as a goal for educational practice or policy.

This conceptualisation of minority languages as barriers to the acquisition of the dominant language has influenced government policy in relation to bilingual programs for speakers of Aboriginal languages in Australia's Northern Territory and has led to the withdrawal of support for these languages in favour of English (Liddicoat 2018a; Liddicoat and Curnow 2014). In 2008, the then Minister for Education introduced an educational reform which required that all schools in the Northern Territory teach in English for the first four hours of schooling. The goal of this policy was to promote English language literacy by increasing the time spent on English in bilingual schools (Devlin 2017a, 2017b). This reform thus explicitly restricted the amount of time that bilingual programs could allocate to students' home languages in order to defend the curriculum space allocated to English-only education. In her media release announcing the policy, the Minister stated: "I support preserving our Indigenous languages and culture – but our Indigenous children need to be given the best possible chance to learn English" (Scrymgour 2008), thus constructing Aboriginal languages and cultures as a limitation on the chances that students have to acquire English. The maintenance of Aboriginal languages is therefore a problem in education, because it conflicts with what is perceived as the main language goal of education – the development of English literacy. Similarly, in the United States, the No Child Left Behind (NCLB) policy emphasized the place of English and in so doing undermined the legitimacy and relevance of bilingual education programs established under the Bilingual Education Act (BEA) of 1968. The BEA has originally created space in education for bilingual programs that would enable minority language speakers to develop literacy in a minority language before transitioning to English medium education. The emphasis in NCLB on moving students into English-medium education as quickly as possible constructed English language acquisition as the main goal of education and undermined the importance of developing students' own languages, even constructing it as an impediment to English learning (Evans and Hornberger 2005). Policies for language maintenance can thus be vulnerable to an ideological position that the teaching of one language is seen as presenting an impediment to the acquisition of another. Liddicoat and Curnow (2014) argue that such discourses normalise limited linguistic repertoires in education and preclude the possibility of conceptualising multilingualism as a normal form of human language use (cf. Agnihotri 2014).

In addition, the way that language-in-education policies position the learning of minority languages in education overall may be problematic. Where LPP constructs minority language learning as transitional, LPP may appear to include minority languages in education, and so promote their maintenance, but may actually ultimately reflect a view of minority languages as having limited utility (Liddicoat 2013). These dynamics can be seen in in the case of a USAID project in Ghana known as the National Literacy Acceleration Program (NALAP) for early childhood education (Rosekrans, Sherris, and Chatry-Komarek 2012; Sherris 2013). NALAP aimed to provide literacy resources and literacy instruction in 11 Ghanaian languages in kindergarten early primary schooling (Grades 1–3) before a transition to English-only education. Ghanaian language literacy was developed alongside English as an additional language in preparation for transition in grade 4. NALAP replaced an earlier English-only approach to education from the beginning of education and so can be considered as potentially contributing to language maintenance work by providing for the development of literacy in local languages and in so doing opening new, valued domains of language use. However, such literacy programs, while they are beneficial for minority language learners, may not support language maintenance in the long term. This is so especially where literacy in local languages lacks value in the local context of family and community, where oral capabilities are more important and opportunities to use literacy for authentic purposes may be very constrained (Kamwangamalu 2010), and lack relevance in the wider context, which operates in the dominant language. If there are no contexts for the application of literacy in minority languages in the valued domains of the market, it is difficult to see how minority languages can enter into the ideologies of value that are held by governing elites. The valued repertoire for many minority students is seen only in terms of the dominant language and their plurilingualism is not seen as something to be developed through education but rather a problem that needs to be resolved for education to be successful (cf. Ruíz 1984). Unless LPP also gives value to the non-dominant language in its own right instead of seeing the value of such languages only in terms of what they contribute to the learning of more valued languages, such programs may perpetuate prevailing ideologies that construct official languages as the sole legitimate languages.

The usual focus of macro-level LPP is on the official, dominant languages of a society. Much LPP is in fact silent about language maintenance efforts, seeing them as private matters for individuals, families or communities. In some cases, such private efforts may receive symbolic support from policy discourses that express a value for maintaining linguistic diversity (e.g. multicultural policy in Australia) and states may even implement policies that provide resources to support community level language maintenance work (e.g. ethnic schools in Australia). Where policy is silent on the role, value or status of other languages, this silence is consequential for the social realities of languages in the nation; explicit policies inevitably construct hierarchies among languages, with languages named in policies being awarded a higher place on the hierarchy than languages that are not mentioned. Silence about languages thus can equate with a perception that 'missing' languages are seen as less useful, less worthwhile or less desirable than languages that are present in policies. Because of this, macro-level policy contexts can frequently provide constraints on language maintenance by representing such activities as less valued by the society and so making the efforts required to maintain a language appear to be less rewarded and less rewarding.

3 Meso-level LPP

Between the macro-level of the state and the micro-level of the family there are a number of LPP actors that can have an influence on language maintenance. Some of the key actors at the meso-level are community cultural and leisure organisations, religious organisations, individual schools, media and other language- and literacy-related services. The LPP of such actors can play a supportive role in language maintenance when attention is given to the use of minority languages and this section will consider how the language decisions of some of these actors can support language maintenance.

3.1 Community organisations as language maintenance policy actors

In many contexts of language maintenance, the linguistic community is the major LPP actor for language maintenance outside the family. Many communities establish organisations for language or cultural maintenance that can provide either contexts of language use or more specific support for maintenance in the form of language schools. As mentioned above, schools are important sites of language maintenance, but such schools are not always supported by macro-level policies and institutions. Where this is the case meso-level actors may provide the only LPP work that directly supports educational development in a minority language (Liddicoat and Baldauf 2008).

Mougeon, Beniak, and Valois (1985) argue that schooling in a community language can be crucial for language maintenance in contexts where children are constantly exposed to the dominant language. However, such education is not often provided by the regular school system and where this is the case, community organisations may play an active role in language maintenance by providing educational programmes to support language and literacy development either alongside or in addition to mainstream schooling provided by government. In some cases, minority language communities may set up schools, usually in the private sector, to cater to their community and to offer education in their home language. Such schools are often associated with institutions that can provide financial support for their establishment. Private sector schools have been a feature of Greek community language maintenance efforts in a number of countries such as Australia (Kalantzis 1985), South Africa (McDuling and Barnes 2012) and the United States (Fishman 1980). Complementary schools may adopt LPP in which the home language is the normal language of instruction, or they may teach in the dominant language but provide the home language as an important subject in the curriculum. Such schools require considerable capital investment and so may not be a viable option for many communities, especially smaller and less wealthy ones.

A common model for schooling is for communities to provide education in the community language as a complement to mainstream schooling as such programs are less demanding in terms of financial resources and do not need to be located within regulatory and bureaucratic mechanisms within the society. Such schools not only open spaces for educational development in languages not offered in mainstream schooling but can also provide an important community resource that supports language maintenance efforts more widely. As Creese argues:

> Complementary schools serve as a social, linguistic, and cultural resource to their respective communities and help counter the expected monolingualising mainstream. Their multilingualism provides an institutional space to connect the languages of the home and community.
> (Creese 2009: 272)

One particularly successful example of a community-based project supporting language maintenance can be seen in the work by Māori to develop Māori medium education in New Zealand, beginning in early childhood education with *Kōhanga reo* (language nests) and then moving into higher levels (Reedy 2000). These institutions represent significant interventions by the community into the educational domain and a reconstruction of the possibilities for language use, development and education within their local context. Such activities have the potential to be instances of what Alexander (1992) calls *language planning from below*, contexts in which successful grassroots community efforts influence macro-level LPP work.

Community organisations outside the domain of education can also be relevant policy actors for supporting language maintenance. Communities may sponsor cultural groups that have as their aim the continuing of folkloric, artistic or performance traditions. Nahirny and Fishman (1965) note that such organisations can play a significant role in language maintenance work because they may function using the community language and in so doing provide a context for language use and open spaces for new language domains. However, for such groups language maintenance is not the key focus and so their contribution to language maintenance will depend very much on their LPP, whether explicit or implicit, and whether use of the community's language is seen as relevant to or facilitative of their non-language goals. The same is true for sporting clubs and other leisure organisations. Where community organisations sponsor sporting clubs for community members, and where the LPP of the clubs includes the community language as the normal language of communication in training and on the field, such clubs may be an important domain for language use and thus contribute to language maintenance efforts. Such sporting clubs have been shown to have had an important role in the maintenance of community languages in Australia (see Janik 1996: for Polish; Martín 1996: for Spanish).

Community organisations often represent a point at which macro and meso level policies may intersect. Australia's Ethnic School's Program, discussed above, is an instance of a macro-level LPP that actively supports such meso-level actors by providing both funding and an institutional structure through which community run complementary schooling can operate. In immigrant contexts, they may also be supported by governments from the immigrants' home countries (Hatoss 2006). Such organisations can therefore provide links between a diasporic community and the core community of language users. They also represent sites at which macro-level LPP of external agencies can find contexts of enactment in other countries.

3.2 Religious organisations as language maintenance policy actors

Spolsky (2009: 43) argues that "religious language planning can play an important role in providing support for the maintenance of a heritage language". The LPP of religious institutions can support language maintenance in a range of different ways. The religious institution can provide a context in which the home language of a community is used for religious services (Liddicoat 2012). The decision to use a minority language for religious purposes is often not taken specifically for language maintenance reasons; it tends to be a response to the needs of adult worshipers. However, the use of a minority language for religious purposes does provide a context for language use outside the home and is often associated with informal communication or activities using the language outside the worship of the church. Thus, the LPP of the institution, in terms of its religious use of a language, can create a hub around which other language practices are used and developed.

Religious institutions also develop LPP in relation to how they teach faith lessons for children (Liddicoat 2012). Souza, Kwapong, and Woodham (2012) discuss the LPP of a number of churches in the UK that cater for immigrant communities and use the communities' languages in their teaching of their faith. They describe contexts where teachers of religion draw on their students' languages in different ways to promote learning, but also implicitly or explicitly contribute to language maintenance. They report on a Catholic church catering for immigrants from Brazil, where catechism is taught in Portuguese as a way of ensuring that Portuguese-speaking parents can have a central role in their children's catechesis. This means that the church's LPP is one that can harmonise with the family LPP of their congregation. This policy does have consequences for how the catechism classes operate as, although they use materials written in Portuguese, the children themselves are not literate in Portuguese and so the classes have to rely on oral language use only. The classes focus mainly on spoken language rather than on teaching literacy and as such they can be considered more as providing opportunities for use of the language in a religious context. At the same time, the classes do provide for the use and development of specific registers of language – the language of religion – that may not be developed in everyday home contexts and also integrate the language into a culturally significant set of social practices. Souza, Kwapong, and Woodham (2012) report that maintaining cultural traditions is an explicit motivation for faith lessons in churches and that this motivation is central in the decision to use the community language rather than English as the usual language of the lessons. Souza, Kwapong, and Woodham (2012) also discuss a different model for supporting language maintenance in the case of a Polish Catholic church in the UK which operates a Polish language school on Saturdays. The school teaches catechism, but this is only a part of the school's curriculum. Most of the work of the school involves teaching literacy and language development in Polish, and in this way the work of the church is similar to other community organisations that take on educational functions.

Where religious practice does not take minority languages into consideration, the result can be a reinforcement of pressures to shift to another, more dominant language. Wang (2016) argues that the decision by Malaysian Catholic churches to use Mandarin rather than Hakka in its liturgy has contributed to the loss of Hakka in the community, as it has influenced local language ideologies about the value and role of Hakka and has affected the linguistic ecology in which Hakka exits.

3.3 Individual schools as language maintenance policy actors

Corson (1999) argues that schools can construct environments of inequality for minority language speakers because they are routinely environments where the dominant group exercises power. Schools therefore can be significant sites operating against language maintenance. In fact, it is often after children begin to attend school that family LPP become difficult to sustain. Even where macro-level policy is supportive of language maintenance, this does not mean that all schools respond in the same way, or that similar support for language maintenance is found at all schools.

It is often the case that where there is macro-level support for maintenance programs in mainstream education, this support is only given where school leaders opt to provide programs for minority language students. Scarino et al. (2013) found that, although there was government funding for first language maintenance programs in schools in South Australia, whether a school offered such a program was dependent on whether or not local school leaders felt that such programmes had educational value for their students and so applied for the money. Thus, school leaders may be important gate-keepers providing or withholding access to language maintenance programs where these are supported by macro-level policy. Similarly, Brown's (2010) study of the Võro language in Estonia describes a situation in which Estonia's policy of elective study of the minorities' languages was operationalised differently in different schools. Some schools maintained the language in a minoritised and devalued position by excluding it from the regular curriculum and offering it after hours. Other schools, however, presented the language as a regular, non-elective, part of the curriculum and enacted structures that gave value to the language and positioned it as important.

Even where macro-level policy does not explicitly support language maintenance, individual schools may do so by providing language programs for minority language students within their curricula. Schools, thus, are not simply institutions that implement policies that have an impact on language maintenance but exercise local agency in ways that can enhance or constrain possibilities for local communities.

3.4 Media as language maintenance policy actors

Fishman (1991) has questioned the significance of the media in LPP, arguing that other domains such as family, community or education played a more important role. However, there is evidence that media LPP can and does have an impact on language maintenance (e.g. Cormack 2007; Riggins 1992), and the significance of media may have become even more important with the widespread use of social media (Cormack 2013; Takam 2017).

Access to media is a key factor for minority language maintenance, and having access to band-width for broadcasting is controlled by governments, whose macrolevel policies may influence access. In some cases, public broadcasting policies may open spaces for minority language presence in the media which can be taken up by community organisations. Minority language media may also be subsidised by government, as for example SBS broadcasting, especially radio services, in Australia (Dreher 2009). The development of public broadcasting has thus been important in giving minority language communities access to the technologies of broadcasting. The development of computer mediated communication and the growth of the internet has had an important impact on language maintenance work by opening new opportunities for communication for minority communities (Arnold and Plymire 2000). Meso-level actors are now likely to use online modes, which are frequently cheaper and easier to manage than other media.

As Cormack (2007) acknowledges, media have a much wider role than language maintenance, but can play a significant role in assisting maintenance efforts, by creating a stronger sense of community identity, showing that the community is modernised and able to participate in contemporary life, and contributing large amounts of language to the public sphere. Media thus can play an important role in language maintenance by creating contexts for language use in valued domains and may give the languages greater status and may encourage speakers to revive and maintain their language (Ó Laoire 2000).

Media LPP that support minority languages are thus forms of prestige or image planning (Ager 2006) – planning to enhance the perceived social value of nondominant language varieties – but they can also contribute to the perceived ethnolinguistic vitality of the language. This was the motivation for the establishment of minority language literary and cultural groups, such as the Catalan *Renaixença*, the Occitan *Félibrige* or the more formally constituted Frisian *Selskip foar Taal- en Skiftekenisse* in the nineteenth century, and thus modern media are continuing and expanding a tradition that has a longer history. One of the key aims of media actors is to provide media communication that is equivalent to that provided by mainstream, dominant language media, and often have materials directed to young people that may provide for motivation to continue using the language rather than shifting to the dominant language in order to access valued aspects of popular culture. For example, the Brezhoweb internet television station, which has broadcast in Breton since 2006, provides Breton language programming across a range of genres, including films, animation, news and current affairs, documentaries, sit coms and sports broadcasts. Programmes are either produced in Breton or existing material is dubbed into Breton, thus creating a wide range of media products for the audience across a broad range of ages (Buannic 2009).

In the case of media organisations, LPP that makes minority languages available is not enough in itself to support language maintenance and the quality of material broadcast is also important. Sepeheri (2010) found that, although media in Azerbaijani is available in parts of Iran, low quality and unattractive content mean that the programs provided are not much used by the local community and that Azerbaijani speakers are more likely to use mainstream media, which has better content and better quality. Thus, an important part of the work of media language planners involves not only decisions about language use but also decisions that allow the language to be used for content that parallels the content and production standards on mainstream media. This means that LPP overlaps with editorial policy and frequently involves a strong level of support for translation as part of media activity.

The development of online media has led to the emergence of new possibilities for using media in language maintenance contexts (Hatoss this vol.) and allows groups and even individuals to become involved in making decisions about the presence and use of languages in the media. Electronic media, including social media thus blur the boundaries between the meso and micro levels of LPP by creating affordances for both groups and individuals to engage in media LPP. Engaging in minority language use on the internet has the potential to bring about changes in language ideologies and challenge existing language regimes (Cru 2015). The availability of social media in a minority language can provide authentic opportunities for using the language and at the same time support the development of social networks of language learners (Lee 2006). Social media have the possibility of extending language use beyond the local community and create peer social networks and popular culture groupings that can provide significant sites for socialization into patterns of language use (Friedman 2011). Because they are not tied to geography, such media may also draw in speakers who may otherwise not have access to a community of language users because of migration (Cru 2015; Lee 2006).

4 Conclusion

Language maintenance takes place in a context that is shaped by the ideologies (Albury this vol.) and language practices of a wider society and these constitute the policy context in which decisions are made about maintaining a language or shifting to another. In any society, the language of the dominant group exerts influence, covertly or overtly, on the language practices of minority language speakers and promotes a shift to the dominant language. Where no explicit policy exists at macro-level or meso-level to support maintenance of minority languages, then micro-level actors maintain languages against the pressure exerted by the discourses that support the dominant language. LPP at macro and meso levels that are supportive of language maintenance provide a context that can make it easier to resist the pressure of dominant languages.

Macro-level policies supporting language maintenance may do little more than shape the context for language maintenance in a positive way by giving positive symbolic value to the continued use of languages and to societal multilingualism. Additionally, they may also provide supportive structures in terms of educational programmes or by officially sanctioning the use of the language in valued domains in the society.

Meso-level policy actors can support language maintenance in two keys ways. Firstly, they can provide resources for language learning or use that the family may not be able to provide. Thus, schools can provide opportunities for developing literate language use and libraries and media can provide resources for entertainment and information. They also play another, and perhaps more important, role in language maintenance work. As institutions, meso-level actors can provide social environments for language use and language socialisation. Thus, a football club, a religious community, or a cultural group may afford opportunities to interact with peers and to develop social relationships through the minority language. By creating contexts where a minority language is required for participation, they may offer tangible social rewards for language use. The LPP of meso-level actors may contribute to the perceived ethnolinguistic vitality of a minority language by providing for an expanded range of domains of use and especially by providing for language use in valued domains.

Ultimately language maintenance depends on decision-making at the micro level as it is at this level that languages are used and transmitted to future generations. Such decision-making is, however, supported or constrained by policies that exist at other levels.

References

Ager, Denis E. 2006. Image and prestige planning. *Current Issues in Language Planning* 6(1). 1–43.
Agnihotri, Rama Kant. 2014. Multilinguality, education and harmony. *International Journal of Multilingualism* 11(3). 364–379.
Albury, Nathan. this vol. Language attitudes and ideologies on linguistic diversity.
Alexander, Neville. 1992. Language planning from below. In Robert K. Herbert (ed.), *Language and Society in Africa*, 56–68. Johannesburg: Witwatersrand University Press.
Annamalai, E. & Tove Skutnabb-Kangas. this vol. Social justice and inclusiveness through linguistic human rights in education.

Arnold, Ellen L. & Darcy C. Plymire 2000. The Cherokee Indians and the Internet. In David Gauntlett (ed.), *Web studies: Rewiring media studies for the digital age*, 186–193. London: Edward Arnold.

Baldauf, Richard B. 2004. Issues of prestige and image in language-in-education planning in Australia. *Current Issues in Language Planning* 5(4). 376–388.

Baldauf, Richard B. 2005. Coordinating government and community support for community language teaching in Australia: Overview with special attention to New South Wales. *International Journal of Bilingual Education and Bilingualism* 8(2–3). 132–144.

Baldauf, Richard B. 2006. Rearticulating the case for micro language planning in a language ecology context. *Current Issues in Language Planning* 7(2&3). 147–170.

Ball, Stephen J. 1993. What is policy? Texts, trajectories and toolboxes. *Discourse: Studies in the Cultural Politics of Education* 13(2). 10–17.

Ben-Ami, Shlomo. 1991. Basque nationalism between archaism and modernity. *Journal of Contemporary History* 26(3/4). 493–521.

Brown, Kara. 2010. Teachers as language-policy actors: Contending with the erasure of lesser-used languages in schools. *Anthropology & Education* 41(3). 298–314.

Buannic, Lionel. 2009. Brezhoweb: Le breton se lâche sur internet. *Ouest-France*. https://www.ouest-france.fr/brezhoweb-le-breton-se-lache-sur-internet-59358 (accessed 5 October 2019).

Castillo Guzmán, Elizabeth. 2016. Etnoeducación afropacífica y pedagogías de la dignificación. *Revista Colombiana de Educación* 71. 343–360.

Chiro, Giancarlo. 2014. Cultural and linguistic diversity in Australia: Navigating between the Scylla of nationhood and the Charybdis of globalisation. *International Journal of Multilingualism* 11(3). 334–346.

Cormack, Mike. 2007. The media and language maintenance. In Mike Cormack & Niamh Hourigan (eds.), *Minority language media: Concepts, critiques and case studies*, 52–68. Clevedon: Multilingual Matters.

Cormack, Mike. 2013. Concluding remarks: Towards an understanding of media impact on minority language use. In Elin Haf Gruyffudd Jones & Enrique Uribe-Jongbloed (eds.), *Social media and minority languages: Convergence and the creative industries*, 255–265. Clevedon: Multilingual Matters.

Corson, David. 1999. *Language policy in schools: A resource for teachers and administrators*. Mahwah, NJ: Lawrence Erlbaum.

Creese, Angela. 2009. Building on young people's linguistic and cultural continuity: Complementary schools in the United Kingdom. *Theory Into Practice* 48(4). 267–273.

Cru, Josep. 2015. Language revitalisation from the ground up: Promoting Yucatec Maya on Facebook. *Journal of Multilingual and Multicultural Development* 36(3). 284–296.

Curdt-Christiansen, Xiao Lan & Jing Huang. this vol. Factors influencing family language policy.

Devlin, Brian. 2017a. Policy change in 2008: Evidence-based or a knee-jerk response? In Brian Devlin, Samantha Disbray & Nancy Devlin (eds.), *History of bilingual education in the Northern Territory: People, programs and policies*, 203–218. Singapore: Springer Singapore.

Devlin, Brian. 2017b. Threatened closure: Resistance and compromise (1998–2000). In Brian Devlin, Samantha Disbray & Nancy Devlin (eds.), *History of bilingual education in the Northern Territory: People, programs and policies*, 165–178. Singapore: Springer Singapore.

Djité, Paulin. 1994. *From language policy to language planning*. Canberra: National Languages and Literacy Institute of Australia.

Dreher, Tanja. 2009. Listening across difference: Media and multiculturalism beyond the politics of voice. *Continuum* 23(4). 445–458.

Dukpa, Lhundup. 2019. Language policy in Bhutan. In Andy Kirkpatrick & Anthony J. Liddicoat (eds.), *The Routledge international handbook of language education policy in Asia*, 355–363. New York: Routledge.

Els, Theo van. 2005. Status planning for learning and teaching. In Eli Hinkel (ed.), *Handbook of research in second language teaching and learning*, 971–992. Mahwah, NJ: Lawrence Erlbaum.

Evans, Bruce A. & Nancy H. Hornberger. 2005. No Child Left Behind: Repealing and "unpeeling" federal language education policy in the United States. *Language Policy* 2. 87–106.

Ferris, M. Roger & Robert L. Politzer. 1981. Effects of early and delayed second language acquisition: English comprehension skills of Spanish-speaking junior high school students. *TESOL Quarterly* 15(3). 263–274.

Fishman, Joshua A. 1980. Ethnic community mother tongue schools in the U.S.A.: Dynamics and distributions. *International Migration Review* 14(2). 235–247.

Fishman, Joshua A. 1991. *Reversing language shift: Theoretical and empirical foundations of assistance to threatened languages*. Clevedon: Multilingual Matters.

Friedman, Debra A. 2011. Language socialization and language revitalization. In Alessandro Duranti, Elinore Ochs & Bambi B. Schieffelin (eds.), *The handbook of language socialization*. 631–647. New York: Wiley-Blackwell.

García, MaryEllen. 2003. Recent research on language maintenance. *Annual Review of Applied Linguistics* 23. 22–43.

Glasgow, Gregory Paul & Jeremie Bouchard. 2019. Introduction. In Jeremie Bouchard & Gregory P. Glasgow (eds.), *Agency in language policy and planning: Critical inquiries*, 1–21. New York & London: Routledge.

Hatoss, Anikó. 2006. Community-level approaches in language planning: The case of Hungarian in Australia. *Current Issues in Language Planning* 7(2&3). 287–306.

Hatoss, Anikó. this vol. Transnational grassroots language planning in the era of mobility and the Internet.

Heugh, Kathleen. 2014. Turbulence and dilemma: Implications of diversity and multilingualism in Australian education. *International Journal of Multilingualism* 11(3). 347–363.

Hornberger, Nancy H. 2006. Frameworks and models in language policy and planning. In Thomas Ricento (ed.), *An introduction to language policy: Theory and method*. Malden, MA: Blackwell.

Hornberger, Nancy H. & Serafín M. Coronel-Molina. 2004. Quechua language shift, maintenance, and revitalization in the Andes: The case for language planning *International Journal of the Sociology of Language* 167. 9–67.

Janik, Janusz. 1996. Polish language maintenance of the Polish students at Princes Hill Saturday School in Melbourne. *Journal of Multilingual and Multicultural Development* 17(1). 3–16.

Kalantzis, Mary. 1985. Community languages: Politics or pedagogy. *Australian Review of Applied Linguistics*. S Series 2. 168–179.

Kamwangamalu, Nkonko M. 2010. Vernacularization, globalization, and language economics in non-English-speaking countries in Africa. *Language Problems & Language Planning* 34(1). 1–23.

Kaplan, Robert B. & Richard B. Baldauf. 1997. *Language planning: From practice to theory*. Clevedon: Multilingual Matters.

Lanza, Elizabeth & Rafael Lomeu Gomes. this vol. Family language policy: Foundations, theoretical perspectives and critical approaches.

Lee, Jin Sook. 2006. Exploring the relationship between electronic literacy and heritage language maintenance. *Language Learning & Technology* 10(2). 93–113.

Liddicoat, Anthony J. 2005. Corpus planning: Syllabus and materials development. In Eli Hinkel (ed.), *Handbook of research in second language teaching and learning*, 993–1012. Mahwah, NJ: Lawrence Erlbaum.

Liddicoat, Anthony J. 2012. Language planning as an element of religious practice. *Current Issues in Language Planning* 13(2). 121–144.

Liddicoat, Anthony J. 2013. *Language-in-education policies: The discursive construction of intercultural relations*. Bristol: Multilingual Matters.

Liddicoat, Anthony J. 2018a. Ideologies of value and the place of Australian indigenous languages in education. In Delombera Negga, Daniel K. G. Chan & Monika Szirmai (eds.), *Language policy, ideology and educational practices in a globalized world*, 59–70. Paris: Editions des archives contemporaines.

Liddicoat, Anthony J. 2018b. National security as a motivation in language-in-education policy. In Catherine K. S. Chua (ed.), *Un(intended) language planning in a globalising world: Multiple levels of players at work*, 113–128. Berlin: de Gruyter.

Liddicoat, Anthony J. 2019. Constraints on agency in micro-language policy and planning in schools: A case study of curriculum change. In Jeremie Bouchard & Gregory P. Glasgow (eds.), *Agency in language policy and planning: Critical inquiries* 149–170. New York & London: Routledge.

Liddicoat, Anthony J. & Richard B. Baldauf. 2008. Language planning in local contexts: Agents, contexts and interactions. In Anthony J. Liddicoat & Richard B. Baldauf (eds.), *Language Planning in Local Contexts*, 3–17. Clevedon: Multilingual Matters.

Liddicoat, Anthony J. & Timothy Jowan Curnow. 2007. Language-in-education policy in the context of language death: Policy and practice in Colombian ethnoeducation. In Jeff Siegel, John Lynch & Diana Eades (eds.), *Language description, history and development*, 419–430. Amsterdam: John Benjamins.

Liddicoat, Anthony J. & Timothy Jowan Curnow. 2014. Students' home languages and the struggle for space in the curriculum. *International Journal of Multilingualism* 11(3). 273–288.

Lo Bianco, Joseph. 2005. Including discourse in language planning theory. In Paul Bruthiaux, Dwight Atkinson, William G. Eggington, William Grabe & Vaidehi Ramanathan (eds.), *Directions in Applied Linguistics: Essays in Honor of Robert B. Kaplan*, 255–264. Clevedon: Multilingual Matters.

Maher, John C. 2001. Ainu Itak – our language, your language – Ainu in Japan. In Joshua A. Fishman (ed.), *Can threatened languages be saved*, 323–349. Clevedon: Multilingual Matters.

Martín, M. Daniel. 1996. *Spanish language maintenance and shift in Australia*. Canberra: Australian National University PhD thesis.

McDuling, Allistair & Lawrie Barnes. 2012. What is the future of Greek in South Africa? Language shift and maintenance in the Greek community of Johannesburg. *Language Matters* 43(2). 166–183.

Miranda, Norbella, Martha Berdugo & Harvey Tejada. 2016. Conflicting views on language policy and planning at a Colombian university. *Current Issues in Language Planning* 17(3–4). 422–440.

Mougeon, Raymond, Edouard Beniak & Daniel Valois. 1985. A sociolinguistic study of language contact, shift, and change. *Linguistics* 23(3). 455–488.

Nahirny, Vladimir C. & Joshua A. Fishman. 1965. American immigrant groups: Ethnic identification and the problem of generations. *The Sociological Review* 13(3). 311–326.

Ó Laoire, Muiris. 2000. Language policy and the broadcast media: A response. *Current Issues in Language and Society* 7(2). 149–154.

Palviainen, Åsa. this vol. Future prospects and visions for family language policy research.

Reedy, Tamati. 2000. Te Reo Māori: The past 20 years and looking forward. *Oceanic Linguistics*, 39(1). 157–169.

Riggins, Stephen H. 1992. Promise and limits of ethnic minority media. In Stephen H. Riggins (ed.), *Minority media: An international perspective*, 277–288. Newbury Park: Sage.

Romaine, Suzanne. 2015. The global extinction of languages and its consequences for cultural diversity. In Heiko F. Marten, Michael Rießler, Janne Saarikivi & Reetta Toivanen (eds.), *Cultural and linguistic minorities in the Russian Federation and the European Union: Comparative studies on equality and diversity*, 31–46. Cham: Springer International.

Rosekrans, Kristin, Arieh Sherris & Marie Chatry-Komarek. 2012. Education reform for the expansion of mother-tongue education in Ghana. *International Review of Education/ Internationale Zeitschrift für Erziehungswissenschaft/Revue Internationale de l'Education* 58 (5). 593–618.

Ruíz, Richard. 1984. Orientations in language planning. *NABE Journal* 8(2). 15–34.

Scarino, Angela, Timothy Jowan Curnow, Kathleen Heugh & Anthony J. Liddicoat. 2013. *Review of the first language maintenance and development program*. Adelaide, Department for Education and Child Development.

Schiffman, Harold F. 1996. *Linguistic culture and language policy*. London: Routledge.

School Education and Research Unit. 2012. *The national education framework: Shaping Bhutan's future*. Thimphu: Royal Education Council.

Schwartz, Mila. this vol. Strategies and practices of home language maintenance.

Scrymgour, Marion. 2008. *Education restructure includes greater emphasis on English*. Press release, 14 October 2008. http://newsroom.nt.gov.au/mediaRelease/4656 (accessed 5 October 2019).

Sepeheri, Mohammed Bagher. 2010. Local radio audiences in Iran: An analysis of Ardeblian people's trust in and satisfaction with 'Sabalan' radio. *Journal of Radio and Audio Media* 17(2). 236–250.

Sherris, Arieh. 2013. Re-envisioning the Ghanaian ecolinguistic landscape: Local illustration and literacy. *Intercultural Education* 24(4). 348–354.

Shohamy, Elana. 2006. *Language policy: Hidden agendas and new approaches*. London & New York: Routledge.

Skutnabb-Kangas, Tove & Desmond Fernandes. 2008. Kurds in Turkey and in (Iraqi) Kurdistan: A comparison of Kurdish educational language policy in two situations of occupation. *Genocide Studies and Prevention* 3(1). 43–73.

Smith-Christmas, Cassie. this vol. Child agency and home language maintenance.

Souza, Ana, Amoafi Kwapong & Malgorzata Woodham. 2012. Pentecostal and Catholic migrant churches in London – the role of ideologies in the language planning of faith lessons. *Current Issues in Language Planning* 13(2). 105–120.

Spolsky, Bernard. 2009. *Language management*. Cambridge & New York: Cambridge University Press.

Takam, Alain F. 2017. Les langues minoritaires dans la communication médiatique. *Linguistica Atlantica* 36(2). 111–139.

Vallverdú, Francesc. 1991. Los estudios sociolingüísticos en España, especialmente la Cataluña. In Carol A. Klee & Luis A. Ramos García (eds.), *Sociolinguistics of the Spanish-speaking world*. Tempe, AZ: Bilingual Press.

Voloshinov, Valentin N. 1929. *Марксизм и философия языка* [Marxism and the philosphy of language]. Leningrad: Priboy.

Wang, Xiaomei. 2016. Language maintenance or language shift? The role of religion in a Hakka Catholic community in Malaysia. *International Multilingual Research Journal* 10(4). 273–288.

Waweru, Nduta. 2014. Kenya: Parents divided over language policy. *The Star (Kenya)*. 13 February. http://allafrica.com/stories/201402130728.html (accessed 5 May 2014).

Nathan Albury
18 Language attitudes and ideologies on linguistic diversity

Beyond the ever-intriguing faculty of humans to acquire and creatively use their linguistic resources, the maintenance of linguistic diversity is ultimately a social phenomenon. Our field acknowledges that a home language, in this case taken to mean a minority or heritage language – such as of immigrant or Indigenous groups whose language differs from the majority but is used in some homes – has a greater chance of ongoing vitality, and indeed transmission, if it is prized and valued by society more broadly, whether this be for social, cultural or economic reasons. Conversely, we may have cause for concern if a language is marginalized through a discursive association with, for example, socioeconomic immobility or oppositional identities. Language behaviours – and the maintenance of home languages in a society – are therefore dialectically related to social, cultural, political and economic circumstances. It is in this perspective that language attitudes and ideologies are pertinent themes in home language research. These, as lines of inquiry, put a spotlight on how individuals, families and communities feel about linguistic diversity and indeed the ongoing use – or not – of specific home languages. With that in mind, this chapter specifically discusses the relevance of researching language attitudes and ideologies vis-à-vis linguistic diversity within the broader framework of home language research. It begins by outlining the place of researching language beliefs in applied linguistics. The chapter then especially seeks to delineate and problematize ideologies and attitudes in theoretical terms, and highlights the theoretical opportunities and challenges that they, as conceptual resources, bring to home language inquiry. In doing the above, the chapter draws on an international library of research on home languages.

1 Language ideology and attitudes in applied linguistics

Since the 1960s with the seminal works of Lambert (1967), Lambert et al. (1960), Hymes (1962, 1972) and Labov (1966), linguists have generally accepted that real-life language behaviours – such as the realization and management of linguistic diversity in the home – are not divorced from their social contexts. Instead, the application of linguistic resources, as they manifest from our cognitive faculties, are mediated through societal norms, beliefs and dispositions. Silverstein (1985: 220) later offered a similar argument that language and society are "irreducibly dialectic" whereby effective meaning-making, through the range of semiotic resources made available by a language, is only made possible through culturally-situated intersubjectivities. The notion is that language behaviours are guided by what a broader community sees as appropriate and expected linguistic practice. Labov's (1966) seminal and oft-cited investigation of New York accents proved this upon detailing phonological shifts which denoted membership to social class and engendered speech stereotypically associated with that class. It is therefore the case that as much as humans are socialized into linguistic competence, so too are we socialized into social, cultural and political constraints and expectations of how language is or should be used. In such thinking, a community's broader milieu – laden with its social, cultural and political views about what is good and what is not good about the social world – informs sociolinguistic practices. For the purposes of this volume, these practices include choices in homes to use and transmit specific languages. A particularly salient influence in that decision-making process is how individuals and communities feel about home languages – and multilingualism more generally – as these feelings manifest in language ideologies and attitudes.

Ideologies and attitudes are pertinent in linguistic research because their impacts can be felt widely across societal domains. Governments pursue language policies that favour certain languages over others based in ideologies of nation-building and perceptions of what constitutes a nation's ethnolinguistic identity (Spolsky 2004). Iceland, for example, is preoccupied with preserving its language to be as close as possible to the ancient Norse language of the Icelandic Sagas. So strong is this concern that the government routinely formulates and promulgates Icelandic neologisms as alternatives to English loanwords and is even resurrecting ancient Icelandic morphology. What is more, public attitudes to this ideological work are by and large very supportive (Hilmarsson-Dunn and Kristinsson 2010). However, this preoccupation means Iceland is largely silent on its emerging multilingualism subsequent to increased immigration, especially from Eastern Europe, under Iceland's regionally integrated economic arrangements. Whereas supporting home languages and their speakers through minority-medium instruction or welfare services has preoccupied western states (cf. May 2014), an Icelandic apprehension about diversity – and the impact this may have on the status of Icelandic – means the state is yet to catch-up with European counterparts on matters of language rights. For example, whereas a child of Polish labour migrants in continental Europe might access education that as an epistemological starting point anticipates multiculturalism and multilingualism in the classroom, her peer in Iceland most likely cannot (Jónsdóttir and Ragnarsdóttir 2010). Iceland's dominant discourse and beliefs about Icelandic as an endangered language therefore have tangible impacts on the status, and broader public perceptions of, home languages.

The impacts of language ideologies and attitudes can also be especially pronounced in the grassroots outside the purview of government but where beliefs hold such power that they nonetheless regulate home language maintenance. Hornberger's (1988) seminal work in Quechua communities of Peru found grassroots ideologies that value Spanish/Quechua multilingualism, with attitudes that on the one hand pedestalized Spanish for socioeconomic mobility but on the other hand positioned Quechua as the preferred code for fostering solidarity. These beliefs guided sociolinguistic arrangements and would be instrumental in determining the future role of Quechua in the face of Spanish as a language of economy (see also Mayer et al. this vol.). My own research amongst Indigenous and non-Indigenous New Zealanders (Albury 2016) revealed ideological enthusiasm, shared by Indigenous and non-Indigenous youths alike, for Māori language revitalization. Fostering the language was seen as pivotal to postcolonial reconciliation, to naming the landscape authentically, and to the formation of a contemporary, quintessentially *Kiwi* identity. Nonetheless, the Māori language was also seen to hold limited instrumental value. In turn, these New Zealand youths offered attitudes that they are more inclined to study languages that are notionally "more useful", such as Mandarin or French, rather than partake in Māori language revitalization.

Language ideologies and attitudes can therefore regulate linguistic diversity at the macro and micro level. Spolsky (2004: 14) even describes community beliefs about language as "policy with the manager left out" because beliefs can – in the absence of any formal law or policy – nonetheless guide a raft of linguistic matters from who gets language rights and who does not, whether someone chooses to study another language and indeed which language, and what language is spoken to whom and in what situations. However, this also raises the pertinent question – one which in my experience muddles junior and senior researchers alike – of what in fact the difference is between language attitudes and ideologies. Applied linguistic literature is prone to using the terms interchangeably, and without necessarily clarifying the theoretical understandings they presuppose when applying these terms (Kroskrity 2004). Some scholars circumvent the dilemma of delineating them by instead capturing ideologies and attitudes collectively as language beliefs, and do so with the perspective that their delineation is perhaps unnecessary or impossible (Spolsky 2004; England 2017). I, however, feel that their delineation is necessary and possible for the purposes of robust scholarship in home language studies. This now becomes the focus of this chapter. What follows is my attempt to explain why that is so, beginning with a discussion of language ideology.

2 Language ideology

The field is awash with competing conceptualizations of what in fact amounts to a language ideology. What unites the different perspectives, however, is the premise that language ideologies are social constructions, that they are products of the human experience and its attempts to regulate social life, that they are shared by some collective, and that they provide a framework of biases about the linguistic world or some part of it. This framework then becomes a reference point for constructing discourses, ideas, dispositions and decisions about language.

Language ideology research has its genesis in the pioneering linguistic anthropological works of Hymes (1977) and of Blom and Gumperz (1972). At a time when their work was at the margins of both linguistics and of anthropology, they argued that local language practices and variation, as they manifest within speech communities, might be best understood through metalinguistic beliefs. Whereas theoretical linguists have rightly argued that languages are all equal, the social turn in linguistics would prove that social realities are more complex. Whether in societies, communities, or homes, beliefs about language – for example about how languages should be used, where they should be used, and their status – mean that different varieties and behaviours are perceived through social filters. They may index different socioeconomic standings or political affiliation, they may diverge from or conform to agreed linguistic norms, or they may challenge notions of ethnic belonging or national cohesion. Adding to this, Silverstein (1979: 193) offered the view that language ideologies are "sets of beliefs about language articulated by users as a rationalization or justification of perceived language structure and use".

It pays to note that a postmodern perspective might warn that ideology research unnecessarily essentializes beliefs and the groups of people deemed to hold these beliefs. Indeed, it is precarious to make definitive correlations between specific groups and specific beliefs, for example that all teachers of bilingual school X uphold ideology Y on multilingualism, or that family Z does or does not value bilingualism. In this regard, language ideology research runs the risk of deemphasizing individual agency – such as how dominant ideologies can be contested, negotiated, (re)interpreted or (re)articulated – in favour of consistency between beliefs and groups of people which would make for neat and tidy research. The question also arises as to what in fact constitutes a collective such that an ideology can be attributed to it. While it is clear that society or social groups may produce and share specific language ideologies, do smaller groups – such as households – also constitute a *collective* that can foster and execute its own ideologies or are they too small, as individual groups, for the purposes of robust ideology research? These questions remain unanswered and their treatment largely depends on individual research enterprises. This is not to say that ideology research is fraught with epistemological anxieties. It is important to be cognizant that language ideologies can exist in parallel and in competition within a given collective. It is also important to note that what constitutes a collective is open for negotiation, that within collectives there can be divergent or minority views, and that approaches to ideology research ought to be made explicit. On this last point, language ideology research can be largely seen as either descriptive or critical.

2.1 A descriptive orientation

A descriptive orientation to language ideology seeks to research, identify and understand the shared beliefs of some collective – where the collective is defined by the researcher – about how language arrangements ought to be and why the collective feels this way. Rumsey (1990: 346), for example, described language ideologies as "shared bodies of commonsense notions about the nature of language in the world". The starting point, as such, is the local contexts and belief systems that make sense of why communities feel and behave the way they do, as these help to contextualize and rationalize ideologies. This was exemplified in Sandel's (2003) work in Taiwan. There, dominant ideologies in the home vis-à-vis the relationship between Mandarin as the community's majority language and Hokkien as a home language were in part rationalized by public histories. Sandel's argument was that language ideologies about the relationship, as they manifested in actual family language practices, could be dialectically traced to different discourses and policies over time that had been sponsored by the Taiwanese government. This political history was essential background to understanding shared commonsense notions about language as they are held in the community and in homes.

For others, descriptive ideological research has especially focused on intersubjectivities within a community that need not be expressed, but nonetheless form an unspoken collective sociocognitive template for dealing with language. For example, Blommaert (2006: 510) defines a language ideology as "the unspoken assumptions that, as some kind of 'social cement', turn groups of people into communities, societies, and cultures". In other words, some beliefs about language are so normative that they need not attract metadiscourse, unless of course this normativity is somehow challenged. Schiffman (1996) speaks of *linguistic culture* as a conceptual tool which, for our purposes, can be considered a descriptive orientation to language ideology. Rather than analyzing language ideologies through epistemological lenses from the outside, researching *linguistic culture* means obtaining an emic view of the collective "ideas, values, beliefs, attitudes, prejudices, myths, religious strictures, and all other cultural 'baggage' that speakers bring to their dealings with language from their culture" (Schiffman 1996: 112). Schiffman's approach was inspired by his ethnographic work in India's Tamil Nadu. He discovered what he believed to be a linguistic culture that did not expect him as an outsider to learn spoken Tamil, and that any Tamil he did speak ought to have been of the formal written variety. So entrenched was this intersubjective belief that Schiffman was approached by local political leaders to cease his ethnographic research. Another item of baggage that can contribute to a *linguistic culture* is religion. From a theoretical linguistic perspective, little difference may be noticed between spoken Hindi, Urdu and Punjabi, but their delineation as separate languages is a local *fait accompli* on the basis of religion rather than linguistics. Whereas Hindi is associated with Hinduism and uses Devanagari script, Urdu is associated with Islam and uses Perso-Arabic script, and Punjabi is associated with Sikhism and uses Gurumukhi script (Schiffman 1996).

At this juncture, I have added folk linguistic knowledge to the mix of constituents that may contribute to language ideology (Albury 2017). The "unspoken assumptions", "social cement", "sets of beliefs about language", and "shared bodies of commonsense notions" that amount to language ideology – as noted above – can also include shared claims of knowledge. I take a Foucauldian view whereby knowledge is socially constructed – and not necessarily empirically reliable – and each instantiation of knowledge contributes to developing or challenging a regime of truth based in the values, beliefs, and world views (Foucault 1980). Language ideology can therefore comprise claims not only of what is desirable, but also of what is true and what is not true about the linguistic world, regardless of the accuracy of such claims. This is because it is discourses, rather than any preordained reality, that construct perceived truths. This especially matters, of course, when claimed knowledge is used to decide whether or not bilingualism is cognitively and socially beneficial, and how it should be managed in the home, in that claimed knowledge in linguistics may help determine whether a home language is at all transmitted (see also Purkarthofer this vol.). My argument is, therefore, that what is claimed by a collective to be true about the linguistic world warrants scholarly attention because this also guides local language discourses, ideas and language policy decisions. Placing local knowledge at the centre of ideology research is also postmodern in that it helps us to decolonize linguistics. It does not herald academic knowledge as a final authority, but validates local knowledge – as part of the human experience – as informing local truths and as guiding local realities. Under such thinking, the academy is not the only source of legitimate truths, if legitimacy is measured by local influence rather than academic qualification. In the case of non-western scholarship, it also helps us to transcend epistemological assumptions about language that may be covertly woven into our research. For example, Fishman (1990) offered pioneering theories about how to stop and reserve language shift in Indigenous communities. His lens did, however, harbour western values, including a direct relationship between language and identity and the ideological salience of literacy. These are being questioned in postmodern terms within emic-oriented language ideology work (cf. Romaine 2006). Placing local ideologies of language at the centre of local sociolinguistic research avoids colonizing local phenomena with epistemologically foreign interpretations and gives voice to knowledge paradigms that do not traditionally feature in mainstream scholarship.

With the preeminence of Western perspectives in sociolinguistics, an oft-described language ideology is the *monolingual assumption* (Cross 2011). The belief here is that individuals and societies – of which the United States is a popular example – are normatively monolingual, irrespective of actual linguistic diversity. Hence the joke "If a man who speaks three languages is trilingual and a man who speaks two languages is bilingual, what do you call a man who speaks only one language? American". Jokes aside, this ideology has been central to the formation of nation-states supported by the standardization of official languages. The genesis of such ideology is in modernism – with its interest in cohesion and uniformity – and in assumptions that ethnicity, language and statehood are directly correlated. Naturally, no state is monolingual in practice and the ideology attracts scholarly discussion. Transnationalism, migration and Indigenous activism mean that even in states that ideologically claim to be monolingual, multilingual realities are increasingly visible. Where homogeneity is challenged, the otherwise unscripted *monolingual assumption* manifests in debates about linguistic orders. In the case of northern Norway, Hiss (2013) discusses the panicked and seemingly racist discourses that emerged among some communities in Tromsø when their town was tagged to be included within the official Indigenous Sámi zone and therefore formally bilingual in recognition of Sámi as an official language. The taken-for-granted Norwegianness of Tromsø had, through political assembly, become open for debate. This created a stage for ideological debate about the linguistic future of Tromsø that harboured a *monolingual assumption* at its core.

In contrast, and in the spirit of looking beyond the West, I would argue that a *multilingual assumption* may be a pertinent ideology on the ground in societies where diversity is normative and where routinely drawing on different language varieties is unmarked. This has been the case in my research on sociolinguistic identities, practices and ideologies in multilingual and multicultural Malaysia (Albury 2018). For those living in a society that hosts only a slight Malay majority, a plethora of Chinese, Indian and Indigenous home languages, as well as prestige for English and Arabic for socioeconomic and religious purposes respectively, day-to-day communication is resourceful. It is defined by meaning-making and fluid multilingual behaviours akin to *translanguaging* (Li 2011). The resultant ideology, as it has especially been expressed by Malaysian youths, sees individual multilingualism as unmarked. Indeed, a Chinese-Malaysian university student I encountered in Penang was at pains to impress upon me the normativity of individual multilingualism in Malaysia and to contrast this with local ideologies in the West. She explained "it's like we are either a bilingual or multilingual, we are *not* monolingual". This is also the case in the Yanyuwa culture in Australia's Northern Territory, where husbands and wives speak different dialects but with a passive understanding of each other's variety (Bradley 2011). In India, daily lives may cross Hindi as a national language, English as a working language, and one or more local languages (Kalra 2017). *The monolingual assumption* can therefore be contrasted with the *multilingual assumption* of other societies.

2.2 A critical orientation

Language ideologies lend themselves not only to description but also to critique because they are sites of power negotiations between speakers on the basis of different languages and the perceived values they hold. A critical approach to language ideology is grounded in criticizing the sociolinguistic world for its inequalities, its injustices, and its systems of domination. For example, Moita-Lopes (2014) refers to Portuguese as an internationalized language and the principled need to reconstruct, for the purpose of late modernity, what *Portuguese* even means as a term and ideology. Doing so would be inclusive of identities, innovations and language changes from Latin America and to be critical of the Eurocentrism – and its implicit power relation embedded in a history of conquest and colonization – that is subsumed within *Portuguese* as a label applied to language realities in Brazil. The goal, in any critical orientation, is to identify such explicit or implicit inequalities and ultimately liberate the marginalized "from the circumstances that enslave them" (Horkheimer 1982: 244). A critical orientation therefore continues the legacy of the pioneering critical social theoretical work of the Frankfurt school (Martin 1996), of Foucault's (1980) concern for social stratifications, and of Bourdieu's (1991) notions of linguistic capital – and language as symbolic power – that advantages some and disadvantages others. Central to these approaches, for our purposes, is an understanding that certain languages come to hold – by virtue of social intervention – greater value or prestige than others (see also Liddicoat this vol.).

On this last point, critical language ideology research has now become widely premised in political economy (cf. Gal 1989; Ricento 2015; Piller and Cho 2013). Political economy is understood to be "the study of the social relations – particularly the power relations – that mutually constitute the production, distribution, and consumption of resources, including communication resources" (Mosco 2017: 13). The starting point is, as Muehlmann and Duchene (2007: 98) explain, that the "expansion of nation-state economies, and the simultaneous strengthening of the private sector, has also resulted in greater articulations between local, national, and supranational identities, as goods, people, and information begin moving across boundaries at a new pace". This has created a new world order, for those in capitalist democracies, that is typified by experiences of globalization including international connectivity through media, migration and liberalized economics. This means that local lives need not be only local, and that languages – and indeed linguistic diversity – become increasingly valorized – or devalorized in the case of home languages – in terms of their efficiency and place within the global order. Oftentimes this is to the detriment of smaller languages and their transmission in homes.

Political economy – especially capitalism, late modernity and neoliberalism – is therefore a framework for discovering and exposing linguistic hegemonies and inequalities subsequent to such valorization. Especially vocal, for example, are Skutnabb-Kangas and Phillipson (2010) who argue that globalization, and the worldwide spread of English that this encompasses, is killing off other languages. Controversially, they add that English and its speakers commit *linguistic genocide* and *linguistic imperialism*, such that globalization amounts not only to homogenization but also to the coordinated spread of Anglo-American culture. They fear that "the 'manifest destiny' that colonial Americans arrogated to themselves has been explicitly linked, since the early nineteenth century, to English being established globally" (Skutnabb-Kangas and Phillipson 2010: 80) and therefore to displacing other languages. Heller and Pavlenko (2010) also approach language ideology through political economy. They propose that the value of specific languages is tied to the linguistic marketplace in capitalist, neoliberal terms, and that this can devalue home languages and their use. For example, the instrumental value of English, but also of other majority languages that are seen to advance socioeconomic mobility, may overshadow the perceived value of home languages that afford less socioeconomic mobility. The concern then is that the world's smaller languages are denied capital, such that their very survival is unduly jeopardized. This creates a need to study language ideologies, vis-à-vis economics and the power relations they create between languages. While these discussions are typically framed in theoretical terms, the rubber hits the road in otherwise bilingual communities, schools and homes where the language of tradition becomes pitted against the language of economy and connectivity, and where parents seek to balance the transmission of culture and heritage with the perceived socioeconomic opportunity inherent to dominant languages.

Political economy therefore necessitates choice between some languages and others on economic lines, and in this respect the critical approach has offered vocabulary that is core to contemporary language ideology research. Two examples that are especially salient are the notion of *language hierarchies* and of *language prestige*, whereby a community attributes specific value or salience to a certain language or variety above others for cultural, economic or social reasons. This builds on seminal works on *diglossia* which sees varieties of a single language stratified for their high or low status (Ferguson 1959), and on the expansion of *diglossia* to include the relative roles and statues given to different languages in a multilingual society. Pervasive examples can be found in postcolonial societies where colonial languages have assumed power and prestige over Indigenous languages. New Zealand is a worthy example in that it is ideologically bicultural and bilingual in the interests of postcolonial reconciliation, but multicultural and multilingual in practice as a result of liberal immigration policy. English is hierarchized above minority languages, but a hierarchy of home languages also seemingly exists. Greater prestige is afforded to Māori as the Indigenous language of the islands, and less prestige to Pacific languages as immigrant languages (de Bres 2015). While prestige can be traced to histories, colonization, education departments and language laws, language ideology becomes especially dynamic in cases of *covert prestige*. Some languages or varieties may not enjoy official or high-culture status, but may be valued for expressing specific, potentially marginalized identities. This has been the case, for example, for Tunisian Arabic. Standard Arabic and French, with their high-status and correlations to religion and culture, generally hold *overt prestige* and occupy official domains. Nonetheless, Tunisian Arabic indexes Tunisian heritage and culture and has attracted a *covert prestige* for the expression of an in-group, quintessentially Tunisian, identity in the postcolonial pan-Islamic world (Stevens 1983; S'hiri 2002).

However, a problem with a political economic orientation to critical language ideology is that it is often applied when analyzing language in a global context with global dynamism. Doing so, however, assumes the operation of free markets or uncensored digital mobility. These, as elements of a new world order, are often taken to be a reality for all. This is not the case for language users outside the reach of competitive capitalism. North Korea is as an obvious example of a closed market with little domestic exposure to English through a transnational economy, meaning the ubiquity of English as ideology and practice, and the alarmist discourse this might entail, hold less clout. In a different example, Iran heavily censors access to digital platforms that represent globalization, such as Facebook and YouTube, meaning contemporary understandings of language practices as increasingly networked and transnational through the affordance of connectivity in technology can be problematized. Instead, linguistic capital and political economy in North Korea and Iran have more domestic orientations than the more internationalized orientations of linguistic capital and political economy in, for example, Europe or North America. As a theoretical presupposition, political economy may therefore be primarily valuable when critiquing language arrangements in free, capitalist environments where languages indeed function as transnational commodities in transnational spaces. What is more, language contact studies show us that political economy is not qualified, in epistemological and cultural terms, to critique all local language arrangements. In the Amazon and in Indigenous Australia, for example, linguistic diversity is in some communities more strongly regulated by cultures of exogamy (Epps 2005) than by economics. Because a critical orientation to language ideology is oriented in exposing and rectifying inequalities, it also presupposes egalitarianism as a social ideal, democracy as a necessary goal, and ethnic rights as a universal value. These are, however, anti-structuralist ideas from the West and not necessarily ones valued in non-Western cultures (Irvine and Gal 2000). We must therefore be cautious in universally applying critical theory in language ideology research. For example, linguistic egalitarianism as a manifestation of multicultural policy is a political, social and economic value in Singapore whereby Malay, Mandarin and Tamil are afforded equal status. In neighbouring Malaysia, which hosts a similar diversity, local political culture has hierarchized race and language under a system of ethnocratic pluralism. There, Malay language and culture are codified as definitive of Malaysia within an ideology that constructs local citizens of Chinese and Indian ancestry as disloyal visitors. A critical orientation to language ideology may wish to criticize Malaysia, but it would do so by presupposing Western values are well-placed to criticize Malaysian values.

The critical approach, and its emphasis on linguistic equality, also tends to assume that personal and collective identities are intrinsically related to language. In practice, however, this relationship is complex rather than a *fait accompli*, and demands critical problematization in itself (cf. May 2000). For example, my research (Albury 2016) in New Zealand suggests that a direct ideological correlation between language and ethnic identity, as is familiar to European societies, may not exist or is at least contestable in the case of Māori. This seems entirely plausible if we agree that identity is relational and we know that beyond dialectal differences, Māori New Zealanders were monolingual prior to the arrival of the British. Instead, Māori sooner identify across tribes in respect to the landscape and ancestry. Language plays a backseat role to other values in identity formation. This all means that applying critical theory outside the cultures from which it epistemologically evolved may at best overlook local value systems, or at worst advance western academic imperialism. This is not to undo the value of critical approaches, but instead to be reflective that critical theory epistemologically biases a western-centric world view.

Other salient notions in language ideology are the *standard language* and *linguistic purism*. Specific language varieties can be codified as the official language of the state, and their grammars, lexica and orthographies are managed centrally. In turn, a collective comes to endorse that variety as normative and correct, including potentially within homes and schools, such that non-conforming behaviours become marked as incorrect or undesirable. In France, standard French was heralded as vital to fostering national cohesion, while divergent practices were seen to threaten unity (Spolsky 2004). In communities that have seen language shift – for example in diaspora communities or Indigenous societies that suffered colonization – language maintenance is often marked by purism in the pursuit of self-determination and the restoration of what was lost (Dorian 1994). As language ideologies, *standard languages* and *linguistic purism* may primarily be the domain of sociolinguists concerned with intra-language behaviours rather than with multilingualism per se. However, their impacts can be detrimental on home languages undergoing revitalization in homes. Zuckermann and Walsh (2011), for example, call on Indigenous communities undertaking language revitalization to embrace rather than reject the hybrid linguistic practices of Indigenous language learners for the sake of language maintenance. Their point is that purism and standards constrict revitalization by ignoring natural language change, interferences that are common to second language acquisition, and the anxieties that purist discourses can inspire.

Not adhering to expected linguistic norms is known to result in *linguistic discrimination* (see also Annamalai and Skuttnab-Kangas this vol.). Rickford and King (2016) offer a compelling analysis of linguistic discrimination under America's standard language ideology. This, they found, can even impede the criminal justice system, as was the case of Jeantel, a witness to a murder trial. She gave evidence in non-standard English, but doing so led the court to deem her evidence unreliable. Her home language was, it was decided, unfit for civil purposes. The standard language ideology was such that it marginalized Jeantel, by way of negative attitudes towards her language, in a domain where equality and justice are supposedly core pursuits. In this situation, language ideology manifested into associated attitudes. This calls on us to also consider what amounts to language attitude and how this is, or is not, different to language ideology.

3 Language attitudes

In our daily lives we confront attitudes, as they are expressed by those connected to us physically and virtually, to various social matters including language. Log on to the Australian franchise of *Student Flights*, and one sees the company's provocative language attitudes woven into its destination marketing. "What's that? You speak French? Excuse me while I remove my pants. The votes are in and it's unanimous: French is the sexiest language in the history of ever". For the same website Russian, on the other hand, is apparently "quite an impressive purr of linguistic chaos. Someone once described Russian speech as existing somewhere between the roar of a walrus and a Brahms lullaby. Sounds about right" (Rigg 2013).

Attitudes are, therefore, subjective. They come to sociolinguistics from social psychology, whereas language ideology scholarship finds its genesis in anthropology. Reliable working definitions of attitude include that it is a "psychological tendency that is expressed by evaluating a particular entity with some degree of favor or disfavor" (Eagly and Chaiken 1993: 1), and that attitude is "a disposition to react favorably or unfavorably to a class of objects" (Sarnoff 1970: 279). In the examples above, the perceived sexiness of French is favourable, whereas the attractiveness of Russian is dubious. However, social psychological responses to linguistic diversity need not only concern specific languages per se. Attitudes may be formed, for example, in respect to a language policy (Baker 2006). In Catalonia, González-Riaño et al. (2019) found that youths seemingly held more positive attitudes towards Catalan than their parents who were more likely to hold positive attitudes towards Spanish. This speaks not only to the support of the younger generation for Catalan language maintenance, but no doubt also to broader sociopolitical biases in the context of Catalan's vexed political situation. In the case of Morocco, Marley (2004) found positive attitudes to French/Arabic bilingual education with the view that these attitudes contributed to the success of that language policy and the maintenance of both languages in Moroccan society. In such cases, attitudes become especially pertinent, and indeed influential in the actual realization of societal multilingualism in places undergoing social and political transformation. In post-Hong Kong, the vexed relationship between Cantonese and Mandarin synonymizes competing political interests under the gradual handover of Hong Kong to China (cf. Lai 2011). Attitudes to the use of Mandarin or Cantonese can be seen as indexing attitudes to Hong Kong's political future, whereby Beijing allegedly supports Hong Kong shifting to Mandarin while most Hong Kong homes remain fervently Cantonese. Attitudes might also form in respect to multilingualism in itself. My work in Malaysia (Albury 2018) has, for example, uncovered attitudes to the multilingual linguistic landscape, linguistic diversity in Malaysian homes and schools, and even to multilingualism as a cognitive phenomenon. These attitudes contributed to the construction of discourses that supported, questioned, or discouraged the maintenance of local diversities. It is through this relationship between attitudes and discourse that attitudinal research is firmly part of the sociolinguistic research enterprise.

Whereas ideologies provide a blueprint for sociolinguistic ideas and behaviours, language attitudes only ever evaluate a specific phenomenon or occurrence. That is to say, language ideologies are a socially-constructed reference point for how things ought to function in society, whereas language attitudes are an evaluation of whether, in what way, and to what extent, a specific language, language practice, or other language matter, is favourable. For example, the *monolingual assumption* discussed earlier may presuppose the normativity of individual and social multilingualism. An attitude, on the other hand, is a person's dispositional reaction to a specific stimulus. Imagine the stimulus is, for example, the use of more than one language in society in a place where the *monolingual assumption* reigns. An associated attitude, held by a person who subscribes to the monolingual assumption, may be that multilingual practices in a specific context or domain are undesirable. Depending on who holds this view, this attitude can influence the maintenance or not of bilingualism in local contexts. In this regard, it could be argued that ideologies tend to be ill-defined whereas attitudes may be more definable. This is because ideologies are typically unmarked and subject to social construction whereas attitudes are dispositions vis-à-vis defined stimuli.

Language attitude research attracts both quantitative and qualitative approaches. Ideological research on the other hand is fundamentally qualitative – making use of discoursal and pragmatic analysis – to the exception of quantitative tools, such as corpus analysis, that help to locate and quantify ideology-laden discourse in texts. Classic attitudinal work is quantitative by tasking participants to rate their levels of agreement to specific notions which serve as stimuli for soliciting a language attitude. This was also the case in my research about the relationship between English and Māori in postcolonial New Zealand. Some 1,300 university students were asked to identify, on a five-point continuum from strongly disagree to strongly agree, how they felt about statements including "revitalising te reo Māori is a good thing, even if it costs time and money" and "it would be better if everyone in the country spoke one language in all situations" (Albury 2016). The total sum of responses would therefore provide a data set on attitudinal trends vis-à-vis these core policy topics. Other quantitative approaches may use a semantic differential scale, whereby participants rate to what extent they endorse certain evaluations of a specific linguistic matter. For example, the *matched guise technique* might ask participants to indicate how intelligent, attractive or kind a speaker is based on that speaker's speech in a specific language or accent (cf. Eisenchlas and Tsurutani 2011). The innovation is that attitudes to language are inferred through evaluations of a speaker, and this is controlled for by the participants also evaluating the speech of a local native speaker but not knowing that this is actually a bilingual who produces both examples.

In qualitative research, attitudes might be identified within discourse or conversational data as stances towards specific topics (Jaffe 2009) where participants use evaluative adjectives to describe specific phenomena or premise their statements as personal opinions. This was the case, for example, in Obojska's (2017) analysis of online metalinguistic talk among Polish teenagers in Norway whose discourses revealed various attitudes towards Polish as a heritage language and to Norwegian as the majority language, including feelings of linguistic shame and obligation that regulate participation in the different language groups, and even attitudes towards the language attitudes of others. It is also the case in research on discourses amongst Serbian users towards Cyrillic and Latin as Serbia's two co-official scripts. Attitudes include, on the one hand, that Cyrillic is valuable because it is intrinsically Orthodox and therefore Serbia's most authentic script, and on the other hand that Cyrillic is undesirable because it indexes Serbian ethnonationalism and conservatism (Jovanović 2018).

Like ideologies, attitudes can be described or be analyzed through a critical lens, but a core distinction is that attitudes need not be held by a collective whereas ideologies are shared beliefs. Attitudes can therefore be the phenomena of individuals and need not constitute shared "commonsense notions" (Rumsey 1990: 345). That is not to say that the same or a similar attitude cannot be shared. To the contrary, attitudes may be held by groups of people who share a world view and researching the prevalence of a particular attitude helps to take the "attitudinal temperature" of the public on specific language issues. The point, however, is that attitudes – with their genesis in psychology – are by definition evaluative dispositions constructed at the point of their expression.

To this extent, language attitudinal research is not without empirical problems. Because attitudes are immediate responses to specific stimuli, their cognitive nature means they may be better described as "an internal state of readiness" (Fasold 1984: 147) at a particular moment in time. These states of readiness may or may not be communicated in such a way they can always be accessed confidently, and may be subject to change. This also means that ideologies, as systematic belief systems that construct social cohesion, are more durable than attitudes. This is because attitudes may be informed by a wide variety of sources such as mood, motivation, individual understanding, ego and personality (Ajzen 2005). Attitudes can also be a logical by-product of what an individual believes to be true about the (socio)linguistic world, such that assumed knowledge becomes a resource for developing an attitude. For example, a pervasive attitude in New Zealand against making Māori language a compulsory subject in schools did not originate in any negative disposition towards the language. Instead, it originated in an assumption that the teacher workforce is too weak to support such policy implementation, entirely separate to matters of linguistics (Albury 2017). Taking an attitude at face value, without further investigation, risks misinterpreting social psychological data.

4 Conclusion: A nexus between language ideology and language attitudes?

So far this chapter has delineated attitudes from ideology for the purposes of home language research. However, the stage they share in sociolinguistics, their often interchangeable use, and their common interest in community perspectives, all imply that they are nonetheless related. The genesis of a specific attitude can indeed sometimes be traced to a systematic language ideology. This dialectical relationship has oftentimes been an empirical conclusion in my own research into discourses about linguistic diversity. Specifically, an individual's attitude may be the obvious articulation of an ideology to which the individual subscribes. For example, Figure 1 shows how that dialectal relationship has manifested within discourses about societal multilingualism in Malaysia. In the first example, a group of youths from the ethnic Malay majority were tasked to discuss the desirability of Malaysia – to which their own heritage language is indigenous – now being multilingual as a result of historic migrations. They were also asked to reflect on the intermittent calls being made by the

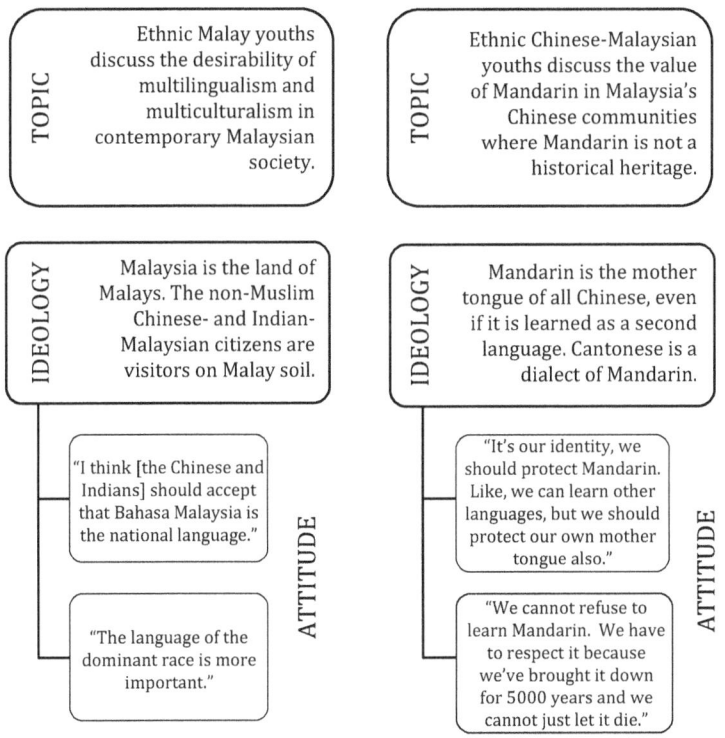

Figure 1: A dialectic relationship between language ideology and language attitudes.

Chinese and Indian minorities for linguistic rights. The second example concerns discussions amongst a group of ethnic Chinese-Malaysian youths about what role Mandarin should play in their community, given that Mandarin was not an historic heritage language brought to Malaysia through migration but is routinely studied as a second language. In both cases, Figure 1 gives examples of different attitudes expressed by individuals being consistent with the prevailing ideology that was identified within that group's discourse more broadly.

Just as commonly, however, ideologies and attitudes may be incongruent. An ideology of a collective may sooner be an idealized world view that does not translate into individual attitudes that advance that ideology. A recurring example of this incongruence results from what May (2014) might call a tension between the Local and the Global. Here, the premise is that in the context of globalization and neoliberalism – with their tendencies towards the homogenization of language and culture – ethnic groups may share a concern for the maintenance of their languages in local communities, schools and homes. However, individual attitudes towards actively participating in that ideology – such as by committing to heritage language learning or raising children bilingually – may be less enthusiastic. That is to say, one may subscribe to an ideology that is good for the collective but not to a congruent attitude if it is seen to place burdens on the individual. For example, research from Ireland shows that Irish holds high ideological value in constructing a sense of nationhood contextualized by memories of English rule. Nonetheless, attitudes to learning and using the language are oftentimes ambivalent, while attitudes to other European languages are positive by seeing them as instrumental and cosmopolitan (Atkinson and Kelly-Holmes 2016). The issue is that socioeconomic ambition and the utility associated with fluency in dominant cultures and languages demotivates individuals and families from committing to home languages. It can also be the case that other cognitive influences simply override the influence of any ideology that might encourage linguistic diversity. For example, the magnitude of linguistic anxiety, negative language learning experiences, or perceived aptitude may result in negative attitudes towards active participation in home language use, acquisition, revitalization or transmission (cf. Sevinç and Dewaele 2018; Sevinç this vol.) despite ideological support for home language development.

I therefore conclude with the view that a nexus between language ideology and language attitudes indeed exists, but it is a complex one that may be both dialectic and incongruent. My interpretation is that they are indeed related, but that how they diverge is as salient as their commonalities. They have different disciplinary and epistemological geneses and offer scholarship different – albeit related – theoretical and methodological concepts. It is therefore futile to seek to theorize attitudes and ideologies as in all cases harmoniously complementary. Nonetheless, and as long as language is seen as a social phenomenon, ideology and attitudes will remain essential concepts for investigating grassroots engagement with matters of linguistic diversity and the multitude of factors that guide the maintenance and development or not, of languages in the home.

References

Ajzen, Icek. 2005. *Attitudes, personality, and behavior*. Milton Keynes: Open University Press.
Albury, Nathan John. 2016. Defining Māori language revitalisation: A project in folk linguistics. *Journal of Sociolinguistics* 20(3). 287–311.
Albury, Nathan John. 2017. The power of folk linguistic knowledge in language policy. *Language Policy* 16(2). 209–228.
Albury, Nathan John. 2018. Multilingualism and mobility as collateral results of hegemonic language policy. *Applied Linguistics*. 1–27. Online First. DOI: https://doi.org/10.1093/applin/amy054
Annamalai, E. & Tove Skutnabb-Kangas. this vol. Social justice and inclusiveness through linguistic human rights in education.
Atkinson, David & Helen Kelly-Holmes. 2016. Exploring language attitudes and ideologies in university students' discussion of Irish in a context of increasing language diversity. *Language and Intercultural Communication* 16(2). 199–215.
Baker, Colin. 2006. Psycho-sociological analysis in language policy. In Thomas Ricento (ed.), *An introduction to language policy: Theory and method*, 210–228. Malden, MA: Blackwell.
Blom, Jan-Petter & John Gumperz. 1972. Social meaning in linguistic structures: Code switching in Norway. In John Gumperz & Dell Hymes (eds.), *Directions in sociolinguistics*, 407–434. Holt: Rinehart & Winston.
Blommaert, Jan. 2006. Language ideology. In Keith Brown (ed.), *Encyclopedia of language & linguistics*, 510–522. 2nd edn. Amsterdam: Elsevier.
Bourdieu, Pierre. 1991. *Language and symbolic power*. Cambridge: Harvard University Press.
Bradley, John. 2011. Yanyuwa: "Men speak one way, women speak another". In Jennifer Coathes & Pia Pichler (eds.), *Language and Gender: A Reader*, 13–20. Malden, MA: Wiley-Blackwell.
Cross, Russell. 2011. Troubling literacy: Monolingual assumptions, multilingual contexts, and language teacher expertise. *Teachers and Teaching* 17(4). 467–478.
De Bres, Julia. 2015. The hierarchy of minority languages in New Zealand. *Journal of Multilingual and Multicultural Development* 36(7). 677–693.
Dorian, Nancy C. 1994. Purism vs. compromise in language revitalization and language revival. *Language in Society* 23(4). 479–494.
Eagly, Alice H. & Shelly Chaiken. 1993. *The psychology of attitudes*. Fort Worth, TX: Harcourt Brace Jovanovich College Publishers.
Eisenchlas, Susana A. & Chiharu Tsurutani. 2011. You sound attractive! Perceptions of accented English in a multi-lingual environment. *Australian Review of Applied Linguistics* 34(2). 216–236.
England, Neil. 2017. Developing an interpretation of collective beliefs in language teacher cognition research. *TESOL Quarterly* 51(1). 229–238.
Epps, Patience. 2005. Areal diffusion and the development of evidentiality: Evidence from Hup. *Studies in Language. International Journal sponsored by the Foundation "Foundations of Language"* 29(3). 617–650.
Fasold, Ralph. 1984. *The sociolinguistics of society*. Oxford: Blackwell.
Ferguson, Charles A. 1959. Diglossia. *Word* 15(2). 325–340.
Fishman, Joshua A. 1990. What is reversing language shift (RLS) and how can it succeed? *Journal of Multilingual and Multicultural Development* 11(1&2). 5–36.
Foucault, Michel. 1980. *Power/knowledge: Selected interviews and other writings, 1972–1977*. Brighton: Pantheon.
Gal, Susan. 1989. Language and political economy. *Annual Review of Anthropology* 18(1). 345–367.

González-Riaño, Xosé Antón, Alberto Fernández-Costales, Cecilio Lapresta-Rey & Ángel Huguet. 2019. Language attitudes towards Spanish and Catalan in autochthonous and immigrant families in Catalonia: Analysing the correlation between student attitudes and their parents'. *International Journal of Bilingual Education and Bilingualism* 22(6). 754–767.

Heller, Monica & Aneta Pavlenko. 2010. Bilingualism and multilingualism. In Jürgen Jaspers, Jan-Ola Ostman & Jef Verschueren (eds.), *Society and language use*, 71–83. Amsterdam & Philadelphia: John Benjamins.

Hilmarsson-Dunn, Amanda & Ari Páll Kristinsson. 2010. The language situation in Iceland. *Current Issues in Language Planning* 11(3). 207–276.

Hiss, Florian. 2013. Tromsø as a "Sámi Town"? – Language ideologies, attitudes, and debates surrounding bilingual language policies. *Language Policy* 12(2). 177–196.

Horkheimer, M. 1982. *Critical theory*. New York: Seabury Press.

Hornberger, Nancy. 1988. Language ideology in Quechua communities of Puno, Peru. *Anthropological Linguistics* 30(2). 214–235.

Hymes, Dell. 1962. The ethnography of speaking. In Thomas F. Gladwin & William C. Sturtevant (eds.), *Anthropology and Human Behavior*, 3–53. Washington D.C.: Anthropological Society of Washington.

Hymes, Dell. 1972. Models of the interaction of language and social life. In John Gumperz & Dell Hymes (eds.), *Directions in sociolinguistics: The ethnography of communication*, 35–71. New York: Holt, Rinehart & Winston.

Hymes, Dell. 1977. Discovering oral performance and measured verse in American Indian narrative. *New Literary History* 8(3). 431–457.

Irvine, Judith T. & Susan Gal. 2000. Language ideology and linguistic differentiation. In Paul V. Kroskrity (ed.), *Regimes of language: Ideologies, polities, and identities*, 35–83. Santa Fe: School of American Research Press.

Jaffe, Alexandra. 2009. Introduction: The sociolinguistics of stance. In Alexandra Jaffe (ed.), *Stance: Sociolinguistic perspectives*, 3–28. New York: Oxford University Press.

Jónsdóttir, Elsa S. & Hanna Ragnarsdóttir. 2010. Multicultural education in Iceland: Vision or reality? *Intercultural Education* 21(2). 153–167.

Jovanović, Srđan M. 2018. Assertive discourse and folk linguistics: Serbian nationalist discourse about the cyrillic script in the 21st century. *Language Policy* 17(4). 611–631.

Kalra, Mani Bhasin. 2017. Preserving heritage languages through schooling in India. In Peter Perciles Trifonas & Themistoklis Aravossitas (eds.), *Handbook of research and practice in heritage language education*, 1–18. Cham: Springer.

Kroskrity, Paul V. 2004. Language ideologies. In Alessandro Duranti (ed.), *A companion to linguistic anthropology*, 496–517. Oxford: Blackwell.

Labov, William. 1966. *The social significance of speech in New York City*. Washington, DC: Center for Applied Lingusitics.

Lai, Mee Ling. 2011. Cultural identity and language attitudes – into the second decade of postcolonial Hong Kong. *Journal of Multilingual and Multicultural Development* 32(3). 249–264.

Lambert, Wallace E. 1967. A social psychology of bilingualism. *Journal of Social Issues* 23(2). 91–109.

Lambert, Wallace E., Richard C. Hodgson, Robert C. Gardner & Samuel Fillenbaum. 1960. Evaluational reactions to spoken languages. *The Journal of Abnormal and Social Psychology* 60(1). 44.

Li, Wei. 2011. Moment Analysis and translanguaging space: Discursive construction of identities by multilingual Chinese youth in Britain. *Journal of Pragmatics* 43(5). 1222–1235.

Liddicoat, Anthony J. this vol. Language policy and planning for language maintenance: The macro and meso levels.

Marley, Dawn. 2004. Language attitudes in Morocco following recent changes in language policy. *Language Policy* 3(1). 25–46.

Martin, Jay. 1996. *The dialectical imagination: A history of the Frankfurt School and the Institute of Social Research 1923–1950*. Vol. 10. Berkley, Los Angeles: University of California Press.

May, Stephen. 2000. Uncommon languages: The challenges and possibilities of minority language rights. *Journal of Multilingual and Multicultural Development* 21(5). 366–385.

May, Stephen. 2014. Justifying educational language rights. *Review of Research in Education* 38(1). 215–241.

Mayer, Elisabeth, Liliana Sánchez, José Camacho & Carolina Rodríguez Alzza. this vol. The drivers of home language maintenance and development in indigenous communities.

Moita-Lopes, Luiz P. 2014. Introduction: Linguistic ideology: How Portuguese is being discursively constructed in late modernity. In Luiz P. Moita-Lopes (ed.), *Global Portuguese: Linguistic ideologies in late modernity*, 1–26. New York: Routledge.

Mosco, Vincent. 2017. Political economy. In Toby Miller (ed.), *The Routledge companion to global popular culture*, 13–22. New York & London: Routledge.

Muehlmann, Shaylih & Alexandre Duchêne. 2007. Beyond the nation-state: International agencies as new sites of discourses on bilingualism. In Monica Heller (ed.), *Bilingualism: A social approach*, 96–110. London: Palgrave Macmillan.

Obojska, Maria A. 2017. "Are you so ashamed to come from Poland and to speak your mother tongue?" – Metalinguistic talk, identities and language ideologies in teenagers' interactions on ASKfm. *Multilingual Margins* 4(1). 27–39.

Piller, Ingrid & Jinhyun Cho. 2013. Neoliberalism as language policy. *Language in Society* 42(1). 23–44.

Purkarthofer, Judith. this vol. Intergenerational challenges: Of handing down languages, passing on practices, and bringing multilingual speakers into being.

Ricento, Thomas. 2015. Political economy and English as a "global" language. In Thomas Ricento (ed.), *Language policy and political economy: English in a global context*, 27–47. Oxford & New York: Oxford University Press.

Rickford, John R. & Sharese King. 2016. Language and linguistics on trial: Hearing Rachel Jeantel (and other vernacular speakers) in the courtroom and beyond. *Language* 92(4). 948–988.

Rigg, Ashton. 2013. The world's sexiest languages. https://www.studentflights.com.au/travel-mag/2013/04/the-worlds-sexiest-languages (accessed 24 April 2019).

Romaine, Suzanne. 2006. Planning for the survival of linguistic diversity. *Language Policy* 5(4). 443–475.

Rumsey, Alan. 1990. Wording, meaning, and linguistic ideology. *American Anthropologist* 92(2). 346–361.

S'hiri, Sonia. 2002. Speak Arabic please!: Tunisian Arabic speakers' linguistic accommodation to Middle Easterners. In Aleya Rouchdy (ed.), *Language contact and language conflict in Arabic: Variations on a sociolinguistic theme*, 149–176. New York & London: Routledge.

Sandel, Todd L. 2003. Linguistic capital in Taiwan: The KMT's Mandarin language policy and its perceived impact on language practices of bilingual Mandarin and Tai-gi speakers. *Language in Society* 32(4). 523–551.

Sarnoff, Irving. 1970. Social attitudes and the resolution of motivational conflict. In Marie Jahodaand and Neil Warren (eds.), *Attitudes*, 279–284. Harmondsworth: Penguin.

Schiffman, Harold. 1996. *Linguistic culture and language policy*. London: Routledge.

Sevinç, Yeşim. this vol. Anxiety as a negative emotion in home language maintenance and development.

Sevinç, Yeşim & Jean-Marc Dewaele. 2016. Heritage language anxiety and majority language anxiety among Turkish immigrants in the Netherlands. *International Journal of Bilingualism* 22 (2). 159–179.

Silverstein, Michael. 1979. Language structure and linguistic ideology. In Paul Clyne, William Hanks & Carol Hofbauer (eds.), *The elements*, 193–248. Chicago: Chicago Linguistic Society.

Silverstein, Michael. 1985. Language and the culture of gender. In Elizabeth Mertz & Richard Parmentier (eds.), *Semiotic mediation*, 219–259. Academic Press.

Skutnabb-Kangas, Tove & Robert Phillipson. 2010. The global politics of language: Markets, maintenance, marginalization, or murder? In Nicholas Coupland (ed.), *The handbook of language and globalization*, 77–100. Malden, MA: Wiley-Blackwell.

Spolsky, Bernard. 2004. *Language policy*. Cambrige: Cambridge University Press.

Stevens, Paul B. 1983. Ambivalence, modernisation and language attitudes: French and Arabic in Tunisia. *Journal of Multilingual and Multicultural Development* 4(2–3). 101–114.

Zuckermann, Ghil'ad & Michael Walsh. 2011. Stop, revive, survive: Lessons from the Hebrew revival applicable to the reclamation, maintenance and empowerment of Aboriginal languages and cultures. *Australian Journal of Linguistics* 31(1). 111–127.

E. Annamalai and Tove Skutnabb-Kangas

19 Social justice and inclusiveness through linguistic human rights in education

> Deprivation of access to quality education is a major factor contributing towards their [indigenous peoples'] social marginalisation, poverty and dispossession.
> (John Henriksen, Chairperson-Rapporteur, UN Expert Mechanism on the rights of indigenous peoples, Henriksen 2009: 10)

> Worldwide, minority children suffer disproportionately from unequal access to quality education. Disadvantaged minorities are far more likely to receive an inferior education than a good one. Disadvantaged minority children are more likely to start school later than the prescribed age, if at all; they are less likely to be ready or well prepared for school; and more prone to drop out or fail to achieve in school. That perpetuates the cycle of poverty, leaving them unable to later fulfil their human potential, to gain meaningful employment and to become respected members of society.
> (Gay McDougall, UN Independent Expert on Minority Issues, McDougall 2009: 7)

1 Introduction: The foundations for social justice and inclusion of the powerless

In this chapter, we will, after a more general introduction to social justice and inclusion of the marginalised, mainly concentrate on educational inequality, because schools are the microcosm of the unjust society; they are the handmaiden of the powerful to maintain their dominance. Educational inequality and discrimination will be presented in relation to the language of instruction in several ways. After this introduction, we consider the following questions: In section 2, we ask what rights people whose first language is not the society's dominant language have in human rights law? Are these rights implemented? In the following section 3, we ask what the role of mother tongues is in education, and what should be done if we follow results from large-scale educational research. In section 4, we compare educational models, showing which ones achieve positive results; it will be clear from Table 1 what some of the central characteristics of the "positive" programs are. Finally, in section 5, we discuss some of the challenges in trying to reach social justice through linguistic human rights in education.

Thinking of the role of education in the inclusion or marginalisation of people, it is axiomatic that justice is a prerequisite for peace and there will be no peace and justice without the inclusion of the powerless; they have to be able to participate on equal terms in the economic, social, political, cultural and educational domains of a nation. Denial of participation on equal terms entrenches inequality in all of the above domains. It engenders violence, physical and psychological, in the relationship between different people. It causes marginalisation of some people, which fences them off from resources and destroys their sense of belonging. A recent United Nations Development Programme (2017; referred to in Deen 2018) report, drawing from extensive empirical analysis, shows that marginalisation is one of the main factors that drive young people in many nations into subscribing to the ideology of violence to solve problems and into taking direct action through violent means. Most of the nations in the world are multi-ethnic and multi-lingual, though they may have different policies in relation to their approach to plurality; they may thus have different perceptions of nationhood. A nation is a state whose citizens share and defend voluntarily the idea of belonging to it in spite of their historical, ethnic and linguistic differences. Such a nation may at a given point in time be in the making, it may be developing from a colony, or it may have been a political formation at an earlier point in time. A just and equitable policy about the ethnic and linguistic differences is one of the cornerstones in building a nation that ensures participation on equal terms for all citizens and, consequently, equal justice. This is social justice, which offsets any historical denial of opportunities. This is what will produce an inclusive nation.

When equal participation is denied for reasons of ethnic and linguistic differences to perpetuate the existing power structure (an example of ethnicism and linguicism), those excluded become the marginalised people who do not have control over their lives. They could be referred to by the term minorities in the sense that they are non-dominant people. People can be marginalised by many other ascriptions as well such as religion, gender, sexual orientation, disability, the amount of formal education or lack of it, etc., but the various kinds of marginalisation need to be treated separately. The term "minority" does not have any official legal definition. But the term includes people marginalised by their historical origin, by their place in technological advancement and/or by their smaller number. We refer to them as ITMs; this stands for **I**ndigenous (such as the Saami in the Nordic countries) / **T**ribal (such as Gond in India) peoples / **M**inority groups (this includes autochthonous, national, immigrant and refugee minorities, the differently abled, and the minoritised/marginalised). The last two are not absolute terms. They refer to people in relation to other people in a power structure. They are appropriately called minoritised people, as "minoritised" carries the semantics of transitivity. They are marginalised by someone denying them agency. This understanding of ITMs as a product of an economic and political process, rather than an independently standing entity, will explain the fact that marginalisation is relative: One people or group, who are marginalised or minoritised in one context of power structure, may be marginalising or minoritising others in another context of power structure. Groups or languages, which have dominant status in a national context, may lack dominance in an international context; those which have dominant status in the regional context of a state or province may lack it in the national context (Mohanty 2019). To give an example, Hindi, being one of the two official languages of India, is a dominant language in the Indian national context of multiple languages, but not in the international context (though Hindi has more speakers than many so-called international languages). Tamil, the sole official language in the state of Tamil Nadu, is dominant in relation to speakers of other languages in the state, but it is not dominant in relation to other languages in the Indian national context. The ITM languages in general do not have a dominant status in any context of a nation; their non-dominant status does not shift in relational terms.

A people which is numerically smaller (thus a demographic minority) may still be dominant because of historical, political, educational and economic reasons. People numerically in the majority are non-dominant in this case. Two different examples of this could be Russian speakers in Estonia, Latvia and Lithuania in the former Soviet Union, or English speakers in many African countries, both during colonisation and after political decolonisation. In ITM the "M" thus also includes such minoritised populations along with demographic minority populations. Inclusiveness in their case with regard to proportional representation in the political structure demands additional attention that largely lies outside the domain of education and requires a democratic polity. Inclusiveness of all in the polity is the means of ensuring that the proportional representation does not tilt dominance in favour of one group over others. Formal education can be and often is one important means of continuing the exclusion of the minoritised people/s. It can also support the means of starting to break the exclusion and enable the marginalised to start or continue the struggle towards social justice. One way of including the excluded is to refer to their legal rights, which is what the next section addresses. Often the powerless are not aware of which rights they may have in national laws or international human rights law; therefore the legal aspect, especially in education, is crucial.

2 Legal foundations

2.1 General and ITM-specific international instruments

While education can be one of the most important means to ensure social justice and inclusion for the powerless, most importantly for the ITMs, there must be a legal foundation[1] to demand rights to education that supports this justice and inclusion at the national and international levels (see UN OHCHR 2018).[2] Therefore we

---

[1] The section *Legal foundations* is to a large extent based on an updated version of Skutnabb-Kangas and Dunbar (2010).
[2] See *Universal Human Rights Index* (https://uhri.ohchr.org), *United Nations Human Rights Treaties* (http://www.bayefsky.com), *Indigenous Peoples' Rights Database* (https://www.chr.up.ac.za/chr_old/indigenous/), and University of Minnesota *Human Rights Library* (http://hrlibrary.umn.edu) for some of the links to human rights documents.

will describe the most important international and regional instruments (legal documents) that grant educational and linguistic rights. The literature about them is vast (see Skutnabb-Kangas and Phillipson's [2017] four edited volumes, *Language Rights*). The various international instruments described here, from different political contexts and pressure groups but with the same goals, work for equity and human rights.

The principle of non-discrimination in both the International Covenant on Economic, Social and Cultural Rights[3] and the Convention on the Rights of the Child,[4] guarantees the right to education for all, thus including ITMs. The *Convention on the Rights of the Child* further stipulates:

1. States Parties recognize the right of the child to education, and with a view to achieving this right progressively and *on the basis of equal opportunity*, they shall, in particular:
   (a) Make primary education compulsory and available free to all;
   [...]
   (e) Take measures to encourage regular attendance at schools and the reduction of drop-out rates.
   (*Convention on the Rights of the Child*, Article 28, paragraph 1, emphasis added)

Article 29 of the *Convention on the Rights of the Child* expands on the basic right to education by stipulating:

1. States Parties agree that the education of the child shall be directed to:
   (a) The development of the child's personality, talents and mental and physical abilities to their fullest potential;
   (b) The development of respect for human rights and fundamental freedoms, and for the principles enshrined in the Charter of the United Nations;
   (c) The development of respect for the child's parents, his or her own cultural identity, language and values, for the national values of the country in which the child is living, the country from which he or she may originate, and for civilizations different from his or her own;
   (d) The preparation of the child for responsible life in a free society, in the spirit of understanding, peace, tolerance, equality of the sexes [a reference not found in the other instruments], and friendship among all peoples, ethnic, national and religious groups *and persons of indigenous origin* [a reference not found in the other instruments, and a very significant one for our purposes; emphasis added];

---

3 ICESCR (https://www.ohchr.org/EN/ProfessionalInterest/Pages/CESCR.aspx); Article 13.
4 CRC (https://www.unicef.org/child-rights-convention/convention-text); Article 28, paragraph 1.

(e) The development of respect for the natural environment [a reference important in relation to the correlational and causal relationship between biodiversity and linguistic and cultural diversity].[5]

Article 30 of the *Convention on the Rights of the Child* makes specific reference to minority and Indigenous children; drawing considerably on Article 27 of the 1966 United Nations *International Covenant on Civil and Political Rights* (ICCPR) – the well-known "minorities" provision – this Article provides as follows:

> In those States in which ethnic, religious or linguistic minorities or persons of indigenous origin exist, a child belonging to such a minority or who is indigenous shall not be denied the right, in community with other members of his or her group, to enjoy his or her own culture, to profess and practice his or her own religion, *or to use his or her own language.*[6] [emphasis added]

In such international instruments (and the regional ones below), every word is important from a legal point of view. Their interpretations fill thousands of pages; the short generalization of these resolutions is that still much more is needed, and implementation of many of the rights leaves much to desire (Skutnabb-Kangas, Phillipson, and Dunbar [2019] call them "criminally inadequate"). Many more court cases than at present are needed to force states to implement what they have signed and ratified.

2.2 Regional instruments

The right to education is also recognized in a number of important regional human rights treaties. For example, Article 2 of the First Optional Protocol of 1952 to the Council of Europe's *Convention for the Protection of Human Rights and Fundamental Freedoms* of 1950 (the *European Convention on Human Rights*, or the "ECHR")[7] provides that "no person shall be denied the right to education", and that the State shall respect the right of parents to ensure that such education and teaching is in conformity with their own religious and philosophical convictions. The right to education is expressed even more categorically than in these European instruments in Article 17 of the *African Charter on Human and Peoples' Rights* of 1981 (the "African Charter")[8]. Its paragraph 1

---

5 See https://www.Terralingua.org; Skutnabb-Kangas and Harmon (2018).
6 Although not specifically directed to education, Article 17 of the *Convention on the Rights of the Child* requires States to "ensure that the child has access to information and material from a diversity of national and international sources, especially those aimed at the promotion of his or her social, spiritual and moral well-being and physical and mental health". It further mentions in (d) a "particular regard to the *linguistic needs of the child who belongs to a minority group or who is indigenous*" [emphasis added].
7 http://conventions.coe.int/treaty/en/Treaties/Html/005.htm
8 http://www.hrcr.org/docs/Banjul/afrhr.html

simply states that every individual shall have the right to education. But in an African context, this basic right is expanded upon in Article 11 of the *African Charter on the Rights and Welfare of the Child* of 1990,[9] which is generally similar to Article 13 of the ICESCR.[10] So, too, is Article 13 of the *Additional Protocol to the American Convention on Human Rights*.[11,12]

In addition to the right to education, many minorities and Indigenous peoples could benefit from additional education rights developed in a range of minority- and Indigenous peoples-specific international instruments. It is important to recognise that Indigenous and tribal peoples benefit from provisions directed at minorities as well as those which are specifically directed at them. It should also be noted, however, that many of the most important minority-specific instruments have been developed in a European context with application primarily to European states. There are relatively few Indigenous peoples in the European states (depending, of course, on how Europe is defined; some "European" instruments also include Russia; see, e.g. Zamyatin 2014, 2016a,b).

The most important of the Indigenous and tribal peoples-specific instruments, the International Labour Organisation's *ILO Convention No. 169* of 1989[13] and the United Nations' General Assembly *Declaration on the Rights of Indigenous Peoples* ("UNDRIP") of 7 September, 2007, are both global in scope, but both suffer from certain limitations: ILO Convention No. 169, as a treaty, creates binding legal obligations for those States which ratify it, but thus far, only 23 states have done so.[14]

While the UNDRIP received very broad support within the UN General Assembly, such support was not universal.[15] Further, as a General Assembly *declaration*, it does

---

9 http://www.africa-union.org/child/home.htm
10 Among the provisions which are not found in Article 13 of the ICESCR but which are found in Article 11 of the *African Charter on the Rights and Welfare of the Child* are that the education of the child shall also be directed to the preservation and strengthening of positive African morals, traditional values and *cultures* (paragraph 2 (c)), and that States Parties shall take special measures in respect of female, gifted and *disadvantaged* children to ensure equal access to education *for all sections of the community* (paragraph 3 (e)).
11 The *American Convention on Human Rights* (http://www.oas.org/juridico/english/sigs/b-32.html) was signed in 1969.
12 https://www.oas.org/dil/1988 Additional Protocol to the American Convention on Human Rights in the Area of Economic, Social and Cultural Rights (Protocol of San Salvador).pdf
13 http://www.humanrights.se/wp-content/uploads/2012/01/C169-Indigenous-and-Tribal-Peoples-Convention.pdf
14 As of December 2019, they include Argentina, Bolivia, Brazil, Central African Republic, Chile, Colombia, Costa Rica, Denmark, Dominica, Ecuador, Fiji, Guatemala, Honduras, Mexico, Nepal, Netherlands, Nicaragua, Norway, Paraguay, Peru, Spain, and Venezuela.
15 143 States voted in favour, four opposed the *Declaration* (Australia, Canada, New Zealand and the United States, all have since accepted it), and eleven States abstained (Azerbaijan, Bangladesh, Bhutan, Burundi, Colombia, Georgia, Kenya, Nigeria, the Russian Federation, Samoa and Ukraine). All but two of the 23 States which have ratified *ILO Convention No. 169* (Colombia, which abstained,

not, strictly speaking, create binding legal obligations; it is part of "soft law" (UN OHCHR 2018: 23). Nevertheless, Paragraph 1 of Article 8 provides that Indigenous peoples and individuals have the right not to be subjected to forced assimilation or destruction of their culture. And Article 13, paragraph 1, states:

> Indigenous peoples have the right to revitalize, use, develop and transmit to future generations their histories, languages, oral traditions, philosophies, writing systems and literatures, and to designate and retain their own names for communities, places and persons.

Article 13, paragraph 2, continues by obliging the states: "States shall take effective measures to ensure that this right is protected." Article 14 continues:
1. Indigenous peoples have the right to establish and control their educational systems and institutions providing education in their own languages, in a manner appropriate to their cultural methods of teaching and learning.
2. Indigenous individuals, particularly children, have the right to all levels and forms of education of the State without discrimination.
3. States shall, in conjunction with indigenous peoples, take effective measures, in order for indigenous individuals, particularly children, including those living outside their communities, to have access, when possible, to an education in their own culture and provided in their own language.

State education (mentioned in 2 above) is at least supposed to be 'free' – involving no payment of fees. But the Article says nothing about who is to finance the establishing and running of Indigenous/tribal peoples' educational systems in their own languages. Which ITMs have the financial resources to establish their own schools?

The 2006 *Convention on the Rights of Persons with Disabilities* (CRPD)[16] further specifies the right to education for persons with disabilities "without discrimination and on the basis of equal opportunity" to "ensure an inclusive education system at all levels" (Article 24). ITMs include all differently abled persons; the *Convention*, however, mentions the Deaf people specifically.

The importance and the implications of these rights for ITMs and their relevance to their education, and the sad stories about their lack of implementation, are presented in hundreds of books (Skutnabb-Kangas and Dunbar 2010, Skutnabb-Kangas, Phillipson, and Dunbar 2019, Skutnabb-Kangas and Phillipson (eds.) 2017). If one wants both formal education and human rights to work for the cause of social justice, ensuring the role of ITM languages in education is a central issue.

---

and Fiji, which was absent), supported the declaration. See http://www.un.org/News/Press/docs/2007/ga10612.doc.htm.
16 https://www.un.org/development/desa/disabilities/convention-on-the-rights-of-persons-with-disabilities.html

3 The role of ITM languages in education

It is noticeable that no direct reference is made in any of the above provisions to a right to education in or through the medium of any particular language or, specifically, to education in or through the medium of the mother tongue or first language of the child, with rare exceptions. It is surprising that there is no separate reference to linguistic groups in the provisions on education (as many human rights treaties do make such a reference). But given the acknowledged close relationship between language and ethnicity, it is unlikely that the omission of linguistic groups would leave such groups outside the protection of rights provision, specifically, in education in or through the medium of the mother tongue of the child.

The issue of the right to a specific medium of education has been addressed in several court cases. Skutnabb-Kangas and Dunbar (2010: 16–17), having examined these court cases, argue that

> where children with limited linguistic skills in a particular language are subjected to education through the medium of that language, this should be considered to be a denial of the substance of the right to education. We are strengthened in this view by the decision of the United States Supreme Court in a very important case involving the provision of education only through the medium of English to about 1,800 children of Chinese ancestry or origin who effectively spoke no English. The case, *Lau v. Nichols*,[17] is relevant to the question of the interaction of the right to education and the principle of non-discrimination. The Supreme Court observed the following about such interactions in educational practices.
>
> Basic English skills are at the very core of what these public schools teach. The imposition of a requirement that, before a child can effectively participate in the educational program, he must already have acquired those basic skills is to make a mockery of public education. We know that those who do not understand English are certain to find their classroom experiences wholly incomprehensible and in no way meaningful.
>
> The case did not involve a consideration of a right to education, but by concluding that the education here was "incomprehensible" to the students and therefore "in no way meaningful" [the court's pronouncement] is clearly suggestive of a complete denial of any right to education.

In most countries, ITMs use in their home a language or languages that is/are different from the one/s used in the public institutions created and controlled by the state. Their languages are commonly used as a pretext for their exclusion from the educational system, which is a prelude to exclude the speakers of these languages from any rightful participation in every sphere, economic, political, social, cultural and aesthetic. The status of their home language/s in schools is central to the policy and practice of exclusion. For reversing this exclusion, the ITM language/s must have a central place in the policy and practice of inclusion. Their languages cannot be peripheral or an appendage to the policy and practice in any spheres, starting

---

17 (1974), 414 U.S. 563 (available at: http://straylight.law.cornell.edu/supct/html/historics/USSC_CR_0414_0563_ZS.html).

crucially from education. But including the language of education (or language in general) has not seemed to be necessary in all inclusion planning.

A recent example is the 2018 UNESCO report *Concept note for the 2020 Global Education Monitoring Report on inclusion*.[18] Even when inclusion is both defined and described in detail in the Concept note, language (as one of the most important causal factors in exclusion in education) is not mentioned even once! This UNESCO report discusses the development of the concept of inclusion and gives its own definition. It takes as its starting point the general comment 4 of the CRPD Committee in 2016, which specifies that inclusive education "'focuses on the full and effective participation, accessibility, attendance and achievement of all students, especially those who, for different reasons, are excluded or at risk of being marginalised.' Inclusive education is a process, not an endpoint." (p. 3) The concept note continues on the same page with:

> Inclusive education has been described in its essence as a statement of political aspiration, an essential ingredient in the creation of inclusive societies, and a commitment to a democratic framework for action. It is both a call for democratic education and an education in democracy. It addresses key questions about the kind of world in which we want our children to live and the role of education in building that world. Accordingly, inclusive education is not restricted to questions about where education takes place (for example, in segregated special schools or regular schools), but also involves a range of *elements* that form educational experiences and outcomes. These elements can include the content of education and learning materials, teaching and teacher preparation, infrastructure and learning environment, community norms, and the availability of space for dialogue and criticism involving all stakeholders (*Concept note for the 2020 Global Education Monitoring Report on inclusion*, p.3)

The mother tongue/home language (or languages) should of course be one of the main elements listed above in the last sentence. It is the language/s through which people have their primary socialisation and relate themselves to the natural and social worlds outside. This role of home languages cannot be ignored for the ITM people, but their significance is often undermined by policy makers, as in the UNESCO report above. Ignoring the home language/s is like valuing life support systems over natural breathing. But "home language" is not a singular notion, it often refers to multiple languages in functionally multilingual societies. A person in these societies is likely to have *a language repertoire* rather than a single language for primary socialization.[19] This is inevitable, and a source of enrichment, in multilingual societies. Every person must have a choice to use her language repertoire for the purposes she considers beneficial to her. One or more than one language from the repertoire could be chosen for social identification of the speaker by the speaker. This is the indexing

---

18 https://unesdoc.unesco.org/ark:/48223/pf0000265329
19 Swain's doctoral thesis in 1972 recognised this – it was called "Bilingualism as a first language". Mohanty's (2019) book describes in detail multilingualism as a first language.

function of language. In "normal" circumstances, the home language(s) are chosen for this function. The sense that these language(s) give to their speakers (and signers) a sense of belonging to a speech community does not exclude a sense of simultaneously belonging to the larger society. Multiple identities coexist and are emphasized and distributed in different social contexts and for different social purposes. Everyone in the larger society has a moral and democratic obligation not to use anybody's home language/s as a tool or pretext for exclusion. Hence social inclusiveness is built fundamentally on home language(s).

Inclusiveness is to have opportunities available to better one's life by free choice. Availing opportunities is accessing without hindrance the economic, political and social capital of the state; being granted, mainly through formal education, the capabilities to choose. According to Jean Drèze and economics Nobel laureate Amartya Sen, "capability" refers to

> the alternative combinations of functionings from which a person can choose [...] freedom – the range of options a person has in deciding what kind of life to lead. Poverty [...] lies not merely in the impoverished state in which the person actually lives, but also in the lack of real opportunity – given by social constraints as well as personal circumstances – to choose other types of living. Even the relevance of low incomes, meagre possessions, and other aspects of what are standardly seen as economic poverty relates ultimately to their role in curtailing capabilities (that is, their role in severely restricting the choices people have). Poverty is, thus, ultimately a matter of 'capability deprivation'.
> (quoted from Misra and Mohanty 2000a: 262–263; see also Drèze and Sen 2002: 35–36)

The loci of poverty, and of intervention, are in Amartya Sen's view, economic, social and psychological, and so measures have to be taken in each of these areas. Misra and Mohanty (2000a: 264) connect this view to education: "Psychological processes, such as cognition, motivation, values and other characteristics of the poor and the disadvantaged are to be viewed both as consequences as well as antecedent conditions which are ultimately related to human capabilities". The central question in reducing poverty is, in their view: "What is the most critical (and cost effective) input to change the conditions of poverty, or rather, to expand human capabilities?" They respond to it themselves: There is "a general consensus among the economists, psychologists and other social scientists that education is perhaps the most crucial input" (Misra and Mohanty 2000a: 265).

What are the consequences for our argumentation for languages here? *If* poverty is understood as "both a set of contextual conditions as well as certain processes which together give rise to typical performance of the poor and the disadvantaged" in school, and *if* of "all different aspects of such performance, cognitive and intellectual functions have been held in high priority as these happen to be closely associated with upward socio-economic mobility of the poor" (Misra and Mohanty 2000b: 135–136), *then* we have to look for the type of division of labour between both/all languages in education that guarantees the best possible development of these "cognitive and intellectual functions" which enhance children's "human capabilities". What is done today when ITM children are instructed with a dominant language as the teaching language in submersion education is not enhancing but rather curtailing these functions, and thus depriving children of the choices and freedom that are, according to Sen, Drèze and others, associated with the necessary capabilities. An ITM child in a submersion programme may be *physically included*, but s/he is certainly *psychologically and cognitively excluded* if she does not understand (most of) what the teachers and the textbook say.

Inclusiveness is also to be a beneficiary in the outcomes of the development of the state. Such inclusiveness means the necessity of investment in *all* languages of the state and in their resources by the policy makers as well as the private citizens. Social justice is served when this investment is made, and the dividends are shared across the peoples. Social justice, in contrast to criminal justice, is often viewed as correcting historical malevolence that has happened through discrimination. But it is more than that. It is also honouring the rights of the sovereign individuals as citizens and as human beings. This also means honouring their right to their languages.

There is the imputed problem of "self-exclusion" by the minorities from their own speech communities if they surrender their linguistic right of using their home language in public domains such as education even when the country's constitution provides it (Annamalai 2000). The larger society, including its policy makers and courts, portrays it as a voluntary choice. Yet it is anything but voluntary, if we understand a voluntary action as one that is without implicit pressures and falsely promised incentives. In the choice of language in education there is no such voluntary action. The formal structure of education makes the option of minority languages as teaching languages either non-existent or a kind of "special education" that is stigmatized. Thus, the structure of education forcibly assimilates ITM children and (tries to) transfer(s) them at least linguistically to another group, namely the dominant-language-using group. Linguistic and often also cultural forced assimilation, in other words.

It bears repetition that the indispensable place for dispensing social justice is education and the place of languages in education. It begins in the school. While school is the microcosm of society, it is also the transformer of society. Language policy in education should prevent the school from reproducing the inequalities of the society; it should explicitly be planned to produce equality in the society. Hence the design of mother-tongue-based multilingual education (MTB-MLE), as described below, is of utmost importance. Education, in other words, can be preventive of social ills, including conflict. It is not just a moral imperative; it is an economic (and political) imperative. Emphasizing the importance of education and its role in eliminating violence in society, Jan Eliasson, a former Swedish Foreign Minister and chairman of SIPRI Board of Governors (SIPRI, the Stockholm International Peace Research Institute) points out that "aside from saving and improving human lives, studies suggest that investing $2 billion in prevention [of conflict] can generate net savings of $33 billion per year from averted conflict" (as reported in Deen 2018).

The importance of education is also highlighted from another angle, namely, the waste of human resources. Globally, over 260 million children and youth do not attend school, and 400 million children quit school after completing primary school education, according to UN estimates (released in mid-February 2018; see UNESCO 2018). This education crisis would by 2030 leave half of the world's 1.6 billion children and youth out of school or without the most basic skills by 2030 (Sanam Naraghi Anderlini, Executive Director of the International Civil Society Action Network, as reported in Deen 2018). A large percentage of these children who do not attend school at all or are pushed out of school early are speakers of ITM languages. Non-use of these languages in school is an important aspect in the push factor (see, e.g. Mohanty 2019). Hence the role of these languages in a well-designed multilingual education system cannot be over-emphasised. Next we describe some aspects of this multilingual education.

4 Multilingual education

Multilingual education emphatically does not mean offering children more than one language as subjects, along with other subjects. There are elite schools that teach selected international languages as subjects besides the national or official language of the state. Schools in India by policy require that students acquire differentiated proficiencies in various languages before they finish school after ten years of schooling (Aggarwal 1991). These schools are not multilingual schools. Multilingual education means using at least two languages as languages of instruction, as media of education, in subjects other than the languages themselves (modifying Andersson and Boyer's [1970/1978] classical definition of bilingual education).

There are many different models of multilingual education, some with "good" results (see Table 1 below), some less successful. For ITM children, the programmes recommended must create an *additive learning situation*: The child learns well both the mother tongue/s and additional languages (for instance a dominant language in the country or state where the child lives, and an "international" language). There are many success stories, as described in the literature in our references. One example is in Ragnarsdóttir (2016) and her team's other publications; these give good overviews of inclusive education and detailed descriptions of how it can be organised.

Unfortunately, most ITM children, if they attend school at all, are in a *subtractive learning situation*. They learn (some of) a dominant language (which is the main teaching language in these *submersion* classes) at the cost of their own language/s, not in addition to it/them. The school subtracts from the linguistic repertoire that the child brings to school; the child is submersed (not immersed) in a foreign teaching language, without any support.[20] But inclusive education should offer both linguistic majority

---

20 See Skutnabb-Kangas and McCarty (2008) for some of the concepts in multilingual education.

Table 1: Some models of bilingual education programmes/models[21] (MIN: minority language, MAJ: majority language).

Programme	Segregation	Submersion	MIN language maintenance	Immersion for "majority"	Dual language/two-way	MIN revitalisation immersion
Linguistic goal	Dominance in L1	Dominance in L2	Bilingualism	Bilingualism	Bilingualism	Bilingualism
Societal goal	Apartheid/Repatriation: prevention of social mobility	(Forced) assimilation, marginalisation	Equity and integration	Linguistic & cultural enrichment	MIN equity Integration MAJ language cultural enrichment	Reconciliation (Indigenous peoples or MIN whose language is endangered)
Child's language	MIN	MAJ + MIN	MIN	MAJ	MAJ+MIN	Min? Maj?
Language of instruction	MIN	MAJ	MIN; MAJ as subject; maybe LOI after gr.8	Min + bilingual later, most often MAJ from gr.7, MIN as subject only	Min + bilingual later (e.g. gr.6: 50-50%; 80-20%) the longer Min. language the better	MIN; MAJ as subject
Teacher	Often mono-lingual in MIN language	Monolingual in MAJ language	Bilingual	Bilingual	Bilingual	Bilingual
Does child know teaching language?	yes	MAJ yes MIN no	MIN yes	Initially no	MAJ not initially; MIN yes	MIN? No, or a little
Programme chosen voluntarily?	no	MAJ? MIN no	MIN yes	yes	Both yes	MIN yes
Are there alternatives?	Often no	MIN no	MIN yes	yes	MAJ yes MIN ?	MIN yes
Results	Poor	MAJ ? MIN poor	Good	Good	Good	Good

[21] Tove Skutnabb-Kangas has used these models since the late 1970s; see, e.g. 1990; this version is from 2019.

children and ITM children a chance to become high-level bi- or multilinguals. Table 1 compares six basic models of educational programmes, with "good" or "poor" results. There are many variants of all of these. There is no one-model-fits-all; every model has to be contextualised.

Table 1 presents comparisons of characteristics of some educational programmes with "good" or "poor" results: 1. Segregation or 2. Submersion (for ITMs, with "poor" results), 3. Minority Language Maintenance (for ITMs, with "good" results), 4. Immersion (for Majority, with "good" results), 5. Dual Language (or Two-Way) (for both ITMs and Majorities, with "good" results), and 6. ITM Revitalisation Immersion (for ITMs, with "good" results). "Poor" results mean that at the group level, children do not reach high levels of bi/multilingualism; they under-achieve at primary school, with negative results for secondary and tertiary education and later life; they may have problems with their identities and self-confidence (see Skutnabb-Kangas, Phillipson, and Dunbar 2019 for detailed statistical descriptions of this from Nunavut, Canada). "Good" results means the opposite: high levels of bi/multilingualism; a good chance of achieving at school and later life, healthy self-confidence and positive often bi/multilingual identities. The order of the programmes reflects their historical developments: Both segregation (e.g. in apartheid Africa) and submersion models (most ITMs in western countries, earlier and still today) were initially common for ITMs. Long struggles by immigrant minorities in the 1960s and 1970s resulted in maintenance programmes, which some national minorities (e.g. Swedish-speakers in Finland, French-speakers in Canada and Afrikaans-speakers in South Africa) had had for a long time. Immersion programmes with French as the main teaching language for English-speakers started in Canada in 1967. Later dual-language programmes combined in the same classroom a maintenance programme for minorities and an immersion programme for majorities. And after long Indigenous struggles, Revitalisation Immersion programmes for Indigenous peoples whose languages are seriously endangered or where children no longer speak them are rapidly growing.

A classical submersion programme where a dominant language is the main teaching language, can have ITM children only, or both ITM children and dominant language speaking children (but the teaching through the medium of the MAJ (Majority) language often happens as if this dominant language were everybody's mother tongue (MT)). The teacher is mostly a monolingual speaker of the teaching language in countries such as the USA, Canada, Australia and Aotearoa/New Zealand. In other countries the teacher may know (some of) the MT of some of the students but is often officially not allowed to use it. The children or parents have not "voluntarily" chosen this kind of education; for it to be voluntary, alternatives should exist, and, very importantly, in most countries parents are not offered enough high-level research-based information on the long-term consequences of the model. Parents often do not speak or read the languages in which the research is communicated. Often submersion programmes through the medium of English have high status, both in ex-colonial situations but also others, and parents are misled into believing that their children learn English well in them (see for examples Mohanty 2019; Rao 2017; Bunce et al. 2016; Skutnabb-Kangas and Heugh 2011). There *are* examples of submersion programmes that work, for instance, programmes for Korean, Chinese, Vietnamese etc. immigrant minority children in the United Kingdom and Canada. But the enrolled children mostly have special support for the mother tongues, such as grandparents living with the family speaking the language, new flows of migrants speaking it, extra private MT teaching, summer camps, books at home in the MT, etc. (for Canadian exemplary ones, see, e.g. Cummins 2000, forthcoming).

Mother-tongue-based multilingual programmes are part of the language maintenance programmes in Table 1. Most research shows that the MT should be the main teaching language minimally for the first 6 years, preferably longer. Thomas and Collier (2002), comparing several programmes in a large-scale quantitative study, write, for instance, that the longer the MT remains the main teaching language, the better the results in not only the MT but in all subjects, and, importantly, the dominant language. The language of instruction is also a more important factor than the social class of the students, i.e. ITM children with low socioeconomic status in these programmes can do as well as middle class children taught through the medium of their language. There are thousands of articles and projects and hundreds of books providing evidence to these claims. The arguments against these programmes are political, not scientific.

Table 1 also shows that UNESCO's (1953) claim that the mother tongue is axiomatically the best teaching language is not that simple. Segregation programmes (such as apartheid teaching in South Africa, or Turkish-medium teaching of Turkish immigrant children in Bavaria, Germany, both in the 1980s and 1990s) have the goal to repatriate the children (for details, see Skutnabb-Kangas 1990). They use the MT of the students, but the teachers do not often have good training, their salaries are low, and the social circumstances are not conducive for positive school achievement for the children. On the other hand, it is perfectly possible to teach some children through the medium of a language that they do not initially know, provided, importantly, that the conditions in Table 1 are met. Again, there are hundreds if not thousands of reports and articles describing these Immersion for Majority (i.e. speakers of a dominant language) programmes. They were initiated in Canada in 1967 and have since spread to many countries.

It is important to compare the features of the Revitalisation Immersion model for ITMs with Immersion for Majority. In both immersion models, the dominant majority language, for instance English, is learned well anyway, even if it is not used as the teaching language for the first years (e.g. not before grade six, most often even later). It is taught as a mother tongue a few hours per week, and the children are surrounded by it in the society where they live. In the Revitalisation Immersion model, many of the children come from families where the mother tongue has ceased to be transmitted from the parent (or even grandparent) generation to the children, and the children are thus either monolingual or very dominant in the majority language.

The ITM language can still be seen as their mother tongue, even if they know only little of it or do not know it at all. In this case the mother tongue is not defined as the language that the child has learned first (often a good definition of an MT) but as a language that the child (and parents) identify with, even if they do not know it (or know only a little of it).[22]

The Table also shows some of the features that the programmes with either "good" or "poor" results have in common; for instance, both social and linguistic goals for these programmes are positive for the "good" group, whereas the programmes with "poor" results in most cases prevent social mobility of the children. The teachers in programmes with "good" results are bi/multilingual. This enables them to support the development of the children's metalinguistic awareness (knowledge of how languages function), because they can compare the languages involved. Metalinguistic awareness is, according to Mohanty's (2019) detailed long-standing studies, probably the main causal factor behind the many benefits that bi/multilinguals as a group have over comparable monolinguals. The teaching with "good" results also has cognitively demanding content.[23]

We do know how various groups of children should be educated for "good" results that add to bi/multilingual skills: a fair chance of succeeding in school and in later life, deep self-confidence, strong sense of identity, ensured social justice and communal inclusion through participation in society. Why are then the solidly research-based recommendations not followed in most ITM education? There are countervailing forces and counter ideologies advanced by those who resist change in education to perpetuate the status quo, which answer this question partially.

5 Countervailing forces against educational justice

Factors presented against using the optimal models of multilingual education include the following. First, policy makers responsible for language in education often come from the elite class with a market-based view of efficiency in terms of monetary cost. From this point of view, to have a variety of educational models appear as inefficient in several ways. The return of financial investment in MT-based

---

[22] Articles in the 521-page Hinton, Huss, and Roche (2018) book describe tens of these revitalisation situations. Olthuis, Kivelä, and Skutnabb-Kangas (2013) describe in detail one revitalisation project where the two missing generations of speakers of Aanaar Saami were recreated, and the whole community (now numbering some 450 speakers) has got new life. Many speakers of very small Indigenous and tribal languages are in a similar situation; the few native speakers are elders. Obviously, it is incredibly wasteful, and criminal, first to almost or completely kill off these languages, and then laboriously recreate or revitalise them.
[23] Many more of them, with comparisons and explanations can be accessed, for instance, in Skutnabb-Kangas (1990), and in Skutnabb-Kangas and García (1995).

multilingual education does not commensurate (measured in terms of GDP), as the policy makers claim. This is an ideological position without empirical support. There is empirical research that suggests the contrary. Walter and Benson (2012) and Grin (2005), among many others, have shown that the costs of good minority education are either marginal, or lower than submersion education. Grin asks both what the costs and benefits are if minority languages *are* maintained and promoted, and what the costs (and benefits) are if they are neither maintained nor promoted.

Some of Grin's conclusions from several publications are as follows:
- diversity seems to be positively, rather than negatively, correlated with welfare
- available evidence indicates that the monetary costs of maintaining diversity are remarkably modest
- devoting resources to the protection and promotion of minority cultures [and this includes languages] may help to stave off political crises whose costs would be considerably higher than that of the policies considered [the peace-and-security argument]
- therefore, there are strong grounds to suppose that protecting and promoting regional and minority languages is a sound idea from a welfare standpoint, not even taking into consideration any moral argument

(Grin 2003: 26).[24]

In addition, the enormous global wastage when children do not attend school or are pushed out early is enormous, also economically.[25]

Secondly, MT-based multilingual education is perceived to be divisive: the claim is that reproducing minorities as "unassimilated" minorities through education is thought to work against national unity (by which policy makers mean uniformity). It is

---

[24] We summarise Grin's economic arguments from an email dated 15 January 2019 (partially presented in Grin 2005): " ... simulation results comparing education through MT versus education through some LWC [languages of wider communication] show that under plausible assumptions (which would also be testable with suitable data), offering MT-medium education 'pays for itself', because it tends to result in lower class *repetition* rates, thus reducing the average per-student cost – and thus freeing up communal resources. ... The positive net effect of offering MT education is further reinforced if one takes into account higher average skills, which gives people access to better jobs – and better jobs, which usually are not just more interesting and more empowering for individuals, also tend to generate higher market value, which in turns gives rise to higher tax revenue. In other words, through this channel too, offering MT-medium education is a sound economic investment, even if you put aside linguistic human rights (LHR) considerations. Putting it another way still, a properly conducted economic analysis of MT education would generally dovetail with and reinforce LHR-based recommendations."

[25] George Monbiot (2018: 109), discussing Universal Basic Income trials in several countries, notes that in "Madhya Pradesh, India – whose levels of poverty ensure that even small payments can make a big difference – strong improvements were seen after six months in health, nutrition and school attendance" (see also SEWA Bharat 2014). If parents can afford it ("small payments") and if they see that children understand what is said in schools and can participate, ITM children attend school and stay there.

believed that it is language differences that cause conflicts, and therefore they should be eliminated through assimilation; education through the dominant languages is supposed to lead to assimilation. But the opposite is true. Where language-based hierarchies dovetail with political and economic hierarchies, it is these rather than language differences that cause conflict; it is often precisely the lack of language rights that leads to conflict, according to several peace-and-conflict researchers. Linguistic Human Rights (LHRs), also in education, may be part of the solution; they can also work to grant ITM languages more status and may enable ITMs to integrate instead of assimilating. Still, most states continue the shortsighted and counterproductive policies of denying ITM children basic linguistic human rights, including proper maintenance-oriented multilingual education. States may find themselves in a position to pay huge reparations if this is continued. Some of those states which are now apologizing for the treatment that Indigenous children have suffered from in residential and other schools (see The Truth and Reconciliation Commission of Canada 2015) are now faced with their obligation; some others are already following (e.g. the Nordic countries). ITMs as groups may also demand reparations for the loss of their livelihood, sacred places and way of life; there are already many court cases. Granting ITMs educational (and other) LHRs is a necessary part of conflict resolution by giving them dignity and opportunities.

Thirdly, a historically and politically determined hierarchical social positioning of languages in a society has more public acceptability than equality between languages; the "acceptance" is hegemonically manufactured by the very elites who are the beneficiaries of linguistic stratification. This is achieved by the elites, who own or control the instruments of communication such as the media and other resources to influence thought, by framing the public discussion in a self-serving narrative and thus wielding enormous influence over government policies.

Fourthly, the pyramidal structure of education from primary to tertiary levels allows less and less local control of education as the levels go up, and this leaves little room for a multiplicity of languages at the higher levels of the pyramid. The pyramidal structure of education arose to meet the needs of a centralised economic and bureaucratic structure needed to sustain an industrial economy. Decentralisation may to some extent flatten this structure.

Fifthly, the ITM mother tongues learned through multilingual education have today no material use in public domains after school and so learning the mother tongues is unproductive. This puts the cart before the horse. A fundamental goal of multilingual education is to effect a change in the existing linguistic organisation of society, which today excludes the languages of the dominated communities from the life of the wider society. With the changes advocated in this chapter, ITM languages would play some roles in public domains, i.e. there would be demands for them. This can create more supply, which in turn can increase the demand, until the situation is "normalised" (a concept used by the Basques and Catalans in Spain) when the languages have their rightful and just space in society. Multilingual education prepares ITM students to make the changes successful. The most important issue, however, is for ITM language speakers to maintain the dignity of their languages and to create a space for them in the public sphere.

Dealing with these counter positions and factors, which make "normalisation" of the status of ITM languages more complex, is not helped by the national and state level governments' subversion of, and indifference to, implementing the good national policies and international agreements that are in place in many countries. The very factors mentioned above probably cause much of the subversion and indifference. The challenge is to cut the circularity in the problem. One way to meet the challenges is through advocacy with and by speakers of ITM languages, so that they might stop believing that these countervailing factors are insurmountable and might not surrender to the forces behind such ideological positions. Instead, they might resist the power of persuasion of these forces through seeing how consent to policies harming their long term interests could be manufactured (see Herman and Chomsky 1988) though various means including education.

This advocacy work with ITM speakers is equally important as advocacy with policy makers at national and international levels. Lo Bianco (2018: 36–37) analyses some of its difficulties in detail. Opponents of minority language advocacy, he writes, "often deploy 'egalitarian' and 'participatory' arguments" against activities which try to reverse language shift (RLS), especially in "societies that prize democratic involvement of citizens". In his analysis of these cases, hostility to revitalisation efforts "originates not just in prejudice or negative judgment against minority communities but, perversely, also from the liberal belief in the overriding importance of public and undifferentiated participation by all citizens" (Lo Bianco 2018: 36). In our view, this is a neoliberal ideology of what inclusion means. Lo Bianco continues:

> [W]hether originating in political ideologies of liberal participationism, or more conventionally, in nationalist demands for cultural assimilation, minority language advocacy must respond to a series of what I call "entrapment rebukes." These are arguments used against RLS advocates that the activity of minority language revitalisation traps the community in poverty and the young in atavistic ethnic identity. I have encountered entrapment rebukes in language policy advising and research in Australia, Asia, Europe, Oceania, and North America. Liberal critics use entrapment logic as a reproach, overtly or subtly, while nationalist interests make recourse to entrapment reasoning as a caution against social fragmentation. Both represent a serious obstacle to public mobilisation for language revitalisation activity. Minorities must regularly display political loyalty to the state/nation, its participatory ideals, or its dominant cultural norms, as they search for sufficient cultural autonomy to cultivate inter-generationally secure language maintenance.
>
> (Lo Bianco 2018: 37–38)

6 To conclude

The strength of a good multilingual education is not limited to its educational success. To successfully achieve linguistic justice for speakers of home languages that are not privileged historically, politically and economically, it is necessary to sustain the use of these languages in life outside and after school in political and economic domains in defined ways which go beyond their use in cultural and social domains. Multilingual education lays the foundation for this, but to erect a structure on it is beyond the field of education; the needed expertise must be trans- and interdisciplinary and has to be organised at the national level and coordinated internationally. It needs to challenge the dominance of globalised growth obsessed market forces and authoritarian political forces that move in the opposite direction. Some positive signs can be seen in the use of communication technology by people who organise against injustice and exclusiveness, and in increasing acceptance of the idea that the global is the local, i.e. multiple locals make the global. Linguistic human rights are a necessary but *not* a sufficient tool in the struggle for social justice, but they do not seem to be forthcoming. It would be rational to reduce poverty through organising ITM education according to research recommendations, i.e. use mother-tongue-based multilingual education. Even if the serious harm of not doing it has been well known for a long time, and the principles for what to do have equally been known, this has not led to mother-tongue-based multilingual education on a large scale. Alexander's review of educational achievements in Africa concludes "[w]e are not making any progress at all" (Alexander 2006: 9); "most conference resolutions were no more than a recycling exercise" (Bamgbose 2002, quoted in Alexander 2006: 10); "these propositions had been enunciated in one conference after another since the early 1980s" (2006: 11); "since the adoption of the OAU [Organisation for African Unity] Charter in 1963, every major conference of African cultural experts and political leaders had solemnly intoned the commitment of the political leadership of the continent to the development and powerful use of the African languages without any serious attempt at implementing the relevant resolutions" (2006: 11). This has led to "the palpable failure of virtually all post-colonial educational systems on the continent" (2006: 16). A similar analysis of other parts of the world would quite probably share Alexander's conclusions.

We need implementation of the existing good laws and intentions (there are many).[26] The sad situation is manifestly not a question of lack of information about what should be done; the political will for that is mostly lacking. Alexander's analysis of reasons for it (2006: 16) states:

> The problem of generating the essential political will to translate these insights into implementable policy [...] needs to be addressed in realistic terms. Language planners have to realize that

---

[26] The United Nations OHCHR (2018) gives many examples from all over the world of Constitutions which not only acknowledge ITM's rights but make states firm duty holders.

costing of policy interventions is an essential aspect of the planning process itself and that no political leadership will be content to consider favourably a plan that amounts to no more than a wish list, even if it is based on the most accurate quantitative and qualitative research evidence.

What Alexander advocates is that the costs of organising or of not organising Mother Tongue based Multilingual (MTM) education are made explicit in economic terms. This necessitates a type of multidisciplinary approach to MTM education that minimally includes expertise of sociolinguists, educators, lawyers and economists. Without that level of engagement, it seems impossible to even start convincing states of rational policies that would in the end be really beneficial not only for ITMs but for the states themselves, including their elites.

When policy makers realize that hierarchical unequal societies are destructive for all, including the rich,[27] when those in power themselves start seriously experiencing the consequences of the human consumption induced climate catastrophe, and when the economic elites accept that the necessary economic de-growth can and must be combined with the growth of necessary human rights for ITMs, some change in education towards social justice and inclusiveness might be possible – unless it is already too late . . .

References

Aggarwal, Santhosh. 1991. *Three language formula: An educational problem*. New Delhi: Gian Publishing House.
Alexander, Neville. 2006. Introduction. In UNESCO (United Nations Educational, Scientific and Cultural Organization), *Intergovernmental conference on language policies in Africa: Harare, Zimbabwe, 17–21 March 1997, Final report*, 9–16. Paris: UNESCO, Intangible Heritage Section.
Andersson, Theodore & Mildred Boyer. 1978. *Bilingual schooling in the United States*. 2nd edn. Austin, TX: National Educational Laboratory Publishers.
Annamalai, E. 2000. Use of language rights by minorities. In Phillipson, Robert (ed.), *Rights to language: Equity, power and education*, 87–91. Mahwah, NJ: Lawrence Erlbaum.
Bamgbose, Ayo. 2002. Launch of the activities of the African Academy of Languages: Mission and vision of ACALAN. *ACALAN Special Bulletin*. 24–25.
Bunce, Pauline, Robert Phillipson, Vaughan Rapatahana & Ruanni Tupas (eds.). 2016. *Why English? Confronting the Hydra*. Bristol: Multilingual Matters.
Cummins, Jim. 2000. *Language, power, and pedagogy: Bilingual children in the crossfire*. Bristol: Multilingual Matters.

---

[27] Wilkinson and Pickett (2010) shows that the most unequal societies where the gap is largest between the richest 20% and the poorest 20% suffer much more of ill health, violence, incarceration, mental illness, drug addiction, teenage pregnancies, infant mortality, and obesity. Life expectancy, social mobility, and levels of trust are lower, likewise school achievement and education levels. Inequality does not affect only the poor, but the vast majority of the population, including the rich. The USA and UK are among the most unequal among the countries studied, the Nordic countries and Japan the most equal.

Cummins, Jim. Forthcoming. *Multilingualism in education: Intersections of research, theory, policy, and practice*. (Linguistic Diversity and Language Rights.) Bristol: Multilingual Matters.

Deen, Thalif. 2018. Can preventive diplomacy avert military conflicts? *Inter Press Service (IPS) News Agency: News and views from the global South*. 21 May. Rome: Inter Press Service. http://www.ipsnews.net/2018/05/can-preventive-diplomacy-avert-military-conflicts/ (accessed 5 Oktober 2019).

Drèze, Jean & Amartya Sen. 2002. *India: Development and participation*. Oxford: Oxford University Press.

Grin, François. 2003. Language planning and economics. *Current Issues in Language Planning* 4(1). 1–66.

Grin, François. 2005. The economics of language policy implementation: Identifying and measuring costs. In Neville Alexander (ed.), *Mother tongue-based bilingual education in Southern Africa: The dynamics of implementation. Proceedings of the Symposium at the University of Cape Town, 16–19 October 2003*, 11–25. Cape Town: Project for the Study of Alternative Education in South Africa (PRAESA).

Henriksen, John B. 2009. Foreword. In Preti Taneja (ed.), *State of the world's minorities and indigenous peoples 2009: Events of 2008*, 10–11. London: Minority Rights Group International (in association with UNICEF).

Herman, Edward S. & Noam Chomsky. 1988. *Manufacturing consent: The political economy of the mass media*. New York: Pantheon Books.

Hinton, Leanne, Leena Huss & Gerald Roche (eds.). 2018. *The Routledge handbook of language revitalization*. New York, NY: Routledge.

Lo Bianco, Joseph. 2018. Reinvigorating language policy and planning for intergenerational language revitalization. In Leanne Hinton, Leena Huss & Gerald Roche (eds.), *The Routledge handbook of language revitalization*, 36–48. New York, NY: Routledge.

McDougall, Gay. 2009. Foreword. In Preti Taneja (ed.), *State of the world's minorities and indigenous peoples 2009: Events of 2008*. 7–10. London: Minority Rights Group International (in association with UNICEF).

Misra, Girishwar & Ajit K. Mohanty. 2000a. Consequences of poverty and disadvantage: A review of Indian studies. In Ajit K. Mohanty & Girishwar Misra (eds.), *Psychology of poverty and disadvantage*, 121–148. New Delhi: Concept.

Misra, Girishwar & Ajit K. Mohanty, 2000b. Poverty and disadvantage: Issues in retrospect. In Ajit K. Mohanty & Girishwar Misra (eds.), *Psychology of poverty and disadvantage*, 261–284. New Delhi: Concept.

Mohanty, Ajit K. 2019. *The multilingual reality: Living with languages* (Linguistic Diversity and Language Rights). Bristol: Multilingual Matters.

Monbiot, George. 2018 [2017]. *Out of the wreckage: A new politics for an age of crisis*. London & New York, NY: Verso.

Olthuis, Marja-Liisa, Suvi Kivelä & Tove Skutnabb-Kangas. 2013. *Revitalising Indigenous languages: How to recreate a lost generation*. Bristol: Multilingual Matters.

Ragnarsdóttir, Hanna. 2016. Building empowering multilingual learning communities in Icelandic schools. In Peter P. Trifonas & Themistoklis Aravossitas (eds.), *Handbook of research and practice in heritage language education*, 1–18. Cham: Springer. https://doi.org/10.1007/978-3-319-38893-9_44-1 (accessed 5 October 2019).

Rao, A. Giridhar. 2017. English in multilingual India: Promise and illusion. In Hywel Coleman (ed.), *Multilingualism and development: Selected proceedings of the 11th Language & Development Conference, New Delhi, India, 2015*, 281–288. London: British Council.

SEWA (Self-Employed Women's Association) Bharat. 2014. *A little more, how much it is … : Piloting basic income transfers in Madhya Pradesh, India*. New Delhi: SEWA Bharat (supported by

UNICEF India). http://sewabharat.org/wp-content/uploads/2015/07/Report-on-Unconditional-Cash-Transfer-Pilot-Project-in-Madhya-Pradesh.pdf (accessed 5 October 2019).

Skutnabb-Kangas, Tove. 1990. *Language, literacy and minorities*. London: The Minority Rights Group.

Skutnabb-Kangas, Tove & Robert Dunbar. 2010. *Indigenous children's education as linguistic genocide and a crime against humanity? A global view* (Gáldu Čála – Journal of Indigenous Peoples' Rights No. 1/2010). Guovdageaidnu [Kautokeino]: Gáldu – Resource Centre for the Rights of Indigenous Peoples. http://www.tove-skutnabb-kangas.org/pdf/Indigenous_Children_s_Education_as_Linguistic_Genocide_and_a_Crime_Against_Humanity_A_Global_View_Tove_Skutnabb_Kangas_and_Robert_Dunbar_grusweb_2010_04_22.pdf (accessed 5 October 2019).

Skutnabb-Kangas, Tove & Ofelia García. 1995. Multilingualism for all? General principles. In Tove Skutnabb-Kangas (ed.), *Multilingualism for all*, 221–256. Lisse: Swets & Zeitlinger.

Skutnabb-Kangas, Tove & David Harmon. 2018. Biological diversity and language diversity: Parallels and differences. In Alwin F. Fill & Hermine Penz (eds.), *The Routledge handbook of ecolinguistics*, 11–25. New York, NY: Routledge.

Skutnabb-Kangas, Tove & Teresa McCarty. 2008. Key concepts in bilingual education: Ideological, historical, epistemological, and empirical foundations. In Jim Cummins & Nancy H. Hornberger (eds.), *Bilingual education. Encyclopedia of Language and Education*, 3–17. 2nd edn. New York: Springer.

Skutnabb-Kangas, Tove, Robert Phillipson & Robert Dunbar. 2019. *Is Nunavut education criminally inadequate? An analysis of current policies for Inuktut and English in education, international and national law, linguistic and cultural genocide and crimes against humanity*. Iqaluit: Nunavut Tunngavik Incorporated. https://www.tunngavik.com/files/2019/04/NuLinguicideReportFINAL.pdf (accessed 5 October 2019).

Skutnabb-Kangas, Tove & Kathleen Heugh (eds.). 2011. *Multilingual education and sustainable diversity work: From periphery to center*. New York, NY: Routledge.

Skutnabb-Kangas, Tove & Robert Phillipson (eds.). 2017. *Language rights*. New York, NY: Routledge.

Swain, Merrill K. 1972. *Bilingualism as a first language*. Irvine, CA: University of California PhD thesis.

Thomas, Wayne P. & Virginia P. Collier. 2002. *A national study of school effectiveness for language minority students' long-term academic achievement*. Santa Cruz, CA: Center for Research on Education, Diversity and Excellence, University of California. http://repositories.cdlib.org/crede/finalrpts/1_1_final (accessed 5 October 2019).

Truth and Reconciliation Commission of Canada. 2015. *Honouring the truth, reconciling for the future: Summary of the final report of the Truth and Reconciliation Commission of Canada*. Ottawa: The Truth and Reconciliation Commission of Canada. http://nctr.ca/assets/reports/Final%20Reports/Executive_Summary_English_Web.pdf (accessed 5 October 2019).

UNDP (United Nations Development Programme). 2017. *Journey to extremism in Africa: Drivers, incentives and the tipping point for recruitment*. New York, NY: UNDP Regional Bureau for Africa.

UNESCO (United Nations Educational, Scientific and Cultural Organization). 1953. *The use of the vernacular languages in education*. Paris: UNESCO.

UNESCO (United Nations Educational, Scientific and Cultural Organization). 2018. *Concept note for the 2020 Global Education Monitoring Report on inclusion*. Paris: UNESCO. https://unesdoc.unesco.org/ark:/48223/pf0000265329 (accessed 5 October 2019).

UNOHCHR (United Nations Human Rights Office of the High Commissioner). 2018. *Human rights and constitution making*. New York, NY, and Geneva: United Nations OHCHR. https://www.ohchr.org/Documents/Publications/HRAndConstitutionMaking_EN.pdf (accessed 5 October 2019).

Walter, Stephen L. & Carol Benson. 2012. Language policy and medium of instruction in formal education. In Bernard Spolsky (ed.), *The Cambridge handbook of language policy*, 278–300. Cambridge: Cambridge University Press.

Wilkinson, Richard and Kate Pickett. 2010 [2009]. *The spirit level. Why equality is better for everyone*. London: Penguin Books.

Zamyatin, Konstantin. 2014. *An official status for minority languages? A study of state languages in Russia's Finno-Ugric republics*. Helsinki: Vammalan Kirjapaino OY, University of Helsinki doctoral thesis.

Zamyatin, Konstantin. 2016a. Russia's minority education and the European language charter. In Reetta Toivanen & Janne Saarikivi (eds.), *Linguistic genocide or superdiversity? New and old language diversities*, 251–284. Bristol: Multilingual Matters.

Zamyatin, Konstantin. 2016b. An ethnopolitical conflict in Russia's republic of Mari El in the 2000s: The study of ethnic politics under the authoritarian turn. *Finnisch-Ugrische Forschungen* 63. 214–253.

Gregory A. Cheatham and Sumin Lim
20 Disabilities and home language maintenance: Myths, models of disability, and equity

1 Introduction

In the United States (U.S.), public schools are increasingly charged with appropriately meeting the educational and social needs of all emergent bilingual students. However, systemic educational inequities exist for students from historically-marginalized backgrounds who are emergent bilinguals (Harry and Klingner 2014). For emergent bilingual students including those diagnosed with or at risk for disabilities, home language maintenance and thus bilingualism are important to language development, academic performance, identity as well as family and community functioning (Cheatham and Hart-Barnett 2017).

Discussion of home language maintenance for emergent bilingual students, who have been diagnosed with or are considered at risk for disabilities, is inherently complex. Social and educational contexts as well as students' academic, functional, and behavioral characteristics, and educators' implementation of effective educational programs (or not) can impact disability diagnosis. By examining key social factors, research has contributed to better understanding of these students and their educational contexts.

2 Statement of purpose

In this chapter, we focus on a critical social variable in the lives of students who are emergent bilinguals – education – in relation to home language maintenance. First, we briefly review myths regarding emergent bilingual students who are labeled as having a disability. Next, we discuss challenges for schools regarding home language maintenance through a nexus of the medical model of disability and deficit discourses for minority students. In so doing, we advance an alternative conception of emergent bilingual students and disability using the social model of disability as an equity-oriented paradigm. This approach holds promise for home language maintenance for emergent bilingual students with and without a disability diagnosis. Here, we focus on students who are emergent bilinguals with reference to learning disabilities (LD), which is the most commonly diagnosed disability for emergent bilingual students in the U.S. (Orosco and Klingner 2010). Additionally, our discussion primarily focuses on

U.S. schools and students although the findings may be of interest for researchers and educators in other geographic contexts.

3 Myths about disabilities and home language maintenance

Myths abound regarding emergent bilingual students diagnosed with disabilities (Cheatham and Hart-Barnett 2017). These myths are likely to have a basis in deficit discourses about minority students and their families, low expectations regarding minority students, and misunderstandings of research. Consequently, these students' capabilities can be underestimated – "If they cannot learn one language, how can they learn two languages?" is a question that educators and researchers may ask. From this viewpoint, maintaining a home language and learning the dominant language of society are expected to yield additional developmental challenges. Indeed, education professionals continue to make recommendations that emergent bilingual students diagnosed with disabilities stop speaking their home language in favor of the dominant language (e.g., English in U.S.) (Jegatheesan 2011; Jordaan 2008). However, emerging research suggests that a positive view of home language maintenance and bilingualism is warranted for students diagnosed with disabilities. Before delving into social contexts of disability and disability models, we begin by refuting two myths about these students.

The first myth is that home language maintenance, and bilingualism more generally, causes or contributes to disability or significant delay (C. Baker, 2017). However, by comparing bilinguals to monolinguals diagnosed with and without disabilities, researchers suggest that bilingualism neither causes nor compounds disability (e.g., Kay-Raining Bird, Genesee, and Verhoeven 2016; Lund, Kohlmeier, and Duran 2017). Notwithstanding limitations of comparison studies (see our discussion in section 5 regarding disability diagnoses), growing evidence indicates that bilingualism is not inherently problematic for, firstly, students with reading disabilities, when investigating reading, language, memory tasks (Abu-Rabia and Siegel 2002), word reading, and working memory (Da Fontoura and Siegel 1995). Secondly, for students diagnosed with autism, language skills (Hambly and Fombonne 2012; Ohashi et al. 2012), language and vocabulary skills (Petersen, Marinova-Todd, and Mirenda 2012), and language and social skills (Reetzke et al. 2015) were largely equivalent to those of monolingual children with autism. Thirdly, for students with language disabilities (i.e., language impairments), it was found that grammatical and morphological skills were not significantly different from those of comparable monolingual students (Paradis et al. 2003). Fourthly, studies suggest that semantic and morphosyntactic skills of students with Down syndrome (Feltmate and Kay-Raining Bird 2008), their expressive and receptive communication, vocabulary, and mean length of utterance (Kay-Raining Bird et al. 2005), as well as their multiple language, memory, and cognitive skills (Edgin et al. 2011) were not significantly different from those of monolingual children with Down syndrome.

A second myth is that emergent bilingual students diagnosed with disabilities should participate in education using only the society's dominant language (e.g., English-only in the U.S.) rather than bilingual instruction (Cheatham and Hart-Barnett 2017). However, while research remains limited, studies illustrate that for bilingual students labeled with a variety of disabilities, instruction incorporating the home language is equally/more effective than second language only (e.g., English) education (Cheatham, Santos, and Kerkutluoglu 2012). For example, students' vocabulary, phonological awareness, writing/reading, appropriate behavior, and narration skills were as high or better with instruction that included the home language compared to dominant-language only instruction. Studies focused on various outcomes for children with autism, speech-language impairment, and intellectual disability (Gutiérrez-Clellen, Simon-Cereijido, and Sweet 2012; Lang et al. 2011; Pham, Kohnert, and Mann 2011; Rohena, Jitendra, and Browder 2002; Simon-Cereijido, Gutiérrez-Clellen, and Sweet 2013; Thordardottir et al. 2015; To, Law, and Li 2012). Most studies investigated language learning for younger emergent bilinguals with language impairments. Studies including emergent bilingual children considered "at risk" (i.e., students thought to be at risk for disability diagnosis) have also illustrated that home language and bilingual instruction tend to result in same or better outcomes compared to instruction without the use of the home language (e.g., Durán, Roseth, and Hoffman 2014). Importantly, evidence suggests that these students can also be included in general education environments rather than being segregated to special education rooms and programs (Cheatham and Hart-Barnett 2017).[1]

Some parents may not want their children to learn their home language, erroneously believing that bilingualism causes or contributes to developmental problems, that two languages are too difficult, or that bilingualism is not needed (Cheatham and Hart-Barnett 2017). Parents from multiple oppressed identities (e.g., low-income, racial/ethnic minority, low English proficiency) and well-educated, high-income families who have been misinformed may readily believe myths about disabilities and home language maintenance. Nonetheless, research illustrates that parents of bilingual students diagnosed with disabilities, including significant disabilities, may recognize the value of the home language for their children's cultural identity and communication needs (e.g., D. Baker 2017; Hampton et al. 2017; Jegatheesan 2011). Emergent bilingual students diagnosed with disabilities, who face challenges of marginalization in schools, need inclusion in family and community life rather than isolation. Daily home activities, such as dinner table conversations, shopping, and religious activities, warrant

---

[1] Studies of bilingualism for students who are deaf/hard of hearing are beyond the scope of this chapter. Interested readers may refer to Willoughby (2012) and Wathum-Ocama and Rose (2002).

home language development (Cheatham and Hart-Barnett 2017). Students' identity as bilinguals requires home language maintenance. Finally, the parent-child bond can be placed at risk when families are convinced to adopt only the dominant society language (Kremer-Sadlik 2005; De Houwer this vol.)

More research is needed regarding home language maintenance and bilingualism for emergent bilingual students diagnosed with disabilities investigating, for example, effectiveness of types of bilingual programs, and students' language and academic skills in relation to their functioning levels. Current evidence suggests that many emergent bilingual students diagnosed with disabilities can be competent bilinguals in accordance with their capabilities and attain positive language, academic, and social outcomes through instruction that includes the home language.

4 Home language maintenance, disability, and social context

While studies address some myths about developmental and instructional outcomes for bilingual students who may have disabilities, another key factor must also be considered: U.S. societal and educational contexts include systemic deficit discourses and educational inequities, which can impact these students' education. Consequently, emergent bilingual students, particularly students who have been labeled as or suspected of having a disability, can face challenges to learning. Within inequitable educational contexts, disability is complex and troubling. For example, disability diagnosis for marginalized students, including students who are emergent bilinguals, is a recognized problem (Artiles et al. 2005). These problems exist despite U.S. educational disability law (i.e., originally PL 94–142 promulgated in 1975) that requires non-discriminatory evaluation to determine student disability and includes a focus on individualized, appropriate education. As a component of discrimination, disability diagnosis and associated educational remedies can assert dominant group power over the students who are marginalized (Turnbull, Stowe, and Huerta 2007), resulting in oppression (Artiles 2013). As such, disability diagnosis and subsequent educational programming can be "disabling" by virtue of social context.

Thus, in this chapter we now turn to relationships between disability and home language maintenance from a sociocultural and critical perspective in which deficit discourses are ascribed to students who have what Crenshaw (1989) noted are multiple, intersecting identities (e.g., language/racial/ethnic/socio-economic minority). Emergent bilinguals in the U.S. are typically immersed in multiple, oppressive, and compounding systems leading to low educational expectations, misunderstandings, and under-education (Harry and Klingner 2014). As such, it is not uncommon that students' home languages are oppressed in favor of dominant language learning (Artiles 2013).

5 Home language maintenance in relation to medical and social models of disability

Emergent bilingual students in U.S. schools can face deficit discourses, misdiagnosis, and inappropriate education. The remainder of this chapter focuses on emergent bilingual students suspected of having or diagnosed with learning disabilities (LD), who constitute the majority of emergent bilingual students participating in the U.S. special education system (Orosco and Klingner 2010). We discuss LD and home language maintenance in relation to the medical model and social model of disability. We focus on social and linguistic factors that contribute to difficulties for emergent bilingual students suspected of and diagnosed with LD within these contrasting viewpoints of disability. For this discussion, we adhere to a strict interpretation of the medical and social model and extend the scope of these models to an analysis of bilingualism. Although the medical model dominates U.S. educational discourse, the social model, originated by disability studies scholars and disability rights activists, appears to be slowly impacting educational research and influencing the U.S. education system.

The medical model of disability, which rests firmly in a clinical perspective on human functioning, is the primary perspective on disability within education (Arehart 2008). Like in medicine, identifying and addressing a biologically-rooted problem relies on diagnosis based on the results of assessments, which lead to "treatment." Here, disability diagnosis and educational planning have appeal, because a disability label opens doors to special education services in the U.S. and can provide students and families with explanations of learning difficulties (Turnbull et al. 2015). In response to disability, schools provide instruction from specially-trained professionals (e.g., special educators, speech-language pathologists, physical therapists). The medical model can be appealing given its simplicity (i.e., test, diagnosis, treatment). With its greatest applicability for disabilities rooted in biology and psychology (Kalyanpur and Harry 2012), disabilities such as LD may involve considerable professional subjectivity and thereby lead to bias against minority students, who may have different learning processes and needs (Harry and Klingner 2014). In contrast, the social model of disability posits that disability is socially is a social construction (Thomas 2004) and thereby accounts for social structures that assign disability to individuals (Oliver 1996).

In sections 5.1–5.3, we continue the discussion of the medical and social model of disability. We critique three key features of the medical model in relation to the social model and home language maintenance: (a) individualization, (b) diagnosis, and (c) remediation. We highlight critiques of the medical model, and present an alternate conceptualization of emergent bilingual students, home language maintenance, and learning disabilities.

5.1 Individualization

5.1.1 The medical model

The medical model of disability focuses on an individual's perceived pathology in relation to "normal" individuals. Students who are different than dominant racial, cultural, linguistic, or ability norms may be viewed in schools as having deficits in comparison to those from dominant racial, cultural, and linguistic backgrounds (Artiles et al. 2010). Thus, individual student differences can be equated with a "problem." This viewpoint reflects and socially constructs what Kachru (1994) characterized as *monolingual bias*, in which bilingualism is conceptualized with reference to monolingualism without acknowledgement of important differences between monolinguals and bilinguals.

For example, in U.S. general education settings, educators tend to compare emergent bilingual students' academic, language, or behavior skills to those of monolinguals, particularly standard American English spoken by White, middle-to-upper class peers, and may presume that emergent bilingual students lack specific intrinsic linguistic or cognitive skills. Moreover, in the individualization process, students' skills are decontextualized from students' social, political, and educational forces (Arehart 2008). In so doing, poverty, societal discrimination, and inequitable educational services are not considered related to students' school performance differences. Consequently, emergent bilingual students' linguistic and communication skills may be deemed by schools as "different" from the norm and, therefore, a "problem", regardless of social and educational contexts and educational services in which home culture and language are ignored or excluded.

Pervasive deficit views can contribute to monolingual English speaking teachers believing that students' home language maintenance while learning the dominant language (e.g., English) causes, or can contribute to disability or significant delay (C. Baker 2017). Moreover, general educators may not want to teach emergent bilingual students and may not know how to teach them (e.g., Bacon 2020; Walker, Shafer, and Liams 2004). Furthermore, teachers may erroneously attribute characteristics of second language acquisition and bilingualism to low motivation, low intelligence, and social problems (Cheatham et al. 2014). Based on deficit discourses about bilingualism and emergent bilingual students, educators may advocate for increased or exclusive English language services at the expense of home language use in hopes of propelling students' English language skills to be more like their monolingual English speaking peers (C. Baker 2017; Mary and Young this vol.).

By placing a problem within the individual, the medical model of disability decontextualizes emergent bilingual students from marginalization and inequity within schools and society (Artiles 2011). For emergent bilingual students, individualization is infused with monolingual bias. Thus, emergent bilingual students' different learning processes and needs can be erroneously conceptualized by school professionals as potential disabilities, which can lead to referral for special education evaluation (i.e., comprehensive assessment to determine whether a student has a disability).

5.1.2 The social model

In contrast to the medical model's individualization, which attributes a disability to an individual's impairments, the social model of disability emphasizes the social, environmental, political, or cultural structure that imposes disability on individuals (Oliver 1996). In fact, this model proposes that disability is socially caused and, therefore, is a social construction (Thomas 2004). The cause of problems for individuals is not inherent mental, physical, or cognitive impairments *per se* but social-structural barriers that prevent people with impairments from fully functioning or participating in the environment (Campbell and Oliver 1996). When society excludes or fails to accommodate individuals' impairments, people with varying needs in relation to their impairments can become socially *disabled* (Oliver 2004). The social model, therefore, results in an innovative understanding of disability that contests dominant social perceptions of disability as an individual's deficit (Campbell and Oliver 1996).

The social model reveals issues of social exclusion, discrimination, and oppression. The social model challenges the medical model's pathologization, decontextualization, and individualization of disability. Therefore, the main contribution of the social model of disability is to provide an alternative conceptualization of the "problem", which leads to a rethinking of ways in which society defines, theorizes, and designates disability (Oliver 2004). Consequently, the field of special education is able to identify problems, such as negative labeling, stigmatization, or rejection of individual differences.

In terms of linguistic diversity and inequity, the social model can promote attention to the socio-politics of monolingualism that oppresses bilingualism and to shift from individual bilingualism to societal bilingualism. For example, the socio-politics of a monolingual English ideology can undervalue and exclude linguistic diversity such as bilingualism (Edwards 2003; Ellis 2006). This marginalizing mechanism reveals the societal aspect of linguistic inequity and how the social model of disability vindicates societal bilingualism. Policies and practices exercised in schools shape a bilingual student's language use, attitude towards language, and relationship to languages and to speech communities of the languages. Societal bilingualism has developed an ecological analysis of language (e.g., language as a social practice) and provides a way to examine emergent bilingual students' home language maintenance or loss at the societal level rather than individual level (García and Baker 2007). Thus, as the social model challenges the problems of decontextualizing disability from surrounding disabling environments, societal bilingualism contextualizes the problem of negative language orientations or internalizing practices within sociopolitical processes.

Both the social model of disability and accounts of societal bilingualism argue that society and its institutions should take the disabling effects and outcomes of social transformation of individual differences into account when considering emergent bilingual students' learning differences. Schools should review monolingual-biased education policies and practices (e.g., the exclusive use of English in teaching, assessing, and educational placements for multilingual students), which discourage home language maintenance. Instead, educators can promote policies allowing for students' bilingual advantages in academic achievement. Additionally, educational environments must be changed to address sociocultural, affective, and familial needs for home language maintenance as discussed below.

5.2 Disability diagnosis

5.2.1 The medical model

Another feature of the medical model of disability that works with deficit viewpoints of emergent bilinguals can be found during special education evaluation (i.e., assessment to determine student disability). Individuals who are different than mainstream norms have long endured misunderstandings and discrimination regarding disability diagnosis. Students considered "different" are often marginalized in schools and are at risk for disability labeling (Artiles et al. 2005; Sullivan 2011). This problem is amplified for students whose identities intersect across several key parameters (i.e., poverty, non-White, other-than-English-speaking, labeled with disability) (González, Tefera, and Artiles 2015; Artiles 2013). Thus, marginalized students are defined not by what they are, but defined by what they are not (Artiles 1998). Kalyanpur and Harry (2012) noted that the medical model sits in conjunction with a clinical/statistical view of disability in which the "norm" for children's skills, behaviors, functioning are measured, compared, and categorized.

Particularly problematic for schools is the diagnosis of LD for emergent bilingual students, because it tends to focus on identifying student deficit. When students in general education are suspected of having a disability, this approach follows a test-diagnose-remediate procedure in which these students' cognitive, linguistic, and academic skills are assessed (typically in English) and compared to other students on the bell curve. However, criteria for LD diagnosis are vague: "A disorder in one or more of the basic psychological processes involved in understanding or in using language, spoken or written, which may manifest itself in the imperfect ability to listen, think, speak, read, write, spell, or do mathematical calculations" (Individuals with Disabilities Education Improvement Act of 2004; IDEIA, 2004). An agreed-upon, precise definition has not been established (Orosco et al. 2016). Without further detail, school bias rooted in deficit discourses and monolingual bias can drive LD diagnosis.

Additionally, U.S. schools traditionally diagnose LD via IQ-academic achievement discrepancy: Students must have an intelligence score within what is considered average, and their intelligence scores must be significantly discrepant from their academic achievement. For emergent bilingual students, this can lead to inappropriate diagnosis, because this approach to diagnosis does not account for critical factors like bilingualism and second language acquisition, particularly in relation to academic achievement. For example, as a consequence of English-only education, home language attrition or loss can occur. This is problematic because of the known importance to learning and cognition between students' home and second language (Lindholm-Leary 2012).

Emergent bilingual students' standardized assessment scores may reveal weaknesses in the home language (due to lack of home language instruction) and in English (as students acquire academic English in classrooms). Home and second language academic vocabulary is critical to a child's developing cognition (Swanson, Orosco, and Kudo 2017). Moreover, when students are tested in both home and second language using translated tests, the two tests are typically not linguistically, functionally, and culturally equivalent (Peña 2007). Additionally, standardized assessments of intelligence and academic achievement do not account for typical characteristics of bilingualism, such as code-switching. Consequently, students may be labeled as "semilingual" (Grosjean 2008: 10; MacSwan and Rolstad 2006) without investigating limitations to special education evaluation and students' social and linguistic learning contexts. Deficit labels do not acknowledge that bilinguals typically have linguistic strengths and weaknesses as a response to the social conditions under which they learn and use each language (e.g., English-only instruction) (C. Baker 2017).

Importantly, compared to emergent bilingual students who participate in bilingual programs, students in English-only immersion programs are nearly three times more likely to be identified as having a disability (Artiles et al. 2005). Additionally, academic achievement skills in subject areas such as reading comprehension and mathematics can erroneously point to disability, because they are intricately linked to students' dynamic English language skills.

A final problem is also found in a contemporary approach to LD diagnosis in U.S. schools using Response to Intervention (RTI).[2] RTI is a movement away from the medical model. It overcomes some weaknesses of the IQ-achievement discrepancy approach and has the possibility for improving LD diagnosis, because RTI focuses on instructional rather than student deficits. However, RTI can also be challenging for emergent bilingual students, because instruction and assessment (e.g., via curriculum based measurement) are often not geared toward emergent bilinguals including their critical need for home language instruction and culturally and linguistically relevant

---

[2] RTI is a student support model in which students receive evidence-based instruction at increasingly intensive levels; if students do not learn in response to instruction, they may be referred for special education evaluation.

instruction (Orosco and Klingner 2010). Moreover, when curriculum-based measures monitor student learning within RTI, emergent bilingual students can be disadvantaged if instruction and curriculum are not culturally and linguistically responsive (Orosco et al. 2016), leading to deficit views of students.

Whether using the IQ-achievement discrepancy or RTI for LD diagnosis, emergent bilingual students' language use is a key aspect of diagnosis. Special education evaluation typically occurs in English for emergent bilingual students (Phuong 2017), and as Kim (2017) noted, monolingual English verbal communication fails to include students who present themselves differently. Even when both languages are assessed, schools tend to measure emergent bilinguals' lack of nativeness in the dominant language (e.g., English) and, thereby, students' failure to be "normal" (Ortega 2014). When schools neither account for the total system for all languages in a bilingual mind nor concede heterogeneous bilingual processing and competencies (Cook 1997), schools are likely to underestimate bilingual abilities and to diagnose nonexistent deficits (Ortega 2016).

Emergent bilingual students are both over- and under-identified as having LD depending on school contexts, individual student characteristics, and student population characteristics (Artiles et al. 2005; Sullivan 2011). Inappropriate referrals to special education and subsequent disability identification may occur because students with language-related disabilities (e.g., LD) and emergent bilingual students can share characteristics, such as poor oral language skills, syntactic and grammatical errors, or comprehension difficulties (Ortiz and Maldonado-Colon 1986; Ortiz 2007). Moreover, the use of standardized assessment tools and LD diagnosis criteria, which are rooted in the medical model of disability, can be problematic. Schools may erroneously assume that the students' language-related difficulties are due to second language acquisition when, in fact, the student has an LD thus leading to underrepresentation of students labeled with LD (Orosco et al. 2016). Furthermore, the vague criteria for LD, the use of inappropriate assessment tools, and a lack of home language instruction can contribute to emergent bilingual students' inappropriate LD labels. Indeed, Ortiz et al. (2011) suggested that 75% of emergent bilingual students diagnosed with reading-related LD may be inappropriately diagnosed. Both under- and over-representation are problematic in that the students do not have opportunities to access appropriate services designed to meet individual needs.

The prescriptive approach to conceptualizing and evaluating emergent bilingual students within schools is dominated by deficit viewpoints, as the medical model of disability may legitimize monolingual biased diagnostic procedures and instruments, which are steeped in inferiority views of non-dominant languages (e.g., other than English). Other consequences of disability diagnosis include stigmatization of students and, as will be discussed below, educational planning that can exclude students from home language/literacy learning, the general education learning environment, and the general education curriculum.

5.2.2 The social model

The social model of disability rejects the practice of localizing a perceived deficit within an individual (i.e., individualization) and questions diagnoses based on the medical model and its biased diagnosis systems. First, the social model challenges the professionalized definitions, knowledge, and practice of an individualizing disability diagnosis. The social model defines disability as "a product of oppositional structures within a socio-political system that produces disablement through inequities and social injustice" (Gabel and Peters 2004: 587). For example, this model raises doubts about the taken-for-granted authority of the diagnosis system and its prescribed remedies. If the traditional education system is able-bodied-people centered, then it attempts to solve the "problems" of people with differences (e.g., impairments) and might merely reflect the biased nature of the education system. The system, then, creates a power asymmetry between the dominant (e.g., able-bodied professionals) and the dominated (e.g., people with differences or impairments) and, consequently, generates social inequities and injustices. Namely, the social model argues that disability is constructed through broad socio-political processes across social and physical environments as well as individuals' experiences functioning within such contexts (Skrtic 1991). The social model, thus, is intended to diagnose not individuals' biological, intellectual, or psychological differences (i.e., impairments), but the extent to which a society is ill-prepared, unwilling, or fails to accommodate those differences. The social model is used to identify societal rather than individual problems.

To counter the problem, the social model of disability recognizes social divisions, structural inequities, and power asymmetries that people with impairments encounter (Barnes, Barton, and Oliver 2002). From this attempt, the field of special education, which legitimizes its diagnostic system and remedial services to address the perceived deficit within students (Harry 2013), is led to recognize the problem of de-contextualizing aspects of such practice. As such, the social model helps schools detect social barriers and conditions that transform minorities into being at risk for disability or being disabled by/in schools.

The social model of disability can positively address various types of diversity. Minority social identities (e.g., social class, race/ethnicity, gender, dis/ability, language status) and associated lived experiences of the disabling environment are, therefore, the objects of analysis (Barnes, Barton, and Oliver 2002). The social model provides implications for linguistic inequity in relation to bilingualism such as identifying how monolingual English society disables bilinguals, for example by promoting "One Language Only" or "One Language at a Time" (Li and Wu 2009: 193) resulting in detrimental effects on emergent bilingual students and their speech communities (Li 2016).

Moreover, the social model demonstrates that the problem is actually education professionals' biased understandings and school practices. As such, the social model points to social disadvantages and inequities that limit bilinguals' linguistic opportunities for home language maintenance in relation to educational, economic, socio-cultural, or political constraints (Frattura and Topinka 2006). Monolingual bias, native superiority, fears of bilingualism establish such social conditions, which prevent bilinguals from becoming multi-competent bilinguals (Beardsmore 2003). The social model of disability, thus, urges the field of special education to scrutinize how such conditions regulate linguistic outcomes (e.g., home language maintenance or loss), availability of options (e.g., English only education that suppresses bilingual education), or (un)equal distribution of alternatives (e.g., limited access to quality bilingual education programs for students diagnosed with disabilities).

5.3 Remediation

5.3.1 The medical model

A final key feature to critique about the medical model of disability that works in parallel with deficit views of minority students is the medical model's focus on remediation. By placing the problem in individual students without reference to social, contextual factors followed by disability diagnosis, schools may implement specialized instruction and professionalized practices to overcome consequences of disability (Arehart 2008; Haegele and Hodge 2016). While typically well intentioned, disability remediation can marginalize and oppress minority students and their home languages. A central focus of special education services should be high quality inclusion for students with diagnosed disabilities (i.e., providing students diagnosed with disabilities with access to general education curriculum with typically-developing peers in natural environments; DEC/NAEYC 2009). Despite legal mandates (e.g., IDEIA 2004), best practice recommendations (e.g., DEC/NAEYC 2009), and research illustrating positive academic and social outcomes for students diagnosed with disabilities and their non-disabled peers (e.g., Odom, Buysse, and Soukakou 2011), schools within the U.S. struggle to successfully implement inclusion, particularly for minority students (Artiles et al. 2010): Many minority students continue to be excluded from general education environments, and even when included, they may not be provided with necessary supports for success.

Notwithstanding U.S. schools' challenges to disability diagnosis for emergent bilingual students, for those students who are diagnosed with LD, the medical model tends to interconnect with deficit discourses as schools plan special education services. U.S. schools struggle to meet the needs of students who have two perceived "pathologies": Disability and limited English language proficiency (LEP) (González, Tefera, and Artiles 2015; Kangas 2017). This is what Cioè-Peña (2017) called an "intersectional gap" in which students' need for educational services for language learning and disability services are inadequate.

Emergent bilingual students are more likely to be segregated from typically developing peers than students who are not emergent bilinguals (Zehler et al. 2003). Additionally, these students are likely to be placed in educational settings in which English is the only instructional language (Zehler et al. 2003). Kangas (2018) found another problem – a service hierarchy for emergent bilingual students such that special education was prioritized over language services.

Moreover, as Kangas (2018) illustrated, there is a lack of professional collaboration and misunderstandings about language education and special education policies. Even in schools where bilingualism is valued, school-level policies and practices can result in emergent bilingual students being prevented from home language maintenance services (Kangas 2017). Furthermore, emergent bilingual students diagnosed with disabilities may not participate in culturally and linguistically responsive instruction, which holds promise for enhanced content as well as home language and dominant language learning (Orosco and Abdulrahim 2017; Ortiz and Robertson 2018). Thus, the medical model is integral to these difficulties, because it aligns with a deficit view of emergent bilingual students who, according to this model, have "problems" with both (dis)ability and English language proficiency (e.g., LEP), which are conceptualized as two distinct pathologies, both requiring distinct remediation.

5.3.2 The social model

The social model of disability has implications for and aligns with particular approaches to providing educational services for emergent bilingual students diagnosed with disabilities (e.g., inclusion, dual language programs for emergent bilingual students diagnosed with disabilities). The importance of individual capabilities and socio-political context to home language maintenance and bilingualism are well known (Ortega 2014). This view embraces the interrelationships among individuals' linguistic systems, cognitive processes, and their socio-cultural experiences (Kramsch 2009). For example, emergent bilingual students' language development can be encouraged or discouraged depending on ways in which their internal resources (e.g., cognitive or linguistic capacities) interplay with external resources (e.g., environmental conditions for language learning and use) (de Bot 2016). This echoes the social model of disability, which views human diversity and associated cognitive or physical functioning as natural phenomena while remaining concerned with environmental (dis)ablement (Baglieri et al. 2011). The social model of disability leads to emphasizing a democratic society's responsibility to optimize educational equity and provisions for *all* students, which extends to emergent bilingual students' academic achievement including home language maintenance.

The social model of disability can liberate individuals diagnosed with disabilities from the myth of (ab)normality (Reindal 2008). This model helps schools view minority students' differences (e.g., race, culture, ability, language) with the intention to provide opportunities to learn the values of inclusion, respect for diversity, equity, and full participation in *all* environments for *all* people (Connor et al. 2008). Therefore, linguistic diversity, as it concerns emergent bilingual students, demands that schools replace the fragmented approach to bilingualism with holistic approaches such as translanguaging pedagogy such that teachers and students can flexibly use their entire language repertoire (e.g., home and majority language) to develop students' language skills corresponding to social, educational demands (López and González-Davies 2015). Furthermore, the new perspective on home language maintenance and bilingualism requires re-envisioning educational goals for emergent bilingual students including those diagnosed with disabilities. Educational goals can include emergent bilingual students becoming unique individuals, who have multilingual repertoires which are unlike monolingual students (Cook 2016), while addressing their unique cognitive, academic, social, and linguistic needs.

Based on the overarching principle that bilingual education is good for all students (Fishman 1976), bilingual education has the potential to reform disabling education (García 2009). For example, bilingual education centers on an inclusive and plural vision of linguistic diversity and variations (e.g., multilingual and multimodal language and literacy) and aims to maximize learning and communication that uses more than one language (García 2009; Escamilla et al. 2014).

The detailed description of the use of two languages in teaching and learning is beyond traditional education programs (e.g., ESL classrooms or English only special education settings). Nevertheless, bilingual education can promote linguistic differences and appreciation of human diversity (García and Kleifgen 2010) so that *all* students can benefit regardless of their dominant languages, socio-economic status, or educational placements. Thus, the vision of bilingual education "as a way of providing meaningful and equitable education" (García 2009: 6) can be extended to inclusive education for students who have been diagnosed with or are considered at risk of having disabilities.

One promising approach to fulfill the vision of the social model of disability is high quality, two-way bilingual immersion (TWBI) programs (i.e., dual language programs) in which language minority and majority students together learn two languages (Lindholm-Leary 2012; Lindholm-Leary and Borsato 2006; Lindholm-Leary and Genesee 2010). Some evidence suggests that dual language programs also can lead to positive outcomes for emergent bilingual students diagnosed with disabilities. For example in one U.S. state, students receiving special education services and who participated in dual language programs, significantly outscored students not participating in dual language programs in reading and math (Thomas and Collier 2014).

Within the TWBI programs, which consider bilingual processing, patterns, or competency as *natural* and *normal*, emergent bilingual students may have less possibility to be misdiagnosed as having a LD. Once emergent bilingual students learn in an inclusive setting that allows for linguistic diversity and learning differences related to bilingualism, those students might have more opportunity for linguistic and educational equity. While TWBI programs provide the inclusive vision, such programs can help emergent bilingual students envision their own goals for bilingualism and biliteracy. In such an accepting and supportive environment, deficit discourses about minority students can be counteracted by culturally/linguistically sustaining pedagogy (Paris and Alim 2014). Furthermore, emergent bilingual students can maintain access to age/grade appropriate curricula and instruction in inclusive TWBI programs. Success requires teacher training in knowledge and instructional skills, for example, teachers should be critical consumers of evidence based practices, which should be adapted to fit emergent bilingual students' culture and language needs (Orosco and Abdulrahim 2017; Ortiz and Robertson 2018). Additionally, teachers should provide support for emergent bilingual students through differentiated instruction based on current understanding of emergent bilingualism and the social model of disability; implement student-centered instructional approaches for language/literacy skills in both languages; support the transfer of linguistic knowledge between students' two languages (Ortiz and Robertson 2018); and provide effective accommodations (e.g., visual cues, provide extra time to complete tasks, clarify multistep directions) (Klingner et al. 2014). Presently, there is a dearth of research about ways educators' can effectively address home language maintenance of students with learning disabilities in classrooms in which students speak multiple languages. In this case, the use of language interpreters, bilingual support personnel, translanguaging, and innovative staffing may be beneficial to support all children's home language maintenance in inclusive environments. Additionally, heritage language schools and educators' support for families' home language maintenance may be effective. For more ideas on supporting multiple languages in single classrooms and schools, please see Paulsrud this vol.

6 Conclusion

In summary, myths about emergent bilingual students and disabilities abound. Emerging research indicates that these students, across a variety of disability labels, can be bilingual and should participate in instruction including their home languages and in inclusive classrooms. Particularly for emergent bilingual students diagnosed with LD, many questions arise about disability diagnosis and educational programming. Deficit discourses about minority students including emergent bilingual students interconnect with the medical model of disability contributing to difficulties with home language maintenance and bilingualism. To secure educational equity including language rights for emergent bilingual students, schools can adopt the lens of the social model of disability. This model can positively reposition bilingualism and, therefore, promotes emergent bilingual students' home language maintenance in society and educational institutions. For emergent bilingual students diagnosed with disabilities, inclusive bilingual education can be implemented to meet their linguistic, academic, and social needs. All these efforts, however, are aimed at going beyond the realm of linguistic or educational benefits. As the social model of disability enables us to challenge the neglected, marginalized, and disabled status of bilingualism, it re-envisions the meaning and value of home language maintenance as a liberating tool, with which linguistic minorities, such as bilinguals, can de/re-construct the monolingual biased society.

References

Abu-Rabia, Salim & Linda S. Siegel. 2002. Reading, syntactic, orthographic, and working memory skills of bilingual Arabic-English speaking Canadian children. *Journal of Psycholinguistic Research* 31(6). 661–678.

Areheart, Bradley A. 2008. When disability isn't 'just right': The entrenchment of the medical model of disability and the Goldilocks dilemma. *Indiana Law Journal* 83(1). 181–232.

Artiles, Alfredo J. 1998. The dilemma of difference: Enriching the disproportionality discourse with theory and context. *Journal of Special Education* 32(1). 32–36.

Artiles, Alfredo J. 2011. Toward an interdisciplinary understanding of educational equity and difference: The case of the racialization of ability. *Educational Researcher* 40(9). 431–445.

Artiles, Alfredo J. 2013. Untangling the racialization of disabilities: An intersectionality critique across disability models. *Du Bois Review* 10(2). 329–347.

Artiles, Alfredo J., Robert Rueda, Jesús J. Salazar & Ignacio Higareda. 2005. Within group diversity in minority representation: English language learners in urban school districts. *Exceptional Children* 71(3). 283–300.

Artiles, Alfredo. J., Elizabeth B. Kozleski, Stanley C. Trent, David Osher & Alba Ortiz. 2010. Justifying and explaining disproportionality, 1968–2008: A critique of underlying views of culture. *Exceptional Children* 76(3). 279–299.

Bacon, Chris K. 2020. "It's not really my job": A mixed methods framework for language ideologies, monolingualism, and teaching emergent bilingual learners. *Journal of Teacher Education* 71(2). 172–187.

Baetens Beardsmore, H. 2003. Who is afraid of bilingualism? In Jean-Marc Dewaele, Alex Housen & Li Wei (eds.), *Bilingualism: Beyond basic principles*, 10–27. Bristol: Multilingual Matters.

Baglieri, Susan, Jan W. Valle, David J. Connor & Deborah J. Gallagher. 2011. Disability studies in education: The need for a plurality of perspectives on disability. *Remedial and Special Education* 32(4). 267–278.

Baker, Colin. 2017. *Foundations of bilingual education and bilingualism*. Tonawanda, NY: Multilingual Matters.

Baker, Diana. 2017. The language question: Considering three Somali American students with autism. *Multiple Voices for Ethnically Diverse Exceptional Learners* 17(1). 20–38.

Barnes, Colin, Len Barton & Mike Oliver (eds.). 2002. *Disability studies today*. Cambridge: Polity Press.

Bot, Kees de. 2016. Multi-competence and dynamic/complex systems. In Vivian Cook & Li Wei (eds.), *The Cambridge handbook of linguistic multi-competence*, 125–141. Cambridge: Cambridge University Press.

Campbell, Jane & Mike Oliver. 1996. *Disability politics: Understanding our past, changing our future*. London: Routledge.

Cheatham, Gregory A. & Juliet Hart-Barnett. 2017. Overcoming common misunderstandings about students with disabilities who are English language learners. *Intervention in School and Clinic* 53(1). 58–63.

Cheatham, Gregory A., Margarita Jiménez-Silva, David L. Wodrich & Masahiro Kasai. 2014. Disclosure of information about English proficiency: Preservice teachers' presumptions about English language learners. *Journal of Teacher Education* 65(1). 53–62.

Cheatham, Gregory A., Rosa M. Santos & Ayfer Kerkutluoglu. 2012. Review of comparison studies investigating bilingualism and bilingual instruction for students with disabilities. *Focus on Exceptional Children* 45(3). 1–12.

Cioè-Peña, María. 2017. The intersectional gap: How bilingual students in the United States are excluded from inclusion. *International Journal of Inclusive Education* 21(9). 906–919.

Connor, David J., Susan L. Gabel, Deborah J. Gallagher & Missy Morton. 2008. Disability studies and inclusive education – Implications for theory, research, and practice. *International Journal of Inclusive Education* 12(5–6). 441–457.

Cook, Vivian. 1997. Monolingual bias in second language research. *Revista Canaria de Estudios Ingleses* 34. 35–50.

Cook, Vivian. 2016. Premises of multi-competence. In Vivian Cook & Li Wei (eds.), *The Cambridge handbook of linguistic multi-competence*, 1–25. Cambridge: Cambridge University Press.

Crenshaw, Kimberle. 1989. Demarginalizing the intersection of race and sex: A black feminist critique of antidiscrimination doctrine, feminist theory, and antiracist politics. *University of Chicago Legal Forum* 1. 138–167.

Da Fontoura, Helena A. & Linda S. Siegel. 1995. Reading, syntactic, and working memory skills of bilingual Portuguese-English Canadian children. *Reading and Writing: An Interdisciplinary Journal* 7. 139–153.

DEC/NAEYC. 2009. *Early childhood inclusion: A joint position statement of the Division or Early Childhood (DEC) and the National Association for the Education of Young Children (NAEYC)*. Chapel Hill, NC: University of North Carolina, FPG Child Development Institute.

De Houwer, Annick. this vol. Harmonious Bilingualism: Well-being for families in bilingual settings.

Durán, Lillian K., Cary J. Roseth & Patricia Hoffman. 2014. Effects of transitional bilingual education on Spanish-speaking preschoolers' early literacy development: Year two results. *Applied Psycholinguistics* 36(4). 921–951.

Edgin, Jamie O., Abhijeet Kumar, Goffredina Spanò & Lynn Nadel. 2011. Neuropsychological effects of second language exposure in Down syndrome. *Journal of Intellectual Disability Research* 55. 351–356.

Edwards, John. 2003. The importance of being bilingual. In Jean-Marc Dewaele, Alex Housen & Li Wei (eds.), *Bilingualism: Basic principles and beyond*, 28–42. Clevedon: Multilingual Matters.

Ellis, Elizabeth. 2006. Monolingualism: The unmarked case. *Estudios de Sociolingüística* 7. 173–196.

Escamilla, Kathy, Susan Hopewell, Sandra Butvilofsky, Wendy Sparrow, Lucinda Soltero-González, Olivia Ruiz-Figueroa & Manuel Escamilla. 2014. *Biliteracy from the start: Literacy squared in action*. Philadelphia, PA: Caslon Publishing.

Feltmate, Krista & Elizabeth Kay-Raining Bird. 2008. Language learning in four bilingual children with Down syndrome: A detailed analysis of vocabulary and syntax. *Canadian Journal of Speech-Language Pathology and Audiology* 32. 6–20.

Fishman, Joshua A. 1976. *Bilingual education: An international sociological perspective*. Rowley, MA: Newbury House.

Franceschini, Rita. 2016. Multilingualism research. In Vivian Cook & Li Wei (eds.), *The Cambridge handbook of linguistic multi-competence*, 97–124. Cambridge: Cambridge University Press.

Frattura, Elise M. & Carol Topinka. 2006. Theoretical underpinnings of separate educational programs: The social justice challenge continues. *Education and Urban Society* 38(3). 327–344.

Gabel, Susan L. & Susan Peters. 2004. Presage of a paradigm shift? Beyond the social model of disability toward resistance theories of disability. *Disability and Society* 19(6). 585–600.

García, Ofelia. 2009. *Bilingual education in the 21st century: A global perspective*. West Sussex: John Wiley.

García, Ofelia & Colin Baker. 2007. *Bilingual education: An introductory reader*. Clevedon: Mutilingual Matters.

García, Ofelia & Joanne Kleifgen. 2010. *Educating emergent bilinguals: Policies, programs, and practices for English language learners*. New York, NY: Teachers College Press.

González, Taucia, Adai Tefera & Alfredo Artiles. 2015. The intersection of language differences and learning disabilities. In Martha Bigelow & Johanna Ennser-Kananen (eds.), *Routledge handbook of educational linguistics*, 145–157. New York, NY: Routledge.

Grosjean, François. (2008). *Studying bilinguals*. Oxford: Oxford University Press.

Gutiérrez-Clellen, Vera, Gabriela Simon-Cereijido & Monica Sweet. 2012. Predictors of second language acquisition in Latino children with specific language impairment. *American Journal of Speech-Language Pathology* 21(1). 64–77.

Haegele, Justin A. & Samuel Hodge. 2016. Disability discourse: Overview and critiques of the medical and social models. *Quest* 68(2). 193–206.

Hambly, Catherine & Eric Fombonne. 2012. The impact of bilingual environments on language development in children with autism spectrum disorders. *Journal of Autism and Developmental Disorders* 42(7). 1342–1352.

Hampton, Sarah, Hugh Rabagliati, Antonella Sorace & Sue Fletcher-Wilson. 2017. Autism and bilingualism: A qualitative interview study of parents' perspectives and experiences. *Journal of Speech, Language, and Hearing Research* 60(2). 435–446.

Harry, Beth. 2013. The disproportionate placement of ethnic minorities in special education. In Lani Florian (ed.), *Handbook of special education*, 73–95. Thousand Oaks, CA: Sage.

Harry, Beth & Janette Klingner. 2014. *Why are so many minority students in special education? Understanding race and disability in schools*. New York, NY: Teachers College Press.

Individuals with Disabilities Education Improvement Act of 2004 (IDEA), P.L. 108–446, 20 C.F.R. § 1400 et. seq. 2004.

Jegatheesan, Brinda. 2011. Multilingual development in children with autism: Perspectives of south Asian Muslim immigrant parents on raising a child with a communicative disorder in multilingual contexts. *Bilingual Research Journal* 34(2). 185–200.

Jordaan, Heila. 2008. Clinical intervention for bilingual children: An international survey. *Folia Phoniatrica et Logopaedica* 60(2). 97–105.

Kachru, Yamuna. 1994. Monolingual bias in SLA research. *TESOL Quarterly* 28. 795–800.

Kalyanpur, Maya & Beth Harry. 2012. *Cultural reciprocity in special education: Building family-professional relationships*. Baltimore, MD: Brookes.

Kangas, Sara E. N. 2017. "That's where the rubber meets the road": The intersection of special education and dual language education. *Teachers College Record* 119. 1–36.

Kangas, Sara E. N. 2018. Breaking one law to uphold another: How schools provide services to English learners with disabilities. *TESOL Quarterly* 52(4). 877–910.

Kay-Raining Bird, Elizabeth, Patricia Cleave, Natacha Trudeau, Elin Thordardottir, Ann Sutton & Amy Thorpe. 2005. The language abilities of bilingual children with Down syndrome. *American Journal of Speech-Language Pathology* 14(3). 187–199.

Kay-Raining Bird, Elizabeth, Fred Genesee & Ludo Verhoeven. 2016. Bilingualism in children with developmental disorders: A narrative review. *Journal of Communication Disorders* 63. 1–14.

Kim, Hyun Uk. 2017. Reflecting on a daughter's bilingualism and disability narratively. *International Journal of Whole Schooling* 13(1). 21–34.

Klingner, Janette, Amy Boele, Sylvia Linan-Thompson & Diane Rodriguez. 2014. *Essential components of special education for English language learners with learning disabilities* (Position Statement 2). Arlington, VA: Council for Exceptional Children.

Kramsch, Claire J. 2009. *The multilingual subject: What foreign language learners say about their experience and why it matters*. Oxford: Oxford University Press.

Kremer-Sadlik, Tamar. 2005. To be or not to be bilingual: Autistic children from multilingual families. In James Cohen, Kara T. McAlister, Kellie Rolstad & Jeff MacSwan (eds.), *ESB4 Proceedings of the 4th International Symposium on Bilingualism*, 1225–1234. Somerville, MA: Cascadilla Press.

Lang, Russell, Mandy Rispoli, Jeff Sigafoos, Giulio Lancioni, Alonzo Andrews & Lilia Ortega. 2011. Effects of language of instruction on response accuracy and challenging behavior in a child with autism. *Journal of Behavioral Education* 20. 252–259.

Li, Wei. 2016. Consequences of multi-competence for sociolinguistic research. In Vivian Cook & Li Wei (eds.), *The Cambridge handbook of linguistic multi-competence*, 164–182. Cambridge: Cambridge University Press.

Li, Wei & Chao-Jung Wu. 2009. Polite Chinese children revisited: Creativity and the use of codeswitching in the Chinese complementary school classroom. *International Journal of Bilingual Education and Bilingualism* 12(2). 193–211.

Lindholm-Leary, Kathryn. 2012. Success and challenges in dual language education. *Theory Into Practice* 51(4). 256–262.

Lindholm-Leary, Kathryn & Graciela Borsato. 2006. Academic achievement. In Fred Genesee, Kathryn Lindholm-Leary, William Saunders & Donna Christian (eds.), 157–179. *Educating English Language Learners*. New York, NY: Cambridge University Press.

Lindholm-Leary, Kathryn & Fred Genesee. 2010. Alternative educational programs for English language learners. In California Department of Education (ed.), *Research on English language learners*, 323–367. Sacramento: California Department of Education Press.

López, Cristina C. & María González-Davies. 2015. Switching codes in the plurilingual classroom. *ELT Journal* 70(1). 67–77.

Lund, Emily M., Theresa L. Kohlmeier & Lillian K. Durán. 2017. Comparative language development in bilingual and monolingual children with Autism spectrum disorder: A systematic review. *Journal of Early Intervention* 39(2). 106–124.

Macswan, Jeff & Kellie Rolstad. 2006. How language proficiency tests mislead us about ability: Implications for English language learner placement in special education. *Teachers College Record* 108(11). 2304–2328.

Mary, Latisha & Andrea Young. this vol. Teachers' beliefs and attitudes towards home language maintenance and their effects.

Odom, Samuel L., Viginia Buysse & Elena Soukakou. 2011. Inclusion for young children with disabilities: A quarter century of research perspectives. *Journal of Early Intervention* 33(4). 344–357.

Ohashi, J. Kaori, Pat Mirenda, Stefka Marinova-Todd, Catherine Hambly, Eric Fombonne, Peter Szatmari, Susan Bryson, Wendy Roberts, Isabel Smith, Tracy Vaillancourt, Joanne Volden, Charlotte Waddell, Lonnie Zwaigenbaum, Stelios Georgiades, Eric Duku & Ann Thompson. 2012. Comparing early language development in monolingual- and bilingual-exposed young children with autism spectrum disorders. *Research in Autism Spectrum Disorders* 6. 890–897.

Oliver, Michael. 1996. *Understanding disability: From theory to practice*. Basingstoke: Palgrave Macmillan.

Oliver, Michael. 2004. If I had a hammer: The social model in action. In John Swain, Sally French, Colin Barnes & Carol Thomas (eds.), *Disabling barriers – Enabling environments*, 7–12. London: Sage.

Orosco, Michael J. & Naheed A. Abdulrahim. 2017. Culturally responsive evidence-based practices with English language learners with learning disabilities: A qualitative case study. *Educational Borderlands* 1. 26–44.

Orosco. Michael J. & Janette Klingner. 2010. One school's implementation of RTI with English language learners: "Referring into RTI". *Journal of Learning Disabilities* 43(3). 269–288.

Orosco, Michael J., Estella Almanza de Schonewise, Carmen de Onís, Janette K. Klingner & John J. Hoover. 2016. Distinguishing between language acquisition and learning disabilities among English learners. In John J. Hoover, Leonard M. Baca & Janette K. Klingner (eds.), *Why do English learners struggle with reading?*, 5–16. Thousand Oaks, CA: Corwin.

Ortega, Lourdes. 2014. Ways forward for a bi/multilingual turn in SLA. In Stephen May (ed.), *The multilingual turn: Implications for SLA, TESOL, and bilingual education*, 32–53. New York, NY: Routledge.

Ortega, Lourdes. 2016. Multi-competence in second language acquisition: Inroads into the mainstream? In Vivian Cook & Li Wei (eds.), *The Cambridge handbook of linguistic multi-competence*, 50–76. Cambridge: Cambridge University Press.

Ortiz, Alba A. 2007. English language learners with special needs: Effective instructional strategies. *Bilingual Education and Bilingualism* 61. 281–285.

Ortiz, Alba A. & Elba Maldonado-Colón. 1986. Recognizing learning disabilities in bilingual children: How to lessen inappropriate referrals of language minority students to special education. *Journal of Reading, Writing, and Learning Disabilities International* 2(1). 43–56.

Ortiz, Alba A. & Phyllis M. Robertson. 2018. Preparing teachers to serve English learners with language- and/or literacy-related difficulties and disabilities. *Teacher Education and Special Education* 41(3). 176–187.

Ortiz, Alba A., Phyllis M. Robertson, Cheryl Y. Wilkinson, Yi-Juin Liu, Belinda McGhee & Millicent Kushner. 2011. The role of bilingual education teachers in preventing inappropriate referrals of ELLs to special education: Implications for response to intervention. *Bilingual Research Journal* 34(3). 316–333.

Paradis, Johanne, Fred Genesee, Martha Crago & Mabel Rice. 2003. French-English bilingual children with SLI: How do they compare with their monolingual peers? *Journal of Speech, Language, and Hearing Research* 46. 113–127.

Paris, Django & H. Samy Alim. 2014. What are we seeking to sustain through culturally sustaining pedagogy? A loving critique forward. *Harvard Educational Review* 84(1). 85–100.

Paulsrud, BethAnne. this vol. The mainstream classroom and home language maintenance.

Peña, Elizabeth D. 2007. Lost in translation: Methodological considerations in cross-cultural research. *Child Development* 78(4). 1255–1264.

Petersen, Jill, Stefka Marinova-Todd & Pat Mirenda. 2012. Brief report: An exploratory study of lexical skills in bilingual children with autism spectrum disorder. *Journal of Autism and Developmental Disorders* 42. 1499–1503.

Pham, Giang, Kathryn Kohnert & Deanine Mann. 2011. Addressing clinician-client mismatch: A preliminary intervention study with a bilingual Vietnamese-English preschooler. *Language, Speech, and Hearing Services in Schools* 42(4). 408–422.

Phuong, Jennifer. 2017. Disability and language ideologies in education policy. *Working Papers in Educational Linguistics* 32(1). 47–66.

Reetzke, Rachel, Xiaobing Zou, Li Sheng & Napoleon Katsos. 2015. Communicative development in bilingually exposed Chinese children with autism spectrum disorders. *Journal of Speech, Language, and Hearing Research* 58(3). 813–825.

Reindal, Solveig M. 2008. A social relational model of disability: A theoretical framework for special needs education? *European Journal of Special Needs Education* 23(2). 135–146.

Rohena, Elba. I., Asha K. Jitendra & Diane M. Browder. 2002. Comparison of the effects of Spanish and English constant time delay instruction on sight word reading by Hispanic learners with mental retardation. *The Journal of Special Education* 36(3). 171–186.
Simon-Cereijido, Gabriela, Vera F. Gutiérrez-Clellen & Monica Sweet. 2013. Predictors of growth or attrition of the first language in Latino children with specific language impairment. *Applied Psycholinguistics* 34. 1219–1243.
Skrtic, Thomas M. 1991. *Behind special education: A critical analysis of professional culture and school organization*. Denver, CO: Love Publishing Company.
Sullivan, Amanda. 2011. Disproportionality in special education and placement of English language learners. *Exceptional Children* 77. 317–334.
Swanson, H. Lee, Michael J. Orosco & Milagros Kudo. 2017. Does growth in the executive system of working memory underlie growth in literacy for bilingual children with and without learning disabilities? *Journal of Learning Disabilities* 50. 386–407.
Thomas, Carol. 2004. Disability and impairment. In John Swain, Sally French, Colin Barnes & Carol Thomas (eds.), *Disabling barriers – Enabling environments*, 21–27. London: Sage.
Thomas, Wayne P. & Virginia P. Collier. 2014. English learners in North Carolina dual language programs: Year 3 of this study: School Year 2009–2010. A research report provided to the North Carolina Department of Public Instruction Fairfax, VA: George Mason University.
Thordardottir, Elin, Geneviève Cloutier, Suzanne Ménard, Elaine Pelland-Blais & Susan Rvachew. 2015. Monolingual or bilingual intervention for primary language impairment? A randomized control trial. *Journal of Speech, Language, and Hearing Research* 58(2). 287–300.
To, Carol K. S., Thomas Law & Xin-Xin Li. 2012. Influence of additional language learning on first language learning in children with language disorders. *International Journal of Communication Disorders* 47. 208–216.
Turnbull, Ann P., H. Rutherford Turnbull, Elizabeth J. Erwin, Leslie C. Soodak & Karrie A. Shogren. 2015. *Families, professionals and exceptionality: Positive outcomes through partnerships and trust*. Boston, MA: Pearson.
Turnbull, H. Rutherford, Matthew J. Stowe & Nancy E. Huerta. 2007. *Free appropriate public education: The law and children with disabilities*. Denver, CO: Love Publishing.
Walker, Anne, Jill Shafer & Michelle Liams. 2004. Not in my classroom: Teacher attitudes towards English language learners in mainstream classrooms. *NABE Journal of Research and Practice* 2. 130–160.
Wathum-Ocama, John C. & Susan Rose. 2002. Hmong immigrants' views on the education of their deaf and hard of hearing children. *American Annals of the Deaf* 147. 44–53.
Wilkinson, Cheryl Y., Alba A. Ortiz, Phyllis M. Robertson & Millicent Kushner. 2006. English language learners with reading-related LD: Linking data from multiple sources to make eligibility determinations. *Journal of Learning Disabilities* 39(2). 129–141.
Willoughby, Louisa. 2012. Language maintenance and the deaf child. *Journal of Multilingual and Multicultural Development* 33(6). 605–618.
Zehler, Anette M., Howard L. Fleischman, Paul J. Hopstock, Todd G. Stephenson, Michelle L. Pendzick & Saloni Sapru. 2003. *Descriptive study of services to LEP students and LEP students with disabilities*. Final report to the U.S. Department of Education, Office of English Language Acquisition. Arlington, VA: Development Associates, Inc.

Topic area 4.2: **Formal education**

Kutlay Yağmur

21 Models of formal education and minority language teaching across countries

1 Introduction

There is scant information on formal education models and minority language teaching in the literature. Minority language education is mostly organized by non-formal education institutions (minority organizations, NGO's, voluntary groups, and so forth) in many countries. Only in a very limited number of national contexts, minority languages, especially immigrant languages, are part of the formal education (Extra and Yağmur 2012). Because the topic "formal education" has multiple dimensions and layers, in this chapter, the focus is on the relationship between the states' integration ideologies and the place of minority languages in formal education institutions. The primary focus of the chapter is on the European context. Even though limited references to Australia and Canada are made, this is just to point out the similarities and differences with the EU practices.

According to a definition by UNESCO, "formal education is institutionalized, intentional and planned through public organizations and recognized private bodies and, in their totality, make up the formal education system of a country" (http://uis.unesco.org/node/334633 last accessed 4 January 2019). Policy makers and national educational authorities decide on formal education programmes. Primary and secondary education programmes have the utmost priority for formal education planners. Vocational education, special needs education and some areas of adult education are often recognized as being part of the formal education system. In terms of language education, the basic primary schooling is the most contested area. The rules and regulations of language use in primary schools are strictly defined. Educational institutions and policy makers do not always tolerate the use of local dialects in schools, let alone immigrant minority languages. Nation-state ideology promotes (and allows) the use of national language/s and chosen foreign languages in formal education.

Depending on the national context and the dominant language ideology, policy makers decide on which languages are to be taught in formal education institutions. The selection criteria might show large variation across countries. In some national contexts, such as Australia or Canada, diversity policies are used to promote the teaching and learning of minority languages but in some other national contexts, such as France or Turkey, the "national" state language has the utmost priority and minority languages have very little place, if any, in the national curriculum (Yağmur 2017). Formal education models are mostly based on the national priorities of nation-states. However, in some decentralized states,

https://doi.org/10.1515/9781501510175-021

like Germany and the Netherlands, local authorities might make decisions in line with supply and demand criteria for offering languages in schools. Even in the same country, there might be different language teaching practices in various levels of formal education. For instance, in the Netherlands, some immigrant minority languages are offered as part of the secondary school curriculum, but immigrant languages are generally not taught in primary schools. Given the complexity and the diverse nature of the topic, it is not always possible to generalize about models of formal education across countries. In line with the historical, demographic, economic and political circumstances, states identify priorities for language teaching. The educational and political considerations in making decisions for teaching regional minority and immigrant minority languages are fundamentally different from foreign language teaching. While foreign languages are taught for instrumental purposes, minority languages are taught mostly for symbolic reasons such as ethnic identity and identification with a group.

The local national circumstances are the most decisive factor in making policy decisions. Even in the case of the teaching national languages, there can be differences in policy and practice. For instance, in South Africa not all the 11 official languages enjoy the same degree of support in formal education. The language education practices in formal education depend on the ideological approach adopted by the national context and language education visions. In the following sections, after a discussion of policy perspectives on state and heritage language education in various forms of formal education (Pluralistic, Civic, Assimilationist and Ethnist), the inclusion or exclusion of minority languages are discussed. Even though the clustering of countries along ideological orientations is common practice (Bourhis et al. 1997), there can be diverse policies for different minority groups in the same national context. Depending on the type of intergroup relations, cultural and the linguistic distance, the host society might adapt various acculturation orientations for different minority groups. Moreover, there can be several policies at different institutions for the same minority group. For instance, both in the Netherlands and France, fundamentally different policies are adopted for immigrant minority languages in the primary and secondary schools. While Turkish and Arabic are not taught in primary schools, these languages are offered in the secondary school curriculum. In order to critically examine the policy differences in primary and secondary schools towards immigrant languages, an assessment of minority language education along nine parameters (such as target groups, arguments for teaching, funding, curricular status and so on) is presented. By using the nine-parameter model developed by Yağmur and Extra (2011), differences in policies across formal education models are evaluated.

2 Growing diversity as a challenge for formal education institutions

As a consequence of growing globalization and large-scale population movements, new social, cultural, and political meanings are attached to languages. Recently, "languages of refugees" was added to the traditional classification of languages as "national, foreign, regional/minority, and immigrant" (Eisenchlas and Schalley this vol.; Mayer et al. this vol.). Nation-states function with "national language/s" construction. Every nation-state has one or more official languages in which all the services, e.g., in education, health care and economy, are provided. Education is primarily provided in the state language. If there are other minority (regional or immigrant) languages spoken by the residents of a country, they are not always taught in educational institutions. In general, some of those minority languages might be used as support for the learning of the state language or might be systematically excluded in the system (Williams, Strubell, and Williams 2013).

As documented by Williams, Strubell and Williams (2013) consolidation of the nation-state is achieved by a national language that is used in all public institutions including the labour market that systematically excludes all other minority languages. The teaching of indigenous minority languages or immigrant minority languages depends on the state policies. Policy makers of the state institutions decide which languages are admissible and which are not in the schools. As indicated by Williams, Strubell and Williams (2013) even the teaching of foreign languages is linked to the state's external relations involving the diplomatic services, foreign trade and intellectual pursuits. Globalization, however, challenges the nation-state institutions and imposes new demands on the economic systems; especially multinational companies challenge the domination of single nation-state languages. Given the global developments and super-diverse societies, the traditional conception of language and society might not be sustained. However, current practice of teaching and learning of minority languages is not in line with global developments. Despite somewhat inclusive European Union (EU) language policies at a macro level, not all member states adhere to multilingual policies at the state level. The EU promotes linguistic and cultural diversity but its vision regarding linguistic diversity has not always been shared by the member states. As reported by Extra and Yağmur (2012), the European Charter for Regional or Minority Languages (ECRML) has been ratified by Parliament in 11 out of the 18 countries surveyed in the Language Rich Europe (LRE) project and only signed by governments in France and Italy. It has been neither signed nor ratified by Bulgaria, Estonia, Greece, Lithuania and Portugal. The concepts of "regional" or "minority" languages are specified in the Explanatory Report to the ECRML (Council of Europe 1992: 3), but immigrant languages are explicitly excluded from it.

The position of minority languages in nation-state institutions show huge variation. Laitin (2000) makes a distinction between a "rationalized" language regime and a "multilingual" regime. If a language is imposed as the only language for educational and administrative purposes, the state has a "rationalized" language regime. According to Laitin (2000: 151), states can achieve language rationalization by three different methods: (a) rationalization through the recognition of a lingua franca (such as Swahili in Tanzania or Bahasa in Indonesia), (b) rationalization through the recognition of the language of a majority group (French in France or Han Chinese in China), and (c) rationalization through the recognition of the language of a minority group (e.g., imposition of Amharic on Ethiopia or Afrikaans in South Africa). If states have not pursued any form of rationalization or were obliged by the social and political circumstances to recognize language rights of minority populations, then these states are said to have multilingual regimes. There are different forms of multilingual regimes with varying numbers of languages. In India, for instance, one can talk of language repertoires of 3 plus/minus 1 language regime. Different languages are used for different purposes in different domains: Hindi for state documents, English for higher civil services and big business, and the state language for state services and education. Besides, an additional language is used for communication in the domestic domain and within a linguistic group. There is also the 2 plus/minus 1 regime, in which in addition to the mainstream language another legalized language is used, e.g. Spanish (with Basque, Catalan) or Russian (with one or two official languages in federal republics plus a variety of minority languages). In some multilingual contexts, some minority group members have neither the regional language nor the mainstream language as their mother tongue. Such speakers are often trilingual. For instance, Turkish speakers in Friesland in the Netherlands may be trilingual in Dutch, Fries, and Turkish. In the case of Berber speakers from Morocco, this might be four languages (Dutch, Fries, a Berber dialect and Arabic). Yet, Turkish or Arabic do not have any formal status in the mainstream society. Most immigrant minority communities within EU countries share this de facto multilingual position.

3 Language education and state ideology

The position of national languages within formal education is undisputed. In some EU countries, most of the indigenous minority languages gained a securer position in formal education. In line with the dominant state ideologies, the practice of heritage/community language teaching shows variation across the globe. The terminology used to denote heritage language teaching (minority, indigenous, immigrant, ethnic, refugee, etc.) and the semantic load of those terms show the prevalent mainstream attitude towards minority groups in each national context (for a comprehensive discussion see Eisenchlas and Schalley this vol.; Yağmur 2019).

In the literature, four clusters of state ideologies shaping integration and language policies of immigrant receiving societies are identified (Bauböck, Heller and

Zolberg 1996; Bourhis 2001; May 2001; Penninx 1996). These ideologies ranging from highly inclusive to highly exclusive comprise pluralist, civic, assimilationist, and ethnist ideologies. This categorization has some limitations as state policies are not static and there are always changes in line with the changing conditions. For instance, Germany was identified as having an ethnist ideology by Bourhis et al. (1997) but some states, such as Berlin, Hamburg and North-Rhine Westphalia, would perfectly fit the profile of a pluralistic ideology. As a matter of fact, heritage language policies of some German states are the most inclusive in the EU. Bourhis et al.'s (1997) grouping is based on citizenship and naturalization laws and this categorization does not reflect the actual practices in formal education. Keeping in mind the limitations of such rigid approaches, models of formal education are assessed in line with the main ideological orientations to minority languages in different countries in this section.

A pluralist ideology proposes duties and responsibilities to be observed by all members of a society. In this ideology, learning the official or mainstream language is the responsibility of the citizens themselves, and the state provides opportunities to facilitate language learning. Despite the inclusive approach to language learning, the emphasis also falls on the full mastery of the state language. Australia is frequently portrayed as fitting the pluralistic model in the literature. As reported by Schalley, Guillemin and Eisenchlas (2015) Australia always promoted multiculturalism and multilingualism by making heritage languages an integral part of the education for all Australian school children. However, following federation, there is a growing emphasis on English only approaches. Concerning the home languages of citizens, the state has no mandate in defining or regulating the private values of its citizens in the domestic domain, nor their political or social affiliation. As different from other ideologies, the state provides financial support for mainstream language classes and for cultural activities to promote home language maintenance. Usually, Australian and Canadian multicultural policies are good examples of the pluralist ideology, but even in these contexts, immigrant languages are in a vulnerable position (Rubino 2010; Burnaby 2008). According to Burnaby (2008), Canadians have considered immigrant languages as *deficit* and encouraged immigrants, especially children, to forget their mother tongue. Formal education has the potential to ameliorate social injustices – not to make everybody equal but to guarantee more equal opportunities (Pöllmann 2009) but at the same time, it has the potential to achieve full linguistic assimilation (and systematic indoctrination) of pupils from minority backgrounds. Even in pluralistic models of formal education, the desired goal for heritage language speakers seems to be the shift to the state language.

Civic ideology expects that immigrants adopt the public values of the mainstream society. Like pluralist ideology, the state does not interfere with the private values of its citizens but unlike pluralism, the state does not provide any provisions for the maintenance or promotion of linguistic or cultural values of immigrant minority groups. A typical example of civic ideology was the Netherlands. However, recent shifts in ideology might characterize the Dutch policies as assimilationist or even ethnist due to exclusionary policies. Especially immigrant minority languages are seen as obstacles before the linguistic assimilation into mainstream society.

Assimilation ideology expects immigrant minority groups to comply fully with the norms and values of the mainstream society. As different from pluralist and civic ideologies, assimilation ideology encourages complete linguistic and cultural shedding of heritage language and culture. In the name of homogenization of the society, assimilationist language policies aim at accelerating the language shift and language loss of immigrant minority groups. With its unitarian approach, Turkish or French policies fit the assimilationist ideology cluster quite well. Basically, most nation-states are assimilationist in nature. According to Waldinger and Fitzgerald (2004: 1179), "as ideology of the nation-state society, the sociology of assimilation necessarily obscures coercive efforts to build a nation-state society by excluding outsiders –via control of external borders- and to distinguish between members and unacceptable residents of the territory – through regulation of the internal boundaries leading to citizenship and legal residence." For most immigrants the link between old-ancestral homeland and new country of residence is an inevitable reality and contributes to the shaping of a transnational identity; but for the nation-state ideology, that link and identity are difficult to accept. Irrespective of the traditional and conservative discourse on immigration and integration, however, immigrant minority groups maintain, build and reinforce multiple connections between their old and new homelands. Identities of minority children are constructed in various ways in mainstream schools reflecting their acculturation experiences. Having their roots in another language and culture, they have to negotiate their identities and reconstruct their linguistic and cultural repertoires. As shown by Yağmur and van de Vijver (2012), linguistic assimilation of Turkish immigrants in France is the highest compared to Turkish immigrants in other countries, such as Australia, Germany and the Netherlands.

Ethnist ideology shares most aspects of the assimilation ideology; yet, it makes it difficult for immigrant minority groups to be accepted legally or socially as full members of the mainstream society. Citizenship and naturalization laws are quite representative for distinguishing ethnist ideologies. The principle of *ius sanguinis* ("law of the blood") underlies acquisition of citizenship in such countries. On the policy level, ethnist ideology seems to favour full linguistic and cultural assimilation of immigrant minority groups but in reality, achieving full membership is not easy. Even though there is variation between the policies of various states in Germany, federal state ideology in Germany is identified as ethnist by Bourhis et al. (1997). As argued earlier in this chapter, German states have divergent policies regarding the teaching and learning of heritage languages and the model of Bourhis et al. (1997) remains simplistic and invalid for the German context.

4 Position of minority languages in formal education

Formal education is highly structured and normative in its organization. It has a rather rigid and prescribed curriculum with its educational objectives, content and pedagogical approach. There is a national curriculum that schools, teachers and students alike must follow. In line with educational objectives, students are evaluated for their learning by means of formal tests so that students can proceed to the next learning stage. Conferring degrees and diplomas pursuant to a quite strict set of regulations is the most common practice in most national contexts. The selection of foreign languages is based on national and international priorities that are socio-historical, cultural and political in nature. Inclusion of minority languages in the national curriculum is not a straightforward enterprise. The most important condition is the willingness of policy makers to adopt inclusive policies, on the basis of which further educational steps can be taken. The EU has been developing the most inclusive language policies in education in the last two decades, but the member states are increasingly reluctant to implement EU policies. Some member states, such as France, Bulgaria and Greece, ignore the EU regulations in order not to offer minority language education in formal education institutions. The discrepancies between pluralistic EU policies and the member-state applications are documented in the Language Rich Europe project by Extra and Yağmur (2012). In this section, first, variable policy developments in member states regarding minority languages are explained, then, to show the complexity of the matter, the contradictory practices within the same national context are discussed. As the discussion of primary and secondary school minority language teaching curricula shows, labelling countries as pluralistic or assimilationist does not always help in understanding policy making.

4.1 Policies on minority languages in formal education

Based on the data derived from the Multilingual Cities Project (MCP) and the Language Rich Europe (LRE) Project, a discussion on the position of immigrant minority languages in formal education institutions is presented in this section. Across Europe, large contrasts occur in the status of immigrant minority languages at formal education institutions, depending on particular nation-states, or even particular federal states within nation-states (as in Germany), and depending on particular minority languages, e.g., being a national language in another European (Union) country or not. Most commonly, immigrant minority languages are not part of the mainstream education system in EU countries. In Great Britain, for example, immigrant minority languages are not part of the so-called "national" curriculum, and they are dealt with in various types of so-called "complementary" education during out-of-school hours (e.g., Martin et al. 2004).

Being aware of cross-national differences in denotation, the concept of *community language teaching* (CLT[1]) is used when referring to immigrant minority language education. The rationale for using the concept of CLT rather than the concepts of *mother tongue teaching* or *home language instruction* is the inclusion of a broad spectrum of potential target groups. First of all, the status of an immigrant minority language as a "native" or "home" language can change through intergenerational processes of language shift. Moreover, in secondary education, both minority and majority pupils are often *de jure* (although seldom *de facto*) admitted to CLT (in the Netherlands, e.g., Turkish is a secondary school subject referred to as "Turkish" rather than "home language instruction"); compare also the concepts of *Enseignement des Langues et Cultures d'Origine* and *Enseignement des Langues Vivantes* in French primary and secondary schools.

In all countries involved in the Multilingual Cities Project, there has been an increase in the number of immigrant minority pupils who speak a language at home other than or in addition to the mainstream language in primary and secondary education. Schools have largely responded to this home-school language mismatch by paying more attention to the learning and teaching of the mainstream language as a second language. A great deal of energy and money is being spent on developing curricula, teaching materials, and teacher training for second-language education. CLT stands in stark contrast to this, as it is much more susceptible to an ideological debate about its legitimacy. While there is consensus about the necessity of investing in second-language education for immigrant minority pupils, there is a lack of support for CLT. Immigrant minority languages are commonly considered sources of problems and deficiencies, and they are rarely seen as sources of knowledge and enrichment. Policy makers, local educational authorities, headmasters of schools, and teachers of "regular" subjects often have reservations or negative attitudes towards immigrant language teaching. On the other hand, parents of immigrant minority pupils, heritage language teachers, and immigrant minority organisations often make a case for including immigrant minority languages in the school curriculum.

From a historical point of view, most of the European countries show a similar chronological development in their argumentation in favour of heritage language teaching. CLT was generally introduced into primary education with a view to family remigration. This objective was also clearly expressed in *Directive 77/486* of the European Community, on 25 July 1977, which is the first and the last Directive on immigrant languages in the EU. The Directive focused on the education of the children of "migrant workers" with the aim "principally to facilitate their possible reintegration into the Member State of origin". As is clear from this formulation, the

---

[1] This abbreviation should not be confused with "communicative language teaching" which is widely referred to CLT as well.

Directive excluded all immigrant minority children originating from non-EU countries, although these children formed a large part of immigrant minority children in European primary schools. At that time, Sweden was not a member of the European Community, and CLT policies for immigrant minority children in Sweden were not directed towards remigration but modelled according to bilingual education policies for the large minority of Finnish-speaking children in Sweden.

Over the years, the demographic developments showed no substantial signs of repatriating families. Instead, a growing immigration came about in many EU countries. This development resulted in a conceptual shift, and CLT became primarily aimed at combating disadvantages. CLT had to bridge the gap between the home and the school environment, and to support school achievement in "regular" subjects. Because such an approach tended to underestimate the intrinsic value of CLT, a number of countries began to emphasise the importance of CLT from a cultural, legal, or economic perspective.

The historical development of arguments for CLT in terms of remigration, combating deficits, and multicultural policy is evident in some German states, in particular North Rhine-Westphalia and Hamburg. In most other countries in the Multilingual Cities Project, cultural policy is tied in with the mainstream language to such an extent that CLT is tolerated only in the margins. Cultural motives have played a rather important role in Sweden. It should, however, be noted that multicultural arguments for CLT have not led to an educational policy in which the status of immigrant minority languages has been substantially advanced in any of the countries involved in the Multilingual Cities Project.

4.2 Evaluation of minority language teaching along nine-parameters

Teaching English, French or German as a foreign language in European secondary schools is common practice. Asking the rationale of schools for teaching these languages would be too odd because policy makers consider these languages as part of the foreign language portfolio. However, in the case of so called "minority" languages, asking for the rationale for teaching indigenous or immigrant minority languages is the default practice. There are many conditions these languages should meet before granting a space in the formal education curriculum. Derived from Yağmur and Extra (2011), a cross-national overview of immigrant minority language teaching in primary and secondary education along nine parameters is presented in this section. Turkish and Arabic classes for primary school children were abolished in the Netherlands as being "in contradiction with integration of immigrant children", which is why, the information presented here is therefore in retrospect.

(1) Target groups

The target groups for CLT in primary schools are commonly children with an immigration heritage, defined as such in a narrow or broad sense. Narrow definitions commonly relate to the range of languages taught and/or to children's proficiency in these languages. The most restrictive set of languages is taught in Spain, i.e., Arabic and Portuguese only, for Moroccan and Portuguese(-speaking) children, respectively. A wide range of languages is taught in Sweden and Germany. The Netherlands, Belgium, and France take an intermediate position. Sweden and France demand from the target groups an active use of the languages at home and a basic proficiency in these languages. Special target groups in Sweden are adopted children; in Germany, ethnic German children (*Aussiedler*) from abroad; and in France, speakers of recognised regional minority languages. Sweden has the most explicit policy for access to CLT in terms of "home language" (nowadays, back to "mother tongue") instead of socio-economic status. The target groups for CLT in secondary schools are commonly those who participated in CLT in primary schools. *De jure*, all pupils are allowed to CLT in the Netherlands, regardless of ethnolinguistic background; *de facto*, most commonly, a subset of immigrant minority pupils takes part. In reality, school directors do not give space to immigrant languages in the school curriculum even if there is demand for these languages from the parents. CLT for secondary school pupils is almost non-existent in Belgium and limited to Arabic and Portuguese in a few secondary schools in Spain.

(2) Arguments

The arguments for CLT are formulated in terms of a struggle against deficits and/or in terms of multicultural policy. Whereas the former type of argument predominates in primary education, the latter type predominates in secondary education. The vague concept of "integration" utilised in all countries under discussion may relate to any of these arguments. Deficit arguments may be phrased in terms of bridging the home/school gap, promoting mainstream language learning, promoting school success in other ("regular") subjects, preventing educational failure, or overcoming marginalisation. Multicultural arguments may be phrased in terms of promoting cultural identity and self-esteem, promoting cultural pluralism, promoting multilingualism in a multicultural and globalising society, and avoiding ethnic prejudice. Whereas in the Netherlands and Belgium deficit arguments dominate(d), multicultural arguments tend to play a greater role in the other countries. Deficit arguments for CLT are almost absent in secondary schools, and multicultural arguments are commonly favoured in all countries.

(3) Objectives

The objectives of CLT in primary schools are rarely specified in terms of the language skills to be acquired. The vague concept of "active bilingualism" has been a common objective in Sweden, whereas in Germany and Spain, reference is made to the development of oral and written language skills, language awareness, and (inter)cultural skills. In none of these cases have more particular specifications been introduced. In contrast, the objectives of CLT in secondary schools are commonly specified in terms of particular oral and written skills to be reached at intermediate stages and/or at the end of secondary schooling.

(4) Evaluation
The evaluation of achievement through CLT may take place informally and/or formally. Informal evaluation takes place by means of subjective oral and/or written teachers' impressions or comments, meant for parents at regular intervals, e.g., once per semester or year. Formal evaluation takes place using more or less objective language proficiency measurement and language proficiency report figures, e.g., once per semester or year. Informal evaluation may occur in lower grades of primary schooling, formal evaluation in higher grades (e.g., in Sweden). In most countries, however, no report figures for CLT are provided throughout the primary school curriculum, and grades in study reports for "language" commonly refer implicitly to proficiency in the mainstream language. If CLT report figures are given (e.g., in France), such figures commonly do not have the same status as report figures for other subjects. The evaluation of achievement through CLT in secondary schools takes place formally through assessment instruments and examinations. Here, grades may have a regular or peripheral status. The former holds in particular for Sweden, Germany, and the Netherlands.

(5) Minimal enrolment
Minimal enrolment requirements for CLT may be specified at the level of the class, the school, or even the municipality at large. The latter is common practice only in Sweden, and the minimal enrolment requirement for children from different classes/schools in Sweden is five (2003/2004). Secondary schools in Sweden may also opt for CLT if at least five pupils enrol; four pupils are required in the Netherlands. All the other countries are more reluctant, with minimal requirements for primary school pupils ranging between 10–20 (Germany, Belgium, France), or without any specification (for the primary school level in the Netherlands and Spain). In the latter case, enrolment restrictions are commonly based on budget constraints.

(6) Curricular status
In all countries, CLT at primary schools takes place on a voluntary and optional basis, provided at the request of parents. Instruction may take place within or outside regular school hours. The latter is most common in Sweden, Belgium, and France. Germany, the Netherlands (until 2004), and Spain allow(ed) for two models of instruction, either within or outside regular school hours, depending on the type of language (in Germany), the type of goal (auxiliary or intrinsic in the Netherlands), and the type of organisation (in integrated or parallel classes in Spain). The number of

CLT hours varies between 1–5 hours per week. If CLT takes place at secondary schools, it is considered a regular and optional subject within school hours in all countries under consideration.

(7) Funding
The funding of CLT may depend on national, regional, or local educational authorities in the country/municipality of residence and/or on the consulates/embassies of the countries of origin. In the latter case, consulates or embassies commonly recruit and provide the teachers, and are also responsible for teacher (in-service) training. Funding through the country and/or municipality of residence takes/took place in Sweden and the Netherlands. Funding through the consulates/embassies of the countries of origin takes place in Belgium and Spain. A mixed type of funding occurs in Germany and in France. In Germany, the source of funding is dependent on particular languages or organisational models for CLT. In France, source countries fund CLT in primary schools, whereas the French ministry of education funds CLT in secondary schools.

(8) Teaching materials
Teaching materials for CLT may originate from the countries of origin or of residence of the pupils. Funding from ministries, municipalities, and/or publishing houses occurs in Sweden, Germany, and the Netherlands, although limited resources are available. Source country funding for CLT occurs in Belgium and Spain. In France, source countries fund teaching materials in primary schools, whereas the French ministry of education funds teaching materials in secondary schools.

(9) Teacher qualifications
Teacher qualifications for CLT may depend on the educational authorities in the countries of residence or of origin. National or state-wide (in-service) teacher training programmes for CLT at primary and/or secondary schools exist in Sweden, Germany, and the Netherlands, although the appeal of these programmes is limited, given the many uncertainties about CLT job perspectives. In Belgium and Spain, teacher qualifications depend on educational authorities in the countries of origin. France has a mixed system of responsibilities: source countries are responsible for teacher qualifications in primary schools, whereas the French ministry of education is responsible for teacher qualifications in secondary schools.

The presented overview of given parameters shows that there are remarkable cross-national differences in the status of CLT. There are also considerable differences between primary and secondary education in the status of CLT. A comparison of all nine parameters makes clear that CLT has gained a higher status in secondary schools than in primary schools. In primary education, CLT is generally not part of the "regular" or "national" curriculum, and, therefore, becomes a negotiable entity in a complex and often opaque interplay between a variety of actors. Another remarkable difference is that, in some countries, CLT is funded by the consulates or embassies of the countries of origin. In these cases, the national government does not interfere in the organisation of CLT, or in the requirements for, and the selection and employment of teachers. A paradoxical consequence of this phenomenon is that the earmarking of CLT budgets is often safeguarded by the above-mentioned consulates or embassies. National, regional, or local governments often fail to earmark budgets, so that funds meant for CLT may be appropriated for other educational purposes.

The higher status of CLT in secondary education is largely due to the fact that instruction in one or more languages other than the national standard language is a traditional and regular component of the (optional) school curriculum, whereas primary education is mainly determined by a monolingual *habitus* (Gogolin 1994). *Within* secondary education, however, CLT must compete with other "foreign" languages that have a higher status or a longer tradition. It should further be noted that some countries provide instruction and/or exams in non-standard language varieties. In France, for instance, pupils can take part in examinations for several varieties of Arabic and Berber (Tilmatine 1997); Sweden offers Kurdish as an alternative to Turkish.

CLT may be part of a largely centralised or decentralised educational policy. In the Netherlands, national responsibilities and educational funds are gradually being transferred to the municipal level, and even to individual schools. In France, government policy is strongly centrally controlled. Germany has devolved most governmental responsibilities to the federal states that developed their own state policies showing large interstate variation. Sweden grants far-reaching autonomy to municipal councils in dealing with educational tasks and funding. With a view to the demographic development of European nation-states into multicultural societies, and the similarities in CLT issues, more comparative cross-national research would be highly desirable.

5 Formal programs and multilingualism

As seen in the previous section, ideological approaches to language and integration alone cannot explain the complex decision-making process in formal schooling. There is a sharp difference in the position of immigrant minority languages in the primary and secondary schools, which cannot be explained by the pluralistic or assimilationist models alone. The most important declarations, recommendations, and directives on language policy in the EU support multilingualism in schools and societal institutions. On numerous occasions,[2] the EU ministers of education declared that the EU citizens'

---

2 In LRE book, Extra and Yağmur (2012) presents an overview of all the relevant communications, directives and reports on the promotion of multilingualism. The following is a selective list of some of the cited reports and communications:

knowledge of languages should be promoted (Extra and Yağmur 2012). Each EU member-state should promote pupils' proficiency in at least two "foreign" languages, and at least one of these languages should be the official language of an EU state. Promoting knowledge of regional minority and/or immigrant minority languages was left out of consideration in these ministerial statements. The European Parliament, however, accepted various resolutions which recommended the protection and promotion of regional minority languages and which led to the foundation of the *European Bureau*

Council resolutions/Conclusions
- Decision of the European Parliament and of the Council on the European Year of Languages 2001 (2000)
- Presidency Conclusions of the Barcelona European Council (2002)
- Conclusions on multilingualism (May 2008)
- Resolution on a European strategy for multilingualism (November 2008)
- Conclusions on a strategic framework for European cooperation in education and training ET 2020 (2009)
- Conclusions on language competencies to enhance mobility (2011)

Conventions
- European Cultural Convention (1954)
- European Charter for Regional or Minority Languages (ECRML) (1992)
- Framework Convention for the Protection of National Minorities (1995)
- European Social Charter (rev 1996)

European Parliament resolutions
- Resolution to promote linguistic diversity and language learning (2001)
- Resolution on European regional and lesser-used languages (2003)
- Resolution on multilingualism: an asset for Europe and a shared commitment (2009)

Recommendations of the Committee of Ministers
- Recommendation N° R (2005)3 concerning teaching neighbouring languages in border regions
- Recommendation N° R (82)18 concerning modern languages (1982)
- Recommendation N° R (98)6 concerning modern languages (1998)
- Recommendation CM/Rec (2008)7 on the use of the CEFR and the promotion of plurilingualism

Communications by the European Commission
- Communication 2005: A new framework strategy for multilingualism
- Communication 2008: Multilingualism: An asset for Europe and a shared commitment
- Green Paper 2008: Migration and Mobility: Challenges and opportunities for EU education systems

Recommendations of the Parliamentary Assembly
- Recommendation 1383 (1998) on linguistic diversification
- Recommendation 1539 (2001) on the European Year of Languages 2001
- Recommendation 1598 (2003) on the protection of sign languages in the Member States of the Council of Europe
- Recommendation 1740 (2006) on the place of mother tongue in school education

for Lesser Used Languages in 1982. Another result of the European Parliament resolutions was the foundation of the European MERCATOR Network, aimed at promoting research into the status and use of regional minority languages. In March 1998, the *European Charter for Regional or Minority Languages* came into operation. The Charter is aimed at the protection and promotion of regional minority languages, and it functions as an international instrument for the comparison of legal measures and other facilities of the EU member-states in this policy domain (Craith 2003). In spite of all the good intentions at the EU level, the policy makers in the member states make a sharp distinction between languages as "national, regional (indigenous) minority, and immigrant minority". Most of the regional minority languages are well protected by legislation (only in some EU countries but not in many others, e.g., France, Greece, Italy and Poland) but immigrant minority languages are excluded in most policy documents (see the outcomes of Language Rich Europe project in Extra and Yağmur 2012).

In general, the policy makers in the EU member states are reluctant to mention "immigrant languages" in policy documents. Explaining the causes of this reluctance is not easy but a number of possible reasons can be suggested. As documented recently by Spolsky (2016), immigrant receiving European governments often considered migrants as guest workers with a temporary status. Even after two generations, the third generation is still identified as "immigrant". For instance, Piller (2001: 260) points out that "it is not uncommon to speak of '*Auslaender in der dritten Generation*,' 'foreigners of the third generation' ", to refer to persons with an immigration heritage. The fact that the third-generation descendants of immigrants are still referred to as being the "foreigners" is the most telling for social inclusion/exclusion of immigrants in the European context. Many European children, who have immigrant grandparents, are still referred to as "immigrant". In many cases, so called "immigrant children" do not even speak the heritage language they are associated with. Gorodzeisky and Semyonov (2009) argue that despite variations in country of origin and ethnic background and despite variations in civil status across countries, immigrants are considered outsiders in their host societies, which leads to exclusion from equal rights. Piller and Takahashi (2011) provide evidence for language being an instrument of social inclusion/exclusion in various immigration contexts. In this respect, it is easier to understand the causes of immigrant languages being excluded in formal education programs.

Another possible reason for exclusion of regional and immigrant minority languages in the formal school curriculum might be the social status attributed to these languages. Ağırdağ (2010) investigated the causes of exclusion of immigrant languages in Flemish schools in Belgium. He argued that bilingual skills of people from an immigrant background are not recognized. Ağırdağ (2010) suggests that immigrants are rarely referred to as "bilingual", but rather as "linguistically different" (*anderstaligen*). In order to show the prevalent mind-set in the society, Ağırdağ (2010) reports the statement of Flemish Minister of Education that the educational inequalities between natives and immigrants are only caused by "language deficiencies" of immigrant pupils. In this type of reasoning, English plus Flemish bilingualism is an asset but Flemish plus Turkish bilingualism is a deficiency. Accordingly, this type of deficiency would lead to lower school achievement among children with an immigration heritage. If bilingualism of immigrant children mean "deficiency" and "lower school achievement", then this type of bilingualism should not be promoted. Holding on to such beliefs, policy makers cannot be expected to give space to immigrant languages in the formal education programs.

Coupling immigrant bilingualism with lower school achievement is a widespread misconception in many European countries. Immigrant languages are seen as obstacles before the learning of the national state language in almost all immigration contexts. Reflecting on the lower school achievement among immigrant children, Ammermüller (2005) argues that the main reason for the low performance of immigrant students in the German context should be searched in their later enrolment in schools and the less favourable home environment for learning. Most German students achieve highly, because they have more home resources as measured e.g. by the number of books at home. He claims that many immigrant children have lower achievement levels because about 40 percent of all immigrant students speak a language other than German at home. According to Ammermüller (2005), differences in parental education and family situation are far less important. As in many national contexts, also in the German context, students' home languages are apparently shown to be the culprits for low achievement in the schools. Most of the educational experts and researchers unwarrantedly blame multilingualism of immigrant children for lower school achievement. International literature on school achievement shows that there are multiple factors that account for school success (e.g. Cummins 2014). The school's language policy, the structure of the curriculum, the teachers' qualifications and experience with language minority children and parental factors account especially for bilingual children's school achievement. Whether the school has a bilingual approach, or a submersion approach would make a huge difference in the language development of minority language speaking children. Even though there is a general reluctance to refer to immigrant students as bilinguals and to develop bilingual programs for them, there is widespread support for bilingual programs (Dutch–English or German–French) for native European students. Bilingual programs in high-status languages find huge public support but strong negative attitudes surround immigrant children's bilingualism. In a typical anti-bilingual fashion, many mainstream teachers believe that immigrant children are overloaded when dealing with two languages, which lowers their proficiency in the national language (Mary and Young this vol.). Preparing language minority children for more successful school careers ideally requires a balanced bilingual approach in which children's greater proficiency in the home language is utilized to promote general cognitive development and the acquisition of the school language (Leseman and van Tuijl 2001). However, given the widespread use of submersion models in most European schools, immigrant children's first language skills cannot be further developed. As reported by Cenoz and Gorter (2010) the idea that non-native speakers are deficient communicators is still widespread in school contexts. The goal for second-language learners and users is often to achieve native-like command of the target language, and this creates a feeling of failure and incompleteness, especially among immigrant children.

Under the socio-political circumstances in Europe these days, it would be unrealistic to expect radical changes in the foreseeable future in the European formal education system regarding immigrant minority languages. However, in other national contexts, for instance in the United States of America and Canada, some formal education institutions incorporate immigrant languages in their curriculums in the form of transitional or full bilingual programs. In the European context, Sweden provides instruction in the home languages of children from an immigrant background. Based on the discussion presented above, it seems logical to suggest that only after full social acceptance of "immigrant" groups, it will be possible to incorporate their languages in school programs as part of school curriculum.

References

Ağırdağ, Orhan. 2010. Exploring bilingualism in a monolingual school system: Insights from Turkish and native students from Belgian schools. *British Journal of Sociology of Education* 31(3). 307–321.

Ammermüller, Andreas. 2005. *Poor background or low returns? Why immigrant students in Germany perform so poorly in PISA*. (Discussion Paper No. 05–18.) http://opus.zbw-kiel.de/volltexte/2005/2908/pdf/dp0518.pdf (accessed 20 November 2006).

Bauböck, Rainer, Agnes Heller & Aristide Zolberg (eds.). 1996. *The challenge of diversity: Integration and pluralism in societies of immigration*. Aldershot: Avebury.

Bourhis, Richard. 2001. Acculturation, language maintenance, and language shift. In Jetske Klatter-Folmer & Piet van Avermaat (eds.), *Theories on maintenance and loss of minority languages: Towards a more integrated explanatory framework*, 5–37. Berlin & New York: Waxmann.

Bourhis, Richard, Léna Céline Moïse, Stéphane Perreault & Sacha Senécal. 1997. Towards an interactive acculturation model: A social psychological approach. *International Journal of Psychology* 32. 369–386.

Burnaby, Barbara. 2008. Language policy and education in Canada. In Stephen May & Nancy H. Hornberger (eds.), *Language policy and political issues in education. Encyclopedia of language and education*, 331–341. New York: Springer.

Cenoz, Jasone & Durk Gorter. 2010. The diversity of multilingualism in education. *International Journal of the Sociology of Language* 205. 37–53.

Council of Europe. 1992. *Explanatory report to the European charter for regional or minority languages*. Strasbourg: Council of Europe.

Craith, Nic M. 2003. Facilitating or generating linguistic diversity. The European charter for regional or minority languages. In Gabrielle Hogan-Brun & Stefan Wolff (eds.), *Minority languages in Europe. Frameworks, status, prospects*, 56–72. Hampshire: Palgrave Macmillan.

Cummins, Jim. 2014. Language and identity in multilingual schools: Constructing evidence-based instructional policies. In David Little, Constant Leung & Piet Van Avermaet (eds.), *Managing diversity in education: Languages, policies, paedagogies*, 3–26. Bristol, Buffalo & Toronto: Multilingual Matters.

Eisenchlas, Susana A. & Andrea C. Schalley. this vol. Making sense of the notion of "home language" and related concepts.

Extra, Guus & Kutlay Yağmur (eds.). 2012. *Language rich Europe: Trends in policies and practices for multilingualism in Europe*. Cambridge: British Council and Cambridge University Press.

Gogolin, Ingrid. 1994. *Der monolinguale Habitus der multilingualen Schule*. Münster & New York: Waxmann.

Gorodzeisky, Anastasia & Moshe Semyonov. 2009. Terms of exclusion: Public views towards admission and allocation of rights to immigrants in European countries. *Ethnic and Racial Studies* 32:3. 401–423.

Laitin, David D. 2000. What is a language community? *American Journal of Political Science* 44(1). 142–155.

Leseman, Paul & Cathy van Tuijl. 2001. Home support for bilingual development of Turkish 4–6-year-old immigrant children in the Netherlands: Efficacy of a home-based educational programme. *Journal of Multilingual and Multicultural Development* 22(4). 309–324.

Martin, Peter, Angela Creese, Arvind Bhatt & Nirmala Bhojani. 2004. *Complementary schools and their communities in Leicester*. Final report. School of Education, University of Leicester.

Mary, Latisha & Andrea Young. this vol. Teachers' beliefs and attitudes towards home language maintenance and their effects.

May, Stephen. 2001. *Language and minority rights: Ethnicity, nationalism and the politics of language*. London: Longman.

Mayer, Elisabeth, Liliana Sánchez, José Camacho & Carolina Rodríguez Alzza. this vol. The drivers of home language maintenance and development in indigenous communities.

Penninx, Rinus. 1996. Immigration, minorities policy and multiculturalism in Dutch society since 1960. In Rainer Bauböck, Agnes Heller & Aristide Zolberg (eds.), *The challenge of diversity: Integration and pluralism in societies of immigration*, 187–206. Aldershot: Avebury.

Piller, Ingrid. 2001. Naturalization language testing and its basis in ideologies of national identity and citizenship. *International Journal of Bilingualism* 5(3). 259–277.

Piller, Ingrid & Kimie Takahashi. 2011 Linguistic diversity and social inclusion. *International Journal of Bilingual Education and Bilingualism* 14(4). 371–381.

Pöllmann, Andreas. 2009. Formal education and intercultural capital: Towards attachment beyond narrow ethno-national boundaries. *Educational Studies* 35(5). 537–545.

Rubino, Antonia. 2010. Multilingualism in Australia: Reflections on current and future research trends. *Australian Review of Applied Linguistics* 33(2). 17.1–17.21.

Schalley, Andrea C., Diana Guillemin & Susana A. Eisenchlas. 2015. Multilingualism and assimilationism in Australia's literacy-related educational policies. *International Journal of Multilingualism* 12(2). 162–177.

Spolsky, Bernard. 2016. The languages of diaspora and return. *Multilingualism and Second Language Acquisition* 1(2–3). 1–119.

Tilmatine, Mohamed (ed.). 1997. *Enseignment des langues d'origine et immigration nord-africaine en Europe: Langue maternelle ou langue d'état?* Paris: INALCO/CEDREA-CRB.

Waldinger, Roger & David Fitzgerald. 2004. Transnationalism in question. *American Journal of Sociology* 109(5). 1177–1195.

Williams, Glyn, Miquel Strubell & Gruffudd O. Williams. 2013. Trends in European language education. *The Language Learning Journal* 41(1). 5–36.

Yağmur, Kutlay. 2017. Multilingualism in immigrant communities. In Jasone Cenoz, Durk Gorter & Stephen May (eds.), *Language awareness and multilingualism: Encyclopedia of language and education*, 1–15. 3rd edn. Cham: Springer.

Yağmur, Kutlay. 2019. The concept of minority/minorities in the European national and supranational EU discourse. *Multilingua* 38(2). 213–229.

Yağmur, Kutlay & Fons van de Vijver. 2012. Acculturation and language orientations of Turkish immigrants in Australia, France, Germany, and the Netherlands. *Journal of Cross-Cultural Psychology* 43(7). 1110–1130.

Yağmur, Kutlay & Guus Extra. 2011. Urban multilingualism in Europe: Educational responses to increasing diversity. *Journal of Pragmatics* 43(5). 1185–1194.

Latisha Mary and Andrea Young

22 Teachers' beliefs and attitudes towards home languages maintenance and their effects

1 Introduction

Research dating back to the 1960s (Rosenthal and Jacobsen 1968) has highlighted the impact that teachers' beliefs and attitudes have on their actions in the classroom, on their interactions with their students and on the extent to which they support students in their learning (see Ashton 2015 for a complete historical review). These beliefs play a role in facilitating or hindering practices "by serving to filter, frame and guide experience, decisions and actions" (Gill and Fives 2015: 1). While this is true with regard to teaching practices in general, much attention has also been given to the role that teachers' beliefs about children's home languages play in classrooms and how these may affect their emergent bilingual and bilingual learners. Beliefs about children's home languages that are not informed by research may compromise teachers' effectiveness with their linguistically diverse students in several ways, including holding low expectations for these children and limiting the educational opportunities which they offer to them (Ullucci 2007). Beliefs and attitudes also inform educational language policies at an institutional level, as well as teachers' practiced language policies in the classroom, which can lead to schools communicating to families, overtly or covertly, the need to give priority to the language of schooling and ultimately to abandon their home languages. Beliefs and attitudes are also an important factor in achieving educational equity and social justice, since they are intertwined with individuals' values, morals and commitment to their students' success (Gay 2015).

In this chapter we will first define the concepts of beliefs, attitudes and ideologies and situate them among the varying terminology used in the literature. We will then discuss the notion of the teacher's image of the child and the ways in which children perceive and integrate the value attributed to their home languages at school and the effect this may have on the children. We pursue this idea by addressing the issue of the use of certain labels to "name" emergent bilingual children and the consequences of their usage. We conclude by examining the possible origins of teachers' beliefs and attitudes and the implications these beliefs have for educational and practiced language policies.

2 Beliefs, attitudes and ideologies – clarifying the concepts

Before reviewing the question of teachers' language ideologies and their beliefs and attitudes towards children's home languages, we would like to start by discussing what these concepts mean to different researchers in the field. The terms which address the constructs of teacher beliefs and attitudes are often used interchangeably and are neither systematically nor clearly defined (Gill and Fives 2015). It is for this reason that some researchers have referred to teacher beliefs as a "messy" construct (Fives and Buehl 2012; Pajares 1992), due to an apparent lack of consistency in the literature in defining what researchers actually mean when investigating these constructs. Although many authors such as Hermans, van Braak, and Van Keer (2008) place knowledge at the heart of their definition of beliefs, stating for example that beliefs are "a set of conceptual representations which store general knowledge of objects, people and events and their characteristic relationships" (Hermans, van Braak, and Van Keer 2008: 128), others (e.g., Fives and Buehl 2012; Pajares 1992; Pettit 2011) have drawn attention to the intertwined relationship between beliefs and knowledge and its problematic nature. Due to this interconnected relationship, Borg (2003) prefers the umbrella term "teacher cognition" – which he defines as "what teachers know, believe and think" (Borg 2003: 81) – a means of embracing "the complexity of teachers' mental minds" (Borg 2003: 86). Pajares (1992) attempted to resolve this problem by focussing on the evaluative component of beliefs and in turn defining beliefs as "an individual's judgement of the truth or falsity of a proposition" (Pajares 1992: 316). In our review of the literature, a number of authors concur on this definition as the basis of an adequate assessment and analysis of teachers' beliefs (Ashton 2015; Fives and Buehl 2012; Richardson 1996).

Attitudes can be seen as expressions of a particular belief or set of beliefs (Eagly and Chaiken 1993) and in this way can be considered as a substructure of belief systems (Pajares 1992). Fishbein (1967: 267) defined attitudes as "learned predispositions to respond to an object or class of objects in a favourable or unfavourable way". Thus, in this chapter we use the term beliefs to refer to propositions held to be true by an individual, whereas our use of the term attitudes refers to an individual's behaviour and response to situations and an expression of their beliefs.

Meta-analyses of the literature on teacher beliefs (Fives and Buel 2012; Hermans, van Braak, and Van Keer 2008) have drawn conclusions with regard to some basic elements concerning the construct of beliefs which are of importance for our discussion on teachers' beliefs about children's home languages and their effects. One important aspect highlighted in the literature is their role as filters (Pajares 1992), frameworks and guides for decision making (Gill and Fives 2015; Rimm-Kaufman et al. 2006). In our context, this means that new information received by teachers is filtered first through their belief systems which in turn determines how the new information, as well as new experiences, will be interpreted (Fives and Buehl 2012). Teacher beliefs are also seen to be generally stable (Fives and Buehl 2012; Skott 2015) and "only likely to change as a result of substantial engagement in relevant social practices" (Skott 2015: 18). Consideration of these two aspects of beliefs, i.e., that they are stable and open to change to a certain degree, will therefore be essential when planning initial and in-service teacher education.

Finally, there is also a general agreement in the literature on the reciprocal relationship between individual beliefs and the context in which the individual finds her/himself. Beliefs are thus situated within larger more central systems and must be understood as being interconnected with such systems (Pajares 1992). Gates (2006) goes so far as to refer to sets of beliefs as "covert systems" situated within ideological stances influencing "how we elaborate meaning, interpret behaviour, and shape our social reality with others" (Gates 2006: 353). Language ideologies, defined by Silverstein (1979: 193) as "sets of beliefs about language articulated by users as a rationalization or justification of perceived language structure and use", encompass both of these constructs. Thus, language ideologies not only concern the beliefs and attitudes that individuals hold about language but also the practices through which these beliefs are enacted (Gal 1998, cited in Razfar 2012), or as Spolsky puts it, "what people do" with language (Spolsky 2004: 14). We will return to this question in section 6.

3 The impact of teachers' beliefs and attitudes towards home languages on classroom practices

Research has identified several ways in which teachers' beliefs and attitudes towards children's home languages may compromise or increase teachers' effectiveness with their linguistically diverse students (Cummins 2000; Saxena and Martin-Jones 2013; Woolard 1998). Borg's research (2003) in the area of teacher cognition and teacher language ideologies points to the link between teachers' beliefs and their practices in the classroom (see also Razfar 2012; Kroskrity 2010; Pettit 2011). Teachers' beliefs about languages, about the children and parents who speak languages other than the language of schooling and about how second languages are acquired have been found to have an impact on the place attributed to children's home languages in the classroom and whether these will be silenced or used as a resource for learning (Hélot 2010; Pulinx, Van Avermaet, and Ağirdağ 2015; Young 2014).

One concern raised by many authors is the effect teachers' beliefs have on the expectations they hold for linguistically diverse children which when either low or unrealistic limit the educational opportunities offered to these students (Fitzsimmons-Doolan, Palmer, and Henderson 2017; Garrity, Aquino-Sterling, and Day 2015; Ullucci 2007). Some studies (Gay 2015; Hernández 2001; Sharkey and Layzer 2000) reveal that when teachers believe bilingual students are not capable of mastering the curriculum, they hold lower expectations for them and take part in what Sharkey and Layzer (2000: 356) call a "benevelont conspiracy", that is to say that teachers do not challenge students, give them easier tasks or avoid calling on them for fear of embarrassing them or putting them under stress. Pulinx, Van Avermaet, and Ağirdağ (2015) also found that negative attitudes towards certain languages or varieties of languages influenced teachers' beliefs about whether students were competent and whether they would achieve academic success. Gay (2015: 447) emphasises the role of beliefs in contributing to self-fulfilling prophesies, in which "teachers get from students what they expect based on what they believe is true".

Another important area for concern are teachers' beliefs about second language learning as these are directly related to the place given to children's home languages within the learning tasks implemented in the classroom. Much research has drawn attention to teachers' lack of knowledge of second language acquisition (Karabenick and Noda 2004; Lucas, Villegas, and Martin 2015; Mary and Young 2018b; Pettit 2011; Reeves 2004) and how this leads teachers to deprive (emergent) bilingual students of support and scaffolding through the use of their home languages and to neglect opportunities for biliteracy development. A common misunderstanding among teachers concerns the nature of second language learning. Many teachers hold the belief that children are able to acquire a second language rapidly through submersion, coupled with a strict language separation policy through which they hear and are exposed solely to the target language in the school context (Pettit 2011; Reeves 2004). Within this idea is that too much exposure to the home language slows the progress of acquisition of the second language (Franceschini 2011; Karabenick and Noda 2004). This belief likens children to "sponges" who are able to "soak up" a second language if immersed in it and if no other languages are present to interfere with this acquisition. It is based on the idea that individuals acquire a second language in the same way as they do their first language, through constant contact and interaction in that language. While sufficient exposure, input, and interaction in the target language are undeniably necessary elements of the process of second language acquisition, research has also emphasised the crucial role an individual's first language plays in their language development, and the importance of cross-linguistic transfer of the knowledge encoded in the first language (Cummins 1981, 2017). Cummins likens this misconception of language development to the image of two separate balloons representing the child's home language and another (second) language. The schema illustrates the unfounded idea held by many teachers that an increased amount of contact with the home language will not allow a sufficient amount of contact in the language of schooling. The fear of failing to equip emergent bilingual learners with the necessary linguistic competences to access the school curriculum leads many teachers to advise parents to "make an effort" to replace the home language with the language of schooling. In so doing, the teacher not only shifts the responsibility for school language development from the school to the home, but also endorses the idea that parents have to make a "choice" between using their home language with their child or prioritising their child's future. We concur with Skutnabb-Kangas and May (2016: 126) that this is "false 'either/or' thinking – there is no need to choose, one can have both".

Finally, regarding the lack of knowledge about language acquisition and bi/plurilingual development, in spite of the instrumental value and cognitive benefits of bi/plurilingualism reported in the literature (e.g., Bialystok 2018; August and Shanahan 2006; Cummins 2008), schools all too often fail to acknowledge minority home language competences and consequently do not develop programmes in collaboration with families to nurture and support multiple language development (Curdt-Christiansen and Lanza 2018).

4 Image of the child: The repercussions of acknowledging or ignoring linguistic and cultural capital

Teachers' attitudes and beliefs are also directly linked to the image they hold of each child present in their classrooms, which contributes over time to the construction of the child's identity. The term "image of the child", taken from the Reggio Emilia approach to early childhood education (Edwards, Gandini, and Forman 1998), encapsulates the powerful impact of the way teachers think about children, or the mental picture of them they have in their mind, on the harmonious development of the child's self-image and well-being. Inherent to this approach, which emerged in Northern Italy in the second half of the 20th century, is the view that children are competent, powerful, creative and curious and that all children possess strong potential for development (Hewett 2001). Malaguzzi (1994), the founder of the movement stressed the foundational nature of the image teachers hold of children and its consequential impact on teachers' behaviour and their relationships with children in the classroom. He advocated the need for teachers to view children as intelligent, strong and beautiful (Malaguzzi 1994), rather than looking for what is lacking in the child and encouraged teachers to strive to draw on the wealth of resources and assets available to the child and what s/he has to offer (Tijnagel-Schoenaker 2017). From this perspective, educators pay particular attention to the child's unique competencies and to the "hundred languages" children may use. The "Hundred languages of children" is a term used by Malaguzzi (1994: 55) to describe the many ways in which children choose to communicate and express themselves (Edwards, Gandini, and Forman 1998). Situated within the socio-constructivist theory, the approach attaches importance to the various, multiple forms of knowing that children may demonstrate and accepts the manifestation of their knowledge through multiple channels (Hewett 2001). As knowledge is viewed to be actively and socially constructed by children, educators are thus called on to shed their role of "transmitters" of knowledge and to endorse new roles such as those of co-researcher, prompter, or designer in a bid to accompany and guide children on their learning paths. Most importantly, in this approach, children are viewed as having not only needs (educational and developmental), but are seen as having specific rights as well (Rinaldi 1998).

Accordingly, teachers holding positive images of students who have knowledge of other languages in addition to the language of schooling, will consequently communicate to them the value of their home languages and will consider them and the knowledge first acquired in the home context as important resources for learning. This means first and foremost that teachers acknowledge the linguistic and cultural capital of individual learners and secondly, that they recognise the right to use the home language(s) in the classroom by allowing and encouraging children to draw on their entire linguistic and cultural repertoires and to be active protagonists of their own learning.

Psychologists have also emphasised the important role of teachers as "significant others" in children's lives and the impact they have on children's self-esteem and self-perceptions as they mature (Burns 1982; Harter 1999; Humphrey 2003; Lawrence 2006; Mruk 1999). Teachers play an important role in the development of academic self-esteem due to their position as "experts" and authority figures and, in addition to feedback from peers, they constitute one of the most important sources of feedback with regard to academic competence and self-worth (Humphrey 2003, 2004). Teachers' verbal and nonverbal communication have a strong impact on children's self-esteem, and specialists have highlighted the important role that communicating acceptance to pupils, including acceptance of their home languages, can play in the development of their self-worth (Humphrey 2003; Lawrence 2006).

Likewise, studies (Cummins et al. 2015, Moons 2010; Thomauske 2011) have revealed the negative effect that deficit beliefs and visions of children's home languages can have on the children themselves and demonstrated that children perceive and integrate very early on the image that their teachers have of them and their home languages. Children's perceptions of the attitudes displayed by their teachers play a role in regulating their behaviour, as these deficit visions are integrated into their self-systems (Harter 1999). Teachers are quite often unaware of the images they construct and communicate to children and parents as these often remain unconscious constructs and are inherently linked to their language ideologies. Gkaintartzi and Tsokalidou (2011), for example, found that despite teachers' prevailing discourses in which they expressed positive views on home language maintenance, the children in their study had in fact integrated and internalised implicit deficit messages communicated to them by teachers/the school concerning the value and legitimacy of their home languages and that they had also understood, even at a very young age, the power relations involved. These teachers had communicated to the children that they had "equal" status in the classroom, that is to say that they were no different from their monolingual peers, and yet they had simultaneously deprived them of access to their most powerful linguistic resource, their home language. As a result, the children were disempowered by the teachers who had implicitly communicated to them that they were lacking, low-achieving and weak as a result of their emergent bilingualism.

In contrast, Rosiers (2017) presents data from Belgium which reveals how some teachers empower their students by valuing their home languages as cognitive tools and allowing spontaneous translanguaging practices in the classroom. Duarte (2018) also observed and documented translanguaging practices in primary and pre-primary classrooms in Luxembourg and the Netherlands whereby teachers were able to value home language competences and use them as scaffolding for learning. Young and Hélot (2003) carried out a longitudinal study which documented how teachers recognised and valued home languages in the context of a primary school project in France and how, as a result of this approach, children found their voices, home school relations improved and previously ignored knowledge and skills were shared.

Other studies (Bensekhar et al. 2015; Di Meo et al. 2015; Dahoun 1995) have highlighted the detrimental effects teachers' negative attitudes towards children's home languages can have on their willingness to speak their home languages at school and whether they view them as legitimate and valued. Moons (2010) presented data showing that not only did emergent bilingual children perceive that their home languages did not have a legitimate place in the classroom, their peers in the classroom had also integrated both negative and positive attitudes communicated to them by the teachers. In classes in which there was openness to languages other than the language of schooling on the part of the teacher, children's peers demonstrated more empathy and understanding towards their emergent bilingual peers, whereas in classrooms in which speaking the home languages was considered socially inappropriate, peers followed the teacher's example in rejecting children's attempts to use their entire linguistic repertoires, resulting at times in peers signalling to the teacher when children were transgressing the classroom or school language policy.

Parents, too, have been shown to be affected by teachers' explicit and implicit attitudes towards home languages. In one study, Thomauske (2011) found that parents in France quickly understood the message, conveyed to them by teachers, that speaking their home languages to their children represented a threat to national unity, would slow the progress of their child's learning of the language of schooling and thus contribute to low academic achievement. In a Turkish immigration context in the Netherlands, Bezçioğlu-Göktolga and Yağmur (2018) also reported on diverging parental beliefs and teacher opinions towards the value of the heritage language, with teachers emerging as the key actors in shaping parental language choices and practices. Failing to acknowledge, value and build upon home language competence can be likened to the amputation of a limb due to the disempowering nature of such actions. Communicating to families that their languages are worthless or even detrimental to their children's educational development not only misinforms parents, but also places them in an unnecessarily stressful situation. De Houwer (2017: 238) reported that "[t]here is overwhelming evidence that parental socio-emotional well-being is negatively affected when young children do not speak the minority language that parents address them in" (see also De Houwer this vol). In a recent study conducted with members of migrant families living in Frankfurt, Germany and Strasbourg, France, Siemushyma and Young (2019) conclude that the use of both the home language and the language of the host country is necessary for the fuller realization of parenting functions. Teachers need to be made aware of the considerable impact their attitudes and actions towards home languages have upon migrant families.

5 What's in a name? Naming students whose home languages differ from the language of schooling

Given the privileged position of teachers as key agents in language education processes and policies (Menken 2008; Menken and García 2010), we would like to turn our attention to the terms used to name students whose home languages differ from the language of the school. Teachers' beliefs about the value of home languages are also reflected in and shaped by the terms employed within their professional contexts to describe learners whose home languages differ from the language of schooling. Some of these terms may insidiously colour the vision of teachers, parents and pupils towards these learners and their competences and therefore warrant a critical examination. Aligning ourselves with García (2009) and Grosjean (2010), we prefer to use the term "bilingual" or "emergent bilingual" when referring to children who function in more than one language in their daily lives. In this section we will explain why we choose to use this term and why it is important to question and reflect upon the terms employed when referring to children who navigate between languages on a regular basis at home and at school (see Eisenchlas and Schalley this vol., for a detailed discussion on the use of terminology).

The ways in which we refer to emergent bilingual children within the mainstream, compulsory education system, the terms used both in official documentation, but more importantly by practitioners themselves reveal much about the dynamics of power and the image of these pupils constructed by schools. For example, in the French context, these children have been referred to in official, ministerial documentation chronologically since the 1970s as: *enfants étrangers* (foreign children), *enfants non-francophones* (non-francophone children), *enfants immigrés* (immigrant children), *élèves de nationalité étrangère* (pupils of foreign nationality), *enfants venus d'ailleurs* (children from elsewhere), *enfants nouveaux venue en France* (newly arrived children in France), *enfants de migrants* (children of migrants), *enfants issus de l'immigration* (children of migrant background), *primo-arrivants* (new arrivals), *élèves nouvellement arrivés en France (ENAF)* (newly arrived pupils in France), *élèves allophones nouvellement arrivés en France (EANA)* (newly arrived allophone pupils in France). For a more detailed discussion of these terms and their use by teachers, see Galligani (2012) and Paul Kister (2016). Many of these terms label these children as outsiders and convey a deficit perspective towards their languages which remain unacknowledged and unnamed.

What is striking about some of the early terms (foreign children, pupils of foreign nationality) is the close association of nationality and language. It should be acknowledged that the terminological move away from associating language with nationality, denoted by the current term "newly arrived allophone pupil" (M.E.N. 2012), is salutary, given that nationality does not automatically confer linguistic competence in a specific language on a national. It is perfectly possible to hold nationality without mastering the official language of the country concerned if, for example, you have inherited your nationality from a parent but never lived in the country of origin of that parent, or if you are a member of a linguistic minority group within a nation for whom either schooling takes place in the minority language or for whom there is little or poor educational provision in the official national language (see Piller 2016 for a detailed discussion and examples). Children do not necessarily speak an official, national language just because they were born in a certain geographical location. Linguistic competence is acquired through socialization within a specific context or contexts (home, school, place of worship, local community etc.) which may be mono-, bi- or multilingual. The complexities of individual, linguistic experiences and competences are not always investigated by teachers who are frequently unaware of the importance of these demographic details, overlooking the opportunities to inform, adapt and individualise their teaching approaches with (emergent) bilingual learners.

The variables associated with migration are numerous and complex and include: reasons for the migration (parents' professional choices/obligations, personal and family ties, instability in the home country ...), conditions of the migration (forced/chosen, direct migration from country A to country B/transit through a number of other countries, accompanied/unaccompanied ...), status of those migrating (legal/illegal, refugee, asylum seeker ...), length of residence in the new country (newly arrived, temporary/permanent, first/second/third generation) etc. The linguistic repertoire of the child will reflect these variables. The complexity of the individual language biography needs to be acknowledged, not oversimplified. Lumping individuals together under a catch-all term is rarely informative, accurate nor useful. Teachers need to be aware of these complexities and to question the terms used to describe learners for whom the language of schooling is an additional language to their language repertoires and to cultivate a positive vision of each child's linguistic resources. These issues need to be addressed during professional development programmes, as discussed in the final section of this chapter.

Clearly, progress has been made since the times when the term *non-francophone* with its visibly negative orientation was used in the official texts published by the French Ministry of Education to the present-day recognition of children's "other" languages, inherent to the term *allophone* (etymologically from Ancient Greek ἄλλος, allos = other and φωνή, phone = sound). However, the term allophone in France, as well as the term *alloglossa pedia* (other language-speaking children) in Greece, have also been criticised (Young 2014; Tsokalidou 2005) – firstly, because they focus on the notion of otherness, consequently facilitating the "othering" of children, i.e. singling them out as different and therefore excluding them from the dominant francophone majority, and secondly, by referring uniquely to the "other" language(s) the term effectively ignores the presence of the developing language of schooling in the child's linguistic repertoire. His/her identity as a learner of the language through which mainstream education is conducted is equally important to the child in terms of being accepted as a member of the dominant group, feeling a sense of belonging (Van Der Wildt, Van Avermaet, and Van Houtte 2017) and envisaging an empowering learning trajectory. In Flanders, Ağirdağ, Jordens, and Houtte (2014) have similarly called into question the term *anderstaligen* (linguistically different). While García (2009) in New York uses the term *emergent bilinguals* as opposed to *ELLs* (English language learners) or *LEPs* (limited English proficient students). Terminology such as (emergent) bilingual or plurilingual would not only reflect the reality of these pupils' linguistic competences but would also present these competences in a more positively connoted light, communicating and reinforcing these children's identities of competence (Manyak 2004) and belonging rather than of deficiency and exclusion (Young 2017).

6 The impact of teacher beliefs on practiced language policies

As we have already discussed, the terminology used to refer to (emergent) bilinguals and whether or not the languages they speak at home are valued has an impact on the learners' self-esteem, self-worth and sense of identity and belonging. Menken (2008) has underlined the strategic position of teachers who interpret and negotiate language policies and as such act as the "final arbiters of language policy implementation" (Menken 2008: 5). Teacher beliefs are a key ingredient in the language policy mix. They interact with all the other components of the classroom recipe and flavour the learning outcomes. Top-down policies can leave teachers feeling disempowered, as they are often viewed as constraints on their professional activities. Sometimes declarative policy is misunderstood by teachers and its enactment exacerbated by a lack of knowledge in a specific domain. A teacher's personal belief system may even conflict with prescribed policy, leaving the teacher feeling guilty due to their inability to put the policy into practice. All these factors render the language policy's journey from paper to classroom a hazardous one, and one which is reliant on the knowledge, understanding and engagement of the professional. The impact of knowledge gained through pre-service teacher education and continued professional development in the areas of bilingualism, second language acquisition and critical language awareness (García 2017) on teachers' beliefs and attitudes toward their (emergent) bilingual pupils and the relevance of this impact for future curriculum development is discussed below.

Language policies are enacted in classrooms on a daily basis. Decisions concerning language and languages are made by teachers and these decisions are not always induced by top-down policy, they may also emanate from teachers themselves, bottom-up. This alternative view of language policy relocates the focus of power and the potential for innovation with the teacher in the classroom. Both Bonacina-Pugh (2012) and Spolsky (2004) maintain that it is doing policy, of the bottom-up variety, i.e. practiced language policy in education, that has the greatest impact on learning due to the reiterative and personalized nature of classroom interactions The teacher is the decision maker about which languages are worthy of interest and which are not, which languages are legitimate tools for learning and which are not, and whether the pupils learn about language and languages or whether they do not.

Such practiced language policies (Bonacina-Pugh 2012; also see Paulsrud this vol.) may be overt, i.e. a teacher may instruct a child to use the language of schooling at school exclusively and banish all home languages from the classroom, but they may equally be covert. A disapproving glance or ignoring the fact that a child knows a language other than the language of schooling, as we have seen, also has profound effects on learners. Research has shown that when learners' identities are reinforced, their well-being and self-esteem increases and they do better at school (Cummins and Early 2011). The language(s) of the home are a key component of our identity, the language(s) through which we initially perceive the world and through which we form key relationships with those closest to us (usually family members). The role of affect in relation to language has been documented by researchers (He 2010) as a key component in learning and well-being. Acknowledging and valuing the language skills of children and their families within the school context plays a key role in pupil well-being and in home-school relations (Dusi and Steinbach 2016).

7 Factors contributing to teachers' beliefs about home languages and cultures

Having discussed the link between teachers' belief systems and their actions, the ways in which these impact on practiced language policies and whether bilingual and emergent bilingual children's learning is supported in the classroom, we now turn to an examination of the factors contributing to these beliefs. In section 3 we discussed how teachers' deficit beliefs about bilingualism and second language acquisition are often based on erroneous notions about second language acquisition (Grosjean 2010; Mary and Young 2018b; Young 2014) and lack of awareness of the important role of language and culture in children's knowledge and identity construction. Below, we detail the four main factors which have been clearly identified in the literature as having an impact on teachers' beliefs with regard to home languages.

The first factor which strongly emerges in meta analyses on the question of teacher beliefs in relation to cultural and linguistic diversity is the link between teachers' prior experience with linguistic and cultural diversity both inside and outside of school (Lucas, Villegas, and Martin 2015; Pettit 2011). Practitioners who have had experiences with language minority populations and bilingual learners express more positive attitudes towards students' home languages and demonstrate a more acute awareness of the positive role children's home languages play in their learning (Fitzsimmons-Doolan, Palmer, and Henderson 2017; Garmon 2004; Lucas and Villegas 2013; Garrity, Aquino-Sterling, and Day 2015). Flores (2001) found that teachers with experience in bilingual classrooms were more aware of the ways in which children's home languages supported their knowledge of the language of schooling than mainstream teachers with no experience in bilingual classrooms and were also conscious of the benefits of cross-linguistic transfer.

The second and equally important factor identified in the literature concerns knowledge gained through teacher education. An important link has been shown between teachers' positive attitudes toward children's home languages and the amount of preparation they receive during their studies and/or training. In particular, teachers who reported having followed courses in multicultural education or linguistic diversity (Flores and Smith 2009; Lucas, Villegas, and Martin 2015; Montero and McVicker 2006; Smitherman and Villanueva 2000) also demonstrated more favourable attitudes towards linguistically diverse learners. Youngs and Youngs' (2001) study of 143 mainstream teachers in the USA found that teachers who had received training in English as a Second Language were significantly more positive about teaching emergent bilingual and bilingual pupils than those who reported having no training. In the same vein, researchers (e.g., Smitherman and Villanueva 2000; Pulinx, Van Avermaet, and Ağırdağ 2015) have also found links between teachers' negative beliefs about children's home languages and their lack of training and/or personal exposure to bi/multilingualism.

The third factor which has been shown to impact on teachers' beliefs toward home languages concerns the language experiences and ethnic backgrounds of teachers themselves. In several studies, teachers who reported being bilingual or proficient in a language other than the language of schooling demonstrated more openness to supporting bilingual learners (García-Nevarez, Stafford, and Arias 2005; Lee and Oxelson 2006).

The fourth and final factor addressed concerns the impact of societal language ideologies on teachers' beliefs. Dominant monolingual language ideologies which are present in many contexts may also cause teachers to struggle to view (emergent) bilingual pupils in a positive light. The association of nationality and language generally reveals a very monolingual vision or monolingual habitus (Gogolin 1994), where a "one language one country" ideology is regarded as the norm. Such monolingual visions tend to be deeply rooted in nation-building ideologies and discourses of national unity. Returning to our French examples, these traces of national language ideology, encapsulated by the adage "*Un pays, une nation, une langue*" (one country, one nation, one language) and enshrined in the constitution as the language of the *République* (article 2 of the Constitution, modified by constitutional law n°95–880 on 4 August 1995) are not only a legacy of France's turbulent political and social history, they are still very much in evidence in twenty-first century French schools where languages other than French, the language of instruction, are often considered as illegitimate and therefore banished from the classroom and sometimes even from the playground, too (Young 2014). Such exclusive, sometimes referred to as glottophobic (Blanchet 2019) or discriminatory, language laws are not only applied in France. Ağirdağ, Jordens, and Houtte (2014), working in the Belgian context, also report on such monolingual policies.

Language ideologies and beliefs about language are extremely powerful forces which influence the implementation of language policies resulting in the support or the undermining of language transmission, development and learning. They filter down to the learners and their families through the education system, with teachers being recognized as key actors in this process (Menken 2008; Menken and García 2010).

8 The importance of deconstructing beliefs and nurturing informed professional attitudes – some concluding remarks

If dominant monolingual ideologies remain unchallenged in our education systems and accepted at face value as common sense in spite of being unsupported by research, not only will the linguistic resources inherent to our multilingual, postcolonial societies be lost, but those who lose them will bear the scars. In the interest of social justice, equity and the realisation of the full potential of all citizens (Annamalai and Skutnabb-Kangas this vol.), teachers need to be equipped with knowledge about language, to develop critical language awareness (García 2017) and informed professional attitudes based on research findings. Publications such as *Big ideas for expanding minds: Teaching English language learners across the curriculum* (Cummins and

Early 2015), *Enacting Multilingualism* (Krulatz, Dahl, and Flogenfeldt 2018) and *What teachers need to know about language* (Adger, Snow, and Christian 2018) are helping to fill gaps in teacher knowledge about language and languages, but these accessible research-supported handbooks need to be supplemented by opening up spaces for professional development where professionals can exchange and confront their beliefs. Belief systems supported by engrained ideologies do not evaporate overnight. Often a prolonged period of reflection and readjustment to new information and alternative visions is necessary before innovative practices can be enacted.

Research has shown that providing (future) teachers with knowledge of first and second language acquisition alone is insufficient (Garmon 2004; Horan and Hersi 2011). Many authors (Crookes 2015; García 2017; Hélot 2018; Lucas, Villegas, and Martin 2015; Mary and Young 2018a; 2018b) emphasise the need for teacher educators to provide opportunities for pre-service and practising teachers to critically examine their beliefs about issues related to language. Several studies have proposed pedagogical interventions in teacher education which allow pre-service and practising teachers to explore and deconstruct their beliefs through reflective writing and discussion tasks. Some examples are the use of blogs or traditional journals (Hsu 2009; Lucas and Villegas 2013), reflection papers (Dolby 2012), Social Perspective Taking (Rios, Trent, and Vega-Castañeda 2003) or Problem Based Learning (Mary and Young 2018b). In addition, García (2017: 272) reminds us that teacher education programmes need to "develop prospective teachers' abilities of how to use this awareness pedagogically to change the world". If teachers are to develop an "advocacy stance" (Lucas and Villegas 2013: 104) in which they recognise their own agency in the classroom (Mary and Young 2018a) and take steps to provide meaningful learning opportunities for children, teacher education programmes need to help (pre-service) teachers better understand the challenges bilingual children and their families face. This can be achieved through access to the personal testimonies of children and parents (Mary and Young 2018b) and by providing community-based learning experiences or field work followed by guided discussion (Lucas and Villegas 2013). As language arbiters (Menken 2008) who interpret, negotiate and do language policy in the classroom, informed and engaged teachers are the key component to supporting and developing multilingual competence amongst pupils and in so doing to making a positive contribution to home language maintenance.

References

Adger, Caroline, Temple, Catherine. E. Snow & Donna Christian. 2018. *What teachers need to know about language*. Clevedon: Multilingual Matters.
Ağırdağ, Orhan, Kathelijne Jordens & Mieke Van Houtte. 2014. Speaking Turkish in Belgian primary schools: Teacher beliefs versus effective consequences. *bilig*. 7–28.

Annamalai, E. & Tove Skutnabb-Kangas. this vol. Social justice and inclusiveness through linguistic human rights in education.

Ashton, Patricia T. 2015. Historical overview and theoretical perspectives of research on teachers' beliefs. In Helenrose Fives & Michele Gregoire Gill (eds.), *International handbook of research on teachers' beliefs*, 31–47. New York: Routledge.

August, Diane & Timothy Shanahan. 2006. *Developing literacy in second-language learners: Report of the national literacy panel on language-minority children and youth*. Mahwah, NJ: Centre for Applied Linguistics.

Bezçioğlu-Göktolga, Irem & Kutlay Yağmur. 2018. The impact of Dutch teachers on family language policy of Turkish immigrant parents. *Language, Culture and Curriculum*. 31(3). 220–234.

Bensekhar, Malika Bennabi, Amalini Simon, Dalila Rezzoug & Marie-Rose Moro. 2015. Les pathologies du langage dans la pluralité linguistique. *La psychiatrie de l'enfant*. 58(1). 277–298.

Bialystok, Ellen. 2018. Bilingual education for young children: Review of the effects and consequences. *International Journal of Bilingual Education and Bilingualism*. 21(6). 666–679.

Blanchet, Philippe. 2019. *Discriminations: combattre la glottophobie*. Paris: Lambert-Lucas.

Bonacina-Pugh, Florence. 2012. Researching "practiced language policies": Insights from conversation analysis. *Language Policy* 11. 213–234.

Borg, Simon. 2003. Teacher cognition in language teaching: A review of research on what language teachers think, know, believe, and do. *Language Teaching* 36. 81–109.

Burns, Robert. 1982. *Self-concept development and education*. Eastborn: Holt.

Crookes, Graham V. 2015. Redrawing the boundaries on theory, research, and practice concerning language teachers' philosophies and language teacher cognition: Toward a critical perspective. *The Modern Language Journal* 99(3). 485–499.

Cummins, Jim. 1981. *Bilingualism and minority-language children*. (Language and Literacy Series.) Toronto: Ontario Institute for Studies in Education.

Cummins, Jim 2000. *Language, power and pedagogy: Bilingual children in the crossfire*. Clevedon: Multilingual Matters.

Cummins, Jim. 2008. Total immersion or bilingual education? Findings of international research on promoting immigrant children's achievement in the primary school. In Jörg Ramseger & Matthea Wagener (eds.), *Chancenungleichheit in der Grundschule: Ursachen und Wege aus der Krise*, 45–55. Wiesbaden: VS Verlag für Sozialwissenschaften.

Cummins, Jim 2017. Teaching for transfer in multilingual school contexts. In Ofelia García, Angel Lin & Stephen May (eds.), *Bilingual and multilingual education*, 103–115. Cham: Springer.

Cummins, Jim & Margaret Early. 2011. *Identity texts: The collaborative creation of power in multilingual schools*. Stoke-on-Trent: Trentham Books.

Cummins, Jim & Margaret Early. 2015. *Big ideas for expanding minds: Teaching English language learners across the curriculum*. Oakville, ON: Rubicon.

Cummins, Jim, Shirley Hu, Paula Markus & M. Kristiina Montero. 2015. Identity texts and academic achievement: Connecting the dots in multilingual school contexts. *TESOL Quarterly* 49(3). 555–581.

Curdt-Christiansen, Xiao Lan & Elizabeth Lanza. 2018. Language management in multilingual families: Efforts, measures and challenges. *Multilingua* 37(2). 123–130.

Dahoun, Zerdalia K. S. 1995. *Les couleurs du silence: Le mutisme des enfants de migrants*. Paris: Calmann-Lévy.

De Houwer, Annick. 2017. Minority language parenting in Europe and children's well-being. In Natasha J. Cabrera & Birgit Leyendecker (eds.), *Handbook on positive development of minority children and youth*, 231–246. Cham: Springer.

De Houwer, Annick. this vol. Harmonious Bilingualism: Well-being for families in bilingual settings.

Di Meo, Stéphane, Claire van den Hove, Geneviève Serre-Pradère, Amalini Simon, Marie Rose Moro & Thierry Baubet. 2015. Le mutisme extra-familial chez les enfants de migrants. Le silence de Sandia. *L'information psychiatrique* 91(3). 217–224.

Dolby, Nadine. 2012. *Rethinking multicultural education for the next generation*. New York: Routledge.

Duarte, Joana. 2018. Translanguaging in the context of mainstream multilingual education. *International Journal of Multilingualism*. Online First. 1–16. DOI: 10.1080/14790718.2018.1512607

Dusi, Paola & Marilyn Steinbach. 2016. Voices of children and parents from elsewhere: A glance at integration in Italian primary schools. *International Journal of Inclusive Education* 20(8). 816–827.

Eagly, Alice H. & Shelly Chaiken. 1993. *The psychology of attitudes*. Orlando, FL: Harcourt Brace Jovanovich College Publishers.

Edwards, Carolyn P., Lella Gandini & George Edwards (eds.). 1998. *The hundred languages of children: The Reggio Emilia approach – advanced reflections*. Greenwich, CT & London: Greenwood Publishing Group.

Eisenchlas, Susana A. & Andrea C. Schalley. this vol. Making sense of the notion of "home language" and related concepts.

Fishbein, Martin. 1967. A behavior theory approach to the relations between beliefs about an object and the attitude toward the object. In Martin Fishbein (ed.), *Readings in attitude theory and measurement*, 389–400. New York: John Wiley & Sons.

Fitzsimmons-Doolan, Shannon, Deborah Palmer & Kathryn Henderson. 2017. Educator language ideologies and a top-down dual language program. *International Journal of Bilingual Education and Bilingualism* 20(6). 704–721.

Fives, Helenrose & Michelle M. Buehl. 2012. Spring cleaning for the "messy" construct of teachers' beliefs: What are they? Which have been examined? What can they tell us. *APA Educational Psychology Handbook* 2. 471–499.

Flores, Belinda Bustos. 2001. Bilingual education teachers' beliefs and their relation to self-reported practices. *Bilingual Research Journal* 25(3). 275–299.

Flores, Belinda Bustos & Howard L. Smith. 2009. Teachers' characteristics and attitudinal beliefs about linguistic and cultural diversity. *Bilingual Research Journal* 31. 323–358.

Franceschini, Rita. 2011. Multilingualism and multicompetence: A conceptual view. *Modern Language Journal* 95(3). 344–355.

Gal, Susan. 1998. Multiplicity and contention among language ideologies. In Bambi Schieffelin, Kathryn A. Woolard & Paul V. Kroskrity (eds.), *Language ideologies: Practice and theory*, 317–331. New York: Oxford University Press.

Galligani, Stéphanie. 2012. Regards croisés sur les enfants venus d'ailleurs et scolarisés en France. *Les Cahiers du GEPE* 4. Les langues des enfants 'issus de l'immigration' dans le champ éducatif français. Strasbourg: Presses universitaires de Strasbourg http://www.cahiersdugepe.fr/index.php?id=2314 (accessed 22 June 2019).

García, Ofelia. 2009. Emergent bilinguals and TESOL: What's in a name? *TESOL Quarterly*. 43(2). 322–326.

García, Ofelia. 2017. Critical multilingual language awareness and teacher education. In Jasone Cenoz, Durk Gorter & Stephen May (eds.), *Language awareness and multilingualism. Encyclopedia of language and education*, 263–280. Cham: Springer.

García-Nevarez, Ana G., Mary E. Stafford & Beatriz Arias. 2005. Arizona elementary teachers' attitudes toward English language learners and the use of Spanish in classroom instruction. *Bilingual Research Journal* 29(2). 295–317.

Garmon, M. Arthur (2004). Changing preservice teachers' attitudes/beliefs about diversity – What are the critical factors? *Journal of Teacher Education* 55(3). 201–213.

Garrity, Sarah, Cristian R. Aquino-Sterling & Ashley Day. 2015. Translanguaging in an infant classroom: Using multiple languages to make meaning. *International Multilingual Research Journal* 9(3). 177–196.

Gates, Peter. 2006. Going beyond belief systems: Exploring a model for the social influence on mathematics teacher beliefs. *Educational Studies in Mathematics* 63(3). 347–369.

Gay, Geneva 2015. Teachers' beliefs about cultural diversity. In Helenrose Fives & Michele Gregoire Gill (eds.), *International handbook of research on teachers' beliefs*, 436–452. New York: Routledge.

Gill, Michele Gregoire & Helenrose Fives. 2015. Introduction. In: Helenrose Fives & Michele Gregoire Gill (eds.), *International handbook of research on teachers' beliefs*, 1–10. New York: Routledge.

Gkaintartzi, Anastasia & Roula Tsokalidou. 2011. "She is a very good child but she doesn't speak": The invisibility of children's bilingualism and teacher ideology. *Journal of Pragmatics* 43(2). 588–601.

Gogolin, Ingrid. 1994. *Der monolinguale Habitus der multilingualen Schule* [The monolingual habitus of the multilingual school]. Münster & New York: Waxman.

Grosjean, François. 2010. *Bilingual: life and reality*. Cambridge, MA & London: Harvard University Press.

Harter, Susan. 1999. *The construction of the self: A developmental perspective*. New York: Guilford Press.

He, Weiyun Agnes. 2010. The heart of heritage: Sociocultural dimensions of heritage language learning. *Annual Review of Applied Linguistics* 30. 66–82.

Hélot, Christine. 2018. A critical approach to language awareness in France: Learning to live with Babel. In Christine Hélot, Caroline Frijns, Koen Gorp & Sven Sierens (eds.), *Language awareness in multilingual classrooms in Europe: From theory to practice*, 117–142. Berlin & Boston: de Gruyter.

Hélot, Christine. 2010. «Tu sais bien parler Maîtresse! » Negotiating language other than French in the primary classroom in France. In Kate Menken & Ofelia García (eds.), *Negotiating language education policies: Educators as policy makers*, 52–71. New York: Erlbaum/Routledge.

Hermans, Ruben, Johan van Braak & Hilde Van Keer. 2008. Development of the beliefs about primary education scale: Distinguishing a developmental and transmissive dimension. *Teaching and Teacher Education* 24(1). 127–139.

Hernández, Anita. 2001. The expected and unexpected literacy outcomes of bilingual students. *Bilingual Research Journal* 25(3). 251–276.

Hewett, Valarie Mercilliot. 2001. Examining the Reggio Emilia approach to early childhood education. *Early Childhood Education Journal* 29(2). 95–100.

Horan, Deborah A. & Afra A. Hersi. 2011. Preparing for diversity: The alternatives to "linguistic coursework" for student teachers in the USA. In Sue Ellis & Elsbeth McCartney (eds.), *Applied linguistics and primary school teaching*, 44–52. Cambridge: Cambridge University Press.

Hsu, Hui-Yin. 2009. Preparing teachers to teach literacy in responsive ways that capitalize on students' cultural and linguistic backgrounds through weblog technology. *Multicultural Education & Technology Journal* 3(3) 168–181.

Humphrey, Neil. 2003. Facilitating a positive sense of self in pupils with dyslexia: The role of teachers and peers. *Support for Learning* 18(3). 130–136.

Humphrey, Neil. 2004. The death of the feel-good factor? Self-esteem in the educational context. *School Psychology International* 25(3). 347–360.

Karabenick, Stuart A. & Phyllis A. C. Noda. 2004. Professional development implications of teachers' beliefs and attitudes toward English language learners. *Bilingual Research Journal* 28(1). 55–75.

Kroskrity, Paul V. 2010. Language ideologies – Evolving perspectives. *Society and Language Use* 7. 192–211.

Krulatz, Anna, Anne Dahl & Mona Evelyn Flogenfeldt. 2018. *Enacting multilingualism: From research to teaching practice in the English classroom*. Oslo: Cappelen Damm.

Lawrence, Denis. 2006. *Enhancing self-esteem in the classroom*. London: Paul Chapman.

Lee, Jin Sook & Eva Oxelson. 2006. "It's not my job": K–12 teacher attitudes toward students' heritage language maintenance. *Bilingual Research Journal* 30(2). 453–477.

Lucas, Tamara & Ana María Villegas. 2013. Preparing linguistically responsive teachers: Laying the foundation in preservice teacher education. *Theory into Practice* 52(2). 98–109.

Lucas, Tamara, Ana María Villegas & Adrian D. Martin. 2015. Teachers' beliefs about English language learners. In Helenrose Fives & Michele Gregoire Gill (eds.), *International handbook of research on teachers' beliefs*, 453–475. New York: Routledge.

Malaguzzi, L. 1994. Your image of the child: Where teaching begins. *Child Care Information Exchange* 3. 52–61.

Manyak, Patrick C. 2004. "What did she say?": Translation in a primary-grade English immersion class. *Multicultural Perspectives* 6(1). 12–18.

Mary, Latisha & Andrea Young. 2018a. Parents in the playground, headscarves in the school and an inspector taken hostage: Exercising agency and challenging dominant deficit discourses in a multilingual pre-school in France. *Language, Culture and Curriculum* 31(3). 318–332.

Mary, Latisha & Andrea S. Young. 2018b. Black-blanc-beur: Challenges and opportunities for developing language awareness in teacher education in France. In Christine Hélot, Caroline Frijns, Koen Gorp & Sven Sierens (eds.), *Language awareness in multilingual classrooms in Europe: From theory to practice*. Berlin & Boston: de Gruyter.

M.E.N. 2012. *Scolarisation des élèves. Organisation de la scolarité des élèves allophones nouvellement arrivés*. Circulaire n° 2012–141 du 2-10-2012. https://www.education.gouv.fr/pid285/bulletin_officiel.html?cid_bo=61536 (accessed 22 June 2019).

Menken, Kate. 2008. *English learners left behind: Standardized testing as language policy*. Clevedon: Multilingual Matters.

Menken, Kate & Ofelia García (eds.). 2010. *Negotiating language policies in schools: Educators as policymakers*. New York: Routledge.

Montero, Miguel & Paula McVicker. 2006. The impact experience of coursework: Perceptions of second language learners in the mainstream classroom. http://radicalpedagogy.icaap.org/content/issue8_1/mantero.html (accessed 23 June 2019).

Moons, Caroline. 2010. *Kindergarten teachers speak: Working with language diversity in the classroom*. Montreal: McGill University MA thesis.

Mruk, Christopher. 1999. *Self-esteem: Research, theory, and practice*. New York: Springer.

Pajares, M. Frank 1992. Teachers' beliefs and educational research: Cleaning up a messy construct. *Review of Educational Research* 62(3). 307–332.

Paul Kister, Stéphanie. 2016. *L'enseignement du français langue seconde / langue de scolarisation (FLS/FLSco) aux élèves allophones arrivants accueillis en classe ordinaire à l'école élémentaire*. Strasbourg: Université de Strasbourg PhD thesis.

Paulsrud, BethAnne. this vol. The mainstream classroom and home language maintenance.

Pettit, Stacie K. 2011. Teachers' beliefs about English language learners in the mainstream classroom: A review of the literature. *International Multilingual Research Journal* 5(2). 123–147.

Piller, Ingrid. 2016. *Linguistic diversity and social justice: An introduction to applied sociolinguistics*. Oxford University Press.

Pulinx, Reinhilde, Piet Van Avermaet & Orhan Ağirdağ 2015. Silencing linguistic diversity: The extent, the determinants and consequences of the monolingual beliefs of Flemish teachers. *International Journal of Bilingual Education and Bilingualism* 5(20). 542–556.

Razfar, Aria. 2012. Narrating beliefs: A language ideologies approach to teacher beliefs. *Anthropology & Education Quarterly* 43(1). 61–81.

Reeves, Jenelle 2004. "Like everybody else": Equalizing educational opportunity for English language learners. *TESOL Quarterly* 38(1). 43–66.

Richardson, Virginia. (1996). The role of attitudes and beliefs in learning to teach. In John Sikula (ed.), *Handbook of research on teacher education*, 102–119. 2nd edn. New York, NY: Macmillan.

Rimm-Kaufman, Sara E., Melissa D. Storm, Brooke E. Sawyer, Robert C. Pianta & Karen M. Laparo. 2006. The Teacher Belief Q-Sort: A measure of teachers' priorities in relation to disciplinary practices, teaching practices, and beliefs about children. *Journal of School Psychology* 44. 141–165.

Rinaldi, Carolina. 1998. Projected curriculum constructed through documentation – Progettazione. In Carolyn P. Edwards, Lella Gandini & George Edwards (eds.), *The hundred languages of children: The Reggio Emilia approach – advanced reflections*, 113–125. Greenwich, CT & London: Greenwood Publishing Group.

Rios, Francisco, Allen Trent & Lillian Vega Castaneda. 2003. Social perspective taking: Advancing empathy and advocating justice. *Equity & Excellence in Education* 36(1). 5–14.

Rosenthal, Robert & Lenore Jacobson. 1968. *Pygmalion in the classroom: Teacher expectation and pupils' intellectual development*. New York: Holt, Rinehart and Winston.

Rosiers, Kirsten. 2017. Unravelling translanguaging. The potential of translanguaging as a scaffold among teachers and pupils in superdiverse classrooms in Flemish education (Belgium). In BethAnne Paulsrud, Jenny Rosén, Boglárka Straszer & Åsa Wedin (eds.), *Translanguaging and education: New perspectives from the field*, 148–169. Bristol: Multilingual Matters.

Saxena, Mukul & Marilyn Martin-Jones. 2013. Multilingual resources in classroom interaction: Ethnographic and discourse analytic perspectives. *Language and Education* 27(4). 285–297.

Skutnabb-Kangas Tove & Stephen May. 2016. Linguistic human rights in education. In Teresa McCarty & Stephen May (eds.), *Language policy and political issues in education. Encyclopedia of language and education*, 125–141. 3rd edn. Cham: Springer.

Sharkey, Judy & Carolyn Layzer. 2000. Whose definition of success? Identifying factors that affect English language learners' access to academic success and resources. *TESOL Quarterly* 34(2). 352–368.

Siemushyma, Maria & Andrea S. Young. 2019. In which language(s) do you parent? How language(s) used by migrant families influence the realization of parenting functions. In Sampson Lee Blair & Rosalina Pisco Costa (eds.), *Transitions into parenthood: Examining the complexities of childrearing*, 149–171. Bingley: Emerald Publishing Limited.

Silverstein, Michael. 1979. Language structure and linguistic ideology. In Paul Clyne, William F. Hanks & Carol L. Hofbauer (eds.), *The elements: A parasession on linguistic units and levels*, 193–247. Chicago: Chicago Linguistic Society.

Skott, Jeppe. 2015. The promises, problems, and prospects of research on teachers' beliefs. In: Helenrose Fives & Michele Gregoire Gill (eds.), *International handbook of research on teachers' beliefs*, 13–30. New York: Routledge.

Smitherman, Geneva & Victor Villanueva. 2000. *Language knowledge and awareness survey conducted by CCCC Language Policy Committee for the National Council of Teachers of English Research Foundation and the Conference on College Composition and Communication*. East Lansing, MI: Michigan State University. https://prod-ncte-cdn.azureedge.net/nctefiles/groups/cccc/committees/langsurvey.pdf (accessed 23 June 2019).

Spolsky, Bernard. 2004. *Language policy*. Cambridge: Cambridge University Press.

Thomauske, Nathalie. 2011. The relevance of multilingualism for teachers and immigrant parents in early childhood education and care in Germany and in France. *Intercultural Education* 22(4). 327–336.

Tijnagel-Schoenaker, Bernadet. 2017. The Reggio Emilia Approach ... the hundred languages. *Prima Educatione* 139–146.

Tsokalidou, Roula. 2005. Raising bilingual awareness in Greek primary schools. *International Journal of Bilingual Education and Bilingualism* 8(1). 48–61.

Ullicci, Kerri. 2007. The myths that blind: The role of beliefs in school change. *Journal of Educational Controversy* 2(1). 1–7.

Van Der Wildt, Anouk, Piet Van Avermaet & Mieke Van Houtte. 2017. Multilingual school population: Ensuring school belonging by tolerating multilingualism. *International Journal of Bilingual Education and Bilingualism* 20(7). 868–882.

Walker, Anne, Jill Shafer & Michelle Iams. 2004. "Not in my classroom": Teacher attitudes towards English language learners in the mainstream classroom. *NABE Journal of Research and Practice* 2(1). 130–160.

Woolard, Kathryn A. 1998. Language ideology as a field of inquiry. In Bambi B. Schieffelin, Kathryn Woollard & Paul Kroskrity (eds.), *Language ideologies: Practice and theory*, 3–47. New York: Oxford University Press.

Young, Andrea S. 2014. Unpacking teachers' language ideologies: Attitudes, beliefs, and practiced language policies in schools in Alsace, France. *Language Awareness* 23(1–2). 157–171.

Young, Andrea S. 2017. "Non, moi je lui dis pas en turc, ou en portugais, ou en, j'sais pas moi en arabe": Exploring teacher ideologies in multilingual/cultural preschool contexts in France. *Bellaterra Journal of Teaching & Learning Language & Literature* 10(2). 11–24.

Young, Andrea & Christine Hélot. 2003. Language awareness and/or language learning in French primary schools today. *Language Awareness* 12(3–4). 234–246.

Youngs, Cheryl S. & George A. Youngs. 2001. Predictors of mainstream teachers' attitudes toward ESL students. *TESOL Quarterly* 35(1). 97–120.

BethAnne Paulsrud
23 The mainstream classroom and home language maintenance

1 Introduction

Due to mobility and migration, many teachers today encounter increasing linguistic diversity in the mainstream classroom as they welcome students from different backgrounds. Students may have home languages that hold high prestige globally or are national languages elsewhere, but they may also have home languages that lack status and recognition. Likewise, their literacy and/or oracy skills in their home languages may be strong or only emerging. Managing multiple home languages in the classroom may be seen as challenging and even problematic in some countries, with policies framed along these lines, such as Australia (e.g. Eisenchlas and Schalley 2019), while some countries that previously merely tolerated home languages now articulate support for them, such as Ireland (e.g. Dillon 2012; Department of Education and Skills 2017). In other countries, policies may also allow more space for the inclusion of home languages in mainstream classrooms, such as Sweden (e.g. Ganuza and Hedman 2018).

Through examples of recent research from a variety of contexts, this chapter aims to explore how home language maintenance may be managed and supported in the mainstream classroom. Here, *home language* refers to languages other than the majority language of instruction in the classroom (see also Eisenchlas and Schalley this vol. for a discussion). The chapter first briefly presents how home language and classroom management have generally been treated in the classroom, and then turns the focus to language orientations (Ruiz 1984) in relation to home language maintenance. The key concepts *ideological and implementational spaces* and *translanguaging* are introduced, followed by the selected studies highlighting the teacher, in relation to policies and to teacher training, and classroom practices. The chapter concludes with final thoughts on how innovative strategies in classroom management may support students' linguistic diversity, and, in the words of Hornberger, encourage multilingualism to "evolve and flourish rather than dwindle and disappear" (2002: 30). Thus, the ambition with this chapter is to take a step away from the deficit perspectives often associated with management of students with other home languages than the majority school language.

2 Background: Home languages in the mainstream classroom

According to Young (2014: 157), "Children for whom the language of instruction is not the language of the home are particularly dependent on their teachers for learning support." The Organisation for Economic Co-operation and Development (OECD), for example, emphasises the need multilingual students have for language support in the classroom as essential to both school achievement and equity in society (Field, Kuczera, and Pont 2007). However, in many educational settings, teachers are not interested in their students' home languages, do not know what they are, or see home language maintenance as the sole responsibility of the parents (Dillon 2012; Young 2014). Some teachers also report that parents do not want home language maintenance to be a part of schooling, but prefer only majority language support (Dillon 2012). Still, in others, teachers allow students to actively use their home languages to support their learning (e.g. Rosiers 2017). How home languages are included or excluded in the mainstream classroom may be related to classroom management choices. Curran (2003: 334) describes classroom management as "of paramount concern for both new and veteran teachers". She maintains that management decisions are "even more complex" when students have different home languages. Curran calls for practical routines (such as designated library days) and prepared classroom environments (such as labels in students' home languages) to give students with limited majority language skills a sense of structure and security. She further argues that mainstream teachers need to affirm linguistic diversity, stating, "Teachers need to model a respect for all languages" (Curran 2003: 338). This focus on linguistic diversity as positive is key to understanding how teachers can support home language maintenance in the mainstream classroom – and policy plays a role in this.

Policies affording or constraining the maintenance of home languages link to the perception of languages other than the majority language as legitimate for learning (Rosén and Wedin 2015). The roles of national policy documents (e.g. in curricula) and the local policies of the school (both implicit and explicit) can be considered in light of Ruiz's (1984) three orientations in language planning: language-as-problem, language-as-right, and language-as-resource. Hornberger (1990: 24) offers a summary of the three orientations:

> Under a language-as-problem orientation, language is seen as an obstacle standing in the way of the incorporation of members of linguistic minorities into the mainstream. Under a language-as-right orientation, the right of linguistic-minority members to speak and maintain their mother tongue is defined as a human and civil right. Under a language-as-resource orientation, the importance to the nation of conserving and developing all of its linguistic resources is emphasized.

While Ruiz wrote about the situation of bilingual education in the 1980's USA when he specified the three orientations, the issues he identified then are still valid today when we consider policy and multilingualism in mainstream schools across contexts. He emphasised the need to explore "what is thinkable about language in society" (1984: 16), with questions related to the ideologies revealed in policy texts, the ways we talk about language in relation to society, and which languages are considered legitimate for whom and when. According to Hult and Hornberger, it is possible to "unpack and reflect upon the ideas aligned with each orientation" (2016: 31) in the implicit or explicit directives in macro and micro policies as well as in the classroom (see also Hult 2013).

2.1 Key concepts

While an understanding of language orientations frames this exploration of the mainstream classroom and home language maintenance, this chapter engages with two related concepts: *ideological and implementational spaces* and *translanguaging*.

2.1.1 Ideological and implementational spaces

Mainstream classrooms are embedded with ideologies that affect a teacher's beliefs and attitudes towards students' home languages (see also Mary and Young this vol.). Politics and policies on the macro level (see Liddicoat and Yağmur, both this vol.) indicate ideologies about language status and hierarchies that should be implemented at the micro level. According to Johnson (2010), official discourses open or close *ideological spaces* and *implementational spaces* in schools (Hornberger 2002). National language and education policies that promote and value multilingualism as a resource open ideological spaces, which in turn allows for implementational spaces in practice (e.g. the school or classroom level). Ideological spaces can also be closed or rejected, thus making implementation difficult. Furthermore, ideological spaces promoting positive attitudes towards home languages are only potential spaces, as "language educators and users must take advantage of this space by implementing multilingual education practices" (Johnson 2011: 129). Likewise, a lack of clear ideological spaces places great responsibility on the individual teacher as well as teacher educators for interpretation and implementation of practices promoting (or not) linguistic diversity. Spaces can be linked to affordances and constraints for multilingualism in the school, with *affordances* defined as "what is available to the person to do something with" (van Lier 2004: 91) or possibilities offering action potential in the environment, and *constraints* defined as obstacles preventing action (van Lier 2004: 4).

Even if the ideology in policy is in place, teachers may need implementational tools. Liddicoat (2014: 121) argues that teachers need to develop their own "pedagogical and linguistic capabilities in order to implement pedagogical change". Teachers have the possibility to resist or support top-down policies – as well as to negotiate their own implementation based on their own ideologies. Furthermore, promoting classroom practices that actually support home language maintenance requires agency, as mainstream teachers need to act on the ideological spaces they perceive in national policy documents such as curricula and in the local policies of the school to create implementational spaces for affirmative practices.

2.1.2 Translanguaging

Translanguaging as pedagogy may play a role in affording home language maintenance, as the recognition of the value of linguistic resources may enhance communication and foster inclusiveness in the spaces of formal education. Translanguaging can be defined as "[...] a process by which students and teachers engage in complex discursive practices that include all the language practices of students in order to develop new language practices and sustain old ones, communicate appropriate knowledge, and give voice to new sociopolitical realities by interrogating linguistic inequality" (García and Kano 2014: 261). As a theoretical perspective, translanguaging offers an ideological stance in support of multilingual pedagogy. The teacher in the mainstream classroom may adopt one of two stances on translanguaging: *scaffolding* or *transformative* (García and Kleyn 2016). A scaffolding stance embraces the view that inclusion of the home language may be necessary for only a certain period, during which the students may use their full linguistic repertoires while becoming proficient in the language of instruction (usually the majority language). A transformative stance, on the other hand, disrupts the language hierarchies in the mainstream classroom, and instead promotes the bilingual development of students "in ways that go beyond how monolinguals perform" (García and Kleyn 2016: 21). Thus, teachers recognize that their students have valuable knowledge and experiences in their use of their home languages that they can bring with them to the classroom.

The potential benefits that a translanguaging stance offers multilingual students in the mainstream classroom have been widely accepted (e.g. Baker 2011; García and Flores 2014), but some question translanguaging as a theory and pedagogy for the minority language speaker (e.g. Ganuza and Hedman 2017; Jaspers 2018). Citing recent research on translanguaging, Jaspers (2019: 84) identifies what he terms as "two technical arguments" of translanguaging: as the natural norm for speakers and as the key to successful instructional practices in the classroom. However, he maintains that the focus on these two arguments is reductionist and creates value assumptions of translanguaging that in turn restrict possibilities to affect policy. Furthermore, Jasper (2019: 89) argues: "Even those teachers who are maximally aware of linguistic diversity and prepared to adapt their curricula will in these circumstances have to strike compromises [with other stakeholders such as the government] and will often not be able to prioritise students' linguistic backgrounds." Instead, he calls for a recognition of languages as desirable, and not only as part of a successful pedagogy, which echoes Ruiz who stated: "the mother tongue is a good thing in itself" (2010: 165). While acknowledging Jasper's concerns, in this chapter, the assumption remains that developing students' home languages may establish the value of those languages as both desirable and as legitimate resources for learning. This can also be related to the Ruizan language orientations, as "teachers with a translanguaging stance have a firm belief that their students' language practices are both a resource and a right" (García, Johnson, and Seltzer 2017: 27). Translanguaging offers a step away from monoglossic norms and monolingual ideologies and instead affords a resistance to language hierarchies and a view of all linguistic resources as valuable.

3 The mainstream classroom and home language maintenance: Selected studies

This section presents selected studies of the mainstream classroom and home language maintenance in primary and pre-primary education. Many studies of multilingual students concentrate on their academic achievement or attainment of the school language (e.g. Broeder and Kistemaker 2015). In this chapter, the focus is instead on studies addressing how classroom language management can adapt to include home languages to greater degrees across a variety of global contexts. This is illustrated with studies focusing on teachers and policy, teacher training, and classroom practices.

3.1 The role of the teacher

Here, I highlight a selection of recent studies of the role of teachers in the mainstream classroom, especially in light of their possibilities to support multilingualism in the mainstream classroom, and to resist preserving schools as monolingual spaces (e.g. Piller 2016). Teachers' beliefs about multilingualism influence how they interpret spaces in policy, influencing their classroom management decisions in relation to home languages. Hult (2013: 168) states that this may allow for "agency, creativity, and the opportunity" to promote support for multilingualism in mainstream education. Ideologies – and subsequently the accompanying practices – may also be changed through increased awareness of students' home language resources, for example through teacher training, although tensions between policy and practice may remain, as seen in the studies below.

3.1.1 Teachers and policy

According to Liddicoat (2014: 127), there can exist a "silence about pedagogy in language policy", which may mean teachers in the mainstream classroom must instead glean directives from implicit policy or rely on the ideologies shaped by their own attitudes, knowledge or beliefs (see also Mary and Young this vol.). A focus on majority languages as the legitimate language for learning may mean that "students' native languages may be tolerated, but not with the intent to develop or maintain [their own] language and develop advanced bilingual skills" (de Jong 2016: 278). *Promoting* should not be confused with *tolerating* (see also May 2015). If home languages are promoted, then measures – whether they be top-down policies or grassroots teaching practices – are in place that entitle students to use all their linguistic resources, and not just the school majority language, in learning. If home languages are merely tolerated, they may instead be seen as an individual resource to be used privately and not within the realm of education. In order to unquestionably promote home languages, school leadership needs to be supportive (Woodley 2016) and school and government policies need to be in place (Varghese and Becerra Lubies 2013), as well as visible and known to teachers (Dillon 2012). Here, studies at the intersection of policy, teachers and the mainstream classroom with linguistic diversity are presented.

In their study of teachers as actors responding to policy (both top-down and bottom-up), Tarnanen and Palviainen (2018) present an investigation of teachers' beliefs and ideologies towards multilingualism in the classroom in response to the most recent Finnish national curriculum (for an overview, see Zilliacus, Paulsrud, and Holm 2017). This national curriculum from 2014 explicitly recognizes the value of home languages. However, Tarnanen and Palviainen acknowledge individual teachers' roles in the reproduction or the resistance of language-in-education policies and highlight the role that teachers' ideologies have in the implementation of policies. Hence, in their meta-ethnography of four synthesized studies, they analysed teacher talk in their aim to create a "comprehensive description of teachers as policy agents and of multilingualism in Finnish schools as it emerges through teachers' beliefs and experiences" (Tarnanen and Palviainen 2018: 6). Their findings indicate that teachers are slow to develop new ideologies, ones that may more clearly support home language maintenance in the classroom, despite the clear directives in the curriculum. Instead, discourses of the separation of school language and home language persist. Accepting other languages may be also limited to symbolic gestures such as knowing about flags or talking about customs. Tarnanen and Palviainen conclude that despite a new curriculum focusing on multilingualism, teachers tend to be reluctant to accept a multilingual turn (e.g. Conteh and Meier 2014), meaning that students' home languages may be valued but still not seen as legitimate languages for learning (see also Coady, Harper, and de Jong 2016).

Sometimes, it is clear that certain language-in-education policies do not support or promote home language maintenance. For example, in Malawi, where the national official language policy stipulates English as the national language, Kamwendo (2016) strongly argues against the ensuing educational policy of mainstream English-medium instruction for Malawian students. Few students have English as a home language, meaning that the legislation does not grant the languages of the students status as legitimate for learning nor as a right or a resource in the classroom. Likewise, home languages would thus lack importance as a resource of expertise for the greater community. In another example, the United States, English-only policies in many states limit the support of bilingual education and subsequently the recognition of home language maintenance in the mainstream classroom (Hopkins 2013). In her study of beliefs, attitudes and prior experiences of teachers in states with different policies (Arizona, California and Texas), Hopkins (2013) found that several factors influence whether or not working teachers see students' home languages as resources to be used for learning in the classroom. One such factor is the teachers' own bilingualism or teacher training in bilingual education (in this case, Spanish). The interviewed bilingual in-service teachers indicated that their teacher training taught them to "think explicitly about how to identify, connect to, and build on students' [linguistic] knowledge and experiences" (Hopkins 2013: 364). This reflects a transformative translanguaging stance, as the teachers created their own local levels of implementation in resistance to policies that did not promote home language use. While Hopkins further maintains that "even bilingual teachers in English-only contexts can leverage their unique skills in their instruction of emergent bilinguals" (Hopkins 2013: 361), García Johnson and Seltzer (2017) would counter that even monolingual teachers working with bilingual students can use translanguaging practices to create spaces that dismantle hierarchies and instead allow students' home languages, as well as family and community practices, into the classroom.

Teachers' knowledge of multilingualism and home language maintenance may vary greatly. For example, some may believe that students should be discouraged from using their home language both at school and in the home, despite research showing that subtractive bilingualism does not benefit learners (Cummins 2007; Varghese and Becerra Lubies 2013). If the home language is relegated to home use only, and schools ban the home language in school, students may not be able to make use of all of their linguistic resources for learning. Pedagogical tensions may also arise if teachers do not feel prepared to work with multilingual students, and thus the role of pre-service and in-service training in forming teachers' attitudes, knowledge and beliefs about multilingual education is key.

3.1.2 Teacher training

To meet the increasing demands of the "linguistic and cultural needs" in classrooms, Coady, Harper, and de Jong (2016: 344) underscore the need for "specialized knowledge and skills in teaching and learning". However, unless there are unambiguous directives in policy paired with a clear focus in pre-service training, there are openings for inconsistent interpretation and unreliable implementation of practices supporting linguistic diversity in the school. Hence, teachers may perpetuate a monolingual ideology in the classroom instead of recognising the needs of a multilingual school. Here, I present four studies of teacher training related to home language maintenance.

In a recent interview study, Paulsrud and Zilliacus (2018) asked Swedish teacher educators and pre-service teachers about the spaces for multilingualism in teacher training. Those interviewed indicated that preparation for how to support linguistic diversity in the mainstream classroom is deficient in teacher education and could be afforded greater attention (see also Dillon 2012). Both teacher educators and pre-service teachers highlighted the importance of multilingualism in the classroom and the need to include multilingual perspectives and working methods in school and education. One teacher educator emphasised the importance of understanding approaches to home language use as a legitimate language for learning: "We need to prepare teacher students to teach in a Swedish school that looks much different than the one they went to themselves" (Paulsrud 2016). This is especially important as teachers' own experiences (e.g. their own schooling, exposure to languages, travels) usually play an important role in their own approach to teaching. Another educator agreed, "I mean, they are all definitely going to end up in a classroom that is multilingual" (Paulsrud and Zilliacus 2018: 37). Paulsrud and Zilliacus (2018) also found that there were uncertainties about the responsibility for multilingualism in teacher education, as seen in one educator's statement, "I think knowledge about multilingualism is important, but it isn't really our responsibility" (p. 41). Language teachers called for more involvement from all subject disciplines, and all educators suggested the need for reforms in teacher education in terms of content and course objectives.

Kolano and King's (2015) study of 43 American pre-service teachers focuses on the completion of one mandatory course on multiculturalism in their teacher education, using written narratives collected over the course term. These pre-service teachers represented a homogenous group of mostly white females. Kolano and King's aim was to determine if a single course could affect these pre-service teachers' attitudes and beliefs towards English language learners (i.e. students with home languages other than the majority school language, English). The pre-service teachers indicated, among other things, the importance of completing practical work experience, called clinical field experiences, in a highly diverse school. Their experiences with diverse learners had particular impact, as most had never spent time in such classrooms before. While the focus of Kolano and King's study was on multiculturalism, linguistic diversity was a key component. One pre-service teacher in their study noted that her previous beliefs about students' home languages was not accurate: "I used to believe that I would need to know a student's primary language in order to effectively teach them" (Kolano and King 2015: 14; see also García and Seltzer 2016). Kolano and King maintain that through targeted teacher training, the pre-service teachers were able "to renegotiate their role to include an understanding of strategies, theories, and practices" (2015: 14) to support students with minority home languages in the mainstream classroom.

In their study of pre-service primary school teachers in Botswana and Swaziland, Kasule and Mapolelo (2013: 265) delve into work with mathematics word problems (described as "mathematical exercises whose content is presented in story form") in light of students' stronger proficiency in a home language. Both Botswana and Swaziland have English-medium education policies for the compulsory school. The 33 participants in the questionnaire study did not themselves have English as a primary home language but were expected to teach mathematics in English. Furthermore, Kasule and Mapolelo saw a mismatch in pre-service teachers' training in English and a national language, when they then later were employed in schools throughout the two countries, where numerous home languages may be spoken. The premise in the study was that students have both oral numeracy and oracy in their home languages. The question was if and how pre-service teachers were aware of this resource, as the use of the home languages for difficult maths problems was "officially discouraged in both countries" (Kasule and Mapolelo 2013: 271). Their results indicate that these pre-service teachers tend to rely on the English-medium school policy, rather than make use of the home languages as a resource when working with difficult mathematics word problems. Two challenges were clear: first, the students often encounter English for the first time in formal schooling, and second, they may not have literacy skills in their home languages. Although they rarely form a part of word problems, "home languages can play a role in solving and teaching mathematics word problems" (Kasule and Mapolelo 2013: 272) but teachers need specific methodologies for teaching to students with any home languages other than English or the national language. This is especially key as teachers often do not share home languages with the young students and pre-service mathematics teachers often lack courses in literacy in their education.[1] Kasule and Mapolelo (2013: 272) conclude, "Raising language awareness in mathematics teaching is important."

In-service training can also be key to forming teachers' practices promoting home language maintenance, as seen in Putjata's (2018) study in the German context. Putjata stresses that teachers need more than theories of second language acquisition. Teachers need training covering three areas: Knowledge, strategies of action, and beliefs about multilingualism in the mainstream classroom. She conducted an intervention study over one year with 12 pre-primary teachers in several German preschools, with an aim to understand how their beliefs about multilingualism may be shaped in a time when "the prevailing political, institutional and professional mind-set in many European countries remains a monolingual one" (Putjata 2018: 260). The four modules studied by the teachers included

---

[1] Compare with Barwell (2014) for a study of an English-speaking mathematics teacher working with young Cree-speaking students in Canada.

the following: (1) Inclusion and cultural diversity; (2) Multilingualism and linguistic diversity management; (3) Multilingualism and fostering second language acquisition; and (4) Cooperation with parents (Putjata 2018: 264). Putjata's questionnaires (both pre- and post-test as well as one year after the training) together with her observations reveal that the teachers did indeed shift their beliefs. A key finding was the teachers' realisation "that allowing languages other than German does not hinder child development; on the contrary, it even leads to positive outcomes" (Putjata 2018: 271). She identifies three crucial moments in the turn: New personal perspectives from experiencing communication in a second language, practical applications of trying new teaching methods, and implementation of said methods together with colleagues. Importantly, Putjata notes that theory alone is not enough (see also Paulsrud and Zilliacus 2018). The teachers needed to learn concrete "methods of language fostering and multilingualism" (Putjata 2018: 271) and then experience and discuss their attempts to incorporate them. Putjata argues, "Including multilingual language awareness in teacher training constitutes the key element for making an educational turn towards multilingualism" (2018: 271).

Coady, Harper, and de Jong (2016: 361) maintain that educators pose a risk to equitable education if they think the usual teaching practices will suit home language speakers who may need more support, as many practices tend to be "unplanned and unmodified". They call for inclusion and inclusive teaching. Creating an inclusive classroom requires teachers to learn "differentiated teaching strategies for students with different learning needs" (Coady, Harper, and de Jong 2016: 363). The pre-service teachers in Paulsrud and Zilliacus's (2018) study emphasised the need for practical teaching experience in working with multilingual students. As one said (Paulsrud 2016), "I have, like, nothing [with multilingual students] at my work placement. I have deficits. I don't know how I will handle it if I end up in a school with multilingual students or, like, multiculturalism." These sentiments echo the lack of focus on multilingual students in the classroom in Putjata's 2018 study of the German context. In order to develop their teaching skills in relation to linguistic diversity in the mainstream classroom, future teachers need to be introduced to both theoretical and practical knowledge. This applies to in-service teachers as well.[2] The four studies above have illustrated that targeted pre-service and in-service teacher training with a focus on attitudes, beliefs, and knowledge may be one way to achieve this (see also Mary and Young this vol.). Changing ideologies may affect how implementational spaces for creating language-as-resource orientations are possible.

---

[2] See Dooly and Vallejo (2020) for a study of an in-service training workshop exploring both *how* to work with multiple home languages in the mainstream classroom and *why*.

3.2 Classroom practices

In the classroom, either teachers choose to reinforce a monoglossic mind-set with teaching and learning through one language only, or they may choose to recognise the potentials of affording the use of all languages as resources for learning (Jones 2017). Bonacina-Pugh (2017: 2) calls the "interactional norms of language choice" in the classroom "practiced language policies"; and she argues that what is legitimate must be seen through both critical and practical lenses. Jones identifies two possibilities for arrangements for using all of the students' home languages: *separate bilingualism* and *flexible bilingualism* (2017: 202). In lessons upholding separate bilingualism, teachers alternate between one or more languages, but still keep them separate, for example in parts of the single lesson or during times of the day, similar to Cummins's description of monolingual instructional assumptions (2007). With flexible bilingualism, however, teachers engage with multiple linguistic resources through the lesson or school day. This section explores three studies of how teachers may do this.

In their study, Falchi, Axelrod, and Genishi (2014) challenge the practice of labelling children who do not speak the majority language at home as "at risk". They argue that due to, for example, having another home language than the school majority language, young students are often viewed as lacking through this moniker alone. They propose the opposite of a deficit perspective, instead seeing the children as possessing skills and knowledge already from home. They choose the term *emergent bilingual*, "to honour the complexity of children's language development and recognize that they are developing their home language(s) as well as English" (Falchi, Axelrod, and Genishi 2014: 346). In their longitudinal study of literacy practices in early primary years, they study the trajectory of emergent bilinguals in an American school in New York City over five years, with special focus on two multilingual children. While one student, Luisa, was a model participant in the lessons, the other, Miguel, was rather distracted and lagged behind in literacy. Miguel's struggles with performance in English literacy skills left him labelled as "at risk", despite his apparent abilities – albeit lack of interest – to write in both English and Spanish. However, the teacher created classroom practices that recognised the multilingual and multimodal capital that Miguel expressed, allowed him to use both his Spanish and English linguistic resources in writing, and praised him for his artistic talent, making "curricular space for herself and her student" (Falchi, Axelrod, and Genishi 2014: 362). Thus, the teacher attempted to afford flexibility within a rather restricted curriculum and literacy discourse; and in doing so, she resisted the dominant discourse of what makes a "good" student. In conclusion, Falchi, Axelrod, and Genishi question assumed norms of literacy, calling for acknowledgement of the many resources that students bring with them to the classroom, including oral storytelling and art, indicating a transformative stance.

In another study, Prosper and Nomlomo (2016) investigate literacy practices in South Africa, where students often have home languages different from the medium of instruction. The South African "Language-in-Education Policy advocates the maintenance of learners' home languages by promoting additive bi- or multilingualism in education" (Prosper and Nomlomo 2016: 80), although there are problems with implementation. Prosper and Nomlomo explored teachers' work with multilingual storybooks (Afrikaans, English and isiXhosa) in a linguistically diverse classroom, focusing on how teachers may support the proficiency their young students have in their home languages. They observed a teacher and her assistant working with literacy tasks following story reading during 17 lessons spread over two terms. The focus was on how reading in students' home languages promotes biliteracy. General findings indicate that while students had access to stories in other languages (albeit not all of the students' languages were represented), their literacy activities following the story time were limited to English only, despite the teacher's awareness of "cognitive benefits of the learners' home languages in literacy learning" (Prosper and Nomlomo 2016: 86). The students spoke at least five home languages other than Afrikaans, English and isiXhosa, but these were "invisible" in the classroom activities (2016: 87). Also, Afrikaans and isiXhosa were relegated to listening activities; and students did not use these languages in their own reading, writing or speaking activities: "the learners were just passive listeners as they were not afforded opportunities to read the stories on their own and to engage with texts in reading and writing in their home languages" (Prosper and Nomlomo 2016: 87). Hence, Prosper and Nomlomo conclude that while multilingual storybooks are a positive part of the classroom practices, teachers need more direct preparation for how to work with home languages together with the medium of instruction, especially if they themselves are not proficient in all of their students' home languages. Simply having materials in different languages in the mainstream classroom is not enough if teachers are to be able to "support and exploit the linguistic and cultural capital embedded in the learners' home languages" (Prosper and Nomlomo 2016: 89).

According to García and Seltzer (2016: 24; see also Curran 2003), while teachers may not know all of their students' home languages, they can still create a classroom environment and classroom practices that allow the home languages to flourish:

> [I]t is possible for teachers to build a classroom ecology where there are books and signage in multiple languages; where collaborative groupings are constructed according to students' home language so that they can deeply discuss a text written in the dominant school language using all their language resources; where students are allowed to write and speak with whatever resources they have and not wait until they have the "legitimate" ones to develop a voice; where all students language practices are included so as to work against the linguistic hierarchies that exist in schools; where families with different language practices are included.

These possibilities are illustrated by Woodley (2016; also García and Seltzer 2016) with her classroom study of Mr. Brown, a 5th grade teacher who teaches 27 students with eight different home languages, including Spanish, Polish, and Arabic. Mr. Brown only speaks his native English and limited Spanish and American Sign Language, but he fills his classroom with the languages of his students (e.g. word walls and labels). He also makes active use of an interactive white board for scaffolding, presenting both content words in different languages and images, and for translation. He "normalizes the classroom's diversity" (García and Seltzer 2016: 27) through his translanguaging stance, and legitimizes the students' home languages as resources for learning and communication.

According to Paulsrud and Rosén (2019), "Keeping languages separate reinforces an ideology that resists a view of linguistic diversity as a resource." They maintain that rather than directing measures for home language support only at students who may be categorised as second language learners or minority language speakers, multilingual pedagogy benefits all students. Allowing and promoting the use of home languages in the mainstream classroom through, for example, translanguaging strategies can increase metalinguistic awareness not only of the bilingual students but also of the so-called monolingual students (Woodley 2016). Falchi, Axelrod, and Genishi's study (2014) show this is possible if a teacher recognises the students as individuals with resources, opening up implementational spaces. However, Prosper and Nomlomo (2016) assert that merely recognising the languages is not enough to create a scaffolding stance. A transformative translanguaging stance is needed to disrupt hierarchies in the mainstream classroom that may limit practices to the majority language (see also Bonacina-Pugh 2017).

4 Conclusion

This chapter aimed to explore how home language maintenance may be managed and supported in the mainstream classroom. Tarnanen and Palviainen (2018: 12) maintain that we are in "times of educational and societal transformations" – and, I argue, that must also lead to a transformative view of language in the mainstream classroom. According to García and Sylvan (2011: 398), "Imposing one school standardized language without any flexibility of norms and practices will always mean that those students whose home language practices show the greatest distance from the school norm will always be disadvantaged. Clearly, monolingual education is no longer relevant in our globalized world." Spaces for this flexibility of practices and norms may be found on the macro level of government policies or the micro level of the school; and they affect teachers' possibilities to promote home languages as valuable resources (e.g. Ruiz 1984) in the mainstream classroom. "Practiced language policies" inform teachers which language/s are appropriate for which situation (Bonacina-Pugh 2017: 9). These on-the-ground policies may be created when ideologies supporting home languages open up implementational spaces in the classroom, just as they may close spaces for such support.

Ideologies are embedded in macro and micro policies, and "schools ideologically construct or disassemble linguistic boundaries" (Paulsrud and Rosén 2019). If these ideologies reinforce language hierarchies and denote only certain languages as legitimate for learning, tensions may arise for primary school teachers if they wish to implement teaching strategies that resist a monolingual mind-set (see also Helmchen and Melo-Pfeifer 2018). In education, a language-as-right orientation aims to ensure equal access to education (de Jong 2016), with both the majority language and the home language included. Thus, this orientation may support the recognition of the right to home language maintenance in the mainstream classroom, resisting the risk that students may instead be given access to the majority language of instruction as the only right. Translanguaging, which affords the inclusion of all students' "ways of knowing and languaging" (García, Johnson, and Seltzer 2017: 13), needs to be a part of teacher education and of the pre-primary and primary school classroom. Educators must understand both the theoretical principles behind a translanguaging stance that supports home language maintenance and development, and the real practices that translanguaging pedagogy can encompass.

The studies in this chapter, however, show that even with policies in place that either potentially constrain home language maintenance (Hopkins 2013) or explicitly afford home language maintenance (Tarnanen and Palviainen 2018), it is up to the individual teacher to act upon the ideological spaces in those policies. Teachers' own education may affect how they exercise their agency. According to Helmchen and Melo-Pfeifer (2018: 11), teacher training is key to "envisaging the implantation of multilingual teaching practice and curricular changes aiming at integrating multilingual strategies as cognitive and affective strategies *de facto*" (original emphasis). This includes understanding how a student's home language may affect learning in the mainstream classroom and subsequently how this may affect the need to differentiate the teaching practices. This understanding is connected to spaces perceived and spaces acted upon in policy and practice, and one way to respond to these spaces is through translanguaging, which may be seen as an implementational strategy in the mainstream classroom. Translanguaging is relevant in this chapter for the possibilities a scaffolding and transformative stance offer practices promoting home language maintenance. For example, a scaffolding stance is clear in the studies by Woodley (2016) and Prosper and Nomlomo (2016), while Falchi, Axelrod, and Genishi (2014) offer a study illustrating a transformative stance.

Several factors related to how mainstream teachers support home language maintenance are not covered thoroughly in this chapter, due to space, although they warrant further exploration. These include an understanding of the role of teachers' identities in forming their attitudes (see Mary and Young this vol.); the role of teachers who are themselves multilingual (although see Hopkins 2013); and the lack of qualified multilingual teachers in many mainstream setting. Regarding the last point, for example, teacher educators in Paulsrud and Zilliacus's (2018) study call for the recruitment of more multilingual students in teacher training. Also, there is a need for more research in understanding exactly how home language maintenance can become a legitimate part of practiced language policies in the classroom, through translanguaging or other practices.

The selected studies presented in this chapter indicate that the relation between mainstream classroom management and home language maintenance depends much on how students' home languages are recognised, promoted, and valued instead of merely tolerated in the mainstream classroom. Returning to the words of Hornberger, how can we see that teachers in the mainstream classroom are finding ways to encourage multilingualism to "evolve and flourish rather than dwindle and disappear" (2002: 30)? Echoing previous calls to move away from the "two solitudes" approach (Cummins 2007), Kleyn (2016: 203) is very clear: "Building a classroom community that is inclusive of all students' languages and cultures is important. Students cannot and should not be asked to leave their home language and cultural practices at the door." An educational policy that affords ideological and implementational spaces for multilingualism in schools also resists systems of social inequality, and thus supports social justice as well as access to democracy (Johnson 2010). In order to create unambiguous spaces for home language maintenance in the classroom, both better preservice and in-service teacher education and solid multilingual educational practices are required. Only then, can educators recognise, promote and value all students' home languages as a right and resource in the mainstream classroom.

References

Baker, Colin. 2011. *Foundations of bilingual education and bilingualism*. 5th edn. North York, Ontario: Multilingual Matters.
Barwell, Richard. 2014. Centripetal and centrifugal language forces in one elementary school second language mathematics classroom. *ZDM Mathematics Education* 46(6). 911–922.
Bonacina-Pugh, Florence. 2017. Legitimizing multilingual practices in the classroom: The role of the "practiced language policy". *International Journal of Bilingual Education and Bilingualism*. Online First. DOI: 10.1080/13670050.2017.1372359
Broeder, Peter & Mariska Kistemaker. 2015. More willingly to school: Tools for teachers to cope with linguistically diverse classrooms. *Intercultural Education* 26(3). 218–234.
Coady, Maria R., Candace Harper & Ester J. de Jong. 2016. Aiming for equity: Preparing mainstream teachers for inclusion or inclusive classrooms? *TESOL Quarterly* 50(2). 340–368.
Conteh, Jean & Gabriela Meier (eds.). 2014. *The multilingual turn in languages education: Opportunities and challenges*. Bristol: Multilingual Matters.
Cummins, Jim. 2007. Rethinking monolingual instructional strategies in multilingual classrooms. *Canadian Journal of Applied Linguistics (CJAL)/Revue Canadienne de Linguistique Appliquée (RCLA)* 10(2). 221–240.
Curran, Mary Elizabeth. 2003. Linguistic diversity and classroom management. *Theory Into Practice* 42(4). 334–340.

Department of Education and Skills. 2017. *Languages Connect: Ireland's strategy for foreign languages in education 2017–2026*. Dublin, Ireland: Department of Education and Skills.

Dillon, Anna Marie. 2012. Supporting home language maintenance among children with English as an additional language in Irish primary schools. *Working Papers in Educational Linguistics* 27(2). 76–94.

Dooly, Melinda & Claudia Vallejo. 2020. Bringing plurilingualism into teaching practice: A quixotic quest? *International Journal of Bilingual Education and Bilingualism* 23(1). 81–97.

Eisenchlas, Susana A. & Andrea C. Schalley. 2019. Reaching out to migrant and refugee communities to support home language maintenance. *International Journal of Bilingual Education and Bilingualism* 22(5). 564–575.

Eisenchlas, Susana A. & Andrea C. Schalley. this vol. Making sense of the notion of "home language" and related concepts.

Falchi, Lorraine T., Ysaaca Axelrod & Celia Genishi. 2014. "Miguel es un artista" – and Luisa is an excellent student: Seeking time and space for children's multimodal practices. *Journal of Early Childhood Literacy* 14(3). 345–66.

Field, Simon, Malgorzata Kuczera, Beatriz Pont & Organisation for Economic Co-operation and Development. 2007. *No more failures: Ten steps to equity in education*. Paris: OECD.

Ganuza, Natalia & Christina Hedman. 2017. Ideology vs. practice: Is there a space for pedagogical translanguaging in mother tongue instruction? In BethAnne Paulsrud, Jenny Rosén, Boglárka Straszer & Åsa Wedin (eds.), *New perspectives on translanguaging and education*, 208–225. Bristol: Multilingual Matters.

Ganuza, Natalia & Christina Hedman. 2018. Modersmålsundervisning, läsförståelse och betyg: Modersmålsundervisningens roll för elevers skolresultat [Mother tongue instruction, reading comprehension and grades: The role of mother tongue instruction for school achievements]. *Nordand. Nordisk tidsskrift for andrespråksforskning* 13(1). 4–22.

García, Ofelia & Nelson Flores. 2014. Multilingualism and common core state standards in the United States. In Stephen May (ed.), *The multilingual turn: Implications for SLA, TESOL and bilingual education*, 147–166. New York: Routledge.

García, Ofelia & Naomi Kano. 2014. Translanguaging as process and pedagogy: Developing the English writing of Japanese students in the US. In Jean Conteh & Gabriela Meier (eds.), *The multilingual turn in languages education: Opportunities and challenges*, 264–281. Bristol: Multilingual Matters.

García, Ofelia & Tatyana Kleyn. 2016. Translanguaging theory in education. In Ofelia García & Tatyana Kleyn (eds.), *Translanguaging with multilingual students: Learning from classroom moments*, 9–33. New York, NY: Routledge.

García, Ofelia & Kate Seltzer. 2016. The translanguaging current in language education. In Björn Kindenberg (ed.), *Flerspråkighet som resurs* [Multilingualism as a resource], 19–30. Stockholm: Liber.

García, Ofelia & Claire E. Sylvan. 2011. Pedagogies and practices in multilingual classrooms: Singularities in pluralities. *The Modern Language Journal* 95(3). 385–400.

García, Ofelia, Susana Ibarra Johnson & Kate Seltzer. 2017. *The translanguaging classroom: Leveraging student bilingualism for learning*. Philadelphia: Caslon Publishing.

Helmchen, Christian & Sílvia Melo-Pfeifer. 2018. Introduction: Multilingual literacy practices at school and in teacher education. In Christian Helmchen & Sílvia Melo-Pfeifer (eds.), *Plurilingual literacy practices at school and in teacher education*, 9–15. Berlin: Peter Lang.

Hopkins, Megan. 2013. Building on our teaching assets: The unique pedagogical contributions of bilingual educators. *Bilingual Research Journal* 36(3). 350–370.

Hornberger, Nancy H. 1990. Bilingual education and English-only: A language-planning framework. *The Annals of the American Academy of Political and Social Science* 508(1). 12–26.

Hornberger, Nancy H. 2002. Multilingual language policies and the continua of biliteracy: An ecological approach. *Language Policy* 1(1). 27–51.
Hult, Francis M. 2013. How does policy influence language in education? In Rita Elaine Silver & Soe Marlar Lwin (eds.), *Language in education: Social implications*, 159–175. London: Bloomsbury Academic.
Hult, Francis M. & Nancy H. Hornberger. 2016. Revisiting orientations in language planning: Problem, right, and resource as an analytical heuristic. *Bilingual Review/Revista Bilingüe (BR/RB)* 33(3). 30–49.
Jaspers, Jürgen. 2018. The transformative limits of translanguaging. *Language & Communication* 58(1). 1–10.
Jaspers, Jürgen. 2019. Authority and morality in advocating heteroglossia. *Language, Culture and Society* 1(1). 83–105.
Johnson, David C. 2010. Implementational and ideological spaces in bilingual education language policy. *International Journal of Bilingual Education and Bilingualism* 13(1). 61–79.
Johnson, David C. 2011. Critical discourse analysis and the ethnography of language policy. *Critical Discourse Studies* 8(4). 267–79.
Jones, Bryn. 2017. Translanguaging in bilingual schools in Wales. *Journal of Language, Identity & Education* 16(4). 199–215.
Jong, Ester de. 2016. Afterword: Toward pluralist policies, practices, and research. *Language and Education* 30(4). 378–382.
Kamwendo, Gregory H. 2016. The new language of instruction policy in Malawi: A house standing on a shaky foundation. *International Review of Education* 62(2). 221–228.
Kasule Daniel & Dumma Mapolelo. 2013. Prospective teachers' perspectives on the use of English in the solving and teaching of mathematics word problems – a brief cross-country survey. *African Journal of Research in Mathematics, Science and Technology Education* 17(39). 265–274.
Kleyn, Tatyana. 2016. Setting the path: Implications for teachers and teacher educators. In Ofelia García & Tatyana Kleyn (eds.), *Translanguaging with multilingual students: Learning from classroom moments*, 202–220. New York, NY: Routledge.
Kolano, Lan Quach & Elena T. King. 2015. Preservice teachers' perceived beliefs towards English language learners: Can a single course change attitudes? *Issues in Teacher Education* 24(2). 3–21.
Liddicoat, Anthony J. 2014. The interface between macro and micro-level language policy and the place of language pedagogies. *International Journal of Pedagogies & Learning* 9(2). 118–129.
Liddicoat, Anthony J. this vol. Language policy and planning for language maintenance: The macro and meso levels.
Lier, Leo van. 2004. *The ecology and semiotics of language learning*. Dordrecht: Kluwer Academic.
Mary, Latisha & Andrea Young. this vol. Teachers' beliefs and attitudes towards home language maintenance and their effects.
May, Stephen. 2015. Language rights and language policy: Addressing the gap(s) between principles and practices. *Current Issues in Language Planning* 16(4). 355–359.
Paulsrud, BethAnne. 2016. Unpublished interview.
Paulsrud, BethAnne & Jenny Rosén. 2019. Translanguaging and language ideologies in education: Northern and Southern perspectives. In Stan Brunn & Roland Kehrein (eds.), *Handbook of the changing world language map*, 1–15. Cham: Springer.
Paulsrud, BethAnne & Harriet Zilliacus. 2018. Flerspråkighet och transspråkande i lärarutbildningen. [Multilingualism and translanguaging in teacher education.] In BethAnne Paulsrud, Jenny Rosén, Boglárka Straszer & Åsa Wedin (eds.), *Transspråkande i svenska*

utbildningssammanhang [Translanguaging in Swedish education contexts], 27–48. Lund: Studentlitteratur.

Piller, Ingrid. 2016. Monolingual ways of seeing multilingualism. *Journal of Multicultural Discourses* 11(1). 25–33.

Prosper, Ancyfrida & Vuyokazi Nomlomo. 2016. Literacy for all? Using multilingual reading stories for literacy development in a grade one classroom in the Western Cape. *Per Linguam* 32(3). 79–94.

Putjata, Galina. 2018. Multilingualism for life – language awareness as key element in educational training: Insights from an intervention study in Germany. *Language Awareness* 27(3). 259–276.

Rosén, Jenny & Åsa Wedin. 2015. *Klassrumsinteraktion och flerspråkighet: ett kritiskt perspektiv [Classroom interaction and multilingualism: A critical perspective]*. Stockholm: Liber.

Rosiers, Kirsten. 2017. Unravelling translanguaging: The potential of translanguaging as a scaffold among teachers and pupils in superdiverse classrooms in Flemish education. In BethAnne Paulsrud, Jenny Rosén, Boglárka Straszer & Åsa Wedin (eds.), *New perspectives on translanguaging and education*, 148–169. Bristol: Multilingual Matters.

Ruiz, Richard. 1984. Orientations in language planning. *NABE Journal* 8(2). 15–34.

Ruiz, Richard. 2010. Reorienting language as resource. In John E. Petrovic (ed.), *International perspectives on bilingual education: Policy, practice, and controversy*, 155–172. Charlotte, NC: IAP – Information Age Publishing.

Tarnanen, Mirja & Åsa Palviainen. 2018. Finnish teachers as policy agents in a changing society. *Language and Education* 32(5). 428–443.

Varghese, Manka M. & Rukmini Becerra Lubies. 2013. How do people use languages differently? In Rita Elaine Silver & Soe Marlar Lwin (eds.), *Language in education: Social implications*, 143–157. London: Bloomsbury Academic.

Woodley, Heather H. with Andrew Brown. 2016. Balancing windows and mirrors. In Ofelia García & Tatyana Kleyn (eds.), *Translanguaging with multilingual students: Learning from classroom moments*, 83–99. New York, NY: Routledge.

Yağmur, Kutlay. this vol. Models of formal education and minority language teaching across countries.

Young, Andrea S. 2014. Unpacking teachers' language ideologies: Attitudes, beliefs, and practiced language policies in schools in Alsace, France. *Language Awareness* 23(1–2). 157–171.

Zilliacus, Harriet, BethAnne Paulsrud & Gunilla Holm. 2017. Essentializing vs. non-essentializing students' cultural identities: Curricular discourses in Finland and in Sweden. *Journal of Multicultural Discourses* 12(2). 166–180.

About the contributors

Nathan John Albury is a policy advisor at Leiden University in the Netherlands following a Marie Curie-Skłodowska Research Fellowship at Leiden University in the Netherlands under the LEaDing Fellows COFUND programme. His research resides in the sociology of language, with a particular emphasis on critical and posthumanist analyses of intersections between language, ethnicity, politics, and economy as macro-level processes that affect societal multilingualism. This also includes how linguistic diversity, as an index of broader diversities, is regulated both through top-down regulatory interventions and through bottom-up agency, linguistic epistemologies, knowledge, and other belief systems. His research has especially focused on Malaysia, New Zealand, Serbia and Iceland.

E. Annamalai, currently Visiting Professor of Tamil at the University of Chicago, was Director of the Central Institute of Indian Languages, Mysore. At the Institute he designed and guided projects on language education for tribal children. His research areas include language policy in education, especially the policy response to the dominance of English, and multilingualism, especially the functional complementation of languages and the emergence of converging grammars. Some of his papers are "Conflict between law and language policy in education: Deliberations of Indian Supreme Court" (2016, *Language Rights*), "Language in political economy and market economy: A case study of India" (2012, *Language & Law*), "Reflections on language policy for multilingualism" (2003, *Language Policy*). He served on the advisory panel on Rausing Endangered Languages Documentation Project, University of London.

José Camacho (University of Illinois-Chicago) is a linguist interested in the structure and use of human languages, particularly Spanish and Amazonian languages. His syntactic research includes topics such as the structure of coordination, null subjects and idiomatic expressions. A second area of interest involves the representation of language among heritage speakers, for example word order patterns and how agreement works. A third area of interest relates to sustainability of minority languages, specifically social factors that negatively affect minority language maintenance in urban contexts.

Gregory A. Cheatham, PhD, is an Associate Professor in the Department of Special Education at University of Kansas, USA. Greg's scholarship focuses on the provision of effective, appropriate, inclusive, and equitable services for children and families from culturally and linguistically diverse and marginalized backgrounds. He has a particular interest in bilingualism for families and children considered at risk for disabilities and children who have diagnosed disabilities. Greg is currently Editor-in-Chief of *Young Exceptional Children*, a practitioner journal from the Division for Early Childhood (DEC) of the Council for Exceptional Children (CEC).

Xiao Lan Curdt-Christiansen is Professor in Applied Linguistics at the Department of Education, University of Bath, UK. Her research interests encompass ideological, sociocultural-cognitive and policy perspectives on children's multilingual education and biliteracy development. She has published widely in the field of applied linguistics. Her recent books include: *Learning Chinese in diasporic communities* (with Andy Hancock); and *Language, ideology and education: The politics of textbooks in language education* (with Csilla Weninger). Her other publications have appeared in academic journals, such as *Language Policy*; *International Journal of Bilingualism and Bilingual Education*; *Journal of Multilingual and Multicultural Development*; *Language and Education*; and *Language, Culture and Curriculum*.

Annick De Houwer is Professor of Language Acquisition and Multilingualism at the University of Erfurt, Germany. Her 1990 CUP book *The acquisition of two languages from birth* constituted pioneering work in bilingual acquisition, and her 2009 textbooks *Bilingual first language acquisition* and *An introduction to bilingual development* are used all over the world. She is co-editor (with Lourdes Ortega) of the 2019 *Cambridge handbook of bilingualism*. Annick De Houwer is the initiator and director of the Harmonious Bilingualism Network, which aims to support and stimulate scientific research into harmonious bilingualism and to make sure the results of that research are widely disseminated both within and outside of academia (www.habilnet.org).

Susana A. Eisenchlas is a Senior Lecturer in Linguistics/Applied Linguistics in the School of Humanities, Languages and Social Science, Griffith University, Australia. She has published extensively in the areas of intercultural communication, gender studies, first/second language acquisition, and more recently, bilingualism and biliteracy. In collaboration with Andrea Schalley, Susana co-chairs the International Association of Applied Linguistics (AILA) Research Network (ReN) on "Social and Affective Factors in Home Language Maintenance and Development". She is on the editorial board of a number of international journals, and co-editor of the open access book series *Current Issues in Bilingualism* published by Language Science Press. In addition to her academic work Susana has been actively involved in promoting the benefits of bi/multilingualism in migrant and refugee communities in Australia through public talks and workshops delivered at schools and libraries.

Anikó Hatoss is a Senior Lecturer in Linguistics at the School of Humanities and Languages, University of New South Wales, Sydney, where she teaches courses in linguistics and applied linguistics. Her research is focussed on diaspora communities, their intergenerational language maintenance and shift, as well as grassroot language planning. To date, she has worked with the Hungarian, South African, German and South Sudanese communities in Australia. Her research monograph, entitled *Displacement, language maintenance and identity* (John Benjamins 2013), explores language use through time and space in South Sudanese refugee-background families. Her research has also contributed to narratives of identity (*Discourse and Society* 2012), agency in grassroots language planning (Routledge 2019) and technology in language maintenance (Deep University Press 2019). Currently she is investigating spatial and temporal dimensions of language use and identity in urban multilingual contexts through the study of linguistic landscapes.

Jing Huang holds an MA in Applied Linguistics from the University of Warwick (UK), and a PhD in Education from the University of Birmingham (UK). She works as a Research Associate in the Department of Education at the University of Bath, UK, and is currently involved in an ESRC-funded multi-level investigation on transnational migration and language policy, which examines how social mobility impacts UK multilingualism at national, community, and family levels. Prior to her academic career, Jing taught English and Chinese for general purposes in China and the UK for several years. Jing's research interests lie in the fields of sociolinguistics and multilingualism in education. She uses ethnography to research multilingual practices of individuals, families, schools, and communities, particularly in relation to ideology, identity, and education.

Päivi Juvonen is Professor of Swedish as a Second Language at Linnæus University, Sweden. Her research interests range from language maintenance and development, language practices in society and education, to language contact and language change. Her recent publications include a co-edited volume *The Lexical Typology of Semantic Shifts* (2016, with Maria Koptjevskaja-Tamm, *Cognitive Linguistics Research* [CLR] 58, de Gruyter Mouton) and articles on recently arrived students. She currently leads the research project "Recently arrived students in Swedish upper secondary school – a multidisciplinary study on language development, disciplinary literacy and social inclusion", funded by the Swedish Science Foundation. She also is part of the project "Attitudes, beliefs, and knowledge: Teachers' views on multilingualism in preschool and primary school".

Elizabeth Lanza is Professor of Linguistics at the Department of Linguistics and Scandinavian Studies, and Director of the Center for Multilingualism in Society across the Lifespan (MultiLing), University of Oslo, Norway, a Centre of Excellence funded by the Research Council of Norway. Lanza's research focuses on bilingualism/multilingualism, with her work appearing in international journals and edited volumes. She has published on language socialization of bilingual children, identity in migrant narratives, language ideology, linguistic landscape, (family) language policy, and research methodology. She is the co-editor of four special journal issues on multilingual families: *Journal of Multilingual and Multicultural Development* (with Li Wei), *International Journal of Bilingualism* (with Kendall King), and *Multilingua* and *International Journal of Multilingualism* (both with Xiao Lan Curdt-Christiansen). She is on the editorial board of the journals *International Journal of Bilingualism, Bilingualism: Language and Cognition, Journal of Multilingual and Multicultural Development, Journal of Multilingual Theories and Practices, Linguistic Landscape, Multilingual Margins,* and the open access book series *Current Issues in Bilingualism* and *Contact and Multilingualism*.

Anthony J. Liddicoat is Professor in the Centre for Applied Linguistics at the University of Warwick. His research interests include language and intercultural issues in education, discourse analysis, and language policy and planning. He has published widely in each of these areas. He is currently co-convenor of the AILA Research Network "Intercultural mediation in language and culture teaching and learning/La médiation interculturelle en didactique des langues et des cultures" and Executive Editor of *Current Issues in Language Planning*.

Sumin Lim is a Ph.D. Candidate in the Department of Special Education, University of Kansas (KU). She specializes in disability and diversity studies and special education policy and systems studies at KU. Her research centers on inclusive, equitable, and intercultural education and practices for culturally and linguistically diverse students and parents. Sumin strives to promote social justice and equity in special education concentrating on the intersection of marginalized racial, cultural, socio-economic, and linguistic identities in relation to a social construction of (dis)abilities. In particular, she addresses issues of educational inequity, such as the persistent disproportionality of language minority students in special education programs, and has promoted bilingualism and biliteracy in her research and teaching.

Sabine Little is a Lecturer in Languages Education at the University of Sheffield. Originally a languages teacher, her research focus now is specifically on notions of identity and belonging as linked to language in multilingual families. As well as working holistically with families, Sabine is working within formal education contexts to help educators and policy-makers understand underlying complexities of identity and belonging in today's "super-diverse" society.

Rafael Lomeu Gomes is a Doctoral Research Fellow at the Center for Multilingualism in Society across the Lifespan (MultiLing), University of Oslo. His research interests include family language practices, sociolinguistics, discourse analysis, and southern theory. He holds a BA in Social Sciences (Pontifícia Universidade Católica de São Paulo, 2010), and an MA in Linguistics (Queen Mary, University of London, 2015). His interdisciplinary background is reflected in his latest research project (2016–2019), an ethnographic investigation of the ways in which situated language practices of Brazilian families raising their children multilingually in Norway intertwine with broader social, cultural, economic and political processes.

Latisha Mary is Associate Professor of English and Language Education at the Faculty of Education and Lifelong Learning (INSPÉ) at the University of Strasbourg where she is involved in initial primary and secondary teacher education. A member of the European plurilingualism research group (GEPE, UR1339 LiLPa), her research focuses on teacher knowledge, attitudes and beliefs about languages, teacher education for the support of second language acquisition, teacher language awareness and the role of language in teacher identity. She is committed to fostering critical teacher language awareness, developing collaborative home–school relationships and helping teachers support bilingual learners in the classroom and has been involved in several national and international research and teacher education projects focusing on language awareness, multilingualism and intercultural education.

Elisabeth Mayer is a Lecturer in Linguistics at Griffith University. Her research interests include language variation and change with a particular focus on dialect syntax in Andean and Amazonian Spanish, second language/dialect acquisition and language policies in relation to Intercultural Bilingual Education. She has published *Spanish clitics on the move: Variation in time and space* (Mouton de Gruyter, 2017), authored and co-authored articles published in *International Journal of Bilingualism, International Journal of Bilingual Education and Bilingualism, Spanish Journal of Applied Linguistics, Languages, Language and Linguistics Compass, Australian Journal of Linguistics,* and co-edited a special issue, "Romance linguistics in the Pacific: Variation in time and space" published in the *Australian Journal of Linguistics* (2013).

Janica Nordstrom is a Lecturer at The University of Sydney, Australia, where she teaches language, literacy, and diversity courses in the teacher education programs. Her research interests are primarily in the fields of ethnography, community language schools and online learning. She is the author of articles and book chapters that focus on ethnographic principles in multilingual research, community language schools, and teaching languages other than English to young children in mainstream classes. Janica is a member of the Sydney Institute for Community Languages, a recently established institute at the University of Sydney. Some of the key work of the institute includes conducting research to inform policy and language teaching in the field of community languages, offering professional development and pathways for community language teachers and developing curriculum and resources to support community language schools.

Åsa Palviainen is Professor of Swedish in the Department of Language and Communication Studies at the University of Jyväskylä, Finland. She completed her PhD in general linguistics at the University of Gothenburg, Sweden, in 2001, and moved to Finland in 2003. Her research interests include bi- and multilingualism, family language policy, technology-mediated language practices, mediated discourse analysis, language education policy, as well as (early) second language learning and teaching. She has been the leader of several externally funded projects and is currently the Principal Investigator of the 4-year research project "Digitally-mediated communication within contemporary multilingual families across time and space (WhatsInApp)" financed by the Academy of Finland (2018–2022).

BethAnne Paulsrud is Senior Lecturer of English at Dalarna University, Sweden. Her research focuses on multilingualism in education policy and practice, and includes studies of translanguaging, teacher education, and English-medium instruction in Sweden. She is co-editor of the volumes *New perspectives on translanguaging and education* (Multilingual Matters, 2017) and *Transspråkande och utbildning i svensk kontext* (Studentlitteratur, 2018), as well as Co-Editor in Chief of the *Journal of Home Language Research* (JHLR). In addition, she studies young multilingual children and family language policy; and she heads the Swedish research in the international project "Attitudes, beliefs, and knowledge: Teachers' views on multilingualism". Dr. Paulsrud's many years of experience as a pre-school teacher, primary school teacher and mother tongue teacher inform her research and her current work with teacher education.

Judith Purkarthofer is a member of the research group for German in Multilingual Contexts/ Language in Urban Diversity (Humboldt University Berlin), after receiving her PhD in sociolinguistics/applied linguistics from the University of Vienna (Austria) and holding the position of post-doctoral research fellow at the Center for Multilingualism in Society across the Lifespan (University of Oslo, Norway). She conducts research in educational contexts with a focus on the construction of multilingual social spaces in schools and preschools and with families and their language practices. Her work is driven by a lifespan perspective on the multilingual subject, embedded in personal and societal networks, and by the urge to find appropriate methods for working with different age groups.

Tim Roberts is a Doctoral Student in English at the Department of Language, Literature, and Intercultural Studies at Karlstad University, Sweden. He previously completed an MA in English Linguistics at Uppsala University. His doctoral project focuses on the language use of parents and children in Swedish-English bilingual families. The project draws on questionnaire, interview, and video data in order to come to an understanding of language practices and their underlying ideologies in these families. Tim teaches and supervises undergraduate students in linguistics, and has also been a research assistant at Uppsala University, the University of Gothenburg, and the Swedish University of Agricultural Sciences.

Carolina Rodríguez Alzza is a Lecturer at Pontificia Universidad Catolica del Perú. She is a researcher in linguistics and anthropological topics at Grupo de Antropología Amazónica (GAA-PUCP). Her work focuses on the Amazon area and indigenous people/languages. She leads a project on documentation and revitalization of language and culture of the Iskonawa people. Her publications include *Rewinki – Canciones de la fiesta de toma de chicha de maíz* (2019), *Entre el 'vivir huyendo' y el 'vivir tranquilos': los contactos de los iskonawa del río Callería* (2017), and *Prefijos de partes del cuerpo en la lengua iskonawa* (2017), *Relaciones gramaticales en la lengua iskonawa* (2015). She has also coedited the book *Tradición oral Iskonawa* (2018).

Liliana Sánchez is a Professor at the University of Illinois at Chicago and Rutgers University. Her publications include *Bilingualism in the Spanish-speaking world*, with Jennifer Austin and Maria Blume (Cambridge University Press, 2015), *The morphology and syntax of topic and focus: Minimalist inquiries in the Quechua periphery* (John Benjamins, 2010), and *Quechua-Spanish bilingualism: Interference and convergence in functional categories* (John Benjamins, 2003). She has published articles in *Bilingualism: Language and Cognition, Glossa, International Journal of Bilingualism, Languages, Linguistic Approaches to Bilingualism, Lingua, Probus*, and *Studies in Second Language Acquisition*, among others.

Andrea C. Schalley is Professor in English Linguistics at the Department of Language, Literature and Intercultural Studies at Karlstad University, Sweden. She is also Co-Director of the Centre for Language and Literature Education at Karlstad University, and Research Affiliate with the Australian Research Council Centre of Excellence for the Dynamics of Language. She has published widely in semantics and ontology-based linguistics as well as on bi/multilingualism and biliteracy. Andrea currently co-chairs the International Association for Applied Linguistics (AILA) Research Network on "Social and Affective Factors in Home Language Maintenance and Development", is editor-in-chief of the open access book series *Current Issues in Bilingualism* (Language Science Press), co-editor of the open access *Journal of Home Language Research*, and leads the international project "Attitudes, beliefs, and knowledge: Teachers' views on multilingualism". She has published with publishing houses such as Mouton de Gruyter, John Benjamins, and Springer, and in outlets such as the *International Journal of Bilingual Education and Bilingualism, International Journal of Multilingualism, Language and Linguistics Compass,* and *Lingua*, amongst others.

Mila Schwartz is a Professor in Language and Education and Head of Language Program (MEd) in Oranim Academic College of Education (Israel). Her research interests include language policy and models of early bilingual education; linguistic, cognitive, and socio-cultural development of early sequential bilinguals; family language policy; and bilingual teachers' pedagogical development. Recently, she has proposed and elaborated on the following theoretical concepts: language-conducive context, language-conducive strategies and child language-based agency. She held the position of Secretary of the Steering Committee of the International Symposium of Bilingualism from 2015 to 2019, and currently she acts as Convenor of the Multilingual Childhoods network. In addition to her academic work, Prof. Schwartz is an Academic Adviser of "Hand in Hand: Center for Jewish-Arab Education" and the Russian-Hebrew-speaking bilingual preschools in Israel.

Yeşim Sevinç is a Postdoctoral Researcher at the Center for Multilingualism in Society across the Lifespan (MultiLing), University of Oslo. Prior to MultiLing, she worked as a Postdoctoral Researcher at the Norwegian University of Science and Technology. Her research interests are interdisciplinary, with a specific focus on multilingualism and emotions in minority contexts. Her recent publications address linguistic, social, psychological, pedagogical and physiological aspects of multilingualism both within and outside the family domain, including a chapter on language contact and emotions in the *Handbook on Language and Emotion* (de Gruyter, 2020). She has published widely in international journals, such as *International Journal of Bilingualism*, *International Journal of the Sociology of Language*, *International Journal of Bilingual Education and Bilingualism*, and *Journal of Multilingual and Multicultural Development*, amongst others.

Tove Skutnabb-Kangas (emerita), bilingual from birth, has been actively involved with Indigenous peoples' and minorities' struggle for language rights for the past six decades. Some research interests include linguistic human rights, linguistic genocide, linguicism (linguistically argued racism), mother-tongue-based multilingual education, revitalisation of endangered languages, English language imperialism, the relationship between biodiversity and linguistic and cultural diversity. She has been published in over 50 languages. She is on editorial boards of more than a dozen international journals. Some of her books include: *Linguistic genocide in education – or worldwide diversity and human rights?* (2000), *Indigenous children's education as linguistic genocide and a crime against humanity? A global view* (2010) with Robert Dunbar; *Language rights* (2017) (ed., with Robert Phillipson, 4 volumes). Tove edits the book series *Linguistic Diversity and Language Rights* for Multilingual Matters. She has received the Linguapax award (2003) and CABEs Vision Award (2013). For more information visit www.Tove-Skutnabb-Kangas.org.

Cassie Smith-Christmas is a Research Fellow at the National University of Ireland, Galway, Ireland. She is the author of *Family language policy: Maintaining an endangered language in the home* (Palgrave, 2016), and is co-editor of two recent volumes: *New speakers of minority languages: Linguistic ideologies and practices* (Palgrave, 2018) and *Gaelic in contemporary Scotland: The revitalisation of an endangered language* (Edinburgh University Press, 2018). Her most recent work has involved working with the family language support programme *Tús Maith* in the Corca Dhuibhne Gaeltacht as part of a Smithsonian Fellowship with the Centre for Folklife and Cultural Heritage. Other previous fellowships include an Irish Research Council Government of Ireland Postdoctoral Fellowship as well as a fellowship at the Institute for the Advanced Studies in the Humanities at the University of Edinburgh.

Amelia Tseng is Assistant Professor of Linguistics and Spanish in World Languages and Cultures at American University and holds a Research Associate appointment at the Smithsonian Center for Folklife and Cultural Heritage. Her work centers on multilingual repertoires and identity in immigrant and diasporic communities. Her recent work has appeared in *Text & Talk*,

Translinguistics: negotiating innovation and ordinariness, The Routledge handbook of Spanish in the global city, and *The Routledge handbook of migration and language* (shortlisted for the British Association for Applied Linguistics 2018 Book Prize).

Kutlay Yağmur is Professor of Language, Identity and Education in the Department of Language and Culture Studies, University of Tilburg. He has published extensively on language contact issues in Australia, Germany, France and The Netherlands. Next to his many research articles in various International Journals, his 2016 book *Intergenerational language use and acculturation of Turkish speakers in four immigration contexts* has been a considerable conceptual and methodological contribution to the study of language and acculturation. He co-ordinated the "Language Rich Europe" project funded by the European Commission and British Council, the findings of which were published by Cambridge University Press and British Council in 2012. Yağmur serves in the editorial board of a number of International Journals, such as *Language, Culture and Curriculum*, *International Journal of the Sociology of Language* and *Language Journal*.

Andrea Young is Professor of English at the Faculty of Education and Lifelong Learning (INSPÉ) of the University of Strasbourg, France. Throughout her career in the French education sector and within the framework of a variety of initial and continuing professional development programmes she has sought to raise language awareness amongst education professionals working in multilingual environments. As a member of the European Plurilingualism Research Group (GEPE, UR1339 LiLPa), her research interests include teacher knowledge, attitudes and beliefs about languages and language, home-school educational partnerships and plurilingual and intercultural education in the school context. She has published in a variety of international journals and contributed to a number of edited books specialising in these areas and has also participated in several European projects, notably with the ECML (European Centre for Modern Languages).

Author Index

Page numbers in italics indicate tables.

Abane, Albert 172
Abdi, Klara 117
Abdulrahim, Naheed A. 413, 415
Abu-Rabia, Salim 402
Adams, Ashley 264
Adger, Caroline 457
Agache, Alexandru 81
Agar, Michael H. 143
Ager, Denis E. 274, 350
Aggarwal, Santhosh 388
Agirdag, Orhan 18, *40*, 439, 446, 447, 453, 455, 456
Agnihotri, Rama Kant 344
Ahearn, Laura M. 178, 218, 224
Ahmed, Aijazuddin 317
Aierbe-Barandiaran, Ana 267
Ajzen, Icek 370
Al-Azami, Salman 311
Albury, Nathan J. 3, 10, 45, 47, 321, 351, 357–376
Alexander, Neville 347, 396, 397
Aliani, Renata 263
Alim, H. Samy 110, 415
Allen, Katherine R. 160
Almanza de Schonewise, Estrella 420
Almér, Elin 239, 248
Alsaker, Françoise 81
Altman, Carmit 222
Alvarez, Steven 206, *208*
Al Zidjaly, Najma 220
Amanti, Cathy 126, 260, 261, 264, 265, 270
Ammermüller, Andreas 440
Anderson, Benedict 110
Andersson, Theodore 388
Andrews, Alonzo 419
Androutsopoulos, Jannis 247, 278
Anisman, Adar 146
Annamalai, E. 11, 45, 47, 53, 282, 312, 341, 367, 377–400, 456
Anthony, Natasha 296
Antón, Xosé 374
Antonini, Rachele 220, 230
Appadurai, Arjun 274–276, 278, 280
Aquino-Sterling, Cristian R. 446, 455

Aravossitas, Themistoklis 303
Archer, Louise 296–298, 301, 303–305
Arguedas, José María 322
Arias, Beatriz 455
Arju, Tahera 146, 215
Armon Lotem, Sharon 232
Arnberg, Lenore 40
Arnold, Ellen L. 350
Arnold, Jane 87
Arriagada, Paula A. 115, 118
Arthur, Jo 296, 297
Arthur, Leonie 260
Artiles, Alfredo 404, 406, 408–410, 412
Ash, Anna 319
Ashraf, Hamid 265
Ashton, Jean 261
Ashton, Patricia T. 444, 445
Atkin, Andrew J. 263
Atkinson, David 372
Aucoin, Katherine J. 82
Auer, Peter 113, 120, 225, 229
August, Diane 448
Axelrod, Ysaaca 474, 476, 477
Azuara, Patricia 206, 211

Backus, Ad 85, 93, 96, 98, 140
Bacon, Chris K. 406
Bae, So Hee 93
Baetens Beardsmore, Hugo 19, 412
Bagga-Gupta, Sangeeta 40
Baglieri, Susan 413
Bailey, Benjamin 111
Baker, Colin 19, 21, 26, 111, 206, 368, 402, 406, 407, 409, 467
Baker, Diana 403
Bakhtin, Mikhail M. 278
Baldauf, Richard B. 186, 275, 282, 303, 337–341, 346
Ball, Arnetha F. 110
Ball, Stephen J. 337
Bamberg, Michael 110
Bamgbose, Ayo 396
Banda, Felix 112
Bango, Andisiwe 172

Author Index

Baquedano-López, Patricia 88, 219
Baraç, Taskin 308
Barakos, Elisabeth 118
Barbarin, Oscar 79
Bardovi-Harlig, Kathleen 20
Barnes, Colin 411
Barnes, Lawrie 346
Bartau-Rojas, Isabel 267
Barton, Len 411
Barwell, Richard 472
Basham, Charlotte 139
Baubet, Thierry 459
Bauböck, Rainer 428
Bayley, Robert 115
Baym, Nancy K. 248
Baynham, Michael 282
Beatty, Michael J. 91
Beauchamp, Catherine 305
Beaver, David I. 55
Becerra Lubies, Rukmini 469, 470
Beck, Ulrich 281
Becker, Ava 89, 100, 114
Begum, Shila 296
Beijaard, Douwe 305
Bello-Rodzen, Ingrid 165
Ben-Ami, Shlomo 342
Beniak, Edouard 346
Benner, Aprile D. 81
Benor, Sarah Bunin 113
Ben-Rafael, Eliezer 39
Bensekhar, Malika Bennabi 450
Benson, Carol 393
Berdugo, Martha 339
Berez-Kroeker, Andrea L. 51, 52
Bergroth, Mari 218, 229, 238, 247
Berkovich, Marina 180
Bezçioğlu-Göktolga, Irem 76, 186, 187, 219, 450
Bhatt, Arvind 304, 308, 310, 442
Bhatt, Rakesh 113, 316, 317
Bhojani, Nirmala 308, 310, 442
Bialystok, Ellen 448
Bigelow, Martha H. 141
Bishop, Russell 319
Björklund, Mikaela 40
Black, Rebecca W. 273
Blackledge, Adrian 40, 110, 143, 177, 278, 296, 299–302, 304

Blackwell, Courtney K. 258
Blanchet, Philippe 456
Blanco, Álvaro 266
Block, David 278, 280
Blom, Jan-Petter 112, 360
Blommaert, Jan 120, 176, 275, 278, 280, 361
Bloomfield, Leonard 19
Blum-Ross, Alicia 165
Boas, Franz 312
Boele, Amy 419
Boivin, Nettie 239, 248
Bonacina-Pugh, Florence 454, 474, 476
Borg, Simon 445
Borjian, Maryam 298
Borland, Helen 130, 140, 296
Bornstein, Marc H. 40
Borsato, Graciela 414
Bot, Kees de 413
Bouchard, Jeremie 282, 338
Bourdieu, Pierre 96, 167, 178, 184, 218, 261, 298
Bourhis, Richard 426, 429, 430
Boutakidis, Ioakim P. 70
Boyd, Robert 261
Boyd, Sally 43, 156, 223, 226, 228, 247, 248
Braak, Johan van 445
Bradley, David 314
Bradley, John 363
Bransford, John 305
Brinkman, Sally 81
Brockevelt, Barbara L. 82
Broeder, Peter 468
Browder, Diane M. 403
Brown, Andrew 475
Brown, H. Douglas 87
Brownlee, Patrick 303, 305
Bruin, Angela de 53
Bryant, Donna 79
Bryson, Susan 419
Buannic, Lionel 351
Bucholtz, Mary 110
Budach, Gabriele 40, 45, 319, 320
Budgeon, Shelley 243
Buehl, Michelle M. 445, 446
Bunce, Pauline 391
Burchinal, Margaret 79
Burnaby, Barbara 429
Burns, Meg 118

Burns, Robert 449
Burstein Feldman, Zhanna 232
Busch, Brigitta 142
Butler, Yuko G. 21
Butvilofsky, Sandra 417
Buysse, Viginia 412

Cable, Carrie 78
Cabo, Diego P. Y. 112
Cacioppo, John T. 104
Caffery, Jo 317
Caldas, Stephen J. 66, 154, 158, 239
Camacho, José 13, 57, 147, 291, 312–331, 375, 442
Campbell, Jane 407
Canagarajah, Suresh A. 51, 89, 165, 222, 276, 277
Cárdenas, Valeska Grau 298, 304
Cardona, Beatriz 294, 296, 303
Carlson, Coleen D. 79
Caron-Caldas, Suzanne 158
Carreira, Maria 26, 304
Carroll, Susanne 157
Carruba-Rogel, Zuleyma N. 113
Carstensen, Laura L. 104
Carter, Bob 282
Cashman, Holly R. 241, 243, 244
Castillo Guzmán, Elizabeth 341
Castro-Gómez, Santiago 163
Cekaite, Asta 72, 158
Cenoz, Jasone 17, 441
Chaiken, Shelly 3, 368, 445
Chambers, Debora 155
Chan, Sarah 134
Chang, Florence 79
Chao, Ruth K. 70
Chatry-Komarek, Marie 344
Chatzidaki, Aspasia 73, 74, 77, 78, 186
Cheatham, Gregory A. 11, 18, 42, 401–421
Chee, Anna 252
Chelliah, Shabhana 55
Cheshire, Jenny 120
Child, Brenda J. 119
Chin, Ng Bee 21
Chiro, Giancarlo 343
Cho, Grace 112–114
Cho, Jinhyun 189, 364
Cho, Kyung-Sook 112–114
Choi, Charles W. 132

Chomsky, Noam 395
Choudhury, Ruhma 296, 299–301, 303, 304
Chow, Henry P. 302, 304
Chrisp, Steven 137, 139
Christensen, Toke H. 242
Christian, Donna 457
Chung, Jeehyae 299, 300, 303, 304
Cioè-Peña, María 412
Ciriza, María del Puy *40*
Clark, Cindy D. 143
Clark, M. Carolyn 92
Cleave, Patricia 418
Clifford, Richard 79
Cloutier, Geneviève 421
Clyne, Michael 20, 84, 112, 284
Coady, Maria R. 469, 470, 473
Coetzee, Frieda 135, 160, 218
Cohenmiller, Anna 239, 248
Collier, Virginia P. 391, 414
Collins, Brian A. 69
Collins, James 278
Comaroff, Jean 166
Comaroff, John L. 166
Connaughton-Crean, Lorraine 2
Connell, Raewyn 163, 166
Connor, David J. 414, 416
Conroy, David 82
Conteh, Jean 293, 296, 469
Conti-Ramsden, Gina 64
Conway, Annie 271
Cook, Vivian 299, 410, 414
Cope, Bill 259
Cope, Joann 91, 92
Copland, Fiona 39, 50, 51
Corbin, Juliet 96
Corder, Kristen 271
Córdova, Paola 323, 324
Cormack, Mike 350
Coronel-Molina, Serafín M. 312, 337
Corson, David 349
Coryell, Joellen E. 92
Costigan, Catherine L. 70
Coupland, Justine 132
Coupland, Nikolas 109, 111, 276
Crago, Martha 420
Craith, Nic M. 439
Crawford, Gisele 79
Creese, Angela 39, *40*, 50, 51, 143, 177, 296, 297, 299–302, 304, 310, 347, 442

Crenshaw, Kimberle 404
Cresswell, Tim 276
Crookes, Graham V. 457
Cross, Russell 362
Crow, Graham 44
Cru, Josep 279, 351
Cruickshank, Ken 283, 303, 305
Crump, Alison 248
Crystal, David 266, 313
Cummings, E. Mark 219
Cummins, Jim 25, 116, 143, 391, 440, 446–449, 454, 456, 470, 478
Cunningham, Clare 29, *40*, 46
Curdt-Christiansen, Xiao Lan 3, 7, *40*, 42, 43, 88, 114–116, 135, 154, 158, 161, 167, 174–193, 194, 199, *202*, 204, 212, 219, 236–238, 246, 247, 264, 301, 304, 339, 448
Curnow, Timothy Jowan 341, 343, 344, 356
Curran, Mary Elizabeth 465, 475
Currie Armstrong, Timothy 77, 119
Custers, Kathleen 240, 242, *245*
Cutas, Daniela 134
Czarniawska, Barbara 247

Da Fontoura, Helena A. 402
Dahoun, Zerdalia K. S. 63, 65, 71, 78, 450
Dailey, René M. 132
Danjo, Chisato 72
Daoud, Annette M. 118
Darling-Hammond, Linda 305
Daubney, Mark 93, 101
Daussa, Eva 165
Davis, Jenny L. 322
Day, Ashley 446, 455
De Angelis, Gessica 175
De Bres, Julia 365
Debski, Robert 295
Deci, Edward L. 258, 268
Deconinck, Julie 136
Deen, Thalif 378, 387, 388
De Fina, Anna 110, 120, 278
De Houwer, Annick 5, 18, *40*, 42, 43, 47, 63–83, 88, 89, 134, 135, 157, 174, 177, 178, 180, 181, 194, 197–200, 205, 212, 214, 219, 239, 240, 248, 404, 451
Dekeyser, Graziela 79
De Korne, Haley 138, 139
De Lannoy, Ariane 172

Della Sala, Sergio 53
De Mejía, Anne-Marie 110
Deters, Ping 220
Devlin, Brian 317, 344
Dewaele, Jean-Marc 85–87, 90–95, 101, 372
Dewaele, Livia 103
Di Biase, Bruno 294, 296, 303
Diebold, A. Richard 19
Diener, Ed 63, 64, 86
Dillon, Anna Marie 464, 465, 469, 471
Dillon, Kathleen 117
Di Meo, Stéphane 450
Dingwall, Robert 51
Dirim, Inci 120
Disbray, Samantha 317
Djité, Paulin 337
Doerksen, Shawna 82
Doerr, Neriko M. 117
Dokis, Daphné P. 70
Dolby, Nadine 457
Dooley, Karen 183, 298
Dooly, Melinda 473
Döpke, Susanne 42, 156, 158, 194, 197, 198, 205, 214, 219
Dorian, Nancy C. 322, 367
Dörnyei, Zoltán 39
Doty, Jennifer 252
Dovalil, Vít *40*
Doyle, Colm *201*
Doyle, Conan 239
Dreher, Tanja 350
Drèze, Jean 386
Drury, Rose 71, 78
Duarte, Joana 450
Dubinsky, Stanley 55
Duchêne, Alexandre 364
Duff, Patricia 109, 117, 299, 301, 302
Dukpa, Lhundup 342
Duku, Eric 419
Dunbar, Robert 379, 381, 383, 384, 390
Durán, Lillian K. 402, 403
Duranti, Alessandro 157, 175, 219
Durkin, Kevin 64
Dusi, Paola 454
Dworkin, Jodi 252
Dyers, Charlyn 119

Eagly, Alice H. 3, 368, 445
Early, Diane 79

Early, Margaret 143, 454, 457
Ebert, Susanne 64
Echu, George 23
Edgin, Jamie O. 403
Edwards, Carolyn P. 448
Edwards, George 448
Edwards, John 17, 19, 20, 407
Edwards, Viv 137, 260, 269
Eisenchlas, Susana A. 1–13, 17–37, 38–58, 67, 85, 88, 109, 112, 116, 131, 146, 156, 166, *203*, 215, 237, 251, 260, 272, 275, 322, 369, 427–429, 451, 464
Eisenlohr, Patrick 279
Ellis, Elizabeth 407
Ellis, Elizabeth M. 320
Ellis, Rod 86
Ellsmore, Marjory 303, 305
Els, Theo van 339, 340
England, Neil 359
Epps, Patience 366
Ericsson, Stina 243, 246, 248
E-Rramdani, Yahya 76
Erwin, Elizabeth J. 421
Es, Elisabeth van 271
Escamilla, Kathy 414
Escamilla, Manuel 417
Evans, Bruce A. 344
Extra, Guus 425–427, 431, 433, 437–439

Falchi, Lorraine T. 474, 476, 477
Fasold, Ralph 370
Fathman, Ann K. 139
Fee, Molly 293
Fefer, Sarah A. 67
Félix, Angela 117
Feltmate, Krista 402
Fennig, Charles D. 314–316
Ferguson, Charles A. 365
Ferguson, Jean 322
Fermino, Jessie Little Doe 319
Fernandes, Desmond 342
Fernández-Costales, Alberto 374
Ferris, M. Roger 343
Fialkova, Larisa *40*
Fillenbaum, Samuel 374
Fiorentino, Alice 239, 241
Fishbein, Martin 445

Fishman, Joshua A. 42, 47, 109, 112, 133, 158, 165, 195, 237, 293–295, 346, 347, 350, 362, 414
Fitzgerald, David 430
Fitzgerald, Michael 295
Fitzsimmons-Doolan, Shannon 446, 455
Fives, Helenrose 444–446
Fleischman, Howard L. 421
Fletcher-Wilson, Sue 418
Flogenfeldt, Mona Evelyn 457
Flores, Belinda Bustos 455
Flores, Nelson 110, 117, 467
Flores, Susana 117
Fogle, Lyn Wright 6, 7, *40*, 42, 88, 89, 115, 134–136, 153–156, 158–160, 167, 174, 178, 180, 183, 196, 212, 213, 218–220, 222, 231, 236, 238, 241, 247, 249
Fombonne, Eric 402, 419
Foucault, Michel 167, 362
Fouces, Oscar Díaz 321
Fox, Sue 122
Franceschini, Rita 447
Francis, Beckly 296–298, 301, 303–305
Francis, David J. 79
Franklin, Glendon 258
Frattura, Elise M. 412
Fredrickson, Barbara L. 86
Frick, Paul J. 82
Friedman, Debra A. 351
Fuligni, Andrew J. 70, 75

Gabel, Susan L. 411, 417
Gafaranga, Joseph 135, 158, 178, 183, 220, 223, 224
Gal, Susan 110, 364, 366, 446
Gallagher, Deborah J. 416, 417
Gallese, Vittorio 259, 264
Galligani, Stéphanie 452
Gallo, Sarah 163, 230
Ganambarr, Banbapuy 331
Gandini, Lella 448
Ganuza, Natalia 464, 467
García, María Elena 120
García, MaryEllen 337
García, Ofelia 20, 26, 109, 112, 113, 166, 206, 277, 293, 298–300, 302, 392, 407, 414, 451, 453, 454, 456, 457, 467, 468, 470, 471, 475–477
García-Nevarez, Ana G. 455

Gardner, Robert C. 374
Gao, Xuesong 233
Garrett, Paul B. 88, 219
Garrett, Peter B. 134
Garrido, María Rosa 116
Garrity, Sarah 446, 455
Gass, Susan M. 213
Gates, Peter 446
Gawne, Lauren 55
Gee, James P. 110, 259
Genesee, Fred 157, 402, 414, 420
Genishi, Celia 474, 477
Georgiades, Stelios 419
Gerber, Livia 88, 136, 165, 188
Ghaffar-Kucher, Ameena 296
Giampapa, Frances 143
Giddens, Anthony 218, 280
Giger, Jarod T. 82
Giles, Howard 112, 132
Gill, Michele Gregoire 444, 445
Ginsburgh, Victor 293
Gkaintartzi, Anastasia 186, 449
Gkonou, Christina 93, 101
Glasgow, Gregory P. 282, 338
Glenberg, Arthur 259, 264
Glick Schiller, Nina 276
Goddard, Cliff 110
Goffman, Erving 223
Gogolin, Ingrid 437, 456
Gogonas, Nikos 73, 186
Goldberg, Abbie E. 160
Goldenberg, Claude 79
Goldfeld, Sharon 68
González, Norma 126, 260, 261, 264, 265, 270
Gonzalez, Taucia 408, 412
Gonzalez, Virginia 117
González-Davies, María 414
González-Riaño, Xosé A. 368
Gooch, Debbe 68
Goodz, Naomi *207*
Gordon, Matthew 243, 244
Gorodzeisky, Anastasia 439
Gorter, Durk 47, 246, 441
Gounari, Panayota 26
Grabowsky, Kirby C. 20
Gram Garmann, Nina 206, *208*
Greenleaf, Floyd I. 91
Gregersen, Tammy 86, 87, 91, 93
Gregory, Eve 140, 213, 215, 311

Grin, François 178, 393
Groff, Cynthia 313, 316
Grosfoguel, Ramón 163
Grosjean, François 18, 21, 111, 117, 409, 451, 455
Grünigen, Renate von 68
Grüter, Therese 157
Gu, Mingyue (Michelle) 119
Guan, Lee H. 315, 316
Guardado, Martin 89, 100, 114
Gubrium, Jay 155
Guilherme, Manuela 166
Guillemin, Diana 429
Gumperz, John J. 111, 112, 142, 360
Gupta, Anthea. F. 24
Gutiérrez-Clellen, Vera F. 403
Gynne, Annaliina *40*
Gyogi, Eiko 218, 220, 226

Habermas, Jürgen 278, 280
Haegele, Justin A. 412
Haimov, Iris 262, 263
Hajek, John 123
Hakuta, Kenji 21
Hale, Ken 315, 319
Hall, Kathy A. 297, 303, 305
Hall, Kira 110
Hambly, Catherine 402, 419
Hamid, Shahela 226, 227, 304
Hamilton, Kyra 265
Hammerness, Karen 305
Hampshire, Kate 172
Hampton, Sarah 403
Han, Wen-Jui 68, 69
Hancock, Andy 294, 300–304
Hannon, Peter 272
Hao, Lingxin 70
Harmon, David 381
Harper, Candace 469, 470, 473
Harris, Roxy 21
Harrison, Barbara 118, 319
Harrison, Linda 81
Harry, Beth 401, 404, 405, 408, 411
Hart-Barnett, Juliet 401–404
Harter, Susan 449
Harvey, David 276
Hasan Amara, Muhammad 55
Hatoss, Anikó 9, 45, 54, 188, 214, 238, 242, 274–292, 295, 321, 347, 351

Haugen, Einar 195, 200
He, Agnes Weiyun 111, 113, 237, 239, 247, 454
Hedman, Christina 464, 467
Heine, Steven J. 42, 160
Heller, Agnes 428
Heller, Monica 111, 365
Helmchen, Christian 477
Helmer, Kimberly A. 118
Hélot, Christine 446, 450, 457
Hemenover, Scott H. 104
Henderson, Kathryn 446, 455
Henrich, Joseph 42, 160, 261
Henriksen, John B. 377
Herman, Edward S. 395
Hermans, Ruben 445
Hernández, Anita 446
Hershfield, Hal E. 88
Hersi, Afra A. 457
Heston, Tyler 55
Heugh, Kathleen 163, 166, 343, 356, 391
Hewett, Valarie Mercilliot 448
Higareda, Ignacio 416
Higgins, Christina 158, 220, 224
Hildebrandt, Neil 222, 223
Hill, Jane H. 94, 115
Hill, Kenneth C. 94, 115
Hilmarsson-Dunn, Amanda 358
Hinkel, Eli 39
Hinnenkamp, Volker 113
Hinton, Leanne 137, 138, 315, 319, 392
Hirsch, Tijana 89, 164, 237–242, 247–249
Hiss, Florian 363
Hjorth, Larissa 252
Hodge, Samuel 412
Hodgson, Richard C. 374
Hoffman, Patricia 403
Hogan-Brun, Gabrielle 110
Holliday, Adrian 111
Holm, Gunilla 469
Holstein, James A. 155
Holton, Gary 55
Hoover, John J. 420
Hopewell, Susan 417
Hopkins, Megan 470, 477
Hopstock, Paul J. 421
Horan, Deborah A. 457
Horkheimer, M. 364
Hornberger, Nancy H. 120, 140, 275, 277, 278, 313, 322, 337, 344, 464–466, 478

Hornsby, Michael 235
Horst, Heather 252
Horwitz, Elaine K. 91, 92, 100
Horwitz, Michael B. 91, 92
Hove, Claire van den 459
Howes, Carollee 79
Howie, Pauline 158
Hsu, Hui-Yin 457
Hu, Guangwei 181, 184
Hu, Shirley 458
Huaman, Elizabeth S. 319
Huang, Chien-Chung 68
Huang, Dang 127
Huang, Jing 3, 7, 43, 115, 154, 174–193, 194, 236, 247, 339
Huerta, Nancy E. 404
Huguet, Angel 374
Hult, Francis M. 3, 39, 43, 154, 313, 466, 468
Humphrey, Neil 449
Huss, Leena 226, 392
Huston, Aletha C. 273
Hyltenstam, Kenneth 166
Hymes, Dell 357, 360

Irvine, Fiona 149
Irvine, Judith T. 110
Izard, Caroll E. 85

Jacobs, Peter 146
Jaffe, Alexandra 300, 369
Jain, Ritu 25
Jäkel, Julia 81
James, Ceri 303
Janik, Janusz 347
Jany, Carmen 279
Jaspers, Jürgen 467
Jee, Min Jung 92
Jegatheesan, Brinda 402, 403
Jenni, Barbara 139
Jessel, John 146, 215
Jiménez, Robert T. 214
Jiménez-Silva, Margarita 417
Jitendra, Asha K. 403
Johnson, David C. 154, 466, 478
Johnson, Patricia 112
Johnson, Susana Ibarra 468, 470, 477
Jones, Bryn 474
Jones, Kathryn 114
Jones, Mari C. 279

Jones, Peter 149
Jong, Ester de 469, 470, 473, 477
Jónsdóttir, Elsa S. 358
Jordaan, Heila 402
Jordens, Kathelijne 453, 456
Jovanović, Srđan M. 370
Juan-Garau, María *202*
Juvonen, Päivi 3, 5, 8, 38–58, 131, 212, 213, 238, 239, 264

Kachru, Yamuna 406
Kagan, Olga 26, 27, 109, 111, 117, 304
Kalaja, Paula 247
Kalantzis, Mary 259, 346
Kalra, Mani B. 363
Kalyanpur, Maya 405, 408
Kamwangamalu, Nkonko. M. 345
Kamwendo, Gregory, H. 470
Kang, Hyun-Sook 181
Kangas, Sara E. N. 412, 413
Kano, Naomi 298, 467
Kaplan, Robert B. 275, 337–339
Karabenick, Stuart A. 447
Kasai, Masahiro 417
Kasuya, Hiroko 219
Katsos, Napoleon 420
Katz, Yaakov 258
Kavanagh, David J. 272
Kaveh, Yalda M. *40*, 73, 74, 76
Kayam, Orly 239, 248
Kay-Raining Bird, Elizabeth 402, 403
Kazuko, Obata 320
Kelly, Barbara F. 55
Kelly-Holmes, Helen 372
Kendrick, Maureen 222
Kenner, Charmian 136, 140, *210*, 211, 311
Kerfoot, Caroline 166
Kerkutluoglu, Ayfer 403
Kern, Richard 266
Kerswill, Paul 122
Khajavy, Gholam H. 132
Kheirkhah, Mina 72, 158, 238, 239
Kidwai, Aysha 316, 317
Kim, Hyun Uk 410
Kim, Jung-In 295, 297–299, 301, 302, 304
Kim, Sujin 120
Kim, Yoon Kyong 69
Kimonis, Eva R. 82
King, Elena T. 471

King, Kendall A. 6, 7, 39, 88, 115, 116, 134, 136, 144, 153–156, 158–160, 164, 167, 168, 174, 175, 196, 218–220, 222, 236, 238, 241, 245–247, 249, 367
King, Su Yeong 70, 81
King O'Riain, Rebecca 241, *245*
Kirsch, Claudine 73, 185, 186
Kistemaker, Mariska 468
Kivelä, Suvi 392
Kleifgen, Joanne 414
Kleyn, Tatyana 467, 478
Klingner, Janette K. 401, 404, 405, 410, 415, 420
Knight, John 13, 271
Kochenderfer-Ladd, Becky 81
Kohl, Katharina 81
Kohlmeier, Theresa L. 402
Kohnert, Kathryn 403
Kolano, Lan Quach 471
Koot, Hans M. 64
Kopeliovich, Shulamit 196, 199, 200, 206, *209*, 212, 214, 224, 225
Kosonen, Kimmo 313, 314, 318
Kostogriz, Alex 296, 303
Kostyuk, Natalia 72
Kotler, Jennifer 273
Kozleski, Elizabeth B. 416
Kral, Inge 320, 321
Kramsch, Claire J. 39, 142, 413
Krashen, Stephen 115
Krauss, Michael 133
Kremer-Sadlik, Tamar 404
Kristinsson, Ari Páll 358
Kroskrity, Paul V. 218, 359, 446
Kruger, Michael W. 91
Krulatz, Anna 457
Kuczynski, Leon 219, 220, 222–224, 228
Kudo, Milagros 409
Kulick, Don 218, 219, 227
Kumar, Abhijeet 417
Kushner, Millicent 420
Kwapong, Amoafi 348
Kwon, Jungmin 278
Kymlicka, Will 282

Labov, William 109, 112, 357, 358
Lacroix, Thomas 274, 275
Lai, Mee Ling 368
Lainio, Jarmo *40*

Laitin, David D. 427, 428
Lam, Wan S. E. 120, 252
Lamb, Terry 276
Lambert, Wallace E. 357
La Morgia, Francesca 264
Lancioni, Giulio 419
Lane, Pia 138, 184, 185
Lang, Russell 403
Lanigan, Jane D. 237, 242, 244
Lansford, Jennifer E. 64
Lanza, Elizabeth 7, 41, 42, 49, 77, 88, 134–136, 153–173, 174, 175, 178, 186, 195, 197, 198, 202, 205, 214, 218–220, 223, 236–238, 243, 244, 249, 257, 275, 339, 448
Laparo, Karen M. 462
Lapresta-Rey, Cecilio 374
Larsen, Jeff T. 88
Larsen-Freeman, Diane 244
Lau, Anna S. 81, 82
Lauricella, Alexis R. 271
Lave, Jean 260, 297
Law, Thomas 403
Lawler, Michael J. 82
Lawrence, Denis 449
Layzer, Carolyn 446, 447
Leap, Willian L. 2
Leclerc, Jacques 47
Lee, Carmen 241
Lee, Jamie S. 113
Lee, Jin Sook 89, 111, 164, 237, 238, 240, 241, 249, 296, 351, 455
Lee, Kiri 117
Lee, Tiffany S. 117, 319
Leeman, Jennifer 112, 116, 117
Lefebvre, Henri 165
Léglise, Isabelle 136, 166
Leikin, Mark *207*
Leist-Villis, Anja 66, 71–74, 76, 78
Le Page, Robert 109
Lerea, Louis 91
Leseman, Paul 440
Leung, Constant 21
Levin, Irene 241, 246
Levitt, Peggy 276, 277, 281
Lewis, Margaret 272
Lewis, Paul M. 133, 314–316
Lewis, Tania 252
Lexander, Kristin V. 136, 153, 154, 158, 164, 247

Leyendecker, Birgit 77
Liams, Michelle 406
Liddicoat, Anthony J. 10, 45–47, 275, 293, 337–356, 364, 466, 469
Li, Duanduan 109, 117, 302
Li, Wei 19, 39, 87, 88, 89, 113, 115, 119, 135, 154, 155, 158, 166, 174, 178, 181, 206, 238, 239, 246, 247, 277, 300–302, 304, 363, 411
Li, Xiaoxia 114
Li, Xin-Xin 403
Li, Xuemei 181
Lier, Leo van 220, 466
Lier, Pol A. C. van 64
Lim, Sumin 11, 18, 42, 401–421
Lim, Sun S. 239, 242, *245*
Lim, Tae-Seop 146
Limacher-Riebold, Ulrike 165
Lin, Angel 88
Lin, Xiaobing 39
Linan-Thompson, Sylvia 419
Lindholm-Leary, Kathryn 409, 414
Lindquist, Hein 206, *208*
Ling, Teck-Yee 315
Litosseliti, Lia 246
Little, Sabine 8, 9, 45, 54, 73, 135, 177, 178, 180, 182, 204, 214, 242, 247, 257–273, 296
Littlebear, Richard E. 115
Liu, Lisa L. 70, 82
Liu, Yi-Juin 420
Liu, Yongbing 39, 116
Livingstone, Sonia 165
Lo Bianco, Joseph 312, 316, 338, 395
Logan-Terry, Aubrey 6, 7, 39, 115, 153, 155, 159, 160, 167, 174, 218, 222, 236, 238
Lomeu Gomes, Rafael 7, 41, 42, 49, 134, 153–173, 175, 195, 218, 220, 236–238, 243, 244, 249, 257, 275, 339
López, Cristina C. 414
López, Luis E. 119
Lou, Nigel M. 84, 89, 101
Lourie, Megan 138
Lucas, Richard E. 86, 80
Lucas, Tamara 447, 455, 457
Lucero, Milagros 323, 324
Luke, Kang-Kwong 113
Lund, Emily M. 402
Lundberg, Adrian *40*, 47

Lunkenheimer, Erika S. 82
Luykx, Aurolyn 153, 218, 220, 238
Lynch, Andrew 112
Lytra, Vally 115, 304, 308

Macalister, John 158, 174
Machan, Tim W. 98
MacIntyre, Peter D. 85–87, 90, 91, 93
Mackey, Alison 213
Mackey, Margaret 262
Madianou, Mirca 164, 239–241, *245*
Mahajan, Anup P. 296
Mahboob, Ahmar 316, 317
Maher, John C. 341
Malaguzzi, L. 448
Maldonado-Colón, Elba 410
Maligkoudi, Christina 73, 74, 77
Makoni, Sinfree 132, 282, 283, 302
Manigand, Alain 71
Mann, Deanine 403
Manyak, Patrick C. 453
Mapolelo, Dumma 472
Mård-Miettinen, Kartia 187
Marinova-Todd, Stefka 402, 419
Markham, Annette N. 248
Markus, Paula 458
Marley, Dawn 368
Marmion, Doug 320
Mar-Molinero, Clare 110
Marsh, Jackie 257, 260, 264
Martin, Adrian D. 447, 455
Martin, Alex 270
Martin, Deidre 163, 167
Martin, Jay 364
Martín, M. Daniel 347
Martin, Peter 304, 308, 431
Martin-Jones, Marilyn 163, 167, 446
Mary, Latisha 12, 46, 47, 138, 154, 406, 440, 444–463, 466, 469, 473, 477, 479
Massey, Doreen 165
Matras, Yaron 279
Mau, Ada 296–298, 301, 303–305
May, Stephen 46, 282, 332, 358, 366, 372, 429, 438, 448, 469
Mayall, Berry 143
Mayer, Elisabeth 9, 10, 45, 137, 275, 312–331, 427
Mazzaferro, Gerardo 278

McCarty, Teresa L. 17, 22–24, 27, 28, 119, 275, 277, 278, 312, 316, 319, 327
McConvell, Patrick 316, 317
McDougall, Gay 377
McDuling, Allistair 346
McGhee, Belinda 420
McIvor, Onowa 146
McKay, Penny 315, 317
McLeod, Sharynne 68, 75
McPake, Joanna 303
McVicker, Paula 455
Meek, Barbra A. 133, 218
Mehta, Paras D. 79
Meier, Richard P. 55
Meisel, Jürgen 157
Melo-Pfeifer, Sílvia 114, 477
Ménard, Suzanne 421
Méndez López, Mariza G. 87, 100
Menken, Kate 110, 314, 451, 453, 456, 457
Menting, Barbara 64
Mercer, Sarah 86, 87
Meskill, Carla 296
Messer, Chris 237, *245*
Mesthrie, Rajend 2
Meyer, Michael 246
Meza, Mario D. 93
Mignolo, Walter D. 163, 167
Milani, Tommaso M. 163
Miller, Elizabeth R. 233
Miller, Daniel 164, 239–241, *245*
Miller, Jane 19
Mills, Jean 29, 30, 72, 74, 76
Milroy, Lesley 243, 244
Minkov, Miriam 213
Miranda, Norbella 339
Mirenda, Pat 402, 419
Mirvahedi, Seyed. H. 158, 174
Misra, Girishwar 386
Mithen, Johanna 81
Mohanty, Ajit K. 120, 378, 386, 388, 391
Moin, Viktor *207*
Moïse, Léna C. 441
Moita-Lopes, Luiz P. 364
Moll, Luis C. 118, 195, 260, 261, 264, 265, 270
Monaghan, Frank 13, 271
Monbiot, George 393
Mondada, Lorenza 247
Montanari, Simona 157

Monterescu, Daniel 188
Montero, M. Kristiina 458
Montero, Miguel 455
Montrul, Silvina 27
Moons, Caroline 449, 450
Moore, Helen 316
Moriarty, Máiréad 235, 274
Moro, Marie-Rose 458, 459
Morris, Delyth 114
Morrow, Virginia 219
Mortimer, Katherine S. 332
Morton, Missy 417
Mosco, Vincent 364
Motha, Suhanthie 88
Motlagh, Fateme G. 265
Mougeon, Raymond 346
Moyer, Melissa G. 39
Moyes, Gordon 260
Mruk, Christopher 449
Mu, Guanglun M. 177, 182, 183, 298
Muckpaloo, Igah 40, 45, 319, 320
Muehlmann, Shaylih 364
Mühlhäusler, Peter 282
Muñóz, Luna C. 64
Munthali, Alister 172
Munuŋgurr, Dhuŋgala 331
Munuŋgurr, Multhara 331
Murillo, Enrique 117
Murphy, Elizabeth 51
Murphy, Kimberlee C. 273
Murray, Garold 276
Myers-Scotton, Carol 227

Nadel, Lynn 417
Nahirny, Vladimir C. 347
Nakamura, Janice 42, 73
Nandi, Anik 40
Nap-Kolhoff, Elma 72
Nava, Monica 127
Neff, Deborah 126
Nelde, Peter 22
Nelissen, Sara 240, 242, *245*
Newland, Lisa A. 64
Ng, Sik 146
Nicholas, Sheilah E. 275, 312, 319, 327
Nicholls, Christine 119
Nieto-Castañón, Alfonso 79
Noble, Greg 294, 296, 303

Noda, Phyllis A. C. 447
Noels, Kimberly A. 84, 89, 101, 146
Noguerón-Liu, Silvia 279, 280, 287
Nomlomo, Vuyokazi 474–477
Noppari, Elina 248
Nordstrom, Janica 9, 45, 141, 283, 293–311
Norenzayan, Ara 42, 160
Norris, Catherine J. 104
Norst, Marlene 293, 294
Norton, Bonny 88, 142
Nuenen, Tom van 277
Nussbaum, Jon F. 132
Nyikos, Martha 229

Obojska, Maria A. 135, 229
Ochs, Elinor 157, 175, 218, 219
O'Connor, Erin 79
O'Connor, Meredith 81
Odeh, Wael 92
Odom, Samuel L. 412
Ó Duibhir, Pádraig 2
Ohashi, J. Kaori 419
Ó hIfearnáin, Tadhg 116, 219
Öhman, Arne 90
Oikonomakou, Marianthi 303
Oishi, Shigehiro 64
Okita, Toshie 158, 177, 180, 196, *201*
Ó Laoire, Muiris 350
Oliver, Mike 405, 407, 411
Olson, Tucker 93
Olthuis, Marja-Liisa 392
Olwig, Karen F. 240
Ó Murchadha, Noel P. 235
Onís, Carmen de 420
Oregui-González, Eider 267
Oregui-González, Marjorie F. 208, 239–241, 260, 264
Orellana, Marjorie F. 208, 239–241, 260, 264
Oriyama, Kaya 40, 179
Orosco, Michael J. 401, 405, 408–410, 413, 415
O'Rourke, Bernadette 40, 322
Ortega, Lilia 419
Ortega, Lourdes 18, 410, 413
Ortiz, Alba A. 410, 413, 415, 416
O'Shannessy, Carmel 139
Osher, David 416
Ota, Hiroshi 146
Otcu, Bahar 26, 293, 296, 298–301, 303, 304

Otcu-Grillman, Bahar 299, 304
Otheguy, Ricardo 20
Otsuji, Emi 166
Owusu, Samuel 172
Owusu, Thomas 278
Oxelson, Eva 455
Oxford, Rebecca 86, 87, 102
Özerk, Kamil 309

Pahl, Ray 243, 244
Pakir, Anne 39
Palmer, Deborah K. 118, 446, 455
Palviainen, Åsa 8, 29, 41, 43, 45, 54, 67, 155, 156, 164, 175, 187, 188, 214, 218, 220, 223, 228, 236–253, 257, 321, 339, 469, 476, 477
Pandharipande, Rajeshwari 316, 317
Papa, Rahul 118, 319
Parada, Maryann 239
Paradis, Johanne 157, 402
Paris, Django 415
Park, Heejung 73
Parreñas, Rachel S. 239, 241, *245*
Patkin, John 119
Patrick, Donna *40*, 45, 312, 319, 320
Patten, Alan 282
Paul Kister, Stéphanie 452
Paulsrud, BethAnne 12, 47, 138, 206, 415, 454, 464–481
Paulus, Markus 64
Pauwels, Anne 277
Pauwels, Luc 247
Pavlenko, Aneta 87, 88, 110, 174, 177, 178, 180, 302, 365
Pekrun, Reinhard 86
Pelland-Blais, Elaine 421
Pelliccia, Andrea 280
Pemberton, Lyn 13, 271
Peña Aguilar, Argelia 87, 100
Peña, Elizabeth D. 409
Penninx, Rinus 429
Pennycook, Alastair 166, 277, 282, 302
Pérez Báez, Gabriela 89, 181
Pérez-Milans, Miguel 154, 275
Pérez-Vidal, Carmen *202*
Perreault, Stéphane 441
Perren, Sonja 81
Perrino, Sabina 120, 278
Peters, Susan 411

Petersen, Jill 402
Petrides, Konstantinos, V. 92
Pettit, Stacie K. 445–447, 455
Pham, Giang 403
Phillipson, Robert 282, 364, 365, 381, 383, 390
Phinney, Jean S. 114
Phipps, Heather 248
Phuong, Jennifer 410
Pianta, Robert C. 79, 462
Pickett, Kate 397
Piedra, María Teresa de la 205, *209*
Pietikäinen, Sari 120
Piller, Ingrid 88, 136, 165, 174, 188, 189, 282, 364, 439, 452, 468
Pimienta, Daniel 266
Pink, Sarah 247
Piñon, Marites 273
Pitkänen-Huhta, Anne 247
Plymire, Darcy C. 350
Polinsky, Maria 26, 27
Politzer, Robert L. 343
Pöllmann, Andreas 429
Porter, Gina 164
Portes, Alejandro 70
Postill, John 252
Potowski, Kim 117
Potter, John 258, 261, 268
Prado, Daniel 266
Prasad, Gail Lori 143
Preston, Dennis R. 96, 110
Prieto-Blanco, Patricia 246
Prior, Matthew T. 88
Pritchard Newcombe, Lynda 137
Prosper, Ancyfrida 474–477
Prout, Alan 239
Prys Jones, Sylvia 26, 111
Pujolar, Joan 322
Pulinx, Reinhilde 18, *40*, 446, 447, 455
Pulsifer, Peter 55
Purkarthofer, Judith 6, 42, 89, 112, 130–149, 154, 165, 220, 229, 362
Putjata, Galina 140, 472, 473

Quay, Suzanne 157
Quiocho, Alice M. 118

Rabagliati, Hugh 418
Rabinowitz, Dan 188
Ragnarsdóttir, Hanna 358, 388

Ram, Nilam 67
Rama, Paul S. 267
Ramallo, Fernando 322
Rampton, Ben 21, 26, 120, 278
Rao, A. Giridhar 391
Rapatahana, Vaughan 397
Razfar, Aria 446
Razz, Moonis 317
Reath Warren, Anne 141, 304
Reedy, Tamati 347
Reershemius, Gertrud 279
Reetzke, Rachel 402
Reid, Wallis 20
Reindal, Solveig M. 413
Ren, Li 181, 184
Restrepo, Ma Adelaida 264
Revis, Melanie 167, 174, 178, 183, 218, 220, 221, 225, 230, 241
Reyes, Illiana 206, *210*, 211
Rezzoug, Dalila 458
Rhodes, Nancy C. 293
Riasat, Saiqa 296
Rice, Keren 55
Rice, Mabel 420
Ricento, Thomas 280, 282, 288, 364
Richards, Martin 67, 69
Richardson, V. 445
Richerson, Peter J. 261
Riches, Caroline 199, 204, 212
Rickford, John R. 110, 367
Rienzner, Martina 141
Rigg, Ashton 386
Riggins, Stephen H. 350
Rimm-Kaufman, Sara E. 445
Rinaldi, Carolina 449
Rios, Francisco 457
Rispoli, Mandy 419
Ritchie, Louise 272
Roberts, Gwerfyl 149
Roberts, Tim 13, 38–58, 146, 215, 251, 272
Roberts, Wendy 419
Robertson, Leena H. 78
Robertson, Phyllis M. 413, 415, 420
Robinson, Muriel 262
Robson, Elsbeth 172
Roche, Gerald 392
Rodríguez, Diane 419
Rodríguez, James L. 70
Rodríguez, Richard 72

Rodríguez Alzza, Carolina 13, 57, 147, 291, 312–331, 375, 442
Roh, Soonhee 82
Rohena, Elba I. 403
Rolstad, Kellie 409
Romaine, Suzanne 24, 110, 342, 362
Romero, Irma 127
Ronjat, Jules 156
Rosa, Jonathan 110, 117
Rose, Elisabeth 64
Rose, Susan 403
Rosekrans, Kristin 344
Rosén, Jenny 465, 476, 477
Roseneil, Sasha 243
Rosenthal, Robert 444
Roseth, Cary J. 403
Rosiers, Kirsten 450, 465
Rothman, Jason 112
Rubino, Antonia 429
Rubio-Alcalá, Fernando D. 91
Ruby, Mahera 140, 146, 160, 215, 303
Rudi, Jessie *245*
Rueda, Robert 416
Ruiz, Richard 9, 27, 313, 326, 345, 464, 466, 468, 476
Ruiz-Figueroa, Olivia 417
Rumsey, Alan 361, 370
Rvachew, Susan 421
Ryan, Ellen 146
Ryan, Richard M. 258, 268

Said, Fatima 135, 178, 182, 183, 196, 218, 226, 238
St. Peters, Michelle 273
Saito, Kazuya 103
Salami, Maryam 265
Salazar, Jesús J. 416
Sánchez, Liliana 13, 57, 147, 291, 312–331, 375, 442
Santos, Boaventura de Sousa 163, 166, 167
Santos, Rosa M. 403
Sapir, Edward 64
Sapru, Saloni 421
Sarnoff, Irving 3, 368
Sarroub, Loukia K. 213
Sawyer, Brooke E. 462
Saxena, Mukul 446
Sayers, Mary 81
Scantlin, Ronda 273

Scarino, Angela 349
Schalley, Andrea C. 1–13, 17–37, 38–58, 67, 85, 88, 109, 116, 131, 146, 156, 166, *203*, 215, 237, 251, 260, 272, 275, 322, 427–429, 451, 464
Schecter, Sandra R. 115
Scheibe, Susanne 104
Schermerhorn, Alice C. 219
Schieffelin, Bambi B. 157, 175
Schiffman, Harold F. 337, 339, 361, 362
Schiffrin, Deborah 110
Schmidt, Annette 133
Schutz, Paul A. 86, 133
Schwartz, Mila 7, 43, 134, 158, 187, 194–217, 222, 236, 339
Schwarzer, David 206
Schweinle, Amy 82
Scollon, Ron 237, 239, 246
Scollon, Suzie W. 237, 239, 246
Scott, Jacqueline 67
Scrymgour, Marion 344
Sealey, Alison 282
Selleck, Charlotte 118
Seltzer, Kate 468, 470, 471, 475–477
Semyonov, Moshe 439
Sen, Amartya 386, 387
Senécal, Sacha 441
Sepeheri, Mohammed B. 351
Serafini, Ellen J. 117
Serrano, María-Sierra Córdoba 321
Serre-Pradère, Geneviève 459
Sevinç, Yeşim 6, 30, 34, 42, 66, 72, 74, 84–108, 113, 115, 134, 140, 185, 200, 372
Shafer, Jill 406
Shanahan, Timothy 448
Sharkey, Judy 446, 447
Sharp, Stephen J. 271
Sheng, Li 420
Sherris, Arieh 344
Shin, Sarah J. 89, 114, 241
Shirazi, Roozbeh 298
S'hiri, Sonia 365
Shiyko, Mariya 82
Shogren, Karrie A. 421
Shohamy, Elana 46, 55, 110, 338
Showstack, Rachel E. 117
Schüpbach, Doris 123
Shulist, Sarah 322

Siegel, Linda S. 402
Siemushyma, Maria 451
Sigafoos, Jeff 419
Sikoli, Mark A. 282
Silverstein, Michael 110, 357, 360, 446
Šimičić, Lucija 282
Simon, Amalini 458, 459
Simon, Amanda 293, 295
Simon-Cereijido, Gabriela 403
Simons, Gary F. 133, 314–316
Simpson, Jane H. 116, 312, 314, 317
Sims, Tamara L. 104
Singer, Ruth 139, 143, 312
Skott, Jeppe 446
Skrtic, Thomas M. 411
Skutnabb-Kangas, Tove 11, 17, 21–24, 27, 28, 45, 53, 166, 277, 282, 312, 342, 364, 365, 377–400, 448, 456
Slaughter, Yvette 123
Slaughter-Defoe, Diana T. 112, 114
Slavkov, Nikolay 75
Slembrouck, Stef 278
Sluijs, Esther M. F. van 271
Smith, Heidi L. 80
Smith, Isabel 419
Smith-Christmas, Cassie 7, 30, *40*, 43, 134, 139, 154, 158, 160, 167, 174, 175, 177, 178, 180, 182, 183, 186, 196, 218–235, 236, 238, 241, 247, 249, 259, 260, 269
Smitherman, Geneva 455
Smythe Kung, Susan 55
Snow, Catherine. E. 157, 457
Soehl, Thomas 136
Solomon, Richard L. 85
Soltero-González, Lucinda 417
Somera, Lilnabeth 146
Song, Juyoung 277, 278
Soodak, Leslie C. 421
Sorace, Antonella 418
Soukakou, Elena 412
Souza, Ana 166, 348
Spanò, Goffredina 417
Sparrow, Wendy 417
Spencer, Liz 243, 244
Spencer, Llinos 149
Spiegler, Olivia 81
Spielberger, Charles D. 90
Spinks, Teagan 272
Spitulnik, Debra 113

Spolsky, Bernard 42, 88, 114, 115, 153, 166, 174, 175, 178, 196, 199, 237, 238, 321, 348, 358, 359, 367, 439, 446, 454
Springhorn, Ron G. 91
Stafford, Mary E. 455
Stanley, Phiona 51
Steien, Guri B. 136, 154, 220
Steinbach, Marilyn 454
Steinberg, Faith S. 91, 100
Stephenson, Todd G. 421
Stern, Alissa J. 279
Stern, Michael J. 237, *245*
Stevens, Gillian 79
Stevens, Paul B. 365
Stevenson, Patrick 110
Storm, Melissa D. 462
Stowe, Matthew J. 404
Strauss, Anselm 96
Strauss, Claudia 219
Stroud, Christopher 163
Strubell, Miquel 22, 427
Suárez-Orozco, Carola 79
Suh, Euncook M. 80
Suldo, Shannon M. 67
Sullivan, Amanda 408, 410
Sundqvist, Pia 265
Suslak, Daniel F. 132
Sutton, Ann 418
Svendsen, Bente A. 244
Swain, Merrill K. 385
Swanson, H. Lee 409
Sweet, Monica 403
Sylvan, Claire E. 476
Szatmari, Peter 419
Szecsi, Tunde 136
Szilagyi, Janka 136
Sznaider, Nathan 281

Tabouret-Keller, Andreé 109
Tacchi, Jo 252
Taeschner, Traute 156
Taipale, Sakari 242, 244
Takam, Alain F. 350
Tallon, Michael 92
Tan, Jon E. C. 309
Tanle, Agustine 172
Tannen, Deborah 135
Tannenbaum, Michal 88, 89, 100, 158, 166, 174, 177, 180, 237, 240, 241, 244, 248

Tarnanen, Mirja 469, 476, 477
Tay, Louis 64
Taylor, Charles 218
Taylor, Denny 257
Taylor-Leech, Kerry 293
Teague, Brad L. 214
Tefera, Adai 408, 412
Tejada, Harvey 339
Tereshchenko, Antonia 298, 304
Thieberger, Nicholas 51, 55, 58, 316
Thomas, Carol 405, 407
Thomas, Lynn 305
Thomas, Wayne P. 391, 414
Thomauske, Nathalie 449, 450
Thompson, Ann 419
Thordardottir, Ellin 418
Thorne, Barrie 252
Thorpe, Amy 418
Tijnagel-Schoenaker, Bernadet 448
Ting, Su-Hie 315
Tinsley, Teresa 303
To, Carol K. S. 403
Todal, Jon 138
Tollefson, James W. 154, 178, 275, 282
Tom, Miye N. 319
Topinka, Carol 412
Toppelberg, Claudio O. 79
Torgersen, Elvind 122
Torres-Guzmán, María 277
Tov, William 64
Tranter, Siobhan 137
Treas, Judith 67
Treccani, Barbara 53
Trent, Allen 457
Trent, Stanley C. 416
Trofimova, Ira 64
Trudeau, Natacha 418
Trudell, Barbara 282, 283
Trumper-Hecht, Nira 55
Tsai, Kim M. 82
Tse, Lucy 112–114, 116, 179
Tseng, Amelia 6, 42, 109–129, 177, 258
Tseng, Vivian 70, 75
Tsokalidou, Roula 186, 449, 453
Tsolidis, Georgina 296, 303
Tsui, Amy 178
Tsurutani, Chiharu 369
Tuijl, Cathy van 440

Tuominen, Anne 218, 224
Tupas, Ruanni 397
Turnbull, Ann P. 405
Turnbull, H. Rutherford 404, 421
Turner, Jonathan 218
Tyrrell, Naomi 44, 238
Tzischinsky, Orna 262, 263

Unsworth, Sharon 157
Urciuoli, Bonnie 115
Uusitalo, Niina 248

Vaillancourt, Tracy 419
Valdés, Guadalupe 25, 27, 109, 112, 117, 138, 322
Valk, Helga A. G. de 40
Valle, Jan W. 416
Vallejo, Claudia 473
Vallverdú, Francesc 342
Valois, Daniel 346
Van Avermaet, Piet 18, 40, 69, 446, 447, 453, 455
Van den Bulck, Jan 240, 242, *245*
Van Der Wildt, Anouk 69, 453
Van Deusen-Scholl, Nelleke 25
Van Houtte, Mieke 453
Van Keer, Hilde 445
Van Mensel, Luk 135, 136, 229
Van Mol, Christof 40
Varghese, Manka M. 469, 470
Varis, Piia 277
Vaughan, Jill 312
Vedder, Paul 69
Vega Castañeda, Lillian 457
Venables, Elizabeth 156, *203*
Verdon, Sarah 75
Verhoeven, Ludo 402
Verloop, Nico 305
Vermunt, Jan D. 305
Verschik, Anna 158, 222
Vijver, Fons van de 430
Villanueva, Victor 455
Villegas, Ana María 447, 455, 457
Vincze, Laszlo 85–87
Vitanova, Gergana 233
Volden, Joanne 419
Voloshinov, Valentin N. 338
Volterra, Virginia 156

Waddell, Charlotte 419
Waldinger, Roger 430
Walker, Anne 406
Walker, Sue 81
Walker, Susan 252
Walls, Francesca 184
Walsh, Anne M. 272
Walsh, Catherine E. 163, 167
Walsh, Michael 367
Walter, Stephen L. 393
Walters, Joel 232
Walters, Sue 296, 297, 302, 303
Wang, Nan 294
Wang, Weihong 174, 178, 184
Wang, Xiaomei 184, 185, 349
Warriner, Doris S. 277
Warschauer, Mark 273
Wartella, Ellen 271
Wathum-Ocama, John C. 403
Waweru, Nduta 343
Weame, Greg 331
Weaver, Scott R. 70
Weber, Shlomo 293
Wedin, Åsa 465
Wee, Lionel 25
Weinert, Sabine 64
Weisskirch, Robert S. 115
Wenger, Etienne 158, 260, 297
White, Katherine M. 272
White, Leon 331
Whiteford, Chrystal 81
Whiteley, Peter 119
Whiteside, Katie E. 68
Whitton, Nicola 259
Wierzbicka, Anna 110
Wigglesworth, Gillian 21, 312, 317, 319, 327
Wiley, Terrence G. 4, 25, 293
Wilkinson, Cheryl Y. 420
Wilkinson, Richard 397
Willard, Jessica 81
Williams, Angie 146
Williams, Colin H. 112
Williams, Glyn 22, 427
Williams, Gruffudd O. 427
Willoughby, Louisa 403
Winsler, Adam 69, 75
Winter, Joanne 277
Witney, John 103

Wodak, Ruth 246
Wodrich, David L. 417
Wong, Ka F. 92, 117
Wong Fillmore, Lily 72, 76, 77, 114, 177
Woodbury, Anthony C. 55
Woodham, Malgorzata 348
Woodley, Heather H. 469, 475–477
Woodrow, Lindy 92
Woolard, Kathryn A. 446
Wright, John C. 262
Wright, Lyn 243, *see also* Fogle, Lyn Wright
Wright, Wayne E. 19, 21
Wu, Chao-Jung 296, 299–304, 411
Wunuŋmurra, W.W. 331
Wyman, Leisy T. 275, 277, 312

Xiao, Yang 92, 117

Yagcioglu-Ali, Dilek 308
Yağmur, Kutlay 11, 12, 27, 47, 76, 138, 186, 187, 219, 425–443, 450, 466
Yamamoto, Masayo *203*, 205, 212
Yelenevskaya, Maria *40*
Yitzhaki, Dafna 89, 100, 166, 232
You, Byeong-Keun 112
Young, Andrea S. 12, 46, 47, 138, 154, 406, 440, 444–463, 465, 466, 469, 473, 477

Young, Catherine 313, 314, 318
Young, Dolly J. 91
Young, Richard F. 88
Youngs, Cheryl S. 455
Youngs, George A. 455
Yuill, Nicola 270
Yunupiŋu, Yalmay 331

Zajíková, Lenka 314
Zakharia, Zeena 26, 293, 298
Zamyatin, Konstantin 382
Zehler, Anette M. 413
Zentella, Ana C. 111, 113
Zhang, Donghui 112, 114
Zhao, Shouhui 116
Zhu, Hua *40*, 89, 112, 135, 154, 177, 178, 181–183, 196, 218, 226, 231, 238, 239, 246, 247, 277
Zilliacus, Harriet 469, 471, 473
Zolberg, Aristide 428
Zou, Xiaobing 420
Zouhir, Abderrahman 318
Zuckermann, Ghil'ad 367
Zulfiqar, Mohsin 309
Zwaigenbaum, Lonnie 419

Subject Index

Page numbers in bold type indicate figures, in italics, tables.

academic achievement 409, 413, *see also* educational success
acculturation 74, 426, 430
acquisition, *see* language acquisition
action research, *40*, 45, 209
active bilingual, *see* bilingual
actors 39, 44, 46, 165, 239, *281*, 337–339, 352, 450, 469, *see also* policy actors
affect 6, 26, 42, 64, 114, 260, 454
affective factors 1, 20
affective relationship 89
affiliation 21, 25, 26, 30, 110, 296
age of acquisition 19, 32, 95, *see also* age of onset
age of onset 8, 21, *31*
agency 26, 29, 119, 282, 286–288, 349
– child agency 7, 8, 133, 135, 157, 158, 167, *176*, 178–180, 181–183, 196, 198, 208, 212, 218–235, 238–240, 245, 268
– community agency 281–283, 320
– teacher agency 457, 467, 477
ambilingual, *see* bilingual
ancestral language 17, 25, 26
anxiety, *see* language anxiety
aphasia 64
assessment (disability) 405, 407–410
assimilation 110, 112, 115, 121, 383, 387, *389*, 394, 395
assimilationist (formal education) 429–431, 437
asymmetrical bilingual, *see* bilingual
attitudes, *see* language attitudes
authorities 39, 46, 230, 282, 425, 426, 436
awareness, *see* language awareness

background speaker 25
balance 21, 156
balanced bilingual, *see* bilingual
beliefs 46, 84, 100, 110, 111, 114, 175, 176, 179, 187, 196, 199, 200, 299, 300, 338, 343, 357–362, 370
– (parental) impact beliefs 7, 77, 174, 177–181, 184
– teacher beliefs 12, 444–463, 468–473

belonging 65, 69, 139, 166, 238, 260, 286, 296–298, 300, 301, 378, 453
bidirectional reciprocal learning *210*, 211
bilingual 2, 5, 6, 8, 10, 17–22, 27, 28, 38, 66–69, 74, 88, 89, 91, 94–96, 98, 101, 109, 111, 116–118, 198, 200, 220, 222, 298, 300, 322, 362, 363, 369, 401–404, 406, 408–414, 416, 439, 440, 444, 451, 453, 470, 474
– active bilingual 19, 20, 264, 269, 270, 434
– ambilingual 20
– asymmetrical bilingual 20
– balanced bilingual 20, 109, 440
– emergent bilingual 11, 68, 69, 401–415, 444, 447, 450–456, 470, 474
– equilingual 20
– passive bilingual 19, 20, 264, 270
– semilingual 20, 117, 409
– symmetrical bilingual 20
– unbalanced bilingual 20
bilingual education 17, 116, 119, 121, 187, 312, 314, 316, 317, 319, 323–326, 344, 368, 388, *389*, 412, 414, 416, 433, 466, 470
bilingual speaker, *see* bilingual
bilingualism 1, 17–21, 24, 26, 30, 33, 34, 49, 52, 53, 54, 63, 66, 72, 78, 88, 89, 98, 110, 115–117, 140, 156, 182, 186, 187, 197, 200, 202, 206, *209*, 213, 298, 300, 360, 362, 369, 389, 401–409, 411–416, 434, 440, 450, 454, 455, 470, 474
– ascendant bilingualism 20, 21
– conflictive bilingualism 63, 73
– Harmonious Bilingualism, *see* Harmonious Bilingualism
– recessive bilingualism 20, 21
biographical research 39, 131, 136, 142–143

CALD (Culturally And Linguistically Diverse) 28
child agency, *see* agency
choice of language, *see* language choice
civic (formal education) 426, 429, 430
classroom practices 12, 117, 303, 304, 446–448, 453, 454, 474–476
co-constructed data collection 247, 248

code-mixing 198, *202*, 206, *207*
code-switching 96, 111, 198, 200–*202*, 206, *207*, 212, 223, 225–227, 267, 409
communication 29, 44, 54, 75, 76, 91, 98, 101, 113, 114, 120, 132, 139–141, 164, 177, 198, 199, *208*, 214, 222, 230, 241, 242, *245*, 267, 270, 288, 348, 350, 363, 364, 394, 402, 403, 406, 414, 449, 467, 476
communicative competence 20, 24, 117, 138
community 8, 9, 39, 43–46
community initiative 3, 323
community language 17, 109, 116, 284, 300, 347, 348
community language school 9, 44–46, 293–311
community of practice 158, 297
community organisation 346–350
competence, *see* linguistic competence
complementary school, 293, 341, 346, 347, 431, *see also* community language school
compliance 8, 221–225, 227–229, 231, 232
computer-mediated communication 188, 241, 244, 295, 301, 350
concept of self 5, 6, 109, *see also* identity
confidence 91, 259, 267, 268, *see also* self-confidence
conflictive bilingualism, *see* bilingualism
control of home language environment 196, 206, 267
convenience sampling 44
conversation analysis 219, 247
cosmopolitanism 116, 120, 280, 281, 288
critical theory 366, 367
cross-disciplinarity 53, 54, 154, *245*, 246, 248, 249, 396
cultural capital 230, 261, 448, 449, 475
cultural diversity 12, 288, 312, 381, 427, 455, 473
cultural heritage/background 26, 27, 84, 85, 131, 194–196
culture 21, 26, *31*, 44, 45, 84, 99, 110–112, 121, 131, 154, 176–179, 206, 261, 301, 320, 321, 324, 346, 347, 361, 383, 430, 434
curriculum 117, 141, 301–303, 324, 343, 412, 431, 435, 437, 441, 469, 474
cyberspora 278, 284, 288

data management 51, 52
decoloniality 163, 166

deficit perspective 11, 12, 18, 25, 27, 28, *31*, 32, 116, 117, 343, 401–415, 429, 434, 440, 449, 452, 464, 474
dementia 64
depression 70
development (language), *see* language development
diary study 39, 155, 156
diaspora 137, 140, 160, 163, 181, 184, 223, 224, 278, 284, 286, 288, 367
digital communication 8, 120, 135, 164, 188, 238, 242, 244, 247, 267, 279, 321
digital practices 136, 164, *209*, 238, 244, 257, 258, 260, 265
digital resources and technologies 51, 54, 188, *204*, 241, 242, 248, 257, 278, 279, 287, 366
dimensions (bilingualism terms) 20, 21, 30–34
dimensions (child agency) 221, 222, 230, 231
disability 11, 383, 401–421
– medical model, *see* models of disability
– social model, *see* models of disability
disability diagnosis 11, 117, 401–405, 408–415
discourse analysis 246, 247
discrimination 74, 88, 110, 112, 116, 119, 121, 323, 324, 380, 383, 404, 406, 408, *see also* linguistic discrimination
disorder 408
distress 51, 63, 230
domain of language usage 2, 21, 23, 28–32, 34, 133, 237, 238, 278, 313, 317, 321, 327, 344, 345, 347, 350, 352, 367, 387, 394, 396, 428
dominant language (of group) 17, 22, 115, 213, 322, 343, 345, 350, 352, 377, 378, 379, 387, 388, 390, 391, 402, 403, 413
dominant language (of individual) 17, 23, 27, 195, *389*
dual language proficiency 69, 76, 77
dual language programs 116, 118, *389*, 390, 413, 414
dynamic model of family language policy (FLP) 7, 175–179

EAL/D (English as an Additional Language or Dialect) 28, 265, 267
education model 11, 12, 346, 388–392, 425–443

education system 46, 97, 186, 187, 283, 293, 303, 314, 317, 319, 383, 384, 388, 411, 425, 431, 441, 451, 456
educational institution 2, 53, 138, 157, 415, 425, 427, 431, 441
educational outcome, *see* educational success
educational policy 39, 117, **176**, 324–325, 342, 433, 437, 470, 478
educational program 294, 314, 340, 344, 346, 352, *389*, 390–392, 401, 404, 412, 414, 415, 425, 439, 440
educational success 1, 175, 339, 396
edutainment 259
ELL (English Language Learner) 28, 453, 471
emergent bilingual, *see* bilingual
emotions 6–8, 63, 68, 84–108, 174, **176**, 177, 180, 182, 213, 240, 241, *245*, 247
– negative emotions 6, 84–108, 200, 267
– positive emotions 85–87, 90, 100, 101, 200, 206, 209
endangered language, *see* language endangerment
English as an Additional Language or Dialect, *see* EAL/D
English Language Learner, *see* ELL
environment language 17
equilingual, *see* bilingual
equity 11, 53, 259, 281–283, 287, 288, 378, 380, *389*, 401, 404, 407, 411, 413–416, 444, 465, 473
ethics 50–51, 76, 248, 283
ethnic group/identity 24, 28, 69, 97, 114, 177, 194, 199, 283, 286, 297, 341, 360, 372, 380, 426, 434, 455
ethnic language 26, 69, 70, 183
ethnic school 9, 116, 283, 293, 294, 341, 345, 347, *see also* community language school
ethnicism 378
ethnicity 26, 111, 117, 118, 143, 166, 363, 384, 411
ethnist (formal education) 426, 429, 430
ethnography *40*, 45, 49, 72, 93, 134, 157–159, 163, 167, 199, *202*, *204*, *208*, *210*, 211, 214, 239, 246–248, 284, 469, 284, 361, 469
European Union 46, 338, 427
expressed guess strategy 198, 200, *202*
external factors 7, 116, 174, 176, 178, 179, 181, 186, 188, 189, 237, 244

family 41, 42, 67, 222, 237, 238, 242–246
family language policy (FLP) 6–8, 29, 85, 88–90, 99–102, 115, 116, 134, 135, 153–173, 174–193, 195, 200, 218, 220, 223, 227, 230, 232, 236–253, 257
family relationship 6, 75, 90, 134, 180–182, 280
familylect 229
father 43, 74, 243
fieldnotes 40, 134, *208*, 210
first language (L1) 22–24, *31*–33, 88, 133, 156, 180, 182, 194, 299, 300, 384, 385, 441, 447
fixed language mindset 84, 89, 96, 99–101
FL (foreign language), *see* foreign language
FLP (family language policy), *see* family language policy (FLP)
focus group *40*, 159
folk linguistics 362
foreign language (FL) 23, 87, 91, 92, 117, 265, 305, 388, 425–427, 431, 437, 438
formal education 11, 34, 46, 47, 293, 319, 378, 379, 386, 425–443, 467
frustration 78, 99, 115
funds of knowledge 118, 195, 205, *210*, 211, 214, 261, 264, 270

gaming/games *204*, 205, *209*, 258–260, 262, 263, 265–267, 269, 270
generalisability 5, 46, 48, 49, 52, 54
generation 6, 84, 94, 95, 97, 98, 100, 112–115, 121, 130–149, 177–181, *210*, 242, *245*, 270, 286, 320, 383, 391, 439
geographical space 44, 54, 132, 137, 160, 161, 164, 166, 242, 276, 279, 285, 295
globalisation 7, 120, 121, 155, 163, 213, 274–276, 288, 364, 372, 427
government body 222
grammar 20, 98, 286, 339, 367, 402, 410
grandparent 72, 95, 114, 133, 135, 136, 140, 160, 206, *210*, 211, 286, 391, 439
grassroots initiative 8, 9, 46, 154, 293, 358, *see also* grassroots language planning
grassroots language planning 9, 274–292
group context 30, *31*, 32
group influence *31*, 32
group status *31*, 32
guilt 51, 72, 87, 180, 454

habitus 183, 298, *see also* monolingual habitus
Happylingual approach 200, 206, *209*, 214
Harmonious Bilingualism 6, 63–83, 88, 182
hegemony, *see* linguistic hegemony
heritage language 4, 17, 22, 25–27, 30–34, 54, 85, 92, 94, 109, 111, 112, 117, 121, 140, 158, 168, **176**, 180, 182, 183, 194, 249, 283, 284, 322, 348, 357, 370, 372, 426, 439, 450
heritage language education 182, 426, 428, 430, 432, *see also* home language education
heritage language school 9, 117, 293, 295, 415, *see also* community language school
heritage speakers 112, 113, 115, 117, 121, 322
heterogeneity 155, 281, 283, 284, 287, 288
home language 2, 4, 5, 6, 9–12, 17, 23, 28–35, 47, 54, 67, 109, 166, 385, 432, 434, 440
home language development 1–13, 38–58, 71, 85, 86, 90, 155, 167, 168, 176, 181–184, 187, *203*, 205, 262, 269, 312, 327, 372, 404
home language education 11, 117, 182, 409, 410, 432, *see* mother tongue instruction
home language environment 195, 196, 200, 204, 205, 206
home language maintenance 1–13, 38–58, 63, 75, 77, 78, 84–108, 109, 112–116, 119, 121, 168, 180, 194–217, 220, 276, 286, 317, 327, 342, 358, 401, 402, 408, 416, 464–481
human rights, *see* linguistic human rights
hypermobility 164, 220

identification 21, 25, 27, 30–35, 139, 181, 385, 426
identity 6, 9, 26, 30, 97, 109–129, 143, 154, **176**, 177, 181, 182, 245, 258, 260, 261, 277, 286, 342, 358, 366, 367, 380, 386, 404, 430, 448, 453, 454
– ethnic identity, *see* ethnic group/identity
– (trans)national identity 6, 115, 116, 120, 278, 288, 314, 315, 342, 343, 358, 364, 430
ideological space 466, 467, 477

ideological underpinning 30–32, 34, 188, 243
ideology
– language ideology, *see* language ideology
– societal ideology, *see* societal ideology
image of the child 444, 448–451
immersion 231, 319, *389*–391, 409, 414
impact beliefs, *see* beliefs
implementational space 466, 467, 473, 476, 478
in-service training, *see* professional development
inclusive education 47, 383, 385, 388, 412, 414, 415, 416, 431, 473, 477, 478
inclusiveness 10, 28, 45, 288, 316, 318, 377–400, 415, 429, 467
indigenous community 6, 109, 116, 119, 120, 160, 278, 312–331, 341, 357, 362, 367, 378, 382, 383
indigenous language 9, 23, 47, 75, 119, 121, 139, 275, 282, 312–327, 341, 344, 363, 365, 367, 371, *389*, 390, 392, 427, 428, 433
inequity, *see* equity
input, *see* language input
integration 144, 320, 343, *389*, 394, 425, 428, 430, 432, 433, 434, 437
interaction order 228, 246
interdisciplinary, *see* cross-disciplinary
intergenerational challenges 6, 42, 89, 130–149
intergenerational communication 75, 114, 132, 134–136
intergenerational conflict 70, 72, 84, 89, 100, 101, 141, 182
intergenerational relations 6, 136, 141, 144
intergenerational transmission 24, 42, 130, 133, 134, 136, 137, 140, 177, 183, 185, 186, 195, 198, 205, *209*, 212, 244, 283, 293, 320, 326, 432
internal factors 7, 174, 176–178, 179–183, 188
international covenant 11, 341, 342, 380, 381
Internet 9, 188, 242, 266–268, 274, 277–280, 287, 288, 295, 303, 351
interpersonal relationship 64, 68, 73, 93, 135, 164, 243, 244
intervention 102, 341, 347, 364, 386, 409, 410, 457, *see also* language intervention
intervention study 45, 472

interview study 40, 43, 45, 71, 72, 74, 89, 93, 96, 101, 136, 159, 185, *201*, *203*, *204*, *207–209*, 212, 239, 246–248, 296, 298, 305, 470, 471

joint action 4, 8, 9, 39, 44, 45

L1, *see* first language (L1)
L2, *see* second language (L2)
language acquisition 2, 134, 153, 154, 156, 157, 297, 343, 344, 447
language acquisition context 19, 21
language acquisition history, *see* linguistic history
language acquisition sequence 23, 27, 30–32, 34
language acquisition type *31*, 32
language anxiety 6, 30, 84–108, 115, 140, 372
language-as-problem orientation 9, 18, 27, 28, *31*, 32, 35, 179, 313–315, 318, 343, 429, 465
language-as-resource orientation 9, 300, 313, 314, 316, 320, 465, 470, 472–474, 476, 478
language-as-right orientation 9, 313, 315–316, 465, 477, 478
language attitudes 10, 11, 12, 46, 47, 76, 87, 117, 179, 180, 182, 298, 321–323, 357–376
language awareness 88, 205, 206, 392, 435, 454–456, 468, 472, 473, 476
Language Background Other Than English (LBOTE), *see* LBOTE
language brokering 115, *208*, 230, 231
language choice 11, 21, 65, 70, 73, 75–79, 88, 136, 186, 187, 198, 223–229, 231, 232, 264, 276–278, 385, 474
language competence, *see* linguistic competence
language development 19, 21, 63, 77, 88, 91, 100, 101, 153, 155, 157, 175, 200, *202*, *204*, 212–214, 238, 240, 242, 260, 263–265, 268, 270, 295, 413, 440, 447, 448, 474, *see also* home language development
language discrimination, *see* linguistic discrimination
language diversity, *see* linguistic diversity
language ecology 195, 200, 214, 218, 241, 247, 275–278, 287, 342, 349
language endangerment 119, 132, 133, 160, 213, 275, 312, 317, 358, *389*, 390
language expertise 21, 293

language function 21, 33, 137, 264, 317, 318, 322, 339, 340, 386
language hierarchy 116, 117, 143, 161, 185, 345, 365, 366, 394, 466–468, 470, 475, 476, 477
language ideology 10–12, 28, 99, 109–111, 121, 142, 153, 154, 161, 175, 176, 185, 189, 196, 199, *201*, *202*, *208*, 212, 219, 238–240, 242, 286, 299, 300, 318, 321, 327, 338, 339, 345, 349, 357–376, 425, 428–430, 445, 446, 449, 456, 466–469, 471, 473, 476, 477
language indexicality 6, 109, 111, 121, 278, 279
language inheritance, *see* linguistic inheritance
language input 77, 78, 135, 139, 156, 157, 196, 197, 199, *203*, 205, 212, 219, 238, 240, 257, 322, 386, 447
language instruction 24, 27, 69, 403, 409, 410, 415, 432, 435, 437, 441, 467
language intervention **176**, 196
language investment 176, 178, 387
language learning 2, 10, 87, 142, 154, 155, 157, 160, 165, 182, 183, 188, 240, 259, 267, 293, 304, 306, 337–339, 352, 403, 412, 413, 429, 434
language log 39
language loss 73, 112, 114, 116, 139, 178, 179, 183, 187, 213, 300, 320, 340, 407, 409, 430
language maintenance 2, 3, 7, 9, 114, 120, 130, 135, 154, 158, 195, 236, 239, 240, 279, 322, 337–356, 367, *389*–391, 395, *see also* home language maintenance
language management 7, 89, 135, 153, 167, 175, 176, 186, 196, 200, *201*, 205, 206, *208*, 211–214, 236, 242, 260, 316, 326, 468, 473
language mode 21
language of instruction 11, 22, 71, 186, 346, 358, 377, 384, 388, *389*, 390, 391, 413, 456, 464, 465, 467, 470, 475, 477
language planning 6, 9–11, 29, 39, 47, 52, 153, 160, 163, 166, 188, 189, 196, 236, 238, 240, 274–292, 313, 314, 322–324, 326, 337–356, 465
language policy 10–12, 18, 27, 34, 39, 47, 54, 137, 140, 153, 154, 163, 166, 174, 175, 178, 180, 189, 196, 222, 236, 275, 282, 304,

312–320, 324, 326, 337–357, 358, 362, 368, 387, 427–431, 437, 440, 444, 450, 453, 454, 456, 457, 469, 470, 474, 476, 478
- family language policy, see family language policy (FLP)
- local policy 11, 465, 467
- national policy 116, 283, 314–316, 319, 327, 395, 465, 467
- practiced language policy 12, 444, 453, 454, 474, 476, 478
- stated language policy 43

language practices 3, 7, 43, 48, 89, 100, 111, 113–115, 130, 135, 136, 153–155, 158, 163, 164, 166–168, 174–176, 179, 181, 185–187, 194–217, 219, 220, 232, 236, 238–242, 244, *245*, 248, 249, 274, 277, 278, 296, 299, 300, 319, 320, 326, 342, 348, 351, 360, 361, 366, 369, 450, 467, 468, 475, 476
- communicative/conversational practices 29, 77, 112, 227
- ritual language practices 196, 206, *209*, 211

language prestige 99, 109, 110, 116, 118, 121, 179, 279, 283, 318, 321, 339, 350, 363–365, 464

language profile 21, 115, 117

language regime 43, 220, 221, 224, 227, 229, 351, 427, 428

language repertoire, see repertoire

language resources 9, 112, 133, 142–144, 176, 181, 186, 188, *204*, 206, 220, 229, 276, 277, 282, 286, 357, 450, 456, 465, 467–469, 474, 475

language rights 24, 47, 54, 119, 120, 167, 282, 312, 315, 317, 323–325, 327, 341, 358, 359, 372, 377–400, 415, 428, 449, 465, 477

language segregation 297, 317, *389*–391, 413

language separation 447, 469

language services 346, 406, 413

language shift 6, 10, 42, 88, 92–94, 100, 116, 142, 158, 179, 181, 184, 187, 195, 219, 224–226, 300, 326, 349–351, 362, 367, 368, 395, 429, 430, 432

language socialisation 6, 73, 78, 109, 134, 154, 156–158, 175–178, 182, 188, 195, 198, 219, 220, 230, 238, 240, 351, 352, 358, 452

language status 7, 132, 160, 174, 183–185, 286, 312–318, 321, 327, 339, 340, 345, 350, 358, 360, 365, 366, 379, 384, 394, 395, 411, 416, 428, 431–433, 439, 440, 464, 466, 470

language teaching 1, 2, 10, 11, 188, 197, 198, 285, 287, 293–297, 301–306, 324, 339, 341, 344, 425–443, see also home language education

language transmission 6, 10, 42, 114, 130, 135, 137, 138, 141, 142, 186, 200, 205, 218, 238, 242, *245*, 247, 249, 340, 357, 364, 365, 372, 456, see also intergenerational transmission

language use 1–3, 6, 7, 9, 10, 18, 21, 29, 34, 43, 47, 64, 67, 70, 73, 75, 77, 88, 94–101, 114, 115, 121, 134–141, 144, 153, 156–158, 160, 161, 163–165, 174, 176, 178, 182, 187–189, 196, 199, 200, *202*, 206, *208*, 212, 214, 219, 220, 237, 238, 260, 264, 266–268, 274, 276, 278, 285, 288, 295, 300, 302, 337–340, 342, 344, 346–348, 350–352, 372, 406, 407, 410, 425, 470, 471

language vitality 10, 279, 312, 320, 321, 350, 352, 357

Languages Other Than English, see LOTE

law 46, 324, 339–341, 359, 365, 379, 404, 429, 430, 456, see also legislation

LBOTE (Language Background Other Than English) 28

learning difficulty 18, 405

learning disability, see disability

legislation 47, 117, 314–316, 323, 439, 470

legitimacy 121, 279, 300, 305, 306, 344, 345, 362, 432, 449, 450, 454, 465, 466, 468–471, 477, 478

LEP (Limited English Proficiency) 28, 412, 413, 453

levels of planning
- macro level, see macro level
- meso level, see meso level
- micro level, see micro level

Limited English Proficiency (LEP), see LEP

lingua franca 22, 184, 266, 315, 428

linguicide 119

linguicism 378

linguistic ability 21, 93, 322, 343

linguistic capital 178, 184, 230, 364, 366, 474, 475
linguistic competence 8, 19–21, 27, 29, 69, 89–91, 98, 142, *201*, 220, 221, 225–227, 229–232, 358, 414, 447, 448, 450, 452, 453
linguistic development, *see* language development
linguistic discrimination 27, 88, 96, 109, 110, 112, 117, 312, 367, 384
linguistic diversity 10, 12, 39, 65, 111, 166, 275, 282, 288, 293, 295, 312, 343, 345, 357–376, 393, 407, 414, 427, 455, 464–467, 469, 471, 473, 476
linguistic ecology, *see* language ecology
linguistic factors 66, 74, 90, 93, 179, 405
linguistic hegemony 6, 109, 116, 300, 364, 394
linguistic history 21, 32, 34, 88
linguistic human rights 11, 282, 327, 341, 377–400
linguistic inheritance 21, 26, 29, 182
linguistic landscape 39, *40*, 246, 275, 316, 317, 368
linguistic norms 8, 111–113, 118, 121, 158, 175, 183, 221, 222, 227–232, 278, 360, 367, 468, 474
linguistic preference 179, 182, 200, 206, 225–227, 269, 270
linguistic purism 367
linguistic resources, *see* language resources
linguistic rights, *see* language rights
linguistic stability 21
listening 19, 20, 475
literacy 78, 136, 140, 141, 154, 176, 186, 200, *204, 209*–213, 238, 257, 259–262, 265–267, 278, 279, 284–288, 315, 319, 320, 339, 344–346, 348, 362, 410, 414, 415, 447, 464, 472, 474, 475
longitudinal study 43, 48, 73, 75, 184, 200, *202, 209, 210*, 242, 247, 450, 474
LOTE (Languages Other Than English) 28, 283

macro level 3, 4, 8, 10, 18, 33, 34, 38–41, 45, 46–49, 52–54, 121, 134, 174, 180, 184, 275, 280, 293, 325, 338–347, 349, 350, 352, 359, 427, 466, 476, 477
macro skills 20
– listening, *see* listening
– reading, *see* reading
– speaking, *see* speaking
– writing, *see* writing
mainstream classroom 12, 138, 464–481
mainstream language 17, 23, 26, 28, 29, 179, 182, 183, 185, 299, 300, 317, 318, 428, 429, 432–435, *see also* majority language
majority language 2, 12, 17, 22, 26, 85, 89, 94, 95, 100, 115, 116, 131, 133, 137, 138, 140, 142, 185, *203*, 205, 212, 220, 225, 231, 260, 315, 319, 321, 322, 361, 365, 370, 388–391, 414, 464, 465, 467, 469, 471, 474, 476, 477
marginalisation 120, 160, 302, 303, 305, 312, 314, 316, 357, 364, 367, 377–379, *389*, 403, 404, 406, 407, 408, 416, 434
matched guise technique 369
maximal engagement strategy 196, 200, *203*, 205, 212
medical model of disability, *see* models of disability
mediated communication 136, 164, 188, 241, 242, 244, *245*, 247, 295, 301, 350, *see also* computer-mediated communication; digital communication
medium of instruction, *see* language of instruction
mental health 64, 381, 397, 407
meso level 3, 4, 8–10, 33, 34, 38–41, 43–46, 49, 54, 275, 293, 337–340, 345–347, 350–352
meta-analysis 48, 52, 194, 445, 455, 469
metalinguistic awareness/knowledge 142, 182, 183, 205, 206, 225, 226, 360, 392, 476
meta-study, *see* meta-analysis
methodology 5, 38–58, 93, 101, 142–143, 200, 213, 214, 236–239, 243–249, 280–282, 319
– action research, *see* action research
– biographical research, *see* biographical research
– conversation analysis, *see* conversation analysis
– diary study, *see* diary study
– discourse analysis, *see* discourse analysis
– ethnography, *see* ethnography
– fieldnotes, *see* fieldnotes
– intervention study, *see* intervention study
– interview study, *see* interview study

- linguistic landscape, see linguistic landscape
- longitudinal study, see longitudinal study
- matched guise technique, see matched guise technique
- mixed methods, see mixed-methods
- moment analysis, see moment analysis
- narrative study, see narrative study
- nexus analysis, see nexus analysis
- observation, see observation
- physiological reaction, see physiological reaction
- qualitative study, see qualitative study
- quantitative study, see quantitative study
- questionnaire, see questionnaire
- school certificate data, see school certificate data
- single-point study, see single-point study
- skin conductance study, see skin conductance reaction
- survey, see survey
- testing, see testing
- thematic analysis, see thematic analysis

micro level 3–8, 29, 34, 38–43, 45, 46, 49, 54, 134, 158, 184, 194, 196, 214, 236, 237, 275, 280, 293, 338, 339, 345, 351, 352, 359, 446, 466, 476, 477
minimal grasp strategy 198, 200
minoritisation 9, 17, 22, 23, 109–112, 116, 117, 121, 131, 137–139, 144, 312, 313, 322, 323, 349, 378, 379, see also marginalisation
minority language 2, 4, 17, 22–24, 30–34, 47, 112, 120, 133, 137–139, 153, 184, 194, 199, 200, *202*, *203*, 205, 231, 236, 267, 275, 279, 282, 288, 313–318, 321, 322, 340–346, 348–352, *389*, 393, 425–434, 437–439, 441, 451, 452
minority language teaching 46, 341, 425–443
mixed methods 39, 53, 213
- mixed qualitative 39, *40*, 49
- mixed qualitative–quantitative 39, *40*, 54
- mixed quantitative 39, *40*
mobility 9, 93, 120, 164, 166, 188, 220, 274, 275, 279, *281*, 322, 359, 365, 366, 386, *389*, 392, 397, 464
models of disability
- medical model 11, 401, 405, 406, 408–410, 412, 413, 415
- social model 11, 401, 405, 407, 408, 411, 412, 413–416

moment analysis 246
monoglossic 9, 54, 141, 299–301, 468, 474
monolingual 20, 64, 68, 69, 88, 111, 112, 117, 198, 199, 362, 363, 367, 389–392, 402, 403, 406, 414, 450, 467, 470, 476
monolingual assumption 362, 363, 369, 474
monolingual bias 111, 406, 408, 410, 412, 416
monolingual habitus 437, 456
monolingual mindset 84, 88–90, 96, 97, 100, 101, 472, 474, 477
monolingualism 84, 97, 100, 187, 406, 407
mother 24, 43, 66, 70–74, 76, 78, 97, 114, 141, 160, 180, 196, *201*, *202*, *209*, 226, 239, 242, 243
mother tongue 4, 17, 22–25, 31–33, 109, 119, 133, 186, 194, **371**, 377, 384, 385, 388, 390–392, 394, 428, 429, 434, 465, 468
mother tongue instruction 24, 29, 141, 432, see also minority language teaching
move-on strategy 198, 200–*202*, 212
multidisciplinary, see cross-disciplinary
multilingual 17, 130–149, 157, 160, 162, 167, 168, 185, 244, 258, 363, 371, 390–392
multilingual assumption 363
multilingual education 11, 320, 387, 388–394, 396, 397, 466, 470
multilingual speaker, see multilingual
multilingualism 1, 88, 116, 118, 120, 121, 134, 144, 163, 166–168, 206, 242, *245*, 278, 312, 313, 315, 344, 347, 352, 358–360, 363, 367–369, 371, 390, 429, 434, 437, 440, 441, 464, 466, 468–473, 475, 478
multimedia 260, 261
multimodality 47, 120, 214, 242, 414, 474

narrative study 39, 87, 88, 246, 471
nation state 22, 46, 274–276, 280, 281, 313, 326, 337, 364, 425, 427, 430, 431, 437
national language 109, 116, 121, 313–316, 318, 319, 322, 340, 342, 363, 425–428, 431, 440, 452, 456, 464, 466, 470, 472
nationalism 121, 275, 280, 281, 370, 395
native language 17, *207*, 319, 432, 469
native speaker 24, 25, 27, 95, 96, 111, 112, 184, 265–268, 296, 297, 303, 322, 369, 392
native-like proficiency 19, 20, 29, 84, 441

NESB 28
new speakers 139, 224, 322
nexus analysis 246, 247
Non-English Speaking Background (NESB), see NESB
non-formal education 425
non-instructional acquisition 23, *31*, 32
non-mainstream language 18, 21, 22–30, 195, see also terms for non-mainstream languages/speakers
norms 3, 10, 17, 44, 45, 84, 89, 99, 112, 177, 178, 183, 219, 222, 261, 357, 385, 395, 406, 408, 430, 476 see also linguistic norms

observation 40–42, 45, 51, 71, 73, 138, 163, 185, *202*, *204*, *208*, 210–213, 243, 247, 248, 304, 473
official language 22, 24, 25, 184–186, 213, 313–316, 322, 340, 345, 363, 367, 378, 379, 388, 426–429, 438, 452, 470
One Person–One Language approach (OPOL), see OPOL
OPOL 153, 156, 197–203, 205–207, 212, 214, 223, 228, 229
oracy 20, 24, 199, 206, 320, 321, 345, 348, 410, 435, 464, 472
origin 21, 177, 188, 287, 378, 380, 381, 432, 436, 437, 439, 444, 452

parent-child interaction 73, 76, 77, 157, 197, 198, 205, 239, 262, 268
parent 5–7, 9, 24, 25, 30, 39, 41–43, 63, 66, 67, 69–78, 90, 94–99, 101, 112–116, 118, 119, 121, 130, 133–138, 140, 141, 144, 155, 160, 161, 165–167, 175–189, 196–200, 205, 206, 211, 212, 218, 219, 223, 224, 227–230, 238–242, 246, 247, 257–259, 261, 263–270, 277, 285–287, 295–298, 301, 303, 304, 318, 325, 348, 365, 368, 380, 381, 390–392, 403, 404, 432, 434, 435, 439, 446–452, 457, 465, 473
parental language 157, 160, 183, 187, 212, 240, 450
participant (research) 38, 39, 41, 43, 44, 46, 48–51, 53, 54, 135, 136, 141, 143, 247, 248, 369

participation 6, 91, 118, 130, 131, 218, 220, 257, 260, 261, 266–268, 277, 299–301, 324, 352, 370, 372, 377, 378, 384, 385, 392, 395, 414
passive bilingual, see bilingual
pedagogy 300–302, 304, 305, 414, 415, 457, 467–469, 476, 477
physiological reaction 93, 96, 101
pluralism 366, 429, 434
pluralistic (formal education) 11, 426, 429–431, 437
plurilingual 453
plurilingualism 1, 345, 438, 448
policy, see language policy
policy actors 180, 337, 346–350, 352
policy documents 28, 47, 48, 339, 340, 439, 465, 467
policy makers 52, 53, 214, 237, 294, 385, 387, 392, 395, 425, 427, 431–433, 439, 440
policymaking 26, 27, 236, 246, 249, 431
political discourse 185
polymedia 164
power relations/dynamics 8, 17, 33, 72, 87, 96, 101, 118, 120, 143, 179, 185, 221, 230, 231, 240, 241, *245*, 282, 303, 363–365, 378, 411, 449
powerful language 2, 26, 113, 184, 185, 278
powerful speaker group *31*, 33, 34, 282, 349, 377, 397, 404
powerless language 2, 32
powerless speaker group 22, 23, 377–379
pragmatics 20, 64, 93, 112, 206, 369
pre-service teacher training 454, 457, 470–473
professional development 18, 302, 305, 306, 436, 446, 452, 454, 457, 470, 472, 473
proficiency 6, 20, 21, 23–26, 29, 30–34, 66, 68–71, 73, 76–79, 95, 96, 98, 101, 111, 113, 115, 181, 200, 297, 299, 302, 303, 388, 434, 435, 438, 440, 472, 475
pronunciation 98, 304
public discourse 26, 27, 185, 342
publication bias 53
purism, see linguistic purism

qualitative study 39–41, 43, 48, 49, 52–54, 66, 72, 75, 93, 158, *201*, 213, 246, 247, 264, 267, 369, 397

quality (input) 78, 157, 196, 197, 205, 219, 238
quantitative study 39–41, 43, 48, 49, 52, 53, 66, 67, 70–72, 75, 93, 95, 136, 158, 213, 246, 248, 263, 369, 391, 397
quantity (input) 157, 196, 197, 219, 238
quasi-speaker 25
questionnaire 64, 71, 92–95, 101, 136, 159, 204, 213, 472, 473

reading 19, 20, 78, 92, 204–206, 209, 211, 213, 262, 285, 402, 403, 409, 410, 414, 475
regime, see language regime
regional minority 137, 426, 427, 434, 438, 439
register 112, 139, 142, 320, 339, 348
rejection 47, 64, 73, 74, 79, 86, 115, 180, 238, 367, 407, 450, 466
religion 143, **176**, 211, *245*, 277, 296, 345, 348, 349, 352, 361, 365, 378, 381
repertoire 18, 20, 22, 23, 25, 26, 111, 112, 117, 130, 133, 134, 136, 137, 140, 142, 144, 162, 181, 182, 196, 230, 278, 326, 344, 345, 385, 388, 414, 428, 430, 449, 450, 452, 453, 467
repetition strategy 198, 200, *202*
replicability 50, 52
reporting 5, 41, 44, 48–50, 53, 54
reproducibility 52
research bias 44, 49, 53, 109, 119, 367
research coverage 49
research designs 5, 38, 41, 43, 45, 47, 48, 50, 51, 53
resistance 87, 112, 113, 118, 119, 135, 179, 183, 219–224, 226, 229, 236, 301, 342, 352, 395, 467–470, 474, 476–478
respect 70, 72, 78, 79, 112, 200, 206, 377, 380, 381, 414, 465
revitalisation 47, 119, 130, 132, *138*, 139, 240, 279, 313, 316, 322, 326, 359, 367, 372, 395
revitalisation immersion *389*–391
routine 135, 163, 189, 198, 206, 211, 242, 302, 465
rural context 9, 130, 279, 317, 319–323, 327

safe space 165, 305
Saturday school 283, 284, 293, 348, *see also* community language school

scaffolding 206, 211, 213, 270, 304, 447, 450, 467, 476, 477
school certificate data *40*
screen time 257, 261–264
second language (L2) 17, 23, 91, 110, 182, 313, 372, 403, 409, 432, 446, 447, 473
second language acquisition (SLA) 85, 91–93, 100, 101, 156, 220, 238, 367, 406, 409, 410, 447, 454, 455, 457, 472, 473
second language learners/speakers 25, 112, 304, 322, 441, 476
segregation, *see* language segregation
self-conception, *see* concept of self
self-confidence 19, 91, 97, 248, 258, 390, 392
self-control 69
self-esteem 51, 91, 113, 117, 211, 249, 305, 434, 449, 453, 454
semilingual, *see* bilingual
SES, *see* socioeconomic status (SES)
shame 6, 76, 89, 113, 115, 185, 297, 370
siblings 115, 197, *208*, 210, 211, 237, 239
single-point study 43, 48
skin conductance level 93, 95, 108
skin conductance response 93, 95, 108
SLA, *see* second language acquisition
social capital 261, 386
social context 3, 23, 89, 95, 110, 120, 258, 295, 317, 357, 386, 404, 412
social exclusion 74, 96, 101, 110, 317, 379, 407, 439
social factors 3, 54, 64, 96, 99, 134, 401, 412
social group 5, 110, 118, 360
social justice 10, 11, 45, 47, 53, 276, 282, 288, 377–400, 411, 429, 444, 456, 478
social media 8, 9, 135, 136, 164, 165, 188, 220, 238, 242, 247, 257–273, 275, 278, 279, 325, 350, 351
social model of disability, *see* models of disability
social network 71, 120, 238, 239, 243, 244, 246, 247, 267, 280, 351
societal ideology 22, 32, 46–48, 115, 116, 118, 121, 179, 183, 238, 246, 274, 318, 343, 351, 358, 369, 370, 395, 425, 426, 428–430, 456
societal influence 2, 32
societal language 5, 42, 67–78, 175, 183, 198, 199, 456

societal norms, *see* norms
society 2, 3, 10, 22, *31*, 32, 46–48, 67, 74, 76, 84, 89, 90, 99, 109, 113, 116, 120, 136, 155, 160, 167, 174, 177, 178, 182, 183, 185, 188, 194, 221, 238, 261, 281, 293, 312–314, 326, 337–339, 345, 346, 351, 357, 360, 362, 363, 365–367, 369, 377, 385–387, 392, 394, 395, 397, 406–408, 413, 416, 426–430, 434, 439, 466
socioeconomic status (SES) 18, 64, 116, 194, 391, 414, 434
southern theory 163,166, 167
speaking 5, 19, 20, 72, 75, 88, 111, 117, 158, 175, 180, 222, 224, 243, 268, 440, 450, 475
special education 387, 403, 405, 407–414
speech style 142, 320
standard language variety 27, 28, 117, 213, 365, 367, 406, 437
strategy (classroom teaching) 464, 472, 473, 476, 477
strategy (home language maintenance) 7, 43, 45, 72, 73, 77, 78, 134, 135, 139, 140, 154, 194–217, 223–228, 238, 240, 242
– expressed guess, *see* expressed guess strategy
– maximal engagement, *see* maximal engagement strategy
– minimal grasp, *see* minimal grasp strategy
– move-on, *see* move-on strategy
– repetition, *see* repetition strategy
stress 51, 71, 74, 96, 98–100, 113, 447, 451
submersion 387–391, 393, 440, 441, 447
supplementary school 9, 293, 294, *see also* community language school
survey 39, *40*, 43, 45, 64, 75–77, 111, 136, 159, 199, *201*, *203*, 239, 243, 246, 248, 285, 286, 302, 320
symmetrical bilingual, *see* bilingual

teacher education 12, 446, 454, 455, 457, 471, 477, 478
teacher training 18, 305, 320, 325, 326, 415, 432, 436, 464, 468, 470, 471, 473, 477
technologies 7–9, 45, 51, 54, 163, 164, 174, 188, *204*, 214, 220, 237, 238, 241, 242, 244, 245, 248, 257–273, 276–280, 283, 284, 286–288, 321, 350, 366, 378, 396

television 262–264, 321, 350
tension 9, 72, 84, 90, 92–94, 96, 98, 100, 101, 167, 259, 265, 321, 372, 468, 470, 477
terminology 4, 17–37, 52, 196, 313, 428, 444, 451–453
terms for non-mainstream languages/ speakers
– abbreviations 27–28, *31*–33
– acronyms 27–28, *31*–33
– ancestral language, *see* ancestral language
– background speaker, *see* background speaker
– Culturally And Linguistically Diverse (CALD), *see* CALD
– English as an Additional Language or Dialect (EAL/D), *see* EAL/D
– English Language Learner, *see* ELL
– first language, *see* first language
– heritage language, *see* heritage language
– home language, *see* home language
– Language Background Other Than English, *see* LBOTE
– language other than X 17
– Languages Other Than English, *see* LOTE
– Limited English Proficiency (LEP), *see* LEP
– minority language, *see* minority language
– mother tongue, *see* mother tongue
– Non-English Speaking Background (NESB), *see* NESB
territory 22, 23, 30, *31*, 110, 281, 294, 314, 315, 323, 430
testing 20, *40*, 142
thematic analysis 50
transformation 45, 120, 154, 163, 368, 408, 467, 470, 474, 476, 477
transition 116, 132, 314, 341, 342, 344, 441
translanguaging 12, 20, 111, 112, 118, 120, 162, 166, 167, 206, *208*, 300, 304, 363, 414, 415, 450, 464, 466–468, 470, 476–478
translocal 9, 44, 45, 54, 274, 276, 277, 280, 284, 286–288
transmission, *see* language transmission
transnational 6, 9, 42, 84–96, 98–102, 120, 130, 135–137, 153–155, 160, 163, 164, 167, 174, 186, 188, 213, 220, 230, 236, 237, 239, 241, 246, 247, 274–288, 366, 430
transnational network 135, 188, 276, 279

transnationalism 6, 109, 119–121, 164, 213, 278, 363
triangulation 49
tribal 312, 317, 378, 382, 383, 392

unbalanced bilingual, *see* bilingual
upbringing 130, 136, 154, 178
urban context 9, 113, 144, 188, 189, 317–327
usage domain, *see* domain of language usage

virtual community 9, 45, 279
virtual connectedness 9, 368
virtual space 44, 54, 279

vitality, *see* language vitality
vocabulary 20, 64, 98, 198, 259, 261, 265, 287, 295, 304, 365, 402, 403, 409

WEIRD (Western, Educated, Industrialised, Rich, and Democratic) 41, 42, 49, 160
well-being 5, 6, 51, 63–83, 86, 88, 90, 139, 180, 195, 248, 282, 381, 448, 451, 454
Western, Educated, Industrialised, Rich, and Democratic, *see* WEIRD
writing 19, 20, 92, *210*, 269, 403, 457, 474, 475

Language Index

Page numbers in bold type indicate figures, in italics, tables.

Afrikaans *162*, 390, 428, 475
Albanian 73, 77, 78, *162*
Amharic *162*, 428
Arabic 65, 79, 92, 136, *162*, 182, 226, 227, 293, 294, 318, 363, 365, 368, 426, 428, 433, 434, 437, 475
Ashaninka 325
Assyrian 294
Aymara 153, 323, 325
Azerbaijani *162*, 351

Bahasa 315, **371**, 428
Basque 428
Bengali 25, 136, *162*, *210*, 211, 297, 301, 304, 317
Berber 318, 428, 437
Breton 350, 351
Burmese 315

Cameroon Pidgin English 22, 23
Cantonese 73, 119, *162*, 293, 368, **371**
Castilian *162*, 184
Catalan *162*, 184, *202*, 350, 368, 428
Chinese 70, 92, 111–114, 116, 117, 119, 161, *162*, 181, 184, 186, 187, *202*, *204*, 231, 294, 297, 298, 301, 302, 304, 363, 384, 391, 428
Cree 472
Czech *162*

Dari 294
Dinka 284–288
Dutch 69, 75, 84, 94, 95–98, 108, *162*, 180, 187, 229, 230, 428, 430, 440
Dzongkha 342

Efik *162*
English 19, 22, 25, 28, 42, 64–66, 68–70, 72, 73, 75, 76, 84, 92, 96, 110, 112, 114, 115, 117, 119, 136, 139–141, 156, 160, *162*, 180, 181, 184–187, 197, 198, *201*–*204*, *207*, *210*, 213, 223–226, 228, 231, 264–267, 283, 285, 293, 296, 298–300, 314–317, 342–344, 348, 358, 363–367, 369, 372, 379, 384, 390, 391, 402, 403, 406–414, 428, 429, 433, 440, 453, 455, 456, 470–472, 474, 475
Estonian *162*, *201*

Farsi 73, *162*
Filipino *162*, 294
Finnish *162*, 228, 294, 433, 469
Flemish 440
French 22, 65, 66, 78, 136, 142, 156, *162*, 181, *203*, *204*, *207*, 219, 223–225, 227, 318, 359, 365, 367, 368, 390, 428, 430, 433, 436, 440, 456
Fries 428
Fulfulde *162*

Gaelic 114, 225–227, 231
Galician *162*
German 66, 71, 78, 133, 141, 142, 156, *162*, 197, 260, 278, 279, 294, 433, 440, 472, 473
Greek 66, 71, 78, *162*, 280, 346
Guaraní 315, 322
Gujarati 25, *162*, 277, 304

Hakka *162*, 349
Haryanvi *162*
Hawaiian 224, 319
Hebrew 89, *162*, *207*, *209*, 224, 225
Hindi 25, *162*, 316, 317, 361, 363, 378, 379, 428
Hokkien 161, *162*, 361
Hungarian *162*, 294

Ibibio *162*
Igbo *162*
Indonesian *162*
Inuktitut *162*, 319
Iquitu 324
Irish *162*, 228, 340, 372
Isconahua 324
isiXhosa 475
Italian 73, *162*, 186, 264, 280

Japanese 73, *162*, 180, *201*, *203*, 226, 294, 298
Jaqaru 324
Javanese *162*, 315
Judeo-Spanish *162*

Kalanga *162*
Kaska 133

Keres 319
Khmer *162*, 315
Kinyarwanda 219, 223–225, 227
Konkani 317
Korean 72, 92, 93, 111, 113, 114, *162*, 295, 297, 304, 391
Kriol 139
Kukama 324, 325
Kurdish *162*, 342, 343, 437
Kutchi *162*
Kven 138, 184, 185

Lao *162*, 315
Latvian *162*, 294
Lithuanian *162*
Lokaa *162*
Luganda *162*
Luxembourgish *162*, 185

Malacca Portuguese Creole *162*
Malay 25, *162*, 185, 186, 315, 363, 366, 371
Malayalam *162*
Maltese 140, 213
Mandarin 25, 73, 112, 161, *162*, 179, 185, 186, 293, 316, 349, 359, 361, 366, 368, **371**, 372
Māori 137, 138, *162*, 319, 340, 347, 359, 365, 367, 369, 370
Marathi *162*
Marwari *162*
Mayan 279
Mayangna 314
Mískito 314
Mohawk 319
Muchik 325

Navajo 319
Ndebele *162*
Nigerian Pidgin *162*
Norse 358
Norwegian 138, *162*, 164, 165, 198, *208*, 223, 370

Ojibwe 319
'Ōlelo Hawai'i *162*
Oromiffa 65, 78

Persian *162*, 298, *see* Farsi
Polish 135, *162*, 229, 348, 349, 370, 475
Portuguese 114, 136, *162*, 294, 348, 364, 434
Punjabi 25, *162*, 361, 362
Putonghua *162*, 213

Quechua 323, 325, 358, 359

Romani 279, 283, 284
Russian 140, *162*, 200, *207*, *209*, 220, 224, 225, 368, 379, 428

Sámi 120, 340, 363
Scottish Gaelic *162*, 225
Shipibo 322, 325, 326
Shiwilu 324
Sinhala *162*
Slovak *162*, 229
Slovene 133, 139
Somali 141, 294, 297
Southern Saami 138
Spanish 68, 69, 72, 76, 92, 94, 110, 111, 113, 115, 117, 118, *162*, 184, *203*, *208–210*, 229, 264, 279, 280, 294, 314, 315, 323, 324, 326, 341, 359, 368, 428, 474, 475
Swahili *162*, 428
Swedish 29, *162*, 226, 228, 294, 297, 298, 303, 304, 390, 471
Sylheti *210*

Tagalog *162*, 315
Taiwanese *162*
Tamil 25, *162*, 185, 186, 224, 361, 366, 379
Telugu *162*
Teochew *162*
Tetum *162*
Thai *162*, 315
Tibetan *162*
Turkish 69, 70, 84, 85, 94–99, 101, 115, 140, *162*, 187, 301, 304, 391, 426, 428, 430, 430, 432, 433, 437, 440, 450

Ukrainian *162*, 304
Urdu 25, 72, *162*, 186, 264, 361, 362
Uro 324

Vietnamese *162*, 293, 304, 391
Võro 349

Wampis 325
Warlpiri 139
Welsh 112, 114, 138

Zapotec 138, 139, *162*, 181

www.ingramcontent.com/pod-product-compliance
Lightning Source LLC
Chambersburg PA
CBHW080922300426
44115CB00018B/2913